OECD Employment Outlook
2018

This work is published under the responsibility of the Secretary-General of the OECD. The opinions expressed and arguments employed herein do not necessarily reflect the official views of OECD member countries.

This document, as well as any data and any map included herein, are without prejudice to the status of or sovereignty over any territory, to the delimitation of international frontiers and boundaries and to the name of any territory, city or area.

Please cite this publication as:
OECD (2018), *OECD Employment Outlook 2018*, OECD Publishing, Paris.
http://dx.doi.org/10.1787/empl_outlook-2018-en

ISBN 978-92-64-30178-8 (print)
ISBN 978-92-64-30179-5 (PDF)

Series: OECD Employment Outlook
ISSN 1013-0241 (print)
ISSN 1999-1266 (online)

The statistical data for Israel are supplied by and under the responsibility of the relevant Israeli authorities. The use of such data by the OECD is without prejudice to the status of the Golan Heights, East Jerusalem and Israeli settlements in the West Bank under the terms of international law.

Photo credits: Cover © Ikoneimages/Inmagine.

Corrigenda to OECD publications may be found on line at: *www.oecd.org/about/publishing/corrigenda.htm*.

Foreword

The *OECD Employment Outlook* provides an annual assessment of key labour market developments and prospects in OECD member countries. Each edition also contains several chapters focusing on specific aspects of how labour markets function and the implications for policy in order to promote more and better jobs. This year's chapters cover recent wage developments, drivers of the decline in the labour share, the impact of collective bargaining on labour market performance, policies to smooth the transition back into employment for workers who lost their job due to economic change, causes and consequences of recent trends in unemployment benefit coverage, and an investigation of the reasons why the gender gap in labour income increases over the working life.

The 2018 *OECD Employment Outlook* is the joint work of staff of the Directorate for Employment, Labour and Social Affairs. The staff of the Economics Department and Statistics and Data Directorate contributed to the preparation of Chapter 2. The whole *Outlook* has also greatly benefited from comments from other OECD directorates and contributions from national government delegates. However, its assessments of each country's labour market prospects do not necessarily correspond to those made by the national authorities concerned.

This report was edited by Andrea Bassanini, and is based on contributions from Alexandre Georgieff (Chapter 1), Cyrille Schwellnus, Mathilde Pak, Pierre-Alain Pionnier and Elena Crivellaro (Chapter 2), Oliver Denk, Andrea Garnero, Alexander Hijzen and Sébastien Martin (Chapter 3), Paul Swaim (Chapter 4), Rodrigo Fernandez, Herwig Immervoll and Daniele Pacifico (Chapter 5) and Gwenn Parent (Chapter 6). Research assistance was provided by Sylvie Cimper, Thomas Manfredi, Sébastien Martin and Agnès Puymoyen. Pascal Marianna prepared the Statistical Annex with the assistance of Dana Blumin and Sylvie Cimper. Editorial assistance was provided by Brigitte Beyeler, Natalie Corry, Liv Gudmundson and Lucy Hulett.

Table of contents

Tables

Figures

Boxes

Follow OECD Publications on:

 http://twitter.com/OECD_Pubs

 http://www.facebook.com/OECDPublications

 http://www.linkedin.com/groups/OECD-Publications-4645871

 http://www.youtube.com/oecdilibrary

 http://www.oecd.org/oecddirect/

This book has...

StatLinks
A service that delivers Excel® files from the printed page!

Look for the *StatLinks* at the bottom of the tables or graphs in this book. To download the matching Excel® spreadsheet, just type the link into your Internet browser, starting with the *http://dx.doi.org* prefix, or click on the link from the e-book edition.

Editorial

Wageless growth: Is this time different?

For the first time since the onset of the global financial crisis in 2008, there are more people with a job in the OECD area than before the crisis. Unemployment rates are below, or close to, pre-crisis levels in almost all countries. Job vacancies have reached record highs in the euro area, the United States and Australia. A growing number of them remain unfilled for many months as labour market conditions get tighter.

Yet, wage growth is still missing in action. As highlighted in this edition of the *Employment Outlook*, OECD countries are now a long way into the growth cycle, but wage growth remains remarkably more sluggish than before the crisis (Chapter 1). At the end of 2017, nominal wage growth in the OECD area was only half of what it was just before the Great Recession for comparable levels of unemployment. And even when inflation is taken into account, real wage growth is a long way off pre-crisis trends. True, in some countries with a long-standing recovery, a few wage agreements entailing significant pay increases have been signed recently, but these remain sparse.

Even more worrisome, this unprecedented wage stagnation is not evenly distributed across workers. Real labour incomes of the top 1% of income earners have increased much faster than those of median full-time workers in recent years, reinforcing a long-standing trend. This, in turn, is contributing to a growing dissatisfaction by many about the nature, if not the strength, of the recovery: while jobs are finally back, only some fortunate few at the top are also enjoying improvements in earnings and job quality.

As labour market tightens up and a growing number of vacancies remain unfilled, why is wage pressure not increasing?

A first answer lies in the slowdown in productivity growth. All else equal, low productivity growth puts a brake on wage growth. While in the years before the crisis hourly labour productivity was growing at 2.3% per year on average in the OECD area, it slumped during the recession. And the chasm, which opened in the early years of the global financial crisis, has not been filled yet: productivity growth levelled off at 1.2% on average over the past five years, and at less than 1% in several countries, including France, Italy, Japan, the United Kingdom and the United States.

While the reason behind this slowdown is currently one of the most hotly debated issues in macroeconomics, productivity trajectories have however been very heterogeneous across firms. Leading firms, at the technological frontier, have enjoyed strong productivity growth similar to that of the pre-crisis period, but follower firms have experienced sluggish productivity growth, widening the gap from the top performers. In other words, productivity growth has become even more concentrated, with limited spillovers from the frontier to follower firms. Aggregate productivity gains are now led by highly-technological, innovative firms that enjoy increasingly large market shares due to their competitive advantage. Even though these dominant positions tend to be temporary, as firms at the technological frontier are continually being challenged by new and better innovators, this process drives down the labour share – the share of national income going to labour. Frontier companies invest massively in capital-intensive technologies and thus tend to have lower labour shares, while reallocation of market shares towards these "superstar" firms further contributes to a lower part of value added that goes to workers (Chapter 2).

The second answer relates to the changing nature of skills demand and its relationship to the skills available in the workforce. The jobs destroyed during the crisis are not the same as those created in the recovery. Leading firms are in great demand of highly-qualified personnel, with high-level cognitive skills – such as complex problem solving, critical thinking and creativity – and social intelligence – social perceptiveness needed when persuading, negotiating and caring for others. These skills are in short supply in many countries and people who possess them have been the main beneficiaries of wage growth. However, many workers are not well equipped to meet the emerging demand for these high-level skills. According to the *Survey of Adult Skills*, almost one-in-four adults lack even basic information-processing skills (digital skills) and can only do simple tasks on computers, which prevents them from accessing jobs in which pay is increasing.

As a result, recent wage developments have not been the same for everybody, with significant differences not only across countries but also within countries, and within firms. While returns to high-level skills have been rising, there is evidence that the number of lower paid jobs is on the rise. For example, involuntary part-time employment has risen significantly in a number of countries since the crisis, and this has been accompanied by a deterioration in the relative earnings of part-time workers.

Declining coverage of unemployment benefits in many countries and mounting long-term unemployment in the aftermath of the crisis (Chapter 5) may also have contributed to low wage growth. Jobseekers may have become less selective when nearing exhaustion of their benefit rights and may tend to accept jobs not matching their expectations in terms of hours worked contractual arrangements and, especially, wage levels. In a number of OECD countries, particularly those hit hard by the financial crisis and then by the sovereign debt crisis, the overall annual growth of real monthly wages would have indeed been higher had the number of those newly hired after an unemployment spell not increased so much and their wage evolved along the lines of other workers. For example, in Spain average real wages would have been 3.1% higher by 2014 had average wages grown at the same rate as the wages of those continuously employed since 2007. Many of the workers who lose their jobs for economic reasons typically face structural challenges that put them at risk of long-term unemployment, unless skills profiling, re-training and counselling are provided early enough (Chapter 4).

In this context, it is crucial that countries develop high-quality education and training systems that provide learning opportunities throughout the life course. Children and youth need to acquire valuable job-specific skills and develop their creativity, problem solving and social perceptiveness, as well as the ability and interest to learn new things. But learning opportunities cannot stop at school and university. Adults must be given continuous opportunities to develop, maintain and upgrade skills at all ages, with a view to preventing as much as addressing skills obsolescence and depreciation. Yet, workforce groups at greater risk of labour market disadvantage receive less training, both formal and informal, which compounds their disadvantage. Across all OECD countries, the low skilled have indeed a probability of being involved in training which is only one-third of that of the high skilled. More needs to be done to overcome this gap, with better targeted training measures but also greater involvement of employers, especially in small and medium-sized enterprises that struggle to offer training.

More generally, in a world where technologies and employers' needs are changing rapidly, the challenge for policy is to ensure that current and future skill demands are well identified. Systems and tools to produce this information exist in most countries. They usually provide reliable evidence that can be used to address skill imbalances but their predictions are rarely well-integrated into policy and practice. Doing so requires good co-operation and co-ordination between key stakeholders in several different areas ranging from employment to education and training to migration policy.

Co-operation and co-ordination among social partners have a key role to play in addressing these challenges, but this requires addressing the long-term trend decline in union membership and eroding role of collective bargaining in a number of countries. Social dialogue makes it easier to anticipate future needs and opportunities, find solutions and manage change proactively, but to be effective social partners should work together in a spirit of co-operation and mutual trust. New evidence provided in this *Outlook* clearly shows that co-ordinated collective bargaining systems, with strong and self-regulated social partners and effective mediation bodies, contribute to high levels of employment, better quality of the work environment, including more training opportunities, and greater resilience of the labour market to shocks (Chapter 3). In a rapidly changing labour market, there is even more need for effective social dialogue. Social partners can and should play an important role in ensuring that the provision of training is consistent with current and future demand for skills, achieving an equitable distribution of productivity gains and supporting individuals who lose their job as a result of technological change or trade.

To sum up, the persistent overall degree of wage moderation masks large differences between workers, but also reflects structural changes in our economies that the global financial crisis has deepened and accelerated. Some stronger wage rises are expected as the labour market tightens further. But the earnings prospects of many workers may well remain meagre as they struggle to adapt to a rapidly evolving world of work. Well-targeted policy measures and closer collaboration with the social partners can and should help these workers address their growing disadvantages by providing them with training and retraining opportunities as well as career guidance and information to foster mobility.

Stefano Scarpetta,
OECD Director for Employment, Labour and Social Affairs

Acronyms and abbreviations

ALMP	Active labour market programme
CASEN	*Encuesta de Caracterizacion Socioeconomica Nacional*
CAWIE	Collectively Agreed Wages In Europe
CNEF	Cross-National Equivalent File
CPS	Current Population Survey
ECB	European Central Bank
ECEC	Early childhood education and care
ENIGH	*Encuesta Nacional de Ingresos y Gastos de los Hogares*
ENOE	*Encuesta Nacional de Ocupación y Empleo*
EPL	Employment protection legislation
ERM	European Restructuring Monitor
EU-KLEMS	EU-level analysis of capital, labour, energy, materials and service inputs data
EU-LFS	European Union Labour Force Survey
EU-SILC	European Union Statistics on Income and Living Conditions
GDP	Gross domestic product
GGLI	Gender gap in labour income
GSOEP	German Socio Economic Panel
GVC	Global value chain
HG	Hours gap
HILDA	Household, Income and Labour Dynamics in Australia
HWG	Hourly wage gap
ICT	Information and communication technology
ICTWSS	Institutional Characteristics of Trade Unions, Wage Setting, State Intervention and Social Pacts Database
IDD	OECD Income Distribution Database
ILO	International Labour Organization
IMF	International Monetary Fund
INPS	*Istituto Nazionale Previdenza Sociale*
ISIC	International Standard Industry Classification
KHPS	Japan Household Panel Survey
KLIPS	Korean Labor and Income Panel Study
LFS	Labour Force Survey
NRR	Net replacement rate
OECD	Organisation for Economic Co-operation and Development
OLS	Ordinary Least Squares

PES	Public employment service
PIAAC	Programme for the International Assessment of Adult Competencies
PISA	Programme for International Student Assessment
PPP	Purchasing power parity
SES	European Union Structure of Earnings Survey
SHARE	Survey of Health, Ageing and Retirement in Europe
STAN	OECD Structural Analysis Database
STEM	Science, technology, engineering and mathematics
STW	Short-time work
UA	Unemployment assistance
UI	Unemployment insurance
UB	Unemployment benefit
WTO	World Trade Organization

Executive summary

Wage growth remains sluggish despite the fall in unemployment

While the impact of the global financial crisis on job quality and inclusiveness persists, employment rates are historically high in most OECD countries and the average unemployment rate is back to its pre-crisis level. In spite of this, nominal wage growth remains significantly lower than it was before the crisis for comparable levels of unemployment, and the downward shift in the Phillips curve – the relationship between unemployment and wage growth – has continued during the recovery. Low inflation expectations and the productivity slowdown, which accompanied the Great Recession and have not fully recovered yet, have both contributed to this shift. Low-pay jobs have also been another important factor. In particular, there has been a significant worsening of the earnings of part-time workers relative to that of full-time workers associated with the rise of involuntary part-time employment in a number of countries. Moreover, the comparatively low wages of workers who have recently experienced spells of unemployment, combined with still high unemployment rates in some countries, have pushed up the number of lower-paid workers, thereby lowering average wage growth.

Labour share declines partly reflect the emergence of "superstar" firms

Real median wage growth in most OECD countries has not kept pace with labour productivity growth over the past two decades, partly reflecting declines in the share of value added going to labour – i.e. the labour share. Technological progress in the sectors producing equipment goods and the expansion of global value chains have reduced labour shares within firms and increased the share of value added accounted for by firms with lower labour shares. Moreover, the dampening effect of technological progress on the labour share tends to be particularly large in countries and industries with a high proportion of low-skilled and high-routine jobs. Countries with falling labour shares have witnessed both a decline in the labour share at the technological frontier and a reallocation of market shares towards firms at this frontier ("superstar" firms) with low labour shares. The labour share decline at the technological frontier reflects the enhanced "creative destruction" process brought about by the technological dynamism of new entrants with lower labour shares rather than anti-competitive forces. These results suggest that the way to help workers make the most of ongoing technological advances is to effectively raise their skills. It is therefore crucial that countries develop high-quality education and training services and provide accessible learning opportunities while developing systems for anticipating skill demands.

Collective bargaining institutions play a key role for labour market performance

The pay and working conditions of one-in-three workers in the OECD are governed by a collective agreement. Bargaining systems that co-ordinate wages across sectors tend to be linked with lower wage inequality and better employment outcomes, including for vulnerable groups. Wage co-ordination increases solidarity between workers in different sectors and helps ensure that collective bargaining improves employment by taking due account of macroeconomic conditions. However, in centralised systems, lower inequality and higher employment may come at the expense of lower productivity growth. The experience of several countries suggests that it can be important to provide employer and worker representatives in the firm with sufficient room to refine or adjust sector-level agreements to take account of company conditions ("organised decentralisation"). Overall, co-ordination and organised decentralisation with broad-based social partners help attain better labour market outcomes, combining good levels of inclusiveness and flexibility. Social dialogue in the workplace is also associated with a higher-quality work environment.

Labour market programmes help workers who lose their jobs for economic reasons

The "creative destruction" process that underlies economic growth and rising living standards causes a considerable number of workers to lose their jobs to economic change every year and many of these workers experience significant income losses and other hardships. The starting point for improving the re-employment prospects and income security of workers who have been made redundant is to make further progress at developing effective national activation strategies that address the barriers faced by this group and their particular advantages when searching for a new job. Two of the most important differences between workers who lose their job for economic reasons and other jobseekers are the greater scope for proactive measures, beginning during the notice period before the layoff occurs, and the large contribution that employers can make to fostering successful mobility for workers they dismiss, ideally in close collaboration with unions and labour market authorities. An important issue for income support is how, if at all, workers who become re-employed at a significantly lower wage should be compensated for their loss of earnings power. Conditions of access to unemployment benefits during the whole unemployment spell also play a crucial role.

Most jobseekers do not receive unemployment benefits

Discussions of the labour market effects of unemployment benefits commonly assume that jobseekers have ready access to such transfers. Accessible unemployment support is a crucial ingredient of an inclusive labour market policy that protects workers rather than jobs. But fewer than one-in-three jobseekers receive unemployment benefits on average across the OECD, and the longer-term downward trend of benefit coverage has continued in many countries after the financial and economic crisis. The reasons behind the decline in coverage rates provide an indication of whether this might be a policy concern, and which measures may be suitable for maintaining benefit accessibility at desired levels. Since the onset of the crisis, changes in the characteristics of jobseekers, such as migration flows or sizeable changes in the shares of the long-term unemployed, have been important drivers of coverage trends. But part of the recent widening of what might be called the "coverage gap" can be clearly ascribed to policy reforms that aimed at reducing unemployment benefit generosity either in search of fiscal restraint or in order to dampen job-search disincentives for the unemployed.

Why does the gender gap in labour income increase over the working life?

Even if the gap in annual average labour income between men and women has gone down significantly, women's annual labour income was still 39% lower on average than that of men in 2015. Comparable estimates of the gender gap in labour income throughout the lifecycle indicate that most of it is generated in the first half of the career. The smaller number of job changes experienced by women in the early stages of their working life and the effect of childbirth and child rearing on mothers' participation in the labour market have a long-lasting impact on women's careers and, therefore, the way the gender gap evolves over the working life. Part-time work plays a less clear-cut role, as it can prevent withdrawal from the labour force but may also represent a career trap for women. The relative importance of each dimensions of the gender gap in labour income – gender differences in employment rates, hours worked and hourly earnings – provides valuable guidelines for policy action. Family policies, measures to encourage behavioural changes among both men and women, and actions promoting changes in the workplace, such as increased take-up of part-time and flexible working time arrangements by both fathers and mothers, can play a key role in helping women to successfully navigate the crucial childbirth phase of their career, stay attached to the labour market and seize the same career opportunities as men.

Chapter 1. Still out of pocket: Recent labour market performance and wage developments

This chapter examines the evolution of labour market performance since the onset of the global financial crisis. OECD labour markets are back to pre-crisis levels in terms of job quantity, with only few notable exceptions, while a more mixed picture emerges as regards job quality and inclusiveness. In spite of this, nominal wage growth remains remarkably lower than it was before the crisis for comparable levels of unemployment, and the shift of the relationship between unemployment and wage growth has continued during the recovery. The chapter investigates the factors accounting for the persistent wage growth slowdown. While low inflation expectations and productivity growth deceleration remain the main drivers of observed patterns, the dynamics of low-pay jobs and the wages associated to them have also been key factors accounting for the overall decline in wage growth.

Key findings

The recovery from the global financial crisis and the subsequent European debt crisis that affected a number of euro area countries is largely complete. At 2.6 % per year in 2017 and 2.5% projected for 2019, OECD economic growth, while not at a record high, appears stable and even the euro area is experiencing the strongest growth of real gross domestic product (GDP) of the past ten years (OECD, 2018[1]). Employment rates are, on average, above pre-crisis levels, with the strongest improvements occurring among under-represented groups. Yet wage growth appears to be lagging behind employment growth, with some signs of acceleration appearing in some countries only towards the end of 2017 or the first quarter of 2018 (OECD, 2018[2]). This soft wage growth suggests that the recovery remains fragile.

This chapter provides an overview of labour market developments since the onset of the global financial crisis with a special emphasis on the possible reasons for unexpectedly low wage growth. The main findings of this chapter are:

- OECD labour markets are back to pre-crisis levels in terms of job quantity, with only a few notable exceptions. Yet, a more mixed picture emerges as regards job quality and inclusiveness, the other two main pillars of the OECD *Jobs Strategy* together with job quantity. Improvements have occurred over the past decade in many countries as regards the gender gap in labour income, the labour market prospects of disadvantaged groups, and the incidence of job strain – excessive job demands combined with insufficient resources. However, labour market insecurity – the risk of unemployment and its economic cost for workers – is not yet back to pre-crisis levels and poverty has grown amongst the working-age population.

- Wage growth also remains remarkably lower than it was before the crisis. The OECD average of hourly wage growth rates was between 1.5 and 2 percentage points lower during the Great Recession than it was before for comparable levels of unemployment, and this shift in the relationship between unemployment and wage growth (the so-called Phillips curve) has continued during the recovery. It is visible even in countries where wage growth seems to be finally picking up a number of years into the recovery, such as the United States.

- All in all, in OECD countries, nominal hourly wage growth dropped from 4.8% in the pre-crisis period to 2.1% in recent years on average. Real wage growth decreased by 1 percentage point over the same period.

- The low-inflation environment and the productivity slowdown have both contributed to the marked deceleration in wage growth. On average, hourly labour productivity growth slowed from 2.3% prior to the crisis to 1.2% in the recent period, while inflation decreased from 2.6% to 0.8%, likely lowering inflation expectations.

- The dynamics of low-pay jobs and the wages they pay have also been key factors accounting for the overall decline in wage growth. In particular, there has been a significant worsening in the average earnings from part-time jobs relative to that of full-time jobs, which is associated with the rise of involuntary part-time employment in a number of countries.

- Comparatively poor working conditions among workers regaining employment after an unemployment spell, combined with a large number of transitions from unemployment to employment in some countries, pushed up the number of lower-paid workers, thereby lowering average wage growth.

Introduction

This chapter provides an overview of labour market developments since the onset of the global financial crisis. After presenting the evolution of the key indicators of labour market performance, developed in the context of the OECD Jobs Strategy in OECD (2017[3]; 2018[4]), special attention is given to wage growth, which appears to be the missing element of the current recovery. Indeed, while unemployment has been on a declining path for a number of years in most OECD countries (OECD, 2016[5]), wage growth remains remarkably lower than it was before the Great Recession for comparable levels of unemployment. This recent downward shift of the wage-unemployment relationship in a number of countries has raised an increasing interest and concern in the academia and policy fora – see for example (IMF, 2017[6]; Bulligan and Viviano, 2017[7]; OECD, 2016[5]; ECB, 2016[8]; Shambaugh et al., 2017[9]). Beyond the factors typically pointed out in the literature, such as the productivity slowdown and fall of inflation expectations, low-pay jobs are considered here as an important channel accounting for the disappointing wage growth deceleration.

The remainder of the chapter is divided as follows: Section 1.1 briefly examines the evolution of labour market performance, using a number of standardised indicators; Section 1.2 investigates the statistical factors accounting for the persistent wage growth slowdown; and Section 1.3 presents concluding remarks.

1.1. Recent developments in key indicators of labour market performance

Labour market conditions continue to improve. In 2017, the OECD average employment rate was almost 2 percentage points above its pre-crisis level, (Figure 1.1, Panel A).[1] Similarly, unemployment rates continue their slow descent, although in a few countries remain somewhat above their pre-crisis levels because employment has not increased enough to fully offset rising trends in participation rates (Figure 1.1 Panel B). Yet, in 2016, broad labour underutilisation – adding up inactive and unemployed people as well as involuntary part-timers – was still, at 28.1%, 1.5 percentage points above 2006 levels (Figure 1.1, Panel C).

The recent performance of OECD countries as regards job quantity has been quite heterogeneous. In 2016, employment rates were more than 8 percentage points above their 2006 levels in Germany, Hungary and Poland. In these countries, these positive employment trends are typically matched by significant reductions in both unemployment and broad labour underutilisation. By contrast, contractions of employment rates as large as 2 percentage points or more occurred in this period in a number of countries hit hard by the Great Recession and the euro debt crisis (Greece, Ireland and Spain) and Denmark. In these countries, negative employment trends are matched by large increases in unemployment and broad underutilisation.

Figure 1.1. Employment performance is back to pre-crisis levels

Employment, unemployment and broad labour underutilisation, 2006 and latest available data

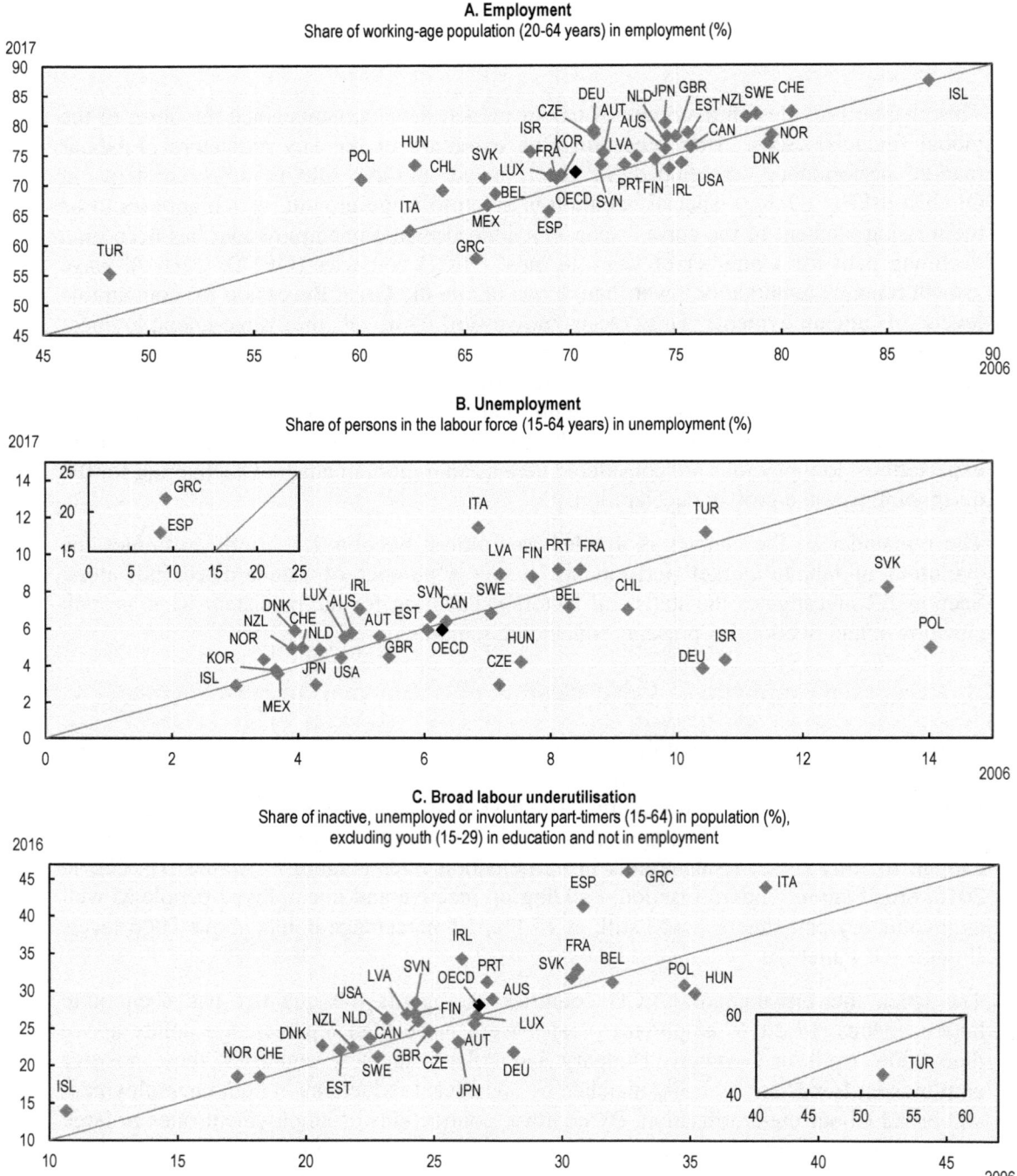

Note: Following OECD (2018[4]), broad labour underutilisation is defined in the chart as the sum of inactive, unemployed and involuntary part-time people.
Source: *OECD Employment Database,* www.oecd.org/employment/emp/ onlineoecdemploymentdatabase.htm; OECD (2018[4]), *Good Jobs for All in a Changing World of Work: The OECD Jobs Strategy,* http://www.oecd.org/mcm/documents/C-MIN-2018-7-EN.pdf.

StatLink ᵃ🔢🗒️ http://dx.doi.org/10.1787/888933777604

The United States is another country in which the employment rate is still significantly below the pre-crisis level, despite the longest job recovery in the post-war period: the unemployment rate is now below the pre-crisis level but broad labour underutilisation is up by 3.2 percentage points. Despite a relatively stable employment rate, in Italy both the unemployment and labour underutilisation rates were higher in 2016 than in 2006 by 4.6 and 6 percentage points, respectively, due to the opposite effects of increasing labour force participation and soaring involuntary part-time. Last but not least, the latest available data show a significantly higher labour underutilisation also in Iceland (by 3 percentage points) as well as in Portugal and Slovenia (by 4 percentage points).

The OECD Job Quality framework measures job quality along three dimensions: i) *earnings quality*, which refers to the extent to which the earnings received by workers in their jobs contribute to their well-being by taking account of both the average level as well as the way earnings are distributed across the workforce; ii) *labour market insecurity*, which is measured as the ex-ante expected monetary loss associated with becoming and staying unemployed as a share of previous earnings; and iii) the *quality of working environment*, measured as the incidence of job strain that is characterised by a combination of high job demands and few job resources to meet those demands.

Trends in job quality since the mid-2000s have been contrasted (Figure 1.2). On the one hand, earnings quality has increased, albeit in a limited way, and job strain decreased almost everywhere. On the other hand, labour market insecurity in 2016 was still above 2006 levels in many countries.

Gross hourly earnings expressed in 2010 USD purchasing power parity adjusted by inequality[2] have increased modestly in most countries, from 15.59 USD to 16.87 USD between 2006 and 2015. This increase is mainly due to limited growth in real wages (see Section 1.2) and an extremely small reduction in earnings inequality. Earnings quality fell significantly in Greece in this period (with a slump of 1.39 USD), and to a limited extent in Mexico, Turkey and the United States (where adjusted gross hourly earnings decreased by 0.15 to 0.35 USD). Large increases (above 3 USD) occurred in Norway only.

Among the countries for which data are available, the incidence of job strain was 27.5% on average in 2015, against 34.5% in 2005 (Figure 1.2, Panel C). The largest drop, albeit from very high values, occurred in Germany (about 16 percentage points), where job strain incidence is now close to the OECD average. By contrast job strain increased only in Sweden (about 2 percentage points) although, at 25.5% in 2015, the country remains among those with the lowest incidence. It must be kept in mind, however, that these trends may not only be driven by structural improvement but also reflect business-cycle-related factors affecting the composition of jobs.[3]

The increase in labour market insecurity (Figure 1.2, Panel B) is largely driven by the fact that, despite higher employment rates, unemployment in a number of countries in 2016 was not yet at its pre-crisis levels – see OECD (2018[1]). Reduction in unemployment-benefit coverage during this period (see Chapter 5), however, played a role in many countries as well. The ex-ante expected monetary loss associated with becoming and staying unemployed increased by more than one percentage point between 2006 and 2016. The largest increase in labour market insecurity (above 10 percentage points) occurred in Greece and Spain. By contrast, in Germany and the Slovak Republic, labour market insecurity fell by more than 1.5 percentage points.

Figure 1.2. Contrasting trends in job quality

Earnings quality, labour market insecurity and incidence of job strain, mid-2000s and latest available data

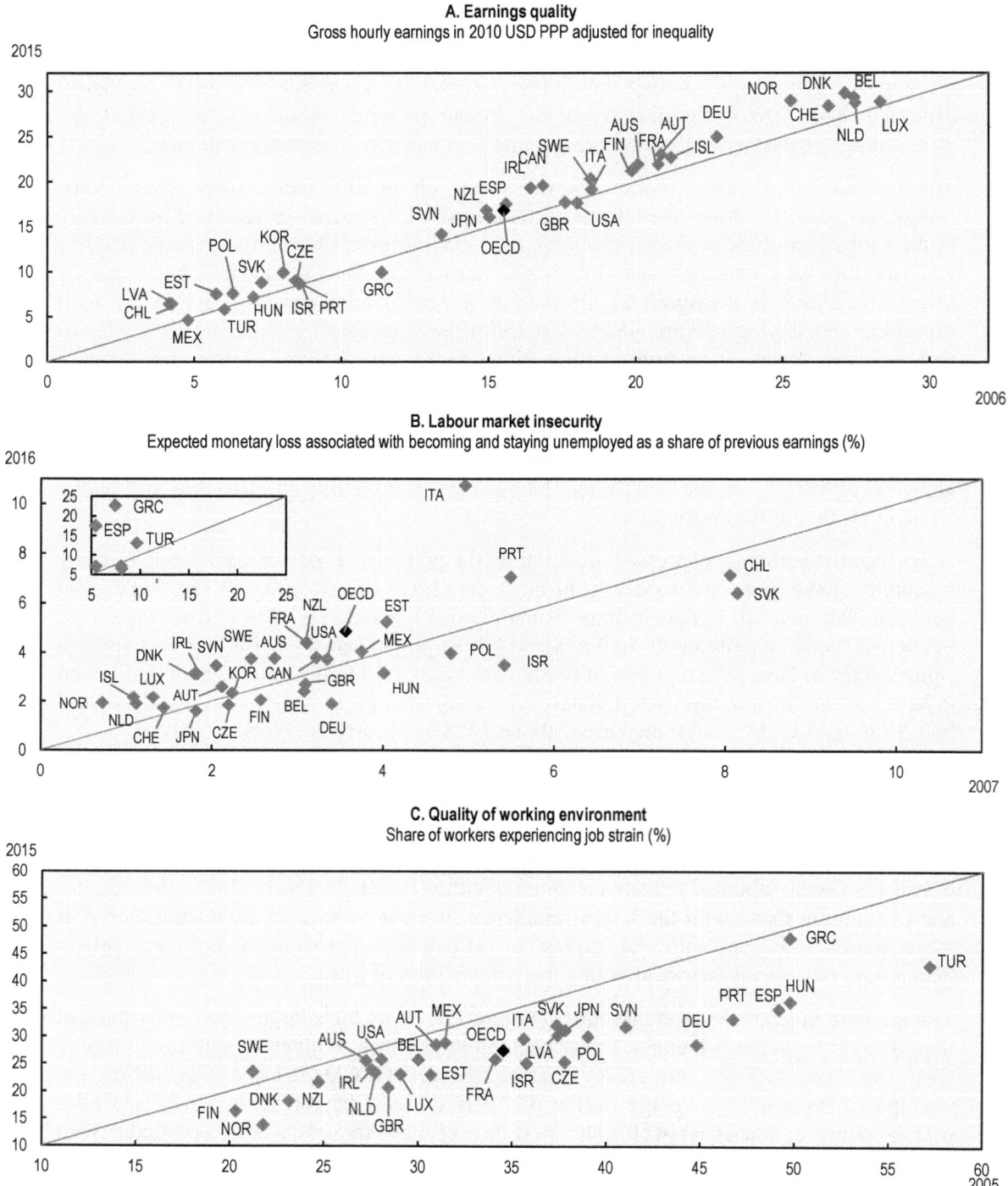

A. Earnings quality
Gross hourly earnings in 2010 USD PPP adjusted for inequality

B. Labour market insecurity
Expected monetary loss associated with becoming and staying unemployed as a share of previous earnings (%)

C. Quality of working environment
Share of workers experiencing job strain (%)

Note: Average earnings adjusted for inequality are obtained as a generalised mean of individual earnings with coefficient -3.
Source: OECD (2018[4]), *Good Jobs for All in a Changing World of Work: The OECD Jobs Strategy*, http://www.oecd.org/mcm/documents/C-MIN-2018-7-EN.pdf.

StatLink ᘯ᠍ᡗᡅ http://dx.doi.org/10.1787/888933777623

Figure 1.3. In spite of more inclusive labour markets, poverty remains a concern

Low-earnings rate, gender gap in labour income and employment gap of disadvantaged groups, 2006 and latest available data

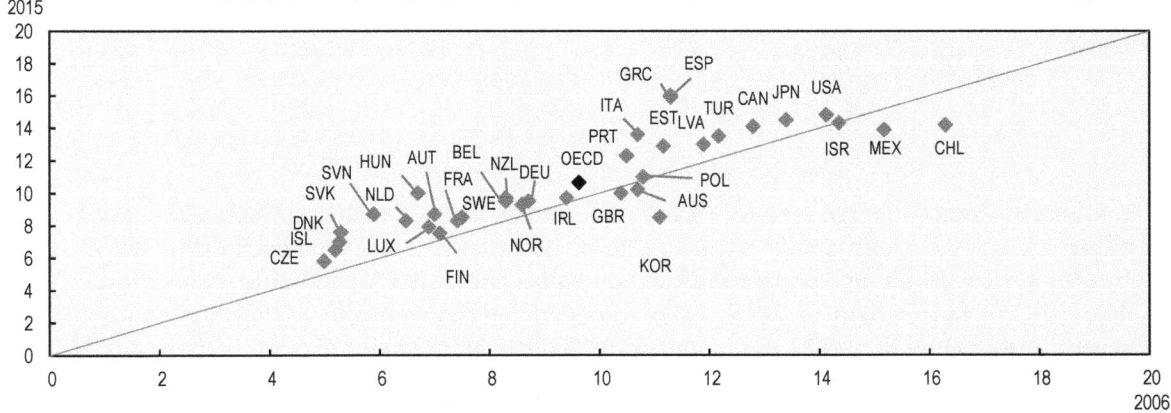

A. Low-income rate
Share of working-age population (18-64 years) with equivalised household disposable income below 50% of the median income (%)

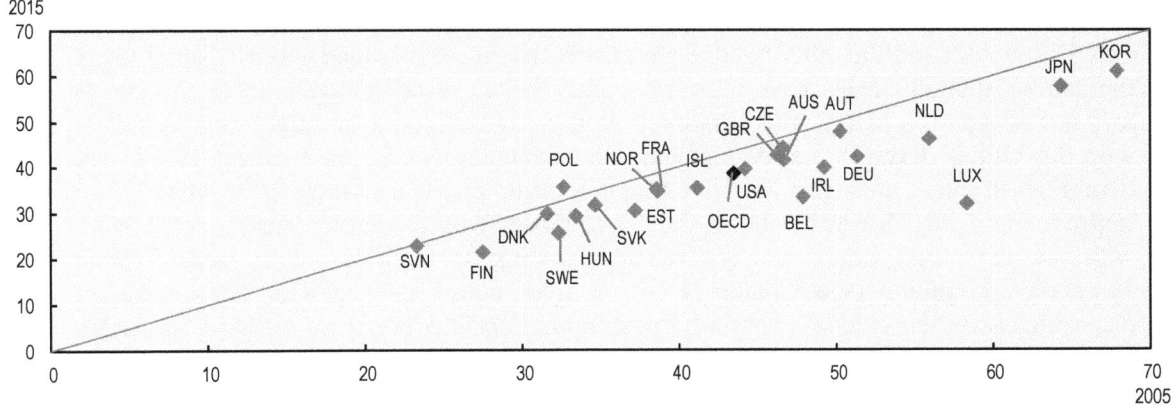

B. Gender labour income gap
Difference between average annual earnings of men and women divided by average earnings of men (%)

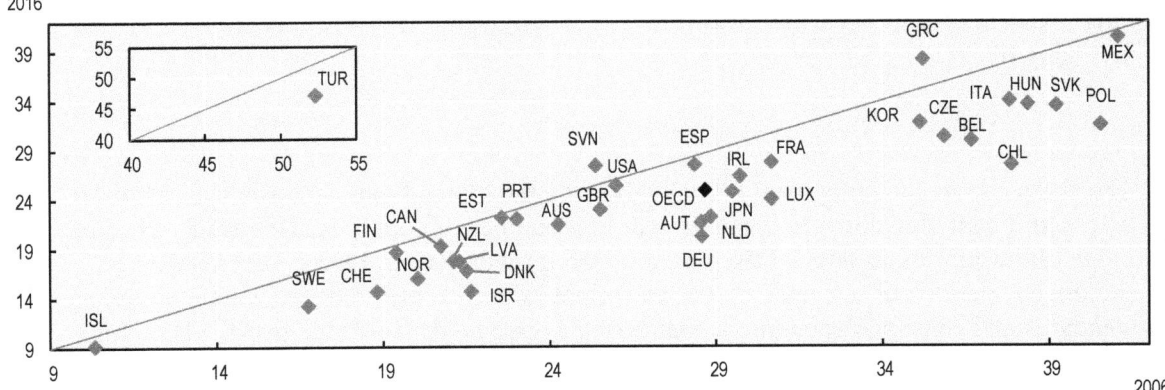

C. Employment gap for disadvantaged groups
Average employment gap as a percentage of the employment rate of the benchmark group (prime-age male workers)

Note: Data on low-income rate refer to 2015 except for Costa Rica and Israel (2016); Denmark, Germany, Hungary, Iceland, Ireland, Italy, Luxembourg, Mexico, New Zealand (2014); Japan (2012), Data on gender labour income gap refer to 2015 except for the United States (2016); Iceland, Ireland, Italy, Luxembourg and Switzerland (2014); Korea (2013). Data on employment gap for disadvantaged groups are a weighted average of the employment gap for mothers with young children, youth (excluding those in education and not in employment), older workers, non-natives and people with disabilities.

Source: Low-income rate: Estimates and calculations based on the *OECD Income Distribution Database* (IDD), http://oe.cd/idd. Gender labour income gap per capita: OECD calculations based on the European Union Statistics on Income and Living Conditions (EU-SILC) for European countries except Germany, Household, Income and Labour Dynamics in Australia (HILDA) for Australia, German Socio Economic Panel (GSOEP) for Germany, Basic Survey on Wage Structure combined with Labour Force Survey results for Japan, Korean Labor and Income Panel Study (KLIPS) for Korea, and the Current Population Survey (CPS - Annual Social Economic Supplement), for the United States. Employment gap for disadvantaged groups: OECD calculations from the *OECD Employment Database*, http://www.oecd.org/employment/emp/onlineoecdemploymentdatabase.htm and *OECD International Migration Database*, http://www.oecd.org/els/mig/oecdmigrationdatabases.htm; for details see footnotes to Figure 1.7 in OECD (2017[3]), *OECD Employment Outlook 2017*, http://dx.doi.org/10.1787/empl_outlook-2017-en.

StatLink ⟪ https://dx.doi.org/10.1787/888933777642

Contrasting trends emerge also as regards labour market inclusiveness. On the one hand, poverty has risen significantly since the onset of the crisis: on average, in the OECD, 10.6% of the working-age population had equivalised household disposable income lower than 50% of the median in 2015 – the so-called low-income rate – against 9.6% one decade before (Figure 1.3).[4] Low-income rates have decreased significantly only in Korea as well as Mexico and Chile – albeit from very high levels in the latter two. By contrast, they have increased by more than 2 percentage points in most of the countries that were hit hard by the euro crisis (Greece, Italy, Spain and Slovenia), as well as in a few Eastern European countries (Hungary and the Slovak Republic).

OECD countries, on the other hand, have clearly managed to reduce gender disparities in the labour market. They have also integrated better disadvantaged groups, such as low-skilled youth, older workers, mothers with young children, immigrants and people with disabilities. Even if women's annual labour income is still, on average, 39% lower than that of men, this gap fell by 4.5 percentage points between 2006 and 2015.[5] Improvements are observable in all OECD countries with available data except Poland, with Luxembourg, Belgium and Ireland showing a reduction even greater than 10 percentage points (see Chapter 6 for a finer analysis of gender labour market disparities and their causes). Similarly, despite the fact that the crisis hit hard on certain groups, the average employment gap of disadvantaged groups[6] has decreased in all OECD countries except in Greece and Slovenia, thanks also to a sufficiently long period of restored growth. While the average employment rate of these groups was, on average, 29% lower than that of prime-age men in 2006, this gap was reduced to 25% ten years later. Remarkable progression was experienced by Chile (10.4%), Poland (9%) and Germany (8.4%).

1.2. Wage growth trends since the onset of the crisis

The sharp rise in unemployment brought about by the global financial crisis was followed by a significant slowdown in wage growth in a number of countries. This wage restraint helped limit job losses and set the stage for job growth during the recovery. However, a prolonged period of stagnating wages might significantly reduce worker's living standards and consumer spending, endangering aggregate demand and growth. Therefore, the decline in unemployment during the recovery should be accompanied by a rebound in wages to allow for it to gain full strength.

1.2.1. The recovery in wage growth lags behind the decline in unemployment

While unemployment has been on a declining path for a number of years in most OECD countries (OECD, 2016[5]), wage growth remains remarkably lower than it was before the recession for comparable levels of unemployment. Underemployment, the productivity slowdown and low inflation expectations are natural candidates to explain this shift of the Phillips curves[7] (IMF, 2017[6]; ECB, 2016[8]; Hong et al., 2018[10]). Some additional country specific explanations have been put forward, such as reduced profitability due to the fall in the terms of trade or the high real exchange rate in Australia (Bishop and Cassidy, 2017[11]; Connolly, 2016[12]; Jacobs and Rush, 2015[13]).

The wage-Phillips curves presented in Figure 1.4 show how nominal hourly wages and unemployment co-varied, both during the previous cycle (in grey) and during the post-crisis period (in blue). A rising unemployment gap – defined as the percentage-point change in unemployment since the start of the global financial crisis – increases competition among workers for jobs and allows employers to lower their wage offers.[8] Provided that inflation expectations, productivity growth and the composition of the workforce do not change significantly, that wage adjustments are not made only on the extensive margin (that is for new hires only), and that labour market slack is well proxied by unemployment, the relationship between the change in unemployment since the start of the crisis and wage growth should follow a stable pattern, at least in the short run: wage growth should decline as unemployment rises and then increase back to its previous levels as the unemployment gap shrinks.

OECD-wide, there has been a clear shift of the Phillips curve following the crisis (top-left panel of Figure 1.4). During the recession, the average hourly wage growth was between 1.5 and 2 percentage points lower than it was before the recession for comparable levels of unemployment. There is also a gap between the pre-recovery and post-recovery curves, showing that this shift has even deepened during the recovery. On average, hourly wage growth in OECD countries was still 0.4 percentage points lower in the last quarter of 2017 than it was in late 2008, while unemployment was at a similar level.

Even in Ireland, the United Kingdom and the United States, where no downward shift of the Phillips curve was observed in the early recovery phase, a softer wage growth with respect to pre-recovery Phillips curves was observed in 2017. In Germany, the continuous decline in unemployment since 2010 has been accompanied by successive shifts of the Phillips curve. These observations highlight that even in those countries where wage growth seems to be picking up the recovery might be fragile.

Full-time wage growth has decreased uniformly across the wage distribution between the previous and the current cycle in a number of countries. Figure 1.5 compares the slowdown in nominal wage growth of full-time employees at the lower decile, the median and the upper decile of the earnings distribution between the periods 2000-07 and 2007-16. Average annual growth of median full-time wages fell by 1.5 percentage points in the OECD area, and slumped by more than 3 percentage points in Ireland, Greece and Portugal as well as many Eastern European countries. Noteworthy, with the only exception of Mexico, in all the countries where wage growth at the median of the wage distribution decelerated by at least one percentage point per year, the wage growth slowdown was significant also at the top decile. Moreover, with the additional exceptions of Latvia and Slovenia, wage growth fell significantly also at the bottom. Yet, the lower deceleration of the bottom decile in a number of countries is by and large a statistical artefact due to composition effects in the context of rising unemployment, particularly strong amongst the low skilled, and should not be taken as evidence that inequality in labour income has decreased since the onset of the crisis. In fact, market income inequality has rather increased over recent years – see OECD (2018[1]).

Figure 1.4. The recovery in wage growth lags behind the decline in unemployment

Wage-Phillips curves: Relationship between nominal wage growth and change in the unemployment rate,[a] selected OECD countries, Q1 2000-Q4 2017

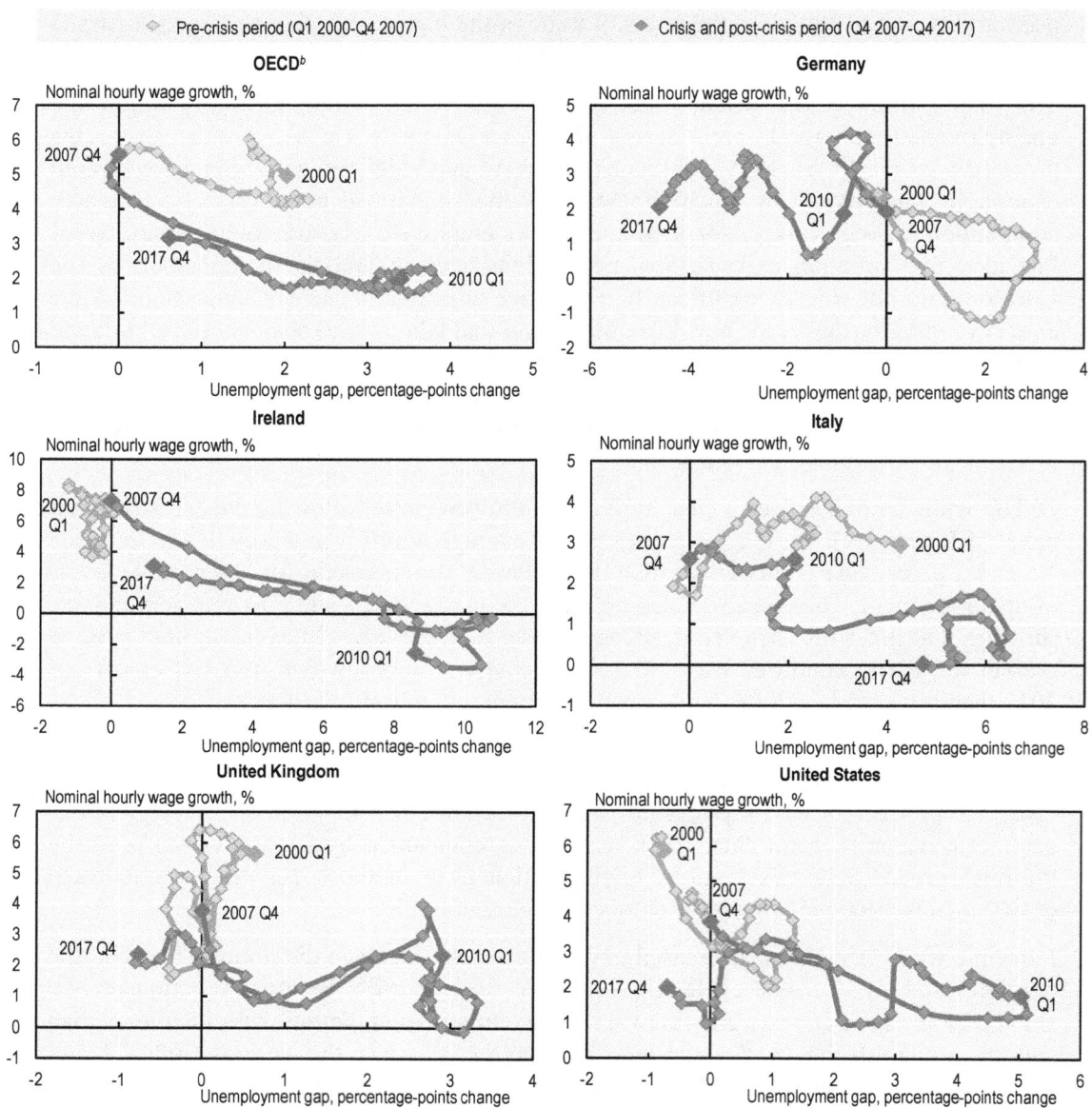

Note: For ease of interpretation series have been trended using a Hodrick-Prescott filter.

a) Nominal wage growth: year-on-year percentage change in nominal hourly wage (defined as total wages divided by hours worked by employees); unemployment gap: percentage-points change in the unemployment rate since the start of the crisis in Q4 2007.

b) Unweighted average of 29 OECD countries (excluding Chile, Iceland, Korea, Mexico, New Zealand and Turkey).

Source: OECD calculations based on quarterly national accounts, and the *OECD Short-Term Labour Market Statistics Database*, http://dx.doi.org/10.1787/data-00727-en.

StatLink 🖵 http://dx.doi.org/10.1787/888933777661

Figure 1.5. The slowdown in wage growth was widely spread

Percentage-point difference in the average annual growth rate of nominal earnings of full-time wage and salary workers between 2000-07 and 2007-16[a]

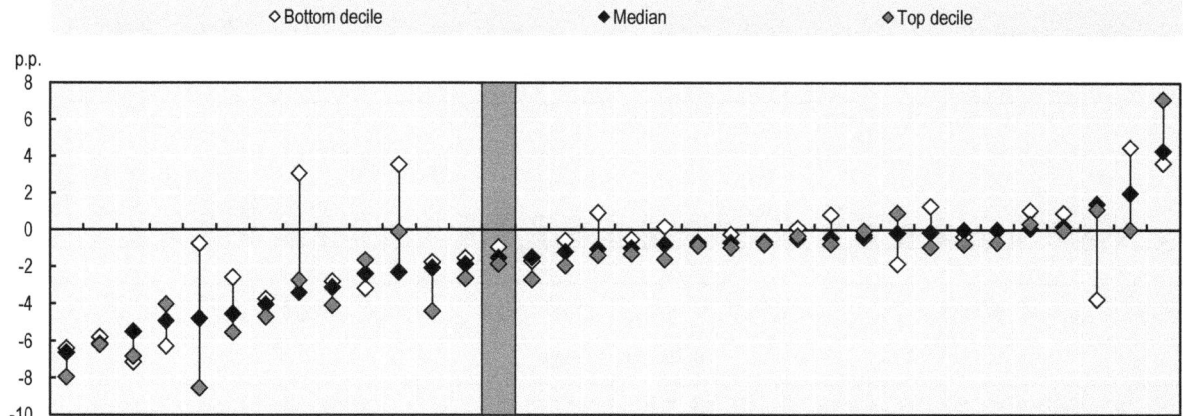

Note: Estimates based on gross earnings of full-time wage and salary workers. However, this definition may vary from one country to another. Further information on the national data sources and earnings concepts used in the calculations can be found at http://dx.doi.org/10.1787/data-00302-en. Results for Estonia, France, Latvia, Lithuania, Luxembourg, Portugal, Spain and Slovenia are based on the European Structure of Earnings Survey (SES).

a) 2000-07 refers to 2000-06 for Chile, Italy and Switzerland; 2001-06 for Poland; 2001-07 for the Czech Republic and Israel; 2002-06 for Estonia, France, Latvia, Lithuania, Luxembourg, Portugal, Spain and Slovenia; 2002-07 for Denmark and the Slovak Republic; 2004-07 for Austria and Greece; and 2005-07 for Mexico. 2007-16 refers to 2006-14 for Estonia, France, Latvia, Lithuania, Luxembourg, Poland, Portugal, Spain, Slovenia and Switzerland; 2006-15 for Chile; 2006-16 for Italy; 2007-13 for Sweden; and 2007-15 for Austria, Belgium, Denmark, Finland, Ireland, Israel, Japan and Norway.

b) Unweighted average of the 32 OECD countries shown (not including Iceland, the Netherlands and Turkey).

Source: OECD calculations based on the *OECD Earnings Distribution Database*, http://dx.doi.org/10.1787/data-00302-en.

StatLink ᠁᠍ᢖᩗ http://dx.doi.org/10.1787/888933777680

1.2.2. The low-inflation environment and the productivity slowdown have both driven wage growth down

In line with the shift of the Phillips curves, Figure 1.6 (Panel A) shows that the average nominal growth of hourly wages in the OECD experienced a significant decline, from 4.8% prior to the crisis to 2.1% in recent years. However, this decline only partially affected the living standards of workers, due to lower inflation, which decreased from 2.6% to 0.8% (Panel C). As a result, real wage growth decreased by 1 percentage point over this period, from 2.2% to 1.2% (Panel B).

Figure 1.6. Low inflation and the productivity slowdown have both driven wage growth down since the crisis

Average annualised percentage growth rate

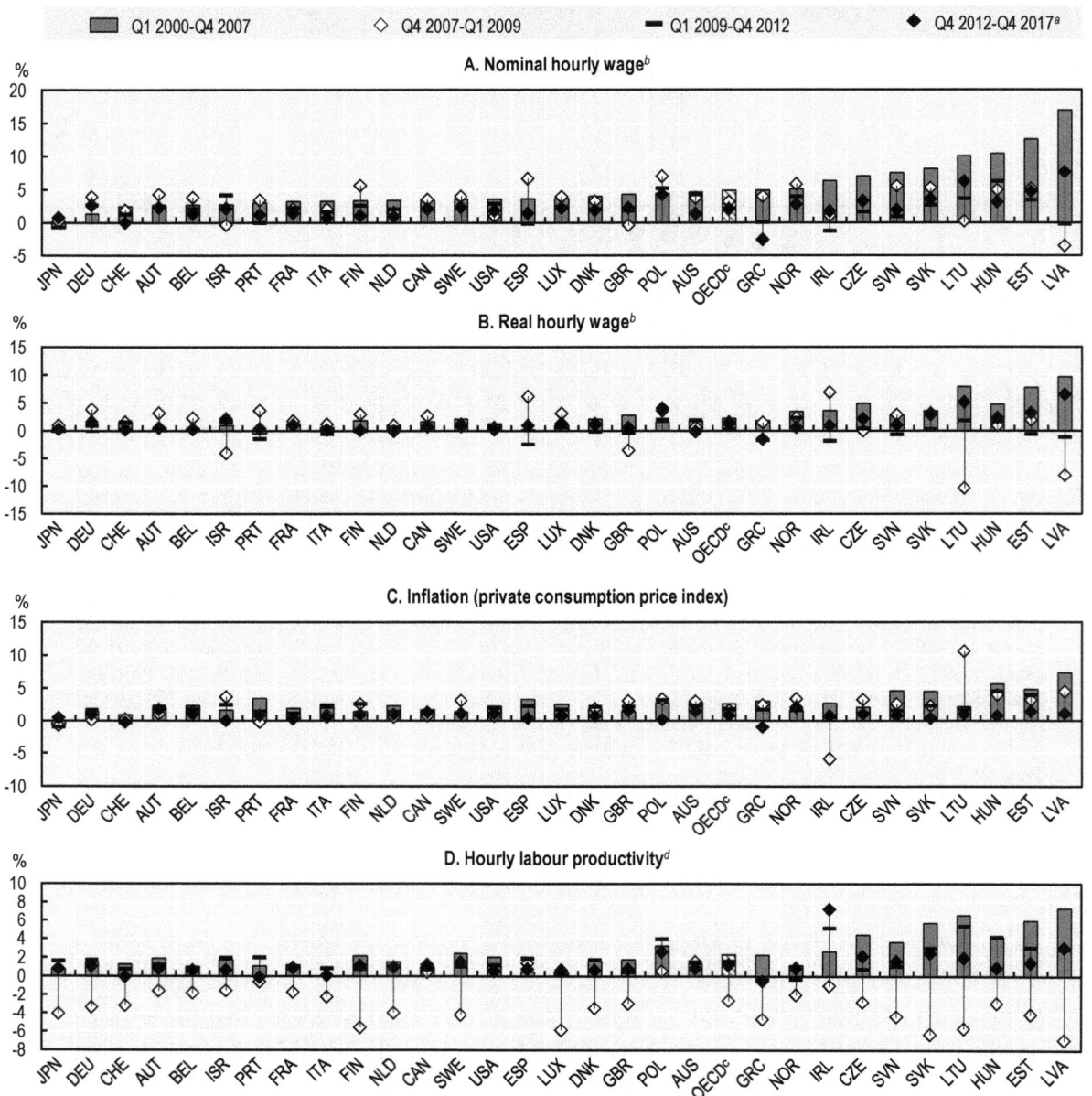

Note: Countries are ordered by ascending order of the average annualised growth rate in nominal hourly wages in Q1 2000-Q4 2007.

a) Q4 2012-Q4 2016 for Switzerland.

b) Total wages divided by total hours worked of employees (and deflated using the private consumption price index in Panel B).

c) OECD is the unweighted average of the 29 OECD countries shown (not including Chile, Iceland, Korea, Mexico, New Zealand and Turkey).

d) Hourly labour productivity refers to real gross domestic product (GDP) divided by total hours worked.

Source: OECD calculations based on quarterly national accounts.

StatLink ⬛🔗 http://dx.doi.org/10.1787/888933777699

Most of the OECD countries experienced a significant slowdown in wage growth at the depth of the crisis. Real wages even declined in some countries, mostly in the euro area, and especially in countries that were hit hard by the sovereign debt crisis, such as Portugal, Spain, Italy and Greece. The dramatic wage reductions in the Baltic States can be related to the high wage growth that occurred in these countries prior to the crisis and by soaring unemployment at the crisis trough. Outside the euro area, real wages declined in Israel and the United Kingdom, while real wage growth considerably slowed down in the United States, to reach 0.3%, on average, between the fourth quarter of 2007 and the first one of 2009.

While real wages rebounded in most countries after the crisis trough, at about 1.2%, on average, real wage growth remained surprisingly stagnant in the OECD area after the end of the recession despite the progressive reabsorption of labour market slack. In most countries, wage growth did not change much after 2010. Between 2009-12 and 2012-17, real wage growth decelerated in Australia, Norway, Switzerland, the Netherlands, the United States and France; and accelerated by less than 0.5 percentage points in Japan, Belgium, Sweden, Greece, Finland, Canada, Austria. More impressive, real wages decreased during the recovery not only in Greece, but also in the Netherlands and Australia.

The low-inflation environment and the productivity slowdown have both contributed to this deceleration of wage growth (IMF, 2017[6]; Shambaugh et al., 2017[9]). Inflation deceleration has lowered inflation expectations, thereby driving down growth of negotiated wages (see also Chapter 3). Similarly, hourly labour productivity growth has only partially recovered from the negative levels reached during the first phase of the crisis[9]: it went down from 2.3%, on average, prior to the crisis to 1.2% in the recent period (Figure 1.6, Panel D). In a context of stagnating workers' bargaining power and strong capital-labour substitution (see Chapters 2 and 3), this inevitably put a limit to the possibility of raising wages.

1.2.3. Low-pay jobs have played a role in sluggish wage growth

The recent literature suggests an additional explanation for the recent shift to the left of the wage-Phillips curve: labour market slack would be greater than what measured by headline unemployment because of greater labour underutilisation due to higher inactivity (Blanchflower and Posen, 2014[14]) and more involuntary part-time employment (IMF, 2017[6]; Smith, 2014[15]), in particular due to those working part-time for economic reasons (Altig and Higgins, 2014[16]). For example, Figure 1.7 shows an upsurge of involuntary part-time in many countries following the recession. Aggregate regressions seem to confirm an impact of the share of involuntary part-timers on the Phillips curve (IMF, 2017[6]), and the contribution of this effect is particularly large in countries where the unemployment rate is still above pre-crisis averages. More generally, this additional slack would be related to the stylised fact that, in the aftermath of the recent, long crisis, many jobseekers have been forced to accept jobs that they consider to be worse in terms of working conditions with respect to their expectations and the job they had before the crisis. These workers are still intensively searching for better jobs, thereby raising the number of applications per vacancy for these jobs and exerting downward pressure on wages.

Figure 1.7. The incidence of involuntary part-time employment increased following the crisis until the early recovery, but then started to decline

A. Involuntary part-time employment as a proportion a total dependent employment

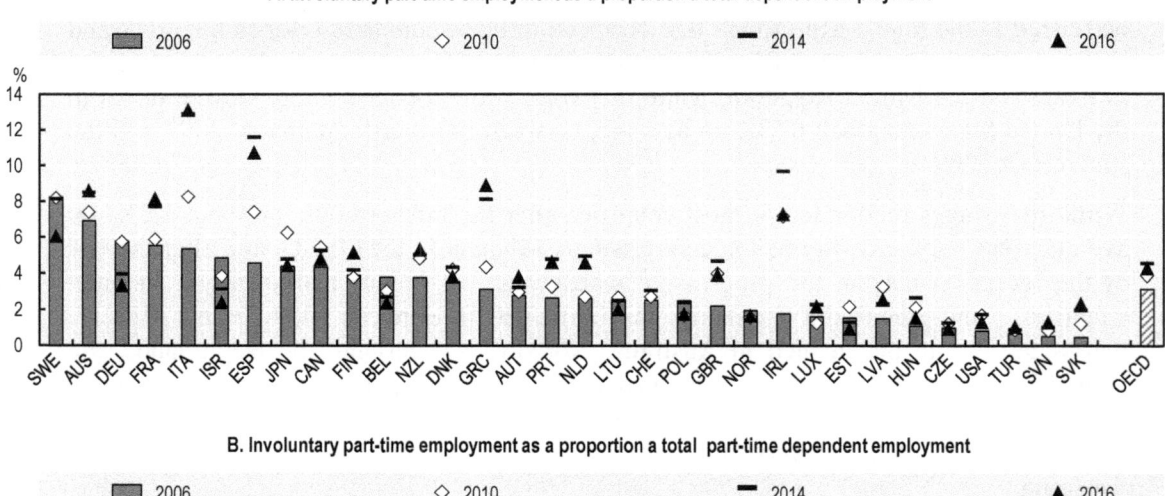

B. Involuntary part-time employment as a proportion a total part-time dependent employment

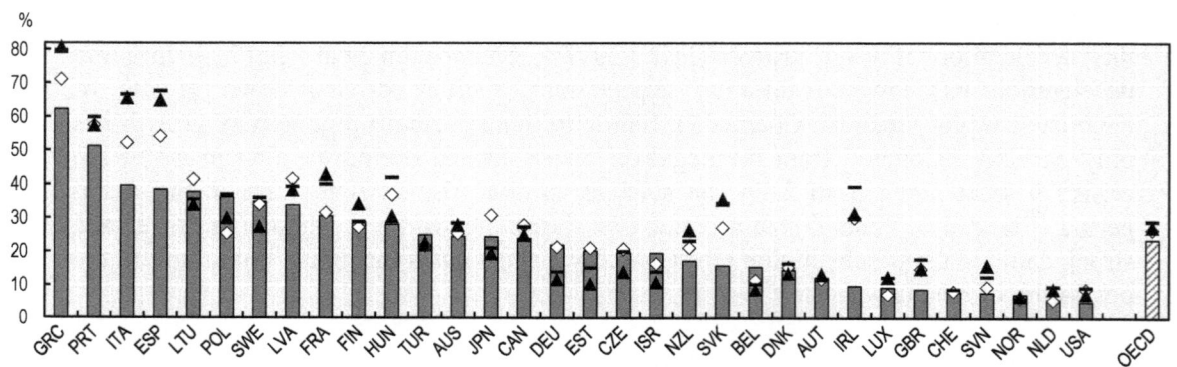

Note: Data refer to the share in total employment in Panel A or total part-time employment in Panel B for Canada, Czech Republic, Israel, Japan, Norway and the United States. Part-time employment is based on national definitions.

OECD is the unweighted average of the 29 OECD countries shown at each period (excluding Chile, Iceland, Korea, Mexico, Switzerland and the United Kingdom).

Source: OECD Employment Database. http://www.oecd.org/employment/emp/employmentdatabase-employment.htm.

StatLink ⬛🔗 http://dx.doi.org/10.1787/888933777718

This line of reasoning relies on conjecturing an aggregate phenomenon, by which workers who could find only low-pay jobs (e.g. those in involuntary part-time jobs), by searching for higher-pay jobs (e.g. full-time jobs), would drive pay on these jobs down due to labour supply in excess of labour demand, resulting in lower average wages. It is possible, however, that part of the slowdown in *average* wages is only driven by the dynamics of low-pay jobs and their specific wages. This might occur either because the wages associated with these jobs grow more slowly than those of other jobs (this effect is called *heterogeneity effect* hereafter), or simply because they are lower and the incidence of the corresponding jobs increases (hereafter called *standard composition effect*). As opposed to the aggregate story, this scenario involves no effect on remaining jobs. For example, if part-timers are less paid than full-timers, then the shift in employment composition towards part-time jobs would result in lower aggregate wage growth, even with no effect on within-group wage growth (standard composition effect). Similarly, a decline in the average growth of part-time wages would result in a slowdown in average wage growth, even in the absence of an effect on the average growth of full-time wages (heterogeneity effect). The latter effect may even result from an increase in the number of lower-pay jobs among part-time jobs (e.g. an increase in the share of involuntary part-time in total part-time). The sum of the composition and heterogeneity effects (hereafter called *broad composition effect*) can be obtained as the difference between the growth rates of the average hourly wage of all workers and of workers in the relatively higher-pay group of jobs – e.g. full-timers (OECD, 2018[1]).

Figure 1.8 shows significant broad composition effects of part-time employment on wage growth in a number of the euro area countries, i.e. the Netherlands, Greece, Germany, Belgium, Italy, Spain and Portugal in the period 2006-14.[10] For example, in Germany, the growth of average hourly real wages for all employees would have been 0.67 percentage point per year greater had it been the same as that of full-timers. The differential growth of full-time and part-time wages (heterogeneity effect) generally played a bigger role in these countries than the standard composition effect – see OECD (2018[1]). This highlights a significant worsening of the earnings of part-time jobs relative to that of full-time jobs. Spain and Italy were exceptions, however: most of the significant broad composition effect observed in these two countries was simply driven by the increasing share of part-time employment and the lower average pay of part-timers. Such standard composition effects were also at play in Iceland, Norway and Ireland, although the broad effects were mitigated by very weak (or even positive) heterogeneity effects – that is by a relatively dynamic growth of part-time wages.

The picture is similar when focusing on the early recovery period only (2010-14): Germany, Greece, Italy, the Netherlands, and Spain still exhibit significant broad composition effects, mainly because of low growth of part-time wages relative to full-time wages (with the exception of Italy), which explains part of the stagnation in overall wage growth observed during the early recovery years. Similarly, this type of effects significantly contributed to the wage growth slowdown during the crisis period (2006-10) in Belgium, Greece, the Netherlands and Portugal.[11] By contrast, there is little evidence of significant broad composition effects of part-time employment during the recovery phase of the previous business cycle (2002-06)[12], thereby highlighting the specific influence of these effects in the post-crisis sluggish wage growth (OECD, 2018[1]).

In turn, the contribution to the wage growth slowdown of the differential growth between full-time and part-time wages (i.e. the heterogeneity effect of part-time employment) appears to have been significantly associated with the growth of the share of involuntary part-time in part-time employment during the early recovery period (Figure 1.9). For example, in Austria, Belgium, Czech Republic, Estonia, Lithuania and Latvia a stable or declining involuntary part-time employment was coupled with an increase in the wages of their part-time jobs relative to full-time wages. By contrast, involuntary part-time employment grew significantly in many other countries, while part-time jobs experienced a relative decline in their wages. Rising involuntary part-time employment might therefore have played a role in the relative decline in part-time wages that drove overall wage growth down between the onset of the crisis and the early recovery.[13]

Figure 1.8. Broad composition effects of part-time employment have continuously driven wage growth down since the crisis

Annualised growth rate of overall and full-time real hourly earnings, in percentage

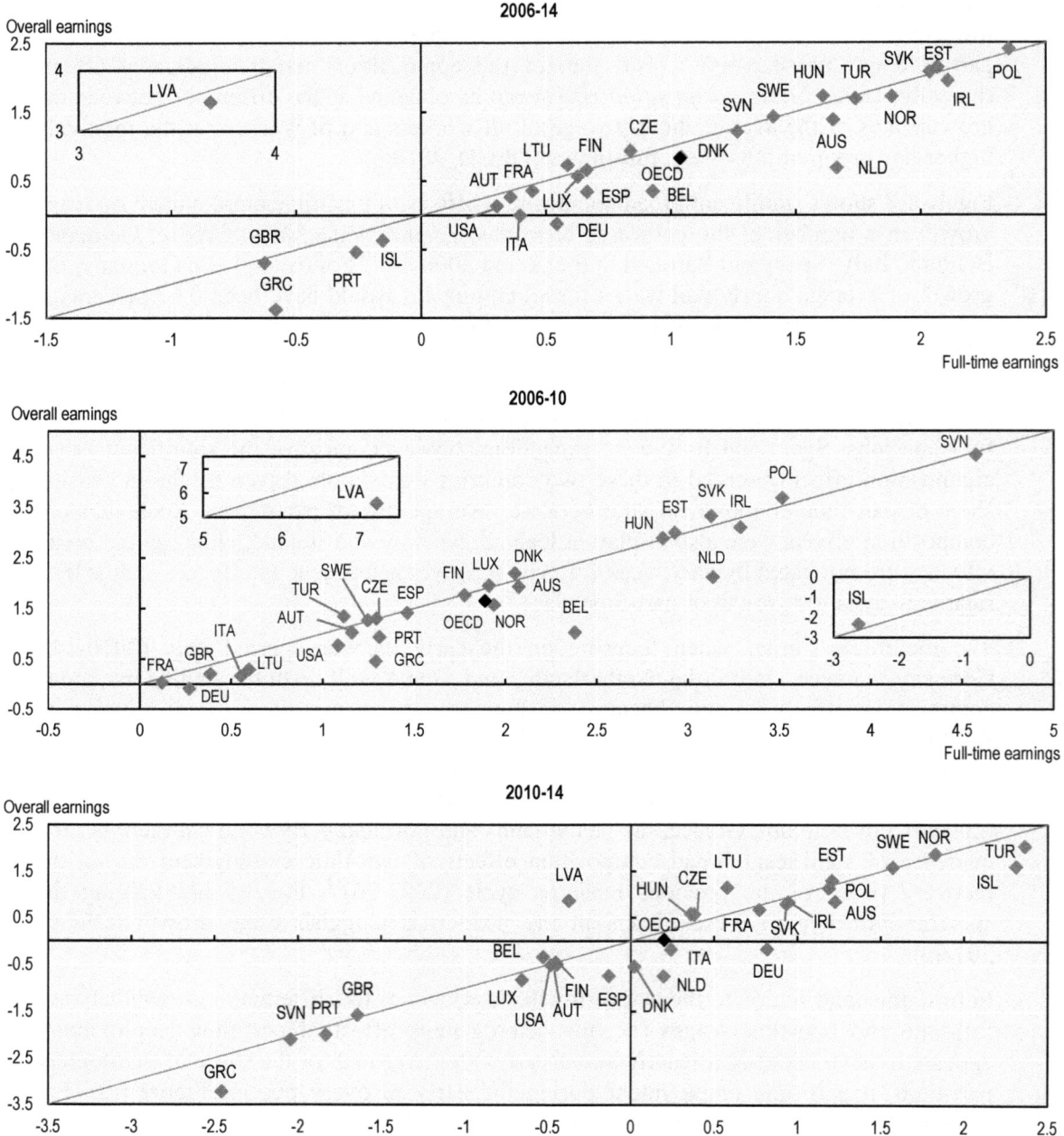

Note: Earnings are deflated using the private consumption price index.

European countries: Data refer to enterprises with at least ten employees in industry, construction and services (except public administration, defence and compulsory social security). OECD is the unweighted average of the 27 OECD countries shown (excluding Canada, Chile, Israel, Japan, Korea, Mexico, New Zealand and Switzerland).

Source: OECD calculations based on Household, Income and Labour Dynamics in Australia (HILDA) for Australia, Labour Force Survey for the United States (CPS - Annual Social Economic Supplement) and Structure of Earnings Survey (SES), Eurostat for other countries.

StatLink ⧉ http://dx.doi.org/10.1787/888933777737

Figure 1.9. The lower differential growth between full-time and part-time wages reflected the expansion of involuntary part-time employment in the early recovery

Annualised heterogeneity effect of part-time employment and annualised growth rate of the incidence of involuntary part-time in part-time employment, 2010-14

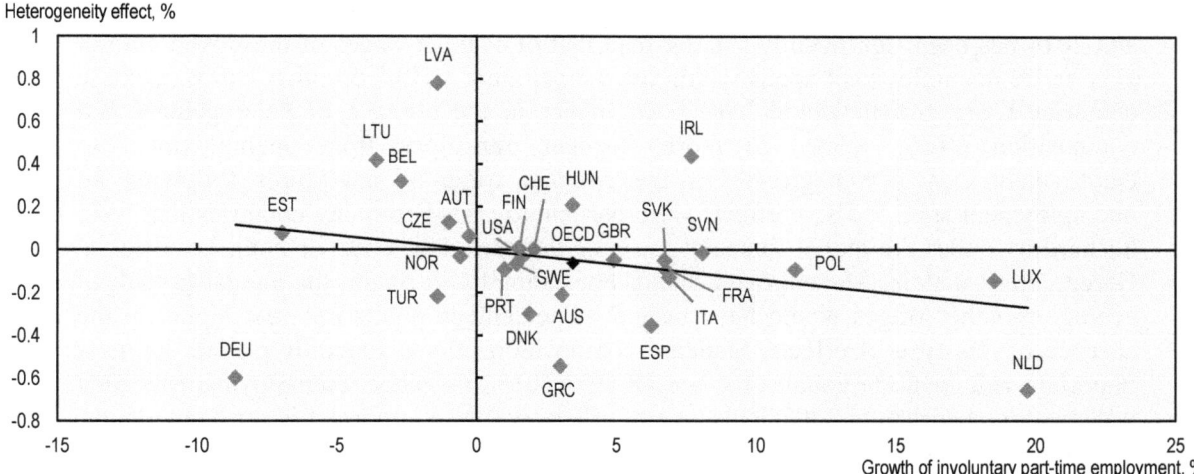

Note: The heterogeneity effect reflects the contribution of the differential growth between full-time and part-time wages to average wage growth. European countries: Data refer to enterprises with at least ten employees in industry, construction and services (except public administration, defence, compulsory social security). OECD is the unweighted average of the 27 OECD countries shown (excluding Canada, Chile, Iceland, Israel, Japan, Korea, Mexico and New Zealand).
Source: Heterogeneity effect: OECD calculations based on Household, Income and Labour Dynamics in Australia (HILDA) for Australia, Labour Force Survey for the United States (CPS - Annual Social Economic Supplement) and Structure of Earnings Survey (SES), Eurostat for other countries. Growth of involuntary part-time employment: *OECD Employment Database*, (www.oecd.org/employment/emp/employmentdatabase-employment.htm).

StatLink 🔗 http://dx.doi.org/10.1787/888933777756

In a symmetric way, it is possible to conjecture that the role of those heterogeneity effects that are associated with the different wage dynamics of part-time and full-time jobs has become less important in the most recent years, due to the recent decline in involuntary part-time employment in many countries (Figure 1.7).[14] One can also expect that this reduction of involuntary part-time might finally result in wage growth picking up. In fact, there have been recently some timid signs that wage growth has begun to recover (OECD, 2018[2]).[15]

The effects of the global financial crisis – or the subsequent sovereign debt crisis – were particularly protracted in many countries. As a result a greater number of workers starting a new job spell either just left unemployment or had recent unemployment experiences, likely originated from job loss coupled, in some cases, with subsequent spells of precarious jobs. To the extent that previous research has shown that workers who suffered an unemployment spell are likely to experiment a wage penalty at re-employment on average – see OECD (2010[17]) and Chapter 4 – or to obtain job offers more frequently in non-standard forms of employment (Katz and Krueger, 2017[18]), it can be expected that the larger the increase in the share of job-finders with recent unemployment experience, the lower the growth rate of average wages, even in the absence of a wage growth slowdown for other workers (giving rise to another standard composition effect). In addition, if in the recovery job-finders tend to accept more frequently lower paid jobs than what they used to do before the crisis, it is likely that the growth of hourly wages of those with recent unemployment experience would be lower, which could again result in lower aggregate wage growth even in the absence of an effect on the growth of average wages of other workers (heterogeneity effect).[16]

In a number of countries, the overall growth rate of real monthly wages between 2007 and 2014 has been significantly smaller than that of average wages of those who did not experience unemployment spells within the year (Figure 1.10).[17] In other words, in these countries wage growth would have been higher in the absence of heterogeneity and composition effects related to more frequent transitions from unemployment to employment and slower growth of the average wage of new hires following an unemployment spell.[18] These effects were particularly large in many countries that were hit hard by either the global financial crisis or the euro debt crisis or both, i.e. Estonia, Greece, Italy, Latvia, Slovenia and Spain. For example, in Spain, the annual growth of average monthly wages would have been 0.45 percentage points per year higher in the absence of this type of effects. Standard composition effects generally played the most important role in these countries – see OECD (2018[1]) – since unemployment in 2014 was much higher than in 2007. This type of effects was also important in the Netherlands. In Estonia and Greece, however, a significant part of the impact of this type of broad composition was driven by the relative decline in the wage of those who had a recent unemployment experience, highlighting the relative worsening of the working conditions accepted by job seekers after an unemployment spell compared to those of other workers. Finland and Iceland were also characterised by significant standard composition effects, but their negative impact on average wage growth was mitigated by a relative improvement of the working conditions of those recently unemployed.

Other types of composition effects than those presented here might also have played a role. Additional analysis was therefore carried out to investigate the impact of the changes in the composition of the workforce in terms of age, type of contract or educational attainment. The results of this analysis, however, suggest that all these additional dimensions played a minor role in the wage growth slowdown, on average,[19] suggesting that they are at best important only for specific countries.[20]

Overall, broad composition effects appear to play a significant role. This is particularly the case in countries where unemployment rates are still significantly above pre-crisis levels. These are the countries where the additional slack effect was found more important in previous research (IMF, 2017[6]). The evidence presented in this chapter suggests that the additional slack effect should not – or at least not completely – be interpreted as an aggregate effect impacting all wages in the same way. The fact that low-pay jobs have been characterised, in recent years, by increasing incidence and/or lower wage growth mechanically results in lower average wage growth.

1.3. Concluding remarks

Employment rates have reached historically high levels in most OECD countries, and the average unemployment rate is back to pre-crisis level. Yet, the impact of the global financial crisis is still quite visible when one zooms in job quality and inclusiveness. Moreover, wage growth remains significantly subdued compared with pre-crisis trends and for comparable levels of unemployment; that is to say, the so-called Phillips curve has shifted during the recession and subsequent recovery.

Figure 1.10. Broad composition effects of unemployment experience have driven wage growth down since the crisis

Annualised growth rate of overall real monthly wages and real monthly wages of those without unemployment spells within the year, 2007-14[a], in percentage

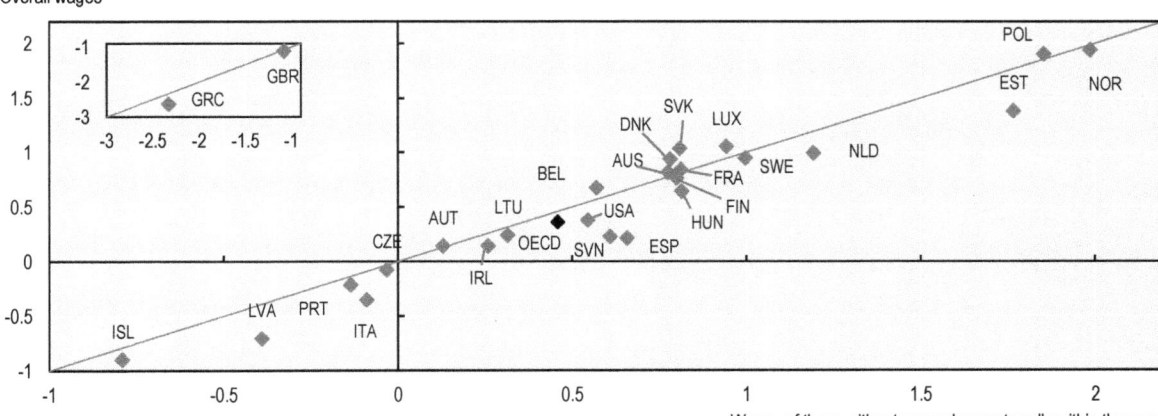

Note: Wages are deflated using the private consumption price index.
a) 2007-13 for the United Kingdom and Ireland, 2008-15 for Australia and the United States. OECD is the unweighted average of the 25 OECD countries shown (excluding Canada, Chile, Germany, Israel, Japan, Korea, Mexico, New Zealand, Switzerland and Turkey).
Source: OECD calculations based on national accounts combined with the European Union Statistics on Income and Living Conditions (EU-SILC) for European countries, Household, Income and Labour Dynamics in Australia (HILDA) for Australia, Labour Force Survey for the United States (CPS - Annual Social Economic Supplement).

StatLink ⬛ http://dx.doi.org/10.1787/888933777775

While declining productivity growth as well as lower inflation expectations remain among the primary explanations for the shift in the Phillips curve, this chapter has singled out low-pay jobs as an important channel accounting for the wage growth deceleration. In particular, earnings of part-time workers have worsened relative to those of full-time workers, largely reflected in the rise of involuntary part-time employment in a number of countries. Moreover, comparatively poor working conditions among those who have regained employment after a joblessness spell, combined with still high unemployment in some countries, pushed up the number of lower-paid workers, thereby lowering average wage growth. This pattern is probably linked to the fact that, as a result of the protracted economic crisis, many workers were forced to accept low-pay jobs.

The overall wage growth deceleration therefore hides significant heterogeneity between workers, with a greater impact on vulnerable individuals who are more prone to experience spells of unemployment and/or precarious jobs. In fact, while wages of top 1% income earners have never been so high (Schwellnus, Kappeler and Pionnier, 2017[19]), the share of households at the bottom of the distribution of disposable income is steadily on the rise.[21] Wageless growth exacerbates existing inequalities in the labour market, making the need for a more inclusive approach to labour policy – as recommended in the new OECD Jobs Strategy (OECD, 2018[4]) – even more relevant. In this regard, skills policies have a major role to play to ensure that no one is left behind in the context of rapidly evolving skill needs. Indeed, many workers lack basic information-processing skills that are in high demand in all OECD labour markets, which prevents them from accessing better paid jobs (OECD, 2017[20]). A greater policy effort is therefore required to ensure that every worker is provided with opportunities to develop, maintain and upgrade his/her skills at all ages, thereby reducing the risk of becoming trapped in low-quality jobs and joblessness, as well as enhancing the ability to adapt to the rapidly changing demand for skills in existing and new jobs.

Notes

[1] See OECD (2018[1]) for a table covering all indicators presented in this section.

[2] Consistent with the OECD Job Quality Framework, average earnings adjusted for inequality are obtained as a generalised mean of individual earnings with coefficient -3 – formally this can be written as $W_{GM} = [(y_1^{-3} + y_2^{-3} + \cdots + y_N^{-3})/N]^{-3}$, where W_{GM} stands for average earnings adjusted for inequality, y_i for income of individual i and N for employment headcount; see OECD (2014[21]) for more details.

[3] For example, during recession years, bad quality jobs are likely to have been destroyed more rapidly, while they might have been more intensively created in the first stage of the recovery. Moreover, work intensity for the same job is likely to vary over the business cycle, with effects on job strain and health – see e.g. Bassanini and Caroli (2015[22]).

[4] See OECD (2017[3]) for a discussion of indicators of labour market inclusiveness.

[5] The gender gap in labour income is computed here as the difference between average annual earnings of men and women as a percentage of those of men. Average earnings are computed by considering the whole working age population, independently of whether effectively working or not during the year. A person with no labour income, therefore, contributes to the denominator of average earnings but not to the numerator (see also Chapter 6).

[6] Defined here as older workers, mothers with young children, youth (excluding those in education and not in employment), immigrants and people with disabilities – see OECD (2017[3]) for more details.

[7] In the long run, wage growth tends to follow labour productivity growth in the absence of changes in inflation expectations, capital intensity or workers' bargaining power (see Chapters 2 and 3). Underemployed workers might be still intensively searching for jobs, thereby raising the number of applications per vacancy and exerting downward pressure on wages.

[8] The unemployment gap is preferred here to the unemployment rate because it allows controlling for cross-country differences in the structural rate of unemployment.

[9] Only a few countries did not experience a fall in hourly labour productivity levels just after the crisis: Australia, Canada, Poland, Spain and the United States.

[10] European Structure of Earnings Survey (SES) data are available only until 2014, which does not allow investigating the role of broad composition effects beyond 2014.

[11] The same is true for Latvia, although the effects in the longer run (2006-14) were mitigated by a strong relative increase of part-time wages relative to full-time wages in 2010-14.

[12] This analysis is undertaken on a restricted set of countries, due to limited data availability.

[13] Although Figure 1.9 focuses on the 2010-14 period only, the same pattern can be observed for the 2006-10 period. However, a few countries are far from the correlation line, making the graph more difficult to read. The graph is therefore not shown here, but is available on request.

[14] A number of countries, such as Germany and Ireland, are off the correlation line in Figure 1.9, which highlights the role played by the specific institutional contexts in the differential growth of full-time and part-time wages.

[15] This is especially the case in Canada, the Czech Republic, Germany, Hungary, Poland and the United States. For the OECD as a whole, real wages are projected to increase by 1% per year on average in 2018 and 2019 (OECD, 2018[2]). Yet, this is still below pre-crisis trends for comparable levels of unemployment.

[16] Job-seekers may be particularly keen to accept lower wages (and worse working conditions) at re-employment when they are not entitled to unemployment benefits or when they are approaching maximum potential duration – e.g. Nekoei and Weber (2017[23]) and references cited therein. The negative trend in unemployment benefit coverage in the recovery years (see Chapter 5), by resulting in lower choosiness of jobseekers, could therefore be one factor behind the increase in lower-paying jobs. To avoid that workers made redundant are exposed to heightened risk of long-term unemployment, early interventions in the unemployment spells, with appropriate counselling and retraining services, are key. These issues are examined in Chapter 4.

[17] Overall wage growth rates in Figure 1.8 and Figure 1.10 can hardly be compared, due to differences in the data sampling methodology (SES data refer to firms with more than ten employees only), the definition of wages (hourly earnings versus monthly wages) and the reference period.

[18] Statistics are constructed from EU SILC, CPS and HILDA microdata. Given that the earnings information available in EU SILC refers to one full calendar year, it is not possible to compute directly the wage growth of those with an experience of unemployment immediately before the job spell. Unemployment experience within the year is therefore used as a proxy. The overall average of monthly wages is trivially equal to the weighted average of monthly wages of those without unemployment spells and of those with some unemployment experience.

[19] Results are available from the OECD Secretariat upon request. IMF (2017[6]) reaches a similar conclusion as regards industry compositional effects. Further analysis will be carried out in the next editions of the Employment Outlook.

[20] For example, Daly, Hobijn and Pyle (2016[24]) argue that increased retirement of high-wage baby-boomers played a significant role in reducing aggregate wage growth in the United States in recent years.

[21] See for example Figure 1.3 in Section 1.1 above.

References

Altig, D. and P. Higgins (2014), *The Wrong Question?*, Federal Reserve Bank of Atlanta, Macroblog, http://macroblog.typepad.com/macroblog/2014/06/the-wrong-question.html. [16]

Bassanini, A. and E. Caroli (2015), "Is Work Bad for Health? The Role of Constraint versus Choice", *Annals of Economics and Statistics* 119/120, pp. 13-37, http://dx.doi.org/10.15609/annaeconstat2009.119-120.13. [22]

Bishop, J. and N. Cassidy (2017), "Insights into Low Wage Growth in Australia", *RBA Bulletin* March, pp. 13-20, https://www.rba.gov.au/publications/bulletin/2017/mar/pdf/bu-0317-2-insights-into-low-wage-growth-in-australia.pdf. [11]

Blanchflower, D. and A. Posen (2014), "Wages and Labor Market Slack: Making the Dual Mandate Operational", *Working Paper Series*, No. 14-6, Peterson Institute for International Economics, https://ideas.repec.org/p/iie/wpaper/wp14-6.html. [14]

Bulligan, G. and E. Viviano (2017), "Has the wage Phillips curve changed in the euro area?", *IZA Journal of Labor Policy*, http://dx.doi.org/10.1186/s40173-017-0087-z. [7]

Connolly, G. (2016), "The Effects of Excess Labour Supply and Excess Labour Demand on Australian Wages", Paper presented to the 45th Australian Conference of Economists, Flinders University of South Australia, Adelaide, http://esacentral.org.au/images/ConnollyG.pdf. [12]

Daly, M., B. Hobijn and B. Pyle (2016), "What's Up with Wage Growth?", *FRBSF Economic Letter*, No. 2016-07, Federal Reserve Bank of San Francisco, San Francisco, CA, https://www.frbsf.org/economic-research/files/el2016-07.pdf (accessed on 30 March 2018). [24]

ECB (2016), "Recent wage trends in the euro area", *ECB Economic Bulletin* 3, pp. 21-23, https://www.ecb.europa.eu/pub/pdf/ecbu/eb201603.en.pdf. [8]

Hong, G. et al. (2018), "More Slack than Meets the Eye? Recent Wage Dynamics in Advanced Economies", *IMF Working Paper*, No. 18/50, IMF, Washington, D.C., https://www.imf.org/~/media/Files/Publications/WP/2018/wp1850.ashx. [10]

IMF (2017), "Recent Wage Dynamics in Advanced Economies: Drivers and Implications", in *World Economic Outlook*, International Monetary Fund, Washington, D.C., https://www.imf.org/en/Publications/WEO/Issues/2017/09/19/world-economic-outlook-october-2017. [6]

Jacobs, D. and A. Rush (2015), "Why is wage growth so low?", *RBA Bulletin*, pp. 9-18, https://www.rba.gov.au/publications/bulletin/2015/jun/pdf/bu-0615.pdf#page=11. [13]

Katz, L. and A. Krueger (2017), "The Role of Unemployment in the Rise in Alternative Work Arrangements", *American Economic Review, Papers and Proceedings*, Vol. 107/5, pp. 388-392, http://dx.doi.org/10.1257/aer.p20171092. [18]

Nekoei, A. and A. Weber (2017), "Does extending unemployment benefits improve job quality?", *American Economic Review*, Vol. 107/2, pp. 527-561, http://dx.doi.org/10.1257/aer.20150528. [23]

OECD (2018), *Good Jobs for All in a Changing World of Work: The OECD Jobs Strategy*, OECD Publishing, Paris, http://www.oecd.org/mcm/documents/C-MIN-2018-7-EN.pdf. [4]

OECD (2018), *OECD Economic Outlook, Volume 2018 Issue 1*, OECD Publishing, Paris, http://dx.doi.org/10.1787/eco_outlook-v2018-1-en. [2]

OECD (2018), "Supplementary material for Chapter 1", in *OECD Employment Outlook 2018*, OECD Publishing, Paris, http://dx.doi.org/10.1787/empl_outlook-2018-12-en. [1]

OECD (2017), *Getting Skills Right: Skills for Jobs Indicators*, OECD Publishing, Paris, http://dx.doi.org/10.1787/9789264277878-en. [20]

OECD (2017), *OECD Employment Outlook 2017*, OECD Publishing, Paris, http://dx.doi.org/10.1787/empl_outlook-2017-en. [3]

OECD (2016), *OECD Employment Outlook 2016*, OECD Publishing, Paris, http://dx.doi.org/10.1787/empl_outlook-2016-en. [5]

OECD (2014), *OECD Employment Outlook 2014*, OECD Publishing, Paris, http://dx.doi.org/10.1787/empl_outlook-2014-en. [21]

OECD (2010), *OECD Employment Outlook 2010: Moving beyond the Jobs Crisis*, OECD Publishing, Paris, http://dx.doi.org/10.1787/empl_outlook-2010-en. [17]

Schwellnus, C., A. Kappeler and P. Pionnier (2017), "Decoupling of wages from productivity: Macro-level facts", *OECD Economics Department Working Papers*, No. 1373, OECD Publishing, Paris, http://dx.doi.org/10.1787/d4764493-en. [19]

Shambaugh, J. et al. (2017), "Thirteen facts about wage growth", *The Hamilton Project - Economic Facts*, September 2017, The Brookings Institution, Washington, D.C., http://www.hamiltonproject.org/assets/files/thirteen_facts_wage_growth.pdf. [9]

Smith, C. (2014), "The Effect of Labor Slack on Wages : Evidence from State-Level Relationships", *FEDS Notes*, No. 2014-06-02, Board of Governors of the Federal Reserve System, Washington, D.C., https://www.federalreserve.gov/econresdata/notes/feds-notes/2014/effect-of-labor-slack-on-wages-evidence-from-state-level-relationships-20140602.html. [15]

Supplementary material for Chapter 1

Supplementary material for Chapter 1 is available online only in English at the following DOI: http://dx.doi.org/10.1787/empl_outlook-2018-12-en.

Chapter 2. Labour share developments over the past two decades: The role of technological progress, globalisation and "winner-takes-most" dynamics

Over the past two decades, real median wage growth in many OECD countries has decoupled from labour productivity growth, partly reflecting declines in labour income shares. This chapter analyses the drivers of aggregate labour share developments using a combination of industry- and firm-level data. Technological change in the investment goods-producing sector and greater global value chain participation have compressed labour shares, but the effect of technological change has been significantly less pronounced for high-skilled workers. Countries with falling labour shares have witnessed both a decline at the technological frontier and reallocation of market shares toward "superstar" firms with low labour shares ("winner-takes-most" dynamics). The decline at the technological frontier mainly reflects the entry of capital-intensive firms with low labour shares into the frontier rather than a decline of labour shares in incumbent frontier firms, suggesting that thus far this process is mainly explained by technological dynamism rather than anti-competitive forces.

Key findings

For the OECD as a whole, real median wages have decoupled from productivity over the past two decades. If real median wages had perfectly tracked productivity growth over 1995-2014, they would have been 13% higher at the end of the period. Developments in the labour share – the share of national income accounted for by labour compensation in the form of wages, salaries and other benefits – explain around one-half of this decoupling, with the other half explained by rising wage inequality, evidenced by declines in the ratio of median to average wages. In the light of this, Chapter 2 analyses the drivers of recent labour share developments. The main findings are as follows:

- The labour share has declined significantly over the past two decades. The aggregate labour share in the 24 OECD countries covered in this chapter fell by around 3.5 percentage points between 1995 and 2013 (from around 71.5% to 68%).

- There have been large differences in labour share developments across countries. While the labour share fell around 8 percentage points in the United States, it remained broadly constant or increased in about half of the covered OECD countries, including France, Italy and the United Kingdom. These differences partly reflect cross-country differences in business cycle developments

- Consistent with the findings in OECD (2012[1]), technological change and globalisation can explain most of the contraction of the labour share. Technology-driven declines in relative investment prices and, to a lesser extent, the expansion of global value chains (in which different stages of production are spread across countries or regions) account for about two-thirds of the aggregate labour share decline in the OECD.

- The substitution of capital for labour in response to declines in relative investment prices is particularly pronounced in industries with a predominance of high routine tasks.

- High shares of high-skilled workers reduce the substitution of capital for labour even in industries with a higher level of routine tasks. High-skilled workers, especially those with high numeracy and problem-solving skills, may be more difficult to replace by machines or may be more easily re-deployed to non-routine tasks than low-skilled workers.

- Declines in relative investment prices affect aggregate labour shares partly by reducing labour shares within firms (labour costs as a proportion of a firm's total value added).

- Global value chain expansion does not affect labour shares within firms, suggesting that such expansion therefore reduces the labour share by reducing the proportion of firms with high labour shares.

- Countries with falling labour shares have witnessed both a decline at the technological frontier and a reallocation of market shares toward capital-intensive "superstar" firms with low labour shares ("winner-takes-most" dynamics).

- The labour share decline at the technological frontier mainly reflects the entry of capital-intensive firms with low labour shares into the frontier rather than a decline in incumbent frontier firms, suggesting that thus far "winner-takes-most" dynamics are mainly explained by technological dynamism rather than anti-competitive forces.

Looking ahead, ongoing advances in automation and artificial intelligence may not only continue to reduce the relative price of investment goods, but also make capital fundamentally more substitutable for labour. These technological advances may allow some firms to temporarily pull ahead. While product market regulation and competition policies will need to prevent emerging dominant players from engaging in anti-competitive practices, this chapter suggests that skills policies will be key to help workers make the most of ongoing technological advances.

Introduction

Real wage gains are the most direct mechanism through which productivity gains are transmitted to workers, but over the past two decades real median wage growth in most OECD countries has decoupled from labour productivity growth. This reflects declines in labour shares – the decoupling of average wages from productivity – and increases in wage inequality – the decoupling of median wages from average wages. In contrast to previous decades, productivity gains no longer appear to translate into broadly shared wage gains for all workers (Schwellnus, Kappeler and Pionnier, 2017[2]). Since wages are typically the main source of market income for low- and middle-income households, this decoupling also tends to increase inequality in market incomes (total pre-tax incomes excluding income from government sources). Since redistribution through taxes and benefits is constrained by efficiency considerations and has declined in many countries, the decoupling of real median wages from labour productivity is a key public policy issue.

This chapter focuses on the decoupling of real average wages from productivity by analysing labour share developments using a combination of aggregate and disaggregate data.[1] Aggregate data provide descriptive evidence on recent labour share developments, while disaggregate data at the industry and firm levels are used to analyse the role of technology and global value chain (GVC) expansion in aggregate labour share developments. The disaggregate analysis further provides insights into the mechanisms underlying aggregate labour share developments, including the roles of substitution of capital for labour (henceforth capital-labour substitution) and firm-level dynamics.

Apart from extending the sample to the post-crisis period, the main innovations of this chapter with respect to the recent analysis of labour share developments in the OECD Employment Outlook (OECD, 2012[1]) are as follows. First, this chapter focuses on the change in relative investment prices as a specific measure of technological change in the investment goods-producing sector rather than multi-factor productivity as an overall measure of technological change. Over the sample period, technological progress in the investment goods-producing sector is mainly reflected in the falling price of information and communication technology (ICT) goods which are likely to be highly substitutable for some types of labour. Second, the chapter analyses the different effects of this type of technological progress on workers in routine- and non-routine occupations as well as the role of skills in limiting capital-labour substitution. Third, it analyses the extent to which aggregate labour share developments are related to "winner-takes-most" dynamics – the best firms capturing an overwhelming share of the market – and provides suggestive evidence on whether such dynamics reflect technological dynamism or anti-competitive forces.

The remainder of the chapter is organised as follows. Section 2.1 describes the conceptual framework for breaking down the decoupling of median wages from productivity into contributions from labour share and wage inequality developments. It also provides descriptive evidence on labour share developments for the covered OECD countries. Section 2.2 uses a combination of industry- and firm-level data to analyse the effects of technological progress and the expansion of GVCs on labour shares, with a special emphasis on recent firm-level dynamics. Section 2.3 analyses the role of skills in promoting the sharing of productivity gains with workers.

2.1. The link between productivity and wages over the past two decades

Conceptually, macro-level decoupling between the growth rate of real compensation of the typical worker and labour productivity growth can be decomposed into the growth differential between real average compensation and labour productivity and the growth differential between median and average compensation. In this chapter, compensation and value added are deflated by the same value added price index so that decoupling of real average compensation from labour productivity reflects declines in labour shares (Box 2.1).[2] Decoupling of real median compensation from real average compensation reflects declines in the ratio of median to average wages, a partial measure of wage inequality.

For the covered OECD countries as a whole, there has been significant decoupling of real median wages from productivity over the past two decades as real median wages have grown at a lower average rate than labour productivity (Figure 2.1). Based on the total economy measure, median compensation would have been around 13% higher than observed in 2013 if it had perfectly tracked labour productivity since 1995. Based on the measure excluding the primary, housing and the non-market sectors, decoupling implies a 12% loss in compensation for the median worker over the period 1995-2013.

The decoupling of real median wages from labour productivity reflects both declines in labour shares and increases in wage inequality. In line with previous studies on decoupling (Pessoa and van Reenen, 2013[3]; Bivens and Mishel, 2015[4]; Sharpe and Uguccioni, 2017[5]) this chapter uses as a starting point compensation and value added in the total economy (Figure 2.1, Panel A). This measure of decoupling suggests similar contributions of declines in labour shares and increases in wage inequality to decoupling. However, the total economy includes sectors for which labour shares are largely determined by fluctuations in commodity and asset prices, such as the primary and housing sectors, or for which labour shares are driven by imputation choices, such as the non-market sector. Labour share fluctuations in these sectors may have different distributional implications from those in the production sector. Once the primary, housing and the non-market sectors – which on average account on for around 30% of value added in OECD countries – are excluded from the analysis, the contribution of the labour share to decoupling becomes smaller (Figure 2.1, Panel B).

Box 2.1. The link between decoupling of median wages from productivity and labour shares

Using the notation $\Delta\% X$ to denote the per cent growth rate of X, decoupling of real median wages from labour productivity in this chapter is defined as follows:

$$Decoupling \equiv \Delta\% \left(\frac{Y/P^Y}{L}\right) - \Delta\% \left(\frac{W^{med}}{P^Y}\right) \qquad (1)$$

where Y denotes nominal value added, P^Y denotes the value added price, L denotes number of workers and W^{med} denotes the nominal median hourly wage. The first term on the right-hand-side is labour productivity growth and the second term is real median wage growth in terms of the value added price. By adding and subtracting real average wage growth $\Delta\% \left(\frac{W^{avg}}{P^Y}\right)$ equation (1) can be re-written as follows:

$$Decoupling \equiv \left[\Delta\% \left(\frac{Y/P^Y}{L}\right) - \Delta\% \left(\frac{W^{avg}}{P^Y}\right)\right] + \left[\Delta\% \left(\frac{W^{avg}}{P^Y}\right) - \Delta\% \left(\frac{W^{med}}{P^Y}\right)\right] \qquad (2)$$

where the first term in square brackets denotes the growth differential between labour productivity and the real average wage and the second term in square brackets denotes the growth differential between the real average and median wage.

The growth differential between labour productivity and the real average wage can be approximated as $-\Delta\% \left(\frac{W^{avg} \cdot L}{Y}\right)$, i.e. the per cent decline in the labour share. The growth differential between the real average and median wage can be re-written as $\Delta\% \left(\frac{W^{avg}}{W^{med}}\right)$, i.e. the per cent increase in the ratio of the average to the median wage. A high ratio of the average to the median wage typically reflects high compensation at the top of the wage distribution, so that it can be interpreted as a partial measure of wage inequality.

Source: The data underlying the above decomposition at the country level are described in Schwellnus, Kappeler and Pionnier (2017[2]), "Decoupling of wages from productivity: Macro-level facts", http://dx.doi.org/10.1787/18151973.

The aggregate labour share in the countries covered by the analysis declined by around 3.5 percentage points over the past two decades, which coincided with falls in relative investment prices and the expansion of GVCs (Figure 2.2). While the coincidence of these trends does not imply causation, it is consistent with results from previous studies suggesting that relative investment price declines may have triggered capital-labour substitution (Karabarbounis and Neiman, 2014[6]; IMF, 2017[7]) while increased GVC participation may have led to the offshoring of the most labour-intensive tasks (Elsby, Hobijn and Sahin, 2013[8]; IMF, 2017[7]) If capital and labour are highly substitutable, the resulting increase in capital intensity may reduce the labour share.

Figure 2.1. Real median wages have decoupled from labour productivity

Indices, 1995 = 100

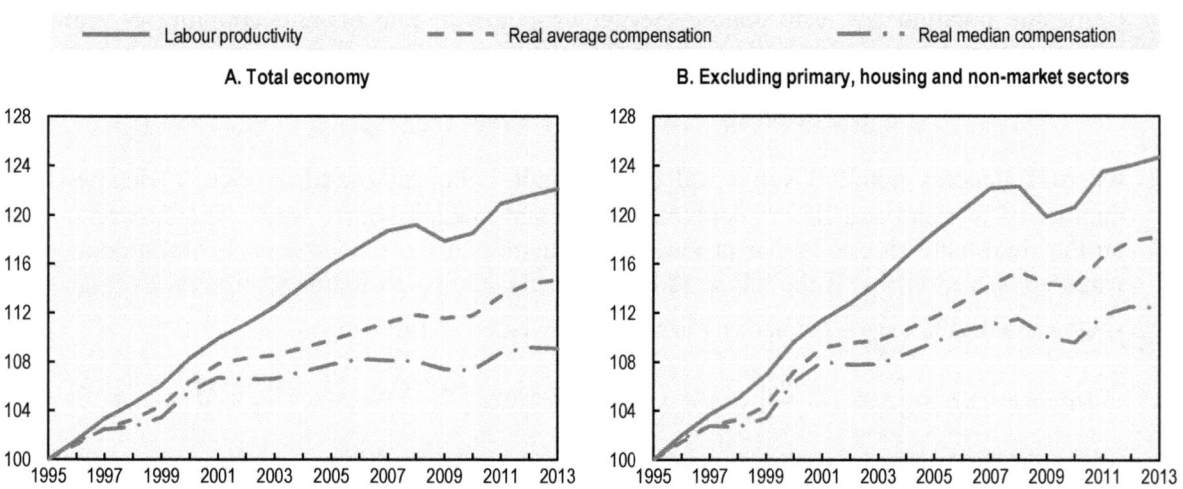

Note: Gross domestic product (GDP) weighted average of 24 countries (two-year moving averages ending in the indicated years). 1995-2013 for Finland, Germany, Japan, Korea and the United States; 1995-2012 for France, Italy and Sweden; 1996-2013 for Austria, Belgium and the United Kingdom; 1996-2012 for Australia and Spain; 1997-2013 for the Czech Republic, Denmark and Hungary; 1997-2012 for Poland; 1996-2010 for the Netherlands; 1998-2013 for Norway; 1998-2012 for Canada and New Zealand; 1999-2013 for Ireland; 2002-11 for Israel; 2003-13 for the Slovak Republic. In Panel A, all series are deflated by the total economy value added price index. In Panel B, all series are deflated by the value added price index excluding the primary, housing and non-market industries. The industries excluded in Panel B are the following (International Standard Industry Classification – ISIC – rev. 4 classification): (1) Agriculture, Forestry and Fishing (A), (2) Mining and quarrying (B), (3) Real estate activities (L), (4) Public administration and defence, compulsory social security (O), (5) Education (P), (6) Human health and social work activities (Q), (7) Activities of households as employers (T), and (8) Activities of extraterritorial organisations and bodies (U).
Source: *OECD National Accounts Database*, http://dx.doi.org/10.1787/data-00727-en, *OECD Earnings Distribution Database*, http://dx.doi.org/10.1787/data-00302-en.

StatLink ᵐˢ🔗 http://dx.doi.org/10.1787/888933777794

While the aggregate OECD labour share has declined over the past two decades, there have been conflicting cross-country developments (Figure 2.3). OECD countries with significant declines in labour shares include large countries such as Japan and the United States. For instance, in the United States labour shares declined by around 8 percentage points over the sample period, explaining around 0.6 percentage points of the 1.3 percentage annual decoupling of real median wages from productivity. In a number of other OECD countries, labour shares have remained broadly constant or have increased. These include a number of large countries, such as France, Italy and the United Kingdom.

Figure 2.2. Falls in labour shares coincided with falls in relative investment prices and the expansion of global value chains

Percentage point changes, excluding the primary, coke and refined petroleum, housing and non-market industries, 1995 = 0

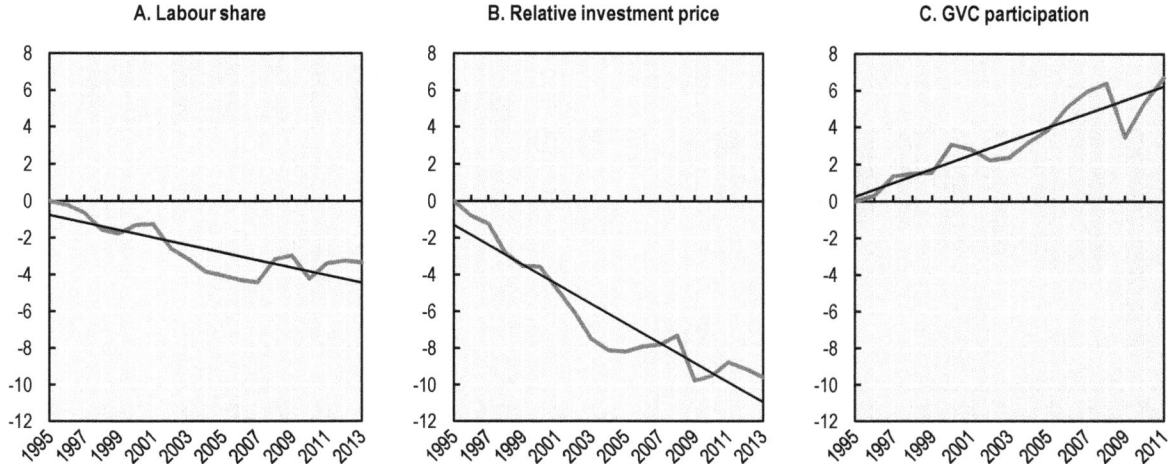

Note: Gross domestic product (GDP) weighted average of 24 countries (Australia, Austria, Belgium, Canada, the Czech Republic, Denmark, Finland, France, Germany, Hungary, Ireland, Israel, Italy, Japan, Korea, the Netherlands, New Zealand, Norway, Poland, the Slovak Republic, Spain, Sweden, the United Kingdom and the United States). GVC: global value chain.
Source: Schwellnus et al. (forthcoming[9]), "Labour share developments over the past two decades: The role of technological progress, globalisation and "winner-take-most" dynamics".

StatLink ᵐˢᵖ http://dx.doi.org/10.1787/888933777813

To some extent, large cross-country differences in labour share developments may be explained by differences in business cycle developments as well as policies and institutions. Background analysis conducted for this chapter suggests that an increase in the output gap of 1% – an increase in output relative to potential – reduces the labour share by 0.5 percentage points (Schwellnus et al., forthcoming[9]). Reforms in a number of areas of product and labour market policies as well as changes in collective-bargaining institutions also emerge as significant determinants of labour share developments (Pak and Schwellnus, forthcoming[10]) – see also Chapter 3. But large cross-country differences in labour share developments may also reflect differences in the nature and the pace of technological progress and the integration into GVCs, which may give rise to different firm dynamics across countries.

2.2. Technological progress, globalisation and the emergence of "winner-takes-most" dynamics

2.2.1. Technological progress and globalisation

Capital-augmenting technological change or technology-driven declines in relative investment prices may reduce the labour share by raising capital intensity. Even if factor prices are determined competitively, the labour share declines with capital intensity if the elasticity of substitution between capital and labour is above unity.[3]

Figure 2.3. Large cross-country heterogeneity in labour share developments

Percentage point changes over the 1995-2013 period, excluding the primary, housing and non-market industries

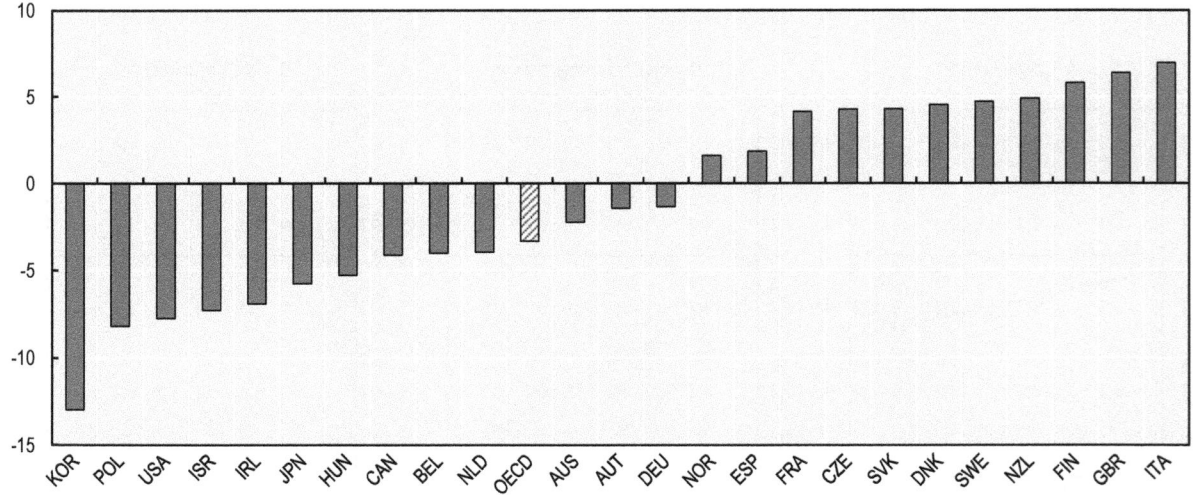

Note: Two-year averages ending in indicated years. The OECD average is the GDP-weighted average of changes in labour shares over the 24 countries included in the figure. 1996-2013 for Austria, Belgium, the Czech Republic, Hungary, Israel, the Netherlands, Poland, the Slovak Republic, Spain and the United Kingdom; 1996-2012 for New Zealand; 1998-2012 for Canada; 1999-2013 for Ireland.
Source: *OECD National Accounts Database*, http://dx.doi.org/10.1787/data-00727-en.

StatLink ᴧᴦᴤᴘ http://dx.doi.org/10.1787/888933777832

Most estimates of the elasticity of substitution are based on within-country time series variation of factor shares and factor prices. These estimates generally imply an elasticity of substitution below one (Chirinko, 2008[11]). By contrast, Karabarbounis and Neiman (2014[6]) use cross-country and cross-industry variation in labour shares and relative investment prices to obtain an elasticity of substitution in the range of 1.2-1.5. According to their estimations, large declines in investment prices across a broad range of high-income and emerging economies explain around 50% of the global decline of the labour share.

Over time, capital may have become more easily substitutable for labour. On the one hand, new technology extends the range of existing tasks that can be carried out by machines, thereby displacing workers and reducing the labour share (Acemoglu and Restrepo, 2018[12]). On the other hand, new technology also creates new tasks that cannot be carried out by machines. As the nature of technological progress changes, the balance between labour displacement and task creation from new technologies may shift. Evidence for the United Kingdom and the United States, for instance, suggests that the elasticity of substitution between ICT capital and labour is significantly higher than for other capital goods and is well above one (Tevlin and Whelan, 2003[13]; Bakhshi, Oulton and Thompson, 2003[14]). In line with this finding, recent evidence on labour share developments for the United States suggests that technological progress has become more labour displacing over time, with particularly large labour-displacing effects in the 2000s (Autor and Salomons, 2018[15]).

Previous research suggests that capital-labour substitution in response to declines in investment prices is particularly pronounced for low-skilled workers. Krusell et al. (2000[16]) find that in the United States the elasticity of substitution between capital and low-skilled labour is around 1.7, well above the estimated elasticity between capital and high-skilled labour of 0.7. This is consistent with cross-country evidence in IMF (2017[7]) of particularly negative effects of declines in relative investment prices on labour shares in countries with high initial shares of routine jobs. Moreover, using cross-country cross-industry data, IMF (2017[7]) find that the elasticity of substitution between capital and labour increases with industries' routine task exposure and is above unity in about half of the industries covered by their analysis.

Globalisation in the form of increased trade integration may have similar effects on the labour share as it increases in capital intensity (Acemoglu and Autor, 2010[17]). For instance, offshoring of the most labour-intensive stages of production or increased import competition may lead to worker displacement and an increase in capital intensity. If the aggregate elasticity of substitution between capital and labour is above unity, this would reduce the labour share. The cross-country evidence in Harrison (2005[18]) and the cross-industry evidence for the United States in Elsby et al. (2013[8]) are consistent with this hypothesis. In a cross-country, cross-industry study IMF (2017[7]) find that increased participation in GVCs has reduced the labour share in low-income countries but that there is no effect in high-income countries.[4]

The analysis of the roles of technological progress and GVC expansion for labour share developments in this chapter is based on an industry-level approach (Box 2.2). From a conceptual standpoint, the fact that changes in aggregate labour shares overwhelmingly reflect developments within industries rather than cross-industry reallocation justifies focusing on industry-level labour shares to explain aggregate developments (Schwellnus et al., forthcoming[9]).[5] From an econometric standpoint, the industry-level approach has the advantage that country- and industry-specific trends can be controlled for through an appropriate fixed effects structure.

The empirical analysis suggests that declines in relative investment prices and increases in GVC participation reduce the labour share. Both in a model with country fixed effects that allows estimating the effect of the business cycle on the labour share and in a model with a more demanding country-period fixed effects structure, the estimated semi-elasticity of the labour share to the relative investment price is 0.19, which suggests that on average across industries a decline in relative investment prices of 10% (approximately the average decline observed in the OECD over 1995-2013, see Figure 2.2) reduces the labour share by approximately 1.8 percentage point. The estimated semi-elasticity of the labour share to GVC participation is around -0.1, which suggests that an increase of backward and forward linkages of 10 percentage points of value added reduces the labour share by 1 percentage point (the average increase observed in the OECD over 1995-2013 was around 6 percentage points of value added, see Figure 2.2).[6]

Box 2.2. Methodology underlying the industry-level analysis

The baseline empirical specification is motivated by the theoretical model in Schwellnus et al. (forthcoming[9]) linking the cost of capital, offshoring and the labour share. The model introduces capital into the two-factor model of offshoring in Grossman and Rossi-Hansberg (2008[19]) and explicitly models factor shares under the assumption of an elasticity of substitution between capital and routine labour above unity. The main predictions are as follows: i) a decline in the relative investment price reduces the labour share, with the reduction being larger in industries using a larger share of routine labour; and ii) a decline in the cost of offshoring has an ambiguous effect on the labour share.

The estimated baseline empirical specification is as follows:

$$\Delta LS_{ijt} = \beta_1 \Delta P_{ijt}^{Inv} + \beta_2 \Delta T_{ijt} + \beta_3 \left(RTI_{ijt}^0 \times \Delta P_{ijt}^{Inv} \right) + \beta_4 \left(RTI_{ijt}^0 \times \Delta T_{ijt} \right) + $$
$$ + \beta_4 X_{ijt} + \alpha_{it} + \alpha_{jt} + \varepsilon_{ijt} \tag{1}$$

where subscripts i, j and t denote, respectively, countries, industries and periods; ΔLS_{ijt} denotes the medium-term (5- or 6-year) change in the labour share; RTI_{ijt}^0 denotes initial routine task intensity; ΔP_{ijt}^{Inv} denotes the medium-term change in the relative investment price; ΔT_{ijt} denotes the medium-term change in participation in GVCs; X_{ijt} denotes control variables that vary at the country-industry-period level, including the initial routine task intensity RTI_{ijt}^0; α_{it} and α_{jt} denote country-by-period and industry-by-period fixed effects. Given that the model is estimated in differences, the fixed effects pick up country-period and industry-period specific trends.

The econometric model is estimated on a sample of 20 OECD countries and 19 industries over the period 1995-2011 for which the dependent and all explanatory variables can be constructed.[1,2] In order to focus on medium-term changes, the sample is split into three periods of approximately five years (1995-2000, 2000-05 and 2005-11). The analysis of medium-term changes rather than long-term changes over the entire period permits a more precise estimation of the effects of structural and policy drivers of labour shares while allowing labour shares sufficient time to adjust given that the elasticity of substitution between labour and capital is likely to be higher in the medium term than in the short-term. Depending on the specification, business-cycle effects are controlled for by including country-period fixed effects or changes in the output gap as explanatory variables.

Source: The detailed description of the data underlying the industry-level analysis and the detailed regression results can be found in Schwellnus et al. (forthcoming[9]), "Labour share developments over the past two decades: The role of technological progress, globalisation and "winner-take-most" dynamics".

Notes:

1. The countries covered by the industry-level analysis are: Australia, Austria, Belgium, Czech Republic, Denmark, Estonia, Finland, France, Germany, Ireland, Italy, Japan, Korea, the Netherlands, Norway, Slovak Republic, Spain, Sweden, the United Kingdom and the United States. Canada, Hungary, Israel, New Zealand and Poland are covered in the aggregate analysis in Section 2.1 of this chapter, but data on labour shares, relative investment prices or routine-task intensity are not available at the level of disaggregation required for the industry-level analysis.

Estonia is not covered in the aggregate analysis in Section 2.1 of this chapter because data on the aggregate wage distribution are not available, but industry-level data on labour shares, relative investment prices and routine-task intensity are available so that it can be included in the industry-level analysis.

2. The industries covered by the industry-level analysis are the following (International Standard Industry Classification – ISIC – rev. 4): manufacture of food (CA), of textile (CB), of wood and paper (CC), of chemicals and chemical and pharmaceuticals (CE+CF), of non-metals (CG), of metals (CH), of electrical equipment (CI+CJ), of machinery (CK), of transport equipment (CL), other manufacturing (CM), utilities (D+E), construction (F), trade (G), transportation (H), accommodation (I), ICT services (J), finance (K), professional services (M+N) and other services (R+S). The primary, coke and refined petroleum, housing and non-market industries are not covered because labour shares in these industries are largely determined by fluctuations in commodity and asset prices or imputation choices rather than structural developments such as technological progress and globalisation.

The econometric results are consistent with macro-level evidence that the labour share is counter-cyclical. The coefficient on changes in the output gap – i.e. the difference in business cycle conditions in the initial year and the final year of each five-year period – is negative and statistically significant at the 1% level, with the estimated semi-elasticity suggesting that a 1 percentage point increase in the output gap (observed GDP growth exceeding potential GDP growth by 1 percentage point) reduces the labour share by 0.5 percentage point.

Taking the estimated elasticities of the baseline model at face value, the observable variables included in the model can account for most of the aggregate labour share decline in the covered OECD countries over the sample period. The observed average decline in the relative investment price across countries and industries over the sample period was around 10% and the average increase in GVC participation around 7 percentage points (see Figure 2.2). Assuming that the elasticities estimated at the industry level are similar to those at the aggregate level, over the period 1995-2013 the baseline results suggest that investment price declines reduced the labour share by around 1.8 percentage points and increased GVC participation by around 0.7 percentage point.[7] Over the same period, business cycle effects raised the labour share by around 0.3 percentage point as the average output gap fell by around 0.7 percentage point. The net effect of changes in the relative investment price, GVC participation and business cycle conditions was around -2%, about 65% of the observed decline in the labour share (Figure 2.4).

Firm-level analysis conducted for this chapter suggests that declines in the relative investment price affect industry-level labour shares at least partly through changes within firms (Box 2.3). The average estimated firm-level semi-elasticity of firm-level labour shares to relative investment prices is around 0.15, remarkably similar to the estimated industry-level semi-elasticity of around 0.19. The estimated semi-elasticity is significantly larger in highly productive firms (around 0.3) that may be better able to adopt new technologies embodied in capital goods if adoption requires complementary know how. However, the firm- and industry-level results are not directly comparable as high-productivity firms are over-represented in the firm-level dataset used in this chapter and the firm-level analysis is based on a more limited country and year sample.[8] Consequently, the similarity in estimated semi-elasticities across the firm- and industry-level analyses cannot be interpreted as ruling out composition effects.

Figure 2.4. Estimated contributions to aggregate OECD labour share decline

1995-2013, percentage points

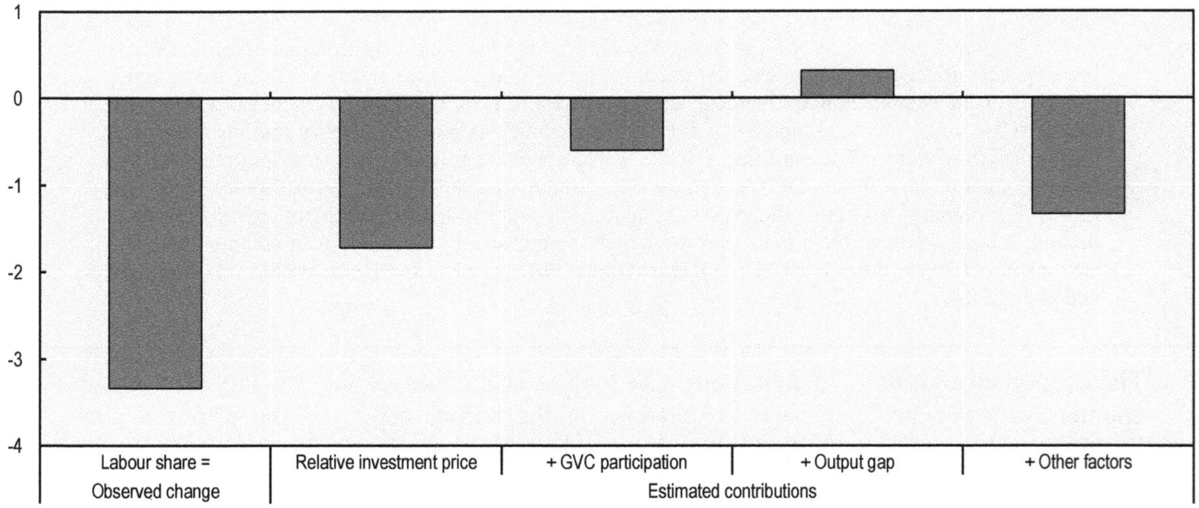

Note: GDP-weighted average of 24 OECD countries (Australia, Austria, Belgium, Canada, the Czech Republic, Denmark, Finland, France, Germany, Hungary, Ireland, Israel, Italy, Japan, Korea, the Netherlands, New Zealand, Norway, Poland, the Slovak Republic, Spain, Sweden, the United Kingdom and the United States). GVC: global value chain.
Source: Schwellnus et al. (forthcoming[9]) "Labour share developments over the past two decades: The role of technological progress, globalisation and "winner-take-most" dynamics".

StatLink 🔗 http://dx.doi.org/10.1787/888933777851

In contrast to the effects of relative investment prices on industry-level labour shares, the effects of increased GVC participation appear to mainly operate through the reallocation of production from high-labour share to low-labour share firms. The insignificance of the estimated coefficient on GVC participation at the firm-level is consistent with the theoretical model in Schwellnus et al. (forthcoming[9]) that shows that GVC expansion has offsetting effects on firm-level labour shares. On the one hand, the decline in the cost of offshoring leads to the substitution of imported intermediate goods for domestic routine labour and thereby to a reduction in the domestic wage bill as a share of gross output. On the other hand, offshoring of previously domestically produced output leads to a reduction in domestic value added as a share of gross output.

In sum, the econometric analysis suggests that technological progress and – to a lesser extent – the expansion of GVCs tends to reduce labour shares. This is broadly in line with the findings in OECD (2012[1]) of negative effects of technological change and intra-industry offshoring on labour shares in high-wage countries.[9] The effects of technological progress appear to operate partly by reducing firm-level labour shares, with large differences across low- and high-productivity firms. By contrast, the effect of GVC expansion appears to operate exclusively by shifting the composition of firms to those with the lowest labour shares.

Box 2.3. Methodology and data underlying the firm-level analysis

In order to assess whether within-firm labour shares respond to changes in industry-level relative investment prices and GVC participation, the following baseline equation is estimated:

$$\Delta LS_{cjit} = \beta_1 \Delta P_{ijt}^{Inv} + \beta_2 \Delta T_{ijt} + \gamma' X_{cji0} + \alpha_{cj} + \alpha_t + \varepsilon_{cji}$$

where subscripts c, j, i, t denote, respectively, countries, industries, firms and time; ΔLS_{cji} denotes the annualised long difference in the firm-level labour share, with long differences computed over the longest period a firm is observed and the sample is constrained to firms that are observed for at least eight years over the period 2001-13; ΔP_{cjt}^{Inv} denotes the annualised long difference of the log relative investment price; ΔT_{ijt} is the annualised change in GVC participation; X_{cji} is a set of firm-level controls that include: initial values of the firm's age, size (as measured by employment) and the initial labour share;[1] α_{cj} denotes country-industry fixed effects and α_t are period-fixed effects that cover all permutations of possible start and end years over the period 2001-13.

The model is estimated using firm-level data from Orbis – a dataset provided by Bureau van Dijk – and industry-level relative investment price indices for nine countries for which long differences in labour shares can be computed for a sufficient number of firms.[2] The Orbis dataset contains information from firms' income statements and balance sheets, including on revenues, value added, employment and compensation. In order to limit the influence of erratic or implausible firm-behaviour, the dataset is cleaned by removing extreme outliers using the procedure described in Andrews et al. (2016[20]). For the purpose of the labour share analysis in this chapter the dataset is additionally cleaned by removing observations with extreme values for labour shares. High-productivity firms are defined as the top 5% of firms within an industry with the highest labour productivity across the countries covered by the analysis.

Source: The detailed description of the data underlying the firm-level analysis and the detailed regression results can be found in (Schwellnus et al., forthcoming[9]), "Labour share developments over the past two decades: The role of technological progress, globalisation and "winner-take-most" dynamics".

Notes:

1. Given that the above specification of the firm-level regressions considers only one long difference per firm, firm fixed effects cannot be included. Including the initial values of the dependent variable allows controlling for unobserved firm characteristics in the absence of firm fixed effects (Angrist and Pischke, 2009[21]).

2. The analysis is limited to the same industries as the industry-level analysis. The included countries are Belgium, Finland, France, Germany, Italy, Korea, Spain, Sweden and the United Kingdom. In order to ensure that results are not driven by firms with extreme values in long differences in labour shares, firms with long differences outside the [-40,+40] percentage point interval are removed from the analysis in this section. The analysis is further restricted to country-industry cells with more than 30 firms in order to ensure that the industry-level variables are identified by a sufficient number of firms. The results are robust to alternative sample restrictions.

Overall, these results are consistent with "winner-takes-most" dynamics in the sense that only a subset of highly productive firms ("superstars") with low labour shares may be fully able to reap the benefits of new technologies and globalisation.

2.2.2. Firm-level dynamics: Does the winner take it all?

Technology and globalisation strengthen supply- and demand-side economies of scale, which may in turn give rise to "winner-takes-most" dynamics – the process through which the most productive firms capture an overwhelming share of the market, see Rosen (1981[22]); Frank and Cook (1995[23]); and Autor et al. (2017[24]). While the relevant market for the best manufacturing firms used to be primarily national or regional, the fall in transport costs and tariffs implies that these firms can now serve significant shares of the global market, strengthening supply side economies of scale. The trend toward larger market size has been reinforced by rapid progress in information and communication technologies (ICT) that allow matching sellers and buyers across geographically distant locations.[10] Rapid progress in ICT has also facilitated the emergence of markets with a global scale in a number of traditional service industries, such as retail and transport, as well as new ICT services with near zero marginal cost of scaling up operations.[11] In some of these industries, including ICT services, retail and transport, network externalities (demand side economies of scale) that favour the emergence of a dominant player have become more important.[12]

Standard economic theory suggests that "winner-takes-most" dynamics imply both falling labour shares in the technologically most advanced firms and reallocation of market shares toward these firms. In a standard model with heterogeneous firms, the best firms have low labour shares because the fixed overhead labour cost needed for production is distributed over a larger output and/or because large market shares allow these firms to charge higher markups (Autor et al., 2017[24]). "Winner-takes-most" dynamics implies that as technology and globalisation raise the relevant market size the best firms become larger, which implies that: i) the labour share in these firms declines as the value added share of fixed overhead labour cost declines and/or their markup increases; and ii) production is reallocated toward low labour share firms as the market share of the best firms increases.

The analysis below provides descriptive evidence on these hypotheses using the Orbis dataset. The sample underlying the analysis covers firms in the non-primary and non-financial business sector of 17 OECD countries with satisfactory firm coverage. To minimise issues related to the under-representation of small firms in the dataset, the analysis in this section is restricted to firms with more than 20 employees.

Decoupling of wages from productivity: Superstar firms or the rest?

In countries that experienced declines in labour shares over the period 2001-13, wages in technologically leading firms decoupled from productivity but closely tracked productivity in the remaining firms (Figure 2.5). This implies that in these countries labour shares within the group of leading firms declined while they remained constant in the remaining firms, which is consistent with "winner-takes-most" dynamics.[13] The best firms in these countries diverged from the remaining firms in terms of both productivity and wages, but wage divergence was much less pronounced than productivity divergence.[14]

In countries that did not experience declines in labour shares, real wage growth outpaced labour productivity growth in both leading firms and the remaining firms. Productivity and wages in leading firms diverged from those of the remaining firms, but labour shares were broadly constant before the crisis of 2008-09 and increased in both groups thereafter. This suggests that in countries with increases in labour shares over the period 2001-13 cross-firm heterogeneity in labour share trends was less pronounced. One possible explanation could be that there was less technological dynamism in countries with increases in labour shares, which is consistent with the fact that productivity growth of the leading firms in these countries was similar to that of the non-leading firms in countries that experienced labour share declines.

The decoupling of wages from productivity in technologically leading firms is overwhelmingly explained by the entry of capital-intensive firms with low labour shares into the technological frontier (Figure 2.6). The decoupling of wages from productivity in leading firms can be decomposed into contributions from firms staying at the technological frontier ("incumbent leaders") and firms entering and exiting it ("net entry"). While productivity and wages remained closely linked in incumbent technological leaders, net entry into the frontier drove a large wedge between wage and productivity growth, implying that labour shares of firms entering the technological frontier were significantly lower than those exiting it. Thus, the decline of labour shares at the technological frontier was not driven by increasing markups or capital intensity in firms remaining at the technological frontier but rather by the entry of firms with higher markups or higher capital intensity into the technological frontier. Empirical analysis suggests that firms entering the technological frontier were about 60% more capital intensive than those exiting it (Schwellnus et al., forthcoming[9]).

Figure 2.5. Average wages and productivity in the best firms and the rest

Indices, 2001 = 100

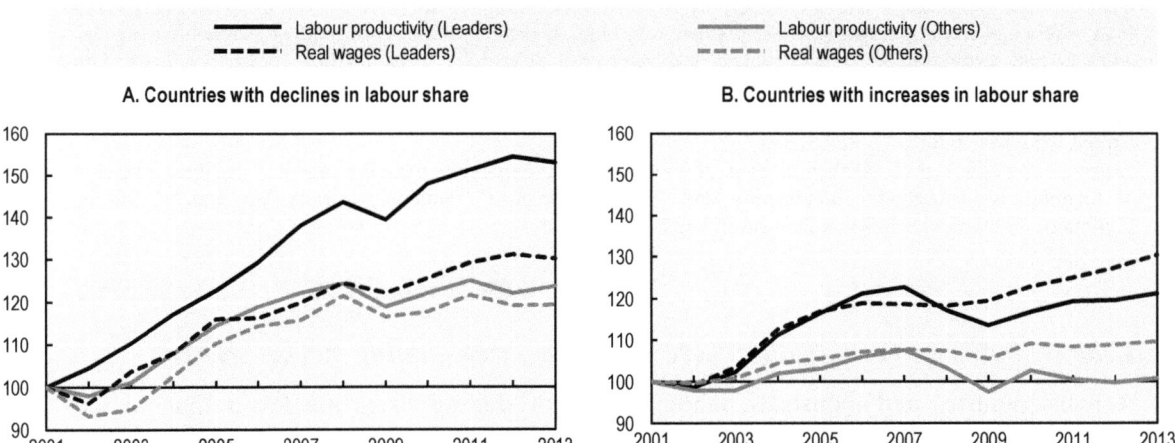

Note: Labour productivity and real wages are computed as the unweighted mean across firms of real value added per worker and real labour compensation per worker. Leaders are defined as the top 5% of firms in terms of labour productivity within each country group in each industry and year. The countries with a decline in the labour share excluding the primary, housing, financial and non-market industries over the period 2001-13 are: Belgium, Denmark, Germany, Ireland, Japan, Korea, Sweden, the United Kingdom and the United States. The countries with an increase are: Austria, the Czech Republic, Estonia, Finland, France, Italy, the Netherlands and Spain.
Source: Schwellnus et al. (forthcoming[9]), "Labour share developments over the past two decades: The role of technological progress, globalisation and "winner-take-most" dynamics".

StatLink ⫸ http://dx.doi.org/10.1787/888933777870

Figure 2.6. Net entry fully explains the decoupling of wages from productivity in leading firms

Contributions to labour productivity and real wage growth at the frontier, countries with declines in labour shares, indices, 2001 = 100

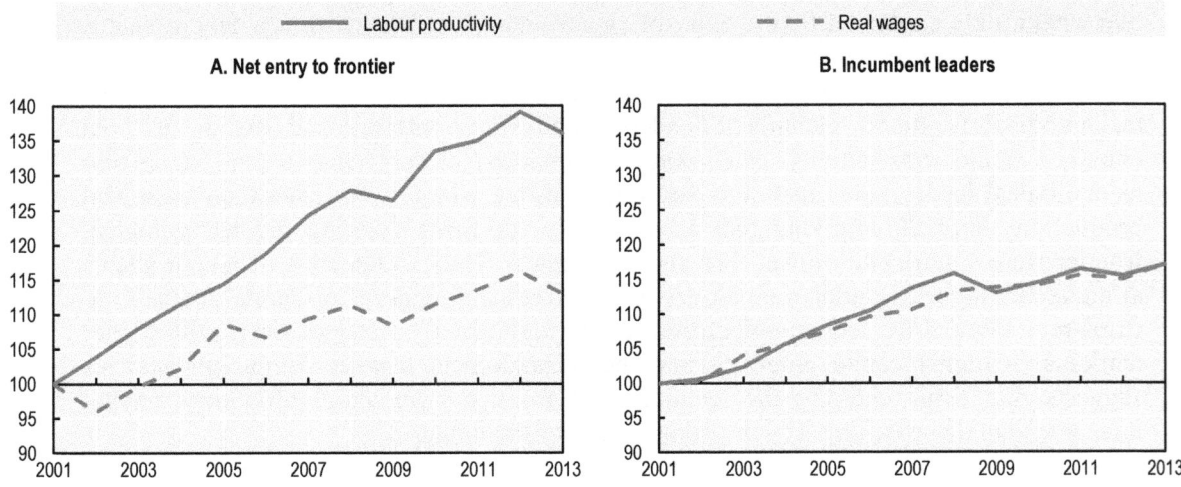

Note: Contributions to real wage growth and labour productivity growth are based on the decomposition

$$\Delta X = [s_2^{st} X_2^{st} - s_1^{st} X_1^{st}] + [s_2^{entry} X_2^{entry} - s_1^{exit} X_1^{exit}] = [s_1^{st} \Delta X^{st}] + [s_1^{exit}(X_2^{entry} - X_1^{exit})] + \varepsilon,$$ where

X denotes the logarithm of labour productivity or real wages; s denotes the share of each group of firms in the total number of leading firms; superscripts denote groups of firms (with *st*, *entry* and *exit* indicating stayers, entrants and exiting firms, respectively); and subscripts denote the period (Baily et al., 1992[25]). The countries with a decline in the labour share excluding the primary, housing, financial and non-market industries over the period 2001-13 are: Belgium, Denmark, Germany, Ireland, Japan, Korea, Sweden, the United Kingdom and the United States.
Source: Schwellnus et al. (forthcoming[9]), "Labour share developments over the past two decades: The role of technological progress, globalisation and "winner-take-most" dynamics". Baily, M. et al. (1992[25]), "Productivity Dynamics in Manufacturing Plants", http://dx.doi.org/10.2307/2534764

StatLink ᕘᘉᔧ http://dx.doi.org/10.1787/888933777889

Labour shares and reallocation: Are superstar firms gaining market shares?

Across countries and industries, labour shares in leading firms are lower than in the remaining firms (Figure 2.7). While labour share developments in leading firms have differed across countries with declining labour shares and those where they increased, labour shares in leading firms are consistently lower than those in the other firms across both country groups. This stylised fact also holds across manufacturing and services, with limited differences across industries at a higher level of disaggregation (Schwellnus et al., forthcoming[9]). Therefore, reallocation of production to firms at the technological frontier tends to reduce the labour share.

In countries with declines in labour shares, value added in leading firms strongly diverged from the remaining firms, implying increasing market shares of firms at the technological frontier (Figure 2.8). Given that labour shares in leading firms are well below those in other firms, in these countries reallocation of value added put further downward pressure on labour shares.

Figure 2.7. Labour shares in leading and other firms, 2001-13

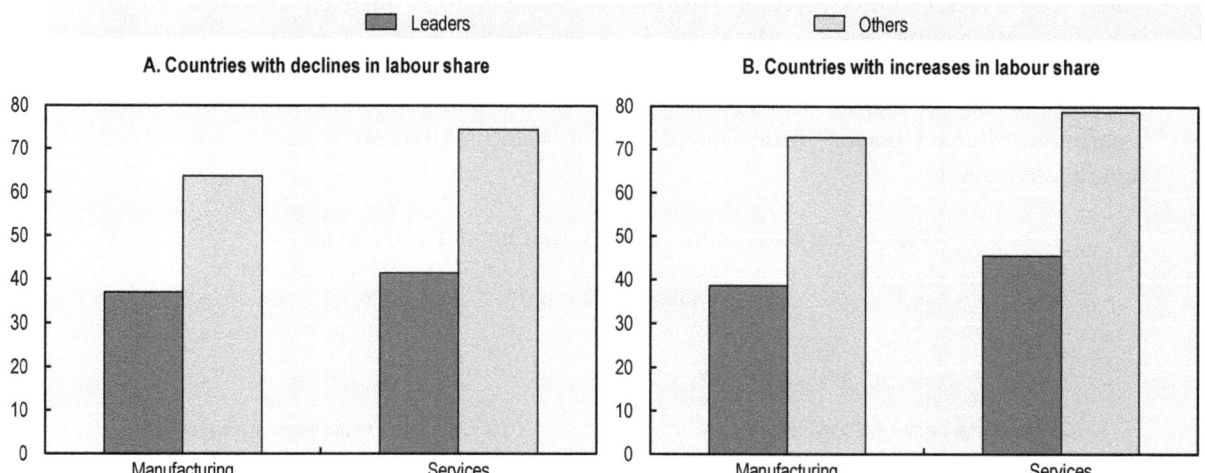

Note: The labour share is computed as the unweighted mean across firms of the percentage ratio of total labour compensation to value added over the period 2001-13. Leaders are defined as the top 5% of firms in terms of labour productivity within each country group in each industry and year. The countries with a decline in the labour share excluding the primary, housing, financial and non-market industries over the period 2001-13 are: Belgium, Denmark, Germany, Ireland, Japan, Korea, Sweden, the United Kingdom and the United States. The countries with an increase are: Austria, the Czech Republic, Estonia, Finland, France, Italy, the Netherlands and Spain.
Source: Schwellnus et al. (forthcoming[9]), "Labour share developments over the past two decades: The role of technological progress, globalisation and "winner-take-most" dynamics".

StatLink http://dx.doi.org/10.1787/888933777908

The labour share effect of production reallocation to firms at the technological frontier is consistent with "winner-takes-most" dynamics but it does not necessarily indicate an increase in anti-competitive forces, such as higher entry barriers. The emergence of new technologies may allow innovating firms to temporarily pull ahead. Autor et al. (2017[24]) find evidence that growing market concentration in the United States occurs predominantly in industries with rapid technological change, consistent with the conjecture that "winner-takes-most" dynamics reflect technological dynamism rather than anti-competitive forces. Nevertheless, there is a risk that over time incumbent technological leaders attempt to reduce the threat of market entry through anti-competitive practices, e.g. through predatory pricing or mergers and acquisitions of competing firms.

In countries with increases in labour shares the pattern of increasing market shares of firms at the technological frontier was more muted. This is consistent with the above conjecture that in these countries "winner-takes-most" dynamics were less prevalent.

Summing up, the firm-level analysis suggests that "winner-takes-most" dynamics have contributed to labour share declines, both through a decline in labour shares within the group of technologically leading firms and the reallocation of market shares toward these firms. The results further suggest that thus far the decoupling of wages from productivity at the technological frontier is not primarily driven by the entrenchment of a small number of superstar firms that raise their markups, but instead by firms with lower labour shares leapfrogging incumbent frontier firms. While low labour shares in firms entering the technological frontier may to some extent reflect high markups, the fact that these firms leapfrog incumbents suggests that high markups likely reflect innovation rents rather than a lack of entry barriers. This interpretation is also consistent with the fact that the share of young and small firms is significantly higher for entrants into the technological frontier than for firms staying at or exiting the frontier.[15] A key challenge for product market regulation and competition policy going forward will be to prevent emerging dominant players from engaging in anti-competitive practices so that markets remain contestable.

Figure 2.8. Real value added in leading and other firms

Indices, 2001 = 100

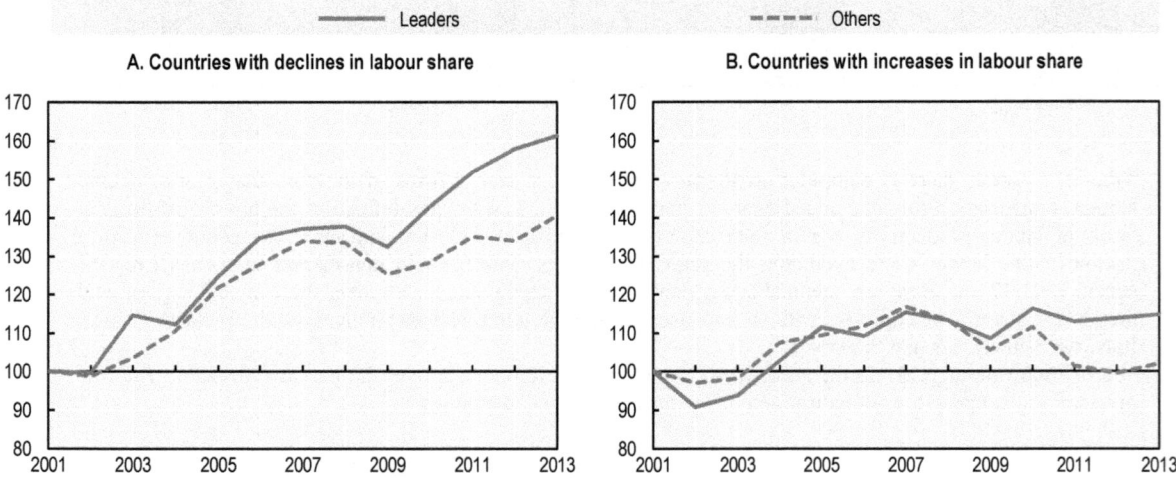

Note: Real value added is computed as the unweighted mean across firms of nominal value added deflated by the industry value added deflator over the period 2001-13. Leaders are defined as the top 5% of firms in terms of labour productivity within each country group in each industry and year. The countries with a decline in the labour share excluding the primary, housing, financial and non-market industries over the period 2001-13 are: Belgium, Denmark, Germany, Ireland, Japan, Korea, Sweden, the United Kingdom and the United States. The countries with an increase are: Austria, the Czech Republic, Estonia, Finland, France, Italy, the Netherlands and Spain.

Source: Schwellnus et al. (forthcoming[9]), "Labour share developments over the past two decades: The role of technological progress, globalisation and "winner-take-most" dynamics".

StatLink ᴍᴸᴵ http://dx.doi.org/10.1787/888933777927

2.3. The central role of skills for broadly shared productivity gains

A large body of evidence suggests that routine task and skill intensity are key determinants of the substitutability of capital for labour. For instance, existing cross-country studies show that declines in labour shares in response to declines in relative investment prices have been more pronounced in countries with higher shares of routine employment (IMF, 2017[7]). The elasticity of substitution between capital and labour is typically estimated to be significantly higher for low-skilled than for high-skilled workers (Duffy, Papageorgiou and Perez-Sebastian, 2004[26]; Krusell et al., 2000[16]). These results suggest that equipping workers with the right skills to carry out non-routine tasks would make them less substitutable with capital and allow them to make the most of ongoing technological advances.

To assess the role of routine-task intensity and skill intensity for capital labour substitution in response to technological progress, the background analysis for this chapter reported in Schwellnus et al. (forthcoming[9]) constructs industry-level measures based on the OECD Survey of Adult Skills - Programme for the International Assessment of Adult Competencies (PIAAC). These measures suggest that the share of high-routine jobs – defined as jobs with limited independence and freedom in planning and organising the tasks to be performed – is particularly high in industries such as transportation and non-metal manufacturing, and particularly low in ICT services and finance (Figure 2.9). While routine and skill intensity are correlated across industries, a high employment share of low-skilled workers does not necessarily imply a high share of high-routine workers, which allows to empirically distinguish between the effects of routine tasks and skills. The accommodation and construction industries, for instance, employ high shares of low-skilled workers but low shares of high-routine workers.

Figure 2.9. High routine intensity does not imply low skill intensity

OECD average, 2012

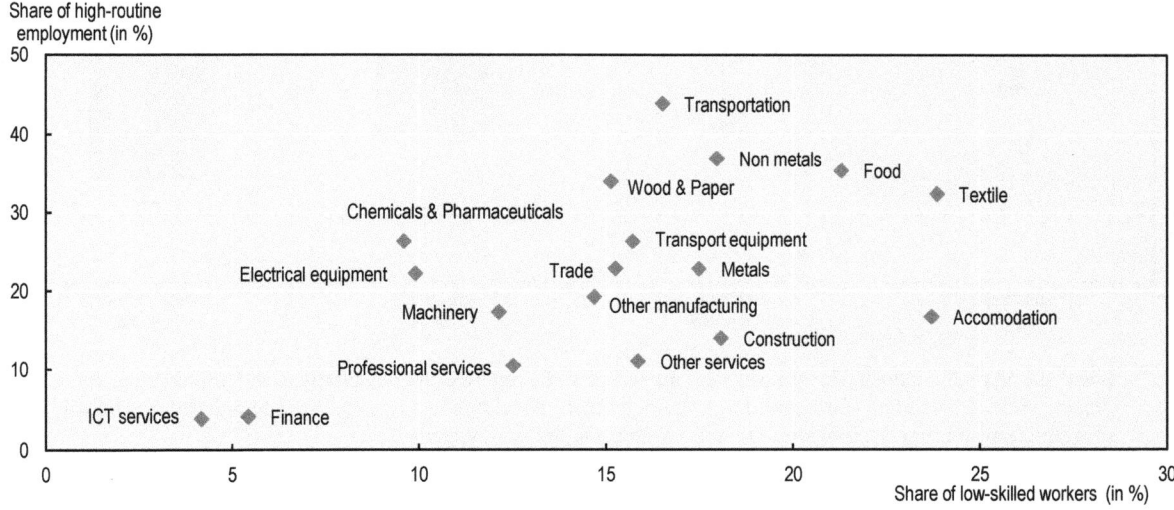

Note: The share of low-skilled workers is defined as the share of workers with numeracy skills below level 2 in the Programme for the International Assessment of Adult Competencies (PIAAC). The share of high-routine employment is defined as the share of workers in an occupation above the 75th percentile of the routine-task distribution.
Source: Schwellnus et al. (forthcoming[9]), "Labour share developments over the past two decades: The role of technological progress, globalisation and "winner-take-most" dynamics".

StatLink ᵅᵅˢᴾ http://dx.doi.org/10.1787/888933777946

The industry-level empirical analysis suggests that a decline in relative investment prices has a lower impact on the labour share in industries with low initial routine intensity. The estimated semi-elasticity is 0.1 for low-routine industries – defined as those industries with initial routine intensity below the median industry – whereas it is around 0.22 for high-routine industries (Schwellnus et al., forthcoming[9]). Similarly, the estimated semi-elasticity is typically significantly lower in industries with high skill intensity, especially problem-solving and numeracy skills.

Even at a given level of routine task intensity, labour share declines in response to relative investment price declines are lower in countries and industries with a high share of high-skilled workers. While high literacy skills do not appear to significantly reduce capital-labour substitution in response to relative investment price declines, numeracy and problem-solving skills are statistically significant when added to the baseline specification separately. The estimated coefficients suggest that even in a high-routine industry a decline in the relative investment price results in an only modest decline in the labour share if the industry employs a high share of workers with high numeracy- or problem-solving skills (Figure 2.10). When all skill indicators are added to the baseline specification simultaneously, only numeracy skills turn out to be statistically significant.[16]

Figure 2.10. High skills reduce capital-labour substitution

Change in the labour share in response to a 10% decrease in the relative investment price, percentage points

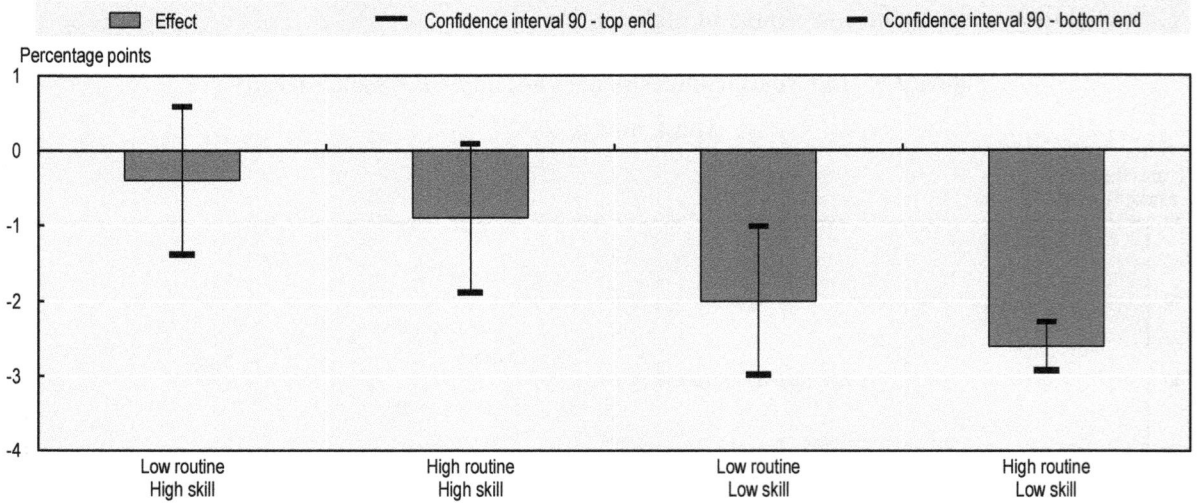

Note: Based on the industry-level results for numeracy skills reported in Schwellnus et al. (forthcoming[9]).
Source: Schwellnus et al. (forthcoming[9]), "Labour share developments over the past two decades: The role of technological progress, globalisation and "winner-take-most" dynamics".

StatLink ᴍᴤᴘ http://dx.doi.org/10.1787/888933777965

Overall these results suggest that high-skilled workers, especially those with high numeracy skills, may be more difficult to replace by machines or may be more easily re-deployed to non-routine tasks than low-skilled workers (see Chapter 4). Basic literacy, numeracy and problem-solving skills remain in high demand in OECD countries and are key to allowing workers to make the most of the opportunities and challenges afforded by technological change and globalisation (Vignoles, 2016[27]; OECD, 2017[28]). The challenge for skill policies is to develop strong skill foundations in youth while also supporting life-long learning, including through strong systems of skills validation and certification (OECD, forthcoming[29]).

2.4. Concluding remarks

This chapter provides evidence suggesting that technological change and greater participation in global value chains have reduced labour shares, including by strengthening "winner-takes-most" dynamics: countries with falling labour shares have witnessed both a decline at the technological frontier and a reallocation of market shares toward capital-intensive "superstar" firms with low labour shares. But technology-induced capital-labour substitution has been significantly less pronounced for high-skilled workers, suggesting that raising skills will be key to reconnecting real median wages to productivity.

Continued technological change is likely to put further downward pressure on labour shares and create new challenges for the broad sharing of productivity gains. Advances in ICT will continue to raise production efficiency for investment goods, further reducing their relative prices and raising capital-labour substitution. But technological progress may also fundamentally change the substitutability of capital and labour. For instance, technological advances in artificial intelligence and robotics could make more human tasks – including cognitive tasks – replaceable by capital in the future. Even though the evidence suggests that the expansion of global value chains stalled in the wake of the global crisis of 2008-09 (Haugh et al., 2016[30]), technological advances may lead to further offshoring of labour-intensive services.

These technological advances may further strengthen "winner-takes-most" dynamics, with wages decoupling further from productivity at the technological frontier and market shares being reallocated to a small number of "superstar" firms with low labour shares. This chapter finds no evidence that the emergence of "superstar" firms indicates the rise of anti-competitive forces rather than technological dynamism. Nonetheless, competition policy will need to find the right balance between preventing anti-competitive practices by incumbent technological leaders and encouraging innovation by allowing entrants into the technological frontier to reap the rewards for their innovations. Irrespective of the source of emerging "winner-takes-most" dynamics, policies that raise human capital through education and training will play a crucial role to broaden the sharing of productivity gains by ensuring that workers can make the most of ongoing technological advances.

Notes

[1] The empirical results reported in this chapter are based on Schwellnus et al. (2017[2]; 2017[33]; forthcoming[9])

[2] Note that the value added price index is different from the GDP price index. GDP includes taxes less subsidies on products whereas value added does not. Value added is thus a more relevant concept to study the relation between labour productivity and wages.

[3] If factor prices are determined competitively real wages are equal to *marginal* labour productivity, but this does not imply equality between real wages and *average* labour productivity. Real wages can decouple from *average* labour productivity even with factor prices that are determined competitively if the elasticity of substitution between capital and labour is non-unitary.

[4] Participation in global value chains is measured by the sum of the share of foreign value added in gross exports (backward participation) and the share of exports consisting of intermediate inputs used by trading partners for the production of their exports to third countries (forward participation).

[5] At the level of industry disaggregation used in this chapter, labour share developments within industries explain around 80% of aggregate labour share developments, which is broadly in line with previous studies (Bassanini and Manfredi, 2012[32]; Karabarbounis and Neiman, 2014[6]; IMF, 2017[7]) . Given that reallocation across industries explains only a small fraction of aggregate labour share developments, weighting industries with shares in aggregate value added in the regression analysis allows making direct statements on aggregate effects.

[6] The value added deflator implicitly enters both the denominator of the labour share and the denominator of the relative investment price. A range of robustness checks reported in Schwellnus et al. (forthcoming[9]) suggest that potential endogeneity of the relative investment price does not bias the results reported here. Changes in GVC participation may partly be driven by labour share developments, e.g. if labour share increases induce offshoring of intermediate goods production. If anything, this could bias the coefficient on GVC participation upwards, but does not call into question the significant negative coefficient on GVC participation.

[7] Industry-level elasticities can plausibly be assumed to be similar to aggregate elasticities because within-industry labour share developments explain aggregate developments (Schwellnus et al., forthcoming[9]) and in the regression analysis industry shares in value added are used as weights.

[8] Moreover, in order to cover a maximum number of firms, the firm-level analysis is based on a single eight-year or longer difference as compared to three non-overlapping five- or six-year differences in the industry-level analysis.

[9] It is also in broadly in line with more recent cross-country studies such as De Serres and Schwellnus (2018[31]), IMF (2017[7]) and Karabarbounis and Neiman (2014[6]).

[10] For instance, the internet has created international marketplaces on which sellers offer a large variety of products and buyers can compare prices globally.

[11] For instance, the marginal cost of replicating and supplying the informational goods provided by digital platforms is near zero.

[12] Network externalities are relevant for digital platforms (e.g. through better matching of suppliers and buyers) but also for retail (e.g. through better access to network of suppliers) and transport (e.g. through more efficient logistics). In some industries, network externalities operate through more subtle channels. For instance, the use of private airlines' computerised reservation systems among travel agents can lead to the emergence of dominant players (Frank and Cook, 1995[23]).

[13] Leaders are defined as the top 5% of firms in terms of labour productivity within each country group in each industry and year, implying that the composition of firms at the technological frontier is allowed to vary over time.

[14] The decoupling of wages from productivity in leading firms does not appear to reflect an increase in stock option compensation. Stock option compensation is typically found to be particularly prevalent in finance and ICT services (Elsby, Hobijn and Sahin, 2013[8]). The finance industry is not covered by Orbis so that the role of increasing stock option compensation can be assessed by removing the ICT industry from the analysis in Figure 2.5. Since the figure remains qualitatively and quantitatively unchanged, increasing non-cash compensation is unlikely to be the main driver of decoupling of wages from productivity in leading firms in countries with declining labour shares (Schwellnus et al., forthcoming[9]).

[15] The share of firms that employ less than 100 workers and have been in existence no more than 5 years is 14% for entrants into the technological frontier, whereas it is 8% for firms staying at the frontier or exiting it (Schwellnus et al., forthcoming[9]).

[16] Although the empirical suggest that numeracy skills are more robustly related to capital-labour substitution in response to relative investment price declines, the insignificance of the literacy and problem solving indicators may to some extent also reflect high collinearity between the three skill indicators. The coefficients on the three skill indicators are jointly significant at the 5% level.

References

Acemoglu, D. and D. Autor (2010), "Skills, Tasks and Technologies: Implications for Employment and Earnings", *NBER Working Paper*, No. 16082, National Bureau of Economic Research, Cambridge, MA, http://dx.doi.org/10.3386/w16082. [17]

Acemoglu, D. and P. Restrepo (2018), "Artificial Intelligence, Automation and Work", *NBER Working Paper*, No. 24196, National Bureau of Economic Research, Cambridge, MA, http://dx.doi.org/10.3386/w24196. [12]

Andrews, D., C. Criscuolo and P. Gal (2016), "The Best versus the Rest: The Global Productivity Slowdown, Divergence across Firms and the Role of Public Policy", *OECD Productivity Working Papers*, No. 5, OECD Publishing, Paris, http://dx.doi.org/10.1787/63629cc9-en. [20]

Angrist, J. and J. Pischke (2009), *Mostly Harmless Econometrics : An Empiricist's Companion*, Princeton University Press, https://press.princeton.edu/titles/8769.html. [21]

Autor, D. et al. (2017), "Concentrating on the Fall of the Labor Share", *NBER Working Paper*, No. 23108, National Bureau of Economic Research, Cambridge, MA, http://dx.doi.org/10.3386/w23108. [24]

Autor, D. and A. Salomons (2018), "Is automation labor-displacing? Productivity growth, employment, and the labor share", *Brookings Papers on Economic Activity Conference Drafts*, https://www.brookings.edu/wp-content/uploads/2018/03/1_autorsalomons.pdf. [15]

Baily, M. et al. (1992), "Productivity Dynamics in Manufacturing Plants", *Brookings Papers on Economic Activity. Microeconomics*, Vol. 1992, pp. 187-267, http://dx.doi.org/10.2307/2534764. [25]

Bakhshi, H., N. Oulton and J. Thompson (2003), "Modelling investment when relative prices are trending: theory and evidence for the United Kingdom", *Bank of England working papers*, No. 189. [14]

Bassanini, A. and T. Manfredi (2012), "Capital's Grabbing Hand? A Cross-Country/Cross-Industry Analysis of the Decline of the Labour Share", *OECD Social, Employment and Migration Working Papers*, No. 133, OECD Publishing, Paris, http://dx.doi.org/10.1787/5k95zqsf4bxt-en. [32]

Bivens, J. and L. Mishel (2015), "Understanding the Historic Divergence Between Productivity and a Typical Worker's Pay: Why It Matters and Why It's Real", *Briefing Paper*, No. 406, Economic Policy Institute, https://www.epi.org/publication/understanding-the-historic-divergence-between-productivity-and-a-typical-workers-pay-why-it-matters-and-why-its-real/. [4]

Chirinko, R. (2008), "σ: The long and short of it", *Journal of Macroeconomics*, Vol. 30/2, pp. 671-686, http://dx.doi.org/10.1016/j.jmacro.2007.10.010. [11]

De Serres, A. and C. Schwellnus (2018), "A general equilibrium (LM and PM reforms) perspective to inequality", in Astarita, C. and G. D'Adamo (eds.), *Inequality and Structural Reforms: Methodological Concerns and Lessons from Policy. Workshop Proceedings, European Economy Discussion Papers No. 71*, European Commission, Brussels, https://ec.europa.eu/info/sites/info/files/economy-finance/dp071_en.pdf. [31]

Duffy, J., C. Papageorgiou and F. Perez-Sebastian (2004), "Capital-Skill Complementarity? Evidence from a Panel of Countries", *The Review of Economics and Statistics*, Vol. 86/1, pp. 327-344, http://dx.doi.org/10.1162/003465304323023840. [26]

Elsby, M., B. Hobijn and A. Sahin (2013), "The Decline of the U.S. Labor Share", *Brookings Papers on Economic Activity*, No. 2013-27, https://www.brookings.edu/bpea-articles/the-decline-of-the-u-s-labor-share/. [8]

Frank, R. and P. Cook (1995), *The winner-take-all society : how more and more Americans compete for ever fewer and bigger prizes, encouraging economic waste, income inequality, and an impoverished cultural life*, Free Press. [23]

Grossman, G. and E. Rossi-Hansberg (2008), "Trading Tasks: A Simple Theory of Offshoring", *American Economic Review*, Vol. 98/5, pp. 1978-1997, http://dx.doi.org/10.1257/aer.98.5.1978. [19]

Harrison, A. (2005), "Has Globalization Eroded Labor's Share? Some Cross-Country Evidence", *MPRA Paper*, No. 39649, https://mpra.ub.uni-muenchen.de/39649/. [18]

Haugh, D. et al. (2016), "Cardiac Arrest or Dizzy Spell: Why is World Trade So Weak and What can Policy Do About It?", *OECD Economic Policy Papers*, No. 18, OECD Publishing, Paris, http://dx.doi.org/10.1787/5jlr2h45q532-en. [30]

IMF (2017), "Chapter 3 : Understanding the Downward Trend in Labor Income Shares", in *World Economic Outlook, April 2017: Gaining Momentum?*, International Monetary Fund, Washington, D.C., https://www.imf.org/en/Publications/WEO/Issues/2017/09/19/world-economic-outlook-october-2017. [7]

Karabarbounis, L. and B. Neiman (2014), "The Global Decline of the Labor Share", *The Quarterly Journal of Economics*, Vol. 129/1, pp. 61-103, http://dx.doi.org/10.1093/qje/qjt032. [6]

Krusell, P. et al. (2000), "Capital-Skill Complementarity and Inequality: A Macroeconomic Analysis", *Econometrica*, Vol. 68/5, pp. 1029-1053, http://dx.doi.org/10.2307/2999442. [16]

OECD (2017), *Getting Skills Right: Skills for Jobs Indicators*, OECD Publishing, Paris, http://dx.doi.org/10.1787/9789264277878-en. [28]

OECD (2012), *OECD Employment Outlook 2012*, OECD Publishing, Paris, http://dx.doi.org/10.1787/empl_outlook-2012-en. [1]

OECD (forthcoming), *Good Jobs for All in a Changing World of Work: The OECD Jobs Strategy*, OECD Publishing, Paris. [29]

Pak, M. and C. Schwellnus (forthcoming), "Labour share developments over the past two decades: The role of public policies", *OECD Economics Department Working Papers*, OECD Publishing, Paris. [10]

Pessoa, J. and J. van Reenen (2013), "Decoupling of Wage Growth and Productivity Growth? Myth and Reality", *CEP Discussion Papers*, No. 1246, http://cep.lse.ac.uk/pubs/download/dp1246.pdf. [3]

Rosen, S. (1981), "The Economics of Superstars", *The American Economic Review*, Vol. 71/5, pp. 845-858, http://dx.doi.org/10.2307/1803469. [22]

Schwellnus, C., A. Kappeler and P. Pionnier (2017), "Decoupling of wages from productivity: Macro-level facts", *OECD Economics Department Working Papers*, No. 1373, OECD Publishing, Paris, http://dx.doi.org/10.1787/18151973. [2]

Schwellnus, C., A. Kappeler and P. Pionnier (2017), "The Decoupling of Median Wages from Productivity in OECD Countries", *International Productivity Monitor*, Vol. 32, http://www.csls.ca/ipm/32/Schwellnus_Kappeler_Pionnier.pdf. [33]

Schwellnus, C. et al. (forthcoming), "Labour share developments over the past two decades: The role of technological progress, globalisation and "winner-take-most" dynamics", *OECD Economics Department Working Papers*, OECD Publishing, Paris, forthcoming. [9]

Sharpe, A. and J. Uguccioni (2017), "Decomposing the Productivity- Wage Nexus in Selected OECD Countries, 1986-2013", *International Productivity Monitor*, Vol. 32, http://www.csls.ca/ipm/32/Uguccioni_Sharpe.pdf, pp. 25-43. [5]

Tevlin, S. and K. Whelan (2003), "Explaining the Investment Boom of the 1990s", *Journal of Money, Credit and Banking*, Vol. 35/1, http://www.jstor.org/stable/3649843. [13]

Vignoles, A. (2016), "What is the economic value of literacy and numeracy?", *IZA World of Labor* 229, http://dx.doi.org/10.15185/izawol.229. [27]

Chapter 3. The role of collective bargaining systems for good labour market performance

This chapter assesses the role of collective bargaining for labour market performance in OECD countries. It builds on the detailed characterisation of collective bargaining systems and practices presented in the OECD Employment Outlook 2017. *Using a rich mix of country-, sector-, firm- and worker-level data, this chapter investigates the link of different collective bargaining settings with employment, wages, working conditions, wage inequality and productivity. It then discusses how broad-based employee and employer organisations, administrative extensions, organised forms of decentralisation and wage co-ordination may contribute to better balance inclusiveness and flexibility in the labour market.*

The statistical data for Israel are supplied by and under the responsibility of the relevant Israeli authorities. The use of such data by the OECD is without prejudice to the status of the Golan Heights, East Jerusalem and Israeli settlements in the West Bank under the terms of international law.

Key findings

Collective bargaining systems in OECD countries are confronted with serious challenges in the face of global competition, technological change and a long-running trend towards decentralisation of bargaining. The shares of workers in trade unions and covered by collective agreements have been declining in many OECD countries and concerns are growing about the ability of collective bargaining to contribute to better labour market performance.

This chapter provides a timely assessment of the role of collective bargaining systems for labour market performance and inclusive growth. It looks at how collective bargaining matters for some of the policy objectives that policy-makers and citizens care most about: employment, wages, quality of the work environment, inequality and productivity. The chapter brings empirical analyses, using the best macro- and micro-data available and the characterisation of collective bargaining systems developed in OECD (2017[1]), together with country experiences and case studies to support policy-makers and social partners themselves in identifying directions for reform.

The analysis builds on a characterisation of collective bargaining systems along four main building blocks:

- The *collective bargaining coverage* – the share of workers covered by collective agreements – which is linked to membership of signatory employer organisations and trade unions, but also to extensions of agreements to other firms and workers in a sector.

- The *level of bargaining* at which collective agreements are negotiated: firm level, sector level or even national level. Multi-level bargaining involves a combination of firm- and higher-level collective bargaining.

- The role of *wage co-ordination* between sector-level (or firm-level) agreements, such as the setting of common wage targets, to take account of macroeconomic conditions.

- The *degree of flexibility* for firms to modify the terms set by higher-level agreements. In *centralised* systems, companies have no or very little scope to modify the terms set in higher-level agreements, in contrast to *fully decentralised* systems where collective bargaining can take place only at the firm level. Between these two extremes, *organised decentralised* systems allow sector-level agreements to set broad framework conditions but leave detailed provisions to firm-level negotiations.

The main empirical findings are as follows:

- Within countries, at the *individual level*, there is a wage premium for workers who are covered by firm-level bargaining compared with those not covered or those covered only by sector-level bargaining. Moreover, the work environment tends to be of higher quality in firms with a recognised form of employee representation (for example a trade union or works council), largely because of lower work intensity, more training options and better prospects for career advancement.

- Comparing collective bargaining systems *across countries*, co-ordinated systems – including those characterised by organised decentralisation – are linked with higher employment and lower unemployment (also for young people, women and low-skilled workers) than fully decentralised systems. Predominantly centralised systems with no co-ordination are somewhat in between.

- Collective bargaining also tends to affect wage dispersion, with greater dispersion in systems with no collective bargaining or where firms set wages independently. By contrast, wage dispersion is on average smallest among workers who are covered by sector-level bargaining. The lower dispersion in wages associated with sector-level bargaining in part reflects lower returns to education, seniority and potential experience for workers covered by collective agreements.

- The effect on wages is also reflected in the relationship of collective bargaining with productivity growth. Centralised bargaining systems tend to be associated with lower productivity growth if coverage of agreements is high. This result suggests that the lack of flexibility at the firm level, which characterises centralised bargaining systems, may come at the expense of lower productivity growth. By contrast, higher co-ordination in systems that are not centralised is not found to have adverse effects on productivity.

- Many OECD countries have taken steps towards decentralisation in the past two decades. Overall, *organised* decentralisation as described above tends to deliver good employment performance, better productivity outcomes and higher wages for covered workers. By contrast, other forms of decentralisation that simply replace sector- with firm-level bargaining, without co-ordination within and across sectors, tend to be associated with somewhat poorer labour market outcomes.

The chapter also provides a detailed discussion of how wage co-ordination works and the features that make organised decentralisation capable to simultaneously achieve good labour market outcomes, provide some flexibility to firms and support adaptability to structural change. The main conclusions are:

- Co-ordination in wage bargaining helps take into account the macroeconomic effects of wage agreements by ensuring that these agreements do not undermine external competitiveness and are set in line with the business-cycle situation. This may be one factor behind the empirical association of co-ordinated systems with higher aggregate employment. The strongest form of wage co-ordination establishes a wage norm that defines the maximum for the collectively-agreed wage increase in every sector.

- In countries where co-ordination works well, it tends to be strongly supported by employer associations (since it moderates wage growth) and trade unions (since it ensures high levels of employment). To be effective, co-ordination requires strong and self-regulated social partners as well as effective mediation bodies.

- The effectiveness of the articulation of firm-level arrangements within framework agreements, which characterises organised decentralisation, hinges to an important extent on the degree of collective worker representation at the firm level.

- In some countries, trade unions and employer organisations engage in sector-level initiatives that aim to enhance labour market adaptability by facilitating job transitions and providing workers with the skills needed in a changing world of work.

Collective bargaining can only contribute to labour market inclusiveness and have a significant macroeconomic effect if it covers a large share of workers and companies:

- Well-organised trade unions and employer organisations with a broad support base tend to be the best way to attain high coverage. At the sector level, they ensure representativeness in wage negotiations. At the firm level, they are the basis for social dialogue between workers and employers.

- Collective bargaining is often confined to large and medium-sized enterprises and workers in standard employment. To promote social dialogue in large and small firms alike and also cover non-standard forms of work, competition and labour law as well as bargaining and organisation practices by social partners may need to adapt.

- In systems with sector-level bargaining and no broad-based representation, administrative extensions can help cover companies and workers not participating in collective bargaining. To avoid harming the economic prospects of start-ups, small firms or vulnerable workers, extensions need to be well-designed to ensure that the parties negotiating the agreements represent the collective interest of a large group of firms and workers. This can be achieved by subjecting extension requests to reasonable representativeness criteria and a meaningful test of public interest and providing well-defined procedures for exemptions and opt-outs of firms in case of serious economic hardship.

Introduction

Collective bargaining is under pressure in many OECD countries. Since the mid-1980s, trade union membership has halved (OECD, 2017[1]).[1] The fall in coverage of collective bargaining has been only a little less marked. In more than half of the countries, collective bargaining now covers less, and in some significantly less, than 50% of the workforce. Where coverage continues to be high, concerns are growing about the ability of collective bargaining to deliver good jobs in a time of global competition, technological change and a trend towards decentralisation of bargaining.

This chapter provides new insights on the role of collective bargaining for good labour market performance. This assessment of collective bargaining also contributes to the new *OECD Jobs Strategy* (OECD, forthcoming[2]), which identifies three main goals for successful labour market policies: i) more and better jobs; ii) labour market inclusiveness; and iii) resilience and adaptability. Collective bargaining has the potential to play a central role in all three. The chapter considers a variety of outcomes related to good labour market performance, including employment, wages, working conditions, inequality and productivity, while the role of collective bargaining for resilience was already investigated in OECD (2017[1]).

The chapter uses a variety of approaches including quantitative analyses and country case studies and mobilises both micro and macro data sources. The next section sets the scene by outlining a framework to illustrate how collective bargaining may matter for labour market performance and inclusive growth. Section 3.2 proceeds with a macroeconomic analysis of the role of collective bargaining for employment and inequality using a novel characterisation of collective bargaining systems. This allows going beyond previous macro-studies, which usually concentrated on the degree of collective bargaining coverage and the level of bargaining, by also taking account of the flexibility of firms to tailor the conditions of sector-level agreements to their needs and of the co-ordination of wages across bargaining units. Section 3.3 uses worker- and sector-level data to study the relationship of collective bargaining with wages, wage distribution and productivity, shedding light on some of the mechanisms behind the relationships found at the macro level. Section 3.4 discusses the role of workplace employee representation for the quality of the working environment. Drawing on a series of country case studies and the broader industrial relations literature, Section 3.5 discusses some policy options that social partners and governments may want to consider to make collective bargaining systems more flexible and more inclusive.

This chapter is part of a broader initiative of the OECD to better understand the role of collective bargaining and social dialogue today and in the future. The first major output of this undertaking was the comprehensive review of collective bargaining systems in OECD and accession countries in the 2017 *Employment Outlook* (OECD, 2017[1]). Subsequent work will analyse the role of collective bargaining for job quality and the future world of work.

3.1. The role of collective bargaining for labour market performance: An overview

Collective agreements signed by employers and unions primarily determine wage levels (or wage increases) and non-wage working conditions, including working time, leave arrangements, training, employment protection, and health and safety provisions (Figure 3.1). Re-negotiations of contracts by particular firms or employees may increase wages above the rate agreed at higher levels (or, in some cases, reduce wages below the negotiated rate). Outcomes such as employment or productivity are usually not part of the collective agreement, although they may be taken into account in the negotiations. The way collective bargaining influences labour market performance depends on the bargaining strategies of social partners, the structure of product and labour markets and the nature of collective bargaining institutions.

The academic literature has focused on two broad classes of bargaining strategies. In the so-called "right-to-manage" model (Leontief, 1946[3]), unions bargain exclusively over wages, leading to lower employment relative to the perfect competition benchmark. Union members, usually referred to as "insiders" in this literature, are viewed as gaining at the cost of "outsiders", unemployed individuals or individuals in vulnerable jobs not covered by collective bargaining (Lindbeck and Snower, 1986[4]). The cause of the presumed inefficiency is that employment is not accounted for in the negotiations. This could have the additional downside of reducing the resilience of the labour market against adverse macroeconomic shocks. In practice, however, unions may not only be concerned about wages but also employment and macroeconomic resilience. This has motivated the "efficient bargaining" model (McDonald and Solow, 1981[5]).[2]

The effect of collective bargaining depends also on the structure of the market and the degree of competition. With perfect competition in product and labour markets, raising wages above the market equilibrium wage induces unemployment. However, when product market competition is imperfect (i.e. when firms have some degree of monopoly or oligopoly power), higher wages may not induce greater unemployment but be simply the result of workers appropriating a greater share of the rents. Moreover, in imperfectly competitive labour markets, higher bargaining power and higher wage floors can increase employment. This would be the case in the presence of monopsony power, which enables firms to offer low wages, for example because workers have limited opportunities to change their employer or would incur high costs if they did so.[3]

Figure 3.1. Collective bargaining, labour market performance and inclusive growth

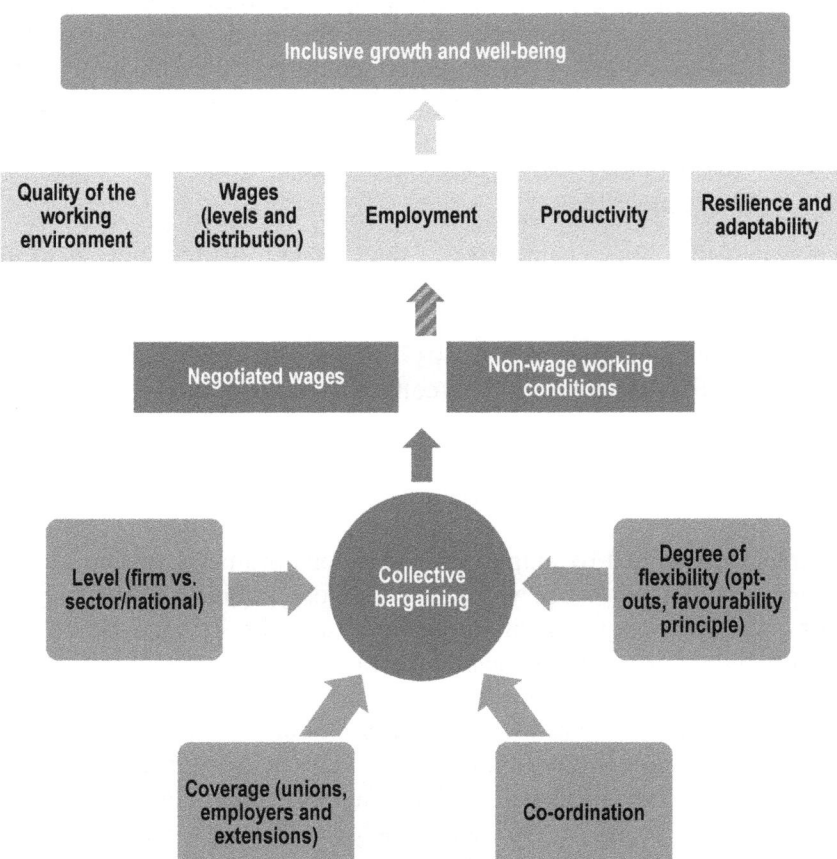

Finally, the role of collective bargaining for labour market performance also depends on the functioning of the institutional system. OECD (2017[1]) documented that collective bargaining systems differ considerably across OECD countries, even among those sharing similar characteristics. For example, the systems in the Netherlands and Portugal,[4] or those in Australia and the United States, although formally similar in many respects, differ substantially in the way they function. The main building blocks of collective bargaining systems are the degree of coverage, the level of bargaining, the degree of flexibility and the role of wage co-ordination:

- *Degree of coverage:* Collective bargaining coverage, rather than only trade union density, is essential to measure the relevance of the system. Collective agreements covering a large share of workers can have a more sizeable macroeconomic effect – positive or negative – on employment, wages and other outcomes of interest than agreements confined to a few firms.

- *Level of bargaining:* This defines the unit at which parties negotiate and may refer to the firm, sector or country. Sector-level or national agreements can be expected to reduce wage inequality relative to decentralised systems, by lowering wage differentials not only between workers in the same firm, but also between workers in different firms and, in the case of national bargaining, in different sectors. Firm-level agreements, by contrast, allow paying more attention to firm-specific conditions, potentially raising productivity.

- *Degree of flexibility:* Sector-level or national agreements may differ substantially in the degree of flexibility they provide to firms. For example, the possibility of opt-outs or leaving the application of the favourability principle to social partners can increase the flexibility of the system and allow for a stronger link between wages and firm performance, with on the upside higher employment and productivity, but on the downside higher wage inequality.

- *Wage co-ordination:* Wage co-ordination between sector-level agreements (or as in the case of Japan between firm-level agreements) helps negotiators internalise the macroeconomic effects of the terms set in collective agreements. This is typically achieved by keeping wage increases in the non-tradable sector in line with what can be afforded by the tradable sector or by strengthening the ability of the system to adjust wages or working time in the face of a macroeconomic downturn. Co-ordination can therefore serve as an instrument for wage moderation and earnings flexibility over the business cycle, with potential benefits for employment and resilience.

Social partners affect labour market outcomes and hence inclusive growth and well-being also by influencing and, sometimes, negotiating or even managing other labour market institutions, such as the minimum wage, labour laws (in particular employment protection legislation), unemployment benefits, active labour market policies, payroll taxes, and family and pension policies. Further, any effects of collective bargaining systems also depend on the other policies and institutions in place. For instance, if decentralisation increases wage inequality, the magnitude of the effect on the broader concept of disposable income inequality depends on the extent to which the tax-and-transfer system offsets the rise in wage inequality. While sometimes important, these issues go beyond the scope of this chapter.

3.2. The role of collective bargaining for employment and wage inequality: New evidence from macro-data

The economic literature has long debated the role of collective bargaining for labour market performance, but paid little attention to the system of collective bargaining as a whole. Studies have mostly examined the presence or relevance of collective bargaining rather than its functioning. For example, many analyses of countries with predominantly firm-level bargaining, such as the United Kingdom or the United States, have focused on the role of trade union membership.[5] Union membership is a reasonable proxy of collective bargaining coverage in countries with predominantly firm-level bargaining. But it is not sufficient for measuring the scope of collective bargaining, as many workers who are not affiliated to a trade union are also covered by collective bargaining – via *erga omnes* clauses and, in countries with sector- or multi-level bargaining, administrative extensions (OECD, 2017[1]).[6] Bargaining coverage is therefore in general a more appropriate proxy for the relevance of collective bargaining.[7]

However, to capture the role of collective bargaining for labour market performance, it is important to go beyond coverage by looking at its main features and actual functioning. Collective bargaining coverage in Italy is comparable to that in the Netherlands or the Nordic countries. Similarly, Australia and Germany have comparable coverage. As OECD (2017[1]) shows, these systems are nevertheless very different. It is therefore important to also consider the characteristics of the system itself. This echoes Aidt and Tzannatos (2008[6]) in their review of trade unions, collective bargaining and macroeconomic performance in which they concluded that, more than trade union density or coverage, what matters most is the functioning of the "entire package".

In terms of main features, most attention has been directed to the role of centralisation, i.e. the predominant level of bargaining. In the early 1980s, the corporatist view suggested that by guaranteeing that wage-setters recognise broader interests, centralisation, intended as national bargaining, can deliver superior outcomes in terms of macroeconomic and labour market performance (Cameron, 1984[7]).[8] However, opponents pointed out that wage increases would be restrained or resource allocation would be more effective if market forces were allowed to play a larger role, bringing the example of the United States or the United Kingdom after Thatcher to support this view.

To reconcile these opposing views, Calmfors and Driffill (1988[8]) proposed the influential "hump-shape" hypothesis, which suggested that both centralisation and decentralisation perform well in terms of employment while the worst outcomes may be found in systems with an intermediate degree of centralisation, i.e. sector-level bargaining. In this intermediate case, organised interests are "strong enough to cause major disruptions, but not sufficiently encompassing to bear any significant fraction of the costs for society of their actions in their own interests" (Calmfors and Driffill, 1988[8]). The paper by Calmfors and Driffill had the merit to suggest that the relationship between the degree of centralisation and performance does not need to be monotonic. This hypothesis was behind the critical stance on sector-level bargaining systems in the 1994 *OECD Jobs Strategy* (OECD, 1994[9]) which recommended decentralising collective bargaining given the impossibility to have full centralisation of bargaining systems.[9] However, later empirical studies did not provide much backing for this hypothesis – see OECD (1997[10]), Traxler, Blaschke and Kittel (2001[11]), Aidt and Tzannatos (2002[12]), Bassanini and Duval (2006[13]) and Eurofound (2015[14]).

Another key feature of collective bargaining systems is the degree of wage co-ordination across bargaining units. Soskice (1990[15]) suggested that co-ordinated systems of sectoral bargaining may be as effective as national bargaining systems at adapting to aggregate economic conditions. Subsequent studies found that co-ordination plays a key role in improving the performance of sector-level bargaining – see the review in Aidt and Tzannatos (2002[12]) as well as the evidence in Elmeskov et al. (1998[16]), OECD (2004[17]), Bassanini and Duval (2006[13]), OECD (2012[18]) and Eurofound (2015[14]). The *Reassessed OECD Jobs Strategy* (OECD, 2006[19]) embraced this "augmented" version of the Calmfors-Driffill hypothesis which entailed that decentralised and centralised or co-ordinated bargaining systems result in better employment performance than sectoral bargaining systems.[10]

More recently, Boeri (2014[20]) revived the debate by suggesting that "two-tier" bargaining systems (i.e. where firm-level bargaining can only top up sector-level bargaining) are worse than fully centralised and fully decentralised systems, as they are not able to respond appropriately either to a microeconomic shock or a macroeconomic one.[11]

All in all, the characterisation and estimation of the economic effects of collective bargaining systems have proven to be a major challenge, leading to a proliferation of indicators for centralisation and co-ordination as well as econometric specifications.

3.2.1. New country-level evidence based on a taxonomy of collective bargaining systems

The role of collective bargaining for labour market performance should be analysed by looking at bargaining systems as a whole, rather than simply at the sum of their components. This section therefore uses a new taxonomy of collective bargaining systems for studying the links with employment and inequality.

The taxonomy of collective bargaining systems is taken from the dashboard in OECD (2017[1]). This proposed a classification scheme based on two main aspects: i) the degree of centralisation as characterised by the predominant level of bargaining as well as the rules and use of extensions, derogations, opt-outs and the favourability principle; and ii) the degree of wage co-ordination between sector-level agreements. OECD (2018[21]) provides further details. The following five categories of collective bargaining systems were identified:[12]

- *Predominantly centralised and weakly co-ordinated collective bargaining systems:* Sector-level agreements play a strong role, extensions are relatively widely used, derogations from higher-level agreements are possible but usually limited or not often used, and wage co-ordination is largely absent. In 2015, France, Iceland, Italy, Portugal, Slovenia, Spain and Switzerland fell in this group.[13]

- *Predominantly centralised and co-ordinated collective bargaining systems:* As in the previous category, sector-level agreements play a strong role and the room for lower-level agreements to derogate from higher-level ones is quite limited. However, wage co-ordination is strong across sectors. In 2015, Belgium and Finland were part of this group.

- *Organised decentralised and co-ordinated collective bargaining systems:* Sector-level agreements play an important role, but they also leave significant room for lower-level agreements to set the standards – either by limiting the role of extensions (rare and never automatic or quasi-automatic), leaving the design of the hierarchy of agreements to bargaining parties or allowing opt-outs. Co-ordination across sectors and bargaining units tends to be strong. In 2015, Austria, Denmark, Germany, the Netherlands, Norway and Sweden were in this group.

- *Largely decentralised collective bargaining systems:* Firm-level bargaining is the dominant bargaining form, but sector-level bargaining (or a functional equivalent) or wage co-ordination also play a role. Extensions are very rare. Australia with its "Modern Awards" (see Box 3.5 for details) and Japan with its unique form of co-ordination (*Shunto*) were in this group in 2015, as well as Greece, Luxembourg and the Slovak Republic. Since the enactment of the Industrial Relations (Amendment) Act of October 2015, which re-introduced "Sectoral Employment Orders", Ireland is also part of this group.

- *Fully decentralised collective bargaining systems:* Bargaining is essentially confined to the firm or establishment level with no co-ordination and no (or very limited) influence by the government. In 2015, Canada, Chile, the Czech Republic, Estonia, Hungary, Korea, Latvia, Lithuania, Mexico, New Zealand, Poland, Turkey, the United Kingdom and the United States were part of this group.

The country classification in 2015 was extended backwards to 1980 using information in the Institutional Characteristics of Trade Unions, Wage Setting, State Intervention and Social Pacts (ICTWSS) database.[14] The time variation in the resulting taxonomy of collective bargaining systems for OECD countries over the period 1980-2015 is considerable – see OECD (2018[21]). It reflects, in large part, the strong trend towards decentralised collective bargaining, but it also captures many country-specific changes in collective bargaining practices. These differences in the time variation are exploited in the analysis to estimate the relationship between systems of collective bargaining and indicators of labour market performance.

The analysis compares labour market outcomes under different collective bargaining systems relative to the fully decentralised system, while controlling for the level of bargaining coverage as well as the possible role of the business cycle, the characteristics of the workforce and persistent country-specific features (using country fixed effects).[15] The results also account for other policy reforms that occurred at the same time, in the areas of labour taxation, product market regulation, job dismissal regulation, minimum wages and unemployment benefits. The relationships estimated in this section may nevertheless be influenced by the state of the labour market over and above the business cycle or other potentially important factors not controlled for; hence, care should be taken not to give the results a strict causal interpretation.

Co-ordinated bargaining systems are associated with higher employment and lower unemployment relative to fully decentralised systems (Panel A of Figure 3.2). This is particularly the case for predominantly centralised systems, while for organised decentralised systems the result on unemployment is somewhat smaller and less robust. Centralised but weakly co-ordinated systems and largely decentralised systems hold an intermediate position, with better employment outcomes than in fully decentralised ones but similar unemployment outcomes. The difference between the employment and unemployment results suggests that such systems are linked with higher employment and labour force participation. On average across all regimes, higher bargaining coverage is associated with lower employment rates (OECD, 2018[21]). Given that in centralised and co-ordinated systems more workers tend to be covered, the extent to which these systems are linked with better employment outcomes could thus be somewhat lower than is displayed in the figure.

Empirically, the relative underperformance of fully decentralised systems is identified from variation in three countries (Ireland, New Zealand and the United Kingdom), which all undertook very significant collective bargaining reforms. The finding does not appear to be specific to these three countries, as it remains unchanged when country fixed effects are omitted from the regression. The results overall are qualitatively robust to two further sensitivity checks – see OECD (2018[21]) for details. First, they are similar when more traditional collective bargaining indicators for centralisation and co-ordination (from the ICTWSS database) are used instead of the new taxonomy indicators.[16] Second, the results with respect to collective bargaining regimes are qualitatively unchanged when collective bargaining coverage is not controlled for.

It is sometimes argued that collective bargaining delivers good labour market outcomes for "insiders" (notably prime-age male full-time workers with a permanent contract) at the expense of jobs for "outsiders", such as youth, women and low-skilled – see Saint-Paul (1996[22]) and Bertola (1999[23]). Moreover, by pushing the interests of "insiders", unions may accept or even contribute to the proliferation of non-standard forms of employment as a buffer for its members, thereby reducing the inclusiveness of the labour market. In particular, unions may make temporary contracts indirectly more attractive for firms, by increasing the labour cost of "insiders", for instance through bargaining over severance pay or assisting workers faced with the risk of dismissal.

The evidence, however, suggests that, in most cases, co-ordinated systems – either centralised or organised decentralised – are associated with better labour market outcomes for vulnerable groups (Panels B and C of Figure 3.2). The unemployment rates of youth, women and low-skilled workers appear to be consistently lower (or at least not higher) in co-ordinated systems than in decentralised ones. Co-ordinated and organised decentralised systems are also associated with a lower share of involuntary part-time workers. Although the share of temporary employment does not vary across different bargaining systems, it is higher in countries with higher bargaining coverage – see OECD (2018[21]). This result, while different from previous evidence on agency work in the United States by Gramm and Schnell (2001[24]) and Autor (2003[25]), is in line with the findings of Salvatori (2009[26]) who shows, looking at 21 European countries, that unionised workplaces are more likely to use temporary employment.

Collective bargaining systems that are not fully decentralised are also correlated with lower wage inequality for full-time employees (Figure 3.3), as measured by the D9/D1-ratio, i.e. the ratio of the wage at the ninth decile of the wage distribution to the wage at the first decile. This association is present both in the lower and upper half of the wage distribution.[17] Similar results are obtained when replacing the taxonomy indicators with indicators for centralisation and co-ordination – see OECD (2018[21]).

Strengthening the bargaining power of low-wage workers is one of the core missions of collective bargaining, so it is not surprising that empirically collective bargaining is associated with lower levels of inequality. Detailed pay scales, where they are defined, can compress wages in the middle and top of the distribution to compensate for higher wages at the bottom; Leonardi, Pellizzari and Tabasso (2015[27]) provide evidence of wage compression within Italian firms. These mechanisms are particularly relevant when bargaining covers a substantial share of the working population. Section 3.3 provides further evidence on the positive role of collective bargaining for wage equality based on matched employer-employee and sector-level data. The inequality results in this chapter complement previous findings that point in the same direction, from earlier studies by Blanchflower and Freeman (1993[28]), Blau and Kahn (1999[29]), Card, Lemieux and Riddell (2004[30]) and DiNardo and Lee (2004[31]) to more recent ones including OECD (2011[32]), ILO (2015[33]) and Jaumotte and Buitron (2015[34]).

In conclusion, using country-level data on labour market outcomes for 35 OECD countries between 1980 and 2016 and a novel characterisation of collective bargaining systems, co-ordinated systems are shown to be associated with higher employment, lower unemployment, a better integration of vulnerable groups and less wage inequality than fully decentralised systems. Weakly co-ordinated, centralised systems and largely decentralised systems hold an intermediate position, performing similarly in terms of unemployment to fully decentralised systems, but sharing many of the positive effects on other outcomes with co-ordinated systems.

Figure 3.2. Collective bargaining systems and employment outcomes

Difference in percentage points with respect to fully decentralised systems

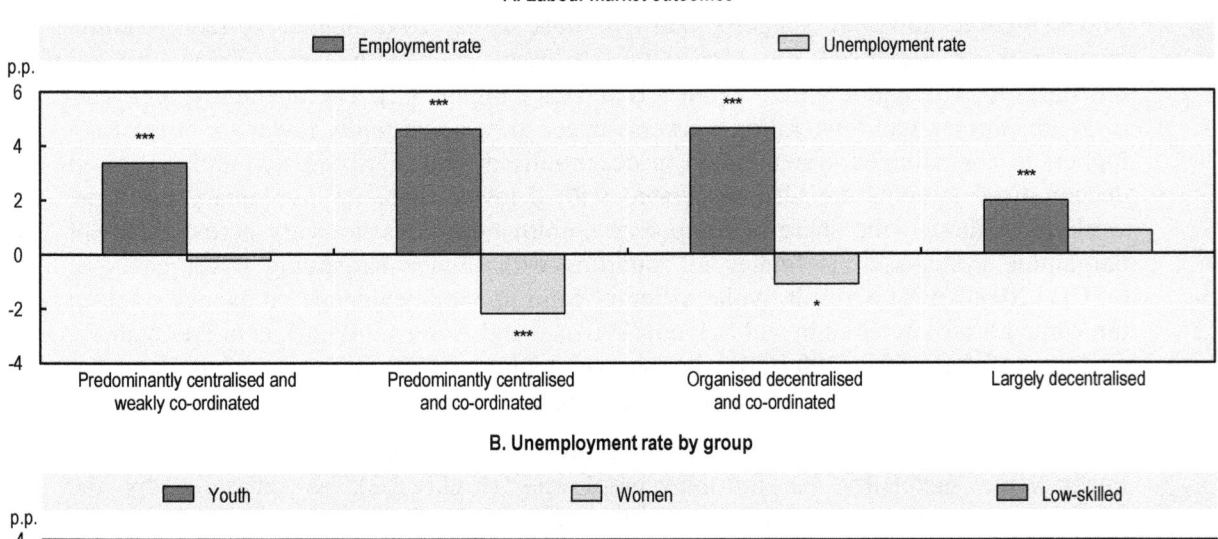

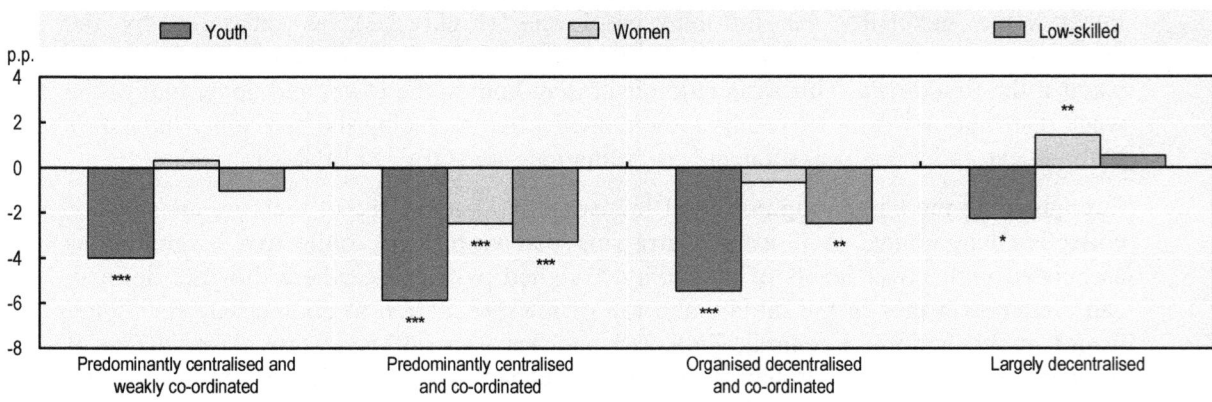

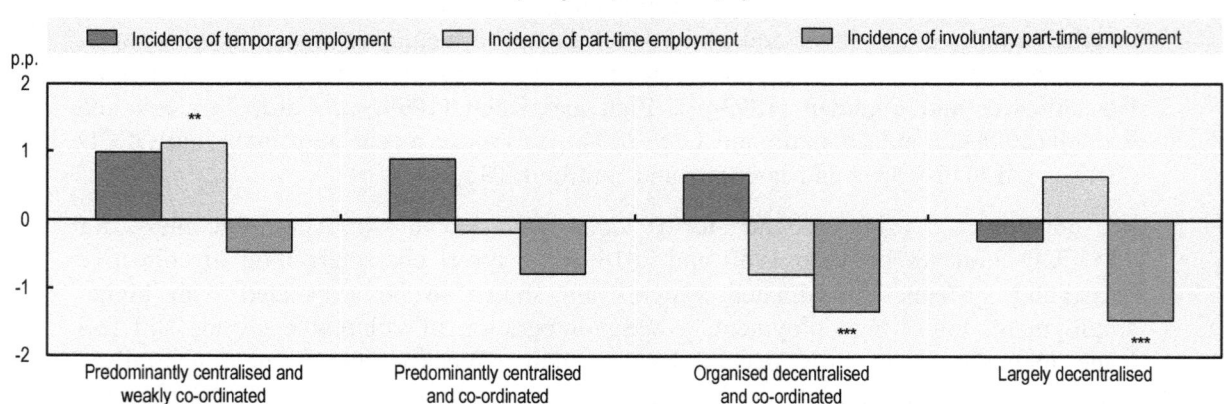

Note: ***, **, *: statistically significant at the 1, 5 or 10% level, respectively. Results are based on Ordinary Least Squares (OLS) regressions including country and year dummies, collective bargaining coverage, log of average years of education, female employment share and institutional variables: tax wedge, product market regulation, employment protection legislation (both temporary and permanent), ratio of minimum wage to median wage and gross unemployment benefit replacement rate. p.p.: percentage points.
Source: OECD estimates. Details on sources and definitions can be found in OECD (2018[21]), "Supplementary material for Chapter 3", *OECD Employment Outlook 2018*, http://dx.doi.org/10.1787/empl_outlook-2018-13-en.

StatLink 🔗 http://dx.doi.org/10.1787/888933778003

Figure 3.3. Collective bargaining and wage dispersion

Point difference with respect to fully decentralised systems

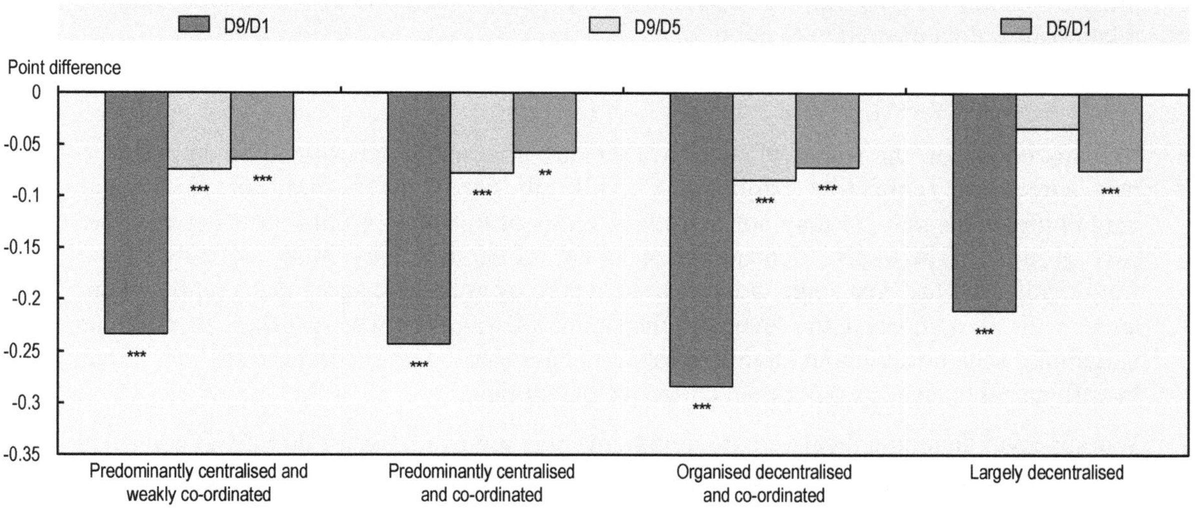

Note: ***, **, *: statistically significant at the 1, 5 or 10% level, respectively. Results are based on Ordinary Least Squares (OLS) regressions including country and year dummies, collective bargaining coverage, log of average years of education, female employment share and institutional variables: tax wedge, product market regulation, employment protection legislation (both temporary and permanent), ratio of minimum wage to median wage and gross unemployment benefit replacement rate. Wage inequality measures are based on the gross wage of full-time wage and salary workers. D1, D5 and D9 stand for the 1st, 5th and 9th decile of the wage distribution.
Source: OECD estimates. Details on sources and definitions can be found in OECD (2018[21]), "Supplementary material for Chapter 3", *OECD Employment Outlook 2018*, http://dx.doi.org/10.1787/empl_outlook-2018-13-en.

StatLink 🖳 http://dx.doi.org/10.1787/888933778022

3.3. The role of collective bargaining for inclusiveness and flexibility: New evidence from micro-data

By centralising or co-ordinating negotiations over wages and working conditions, collective bargaining has a tendency to compress pay differences among workers. As a result, it weakens the link between individual performance, wages and working conditions. In the context of firm-level bargaining, overall firm performance necessarily becomes the main reference for negotiations on pay increases rather than individual performance. Similarly, in the context of sector-level bargaining, overall industry performance becomes the main contextual factor for pay increases. In the same vein, centralisation and co-ordination place a greater emphasis on macroeconomic performance and therefore competitiveness and resilience.

Collective bargaining may manifest itself in a lower dispersion of wages, by defining common criteria for wages of workers, firms or sectors. But by the same mechanism, it may also lead to stronger rigidities in wages over time, as negotiating partners are less flexible to tailor wages to the individual worker, firm or sector. The effects of such rigidities are likely to depend on the context in which they occur. In some cases, they may be benign, for example when they reduce the scope for discriminatory practices or serve a specific economic purpose as in the case of co-ordination, while in others they may raise concerns, for instance when they weaken incentives for skill acquisition.

This section uses worker- and sector-level data to shed further light on the relationship between collective bargaining institutions, wage equality, productivity growth and the way wages are set in line with productivity in firms and sectors. In doing so, the analysis provides useful insights into the mechanisms that may drive some of the macroeconomic relationships documented in Section 3.2.

3.3.1. Collective bargaining and wage dispersion

In many countries, the wages of some workers are principally determined by a collective pay agreement (collective bargaining), while those of others are not (individual bargaining). This may, or may not, introduce forms of injustice or unfairness between the two groups of workers, depending on what collective bargaining actually does. Empirically, the fact that some workers are covered by collective agreements while others are not allows comparing the level and dispersion of wages between workers in different bargaining schemes, without having to rely on country-to-country comparisons that might be influenced by aspects other than collective bargaining.

Worker-level data on collective bargaining coverage are available for 20 OECD countries (plus one accession country, Lithuania). Besides distinguishing workers covered by collective bargaining from those who are not, the micro-data separately identify workers whose wage is primarily determined by a firm- as opposed to a sector-level agreement.[18] This creates the possibility of distinguishing three bargaining levels: i) individual or no collective bargaining; ii) firm-level bargaining; and iii) sector-level bargaining. The three co-exist in the dataset for seven of the 21 countries; in the others two co-exist. Labour earnings are defined per hour and include bonus payments. As in Section 3.2, dispersion is measured as the ratio of wages at the ninth decile to the first decile.

When comparing wage dispersion between workers who are covered by collective bargaining and those who are not, it is important to account for possible sample selection: For instance, if collective agreements cover mainly men, or certain industries, wage dispersion may be lower with collective bargaining because wages tend to be more similar among men only, or among certain industries, than in the entire working population. Different empirical techniques can be applied to adjust for these compositional differences between bargaining groups. The one used in this section goes back to Juhn, Murphy and Pierce (1993[35]) and has been widely used since.[19] For each country and bargaining level separately a standard hourly wage regression is run on a large number of explanatory variables: age, gender, education, firm size, contract type, years employed in the firm, industry and occupation. Differences in composition are then corrected by replacing the coefficients and residuals in each bargaining level with those for the group of workers who are not covered. Box 3.1 describes the empirical approach in detail.

Box 3.1. Empirical approach to adjust wages and wage dispersion for differences in composition

Differences in wages and wage dispersion between workers covered by collective bargaining and those not could, in part, be due to differences in composition. A standard way to adjust for these compositional differences is provided by Juhn, Murphy and Pierce (1993[35]). Applying this method in the present context, for each country and bargaining level b (no collective bargaining, firm-level bargaining, sector-level bargaining) separately, the following regression is run:

$$\log(w_{ib}) = x_{ib}\beta_b + \varepsilon_{ib}.$$

The wage of worker i is measured per hour, and weights in the survey are used to better align the sample with the actual working population. Control variables, x_{ib}, include dummies for age, gender, education, firm size, contract type (permanent or temporary), job tenure, industry and occupation. A few control variables are not available for some countries. Comparing estimated coefficients, $\hat{\beta}$, for the same variables allows examining, for instance, differences in the gender gap or education premium between workers covered by collective bargaining and those who are not.

The empirical approach to adjust a wage statistic, $f(w_b)$, such as the average wage or D9/D1-ratio, for compositional differences is as follows. Workers whose wages are not governed by collective bargaining, b_1, are taken as the benchmark. In Belgium, France and Spain where data for workers not covered are not available, firm-level bargaining is taken as the benchmark. The counterfactual wage of worker i covered by collective bargaining, b_2, is then calculated as

$$\log(w_{ib_2}^x) = x_{ib_2}\hat{\beta}_{b_1} + \hat{\varepsilon}_{ib_1}(\hat{p}_{ib_2}|x_{b_2}),$$

with the last expression denoting the residual from the regression for workers not covered that is at the same percentile $\hat{p}_{ib_2}$ as worker i's residual. The assumption is that, had a covered worker become uncovered while maintaining the same characteristics, the new residual of the worker would have belonged to the same percentile of the distribution of the residuals in the uncovered sector as the percentile the old residual belonged to in the distribution of the covered sector.

The difference in the desired wage statistic using the raw data is

$$f(w_{b_2}) - f(w_{b_1}),$$

which after adjusting for differences in composition becomes

$$f(w_{b_2}) - f(w_{b_2}^x).$$

On average, earnings dispersion is lower with collective bargaining, when accounting for compositional differences (Figure 3.4). In the first group of countries where all three bargaining levels co-exist, wage dispersion is highest among workers not covered by collective bargaining, followed by firm-level and then sector-level bargaining. By contrast, for the second group of countries where there is no sector-level bargaining, wage dispersion among workers covered and those not, at least on average, is the same. A cross-country comparison of the averages for the first two groups suggests that firm-level bargaining is only effective in lowering wage dispersion when it comes on top of sector-level bargaining. One possible explanation for this may be that companies characterised by firm-level bargaining are in most cases also covered by sector-level bargaining. Firm-level bargaining may then not fully undo the inequality reduction due to sector-level bargaining. In five countries (Hungary, Korea, Mexico, Norway and Portugal), the results go in the opposite direction. Nevertheless, overall, they appear consistent with those in the previous section which suggested that the economy-wide distribution of wages is less equal in systems without scope for sector- or higher-level bargaining (see Figure 3.3).

3.3.2. What accounts for the lower wage dispersion with collective bargaining?

Empirically, two categories of factors may account for the lower wage dispersion with collective bargaining: differences in the returns to characteristics (technically, the coefficients) and unexplained differences (the residual). This issue is investigated here by focusing on the two largest country groups for which data are available: the first with seven countries (which have three collective bargaining types) and the second with nine countries (which have two types: firm-level bargaining and no collective agreement).

Four characteristics are studied to analyse the extent to which collective bargaining may compress their returns (Figure 3.5): a higher age, being male, a better education and seniority at work (measured by the number of years in the firm). All four typically exhibit increasing returns in micro-level analyses, meaning that older, male, more educated and more experienced workers tend to earn more.

Compared with uncovered workers, the age premium is lower for people who are covered by firm-level bargaining and even more so for those covered by sector-level bargaining. Collective bargaining thus lowers wage inequality, in part by flattening the distribution of wages among people of different ages. By contrast, no evidence is detected that collective bargaining compresses the gender pay gap on average. If anything, men's wage premium over women is slightly larger among workers covered by collective bargaining than those who are not.

The benefit of better education, in terms of higher pay, is lower with firm- and even more so sector-level bargaining. A lower payoff from education, while reducing inequality, may also negatively affect productivity growth if this leads to lower investment in education. Finally, monetary rewards for seniority are also found to be an explanatory factor for why in countries with firm- and sector-level bargaining wage dispersion is lower with collective bargaining than without, although the picture is the opposite in the group of countries with only firm-level bargaining.

Even if reduced returns to age, education and seniority go some way towards explaining the lower wage dispersion with collective bargaining, overall it is mainly unobserved factors that reduce wage dispersion (Figure 3.6).

Figure 3.4. Composition-adjusted wage dispersion by level of collective bargaining

Ratio of the 9th to the 1st earnings decile

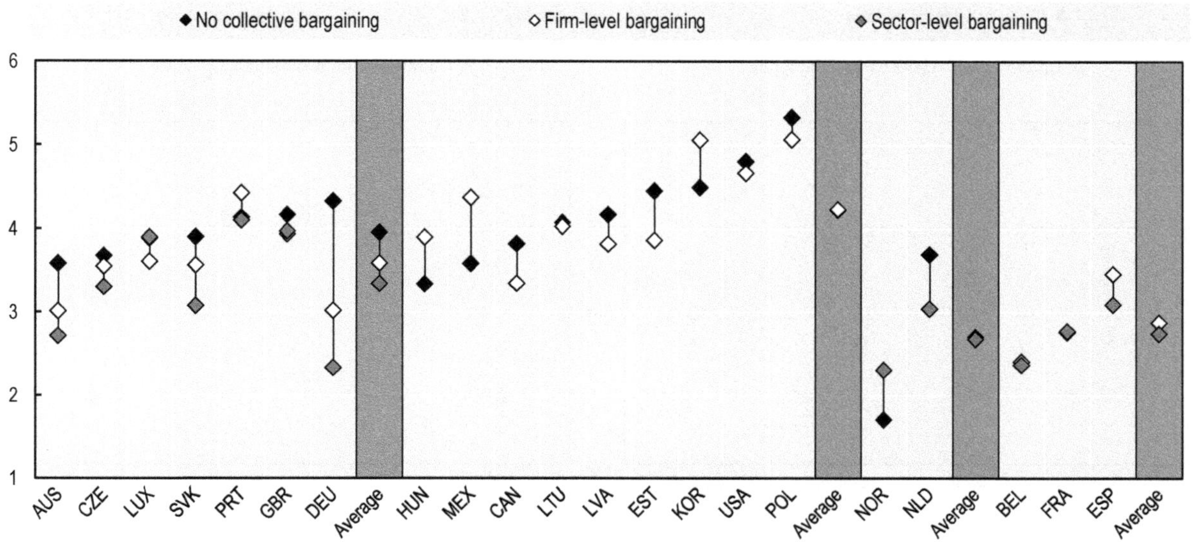

Note: Results are based on Juhn-Murphy-Pierce decompositions using workers without a collective agreement as the reference group and controlling for gender, age, educational attainment, industry, occupation, firm size, type of contract and job tenure. Countries are ordered in ascending order of the D9/D1-ratio for employees not covered by a collective agreement, where D1 and D9 stand for the 1st and 9th decile of the wage distribution. Data are from 2012-16, depending on the country (2006 for Germany). The first group of countries allows comparing wage dispersion among workers not covered by collective bargaining with that among workers covered by firm-level agreements and that among workers covered by sector-level agreements. The second group compares wage dispersion among uncovered workers with that among workers with a firm-level agreement. The third group compares wage dispersion among uncovered workers with that among workers with a sector-level agreement. The final group allows comparing wage dispersion among workers with a firm-level agreement with that among workers with a sector-level agreement. "Sector-level bargaining" for Australia refers to the use of Modern Awards (see Box 3.5). A proper sector-level bargaining does not exist in Australia.
Source: OECD calculations based on the European Structure of Earnings Survey (SES) for European countries, the Household, Income and Labour Dynamics survey (HILDA) for Australia, the Labour Force Survey (LFS) for Canada, the Korean Labor and Income Panel Study (KLIPS) for Korea, the *Encuesta Nacional de Ocupación y Empleo* (ENOE) for Mexico and the Current Population Survey Merged Outgoing Rotation Group (CPS MORG) for the United States.

StatLink ᵐˢᴾ http://dx.doi.org/10.1787/888933778041

3.3.3. Collective bargaining wage premium

This section has so far focused on wage dispersion within each bargaining type, i.e. wage dispersion among workers not covered by collective agreements and wage dispersion among workers covered by collective bargaining. Results can be interpreted as illustrating what would happen to wage inequality if in a country collective bargaining moved from inexistent to full coverage or from full to no coverage. This naturally seems extreme. When considering less extreme scenarios, account should also be taken of pay differences which may exist between workers covered by collective agreements and those not. Such pay differences are sometimes referred to as the collective bargaining wage premium.

Figure 3.5. Wage returns by level of collective bargaining

Unweighted averages across countries, 2014

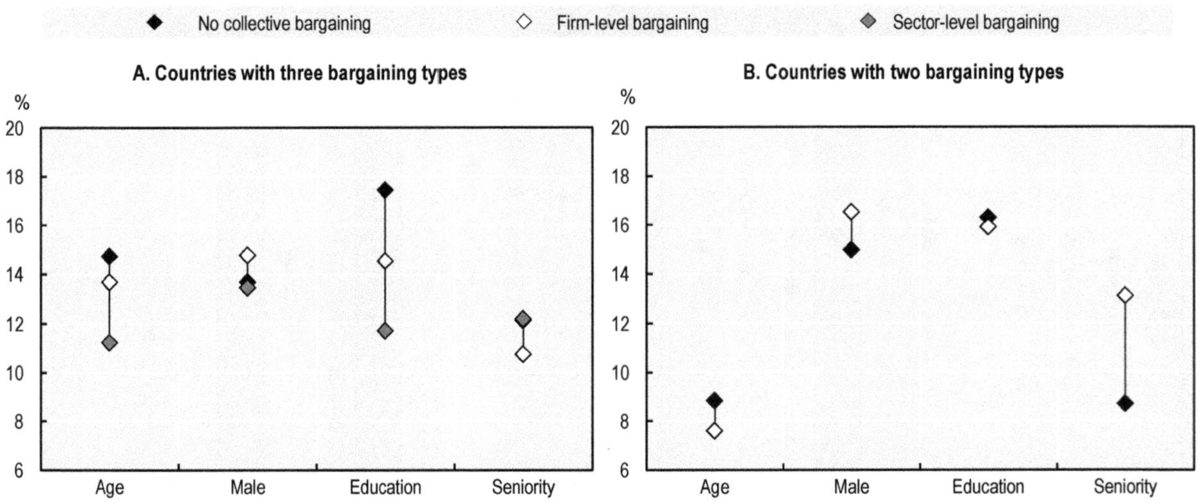

◆ No collective bargaining   ◇ Firm-level bargaining   ◆ Sector-level bargaining

A. Countries with three bargaining types

B. Countries with two bargaining types

Note: Results are based on ordinary least squares (OLS) regressions controlling for gender, age, educational attainment, industry, occupation, firm size, type of contract and job tenure. Data are from 2012-16, depending on the country (2006 for Germany). The age premium is calculated relative to 20-29-year-olds, the education premium relative to workers with no high school education and the seniority premium relative to workers who have worked for their current employer for less than one year. The categories for the comparison groups (different age groups, education categories and brackets for number of years in the firm) are weighted by the proportion of workers in these categories. The countries with three bargaining types are Australia, the Czech Republic, Germany, Luxembourg, Portugal, the Slovak Republic and the United Kingdom. The countries with two bargaining types are Canada, Estonia, Hungary, Korea, Latvia, Lithuania, Mexico, Poland and the United States.

Source: OECD calculations based on the European Structure of Earnings Survey (SES) for European countries, the Household, Income and Labour Dynamics survey (HILDA) for Australia, the Labour Force Survey (LFS) for Canada, the Korean Labor and Income Panel Study (KLIPS) for Korea, the *Encuesta Nacional de Ocupación y Empleo* (ENOE) for Mexico and the Current Population Survey Merged Outgoing Rotation Group (CPS MORG) for the United States.

StatLink ㎙㎱ http://dx.doi.org/10.1787/888933778060

Workers are paid more with firm-level bargaining, while sector-level bargaining is not associated with relatively higher pay on average (Figure 3.7). This is not surprising as firm-level negotiations can often only raise wages relative to sector-level agreements. The differences in wages may also signal higher productivity in companies with firm-level bargaining. The results are in line with a large body of the literature which finds that sector-level bargaining is not linked with higher wages on average – see Dell'Aringa and Lucifora (1994[36]), Hartog, Leuven and Teulings (2002[37]), Rycx (2003[38]) and Cardoso and Portugal (2005[39]). The variation for sector-level bargaining across countries is large, with a positive premium in some countries and a negative one in others. By contrast, wages of workers covered by firm-level agreements are higher than those of uncovered workers in all countries except Latvia. In countries with low collective bargaining coverage, wage inequality can thus rise as firm-level bargaining expands to include more workers, even if wage dispersion is smaller among workers covered by firm-level bargaining than among those who are not.

Figure 3.6. Accounting for the differences in wage dispersion with and without collective bargaining

Change in the ratio of the 9th to the 1st earnings decile relative to employees not covered by collective bargaining (adjusted for composition), 2014

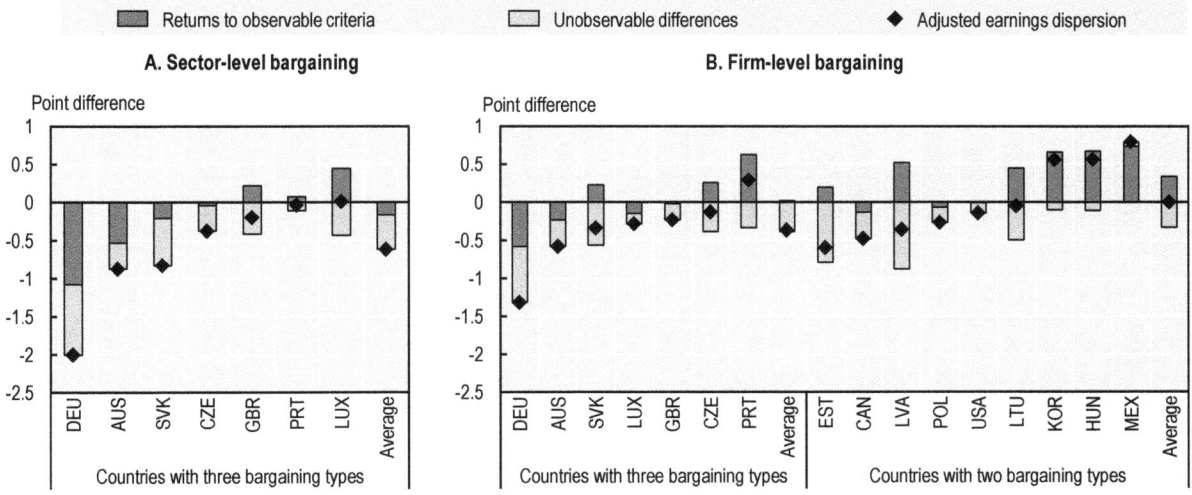

Note: Results are based on Juhn-Murphy-Pierce decompositions using workers without a collective agreement as the reference group and controlling for gender, age, educational attainment, industry, occupation, firm size, type of contract and job tenure. Data are from 2012-16, depending on the country (2006 for Germany). For countries with three bargaining types, data are available for firm- and sector-level bargaining and no collective bargaining. For countries with two bargaining types, data are available for firm-level bargaining and no collective bargaining. "Sector-level bargaining" for Australia refers to the use of Modern Awards (see Box 3.5). A proper sector-level bargaining does not exist in Australia.
Source: OECD calculations based on the European Structure of Earnings Survey (SES) for European countries, the Household, Income and Labour Dynamics survey (HILDA) for Australia, the Labour Force Survey (LFS) for Canada, the Korean Labor and Income Panel Study (KLIPS) for Korea, the *Encuesta Nacional de Ocupación y Empleo* (ENOE) for Mexico and the Current Population Survey Merged Outgoing Rotation Group (CPS MORG) for the United States.

StatLink ᵐˢ᪲ http://dx.doi.org/10.1787/888933778079

3.3.4. Collective bargaining and wage-productivity misalignment

The analysis above has shown that collective bargaining tends to be associated with lower wage dispersion. The stronger wage compression with collective bargaining may reflect a more pronounced misalignment of wages with a firm's or sector's productivity, because centralisation or co-ordination of negotiations makes pay in part determined by factors other than the firm or sector. In this sense, lower wage flexibility at the sub-national level and lower wage dispersion could be seen as two sides of the same coin.[20]

The extent to which wages in a particular firm or sector correspond to the productivity in the firm or sector can be estimated with available data. By comparing countries with one another, the analysis that follows provides suggestive evidence that wages tend to be less aligned with labour productivity in countries where collective bargaining institutions have a more important role.[21]

Figure 3.7. Wage premium by level of collective bargaining

Composition-adjusted difference in average wages relative to no collective bargaining, 2014

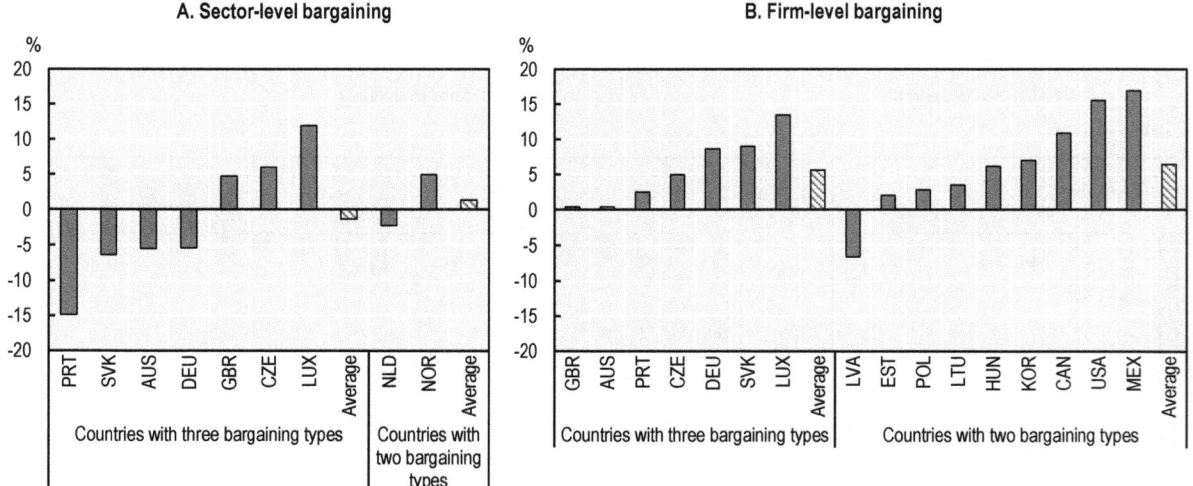

Note: Results are based on Juhn-Murphy-Pierce decompositions using workers without a collective agreement as the reference group and controlling for gender, age, educational attainment, industry, occupation, firm size, type of contract and job tenure. Data are from 2012-16, depending on the country (2006 for Germany). "Sector-level bargaining" for Australia refers to the use of Modern Awards (see Box 3.5). A proper sector-level bargaining does not exist in Australia.
Source: OECD calculations based on the European Structure of Earnings Survey (SES) for European countries, the Household, Income and Labour Dynamics survey (HILDA) for Australia, the Labour Force Survey (LFS) for Canada, the Korean Labor and Income Panel Study (KLIPS) for Korea, the *Encuesta Nacional de Ocupación y Empleo* (ENOE) for Mexico and the Current Population Survey Merged Outgoing Rotation Group (CPS MORG) for the United States.

StatLink ⬛ᵢₗ⬛ http://dx.doi.org/10.1787/888933778098

The analysis relies on insights using sector-level data, examining the correlation between wages and productivity across sectors. Sector-level data have the advantage that they cover the same number of units (i.e. sectors) for many countries over a long period of time. They are available for 27 OECD countries (plus Lithuania) from 1980 to 2014, covering 24 sectors. Box 3.2 describes the estimation approach.

Countries show marked differences in the degree to which wages and productivity are aligned for different sectors (Figure 3.8).[22] The correlation is relatively high in many Eastern European countries (the Czech Republic, Estonia, Hungary, Latvia, Lithuania and Poland). It is also high in Korea, Portugal, Spain and the United Kingdom. By contrast, misalignments of wages with productivity appear to be strong in some Nordic countries (Denmark, Finland, Norway and Sweden), as well as Belgium, Greece, Luxembourg and Slovenia.

Box 3.2. Empirical approach to estimate the role of collective bargaining for wage-productivity alignment

The alignment of wages with productivity is estimated through the strength of the correlation of the hourly wage rate with hourly labour productivity. The baseline regression uses sector-level data and is as follows:

$$\log(w_{sct}) = \beta_c \log(\text{LP}_{sct}) + \alpha_{ct} + \varepsilon_{sct}.$$

If wages, w_{sct}, and labour productivity, LP_{sct}, are positively correlated across sectors in country c, $\beta_c > 0$. The inclusion of the country-year fixed effects, α_{ct}, ensures comparing sector s_1 in a given country and year to other sectors in the same country and year. When investigating the relative roles of wage co-ordination, centralisation and bargaining coverage, productivity is interacted with indicators for co-ordination, centralisation and bargaining coverage.

The approach comes down to studying the role of collective bargaining for the distribution across sectors of the labour share, i.e. the share of value added going to workers. Pak and Schwellnus (forthcoming[40]) use sector-level data to study the role of, among others, collective bargaining for the size of the labour share.

Figure 3.8. Elasticity of wages with respect to productivity across sectors: Country estimates

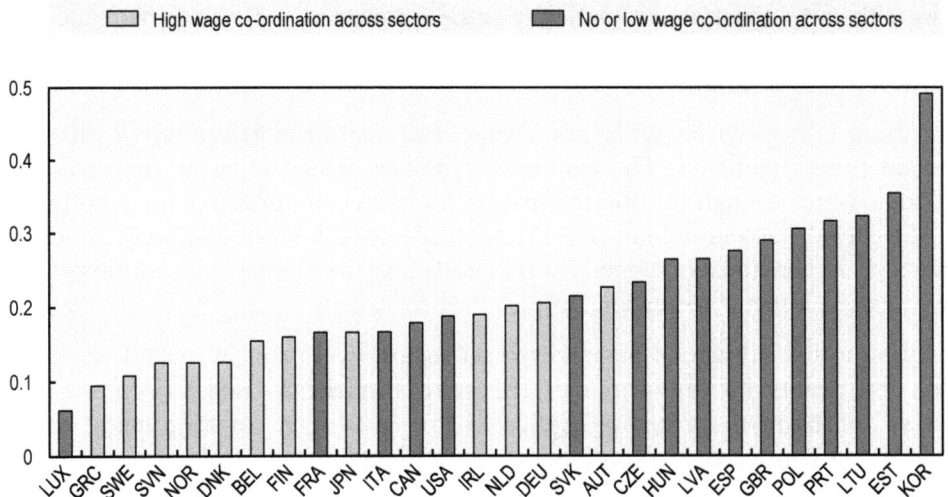

Note: Results are based on Ordinary Least Squares (OLS) regressions of the log hourly wage on log hourly labour productivity across sectors. The regressions include country-year dummies. Co-ordination is classified as high for a country if in the majority of the years in the sample it is classified as high.
Source: OECD estimates based on *OECD Annual National Accounts Database*, http://dx.doi.org/10.1787/data-00727-en, completed with *OECD Structural Analysis (STAN) Database*, http://dx.doi.org/10.1787/data-00649-en, EU-level analysis of capital, labour, energy, materials and service inputs data (EU-KLEMS) and Institutional Characteristics of Trade Unions, Wage Setting, State Intervention and Social Pacts (ICTWSS) database, http://uva-aias.net/en/ictwss.

StatLink ⟨ᵐᶦˢ⟩ http://dx.doi.org/10.1787/888933778117

Several features of collective bargaining could affect the flexibility of firms in a sector to set wages in line with sector-level productivity. Possibly the most natural candidate is wage co-ordination across sectors, which actively seeks to limit differences in pay across sectors by establishing some cross-sectoral wage norm for the purposes of collective bargaining. This is borne out in the data. Wages and productivity at the sector level are more aligned in countries without co-ordination in wage-setting. The difference is stark: On average across countries, the elasticity of wages with respect to productivity is 0.26 without and 0.16 with cross-sector wage co-ordination. This means that if productivity is 10% higher in some sector than another, wages tend to be 2.6% higher in this sector in non-co-ordination countries and 1.6% higher in co-ordination countries.[23]

Wage co-ordination is correlated with other features of collective bargaining such as coverage rates and the degree of centralisation. Centralisation may matter for wage-productivity alignments because in industries with stronger trade unions workers may appropriate a greater share of the production surplus. Coverage may matter since without coverage wage co-ordination and centralisation have no role. Moreover, in countries with no explicit wage co-ordination but high coverage and centralised bargaining, negotiations in one sector may nevertheless serve as an implicit benchmark for others. Thus, some cross-sector co-ordination can happen even if co-ordination is not institutionalised.

Sectoral wages are set less in line with sectoral productivity in systems with cross-sector wage co-ordination, even when differences in coverage rates are accounted, or controlled, for (Figure 3.9). As coverage rates tend to be higher in countries with wage co-ordination, taking account of this reduces the difference in the wage-productivity correlation between countries with and without co-ordination. Centralisation, too, is found to be related with a weaker alignment between wages and productivity across sectors – see (OECD, 2018[21]) for the full regression results.

Co-ordination, collective bargaining coverage and centralisation jointly predict lower wage-productivity alignment. The empirical evidence, which is based on cross-country comparisons, is not enough for proving that such features of collective bargaining are the driving, or causal, factors behind the differences across countries in wage-productivity alignments. It is nonetheless suggestive that collective bargaining has an important role for how wages in a sector correspond to sector performance.

The analysis in this subsection has focused on sector-level data. In related work, and in line with the results in this section, Berlingieri, Blanchenay and Criscuolo (2017[41]) show, based on harmonised micro-aggregated firm-level data covering many countries, that trade union density and co-ordination in wage-setting tend to be associated with a lower dispersion of average wages across firms and a weaker link between productivity and average wage dispersion across firms in the same sector.

This section has used data on actual wages in different sectors in the economy. Typically, however, collective bargaining sets negotiated wages which may depart from actual wages. In the euro area, negotiated wages have grown at a lower rate since 2000 than actual wages and labour productivity (Box 3.3). Negotiated wages have tended to follow productivity only with a considerable lag, which appears to have induced a misalignment of wage and productivity growth rates at the macroeconomic level in the short run.

Figure 3.9. Elasticity of wages with respect to productivity across sectors: The role of collective bargaining

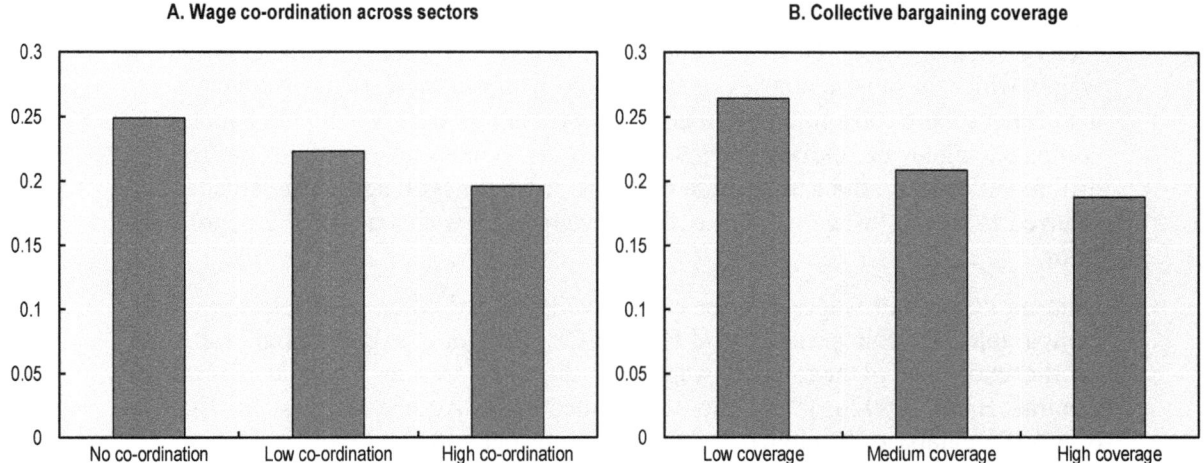

Note: Results are based on Ordinary Least Squares (OLS) regressions of the log hourly wage on log hourly labour productivity across sectors. The regressions include country-year dummies and interactions of log productivity with wage co-ordination dummies and collective bargaining coverage. Low, medium and high collective bargaining coverage are defined by the averages for the bottom third, middle third and top third in the distribution of coverage rates in the sample.

Source: OECD estimates based on *OECD Annual National Accounts Database*, http://dx.doi.org/10.1787/data-00727-en, completed with *OECD Structural Analysis (STAN) Database*, http://dx.doi.org/10.1787/data-00649-en, EU-level analysis of capital, labour, energy, materials and service inputs data (EU-KLEMS), and Institutional Characteristics of Trade Unions, Wage Setting, State Intervention and Social Pacts (ICTWSS) database, http://uva-aias.net/en/ictwss.

StatLink http://dx.doi.org/10.1787/888933778136

Overall, in countries where wage co-ordination has an important role or wages are more centralised at the sector level, the correlation of wages with productivity at the sub-national level is weaker. This suggests that wage co-ordination "works", in the sense that it co-ordinates wages, and by partially delinking wages from productivity may end up in a less dispersed wage distribution. Centralisation and co-ordination may also affect how wages can respond to individual firm performance. In the longer term, such delinking of wages from productivity could have potentially important implications for productivity growth. It could reduce incentives for workers to innovate, work hard and move to a better-paid job. However, stronger misalignments of wages from productivity do not need to have such negative effects; for example, they may even increase innovation incentives, if firms would reap the full benefits of productivity gains. Box 3.4 summarises the existing literature on collective bargaining and productivity. It also provides exploratory evidence that certain forms of sector-level bargaining may come at the expense of lower productivity growth within sectors.

Box 3.3. Negotiated wages in euro area countries

Analyses on wage developments and collective bargaining almost exclusively focus on actual wages. However, collective agreements usually define contractual wages which in most countries apply only to a subset of workers. Actual wages also reflect the trends among non-covered workers as well as supplements at the company, plant or individual level (such as bonus or overtime pay). The difference between the actual wage outcome and the negotiated wage is generally referred to as the "wage drift", i.e. the movement of wages above the negotiated floor.

Data on negotiated wages are not easily available and when available not easily comparable. The European Central Bank (ECB) provides "experimental" statistics on the evolution of negotiated wages for the euro area as a whole (European Central Bank, 2002[42]),[24] while the Collectively Agreed Wages In Europe (CAWIE) database developed by the European network of Trade Union related Research Institutes (TURI) provides the underlying national statistics.[25] Similar data are also collected and published by Eurofound (2017[43]). Figure 3.10 shows the trends in negotiated wages, actual wages and labour productivity in real terms for the euro area as a whole from 2000 to 2016 using the ECB data. The aggregate data show that, on average, negotiated wage growth has been relatively limited, or at least well below productivity growth both before and after the crisis. Actual wage growth exceeded negotiated wage growth but remained below productivity growth, reducing the labour share. Only during 2008-09 negotiated (and actual) wage growth increased above productivity growth due to the unexpected deflationary shock of the crisis and the staggering of collective agreements. Staggering refers to the inability to renegotiate agreements signed under more favourable economic conditions, which can amplify the aggregate shock, as shown by Diez-Catalan and Villanueva (2015[44]) for Spain.

Country-specific data (OECD, 2018[21]) show that in all countries (except in Italy, as a result of dismal productivity growth, not "excessive" wage increases) negotiated wages have grown in line with, or often less than, labour productivity growth, apart from 2008-09. Interestingly, negotiated wages in the Netherlands have barely moved since 2000 – in fact, negotiated wages in the Netherlands are practically unchanged since the 1970s in real terms (de Beer and Keune, 2017[45]) – but thanks to a sizeable wage drift actual wages have grown in line with productivity. By contrast, in Germany actual wages have grown considerably less than productivity and less than negotiated wages, showing a negative "wage drift". This unique trend of negative wage drift (at least among the European countries for which data are available) means that actual wages are not bound by negotiated wages, which is probably the result of decreasing bargaining coverage in Germany and the use of opening clauses which allow companies to deviate from sector-level agreements (Schulten, 2013[46]).

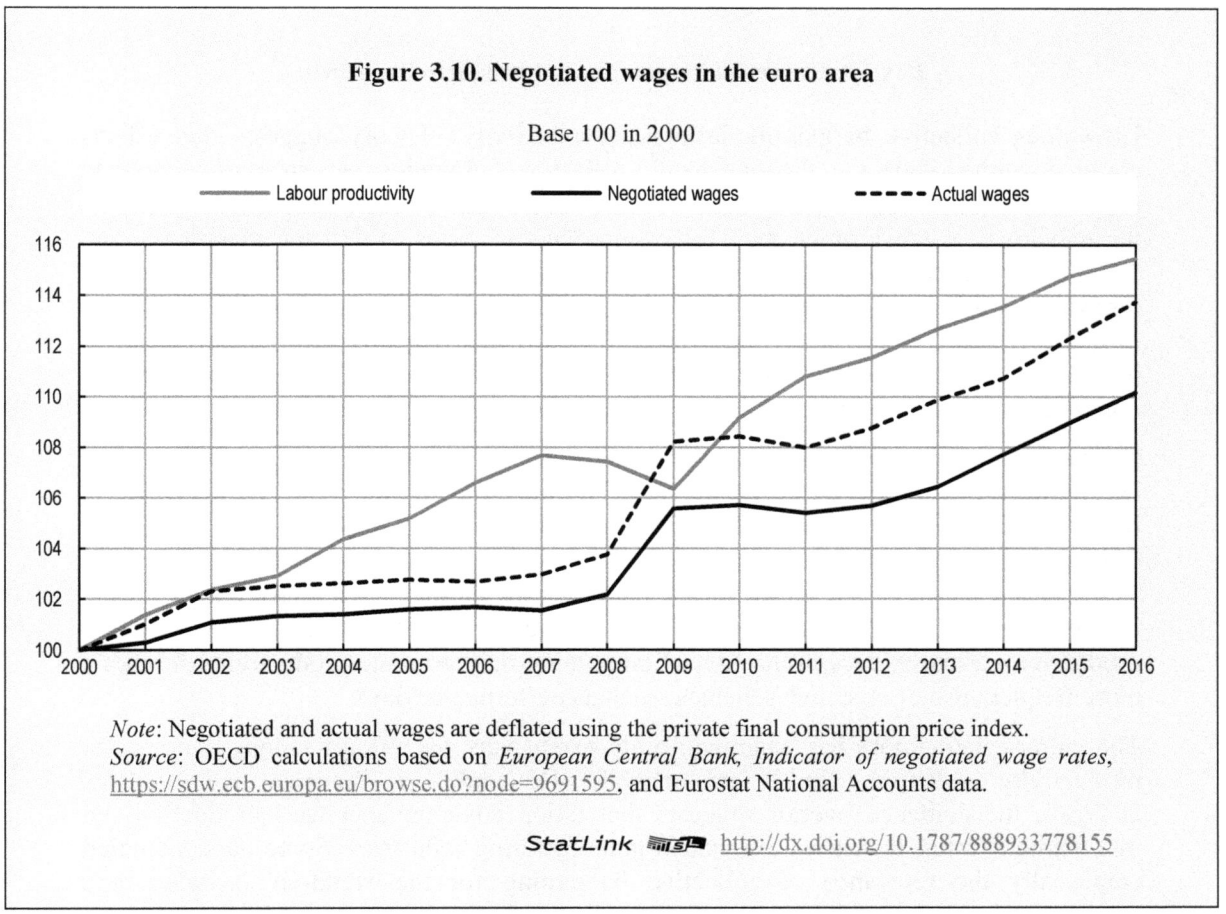

Figure 3.10. Negotiated wages in the euro area

Base 100 in 2000

Note: Negotiated and actual wages are deflated using the private final consumption price index.
Source: OECD calculations based on *European Central Bank, Indicator of negotiated wage rates*, https://sdw.ecb.europa.eu/browse.do?node=9691595, and Eurostat National Accounts data.

StatLink 🔗 http://dx.doi.org/10.1787/888933778155

3.4. The role of workplace representation for the quality of the working environment

While the interest of past work on collective bargaining has to a large extent focused on its role as a "wage-setting institution", much of the content of collective agreements is dedicated to non-wage working conditions, such as employment protection, working time, health and safety, training and social protection. This section provides some empirical evidence on the role of employee representation at the workplace for the quality of the working environment as defined by the OECD/G20 Job Quality Framework (OECD, 2014[47]).

At least since the seminal book "What do unions do?" by Freeman and Medoff (1984[48]), trade unions and collective bargaining are seen not only as institutional means for articulating and pressing demands for higher wages, but also as vehicles for collective communication and exchange between workers and their employers. Unions can influence job quality directly (by negotiating non-wage working conditions in collective agreements) or indirectly (by providing workers with a platform to voice their concerns and requests).

Box 3.4. Collective bargaining and productivity growth

How does collective bargaining influence productivity? Theory suggests that effects could go either way. On the one hand, collective bargaining can increase aggregate productivity by setting higher wage floors (and making it more difficult to cut costs through lower wages) which may force unproductive firms to exit the market (Braun, 2011[49]). More rigid wages may also increase the incentives of the firms' owners to innovate, as they would reap the full benefits of productivity gains – see Acemoglu and Pischke (1999[50]) and Haucap and Wey (2004[51]). Other ways through which collective bargaining could promote productivity growth are higher "efficiency" wages, better non-wage working conditions and the possibility for workers to voice concerns.

On the other hand, a more compressed wage structure may reduce the incentives to work hard and move to a more productive firm, harming firm productivity and the efficient reallocation of workers. Union power could also allow workers appropriating the benefits of investments by employers, giving rise to the so-called "hold-up" problem (Malcomson, 1997[52]) and reducing investment incentives for firms. Further, limitations to adjustments in the organisation of work (such as in working time, shifts or leave) could lower productivity. Finally, decentralisation of bargaining may promote productivity through a more frequent use of incentive schemes (such as performance pay).

The empirical literature has examined quite extensively the role of union coverage for productivity. According to a meta-analysis (Doucouliagos, Freeman and Laroche, 2017[53]), the evidence overall suggests that union coverage increases productivity in non-manufacturing industries, but not in manufacturing industries. Some papers studied empirically the relevance of collective bargaining for the "hold-up" problem and investment, with inconclusive results overall. Card, Devicienti and Maida (2014[54]), using matched employer-employee data from Italy's Veneto region, obtain little evidence of hold-up. Based on sector-level data for OECD countries, Cardullo, Conti and Sulis (2015[55]) find that union coverage reduces investment in sunk-capital-intensive industries relative to others.

The results in this section suggest that certain collective bargaining systems can be associated with stronger misalignments of pay and productivity, with possible consequences for productivity growth. However, few papers have directly studied the role of different features of bargaining systems, such as centralisation or co-ordination, for productivity, in part due to lack of suitable data. Andreasson (2017[56]) finds that in Sweden companies for which wage-setting is more decentralised have higher value added per employee and higher productivity. Similarly, Garnero, Rycx and Terraz (2018[57]) obtain a positive link between decentralised bargaining and productivity, using Belgian firm-level data. For developing countries, Lamarche (2013[58]; 2015[59]) argues that firm- instead of sector-level agreements could yield productivity gains. However, Hibbs and Locking (2000[60]) document that decentralisation in Sweden in the 1980s reduced aggregate productivity growth by slowing down the exit of inefficient firms. Taking the evidence from these papers together, decentralisation appears to improve firm productivity, while it may slow down the cleansing effect of higher wages and therefore, due to composition effects, not translate in higher aggregate productivity growth.

To study the links of centralisation and co-ordination with productivity growth, the following variant of the sector-level approach by Rajan and Zingales (1998[61]) is used.

The premise is that collective bargaining reforms tend to affect sectors more where collective bargaining coverage is high and therefore productivity growth in these sectors should be affected more. The estimating equation is:

$$PG_{sct} = \beta_1 Coverage_{sc} \times Centralisation_{ct} + \beta_2 Coverage_{sc} \times Coordination_{ct} + P_{sct-1} + \alpha_{ct} + \gamma_{sc} + \varepsilon_{sct}.$$

The dependent variable, PG_{sct}, indicates productivity growth in sector s, country c and year t. The lagged level of productivity, P_{sct-1}, accounts for convergence. Regressions are run for total factor and labour productivity. Estimation of the coefficients of interest, β, requires variation in coverage across sectors and centralisation or co-ordination across time. This is the case for seven countries with available data: Austria, Denmark, Finland, France, Germany, the Netherlands and Spain.

Centralisation is linked with lower productivity growth, both for total factor and labour productivity – the full set of empirical results is available in OECD (2018[21]). Productivity growth is higher in high compared with low coverage sectors when collective bargaining is more decentralised. No association is estimated for wage co-ordination. The estimation, which relies on sector comparisons, does not readily allow conclusions on aggregate productivity growth. It also does not rule out issues of endogeneity, despite relying only on within-country variation. Yet, the results suggest that centralised bargaining may come at the expense of lower productivity growth, although analysis beyond these empirical explorations is needed to examine the links between bargaining regimes and productivity further.

The literature has focused mostly on job satisfaction, in particular to understand the apparent puzzle highlighted by Freeman and Medoff of a negative correlation between job satisfaction and unionisation. Ensuing studies confirmed this negative link but came to the conclusion that it is a selection rather than a causal effect – see Doucouliagos, Freeman and Laroche (2017[53]) who review 59 studies on the topic. People enter a union because they are less satisfied; it is not unions that make them unhappy: poor job quality and bad management are strongly linked with the desire for union representation in the United Kingdom and the United States (Bryson and Freeman, 2013[62]). Moreover, as Bryson and Green (2015[63]) note, by offering employees an opportunity to address poor job quality via bargaining and worker voice, dissatisfied union employees are less likely to quit than dissatisfied non-union employees – see also Box 4.6 in OECD (2017[1]). On the other hand, relatively little is known about the role of unions and collective bargaining for intrinsic measures of job quality. Green and Whitfield (2009[64]) find that employees in workplaces with recognised unions are more likely to say that they have no time to complete tasks and are less likely to agree that they have influence over the pace of work and how tasks are done. Bryson and Green (2015[63]) argue that unionised jobs are subject to lower task discretion but higher skill use and increased exposure to a learning requirement.

The analysis in this section takes advantage of the information provided by the European Working Conditions Survey for 25 OECD countries (plus Lithuania) to study the link between the presence of a recognised form of employee representation (trade union, works council or similar committee representing employees) and the quality of the working environment, one of the three dimensions of the OECD/G20 Job Quality Framework. The quality of the working environment captures non-economic aspects of jobs, including the nature and content of the work performed, working-time arrangements and workplace relationships. It is measured as the incidence of job strain, which occurs when workers face high job demands with low job resources. The job demands considered are: i) physical demands; ii) work intensity; and iii) inflexibility of working hours; while job resources consist of: i) task discretion and autonomy; ii) training; and iii) perceived opportunity for career advancement.

The results show that the presence of a recognised form of employee representation, on average, is associated with lower job strain and hence a better quality of the working environment (Figure 3.11). In particular, the effect is the result of a negative link between the presence of a recognised form of employee representation and the intensity of the work (working long hours) and a positive correlation with the number of days spent in training over the last 12 months and the perceived prospects for career advancement. No significant link is found with the physical demands (the probability of carrying or moving heavy loads), the inflexibility of working hours and task discretion. These regressions control for age, education, gender, temporary contract, occupation, tenure, establishment size, industry and country dummies. The industry dummies ensure that the results are not driven by the working environment being of better quality in highly unionised sectors, independent of employee representation.

Although not necessarily providing causal evidence, these results suggest that employee representation at the workplace can play a significant role in improving job quality, in particular by reducing work intensity and increasing training opportunities and prospects for career advancement. Indeed, in all countries, even those where sector-level agreements still play a prominent role, bargaining and consultation at the workplace level are key to voice workers' concern and find viable and pragmatic solutions to improve the quality of the working environment. These results also confirm the importance of looking at collective bargaining beyond its role as a "wage-setting institution". Nevertheless, more research in this area is needed and subsequent OECD work will analyse the role of collective bargaining for job quality in further detail.

3.5. Balancing inclusiveness and flexibility in collective bargaining systems

The future of collective bargaining, its relevance and function, will depend on how it will adapt to changing labour market conditions. Social partners and governments should aim to reap the benefits of collective bargaining for employment and inclusiveness while avoiding that collective bargaining becomes a straitjacket, by ensuring that firms are able to adjust wages and working time when their business situation requires it.

This chapter has put forward new evidence based on a range of data sources (country-, sector-, firm- and worker-level data) that suggests that, to a certain extent, collective bargaining has historically meant a trade-off between inclusiveness and flexibility. In countries and periods when collective bargaining was not confined to firm-level bargaining (or simply absent), wage inequality has been lower and employment, including of vulnerable groups, has been higher. Wage co-ordination can also have the benefit of strengthening the resilience of the economy against business-cycle downturns (OECD, 2017[1]). This chapter and the literature, however, have also provided evidence that more centralised bargaining at the sector or national level may come at the cost of reduced flexibility to adjust pay and working conditions in line with business conditions for the individual sector or firm, with potentially adverse implications for productivity.

Figure 3.11. Employee representation is linked with a higher-quality work environment

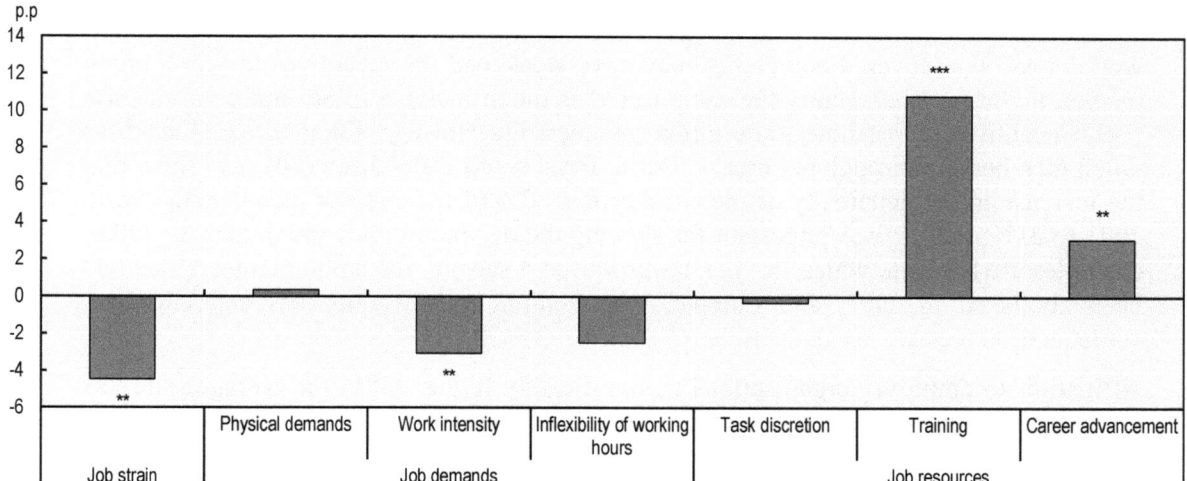

Note: ***, **, *: statistically significant at the 1, 5 and 10% level, respectively. Results are based on Ordinary Least Squares (OLS) regressions. They control for age, education, gender, type of contract, occupation, job tenure, establishment size, industry and country dummies. p.p.: percentage points.
Source: OECD calculations based on the Sixth European Working Conditions Survey (EWCS), 2015.

StatLink ᐯᕈᔕᐳ http://dx.doi.org/10.1787/888933778174

This section discusses possible pathways going forward, through the combined use of tools that help promote inclusiveness (Section 3.5.1) and tools that help promote flexibility (Section 3.5.2). Inclusiveness in this context is to a large extent about being represented; hence, a strong emphasis is placed on broad-based collective bargaining and social dialogue. Flexibility can be attained in many ways, but the challenge is to nest it within systems that deliver broad-based coverage. Organised decentralisation (which leaves space for firm-level agreements to set the terms of employment within a broader framework of sector-level agreements), high levels of representation at the local level and wage co-ordination across sectors are among the elements that hold most promise to effectively balance inclusiveness with flexibility.

3.5.1. Promoting broad-based collective bargaining and social dialogue

Broad-based employer and employee organisations tend to be the best way for countries to attain high collective bargaining coverage

For collective bargaining to have meaningful macroeconomic effects, it needs to involve and cover a large share of workers and companies. Well-organised social partners – unions and employer organisations with a broad support base – are often the condition for attaining high coverage. Declining coverage rates in several countries have reduced the potential role of collective bargaining for promoting earnings equality and social cohesion. In countries where coverage has held up but trade union density has declined, questions about the legitimacy and representativeness of trade unions are sometimes raised.

Currently, the union membership rate is above 50% only in OECD countries with the so-called "Ghent system", i.e. where union-affiliated institutions administer unemployment benefits (Denmark, Finland, Iceland, Sweden and partly Belgium), and in Norway. However, even the Ghent system has been gradually eroded through the development of private insurance funds (OECD, 2017[1]). The use of administrative extensions and *erga omnes* clauses that extend collective agreements to non-unionised workers and non-covered companies may have weakened the incentives to join a union (as non-union members enjoy the same rights as union members). Several countries use fiscal incentives to promote trade union membership. Norway, for instance, subsidises union membership through tax breaks. Barth, Bryson and Dale-Olsen (2017[65]) show that the increase in the generosity of the subsidy from 7% of the average membership fee in 2001 to 21% in 2012 was important for slowing the decline in trade union density. Other examples are Sweden, which has just reintroduced a subsidy for union members that had been abolished in 2007, and Finland, where union membership fees and employer confederation fees are tax-deductible.

Affiliation to employer organisations is significantly higher (50% on average) and has been quite stable over the last few decades, in contrast to the strong decline in union membership. An extreme case is Austria where membership to the sectoral branch of the chamber of commerce (*Wirtschaftskammer Österreich* or WKÖ) in each region (*Bundesland*) is compulsory for all companies. Sector-level agreements signed at the regional or in some cases national level therefore necessarily cover all firms in the sector, obviating the potential need of formal extension measures by the government. Studying the trends in 13 European countries, Brandl and Lehr (2016[66]) argue that employer organisations have been able to remain relatively strong by adapting their organisational structures and activities to the changing needs of businesses. Moreover, the use of administrative extensions of collective agreements in many countries strengthens the incentives for membership to employer organisations since the terms of agreements also apply to non-members (whose objectives may be different to those of members).

Even in countries where company-level bargaining plays a significant role, it is often mostly confined to large and medium-sized enterprises. To extend social dialogue to all segments of society, some governments have tried to promote social dialogue in small firms. One example is the 2017 labour market reform in France. This introduced the possibility for companies with less than 20 employees to have a company-level agreement even in the absence of a union delegate, provided at least two-thirds of employees support the agreement. It also allowed companies with 20 to 50 employees to negotiate with an elected representative even if not explicitly mandated by the unions. Unions fear that these initiatives to promote social dialogue in small businesses will in fact lead to abuses by employers who have stronger bargaining power than employees. However, in France the role of firm-level bargaining remains quite tightly defined by sector-level agreements which, very often (at least until the 2017 reform), explicitly block renegotiations and derogations at the firm level on most topics. Another example comes from Italy, where the government in 2017 increased tax incentives to promote negotiations on performance-related pay and welfare provisions at the firm level with the stated aim of extending firm-level bargaining also to medium and small firms and strengthen the link between productivity and wage increases at the firm level (D'Amuri and Nizzi, 2017[67]).

The rise of non-standard and new forms of work represents a major challenge for collective bargaining systems. The meaning of "employer", "employee" and "place of work" becomes increasingly blurred, impeding the ways in which employers and employees have negotiated traditionally. Unions are making efforts to reach out to workers in new forms of work.[26] Non-union labour movements to defend workers' interests are also emerging.[27] Technology and social media help workers organise by facilitating building communities and engaging in protests, boycotts and petitions. Moreover, direct forms of voice such as regular meetings, team briefings and problem-solving groups may contribute to fill in for unions and representative bodies (Bryson, Forth and George, 2012[68]; Bryson et al., 2017[69]).

Such alternative forms of collective organisation are a tool for preserving some form of workers' voice at times of rapid changes to work relationships. But these new bodies are often not entitled or may not even want to engage in direct negotiations with employers. Hence, some employers fear that these alternative forms of organisation represent a threat to the traditional forms of collective bargaining that have been based on negotiations and industrial peace. Moreover, some restrictions to worker and employer organisation may come from labour and competition laws which are often based on traditional concepts of "employer" and "employee". For instance, in the case of platform workers, but also of the self-employed more generally, a key challenge is that bargaining collectively on wages would be against the traditional interpretation of competition rules which tend to consider them as "undertakings" (Daskalova, 2017[70]). This highlights the importance of legal reform to clarify the scope for collective bargaining and support the emergence of new forms of social dialogue.

Extensions can be an alternative to support wide coverage of collective agreements when social partners are weak, but have to be well regulated

In the absence of broad-based social partners, another way of making collective bargaining coverage more inclusive is through the use of administrative extensions. These extend the coverage of collective agreements beyond the members of the signatory unions and employer organisations to all workers and firms in a sector. Extensions level the playing field across firms in a sector and reduce the burden associated with lengthy and detailed negotiations, which can be particularly relevant for small firms. In addition, they support the sustainability of "public goods", including sectoral training and mobility schemes funded by collective agreements. However, extensions can also have downsides, as they may be used as a tool for unfair competition and harm the economic prospects of those not represented at the negotiation table, such as start-ups, small firms or vulnerable workers – see Haucap, Pauly and Wey (2001[71]), Magruder (2012[72]) and Hijzen and Martins (2016[73]).

To avoid or minimise the potential negative effects, it is important that the parties negotiating the agreement represent the interests of a wide range of firms and workers and leave some "escape valves" for specific cases. This can be achieved by requiring reasonable representativeness criteria and a meaningful test of public interest, while establishing well-defined procedures for exemptions and opt-outs in case of serious economic hardship (OECD, 2017[1]).[28]

As discussed above, extensions may weaken incentives for trade union membership. This, in turn, may have adverse consequences for the quality of labour relations but also make it harder to introduce more flexibility in the system through the use of decentralised organisation (see Section 3.5.2). Extensions therefore can play a useful role for ensuring that all employees in a sector are covered but do not provide a one-to-one substitute for collective organisation.

Extensions of collective agreements can only be used in countries with some form of sector-level agreements. The case of Australia, where a government body determines minimum standards for each sector, represents an alternative approach for ensuring basic terms of employment among all firms in a sector (Box 3.5). The main challenge of this system is the difficulty to establish appropriate sectoral standards, as this presupposes detailed knowledge of the sector which may often require a strong involvement of the social partners.

3.5.2. Ensuring that collective bargaining systems are able to respond to changing and unexpected challenges

Collective bargaining and social dialogue should also support strong economic outcomes, which may require ensuring that working conditions are sufficiently well-aligned with economic conditions. This can be achieved by allowing some degree of flexibility at the firm or worker level or through the use of mechanisms to co-ordinate bargaining outcomes across sectors and firms with a focus on macroeconomic performance. Moreover, social partners can play a key role in supporting job transitions and ensuring that workers are equipped with the skills needed.

Leaving more scope for company-level bargaining does not require disavowing sector-level bargaining

Debates on collective bargaining have largely focused on the level of negotiation. The introduction of flexibility in predominantly sector-level systems has therefore often been considered as requiring a shift from sector- to firm-level bargaining. While such a shift would indeed provide more flexibility to firms, it may also induce a decline in coverage, undermining the inclusiveness of the system.[29] However, experiences from a number of countries show that less radical options, typically referred to under the heading of "organised decentralisation" (Traxler, 1995[74]), are available. These have the advantage of preserving sector-level bargaining, while enabling a closer link between productivity and working conditions at the firm level.

Organised decentralisation occurs within the framework provided by sector-level agreements, while explicitly allowing elements of working conditions and work organisation to be negotiated or determined at the company or even worker level under certain conditions through specific procedures. In principle, the sector-level framework should preserve collective bargaining coverage and give firms and workers more freedom to set working conditions. Decentralisation usually takes place through company collective agreements with trade unions, but in some cases also through agreements by the management with non-union worker representatives (such as works councils) or individual employees. For Traxler (1995[74]), who coined the term, organised decentralisation stands in contrast to "disorganised decentralisation", a system where firm-level agreements entirely replace sector-level agreements and many workers are left without representation.

Organised decentralisation can take several forms – see Ibsen and Keune (forthcoming[75]) for more details. In a first model, sector-level agreements provide a general framework but leave room for lower-level agreements to tailor the terms of employment. This approach is thus predicated on multi-level bargaining and strong local representation (or extensions) and can be found in Denmark, Norway and Sweden, for instance. In these countries, the favourability principle is not set in the law but entirely left to the bargaining parties who decide whether and in which case it applies.

Box 3.5. An alternative to sector-level bargaining? The case of Modern Awards in Australia

Australia[1] does not have sector-level bargaining, but a form of industry- or occupation-wide regulations, so-called Modern Awards, which set industry-specific wage floors that vary by skill level. While some 36% of employees are covered directly by collective agreements, another 23% are covered by awards only. That is, around three-fifths of employees have wages that are not determined by the employer and the individual employee but instead either through collective bargaining or an external regulator. This is well above the average rate of collective bargaining coverage across the OECD. The system has been in place for several decades and a similar organisational arrangement was in place in New Zealand until 1991.

Awards in Australia set sectoral minimum wages that vary according to the skill level of the job, with provisions for night and weekend premiums ("penalty rates"), overtime pay, working time and other dimensions of working conditions. A Modern Award covers a whole industry in most states and territories (some states have retained their workplace relations practices). Australia also has a "national minimum wage", but this is usually fixed at the lowest rate in any award and adjusted every year at the same time as the rest of the award pay structure.

Awards are set by a federal tribunal, the Fair Work Commission, whose members are chosen by the government and selected among employer bodies, unions, lawyers and government officials. Unions and employers make submissions on the content of Modern Awards and then the Fair Work Commission decides. The Commission is also tasked with revising, after consultations, wage rates (recently every four years). Outside these reviews, the relationship between awards is quite stable and award wage increases in one industry rarely outpace, or fall behind, those in other industries.

With the support of employees, employers can deviate from the terms set in the awards, in particular those relating to working hours, through specified processes, but workers should still be better off overall. Mechanisms exist to adjust to temporary, special circumstances, but these are not widely used.

Modern Awards do not represent a form of sector-level bargaining, but they create a set of industry-specific skill-varying wage floors which, while significantly different, can be compared with the use of administrative extensions in countries with sector-level bargaining.

Note:

1. This box has been prepared in collaboration with David Peetz (Griffith University).

In this first form of organised decentralisation, sector-level agreements can take the following forms or a mix of them:

- *Minimum agreements:* They set minimum standards but leave the setting of actual wages and working conditions up to company agreements, with the condition that they respect the minimum standards.

- *Corridor agreements:* They set the boundaries (minimum and maximum) between which the terms of employment in company-level agreements can be set.

- *Default agreements:* They set wages and working conditions, but these come only into force in case local parties do not find an agreement. Hence, company agreements can also set wages and working conditions below the default levels.

- *Figureless agreements:* They contain no wage standards which are entirely left to the company level.

In practice, few "pure" agreements exist, as even default agreements may include some common standards.

Sector-level agreements can also allow for a different type of decentralisation where working conditions are not set by a company agreement but by individual workers. Such *à-la-carte* arrangements offer individuals the option to exchange, within predefined limits, wages, working time and free time. In some cases, company-level agreements introduce this option for the workforce ("mandated *à-la-carte*"). In others, this is done in the sector-level agreement, regardless of a company-level agreement ("un-mandated"). *À-la-carte* arrangements tend to be important in the Netherlands where the scope for bargaining at the firm in addition to the sector level tends to be limited beyond certain industries and larger firms, given relatively low levels of local representation (Visser, 2016[76]).

In a second model of organised decentralisation, notably present in Germany and Austria, sector-level agreements set the standard terms of employment and allow for exceptions to the favourability principle via opt-out or derogation clauses. These clauses, often also known as competition, hardship or opening clauses, allow company-level agreements to deviate downwards from wages and working conditions set in a sector-level agreement. Traditionally, such clauses were intended to apply to companies in serious economic problems for a temporary time period under predefined conditions.[30] Since 2004 in Germany, opening clauses have been used more generally by companies to reduce labour costs. Some clauses allow companies to postpone or cancel parts of the sector-level agreement, notably wage increases, depending on the type or economic situation of the company.

In Germany, opening clauses are usually contingent upon an initial agreement between the signatory social partners in the industry or region. There is some leeway in designing the clause, in terms of what substantive issues it includes (wages, working time, employment guarantees, etc.) and under what conditions and according to which procedures the derogation can be made. According to Schulten and Bispinck (2017[77]), company-level parties (management and works council) usually make a joint application to the signatory parties at the sector level which take the final decision. It is, however, also possible to derogate the final decision-making competence to the company-level parties. According to a recent study (Amlinger and Bispinck, 2016[78]), derogation agreements concern mainly working time (14% of all companies covered by a collective agreement), wages (10%), allowances (10%), annual bonuses (10%) and apprenticeship pay (3%). The clauses in sectoral agreements mainly define the rules and conditions under which the derogation can be made, in particular:

- Companies have to disclose their financial information to justify a derogation.

- Parties at the company and industry level need to have the time to scrutinise the company's financial status and the measures taken.

- The duration of the derogation should be limited to ensure terms and conditions will return to the standards in the sectoral agreement.

- Derogations are conditional on the safeguarding of jobs or investment plans to make the company more viable.

In addition to these bi-partite procedures, unions have instated their own procedural requirements to avoid that derogations are agreed between local parties without workers getting something in exchange. According to Haipeter and Lehndorff (2014[79]) and Schulten and Bispinck (2017[77]), such internal union procedures have helped ensure a controlled use of opt-outs. Baccaro and Benassi (2017[80]) are less optimistic, as control through internal procedures is only strong in some sectors, notably metalworking where unions are still strong locally. In the German retail sector, by contrast, decentralisation has been less "organised", since unions and works councils are less prevalent and employers have rather opted for non-binding membership to the employer association or no membership at all. With limited use of extensions, this has led to a substantial decrease in bargaining coverage.

Although strict conditions on the use of opening clauses help ensure that the decentralisation process remains organised, they may also severely diminish their role. Where opening clauses exist, opt-outs are mostly used by large firms which are not necessarily those most in need. Small firms are often not able to make use of derogations and opt-out clauses because they lack the capacity or worker representation. In a possibly extreme, but not totally unlikely scenario, opt-outs with very strict conditions may become an anti-competitive tool: Large firms could first negotiate relatively generous conditions in sector-level agreements and then opt out to improve the terms in their favour, leaving competitors to bear the brunt of the generous terms they negotiated (OECD, 2017[1]).[31]

Overall, organised decentralisation appears to be able to increase the flexibility of the system, at least to some extent, without being accompanied by a substantial decline in the number of workers being represented. This is the case in countries where well-regulated extensions help attain high collective bargaining coverage (as in the Netherlands), where membership of trade unions is high (as in the Nordic countries) and where employer association density is high (as in Austria). In Germany, the introduction of opening clauses has been accompanied by a reduced use of extensions and a decline in bargaining coverage. Special forms of membership with the employer association (so-called *Ohne Tarifbindung-Mitgliedschaft*), which do not bind companies to collective agreements, have added to the disengagement of employers from bargaining. The experience of Germany exemplifies the difficulty of organised decentralisation in a context where the degree of local representation is relatively weak. In such a context, the scope for opt-out is limited for some firms, increasing incentives for disengaging from employer associations altogether, contributing to the decline in collective bargaining coverage. In the end, decentralisation in Germany represents a combination of organised and disorganised elements, as Visser (2016[76]) and Oberfichtner and Schnabel (2017[81]) also noted.

Several countries, especially in Southern Europe in the wake of the euro area crisis, introduced reforms to increase the flexibility of their collective bargaining systems along the lines of the German model. Examples are Spain (OECD, 2014[82]), Portugal (OECD, 2017[83]) and, to a different extent, Greece (OECD, 2018[84]). Special attention should be paid in the coming years to a careful evaluation of the introduction of opening clauses in countries which did not have them and their possible interaction with other elements of the collective bargaining system. The absence of strong worker representation at the local level in the form of unions or works councils limits the scope of such reforms and may increase incentives for firms to leave an employer association in the absence of extensions or to opt for less organised forms of collective bargaining.

Wage co-ordination can strengthen flexibility to macroeconomic conditions

OECD (2012[18]) and OECD (2017[1]) have found that wage co-ordination across sectors can contribute to labour market resilience in the aftermath of an economic downturn thanks to greater flexibility in earnings (i.e. working time and wages) and better employment outcomes based on wage moderation. The new evidence reported in Section 3.2 on the link between collective bargaining systems and employment provides further support for these results.

Co-ordination works either by having sector- or firm-level agreements following the guidelines fixed by peak-level organisations or a social pact or by identifying a leading sector (or group of companies) which sets the mark for others to follow ("pattern bargaining").

Guidelines by peak-level organisations define norms or objectives that should be followed when bargaining at lower levels. They are present in several countries but they tend to be binding only in countries where peak-level unions or employer organisations are relatively strong and centralised (in the Nordic countries and to a significantly lower extent in France and Italy).

A social pact is a peak-level deal over a comprehensive policy package that is negotiated between the government, trade unions and employer organisations. By bringing all parties to the same table at the national level, it helps devising a widely shared response, especially in the case of macroeconomic shocks. This therefore represents a strong form of co-ordination. As argued in OECD (2017[1]), peak-level co-ordination and social pacts can reduce transaction costs involved in the negotiation of temporary wage and working-time reductions and make these more acceptable to workers by ensuring that they are widely shared.

The objective of pattern bargaining is to support macroeconomic performance based on international competitiveness, both in good and bad times. A concrete example of pattern bargaining is Sweden, where the tradable sector (mainly manufacturing) sets the "cost mark" (an increase in the wage bill for that year), looking at productivity and wage developments in other countries. The cost mark represents a reference ceiling for the other sectors. In this case, the role of firm-level bargaining is mainly called to decide on the distribution of wage increases within the firm (with exceptions).[32] Pattern bargaining, in different forms, is also present in Austria, Denmark, Germany, Japan, the Netherlands and Norway.

A precondition for a well-functioning co-ordination of wage bargaining is to have strong and representative employer and employee organisations. Wage co-ordination requires a high level of trust in and between the social partners and the availability of objective and shared information on the labour market situation. Enforcing maximum wage targets is not straightforward, especially if some non-tradable sectors can afford more than the agreed "cost mark". Ibsen (2016[85]) highlights the role of mediation bodies for the functioning of pattern bargaining in Denmark and Sweden. In Denmark, the mediation institution can call for the approval of all agreements into one majoritarian union ballot, which effectively forces potential defectors into the agreement. In Sweden, the mediation process works rather through persuasion and naming and shaming. Conversely, the lack of effective mediation bodies is considered as one of the reasons behind the decline of pattern bargaining in Germany. The unique degree of self-regulation by the social partners makes co-ordination fundamentally different from centralisation which is commonly written in laws or regulations.

A further consideration is that the share of manufacturing in total employment and GDP has been decreasing in most countries, putting into question its role as leading sector in pattern bargaining and the sustainability of co-ordination through pattern bargaining in the future. In the Swedish context, the Labour Market Policy Council highlighted that, if this situation were to persist, there is a risk of a collapse of the current co-ordination system (Arbetsmarknadsekonomiska rådet, 2017[86]). This could make it more difficult to secure wage moderation. One way to prevent this may be to take account of productivity and price developments in all tradeable sectors beyond just manufacturing when setting the "cost mark".[33]

All in all, co-ordination remains a unique tool to strengthen the resilience of the labour market and increase the inclusiveness of collective bargaining, while safeguarding the competitiveness of the national economy. However, co-ordination not only requires strong social partners at national and local levels, but it also faces increasing challenges to remain effective in a changing economic structure.

Social partners can play an important role in supporting transitions and strengthening the adaptability of the labour market

In several countries, social partners play an important role in supporting workers who move from one job to another, a role that may be particularly important during times of structural change due to globalisation and digitalisation. Chapter 4 in this *Employment Outlook* discusses in detail the role of public policies and social partners in managing labour market transitions. It presents, for example, the case of Job Security Councils in Sweden which are jointly owned by employer organisations and unions (i.e. the government has no role) and play a key role in case of plant closures and other mass layoffs. Similarly, Austria's Outplacement Labour Foundations offer assistance, guidance, reskilling, practical training and direct help to workers who have been dismissed for economic reasons. But in addition they provide extended unemployment insurance, especially to workers in most need. Austria also has In-placement Labour Foundations which are more forward-looking, helping companies obtain qualified personnel in case of shortage.

In some countries with sector-level bargaining, unions and employer organisations collaborate to invest in the skills of the workforce. In the Netherlands, for example, the sectoral training and development O&O funds (*Opleidings- en Ontwikkelingsfonds*) are social partner initiatives that are financed primarily through a payroll levy fixed in collective agreements. They provide learning possibilities to workers to keep them "up-to-date" and ready to find new jobs in the future. Constant exchanges between the social partners allow O&O funds to anticipate skill needs. However, even these models face challenges and need to be adapted to the new world of work. For instance, the sectoral structure of the O&O funds could become less relevant in a world where job-to-job transitions may take place increasingly across sectors.

3.6. Concluding remarks

Collective bargaining systems are at a crossroads in many OECD countries. Technological and organisational change, global competition and a trend towards decentralisation of bargaining through reforms in the 1990s and during the global financial crisis have affected the role of unions and employer organisations and reduced the scope of collective bargaining.

This chapter has shed new light on the role that collective bargaining can play for good labour market performance. By using a mix of available cross-country micro- and macro-data, it has provided evidence on the role of collective bargaining for employment, wages, working conditions, inequality and productivity. The results show that co-ordinated collective bargaining systems are associated with higher employment, lower unemployment, a better integration of vulnerable groups and less wage inequality than fully decentralised systems. Previous evidence also showed that these systems help strengthen the resilience of the economy against business-cycle downturns. Uncoordinated centralised systems hold an intermediate position, performing similarly in terms of unemployment to fully decentralised systems, but sharing many of the positive effects on other outcomes with co-ordinated systems. However, centralised systems may reduce the flexibility of firms to adjust pay and working conditions in line with business-cycle conditions and hamper reallocation across firms and sectors, with potentially adverse implications for productivity.

The world of work is changing rapidly, with workers increasingly having different jobs and even careers over their working life and holding more than one job at the same time. In this context, it is necessary to rethink the role of collective organisation and collective action. These changes to the world of work are especially challenging for social dialogue and collective bargaining which, more than other labour market institutions, are deeply embedded in the social fabric of each country and based on decades of practices and traditions. However, a comparison with countries facing similar challenges can provide useful inspiration to policy-makers, trade unions and employer organisations who are considering how to adapt their systems.

Notes

[1] See OECD (2017[1]) for a detailed portrait of trends in membership in trade union and employer organisations as well as collective bargaining coverage in OECD countries over the past three decades.

[2] In "efficient bargaining" models, employers and unions bargain jointly over wages and employment in a way that maximises the surplus after deduction of their outside options.

[3] Recent evidence from the United States suggests that monopsony power may be higher than previously thought – see Azar, Marinescu and Steinbaum (2017[103]) and Benmelech, Bergman and Kim (2018[101]).

[4] See Hijzen, Martins and Parlevliet (2018[93]) for a detailed comparative analysis of the collective bargaining systems in these two countries.

[5] For OECD countries, Freeman (1988[95]) found no effect of unionisation on unemployment, while Nickell (1997[89]) and Nickell and Layard (1999[90]) found a positive correlation. Scarpetta (1996[88]) suggested that a high unionisation rate tends to reinforce the persistence of unemployment. Other papers exploited policy reforms in particular countries to study the relationship of unionisation with employment: Blanchflower and Freeman (1993[28]) used the Thatcher reforms in the United Kingdom, finding no effect on unemployment and the probability of leaving unemployment. Maloney (1997[92]), by contrast, found that the reform in New Zealand that led to a sharp reduction in unionisation caused a significant increase in employment.

[6] *Erga omnes* (literally in Latin, "towards everybody") refers to the extension of agreements to all workers in the same firm, not only the members of signatory unions. *Erga omnes* differs from the administrative extension of a collective agreement which refers to the extension of a collective agreement at the sector level to workers in firms which have not signed the agreement or are not affiliated to an employer organisation which signed the agreement.

[7] Nickell and Layard (1999[90]), for instance, find a positive effect of coverage on unemployment and a negative one on employment, while Baker et al. (2005[102]) find insignificant effects. At the OECD-level, de Serres and Murtin (2014[100]) find that bargaining coverage, especially if larger than union coverage, can lead to rigid adjustments in wages and may be detrimental to employment. Several studies have also used the difference between bargaining coverage and trade union density, the so-called "excess bargaining coverage", to study the effect of administrative extensions, while in fact this measure mixes *erga omnes* clauses and administrative extensions. For example, Murtin, de Serres and Hijzen (2014[91]) study the interaction of extensions and the tax wedge and find a negative effect of the tax wedge on unemployment in countries with higher "excess coverage". Gal and Theising (2015[94]) find a negative effect of "excess coverage" on employment, but the effect appears to be driven by Germany, New Zealand and Spain. Égert and Gal (2017[97]) also find that higher "excess coverage" is associated with lower employment rates.

[8] Corporatism is a "system of social organisation that has at its base the grouping of men according to their community of their natural interests and social functions, and as true and proper organs of the state they direct and co-ordinate labour and capital in matters of common interest" (Cameron, 1984[7]).

[9] In the original *Jobs Strategy*, centralised or co-ordinated bargaining arrangements were viewed more positively than sector-level bargaining but not explicitly supported. While countries with such systems typically managed to sustain relatively high employment levels, the empirical evidence based on country panels was judged to be weak. Moreover, strong employment performance in those countries reflected, to an important extent, developments in the public rather than the private sector. More fundamentally, the ability to foster fully centralised bargaining

systems or systems that are effectively co-ordinated so as to promote resilience and contain wage spirals was put in doubt.

[10] The *Reassessed Jobs Strategy* also acknowledged that collective bargaining arrangements are deeply embedded in countries' social fabric and this was seen as the main reason why so little progress was made since the original *Jobs Study* of 1994.

[11] However, it is not clear whether the result by Boeri (2014[20]) is driven by the "two-tier" structure of the system or the lack of wage co-ordination in those countries that have a two-tier structure.

[12] Classifying countries in these categories of collective bargaining systems necessarily comes with some simplification. The detailed discussion in OECD (2017[1]) should thus be kept in mind when comparing and assessing the functioning of the different bargaining systems across countries.

[13] In the *Employment Outlook 2017* (OECD, 2017[1]), Spain and Switzerland were mentioned in an intermediate group between the predominantly centralised and organised decentralised ones. The number of observations between 1980 and 2015 for such an intermediate group is, however, too small for it to be used for econometric purposes.

[14] The ICTWSS database is available at http://www.uva-aias.net/en/ictwss.

[15] To avoid a reduction in the sample size, missing values among control variables have been redefined at zero and dummies for missing observations have been included among the controls.

[16] Separately controlling for the degrees of centralisation and co-ordination delivers qualitatively similar results (OECD, 2018[21]): Centralisation is associated with lower employment rates (although the relationship is not monotonic as it becomes weaker for extreme forms of centralisation) and not related with the unemployment rate. Wage co-ordination is linked with higher employment rates and lower unemployment rates.

[17] While decreasing wage inequality among full-time workers, collective bargaining may increase earnings inequality between full-time employees and other workers, in the spirit of an insider-outsider model. Since the data in this analysis are based on hourly wages of full-time workers, they cannot be used to study effects on overall earnings inequality among all workers.

[18] For European countries, the bargaining variable that is reported in the data is a characteristic that is associated with the firm, not the individual. Hence, all workers in one firm are classified in the same way, whether or not this type of bargaining applies to every single worker in the firm. The data only indicate the agreement that is the most relevant, even if both a sector- and a firm-level agreement are in place. For a few other countries, even if the variable is not missing, there is no within-country variation in the data, and the data are therefore not used.

[19] Compared with an OLS regression that includes one or two collective bargaining dummies, the Juhn-Murphy-Pierce (JMP) decomposition has the advantage that it nests all the different parts of the analysis in this section. The alternative to the JMP decomposition would be to employ reweighting methods, such as those popularised by DiNardo, Fortin and Lemieux (1996[98]). These reweighting methods are, however, especially sensitive to the problem of lack of common support, i.e. characteristics being common in one collective bargaining scheme, but not in another. For this reason, they cannot be used in this context.

[20] Misalignment of wages and productivity may come at an efficiency cost, in particular weaker productivity growth. The possible link between efficiency, wage-productivity alignment and wage dispersion gives collective bargaining, potentially, a central role in the productivity-inequality nexus – see OECD (2016[104]) and OECD (2016[106]).

[21] In a frictionless economy, wages in one sector should equal marginal productivity in this sector. The analysis uses average rather than marginal productivity, as marginal productivity is more

difficult to measure. With a standard Cobb-Douglas production function, marginal productivity equals average productivity. In practice, however, the parameters of the production function may not be constant across sectors, competition may be imperfect and the distribution of sectoral wages may not be aligned with that of average productivity also for reasons that have nothing to do with collective bargaining (e.g. because of differences in capital intensity across sectors and over time; see, for example, Chapter 2).

[22] The analysis of cross-sector correlations controls for the level of aggregate productivity in the economy through country fixed effects.

[23] When annual growth rates of wages and productivity are analysed instead of their levels, the results are similar. With growth rates capturing more short-run adjustments, this suggests that collective bargaining may influence the way wages are set both in the short and longer term.

[24] The euro area aggregate statistics are based on non-harmonised data for ten countries which include all larger countries and cover more than 95% of the euro area (Schulten, 2013[46]). The ECB labels as "experimental" those data for which compromises in terms of harmonisation, coverage and methodological soundness of the source data have to be made.

[25] For a methodological note on CAWIE data, see Van Gyes and Vandekerckhove (2015[87]); for policy analyses, see Schulten (2013[46]) and Delahaie, Vandekerckhove and Vincent (2015[99]). Compared to the discussion in this chapter, Schulten (2013[46]) also examines sectoral developments of negotiated wages but does not find clear patterns across European countries.

[26] In Germany, the metalworkers' union IG Metall opened itself to self-employed members in 2016 and set up a website http://faircrowd.work/, which allows platform workers to connect to one another, rate platforms and join the trade union. IG Metall also established an ombudsman office to settle disputes among crowd workers, clients and platforms by mutual out-of-court agreement. Unions in several other countries have taken similar initiatives.

[27] Worker centers in the United States are one example (Fine, 2006[96]): They are non-profit community-based organisations, not unions. This allows them to keep more freedom to engage in collective action and boycotts and to reduce the amount of bureaucracy they are subject to and opens opportunities to alternative sources of funding (including foundations and governments). Worker centers engage in advocacy and aim to improve working conditions through policy change rather than bargaining. Another model is co-operatives which organise self-employed workers and provide a range of services to them. One example of this is SMart, a co-operative originally set up to support artists in Belgium, but now offering services to other atypical workers and operating in nine countries. SMart provides the self-employed with a wide range of services, including: help with invoicing and the declaration of income; getting paid as an employee (and therefore gaining access to social protection); debt collection; salary advancement (through a mutual guarantee fund); and the provision of training and co-working spaces.

[28] See pages 140-145 of the *Employment Outlook 2017* (OECD, 2017[1]) for a detailed discussion of the pros and cons of the different options and OECD (2017[107]) for an application in the context of France, where extensions up to the recent reform used to be semi-automatic.

[29] Last year's *Employment Outlook* (OECD, 2017[1]) showed that in Europe the proportion of workers covered by shop stewards, worker representatives, works councils or other forms of employee representation in the workplace is lower in countries where firm-level bargaining dominates. By contrast, representation tends to be high in multi-level systems characterised by complementarity between sector- and firm-level agreements.

[30] A special type of opening clauses concerns the short-time working scheme *Kurzarbeit* which allows companies in times of economic crisis to put part of their workforce temporarily on unemployment benefits. These measures are meant to preserve valuable personnel for a company

in crisis. It differs from the "normal" opening clauses in that generally the government has a key role in these measures, since it regulates the use of unemployment benefits.

[31] In a few other countries (including France – at least until the 2017 reform –, Italy and Portugal), company-level bargaining plays a sometimes significant role, but either due to a strict application of the favourability principle or the practice of social partners to "lock" the content of sector-level agreements, firm-level agreements can only improve the standards set at the national or sector level. In principle, these two-tier structures could still allow balancing high coverage, macroeconomic stability and some margins of adjustment at the firm level. Indeed, the main advantage of such a system is that it does not rely on local representation in small or less productive firms. However, Boeri (2014[20]) argues that these regimes "combine the rigidity in pay of centralised systems with a lack of consideration of macroeconomic constraints" (Boeri, 2014, p. 17[20]). This may be because those who can afford more favourable agreements at the company level impose generous working conditions on others through their involvement in the negotiation of sector-level agreements. But it could also reflect the absence in those countries of a proper system of wage co-ordination which has been proven to be key for macroeconomic flexibility (OECD, 2017[1]).

[32] For example, during the bargaining round in 2016 the "cost mark" was set at about 2.5% but assistant nurses received an agreed wage raise of about 3.5%. All social partners agreed on this exception due to many years of comparatively small wage increases for assistant nurses despite labour shortages in their profession.

[33] The IMF (2017[105]) in its Article IV review for Sweden called on social partners to find ways to make wages more responsive to Swedish conditions at both the macroeconomic and sector level.

References

Acemoglu, D. and J. Pischke (1999), "The structure of wages and investment in general training", *Journal of Political Economy*, Vol. 107/3, pp. 539-572. [50]

Aidt, T. and Z. Tzannatos (2008), "Trade unions, collective bargaining and macroeconomic performance: a review", *Industrial Relations Journal*, Vol. 39/4, pp. 258-295. [6]

Aidt, T. and Z. Tzannatos (2002), *Unions and collective bargaining : Economic effects in a global environment*, The World Bank, Washington, DC. [12]

Amlinger, M. and R. Bispinck (2016), "Dezentralisierung der Tarifpolitik – Ergebnisse der WSI-Betriebsrätebefragung 2015", *WSI-Mitteilungen*, Vol. 3, pp. 211-222. [78]

Andreasson, H. (2017), "The effect of decentralized wage bargaining on the structure of wages and firm performance", *Ratio Working Paper*, No. 241. [56]

Arbetsmarknadsekonomiska rådet (2017), *The duality of the Swedish labour market: Summary of the Swedish Labour Policy Council report*, Arbetsmarknadsekonomiska rådet, Stockholm. [86]

Autor, D. (2003), "Outsourcing at will: The contribution of unjust dismissal doctrine to the growth of employment outsourcing", *Journal of Labor Economics*, Vol. 21/1, pp. 1-42. [25]

Azar, J., I. Marinescu and M. Steinbaum (2017), "Labor market concentration", *Working Paper*, No. 24147, NBER, Cambridge, MA. [103]

Baccaro, L. and C. Benassi (2017), "Softening institutions: The liberalization of German industrial relations", in Howell, C. (ed.), *European industrial relations: Trajectories of neoliberal transformation*, Cambridge University Press, Cambridge. [80]

Baker, D. et al. (2005), "Labor market institutions and unemployment: Assessment of the cross-country evidence", in Howell, D. (ed.), *Fighting unemployment: The limits of free market orthodoxy*, Oxford University Press. [102]

Barth, E., A. Bryson and H. Dale-Olsen (2017), "Union density, productivity and wages", *IZA Discussion Paper*, No. 11111. [65]

Bassanini, A. and R. Duval (2006), "Employment patterns in OECD countries: Reassessing the role of policies and institutions", *OECD Social, Employment and Migration Working Papers*, No. 35, OECD Publishing, Paris, http://dx.doi.org/10.1787/702031136412. [13]

Benmelech, E., N. Bergman and H. Kim (2018), "Strong employers and weak employees: How does employer concentration affect wages?", *NBER Working Paper*, No. 24307. [101]

Berlingieri, G., P. Blanchenay and C. Criscuolo (2017), "The great divergence(s)", *OECD Science, Technology and Industry Policy Papers*, No. 39, OECD Publishing, Paris, http://dx.doi.org/10.1787/953f3853-en. [41]

Bertola, G. (1999), "Microeconomic perspectives on aggregate labor markets", in Ashenfelter, O. and D. Card (eds.), *Handbook of Labor Economics*, Elsevier. [23]

Blanchflower, D. and R. Freeman (1993), "Did the Thatcher reforms change British labour performance?", *NBER Working Papers*. [28]

Blau, F. et al. (1999), "Institutions and laws in the labor market", in Ashenfelter, O. and D. Card (eds.), *Handbook of Labor Economics*, Elsevier. [29]

Boeri, T. (2014), "Two-tier bargaining", *IZA Discussion Paper*, No. 8358. [20]

Brandl, B. and A. Lehr (2016), "The strange non-death of employer and business associations: An analysis of their representativeness and activities in Western European countries", *Economic and Industrial Democracy*, pp. 1-22. [66]

Braun, S. (2011), "Unionisation structures, productivity and firm performance: New insights from a heterogeneous firm model", *Labour Economics*, Vol. 18/1, pp. 120-129. [49]

Bryson, A., J. Forth and A. George (2012), *Workplace social dialogue in Europe: An analysis of the European Company Survey 2009*, Eurofound, Dublin. [68]

Bryson, A. and R. Freeman (2013), "Employee perceptions of working conditions and the desire for worker representation in Britain and the US", *Journal of Labor Research*, Vol. 34/1, pp. 1-29. [62]

Bryson, A. et al. (2017), "The twin track model of employee voice: An Anglo-American perspective on union decline and the rise of alternative forms of voice", *IZA Discussion Paper*, No. 11223. [69]

Bryson, A. and F. Green (2015), "Unions and job quality", in Felstead, A., D. Gallie and F. Green (eds.), *Unequal Britain at work: The evolution and distribution of job quality*, Oxford University Press, Oxford. [63]

Calmfors, L. and J. Driffill (1988), "Bargaining structure, corporatism and macroeconomic performance", *Economic Policy*, Vol. 3/6, p. 13. [8]

Cameron, D. (1984), "Social democracy, corporatism, labour quiescence and the representation of economic interest in advanced capitalist societies", in Goldthorpe, J. (ed.), *Order and conflict in contemporary capitalism*, Oxford University Press, Oxford. [7]

Card, D., F. Devicienti and A. Maida (2014), "Rent-sharing, holdup, and wages: Evidence from matched panel data", *Review of Economic Studies*, Vol. 81/1, pp. 84-111. [54]

Card, D., T. Lemieux and W. Riddell (2004), "Unions and wage inequality", *Journal of Labor Research*, Vol. 25/4, pp. 519-559. [30]

Cardoso, A. and P. Portugal (2005), "Contractual wages and the wage cushion under different bargaining settings", *Journal of Labor Economics*, Vol. 23/4, pp. 875-902. [39]

Cardullo, G., M. Conti and G. Sulis (2015), "Sunk capital, unions and the hold-up problem: Theory and evidence from cross-country sectoral data", *European Economic Review*, Vol. 76, pp. 253-274. [55]

D'Amuri, F. and R. Nizzi (2017), "Recent developments of Italy's industrial relations system", *Questioni di Economia e Finanza (Occasional Papers)*, No. 416. [67]

Daskalova, V. (2017), "Regulating the new self-employed in the Uber economy: What role for EU competition law?", *TILEC Discussion Paper* , No. 2017-028, Tilburg University. [70]

de Beer, P. and M. Keune (2017), "Dutch unions in a time of crisis", in Lehndorff, S., H. Dribbusch and T. Schulten (eds.), *Rough waters European trade unions in a time of crises*, ETUI, Brussels. [45]

de Serres, A. and F. Murtin (2014), "Unemployment at risk: the policy determinants of labour market exposure to economic shocks", *Economic Policy*, Vol. 29/80, pp. 603-637. [100]

Delahaie, N., S. Vandekerckhove and C. Vincent (2015), "Wages and collective bargaining systems in Europe during the crisis", in Van Gyes, G. and T. Schulten (eds.), *Wage bargaining under the new European Economic Governance*, ETUI, Brussels. [99]

Dell'Aringa, C. and C. Lucifora (1994), "Collective bargaining and relative earnings in Italy", *European Journal of Political Economy*, Vol. 10/4, pp. 727-747. [36]

Diez-Catalan, L. and E. Villanueva (2015), "Contract staggering and unemployment during the Great Recession: Evidence from Spain", *Working Paper*, No. 1431, Banco de Espana. [44]

DiNardo, J., N. Fortin and T. Lemieux (1996), "Labor market institutions and the distribution of wages, 1973-1992: A semiparametric approach", *Econometrica*, Vol. 64/5, p. 1001. [98]

DiNardo, J. and D. Lee (2004), "Economic impacts of new unionization on private sector employers: 1984-2001", *Quarterly Journal of Economics*, Vol. 119/4, pp. 1383-1441. [31]

Doucouliagos, H., R. Freeman and P. Laroche (2017), *The economics of trade unions : A study of a research field and its findings*, Routledge, London. [53]

Égert, B. and P. Gal (2017), "The quantification of structural reforms in OECD countries: A new framework", *OECD Journal: Economic Studies, OECD Publishing, Paris*, Vol. 2016/1, http://dx.doi.org/10.1787/eco_studies-2016-5jg11qspxtvk. [97]

Elmeskov, J., J. Martin and S. Scarpetta (1998), "Key lessons for labour market reforms: Evidence from OECD countries' experience", *Swedish Economic Policy Review*, Vol. 5/2. [16]

Eurofound (2017), *Developments in collectively agreed pay 2016*, Eurofound, Dublin. [43]

Eurofound (2015), *Pay in Europe in different wage-bargaining regimes*, Publications Office of the European Union, Luxembourg. [14]

European Central Bank (2002), "Monitoring wage developments: An indicator of negotiated wages", in *ECB Monthly Bulletin September 2002*, European Central Bank. [42]

Fine, J. (2006), *Worker centers: Organizing communities at the edge of the dream*, ILR Press/Cornell University Press. [96]

Freeman, R. (1988), "Union density and economic performance: An analysis of U.S. States", *European Economic Review*, Vol. 32/2-3, pp. 707-716. [95]

Freeman, R. and J. Medoff (1984), *What do unions do?*, Basic Books, New York. [48]

Gal, P. and A. Theising (2015), "The macroeconomic impact of structural policies on labour market outcomes in OECD countries: A reassessment", *OECD Economics Department Working Papers*, No. 1271, OECD Publishing, Paris, http://dx.doi.org/10.1787/5jrqc6t8ktjf-en. [94]

Garnero, A., F. Rycx and I. Terraz (2018), "Productivity and wage effects of firm-level collective agreements: Evidence from Belgian linked panel data", *IZA Discussion Paper*, No. 11568, IZA, Bonn. [57]

Gramm, C. and J. Schnell (2001), "The use of flexible staffing arrangements in core production jobs", *Industrial and Labor Relations Review*, Vol. 54/2, pp. 245-258. [24]

Green, F. and K. Whitfield (2009), "Employees' experience of work", in Whitfield, K. et al. (eds.), *The evolution of the modern workplace*, Cambridge University Press, Cambridge. [64]

Haipeter, T. and S. Lehndorff (2014), "Decentralisation of collective bargaining in Germany: Fragmentation, coordination and revitalisation", *Economia & Lavoro*, Vol. 45/1, pp. 45-64. [79]

Hartog, J., E. Leuven and C. Teulings (2002), "Wages and the bargaining regime in a corporatist setting: The Netherlands", *European Journal of Political Economy*, Vol. 18/2, pp. 317-331. [37]

Haucap, J., U. Pauly and C. Wey (2001), "Collective wage setting when wages are generally binding: An antitrust perspective", *International Review of Law and Economics*, Vol. 21/3, pp. 287-307, http://dx.doi.org/10.1016/S0144-8188(01)00061-8. [71]

Haucap, J. and C. Wey (2004), "Unionisation structures and innovation incentives", *Economic Journal*, Vol. 114/494, pp. C149-C165. [51]

Hibbs Jr., D. and H. Locking (2000), "Wage dispersion and productive efficiency: Evidence for Sweden", *Journal of Labor Economics*, Vol. 18/4, pp. 755-782. [60]

Hijzen, A. and P. Martins (2016), "No extension without representation? Evidence from a natural experiment in collective bargaining", *IZA Discussion Paper*, No. 10204. [73]

Hijzen, A., P. Martins and J. Parlevliet (2018), "Collective bargaining through the magnifying glass: A comparison between the Netherlands and Portugal", *OECD Social, Employment and Migration Working Papers*, No. 199, OECD Publishing, Paris, http://dx.doi.org/10.1787/06b8e7dd-en. [93]

Ibsen, C. (2016), "The role of mediation institutions in Sweden and Denmark after centralized bargaining", *British Journal of Industrial Relations*, Vol. 54/2, pp. 285-310. [85]

Ibsen, C. and M. Keune (forthcoming), "Organized decentralization: Case studies of Germany, Netherlands and Denmark", *OECD Social, Employment and Migration Working Papers*, OECD Publishing, Paris. [75]

ILO (2015), *Labour markets, institutions and inequality: Building just societies in the 21st century*, International Labour Organization. [33]

IMF (2017), *Sweden - Selected Issues*, International Monetary Fund, Washington, DC. [105]

Jaumotte, F. and C. Buitron (2015), "Inequality and labor market institutions", *Staff Discussion Note*, No. 15/14, IMF. [34]

Juhn, C., K. Murphy and B. Pierce (1993), "Wage inequality and the rise in returns to skill", *Journal of Political Economy*, Vol. 101/3, pp. 410-442. [35]

Lamarche, C. (2015), "Collective bargaining in developing countries", *IZA World of Labor*. [59]

Lamarche, C. (2013), "Industry-wide work rules and productivity: evidence from Argentine union contract data", *IZA Journal of Labor & Development*, Vol. 2/11. [58]

Leonardi, M., M. Pellizzari and D. Tabasso (2015), "Wage compression within the firm", *CEPR Discussion Paper*, No. 10770. [27]

Leontief, W. (1946), "Wages, profit and prices", *Quarterly Journal of Economics*, Vol. 61/1, p. 26. [3]

Lindbeck, A. and D. Snower (1986), "Wage setting, unemployment, and insider-outsider relations", *American Economic Review*, Vol. 76/2, pp. 235-239. [4]

Magruder, J. (2012), "High unemployment yet few small firms: The role of centralized bargaining in South Africa", *American Economic Journal: Applied Economics*, Vol. 4/3, pp. 138-166. [72]

Malcomson, J. (1997), "Contracts, hold-up, and labor markets", *Journal of Economic Literature*, Vol. 35/4, pp. 1916-1957. [52]

Maloney, T. (1997), "Has New Zealand's Employment Contracts Act increased employment and reduced wages?", *Australian Economic Papers*, Vol. 36/69, pp. 243-264. [92]

McDonald, I. and R. Solow (1981), "Wage bargaining and employment", *American Economic Review*, Vol. 71/5, pp. 896-908. [5]

Murtin, F., A. de Serres and A. Hijzen (2014), "Unemployment and the coverage extension of collective wage agreements", *European Economic Review*, Vol. 71, pp. 52-66. [91]

Nickell, S. (1997), "Unemployment and labor market rigidities: Europe versus North America", *Journal of Economic Perspectives*, Vol. 11/3, pp. 55-74. [89]

Nickell, S. and R. Layard (1999), "Labor market institutions and economic performance", in *Handbook of Labor Economics*, Elsevier. [90]

Oberfichtner, M. and C. Schnabel (2017), "The German model of industrial relations: (Where) does it still exist?", *IZA Discussion Paper*, No. 11064. [81]

OECD (2018), *OECD Economic Surveys: Greece 2016*, OECD Publishing, Paris, http://www.oecd-ilibrary.org/economics/oecd-economic-surveys-greece-2016_eco_surveys-grc-2016-en. [84]

OECD (2018), "Supplementary material for Chapter 3", in *OECD Employment Outlook 2018*, OECD Publishing, Paris, http://dx.doi.org/10.1787/empl_outlook-2018-13-en. [21]

OECD (2017), *Labour market reforms in Portugal 2011-15: A preliminary assessment*, OECD Publishing, Paris, http://dx.doi.org/10.1787/9789264269576-en. [83]

OECD (2017), *Les extensions administratives des accords de branche en France: Effets et pistes de réformes*, OECD Publishing, Paris, http://www.oecd.org/fr/economie/extensions-administratives-des-accords-de-branche-en-France.pdf (accessed on 29 January 2018). [107]

OECD (2017), *OECD Employment Outlook 2017*, OECD Publishing, Paris, http://dx.doi.org/10.1787/empl_outlook-2017-en. [1]

OECD (2016), "Promoting productivity and equality: A twin challenge", in *OECD Economic Outlook, Volume 2016 Issue 1*, OECD Publishing, Paris, http://dx.doi.org/10.1787/eco_outlook-v2016-1-3-en. [106]

OECD (2016), *The Productivity-inclusiveness nexus*, OECD Publishing, Paris. [104]

OECD (2014), *OECD Employment Outlook 2014*, OECD Publishing, Paris, http://dx.doi.org/10.1787/empl_outlook-2014-en. [47]

OECD (2014), *The 2012 labour market reform in Spain: A preliminary assessment*, OECD Publishing, Paris, http://dx.doi.org/10.1787/9789264213586-en. [82]

OECD (2012), *OECD Employment Outlook 2012*, OECD Publishing, Paris, http://dx.doi.org/10.1787/empl_outlook-2012-en. [18]

OECD (2011), *Divided we stand: Why inequality keeps rising*, OECD Publishing, Paris, http://dx.doi.org/10.1787/9789264119536-en. [32]

OECD (2006), *OECD Employment Outlook 2006*, OECD Publishing, Paris, http://dx.doi.org/10.1787/empl_outlook-2006-en. [19]

OECD (2004), *OECD Employment Outlook 2004*, OECD Publishing, Paris, http://dx.doi.org/10.1787/empl_outlook-2004-en. [17]

OECD (1997), *OECD Employment Outlook 1997*, OECD Publishing, Paris, http://dx.doi.org/10.1787/empl_outlook-1997-en. [10]

OECD (1994), *The OECD Jobs Strategy*, OECD Publishing, Paris, http://dx.doi.org/10.1787/20743653. [9]

OECD (forthcoming), *Good jobs for all in a changing world of work: The OECD Jobs Strategy*, OECD Publishing, Paris.　[2]

Pak, M. and C. Schwellnus (forthcoming), "Labour share developments over the past two decades: The role of public policies", *OECD Economics Department Working Papers*, OECD Publishing, Paris.　[40]

Rajan, R. and L. Zingales (1998), "Financial dependence and growth", *American Economic Review*, Vol. 88/3, pp. 559-586.　[61]

Rycx, F. (2003), "Industry wage differentials and the bargaining regime in a corporatist country", *International Journal of Manpower*, Vol. 24/4, pp. 347-366.　[38]

Saint-Paul, G. (1996), *Dual labor markets: A macroeconomic perspective*, MIT Press, Cambridge, MA.　[22]

Salvatori, A. (2009), "What do unions do to temporary employment?", *IZA Discussion Paper*, No. 4554.　[26]

Scarpetta, S. (1996), "Assessing the role of labour market policies and institutional settings on unemployment: A cross-country study", *OECD Economic Studies*, No. 26, OECD Publishing, Paris, https://www.oecd.org/eco/growth/2502834.pdf (accessed on 15 January 2018).　[88]

Schulten, T. (2013), "Current trends in collectively agreed wages and wage drift in Europe 2001-2010", *Hans-Böckler-Stiftung Policy Paper*, http://ilera-europe2013.eu/uploads/paper/attachment/148/ilera2013_paperID96b.pdf (accessed on 25 January 2018).　[46]

Schulten, T. and R. Bispinck (2017), "Varieties of decentralisation in German collective bargaining: Experiences from metal industry and retail trade", *CSDLE "Massimo D'Antona" Working Paper*, No. 137/2017.　[77]

Soskice, D. (1990), "Reinterpreting corporatism and explaining unemployment: Co-ordinated and non-co-ordinated market economies", in Brunetta, R. and C. Dell'Aringa (eds.), *Labour relations and economic performance*, Palgrave Macmillan, London.　[15]

Traxler, F. (1995), "Farewell to labour market associations? Organized versus disorganized decentralization as a map for industrial relations", in Crouch, C. and F. Traxler (eds.), *Organized industrial relations in Europe: What future?*, Aldershot, Avebury.　[74]

Traxler, F., S. Blaschke and B. Kittel (2001), *National labour relations in internationalized markets*, Oxford University Press, Oxford.　[11]

Van Gyes, G. and S. Vandekerckhove (2015), "Indicators of collectively agreed wages in the euro zone: A quality report", in Van Gyes, G. and T. Schulten (eds.), *Wage bargaining under the new European Economic Governance*, ETUI, Brussels.　[87]

Visser, J. (2016), "What happened to collective bargaining during the great recession?", *IZA Journal of Labor Policy*, Vol. 5/1, p. 9.　[76]

Supplementary material for Chapter 3

Supplementary material for Chapter 3 is available online only in English at the following DOI: http://dx.doi.org/10.1787/empl_outlook-2018-13-en.

Chapter 4. Back to work: Lessons from nine country case studies of policies to assist displaced workers

This chapter analyses how best labour market programmes can reduce the costs borne by workers who lose their jobs due to business closings or other economic reasons ("displaced workers"). The chapter shows that a considerable number of workers are displaced every year and that many in this group – especially older workers in blue-collar jobs – experience large earnings losses due to both long periods out of work and re-employment at a lower wage. The chapter draws upon detailed case studies of policies to assist displaced workers in nine OECD countries and provides many examples of the effective use of active labour market policies and unemployment benefits to ensure that the labour market adjustment costs inherent to a dynamic economy are kept as low as possible and that these costs are not unfairly concentrated on the displaced workers who have the most limited job mobility.

The statistical data for Israel are supplied by and under the responsibility of the relevant Israeli authorities. The use of such data by the OECD is without prejudice to the status of the Golan Heights, East Jerusalem and Israeli settlements in the West Bank under the terms of international law.

Key findings

A dynamic economy requires a fluid labour market in which workers are continually moving from shrinking to growing firms. Indeed, labour reallocation is an integral part of the "creative destruction" process that underlies economic growth and rising living standards. A considerable number of workers who lose their jobs to economic change ("displaced workers") nevertheless experience significant income losses and other hardships, and these costs need to be kept as low as possible if the net benefits of growth are to be maximised and shared in an equitable manner. One way that governments can reduce the costs of labour market restructuring is by improving the re-employment assistance and income support that labour market programmes provide to displaced workers. This chapter discusses how best that can be achieved, highlighting the general policy lessons from the OECD's *Back to Work* reviews of nine countries which analysed policies to improve the re-employment prospects of displaced workers. The chapter first examines the scale of job displacement and the labour market problems encountered by those affected:

- Job displacement – defined as a permanent economic dismissal affecting a worker who has at least one year of job tenure – is quite common. Between 1% and 7% of the workforce is displaced annually, implying a significant probability that a typical worker will experience displacement one or more times during her working life. Nonetheless, job displacement accounts for only a modest share of all job separations, many of which are voluntarily initiated by the worker.

- A considerable number of displaced workers find a suitable new job rapidly, but the majority experience significant losses of income and potentially would benefit from re-employment assistance and income support. Income losses are particularly large during the period of joblessness that immediately follows displacement in the majority of cases. In certain countries earnings can fall by up to 50% on the year of dismissal and remain up to 10% below pre-displacement years even four years after being laid-off. However, income losses can continue after displaced workers are re-employed, because wages in post-displacement jobs are often lower than those from the lost jobs. The risks of long-term joblessness and large earnings losses after re-employment are particularly significant for older and long-tenure workers in blue-collar jobs.

- Displaced workers find new jobs much more rapidly in some countries than in others. Whereas nearly 90% are re-employed within a year in Finland and Sweden, the corresponding figure for France and Portugal is about 30%. The earnings losses of displaced workers also vary considerably across the countries analysed. These differences suggest that national labour market policies and institutions can have a significant impact on the adjustment costs borne by displaced workers.

- The costs faced by displaced workers are also highly variable within the same country. The re-employment and retraining support offered to each worker therefore needs to be calibrated to reflect individual needs. However, these needs may be difficult to assess in a timely manner in practice.

- There is a surprising scarcity of rigorous evaluation evidence concerning what works for displaced workers. Additional evaluations of the effectiveness of the different policy options that are discussed here would be very helpful.

When feasible, *proactive actions* can play some useful role in limiting the cost of job displacement. These can take the form of:

- *Preventive measures.* There is a potential, albeit limited, role for measures to prevent layoffs that are not socially efficient, either by effectively taxing layoffs (e.g. through higher unemployment insurance contributions for employers who lay off workers or employment protection legislation rules that impose costs on firms dismissing permanent workers) or by using a short-time work scheme to encourage employers facing temporary difficulties to preserve jobs that are viable in the long run. However, a light touch with preventive measures is required, especially as regards employment protection legislation, so as to preserve efficiency in the reallocation process and avoid discouraging job creation.

- *Early intervention measures.* A crucial difference between displaced workers and most other groups served by the public employment service (PES) is that it is often possible to initiate re-employment services during the notice period prior to displacement. Rapid response services, such as setting up a temporary PES office in a factory that will soon close, facilitate the timely delivery of re-employment services which can jump-start the adjustment process. These early intervention services can be quite effective. However, they are not used as widely as would be desirable, often being limited to workers affected by mass layoffs. In Sweden, the job security councils that are operated by the social partners demonstrate the feasibility of offering effective early intervention measures to all displaced workers, including those affected by individual or small-scale layoffs, when employers and unions are constructively engaged. It is important to require that employers provide at least a minimally adequate period of advance notice of layoffs whenever possible, while ensuring that notified workers be the focus of outreach initiatives by the PES or be required to register with the PES as soon as they are notified.

An effective national *activation strategy* to get people into work provides a solid foundation for promoting rapid the re-employment of displaced workers while a well-designed *unemployment benefits scheme* is key to providing adequate income security. However, policy also needs to take into account of the specific barriers to re-employment that often confront displaced workers – such as obsolete skills and the absence of recent job search experience, while also leveraging their advantages – notably a history of stable employment and strong labour force attachment. Adapting re-employment and income supports for this group raises issues in a number of areas:

- *Active labour market programmes (ALMPs).* While all displaced workers should benefit from prompt access to basic job search services, some will require more intensive re-employment services or retraining. One key challenge is to identify this smaller group rapidly and offer them intensive services when these are most effective, rather than only after a long period of unemployment as is frequently the case. Two additional challenges are to reduce the often large inequities in the access of different groups of displaced workers to re-employment help and to rapidly scale-up re-employment services when there is an upsurge in displacement, either locally or nationally. Re-employment services for displaced workers are typically delivered by a combination of general ALMPs and programmes targeted at this specific group and a pragmatic mix of general and targeted programmes is ideal. In countries where many displaced workers can only access unemployment benefits after a long delay (or never), it is important to decouple the initiation of contact with the PES and access to re-employment support from the timing of benefit receipt.

- *Income support.* In most countries with unemployment insurance systems, the benefit entitlements of displaced workers tend to be relatively high because they have more stable employment histories than most other unemployed persons. Nonetheless, benefits only provide compensation for a small proportion of earnings losses, especially for workers who experience a long spell of unemployment or become re-employed at a significantly lower wage or in a part-time job. Providing adequate income support for displaced workers, while also encouraging rapid re-employment, requires good programme design. For example, a temporary wage supplement can be offered to displaced workers who return to work rapidly by accepting a new job at a lower pay level. Much remains to be learned, however, about how best workers can be insured against the earnings losses due to displacement while minimising adverse impacts on job search incentives.

A broader set of policies can contribute to the successful management of labour market restructuring, including by helping to lower the costs of job displacement, although these lie beyond the scope of this chapter. Important examples include policies to foster economic revitalisation in regions that have been hit hard by mass layoffs and an effective national system to anticipate and meet changing job skill requirements.

Introduction

OECD labour markets are characterised by their dynamism. Each year, more than 20% of jobs, on average, are created and/or destroyed, and around one-third of all workers are hired by and/or separate from their employer (OECD, 2009[1]). These large job and worker flows are a reflection of a continuous process of labour reallocation that contributes to productivity gains and rising living standards. However, high job turnover is also a source of insecurity for workers, especially those who lose their jobs because their employer downsizes its workforce or goes out of business altogether, a group that labour market researchers typically label as "displaced workers".[1] An important challenge facing OECD governments is to nurture labour market dynamism while keeping the adjustment costs borne by displaced workers as low as possible. This chapter analyses how labour market programmes can contribute to meeting that policy challenge by improving the re-employment prospects of displaced workers and compensating them for part of their lost earnings.

Assisting displaced workers has long been recognised as being an important policy goal for active and passive labour market programmes. In fact, unemployment insurance (UI) and the active labour market programmes (ALMPs) that are offered by the public employment service (or its private subcontractors), such as job placement and retraining, were developed in large part to assist workers who were laid-off by their employers in response to changing economic conditions. The vast research literature analysing the design and operation of such programmes is highly relevant for assessing how they can assist this group in a cost-effective manner. However, this research rarely assesses the specific situation of displaced workers, as distinct from that of other participants of labour market programmes, making it difficult to draw firm conclusions about which general measures work best for this particular group and whether they also require special support measures. This limitation is particularly unfortunate at a time of heightened public concerns about the uneven distribution of the benefits and costs associated with rapid economic change. Workers who are displaced due to globalisation, technological and other structural change figure prominently among the potential victims of economic restructuring, making it timely to assess how well labour programmes are meeting the re-employment and income support needs of this group.[2]

This chapter documents the labour market services currently offered to displaced workers in OECD countries and assesses how those services could be improved. Policy reforms that reduce the costs associated with job displacement would bring significant overall efficiency and equity benefits, for example by helping workers whose jobs are automated to move quickly into other jobs that make productive use of their skills, while also helping to maintain support for open, innovative and flexible economies.[3]

This chapter provides an overview of the main policy lessons that emerged from a multi-year study of job displacement, and particularly nine country reviews of policies to assist workers displaced by economic change, which the OECD conducted between 2013 and 2017.[4] These *Back to Work* reviews provide new insights into effective policy approaches in different national contexts, while also highlighting several pitfalls to avoid. Since this chapter is intended to provide policy lessons that are general enough to apply to countries that did not participate in the nine reviews, it focuses on issues that arose in the provision of cost-effective support to displaced workers in most or all of the countries reviewed.[5] The chapter also draws upon relevant experience in other OECD countries and updates key parts of the cross-country statistical analysis of the incidence and consequences of job displacement that was originally presented in Chapter 4 of the 2013 issue of this publication (OECD, 2013[2]) .

The remainder of the chapter is organised as follows. Section 4.1 briefly documents the incidence and consequences of job displacement and situates the labour market policies that are analysed in detail in this chapter within the broader range of policies affecting labour market adjustment costs. It also discusses the disappointing paucity of rigorous evaluation evidence concerning the cost-effectiveness of labour market programmes for displaced workers. Section 4.2 then analyses policies that either prevent some displacements or allow the adjustment process to get underway during the notice period. Section 4.3 looks at ALMPs that are intended to assist displaced workers back into suitable jobs, including job-search assistance, counselling and retraining. In Section 4.4, attention turns to unemployment benefits and public and private measures that compensate displaced workers for at least a part of their lost earnings. A concluding section briefly recaps the main lessons for policy while also highlighting issues that require further study.

4.1. The policy challenge

4.1.1. Overview of job displacement and the resulting costs for workers

Much of the public concern about job displacement centres on mass redundancies, such as when a factory closes or a large firm declares bankruptcy and lays off its entire workforce. Many case studies of particular mass layoffs have documented the disruption and economic hardship that result for many of the workers losing their jobs (especially older, long-tenure workers), their families and often also for the broader community where they live, due to spill-over effects on the local economy.[6] A growing number of econometric studies have confirmed that the costs in higher unemployment and inactivity, lower wages and poorer health can be large and persistent for workers in local labour markets that experience a sudden increase in import competition, particularly blue collar workers who are initially employed in industries facing that competition (Autor, Dorn and Hanson, 2016[3]). The evidence from studies of specific mass layoffs and the local impacts of "the China shock" makes it clear that the cost of plant closings and mass layoffs can be very high. However, more comprehensive types of evidence are also required to assess the overall importance of job displacement as a source of insecurity for workers and the implications for labour market policy.

The OECD has collected harmonised statistics on job displacement in 13 OECD countries which help to characterise the overall policy challenge related to assisting displaced workers. These statistics were presented in detail in OECD (2013[2]). A partially updated version of these data are now used to provide a brief overview of the incidence and consequences of job displacement which helps define the policy challenge confronting labour market programmes intended to assist displaced workers.[7]

How large is the risk of displacement and who is most affected?

Figure 4.1 shows that the annual incidence of job displacement has ranged from 1% to 7% of dependent (wage and salary) employment since 2003 in the 13 OECD countries for which harmonised data could be assembled. Unfortunately, the considerable cross-country differences in the estimated displacement rates are difficult to interpret because they reflect a combination of real differences in the incidence of displacement (e.g. due to differences in industry structure or employment protection rules) and measurement issues related to differences in the underlying data sources and definitions.[8] In order to gauge the cyclicality of the displacement rate, the average risk of displacement is shown separately for three periods: the years preceding the global financial crisis, the peak crisis years and the early post-crisis recovery period. Not surprisingly, the displacement rate is counter-cyclical, being highest in almost all countries during the 2009-10 crisis period. Nonetheless, the displacement rate during the pre- and post-crisis periods was approximately two-thirds that during the crisis, indicating that the majority of job displacements reflect on-going structural change and the changing competitive position of different firms, rather than business cycle downturns.[9]

These displacement rates suggest that a typical worker faces a substantial risk of experiencing at least one economic layoff over the course of her working life, helping to explain the political salience of concerns about job displacement.[10] Nonetheless, total job separations considerably exceed the number of workers who are displaced, since many workers voluntarily quit their jobs each year and it is also quite common for low-tenure workers on temporary contracts to leave the firm when their contract expires.[11] Figure 4.2 shows that total separation rates in OECD countries have ranged from between 9% and 32% in recent years (Panel A), with displacements estimated to account for between 9% and 36% of total separations, in the smaller number of countries where both rates could be estimated (Panel B).[12] In sum, job displacement is not a rare phenomenon and it is understandable that the threat of displacement looms large in the minds of many workers, but it also should be borne in mind that these layoffs occur within the context of high labour turnover which sees approximately one-third of all workers being hired and/or separated from their employer each year. Nonetheless, since mid-career job mobility is common and often voluntary, it cannot be assumed that job displacement necessarily results in large and enduring costs for all workers who experience it.

Figure 4.1. Between 1% and 7% of workers lose their jobs to economic change every year

Job displacement rates of workers with at least one year of job tenure in selected countries

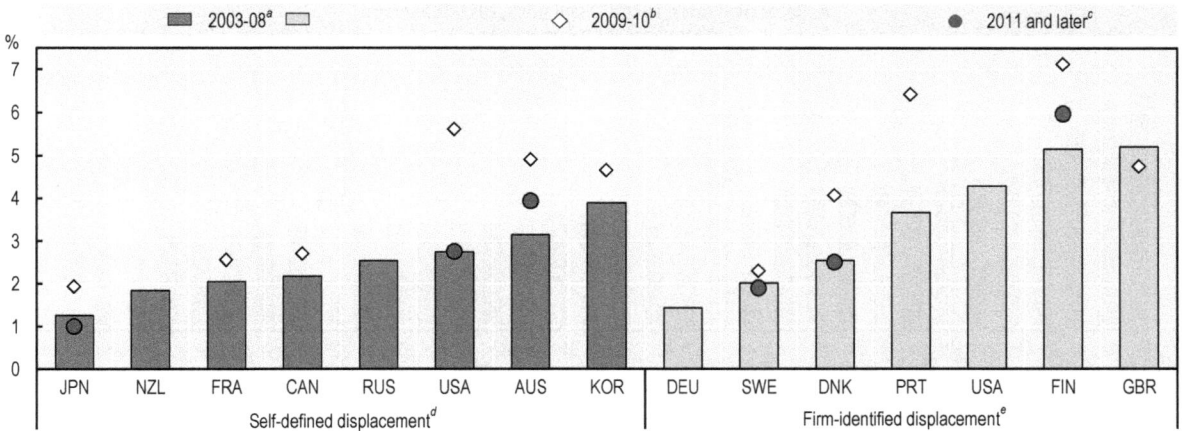

Note: Data refer to percentages of employees aged 20-64 who are displaced from one year to the next, 2003-08, 2009-10 and 2011 and later averages. See Table A1.1 in Annex A.1 of OECD (2013[4]) for details on the samples and definitions used for each country.

a)   Data refer to an average of 2000-04 for Germany, to an average of 2004-08 for France and the Russian Federation, and for the United States to an average of 2003, 2005 and 2007 for self-defined displacement, and to an average of 2003-07 for firm-identified displacement.

b)   Data refer to 2009 for Korea, Portugal and the United States.

c)   Data refer to an average of 2011-13 for Australia and Japan, to an average of 2011-12 for Denmark, Finland and Sweden, and to an average of 2011 and 2013 for the United States for self-defined displacement.

d)   Self-defined displacement (using household Panel data): job separations where the reason given for leaving the previous job is economic reasons (e.g. redundancy, layoff, business slowdown, lack of work, firm closure, mass dismissal, etc.) or dismissal for cause.

e)   Firm-identified displacement (using administrative data): job separations from firms that, from one year to the next, experience an absolute reduction in employment of five employees or more and a relative reduction in employment of 30% or more (mass dismissal) or that ceased to operate (firm closure).

Source: OECD (2013[4]), "Back to Work: Re-employment, Earnings and Skill Use after Job Displacement" http://www.oecd.org/employment/emp/Backtowork-report.pdf and OECD estimates updated from national microdata.

StatLink 🔗 http://dx.doi.org/10.1787/888933778193

Job displacement affects all types of workers, but some demographic groups face a greater risk of involuntary job loss than others.[13] In most of the countries studied, displacement rates are higher for both workers in their 20s and older workers (aged 55-64 years) than for prime-age workers. Workers with less than a secondary education and those whose jobs require largely manual skills also have above-average rates of displacement. Men are displaced more often than women in most countries, but this difference appears to reflect gender differences in the types of jobs held – notably the over-representation of men in manufacturing, construction and manual occupations rather than any discrimination against men when it comes to dismissal. Two of the strongest patterns affecting the incidence of displacement is that lower tenure workers (1-4 years of job tenure) and employees in smaller firms (10-49 workers) face a significantly elevated risk of involuntary job loss.

Figure 4.2. Job displacement is only one (particularly disruptive) form of worker turnover

Total job separation rates and job displacement shares in OECD countries[a]

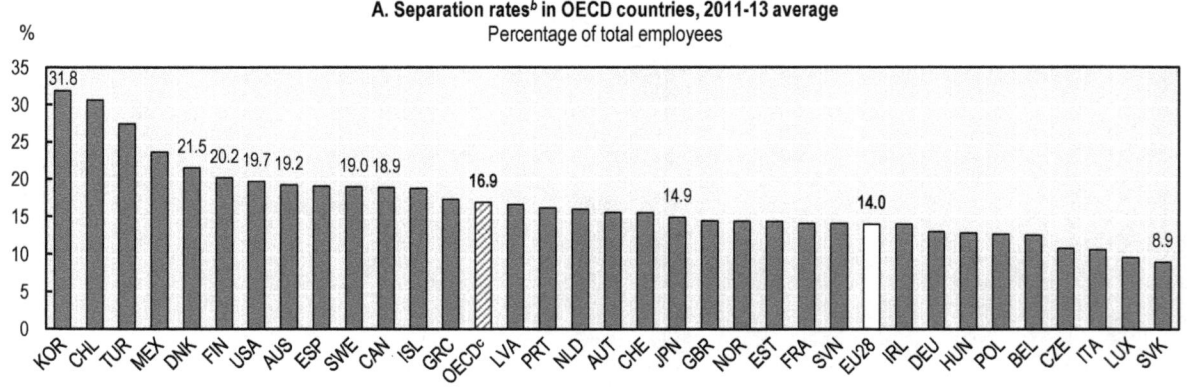

A. Separation rates[b] in OECD countries, 2011-13 average
Percentage of total employees

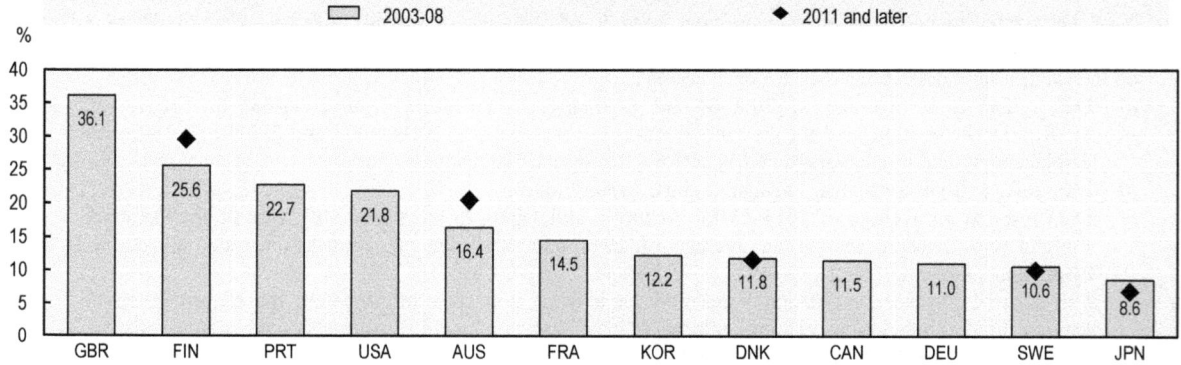

B. Job displacement[d, e] as a share of total separations, selected OECD countries

a) The estimates of total separations and displacement that are combined to calculate the displacement share of total separations are based on different data sources for some of the countries analysed and may not be fully comparable. Thus, the estimated displacement shares of total separations which are displayed in Panel B should be considered as providing only an approximate indication of the contribution of economic dismissals to total separations. The large cross-country differences in this ratio should also be interpreted with caution since they may reflect measurement biases.

b) Data refer to the difference between the hiring rate and the net employment change.

c) Unweighted average of the 33 OECD countries shown in Panel A.

d) Data in Panel B refer to percentages of employees aged 20-64 who are displaced from one year to the next, 2003-08 averages and 2011 and later averages. See Table A1.1 in Annex A.1 of OECD (2013[4]) for details on the samples and definitions used for each country.

e) Firm-identified displacement for Denmark, Finland, Germany, Portugal, Sweden, the United Kingdom and the United States. Self-defined displacement for Australia, Canada, France, Korea, Japan and the United States. For more details about displacement definitions and years referring to countries, see notes to Figure 4.1.

Source: For separations rates in Panel A: Fujii, M. and R. Kambayashi (2014[5]) "Long-term effects of job displacement in Japan: A conservative estimate using the Japanese Longitudinal Survey on Employment and Fertility (LOSEF)", https://hermes-ir.lib.hit-u.ac.jp/rs/bitstream/10086/26917/1/DP634.pdf, and calculations using data from the Survey on Employment Trends (ETS) for Japan; and *OECD Job Tenure Dataset,* a subset of the *OECD Employment Database,* www.oecd.org/employment/database for all other OECD countries. For displacement rates used in Panel B, OECD (2013[4]), "Back to Work: Re-employment, Earnings and Skill Use after Job Displacement", http://www.oecd.org/employment/emp/Backtowork-report.pdf, and OECD estimates updated from national microdata.

StatLink ᠊᠊᠊᠊ http://dx.doi.org/10.1787/888933778212

The finding that job displacement disproportionately affects younger and low-tenure tenure workers, as well as workers employed by smaller firms, suggests that the experience of many displaced workers may not conform to the worst case scenario where one or more large employers close creating a situation of persistently high unemployment in the local labour market, large negative spill-over effects on the local economy and high adjustment costs for the affected workers, many of whom are long-tenure workers in declining occupations and sectors. Indeed, the limited evidence available from other data sources suggests that the majority of displacements are associated with smaller layoff events that are unlikely to be associated with large negative externalities depressing the local labour market, but may nonetheless imply significant adjustment costs for the affected workers:

- The *European Restructuring Monitor (ERM) Database* provides information about large restructuring events in European countries since 2002, as compiled by a network of specialists who monitor various news sources and company announcements. The number of layoffs captured by this database during 2000-08 can be compared with the number of displacements during the same period as captured in the OECD data underlying Figure 4.1, albeit only for seven European countries. In most countries, the mass dismissals captured in the ERM dataset represent less than 15% of all displacements. Similarly, administrative data on mass layoffs that were collected by the US Bureau of Labour Statistics until recently captured only about one-fifth as many layoffs as the Displaced Worker Survey which collected information on all economic dismissals (OECD, 2005[6]). These comparisons suggest that a large majority of all job displacement take the form of small to medium scale layoffs, rather than mass layoffs.

- Two household surveys that are designed to provide comprehensive estimates of job displacement also provide information about whether each displacement occurred as a result of a business or plant closing. The Displaced Worker Survey indicates that 37% of all displacements in the United States represented total closings during 2013-15 (BLS, 2016[7]), while the SHARELIFE data indicate that 48% of the displacements in 13 EU countries represented total closings during 1986-2008 (Andrews and Saia, 2017[8]). While these estimates of the shutdown share of total displacements exceed the estimates of the mass layoff share cited above, it should be noted that many business closings likely involve small businesses and thus relatively few workers.

- Even if the majority of displaced workers do not fit the worst case scenario, the minority who have their working lives upended in such a manner are almost certainly a sufficiently large group to be of considerable policy concern. It should also be noted that some workers affected by individual or small scale displacements may have worked for local subcontractors of a large firm that closed and, hence, are likely to face particularly difficulties in finding a suitable new job where they live.

The consequences of displacement for the affected workers

While a considerable number of workers are displaced each year, the implications for labour market programmes depends crucially on the consequences for the affected workers; in particular, whether most workers experiencing a displacement are able to find new jobs quickly that are comparable to the lost jobs or, instead, experience long periods out of work or significant earnings losses even once re-employed.

Figure 4.3 presents re-employment rates within 1 and 2 years of experiencing an economic dismissal.[14] While some displaced workers return to work relatively rapidly, many remain jobless for an extended period. Dramatic differences in the speed of re-employment are also apparent for the 13 OECD countries that are analysed: At one extreme, only about one in three French and Portuguese workers are re-employed within one year of displacement, whereas nearly 90% of displaced workers are re-employed within a year in Finland and Sweden. Countries with low first year re-employment rates make up some of the ground in the second year following displacement, but international differences still remain large as regards the probability of returning to work.[15] Re-employment rates for the peak crisis years (2009-10) and the early post-crisis recovery are somewhat lower than the pre-crisis rates, while international differences in the speed of re-employment remain quite stable across the three periods considered.[16] OECD (2013[2]) shows that re-employment rates in almost all countries are below-average for women, workers with less than a secondary education and, especially, for older workers (aged 55-64 years). The time spent out of work after displacement reflects a combination of unemployment (i.e. active but unsuccessful job search) and labour force withdrawal and is one of the main sources of lost earnings due to displacement, particularly in the first year or two following a dismissal.

Figure 4.4 shows regression-based estimates of mean earnings impacts of displacement, which are inferred from differences between the evolution of the earnings for workers who are displaced in a given year and a control group of workers who were not displaced in that year.[17] In all of the countries analysed, earnings fall during the year of displacement (DY), sometimes quite sharply (e.g. by nearly 50% in Portugal).[18] The earnings gap created by displacement then declines very substantially during the next three to four years, albeit without having fully disappeared by the end of the observation window. These earnings impacts represent the combined effect of the time required to find a new job, when earnings are zero, and any change in earnings or job stability between the former and new jobs. A number of national studies of the earnings impact of displacement have shown that both the time out of work and lower earnings on the post-displacement job (due to both lower wages and lower hours) make important contributions to overall earnings losses and that these losses can be large and persistent for some displaced workers, even if they are modest on average after the first year or two.[19] The negative consequences of displacement are not limited to reduced earnings. For example, a number of studies have also documented declines in the health status of workers who are displaced, including an increased incidence of depression, hospitalisation for alcohol-related conditions and higher mortality, as surveyed by Bassanini and Caroli (2015[9]).

The mean impact of displacement on earnings, which is presented in Figure 4.4, hides the very large variation in the costs borne by different workers. Figure 4.5 illustrates the heterogeneity of displacement costs. Panel A shows that the economic cost of being displaced tends to increase quite sharply with age, although the age gradient is not equally steep in all countries. OECD (2013[4]) provides additional examples of differences in the average earnings impact of displacement that are associated with observable characteristics, showing that earnings losses generally decline with the level of education, whereas the size and sign of gender differences in earnings losses vary from country to country (e.g. the earnings losses following displacement are higher for women than for men in the United States, but the opposite is true in Finland).

Figure 4.3. Displaced workers find new jobs much more rapidly in some OECD countries than in others

Re-employment rates after displacement in selected OECD countries,[a] 2000-13 percentages

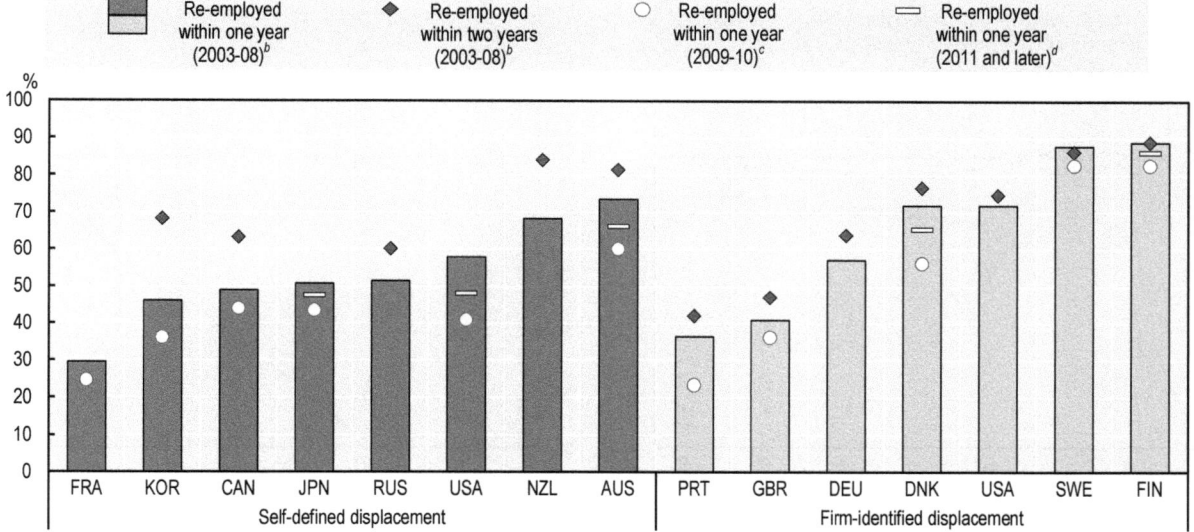

a) For countries with self-defined definition of job displacement, data refer to workers who lose their job for economic reasons, due to the end of a temporary contract or for cause. For countries with firm-identified definition of job displacement, data refer to workers who lose their job due to a mass layoff or firm closure. For full details of the data sources and methodology, see Table A1.1 in Annex A.1 of OECD (2013[4]).

b) Data refer to an average of 2000-08 for Canada, to an average of 2004-08 for France and the Russian Federation, to an average of 2000-04 for Germany, and to an average of 2004, 2006 and 2008 for the United States. There are no data on re-employment within two years for France and the United States.

c) Data refer to 2009 for Korea, Portugal and Sweden, and to 2010 for the United States for self-defined displacement.

d) Data refer to an average of 2011-13 for Australia and Japan, to an average of 2011-12 for Denmark and Finland, and to an average of 2012 and 2014 for the United States for self-defined displacement.

Source: OECD (2013[4]), "Back to Work: Re-employment, Earnings and Skill Use after Job Displacement", http://www.oecd.org/employment/emp/Backtowork-report.pdf, and OECD estimates updated from national microdata.

StatLink ᴍꜱᴾ http://dx.doi.org/10.1787/888933778231

Panel B of Figure 4.5 zeros in on the impact of displacement on wages once workers have become re-employed. Based on data that were collected for four of the countries where policies to assist displaced workers were reviewed, it can be seen that wages on the new job range from being considerably above those on the old job to much lower. While the share of (re-employed) displaced workers experiencing wage increases of 10% or more ranges from 11% in Japan (where the economy was quite stagnant) to 41% in Australia (where economic growth was strong), the shares experiencing substantial wage reductions are more uniform: around 30% experienced a wage cut of at least 10% and around 10% a wage cut of 30% or more.

Figure 4.4. The depth and persistence of the reduction in earnings following displacement varies considerably across OECD countries

Average earnings changes *before* and *after* displacement, percentage of pre-displacement earnings

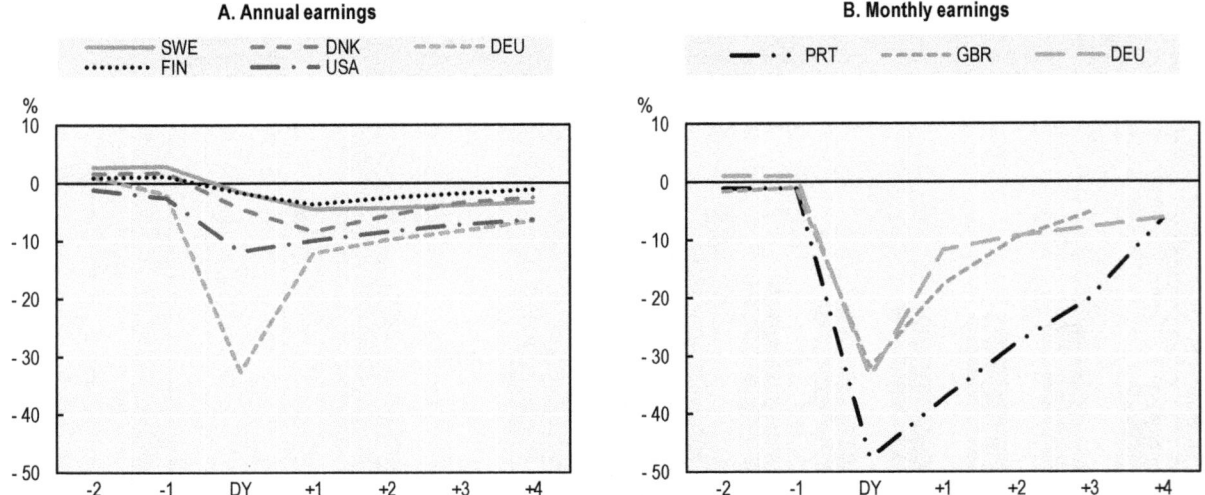

Note: DY: Displacement year. The estimation sample includes displacements that occur between 2000 and 2005. Pre-displacement earnings are the average earnings in the third year prior to displacement. See Annex 4.A1 in OECD (2013[2]) for a full description of the samples, years and definitions used for each country.
Source: OECD (2013[2]), *OECD Employment Outlook 2013*, http://dx.doi.org/10.1787/empl_outlook-2013-en.

StatLink ᴀᵢᵢᴤ￫ http://dx.doi.org/10.1787/888933778250

The estimates presented above reflect relatively short-run wage effects for workers who found a new job within a year of being displaced. However, a number of national studies have looked at wage effects after more time has elapsed and a higher share of displaced workers have found new jobs, generalising the finding that large wage losses are experienced by a sizeable minority of displaced workers, while also showing that these losses are quite persistent. A number of these studies have also shown a concentration of large and persistent earnings losses among older, long-tenure workers, particularly when they are also blue-collar workers lacking a tertiary education. The pre-displacement wages of many workers with this profile tend to reflect, in considerable part, returns to specific human capital that are often lost when these workers are displaced.[20] The polarisation of the labour market in recent years has probably worsened re-employment prospects for experienced workers losing medium-skill production jobs, since relatively few new job openings match well with even the more portable skills possessed by this group (OECD, 2017[10]).

Policy implications

These empirical findings help to define the challenge facing labour market programmes intended to reduce the adverse consequences of job displacement for workers. In particular, they confirm that:

Figure 4.5. The impact of job displacement on earnings is highly variable

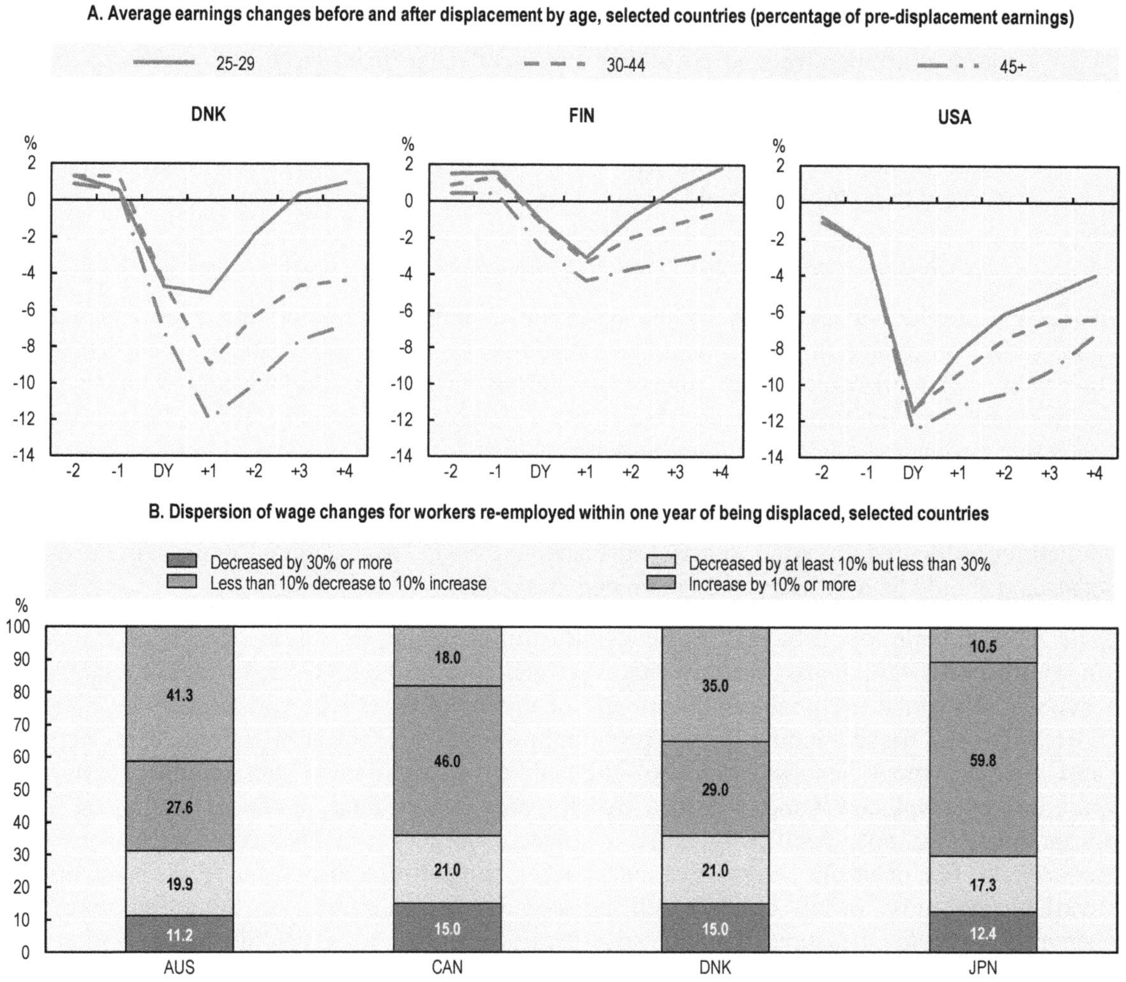
A. Average earnings changes before and after displacement by age, selected countries (percentage of pre-displacement earnings)
25-29
30-44
45+
DNK
FIN
USA
%
2
0
-2
-4
-6
-8
-10
-12
-14
-2
-1
DY
+1
+2
+3
+4
B. Dispersion of wage changes for workers re-employed within one year of being displaced, selected countries
Decreased by 30% or more
Less than 10% decrease to 10% increase
Decreased by at least 10% but less than 30%
Increase by 10% or more
%
100
90
80
70
60
50
40
30
20
10
0
41.3
27.6
19.9
11.2
18.0
46.0
21.0
15.0
35.0
29.0
21.0
15.0
10.5
59.8
17.3
12.4
AUS
CAN
DNK
JPN

Note: The estimation sample includes displacements that occur between 2000 and 2005. Pre-displacement earnings are the average earnings in the third year prior to displacement. DY = displacement year. See Annex 4.A1 in OECD (2013[2]) for a full description of the samples, years and definitions used for each country. Data refer to annual earnings for Denmark, Finland and the United States. For Japan, data refer to the period 2004-12 and workers of 20-64 years of age who were re-employed within one year from displacement in firms with five or more employees.

Source: Compiled by the OECD Secretariat using data sources described in Annex 4.A1 in OECD (2013[2]), *OECD Employment Outlook 2013*, http://dx.doi.org/10.1787/empl_outlook-2013-en for Panel A; and also Japan Ministry of Health Labour and Welfare, calculations using microdata from the Survey on Employment Trends for Panel B.

StatLink http://dx.doi.org/10.1787/888933778269

- Displacement is an important source of unemployment, earnings insecurity and other types of hardship for workers. Cost-effective measures to reduce the adjustment costs borne by displaced workers could thus serve important policy goals.
- The large cross-country differences in the speed of re-employment following displacement and the size of the earnings losses once re-employed suggest that well designed labour market policies and institutions may be able to significantly lower the costs of displacement without undercutting labour market dynamism.

- Providing effective adjustment assistance to displaced workers is complicated by the fact that this is a very heterogeneous group in terms of their personal characteristics and employment histories. Most importantly, the nature and size of the displacement-related costs that they bear range from large and persistent for the hardest-hit individuals to virtually non-existent for workers who move quickly to a new job that is as good as or even better than the lost job. This heterogeneity suggests that how much and which types of assistance displaced workers require is likely to be highly variable.

4.1.2. Overview of measures for reducing the costs borne by displaced workers

Table 4.1 provides a taxonomy of the wide range of public and private measures that potentially can reduce the adjustment costs resulting from job displacement. In particular, the table differentiates between direct and indirect measures (the table columns), and general and targeted measures (the table rows). This taxonomy is intended to illustrate the need to coordinate the labour market measures, which are analysed in detail in this chapter, with other policies that affect the incidence and consequences of displacement. It also highlights several important policy design issues and provides a reminder that many of the policy levers that can be used to lower displacement costs have potentially high efficiency costs and should be used with care or avoided altogether.

The first column of Table 4.1 provides illustrative examples of the types of *direct* measures to assist displaced workers that were the focus of the nine *Back to Work* country reviews and which are analysed in the rest of this chapter. Direct measures include the core active and passive labour market programmes, such as job-search assistance, training and unemployment benefits. Much of the public re-employment and income support received by displaced workers is provided by *general* measures in the sense that these programmes do not specifically target displaced workers and also serve many other jobseekers. For example, unemployment benefits and job-search assistance are typically available to most or all unemployed persons (and, sometimes, to some employed persons). *Targeted* measures that are specifically designed to assist displaced workers also play a role in all nine of the countries that have been reviewed, although their importance and design show considerable variation from country to country. While targeted measures have the potential to be tailored to the particular difficulties encountered by displaced workers, they can also create wasteful duplication of programmes and inequities in the access to adjustment assistance across jobseekers who face similar difficulties.

The last two items in the first column of Table 4.1 illustrate the important role that private actors, particularly employers, can play in limiting the adjustment costs borne by displaced workers. For example, employers providing workers advance notification of layoffs improve the chances of these workers to make a smooth transition to another job, by allowing them to get an early start at searching (or retraining) for a new job. Another example of employers contributing to a successful adjustment is when they offer outplacement services to workers they displace, possibly in collaboration with trade unions. The nine country case studies that this chapter draws upon provide a strong confirmation of the importance of constructive employer and union engagement in assisting displaced workers, especially when these private initiatives are effectively coordinated with public assistance for this group.[21] However, they also highlight how difficult it can be for governments to foster effective employer engagement when it is not spontaneously offered. Difficult co-ordination issues can also arise between public and private measures to assist displaced workers. As will be discussed in Sections 4.3 and 4.4, one important co-ordination issue is how, if at all, the receipt of severance payments should affect the access of displaced workers to public unemployment benefits and active labour market programmes (ALMPs).

Table 4.1. A taxonomy of public and private measures to reduce the labour market adjustment costs borne by displaced workers

Types of measures	Direct	Indirect
General	Unemployment insurance (UI) and other income-replacement benefits available to all unemployed workers under common rules.	Macroeconomic and structural policies conducive to strong growth and high employment.
	Active labour market programmes (ALMPs) available to all unemployed workers under common rules.	Framework conditions for efficient reallocation of labour in response to structural change (e.g. adjustment-friendly EPL and housing policies conducive to geographic mobility).
	Public insurance schemes against unpaid compensation when employers declare bankruptcy without making provision to fully compensate workers.	Education and training policies that anticipate and meet emerging skill demands.
Targeted	Special adjustment assistance or income-replacement benefits available to all displaced workers or to sub-groups of displaced workers (e.g. job losers in specific sectors or workers who lost their job due to a particular natural disaster).	Industry redevelopment or rationalisation programmes.
	EPL rules regulating economic layoffs, such as requirements for advance notification and severance payments, or rules about which workers are selected to be dismissed during a partial layoff.	Local economic development policies (e.g. geographically targeted tax or hiring subsidies, or public-private partnerships to develop new sources of comparative advantage).
	Private outplacement services that employers and/or trade unions offer to certain displaced workers.	Trade policy measures to restrict imports such as tariffs and industry-specific trade safeguards or anti-dumping measures under WTO rules.

Note: EPL: Employment protection legislation. WTO: World Trade Organization. Several of the policy options included in the table are not recommended by the OECD because they are likely to do more harm than good (e.g. overly strict EPL and trade protectionism). They are included because governments have sometimes made use of these measures to protect workers at risk of displacement.

Many public policies have important, albeit indirect, impacts on how well displaced workers fare. The second column of Table 4.1 provides a few examples of the large number of *indirect* measures that potentially could reduce the adjustment costs borne by displaced workers. These include: i) macroeconomic and structural policies that are conducive to high employment and labour mobility; ii) educational and vocational training policies that improve the overall employability of mid-career workers, including their capacity to retrain should they experience displacement; iii) local economic development policies that stimulate job creation in areas affected by mass layoffs and iv) housing policies that are conducive to geographic mobility. While this chapter does not analyse these framework conditions in any detail, it should be borne in mind that the direct measures to assist displaced workers, which are analysed here, are only one component of the broader policy strategy that is required to manage economic restructuring and its potentially disruptive impact on workers.[22] Consideration of the types of indirect measures that are sometimes advocated to reduce the costs borne by displaced workers also highlights the risk that policy responses that undermine economic dynamism, such as trade protectionism, may be adopted if economically efficient measures to assist displaced workers are not put in place.[23]

Rigorous evaluation evidence on what works for displaced workers is surprisingly sparse

Much is now known about the effectiveness of different types of active labour market programmes (ALMPs), thanks to the growing number of rigorous evaluation studies that have been conducted, particularly in Western Europe and North America (Card, Kluve and Weber, 2015[11]; Kluve, 2010[12]). One common finding from these studies is that the effectiveness of any given type of re-employment support is greater for some groups of jobseekers than for others, underlining the importance of tailoring the services offered to each jobseeker to their particular needs. Unfortunately, relatively few evaluation studies have examined the effectiveness of ALMPs specifically for displaced workers, leaving considerable uncertainty about how informative existing evaluation results are for assessing what works for the group that is the focus of this chapter, namely, formerly stable workers who experience an economic dismissal.[24] There is also the added complication that displaced workers are a very heterogeneous group. For example, the types of measures that are cost-effective for a younger displaced worker with good opportunities for labour market mobility are very likely to differ from the types of assistance that would be most cost-effective for an older long-tenure displaced worker whose largely manual skills do not match up well with the current structure of labour demand.

There are a modest number evaluation studies that have estimated programme impacts for displaced workers and which provide useful information about what works for this group. However, they are as yet too few to judge whether their findings generalise beyond the specific programmes and countries that have been studied. Notable examples include:

- The largest number of evaluation studies singling out displaced workers have been conducted in the United States, where the Federal government has targeted funding to programmes that serve this group: both the "dislocated worker" track of the main ALMP funding stream provided by the US Department of Labor and the Trade Adjustment Assistance (TAA) programme for trade-displaced workers. Overall, the evaluation results for measures to assist displaced workers have been very poor and cannot be said to provide consistent evidence that any of the main types of interventions studied have been cost effective.[25] However, there are several reasons to think that these disappointing results may provide an excessively pessimistic picture of the potential effectiveness of ALMPs for displaced workers. First, many of the workers receiving job search, retraining and other assistance in these evaluation studies had already been unemployed for an extended period of time before receiving the assistance that was evaluated, whereas re-employment assistance is likely to be more effective if initiated early in the unemployment spell or even during the notice period. A second reason is that the fragmented nature of the US system of labour market programmes and vocational training means that many members in the control group of "unserved" displaced workers actually received a similar service from another source, causing the estimated impact to understate the difference between receiving the service being evaluated (e.g. retraining) and not receiving it from any source. It is also possible that the relatively limited re-employment impacts of the active measures evaluated reflects, in part, how these services generally were not integrated into a broader activation strategy.[26]

- OECD (2015[13]) highlights key results from several recent evaluations of various types of ALMP measures that were offered to displaced workers in Canada. Quite consistent evidence is found that job-search assistance, targeted wage subsidies and training all increased post-displacement participation, employment and earnings, with the benefits from job search assistance and targeted wage subsidies being larger than those from training. A particularly encouraging result is that older displaced workers benefited even more from most of these measures than their younger counterparts. Another important finding is that post-programme gains in both employment and earnings were larger when the services were offered more quickly following displacement.

- Several evaluation studies in Europe also suggest that ALMPs can reduce the costs borne by displaced workers. In France, displaced workers signing a contract of professional security (*contrat de sécurisation professionnelle*, frequently abbreviated as CSP) are able to access more personalised and intensive re-employment and retraining assistance from the public employment service than is generally available to unemployment insurance benefit recipients. Evaluations have confirmed that displaced workers who sign a CSP receive more intensive assistance than other jobseekers and that this group finds a new job more quickly – and has a higher probability of finding a relatively stable job – than other jobseekers with a similar profile who receive the regular PES services, DARES (2017[14]). A random assignment evaluation of the rapid provision of intensive counselling and job-search assistance for older jobseekers in Switzerland showed that these measures significantly increase re-employment for participants between the ages of 45 and 54 years, but had no effect for participants age 55 or older (Arni, 2012[15]). Intensive job-search counselling appeared to promote re-employment, in part, by convincing displaced workers to adopt more effective job-search strategies, including more realistic wage targets for the new job.

Two additional limitations of the ALMP evaluation literature for the purposes of this chapter, are especially notable. First, few or no studies could be located that evaluate the effectiveness of several types of re-employment assistance that the *Back to Work* country reviews identified as appearing to be particularly effective. In particular, rigorous evaluations of early intervention measures, which are the subject of Section 4.2, appear to be almost completely lacking. Indeed, it is difficult to construct a control group or another type of counterfactual for workers who benefit from these measures, since they typically provide re-employment services and counselling to all of the workers affected by a mass layoff, beginning during the notice period.[27] A second limitation is that there appears to be no evidence about the effectiveness, in terms of speeding up the re-employment of displaced workers, of the behavioural requirements that many OECD countries include among the eligibility rules for unemployment benefits.[28] It appears plausible that the subset of displaced workers with the best re-employment opportunities might be particularly likely to hasten their job search in order to avoid participating in activities that they would be unlikely to value very highly or finding themselves subject to benefit sanctions. However, there does not appear to be any evidence about whether this group really is particularly responsive to the so-called "threat effect" (Filges and Hansen, 2017[16]).

While it is to be hoped that additional rigorous evaluation evidence on the effectiveness of different types of labour market measures for displaced workers will be forthcoming, the more descriptive and qualitative evidence collected in the nine *Back to Work* country reviews already provides much useful guidance concerning potentially effective policy actions to lower displacement costs. The general lessons that emerge are summarised in

Sections 4.2 to 4.4. It should be borne in mind, however, that many of the policy approaches that are identified as promising have not been rigorously evaluated.

4.2. Prevention and early intervention measures

One important difference between displaced workers and most other recipients of public employment services and unemployment benefits is that there is greater scope for *proactive* measures in the case of displaced workers. This is particularly true when employers provide workers and public labour market authorities with a significant amount of advance notice of layoffs, opening up the possibility of taking actions to save jobs that are still economically viable or to help workers to begin the adjustment process before they become unemployed. The columns of Table 4.2 identify the main types of proactive public policies and private initiatives that potentially can lower the costs borne by displaced workers, while the rows indicate whether the potential benefits take the form of avoiding socially-inefficient layoffs or of speeding job search and re-employment for workers whose jobs are no longer economically viable and thus should not be saved.

Table 4.2. Prevention and early intervention measures for displaced workers: Policy goals and types of policy measures

Policy goals	Types of measures				
	Employment protection rules applying to permanent workers and mass layoffs	Experience rated financing of UI benefits	Short-time work schemes	Private outplacement services (prior to layoff)	PES early interventions services (especially rapid response services for mass layoffs)
Prevention: Preserving viable jobs	X	X	X		
Early intervention: Minimising post-displacement adjustment costs by getting an early start on finding a new job	X			X	X

Note: X denotes a major policy goal of the indicated policy measure. PES: Public employment service. UI: Unemployment insurance. Employment protection legislation (EPL) is intended to promote both prevention and early intervention. The EPL components that are most relevant for prevention include those that effectively tax employers for displacing workers and certain procedural requirements (e.g. to consult with workers, unions or public authorities about alternatives to layoffs). EPL requirements for employers to provide advanced notification of layoffs and outplacement assistance to the affected workers are particularly relevant for expanding early intervention measures. While EPL can potentially promote prevention and early intervention, it can also create high efficiency costs.

The main policy measures intended to preserve jobs that pass a social benefit-cost comparison are those that either: i) effectively tax layoffs (e.g. EPL rules that impose costs on employers who dismiss permanent workers and the experience rating of employers' contributions to the UI benefit system); or ii) subsidise firms to preserve jobs, which are viable in the long run, during a short period when the employer has less or no need for those workers (e.g. short-time work schemes). As regards early intervention measures that assist displaced workers to get an early start at finding a new job, the types of assistance that are offered are broadly similar to the ALMPs that public employment offices provide to unemployed jobseekers. However, there is some customisation of the content and organisation of the re-employment and retraining services that are delivered to workers who are still employed but on notice that they soon will be dismissed. Another difference is that employer-provided assistance plays a larger role at this early stage of the post-displacement adjustment process, albeit more so in some countries than in others.

The rest of this section discusses job preservation and early intervention measures in more detail, focussing on the practical issues that arise in making effective use of these tools. Good practice examples are provided in both domains, along with several pitfalls to avoid. In particular, the important limits to the use of both preventive and early intervention measures is emphasised: Overuse of prevention measures impedes efficiency-enhancing labour reallocation while trying to provide too much re-employment assistance prior to displacement can disrupt production, potentially discouraging employer collaboration in early intervention measures, or wasting resources by providing costly re-employment services to workers who are able to find a suitable new job on their own (or largely on their own).

4.2.1. Preventing inefficient layoffs without hampering the creative destruction process

Standard economic theory suggests that displacement rates would be likely to exceed the social optimum in the absence of policies that cause employers to take account of the social externalities associated with layoffs, such as the need to finance the unemployment benefits that will be paid to workers who are displaced (Blanchard and Tirole, 2008[17]). Employment protection legislation (EPL) is the policy instrument that is most commonly used to limit overuse of economic dismissals. Mandatory severance payments and certain procedural requirements (e.g. an obligation to provide re-employment assistance to workers who are dismissed or to reinstate workers who successfully challenge their layoff in a labour court) are particularly likely to increase employer-borne costs associated with job displacement and thus to discourage layoffs when the associated economic gains for the firm would be quite small in the absence of EPL. However, experience has shown that EPL needs to be used cautiously because it has often hindered efficiency-enhancing labour mobility (OECD, 2013[2]). A particular risk is that EPL worsens the re-employment prospects of displaced workers and voluntary job changers, because it causes employers to be more cautious about hiring. A light touch is thus necessary with employment protection measures, placing the emphasis on provisions, such as mandatory advance notification, that facilitate prompt access to re-employment assistance for displaced workers (see the discussion of early interventions measures below), rather than measures that only make it cumbersome or expensive for employers to reduce staffing levels through dismissals.

Unemployment insurance (UI) schemes can be structured so as to discourage excessive layoffs, either through the experience rating of employers' UI contributions or through a short-time work (STW) scheme. Economists have often advocated experience rating as providing a more efficient instrument for forcing employers to internalise the social costs of job displacement than EPL, because it operates as a straightforward tax on layoffs that is tied to an important component of the social costs associated with displacement – see e.g. Albrecht and Vroman (1999[18]); Cahuc and Malherbet (2004[19]). Experience rating has not been widely adopted in practice, but may have considerable potential to discourage excessive layoffs without impeding desirable labour mobility, either on its own or in combination with a STW scheme (Cahuc and Nevoux, 2017[20]).[29] While the evaluation evidence for experience rating is largely limited to the United States and provides mixed results, recent experience suggests that well-designed STW schemes are able to preserve significant numbers of viable jobs during recessions without creating large efficiency costs. This potential is illustrated by the effectiveness of the *Kurzarbeit* programme in Germany during the 2008-09 global crisis (Boeri and Bruecker, 2011[21]). Among the nine countries participating in the *Back to Work* reviews, the experience of

Japan following the global financial and economic crisis provides a good example of how STW can help to preserve jobs during a deep but relatively short recession. In both Japan and Germany, enrolment in the STW scheme expanded rapidly in 2009, when business conditions worsened (and many employers may have faced financial constraints making it difficult to preserve viable jobs), but quickly returned to very low levels as the economy began to recover. By contrast, enrolment in the Finnish STW programme has remained quite high in recent years, even during economic expansions, probably because employers do not bear any of the cost of providing STW benefits.[30] This appears to be a deliberate policy choice in Finland, where STW serves, in part, as an implicit subsidy for sectors where employment is highly seasonal. However, there is a risk that STW may be overused by Finnish employers, with the result that it ends up subsidising jobs that are no longer viable and which end, in any case, once the subsidy payments expire.

In sum, there is some potential scope for prevention measures to reduce displacement costs. However, it is limited and governments need to guard against the danger that excessive recourse to prevention measures creates high efficiency costs by impeding the reallocation of workers toward more productive employments. As regards reducing the costs borne by displaced workers, the main policy focus needs to be on measures to improve the re-employment outcomes of workers whose jobs are no longer economically viable, while also compensating them for some part of the earnings losses that cannot be avoided. Since most of the emphasis should be placed on the promotion of successful job mobility after displacement, it is important to ensure that re-employment measures are as effective as possible, including by initiating them as early as possible.

4.2.2. Early intervention measures

Early-career job transitions are usually a source of career advancement (see Chapter 6). By contrast, mid-career job mobility can be a difficult and time-consuming process, especially when the job transition is involuntary and it affects long-tenure workers who have not searched for a job on the external labour market in many years and have a strong emotional attachment to the type of work they are familiar with. Getting an early start on making this transition can be advantageous for a number of reasons. Even if the total time to become re-employed remains unchanged, beginning during the notice period reduces the amount of time spent out of work and, hence, the earnings losses associated with displacement.[31] However, it may also be possible to speed up the adjustment process and achieve better outcomes by starting the process before workers become unemployed. For example, prospective employers may tend to view job applicants who are still employed more favourably than those who are unemployed and it is well known that the longer a worker is unemployed the more their labour market prospects tend to deteriorate.

Other advantages to early interventions can be cited, particularly in the case of mass layoffs. For example, group counselling and job-search orientation activities can be more easily organised during the notice period, particularly if the employer allows these services to be delivered at the work site.[32] Group activities have two advantages in this context. First, they make it easier to meet the sudden increase in the local demand for re-employment services that can easily overwhelm the service capacity of the local PES, especially when all services are delivered on an individual basis. Group activities can also be more effective in some cases. Since many of the workers affected by a mass layoff are confronting the same issues, group activities can be useful psychologically, for example in helping to overcome the reluctance of many experienced workers in a declining sector or occupation to consider possible career shifts, while also offering good opportunities to bring workers, who are about to be displaced, together with potential employers ("job fairs").

Apart from the greater emphasis on group activities, the substantive content of the early intervention measures that are provided by the PES appear to be quite similar to the re-employment services that are offered to newly registered unemployment benefit recipients. There is typically a focus on orientation activities, such as informing workers of the types of assistance that are available to them and how to access them. Another common focus is to assist workers to develop realistic strategies to find a new job, taking into account their skills and interests, labour market conditions, and the fact that many of them lack recent experience in searching for a job. While intensive measures, such as training, typically do not start during the notice period, considerable attention is often devoted to documenting workers' skills and assessing how they align with employment opportunities in the local and national economy, including whether they should consider retraining.[33]

While there is little hard evidence quantifying the advantages of early intervention measures, the country visits undertaken in connection with the nine *Back to Work* reviews made it clear that practitioners believe that the benefits are considerable and they invest a lot of energy and resources in providing what are sometimes referred to as "rapid response services".[34] However, there is also a lot of variation across OECD countries in the way that early interventions are organised and the barriers they encounter in providing timely services to all of the displaced workers who would benefit from them. While the approach adopted needs to vary depending on national circumstances, such as how actively social partners participate in assisting displaced workers, it is nonetheless instructive to consider the main organisational issues that arise and the strengths and weaknesses of the different approaches that have been used to address them.

How large a role for employers and unions?

The extent to which employers and unions are actively involved in planning and providing re-employment services to displaced workers is highly variable (see also Chapter 3) and can have an important effect on the feasibility and effectiveness of early interventions, as well as on the most effective way to organise public early intervention measures. This diversity is best illustrated by considering a few examples:

- *The Rapid Re-employment and Training Service (RRTS) in Ontario* provides re-employment services for workers affected by larger scale layoffs, beginning during the notice period (see Box 4.1 for a more detailed description). It provides a good example of the public provision of early intervention measures where Employment Ontario (the provincial PES) plays a leading role, but other government agencies are also mobilised, notably Ontario's Ministry of Training, Colleges and Universities. The RRTS illustrates the importance of adapting the level and type of service offered to the severity of the layoff and the capacity of the local employment service providers.[35] For example, a temporary office (an *Action Centre*) is set up at or near the work site, when a large layoff threatens to overwhelm local re-employment services.

Box 4.1. The Rapid Re employment and Training Service in Ontario, Canada

The *Rapid Re-employment and Training Service* (RRTS) in Ontario provides an immediate response to large-scale layoffs with the objective of connecting individuals with *Employment Ontario* (PES) services to help them regain employment. The level and type of support offered is tailored to the severity of the layoff and the capacity of the local employment service providers, which are typically third-party providers, such as non-profit firms, that the PES has engaged to provide employment services in a particular locality. The type of RRTS services offered may vary from:

Tier 1: If local re-employment services have sufficient capacity to assist the affected workers, then the RRTS is limited to delivering information sessions and raising awareness of the employment services available to workers who will lose their jobs. These sessions may take place at the local *Service Canada* office (the agency where workers access Employment Insurance benefits) or by arranging for *Employment Ontario* service providers to go on site or extend their hours of operation so that affected workers can access their services before layoffs occur. Anecdotal evidence suggests that around 90% of the layoffs are dealt with using Tier 1 service, but these tend to be the layoffs affecting relatively few workers.

Tier 2: In a situation where nearby *Employment Ontario* service providers do not have sufficient capacity to meet demand. Supplementary funding is provided for outreach to affected workers, sometimes including the establishment of an *Action Centre* to deal with large scale closures. Through these *Action Centres*, displaced workers can access: i) job-search assistance; ii) financial counselling and personal counselling to deal with the stress of job loss; iii) individual and group needs assessment; iv) vocational and educational counselling; and v) referral to programmes of *Employment Ontario* including the *Second Career* programme for older displaced workers. Every laid-off worker develops an action plan within 15 days of his or her initial assessment and can access customised training, skills upgrading, job placement and relocation services. In general, *Action Centres* should not operate for more than a year.

Tier 3: When displacement occurs on a sufficient scale to have an adverse impact on the local economy or the community, a larger and a broader inter-ministerial approach is taken. A local adjustment committee is established, which is led by an independent chair and is responsible for co-ordinating the implementation of the *Service Action Plan*. This plan is put in place within 30 days of the initial response and outlines the roles of each of the service providers in the community who will be delivering services to displaced workers. A key component of the process is the development of a multi-disciplinary *Rapid Response Team*, which is formed at the local or regional level to provide timely, focused and integrated training and employment solutions to affected workers and communities.

Source: OECD (2015[13]), *Back to Work: Canada – Improving the Re-employment Prospects of Displaced Workers*, http://dx.doi.org/10.1787/9789264233454-en.

- *Job Security Councils (JSCs) in Sweden* provide an example of re-employment services for displaced workers, including early interventions, which are provided by the social partners (i.e. employer federations in close collaboration with union federations), rather than by the PES or other public actors (see Box 4.2 for a more detailed description). The JSCs make productive use of the comparatively long notice period in Sweden to speed the return to work following displacement and are probably a key explanation why nearly 90% of workers are re-employed within a year of being laid-off. This model is particularly successful at extending early intervention measures to individual and small-scale layoffs. One weakness of the JSC system is that there is considerable variation in the level of support the councils provide to different displaced workers.

- *Hybrid models that feature a more even mix of public and private actions* to promote successful adjustment can also be found in OECD countries. For example, the *Change Security* programme in Finland represents a close partnership between the PES, employers and unions in managing displacements (OECD, 2016[22]). Even in countries where the involvement of employers in the provision of re-employment assistance to displaced workers is not strong in general, some employers voluntarily provide outplacement services to workers that they are displacing and these services can represent an important supplement to the services provided by the PES. For example, (OECD, 2015[23]) discusses how large Japanese employers who displace regular workers typically engage private placement firms to assist the affected workers in their search for a new job. While there is no legal obligation for employers to provide outplacement services in Japan, doing so appears to be closely related to the human resources strategies associated with the "lifetime employment" system, which is characterised by a strong employer commitment to providing a high level of employment security to regular workers.[36]

Can governments foster greater employer engagement?

Since constructive employer engagement is of great value in providing prompt and effective re-employment assistance to displaced workers, it is important to assess what governments can do to promote such engagement where it is not already well rooted in national industrial relations institutions and practices.[37] OECD governments make use of two main policy strategies to foster greater employer engagement than is spontaneously offered: i) legal compulsion via EPL; and ii) a softer touch approach relying on incentives and moral suasion. These two approaches can also be used in combination. For example, a requirement in Quebec province in Canada that employers organise outplacement services for displaced workers in the form of an outplacement assistance committee (*Comité d'aide au reclassement*, or CAR) is combined with a 50 % subsidy of the cost of those services (OECD, 2015[13]).

There is a role for EPL rules to require some minimal level of constructive employer engagement in improving the re-employment prospects of workers they displace. In particular, there appears to be a clear case to require at least a minimum level of advance notification to workers, unions and public labour market authorities, since it is a *sine qua non* for early intervention. Figure 4.6 shows that advance notice requirements differ strikingly across OECD countries, ranging from no general requirement in the United States[38] to quite long notice periods in some European countries. Consistent with the findings that displacement costs rise strongly with job tenure, many countries require longer notice periods for workers with greater tenure. In some countries, notice periods also vary between occupational groups, but it is questionable whether there is a good economic rationale for those differences.[39]

Box 4.2. Job Security Councils in Sweden

Job Security Councils (JSCs) were first developed in the 1970s against the backdrop of the deteriorating economic conditions in Sweden in the late 1960s and the massive job losses among white-collar workers in the wake of the oil crisis in 1973. In this context, the public employment service was not regarded by employers as providing sufficient support for white-collar workers to find new jobs (Diedrich and Bergström, 2006[24]).

The councils are based on collective agreements between the social partners in a sector or occupational field, such as white-collar workers in the private sector. JSCs are actively involved in all stages of the process of restructuring, including by providing advice to employers and trade unions at an early stage in the process. They also provide transition services and guidance to workers who are made redundant, through individual counselling, career planning, job-search assistance, outplacement services and retraining. The councils' activities are financed by employer contributions which are fixed as a percentage of their total payroll. The contribution level is determined as part of the collective agreement (currently 0.3% of payroll). As such, the council operates as a form of insurance, spreading the costs of restructuring across all employers who are covered by the collective agreement. A particular strength of the JSCs is that prompt re-employment support is offered to all displaced workers covered by the agreement, including workers in small and medium-sized enterprises (European Commission, 2010[25]).

JSCs appear to make a significant contribution to the unusually rapid re-employment rate of displaced workers in Sweden (cf. Figure 4.3). Indeed, the councils report that around 90% of their participants find a solution within nine months: 78% finding new employment, 8% starting a new business and 6% enrolling in longer duration education or training. This success reflects a strongly proactive orientation, a comparatively long notice period, and JSC staff's intimate knowledge of the workers they serve and their occupational labour markets. However, despite the overall very positive experience with JSCs in Sweden, heavy reliance on the councils to provide re-employment services also raises several concerns. One concern is that the private-sector, white-collar JSC offers considerably more intensive re-employment and, especially, retraining services then the main blue-collar JSC, probably because the former has considerably greater resources per displaced workers. These differences in the level of support offered are reflected in re-employment outcomes: whereas 65% of the white collar workers serviced by their JSC find a new permanent job within six months, this is the case for only 38% of their blue-collar counterparts. Another source of unequal access to re-employment support is that approximately 20% of the workforce is not covered by a JSC. Finally, coordination between the JSCs and the PES is quite limited, making it difficult for the PES to complement the services offered by the JSC in a timely manner.

Source: OECD (2015[26]), *Back to Work: Sweden: Improving the Re-employment Prospects of Displaced Workers*, http://dx.doi.org/10.1787/9789264246812-en; Diedrich, and Bergström (2006[24]), "The job security councils in Sweden", http://imit.se/wp-content/uploads/2016/02/2007_145.pdf; and European Commission (2010[25]), "27 National seminars on anticipating and managing restructuring", http://www.employment-studies.co.uk/resource/27-national-seminars-anticipating-and-managing-restructuring-arenas.

Figure 4.6. Legally mandated notice periods vary widely

Average minimum advance notice periods for individual dismissals in OECD countries
by years of job tenure, 2013

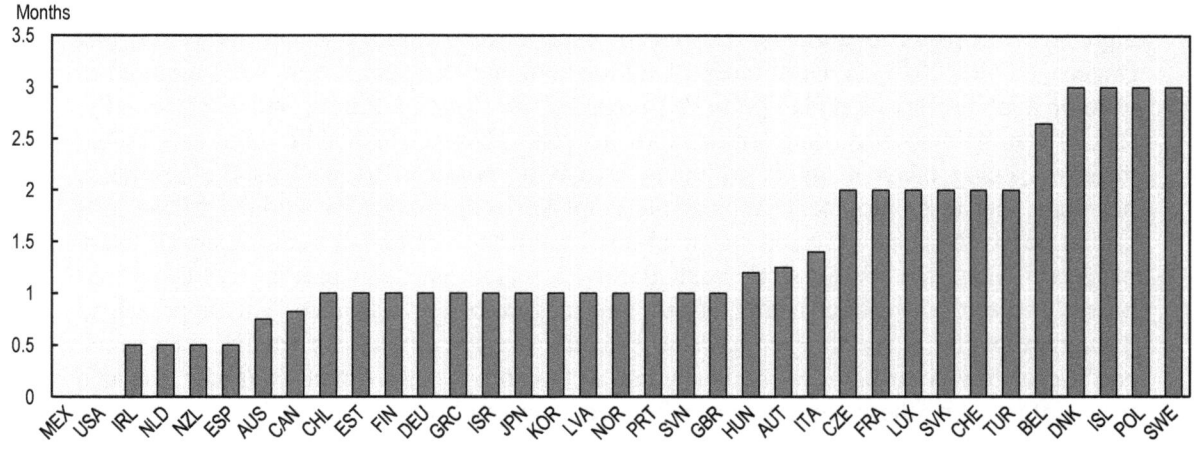

A. Workers with 4 years of tenure

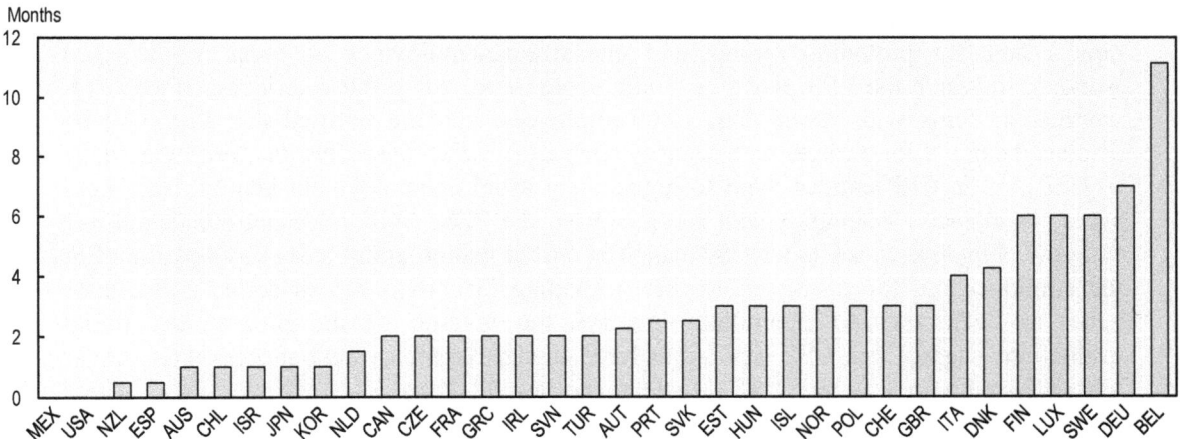

B. Workers with 20 years of tenure

Source: OECD Employment Protection Database, 2013 update, http://dx.doi.org/10.1787/lfs-epl-data-en.

StatLink ᵐˢ🔗 http://dx.doi.org/10.1787/888933778288

Unfortunately, there is little evidence that can be drawn upon to identify the optimal level of notice. In particular, it is not clear when increases in the length of the notice period begin to translate into additional benefits for displaced workers, in terms of easier transitions to new jobs, that are too small to justify the additional costs that result for employers (e.g. in terms of disruptions to production due to low worker morale or increased wariness of credit markets, suppliers and customers to engage with a firm seen to be struggling). Nonetheless, countries with relatively low notice requirements should consider raising them closer to OECD averages, perhaps in combination with relaxing other EPL requirements, such as the level of mandatory severance payments. Another open question is whether advance notification requirements should be combined with an obligation for employers to offer workers a minimum number of days of paid job search leave during the notice period. For example, workers on notice of displacement are entitled to between 5 and 20 days of paid job search leave in Finland, depending on the length of their notice period (OECD, 2016[22]). However, little is known about how much these entitlements contribute to good re-employment outcomes nor about the resulting cost for employers.

EPL requirements that employers provide re-employment services to workers they displace may also be useful in some cases, although experience suggests caution because these types of obligations can impede efficiency-enhancing labour mobility by imposing excessively high layoff costs on employers. The recent experience of France is informative in this respect (OECD, 2015[13]). Until recently, all medium and large employers were required to develop a job preservation plan (*plan de sauvegarde de l'emploi*, PSE or, more colloquially, "social plan") when displacing ten or more workers. These plans need to both specify the measures being taken to avoid as many layoffs as possible, as well as the severance payments and re-employment services the employer will provide to workers whose jobs cannot be saved (often delivered via an ad-hoc local team – *cellule de reclassement*). These plans are submitted to the work council for its review and can also be reviewed and possibly rejected by labour courts, if they are judged to be inadequate. This approach to managing layoffs is widely seen as expensive and overly complex for smaller employers, and it probably contributes to the heavy use of temporary employment contracts (i.e. as a means of avoiding these requirements when reducing employment levels). The process was also often conflictual, delaying the access of displaced workers to re-employment services. Smaller and medium-sized firms were also seen to lack the necessary expertise to organise effective re-employment services. A series of reforms in recent years has shifted towards a new system for providing prompt and intensive re-employment services to displaced workers, in which the PES plays the leading role in providing those services. Since 2011, workers in firms with fewer than 1 000 employees who are notified that they will be displaced can opt for a career path security contract (*contrat de sécurisation professionnelle* or CSP).[40] The CSP entitles them to higher than usual unemployment benefits and rapid access to intensive re-employment services from the PES, while releasing their employer from the obligation to set up a social plan. The cost of this programme is shared by the PES, the employer and the dismissed worker, providing incentives for all actors to facilitate better co-operation and potentially improve the take-up of the programme. Initial evaluations suggest that CSP signatories have greater re-employment success than similar jobseekers who do not sign a CSP (DARES analyses, 2017[14]).

In countries where there are important gaps in constructive employer engagement, it is sometimes possible to encourage broader voluntary engagement through either subsidies or outreach policies. For example, the *Labour Mobility Subsidy* in Japan reimburses part of the costs incurred by employers who contract with a private placement firm to provide re-employment support for workers they are displacing, provided those workers are placed into new jobs sufficiently rapidly (OECD, 2015[23]).[41] The PES in the US states of Michigan and Pennsylvania provide examples of outreach policies. These states operate "early warning" systems to try to identify upcoming plant closings and other mass layoffs, for example by reading the business press and talking with various economic actors (OECD, 2016[27]). If they believe that a firm may be preparing a mass dismissal, they contact it to verify whether that is the case. If a pending layoff is confirmed, then the employer is encouraged to make use of the government's ability to provide re-employment services for its workers, for example by setting up a rapid response plan for them. While these efforts are worthwhile, their effectiveness is undercut when advance notice is often not provided or many employers prefer not to co-operate with the PES. In the worst cases, "run-away firms" close or move out of the country without providing any notice or making any other provision for their workers.

Unequal access to early intervention measures

Another challenge affecting the provision of early intervention measures is that only a relatively small subset of displaced workers have access to these services in most countries: primarily workers who are laid-off as a part of a mass layoff at a large firm, which triggers public rapid response services, or whose employer makes an effort to ensure that good re-employment services are available. One advantage of the Job Security Councils in Sweden is their universal coverage of displaced workers in the sectors where they operate.[42] Quebec province in Canada makes use of an interesting strategy to extend rapid response services to workers affected by small or individual layoffs. Displaced workers whose employer is laying off fewer than 50 workers and hence is not obligated to set-up an outplacement programme of its own (i.e. a CAR), can enrol instead in a continuous enrolment outplacement plan run by the PES (*comités d'aide au reclassement à entrées continues*, CREC). Although the CREC have yet to be subjected to a rigorous evaluation of its effectiveness, it provides an interesting model for expanding access to early intervention services.

Displacement costs are probably above-average for workers who are displaced by mass layoffs that result in chronic excess labour supply in the local labour market.[43] That raises the possibility that the *de facto* concentration of early intervention measures on workers who lose their jobs during a mass layoff, as is the case in most of the countries reviewed, may tend to target additional re-employment assistance to a subgroup of displaced workers who face particularly large barriers to successful job search and thus be a reasonably good way to direct limited budgetary resources. While there is probably some truth to this conjecture, the size of a layoff is likely to be an imprecise indicator of the adjustment difficulties faced by individual displaced workers.[44] Even in instances when a mass layoff has a large ripple effect on the local economy that worsens re-employment opportunities for displaced workers, many of the affected workers are likely to have lost their jobs as a result of small layoffs (e.g. at subcontractor firms or other local businesses), rather than in the initial mass layoff. This suggests that governments should attempt to extend access to early intervention measures to workers affected by small or even individual displacements, whenever cost-effective ways can be found to do so. Resources permitting, it also seems best to provide early intervention services to all displaced workers, rather than only those facing above-average re-employment difficulties. Quite apart from how much re-employment assistance a particular displaced worker requires, it usually will be an advantage to them to be able to access that assistance as soon as they are notified their job is ending, rather than needing to wait until they have become unemployed.

Co-ordination challenges

Early intervention measures, particularly the establishment of rapid response services in anticipation of mass layoffs, raise several coordination challenges for the governments. One concern is illustrated by Australian employers who sometimes complained in the past about having been contacted by multiple government agencies in an uncoordinated manner when they were preparing a mass layoff, with the result that they answer the same questions multiple times and sometimes receive conflicting information about how they should coordinate their planning with the government and what services are available to the employer or the workers who will be displaced (OECD, 2016[28]).[45] When employers (or the social partners) provide substantial re-employment services to displaced workers, another coordination issue arises for the PES, namely, to make sure that public re-employment services complement the private services, avoiding both wasteful duplication and the risk that certain workers fall between the cracks.[46] As much as possible, government agencies should coordinate their interactions with employers and private providers of re-employment services. One way to do this is to establish a formal coordination process, as was done for a recent mass layoff at the Sharp Corporation in Nara Prefecture in Japan (see Box 4.3).

4.3. Re-employment assistance including retraining

After the notice period has ended and workers have been displaced, much of the policy focus should remain on active measures to promote rapid re-employment. This section analyses how best that can be done within a broader national activation strategy (i.e. a co-ordinated system of monitoring, sanctions and employment services that promotes transition to employment). The experience of many OECD countries confirms that enforcing the obligation of unemployment benefit recipients (and some recipients of other income replacement benefits) to search actively for a job or participate in activities that raise their employability, while also providing them with the re-employment supports that they need can significantly speed the transition into suitable jobs – see OECD (2013[2]; 2015[29]).[47] It stands to reason that displaced workers would be more likely to benefit from effective re-employment services in countries that operate a strong overall activation strategy. However, minimising the costs that workers bear following displacement also requires the general principles of activation policy to be applied to displaced workers in a way that addresses their specific needs for re-employment support. This section analyses how best that can be done, drawing upon recent policy experience in OECD countries, particularly the nine countries that participated in the *Back to Work* reviews.

4.3.1. *Overall spending on active labour market programmes*

While the primary focus of this section will be on ensuring that displaced workers receive the right types of re-employment support at the right time, it is useful to begin with a short review of overall spending on active labour market programmes (ALMPs) since this is likely to have an important effect on the services that displaced workers can access. Indeed, a number of cross-country regression studies have concluded that higher ALMP spending is associated with better aggregate labour market outcomes and Andrews and Saia (2017[8]) recently extended that line of research by showing that re-employment of displaced workers tends to be more rapid in countries with relatively high aggregate spending on ALMPs.

ALMP spending per unemployed persons as a percentage share of per capita GDP varies tremendously across OECD countries, including the nine countries participating in the *Back to* Work reviews. Panel A of Figure 4.7 shows that, in Denmark, spending on active measures for each unemployed person was as high as 64% of per capita GDP in 2015, by far the highest value observed in the OECD area. By contrast, in the United States, spending per unemployed was just 4% of per capita GDP, one of the lowest spending levels within the OECD.[48]

There are also striking cross-country differences in the way total spending is divided across the different types of programmes (Panel B of Figure 4.7). This heterogeneity also concerns the nine review countries.

Box 4.3. HQ Sharp in the Nara Prefecture

After a rapid deterioration of business conditions, Sharp announced an early retirement plan on 20 November 2012 that was intended to enrol 2 000 workers, but actually attracted 2 960 enrolees aged 40 and above. A considerable number of those workers lived in Nara Prefecture. In response to this announcement, the Nara Labour Bureau (the PES) and the Nara Prefectural Government jointly organised the *Support for Sharp Related Displaced Employees Headquarters* ("HQ Sharp") in November 2012.

While the headquarters model has been used for other mass displacements in Japan, the composition of participating organisations and their mode of operation vary from case to case. Indeed, HQ Sharp was one of the best instances of a prefectural labour bureau and a prefectural government jointly establishing and managing headquarters' downsizing. This organisation was selected because it reflected the already close working relationship between the *Labor Bureau* and labour market programmes run by the prefectural government, such as its *Job iCenter*. The additional partners in HQ Sharp included the Industrial Employment Stabilization Center (IESC) in Nara – a private agency that facilitates employee transfers between participating firms – and four municipal governments.

HQ Sharp was a co-ordinating committee consisting of managers from the participating organisations. Its mission was to build an integrated support system to offer effective re-employment and livelihood aid for displaced workers. It was also intended to provide support measures for related businesses (e.g. suppliers for Sharp). Much of the work of the headquarters consisted of an extensive consultations process that was used to achieve agreement on the strategy to adopt and eventually the setting up and implementation of actions plans. Another key focus was to set up a system for exchanging relevant information. Finally, a system to provide vocational counselling at the job centre was set up.

The ultimate aim of HQ Sharp was to facilitate smooth transitions into re-employment and to support the living standards of workers who lost their job. As part of achieving this goal, informational meetings were organised for workers who were to be displaced by Sharp. At these meetings, information was provided about various services that were available to these workers, as well as instructions about how to access these services. At these informational meetings, workers were also provided with temporary registration cards that they could fill out, if they wished to register for outplacement assistance from the Nara IESC.

Source: Information presented to the OECD Secretariat when it visited the Nara Labour Bureau, the Nara Prefectural Government, and the Nara office of the IESC in October 2013.

The largest share of spending went to basic case management and job-search assistance ("PES and administration") in Australia, Canada, Japan and New Zealand, while Finland concentrated spending on training. Denmark and the United States allocated large shares of their ALMP spending to both training and sheltered and support employment, while Sweden spent the most on employment incentives and Korea on direct job creation. It is rather remarkable that labour market practitioners in these nine countries described their efforts to support displaced workers back into work in a similar manner, when resource levels and spending priorities for ALMPs appear to be so different. That they do, suggests that many of the issues involved in providing the right services to displaced workers remain relevant at very different levels of overall resources, even if a resource-rich environment is undoubtedly an advantage.

Figure 4.7. The re-employment assistance available to jobseekers is influenced by overall spending on active labour market programmes

The level and composition of ALMP spending in OECD countries, 2015

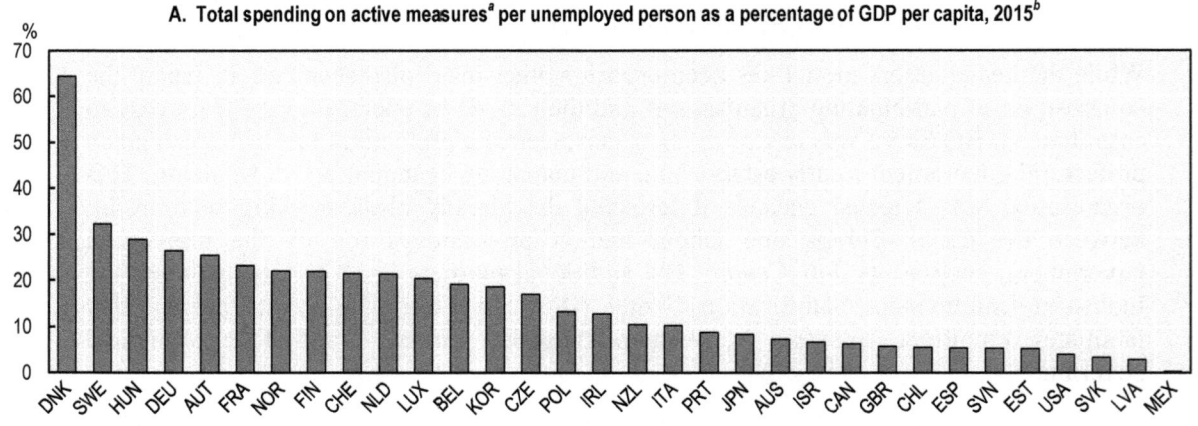

A. Total spending on active measures[a] per unemployed person as a percentage of GDP per capita, 2015[b]

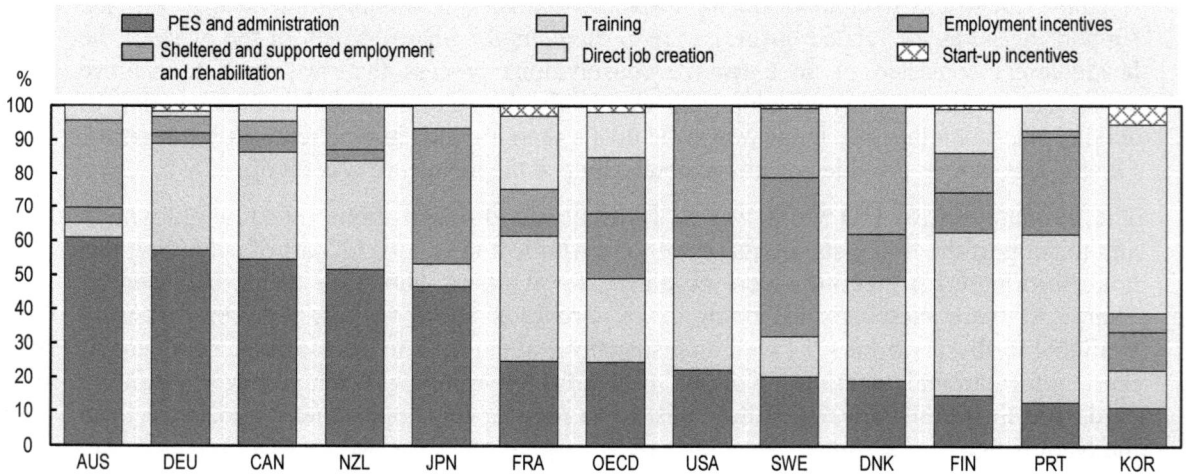

B. Distribution of expenditure by ALMP category, 2015[b]

Note: ALMP: Active labour market programme. FY: Fiscal year. GDP: Gross domestic product. PES: Public employment service. Countries are ranked by decreasing order of public expenditure in active measures (Panel A), and respectively of PES and administration (Panel B).

a) Data cover the categories 1 to 7 in the OECD/Eurostat Labour Market Programme Database (PES and administration, training, employment incentives, sheltered and supported employment and rehabilitation, direct job creation, start-up incentives).

b) Data refer to active measures and to 2014 for Estonia, to FY 2011/12 for the United Kingdom, to FY 2014/15 for New Zealand and to FY 2015/16 for Australia, Canada, Japan and the United States.

Source: OECD/Eurostat Labour Market Programme Database, http://dx.doi.org/10.1787/data-00312-en, for ALMP data; *OECD Employment Database*, www.oecd.org/employment/database for unemployment; and *OECD Annual National Accounts* (ANA) *Database*, http://stats.oecd.org/Index.aspx?DatasetCode=SNA_TABLE1 for GDP.

StatLink 🔗 http://dx.doi.org/10.1787/888933778307

4.3.2. Do displaced workers receive the right types of re-employment services?

How do the needs of displaced workers differ from those of other PES clients?

The empirical findings in Section 4.1 suggest that the job-search aspirations and prospects of displaced workers differ significantly from the jobseekers who have been the primary focus of activation policies in many countries, where emphasis has often been placed on moving benefit recipients who are quite distant from the labour market into usually low-skill and low-pay employment (Immervoll and Scarpetta, 2012[30]).[49] That raises the possibility that it may be difficult for employment services that have a strong focus on supporting relatively disadvantaged persons (e.g. low-skilled individuals with little or no history of stable and reasonably well-paid employment, including early school leavers and persons with partial disabilities) also to serve effectively mainstream displaced workers who had experienced considerable employment security in medium or well-paying jobs prior to being laid-off and hope to find new jobs of a similar quality. If both groups are to be served well, the specific support measures offered to displaced workers will need to differ in important respects from those offered to many of the other jobseekers supported by the employment service.

Immervoll and Scarpetta (2012[30]) and OECD (2015[29]) argue that an effective activation strategy needs to address three basic types of barriers to successful job search by taking measures to: i) strengthen the client's motivation to look for and make use of existing earnings possibilities (e.g. by reinforcing work incentives and enforcing job-search requirements, with benefit sanctions and warnings); ii) address labour-supply side barriers to employment (e.g. by increasing employability with training and rehabilitation); and iii) expand earnings opportunities by connecting clients with suitable job openings or using demand-side instruments, such as wage subsidies, to create employment opportunities. This taxonomy provides a useful framework for delineating the specific re-employment barriers (and advantages) that are characteristic of displaced workers:

- *Motivation.* Since displaced workers have a stable work history, they are usually characterised by strong labour force attachment and are highly motivated to return to work. An off-setting factor is that many displaced workers qualify for relatively generous unemployment benefits and/or large severance payments and may thus be tempted to delay intense job search for a considerable period of time, if their search effort and work availability are not monitored effectively and they are not counselled about the risk that an extended period out of work is likely to be viewed as a bad signal by prospective employers. A history of stable and well-paid employment can also generate overconfidence about how easily a new job can be found or unrealistic aspirations concerning the pay level or the possibility to remain in the same industry and occupation. However, excessive pessimism can also be a problem, particularly for older displaced workers or workers displaced from declining occupations who doubt their capacity to make a career transition. Early engagement with the employment service, including counselling about the adjustment process and encouragement to develop a realistic re-employment strategy as quickly as possible, is thus likely to be especially valuable for displaced workers.

- *Employability.* Familiarity with the world of work and a proven ability to perform on the job are typically not a problem for displaced workers. However, matching their skills with available jobs can be a challenge. This is particularly the case for older blue-collar workers displaced from declining sectors and occupations. This group has typically acquired a lot of skills on the job that are not well documented and which may not match well with the more cognitive and social skills required in growing sectors and occupations. In such cases, skill audits that document the worker's skills (sometimes referred to as recognition of prior learning or RPL) can be very useful, especially when combined with counselling that helps these workers to identify retraining strategies that can supplement their existing skills so as to qualify them for jobs currently in demand ("gap training"). Coaching in job-search methods is also likely to be useful for long-tenure workers who have not looked for a job in many years.

- *Opportunities*. The public employment service may struggle to help place displaced workers who have lost good-quality jobs, even if their occupational specialty is still in demand. Job placement is most effective when PES staff have a good knowledge of the relevant segment of the labour market and good contacts with employers. The widespread perception in the nine countries participating in the *Back to Work* reviews is that the PES is most effective at placing low-skilled workers with relatively little or relatively unstable work histories into low-paying jobs. This suggests that it may make sense for the PES to create a separate track of re-employment services for more skilled displaced workers, possibly making use of private placement agencies that specialise in placing workers into higher paying jobs.[50] When a large number of displacements in a region is associated with persistently depressed labour market conditions, the PES should also facilitate the geographic mobility of job losers who are receptive to the idea of moving to another region with a more buoyant labour market (e.g. through providing information about employment opportunities and subsidising moving costs). However, experience shows that many displaced workers (and their families) have strong ties to their community, implying that the focus often needs to be on promoting successful job placement where they live, possibly including measures such as hiring subsidies for local employers and broader efforts to diversify the local economy.[51]

Individual tailoring of re-employment services for displaced workers

The empirical analysis in Section 4.1 showed that the labour market experience of displaced workers is incredibly varied: while a considerable number of displaced workers move quickly into new jobs that are about as good as or better than the lost job, another sizeable group incurs moderate income losses and a third group experiences a large and lasting decline in their earnings capacity, due to long-term joblessness, large wage reductions on the post-displacement job or a combination of the two. The heterogeneity in displacement costs complicates the provision of re-employment services to displaced workers, since their individual needs for this type of support range from small or even non-existent to large. Clearly, the goal should be to tailor the offered support to individual needs, so as to avoid both unnecessary spending on services for workers who can find a suitable new job with little or no assistance, on the one hand, and delaying access to intensive services to those who need them until they have been unemployed for a long time, on the other. However, this is more easily said than done.

Systematic early needs assessment for displaced workers represents the most straightforward approach to tailoring re-employment services to match individual needs early in the unemployment spell. The focus would be to: i) better identify the jobseeker's skills, relevant experience and opportunities in the labour market; ii) explore options for alternative career paths; iii) identify skills development needs and other barriers to re-employment; and iv) refer to more intensive interventions (e.g. intensive individual counselling or training) only when specific barriers to re-employment have been identified. This needs assessment would be the occasion for displaced workers to discuss their professional plans, retraining options and job-search methods with a case worker. It could also be formalised in an individual action plan, at least in cases where significant barriers to quick re-employment have been identified.

The *Back to Work* reviews show that current PES practice diverges sharply from such an approach. This could indicate that there is considerable scope for improvement. However, this divergence also suggests taking a cautious and incremental approach to introducing systematic early needs assessment for displaced workers, until it has been demonstrated that such an approach has been successful in practice. Among the considerations that arise, the following can be listed:

- When a displaced worker registers at the PES, a profiling instrument and/or case worker judgement typically are used to make an initial assessment of individual needs and, thus, which re-employment services the jobseeker can access early in their jobless spell. In making these determinations, it appears that little or no explicit attention is devoted to trying to differentiate between displaced workers who have good mobility prospects and those requiring more intensive assistance in any of the nine countries reviewed. Indeed, it is rare for the PES to classify its clients according to whether they were displaced or became jobless through another route.[52] This probably reflects, at least in part, the finding in Section 4.1 that the labour market prospects of displaced workers are so varied. In effect, the statistical category that economic researchers have adopted for displaced workers, while useful for studying labour market turnover, is too broad to serve case workers as a useful proxy indicator of individual needs for re-employment support.

- It is possible that the case management practices that are used for all newly registered workers, whether or not they were displaced, implicitly capture the distinction between displaced workers who do and do not require intensive services, at least to some degree. While there is considerable variation in national practice, the logic for determining individual needs tends to be quite similar. Typically, information is collected on a number of factors thought to predict greater barriers to re-employment (e.g. a long period out of work, poor skills or health problems). Whether or not this information is combined into an overall numerical score, it provides the basis for case workers judgements concerning the job seeker's initial needs for re-employment and retraining services.

- Data on which re-employment services displaced workers receive and when are generally lacking. Nonetheless, it seems likely that the needs assessment practices currently in use result in too few newly displaced workers being granted access to intensive re-employment assistance early in the unemployment spell, although they eventually may be offered such services should they remain unemployed for a long enough period of time. This conjecture is based on the observation that newly displaced workers with a stable employment history do not fit the profiles that typically are used by PES offices to identify the persons at the highest risk of long-term unemployment and benefit dependency.[53]

- If displaced workers were assessed as a distinct group among new PES clients, would it be possible to better identify the individuals who would benefit from prompt access to intensive services? The spotty evidence available suggests that it is probably quite difficult to accurately assess the individual needs of newly displaced workers. For example, a random assignment evaluation of a pilot programme in Switzerland, which offers intensive re-employment services to older displaced workers, concluded that the counsellors who worked closely with these jobseekers found it very difficult to anticipate which individuals were at greatest risk of long-term unemployment (Arni, 2012[15]). This experience is consistent with the statistical evidence discussed in Section 4.1. While there are large average differences in displacement costs across groups defined by age, tenure and several other observable characteristics, much of the individual variation in costs remains even after controlling statistically for a considerable number of individual and job characteristics (cf. Figure 4.5).

- While a general solution to individualising the re-employment support that is offered to displaced workers is not yet available, the *Back to Work* reviews highlight how skills validation tied to training support is an area in which important progress has been achieved. The re-employment prospects of displaced workers, particularly older workers whose vocational skills were largely learned on the job, can be greatly improved if their job skills are credibly assessed and documented in a way that makes it possible to ascertain how well they match up with skills credentials that are used in the external labour market. A number of OECD countries have developed recognition for prior learning (RPL) instruments that can be used for this purpose and the closing of a large Bridgestone tire factory in Adelaide in 2010 illustrates how effective RPL can be when the employer cooperates in documenting workers' skills and re-employment counsellors use the results of the RPL exercise to engage the worker in a discussion about whether retraining would be desirable and, if so, which type of training would most efficiently qualify that worker for a suitable new job (OECD, 2016[28]). The payoff to this approach is increased when vocational education and training providers are flexible about providing customized training courses that cover only the material that needs to be learned. Since employers who are recruiting new workers often place a lot of emphasis on work experience, as well as formal qualifications, the PES should also assess whether a temporary hiring subsidy should be used to make it easier for newly trained displaced workers to obtain some initial experience in their new occupation. Good practice examples of applying this general strategy were observed in many of the countries reviewed, but it appears that only a small share of displaced workers have access to these services.

- In light of the difficulty of identifying which individual displaced workers would benefit most from quick access to intensive re-employment services, it seems worthwhile to experiment with different approaches to identifying members of that group early in their unemployment spells. More targeting could also be done at the group level. In particular, greater access to intensive services could be offered to older long-tenure displaced workers. As is illustrated by the Swiss pilot programme evaluated by Arni (2012[15]), the inability of case workers to forecast which older displaced workers in particular faced the greatest re-employment barriers did not prevent the programme from speeding re-employment and raising employment stability.[54] Another group that could be offered greater access to intensive services at the beginning of their unemployment spell is displaced workers whose participation in early intervention measures, such as counselling and skills audits, reveals that they face important re-employment barriers. There could also be some scope for self-selection, such as limiting training access to displaced workers who have developed a credible proposal for retraining as part of a broader plan for career mobility.

4.3.3. Difficulties in providing displaced workers with prompt access to effective re-employment services

Reaching displaced workers who do not immediately qualify for unemployment benefits

Access to even the most basic re-employment services can be delayed when a considerable amount of time elapses between the time when a worker is displaced and the time when she becomes eligible to receive unemployment benefits. As is discussed in Section 4.4, eligibility rules for UI benefits in a number of OECD countries treat severance payments as compensation. For example, a severance award that is equivalent to six months of wages delays eligibility for unemployment benefits by six months in Australia, Canada, Finland and Sweden. This delay in receiving income benefits typically results in an equal delay in registration with the PES and thus of exposure to activation measures, such as job-search requirements and counselling. In some cases, displaced workers are entitled to obtain basic job-search assistance at employment offices even when they are not eligible for an income benefit, but these services tend to be quite limited and take-up low. As regards ensuring displaced workers have prompt access to re-employment services, the implication of these delays is that participation in re-employment measures needs to be decoupled from the receipt of income support.[55]

Two strategies to decouple the initiation of re-employment services from benefit eligibility are practiced by at least a few OECD countries:

- *Outreach.* Some PES services are generally available to all workers, such as self-service use of job search tools (e.g. an online database of job vacancies). Greater use of these resources could be encouraged among displaced workers who are not receiving an unemployment benefit by raising public awareness of the availability of these services and enhancing their value for users. While such measures would be potentially useful for labour market participants more broadly, it seems unlikely that such measures would be very effective in engaging many displaced workers who have received a large severance award. One way to more effectively reach displaced workers is illustrated by the *Jobs and Training Compact* that the Australian government introduced at the beginning of the global financial crisis and which temporarily allowed displaced workers to access an intermediate level of re-employment support, rather than only basic services, even when they were not eligible to receive income benefits (OECD, 2016[28]).

- *Mandatory registration.* In order to minimise unemployment duration and facilitate early contact with employment services, several OECD countries require workers to register with the PES as soon as they are notified that they will be dismissed, even though they are not yet eligible to receive unemployment benefits. For example, Switzerland requires displaced workers to give proof of job-search activities between dismissal notification and the first interview at the PES to receive unemployment benefits (Duell et al., 2010[31]). A similar preventive approach was adopted in Germany as part of the Hartz reforms, with workers being obligated to register as jobseekers three months before their job ends or, for those with shorter notice, within three days of receiving notice of dismissal (Mosley, 2010[32]). This type of registration obligation allows the PES to make referrals of vacancies even before the first unemployment benefit payment. As much as possible, these sorts of requirements should be combined with the early initiation of at least basic re-employment services, including during the notice period (cf. Section 4.2 discussion of early intervention measures).

Meeting sudden upsurges in the number of displaced workers

Another specificity of displaced workers is that the number of job losers requiring re-employment services is quite variable and, in particular, is subject to sudden upward spikes that can overwhelm the capacity of ALMP providers to meet the increased demand. This is most frequent at the local level when one or several mass layoffs create an upsurge in the number of job losers requiring assistance, even as job-search opportunities in the local labour market may worsen. Something similar occurs at the national level during a recession. Finally, natural disasters can cause widespread job displacement in the affected region which needs to be addressed, even as other urgent needs such as rescue, evacuation and rebuilding also require a vigorous response.

The nine *Back to Work* reviews, together with closely related OECD studies of the temporary expansions of ALMPs in response to the upsurge in displacements and unemployment that followed the global financial crisis (OECD, 2009[1]; 2010[33]; 2012[34]) and six recent natural disasters in OECD countries (Venn, 2012[35]), all suggest that labour market programmes have withstood these stress tests surprisingly well overall, albeit at the cost of increased spending and intense efforts by programme managers and the line staff to quickly put those extra resources to good use. Nonetheless, an improved capacity of labour market programmes to rapidly upscale re-employment services for displaced workers remains a priority. One of the biggest challenges is to rapidly expand capacity without compromising quality. Another is to shift the mix of services that are delivered, so as to reflect changes in the composition of workers being served and labour market conditions. Several lessons can be drawn from recent experience:

- There are important limits to how rapidly ALMPs can be up-scaled at the national level, because spending levels typically rise much less than proportionally to the increase in unemployment during recessions and, even when increased funding is available, it is difficult to expand service supply quickly without diluting quality (e.g. it takes time to recruit and train case workers and other skilled staff). For example, ALMP expenditures per unemployed person fell quite sharply as unemployment surged following the global financial crisis, just as the share of displaced workers among the unemployed increased.[56] However, the decline in ALMP spending per unemployed person was less sharp than would have been predicted based on spending patterns in earlier recessions, probably due to the increased priority governments have come to place on activating the unemployed (OECD, 2012[34]).[57] Despite that reduction in resources per person, the more active stance that had gradually been adopted in the years preceding the crisis remained largely intact and the recessionary increases in long-term unemployment and labour force withdrawal were lower than would have been predicted, given the severity of the downturn.

- A rapid upscaling of re-employment support is more feasible at the regional level when this expansion is supported by a national effort. For example, the national government in Australia operates Structural Adjustment Programmes that support regions where structural decline in key industries (e.g. autos, steel, textiles and forestry) has resulted in large-scale displacement (OECD, 2016[28]). The responses to a number of recent natural disasters also illustrate how national governments can support local and regional authorities in responding to a sudden upsurge in the number of displaced workers in a context in which re-employment services need to be closely co-ordinated with other government services, such as those related to arranging housing and schooling for families who were evacuated from the affected areas (Venn, 2012[35]). The 2010-11 earthquakes in Canterbury New Zealand provide an example of the national government ramping up public support for workers displaced by a natural disaster, including measures to save jobs and measures to expand income and re-employment support for workers whose jobs could not be saved (see Box 4.4). The US response to the large-scale economic dislocation that followed Hurricane Katrina in 2005 illustrates the additional complexity of mobilising non-local resources in a Federal system, where each state operates its own unemployment insurance system and re-employment services. Many workers in New Orleans and other hard-hit areas in Louisiana were forced to evacuate their home communities, including large numbers who were evacuated to other states. The Louisiana Department of Labor received important help from their counterparts in surrounding states and the Federal government in making it possible for displaced workers to access UI benefits and re-employment services at evacuation centres.[58]

4.3.4. *What role for targeted re-employment assistance for displaced workers?*

In most OECD countries, displaced workers primarily access public re-employment services through the *general* ALMPs that are operated by the PES and do not treat displaced workers as a distinct client group from other jobseekers. However, *targeted* programmes are sometimes set up for displaced workers or subgroups of displaced workers. Often, these targeted programmes are also operated by the PES as part of their portfolio of services that can be offered to jobseekers, just as they may offer special programmes for unemployed youth, new immigrants, persons with partial disabilities and other groups. In particular, the public early intervention measures that were discussed in Section 4.2 are necessarily organised in this way (e.g. rapid response services for mass layoffs). It is much less evident, however, whether it also makes sense to set up targeted programmes for displaced workers once they have become unemployed and are registered with the public employment service. This is a very heterogeneous group which overlaps considerably, in terms of the re-employment support that they require, with other job seekers served by the PES. As was discussed above, re-employment services should be tailored as much as possible to individual needs, but it is not clear how much that goal is furthered by creating targeted services for displaced workers.

A small number of countries, but also the European Union, have set up separate public programmes to provide re-employment assistance (and sometimes income benefits) to certain subgroups of displaced workers that are considered to require more intensive or somewhat different types of assistance than is provided by general ALMPs. Often, these programmes focus on workers who are adversely affected by increased import competition or were employed in one or a few declining sectors. *Trade Adjustment Assistance* (TAA) in the United States and the more recently established *European Globalisation Adjustment Fund* (EGF) in the European Union are the most prominent examples of programmes targeted on trade displaced workers, while Australia has placed a particular emphasis on sectoral adjustment programmes.[59] Since the sectors that have been chosen to receive this form of support have been characterised by exposure to intense import competition (e.g. autos, steel, and textiles), the focus of these two types of independent targeted programmes have overlapped to a considerable extent. However, the sectoral programmes in Australia have placed much greater emphasis on measures to enhance sectoral competitiveness and economic redevelopment in local labour markets that are hard-hit by the sharp erosion of their comparative advantage, whereas EGF and TAA, have emphasised the provision of re-employment assistance to individual displaced workers.[60]

Targeted programmes for displaced workers have a number of potential benefits, whether organised as distinct services within the range of ALMPs operated by the PES, or as an entirely separate programme. The main benefit is that targeted programmes can provide a mix of services that is optimised to address the needs of displaced workers, such as the rapid response services offered to a group of workers on notice they will lose their job in a mass layoff. Operating a separate ALMP stream of re-employment services for displaced workers also makes it easier to develop a group of case workers and counsellors who specialise in working with displaced workers and become expert in the specific issues this group faces. Additional potential benefits of setting up an entirely separate programme for displaced workers are that this approach makes it easier to offer this group more intensive services than are available to unemployed persons generally through the PES, while also being more visible. Increased visibility of public programmes that assist trade displaced workers could be useful for assuaging popular concerns about the adverse impact of globalisation on workers.[61]

Targeted measures, especially those operated as independent programmes, also have potential drawbacks. These disadvantages have been clearly documented in the case of TAA, which has been the object of a number of careful evaluations since it was established in 1960 (OECD, 2016[27]).[62] In particular, running a separate and better resourced programme for a subset of displaced workers, such as trade displaced workers, can create both inefficiencies and inequities:

- Inefficiencies can result from the duplication of programmes and administrative processes. In particular, eligibility determination has proven to be a cumbersome and often rather arbitrary process, although it has improved over time. One difficulty is the conceptual and practical difficulty of distinguishing between workers who are displaced because of international trade and those displaced for other reasons, since the extent to which import competition is a causal factor in a particular economic dismissal is both difficult to assess and varies along a continuum from not being a factor to being the only factor. This complexity, together with the concern to effectively control access to an expensive package of government-financed benefits has led to a burdensome application and review process that has often meant that benefits only became available long after the displacement occurred, reducing their effectiveness.

- A second drawback to operating an independent programme for a subset of displaced workers is that it is very likely to create inequities because more intensive support is offered to job losers who qualify for the targeted programme than is offered to other displaced workers (and other jobseekers more generally who face similar barriers to successful adjustment.)

Box 4.4. Assisting workers displaced by the Canterbury earthquakes in 2010-11

In 2010 and 2011 significant earthquakes struck Christchurch, New Zealand's second largest city, and its rural hinterland causing rock falls and land damage, widespread building and infrastructure damage and, in the 2011 case, loss of life. The financial cost of the damage, excluding business disruption and clean-up costs is estimated at 10% of New Zealand's Gross Domestic Product (APEC, 2013[36]). Following these disasters, population size in Christchurch City fell about 6%, whereas nearby districts in the Canterbury region experienced population increases, partly due to movement out of the city (Reserve Bank of New Zealand, 2016[37]).

Employment in Canterbury initially declined by 5% after the Earthquakes, but has since risen by about 16%, with that rise almost exclusively accounted for by rapid growth in the construction industry, which encountered labour shortages during the rebuilding period.

The national government took a number of initiatives to expand both income and re-employment support for workers who were displaced by the earthquakes, while also helping local employers to recover.

As concerns income support, people who lost income because they could not get to work or because their workplace closed could get a Civil Defence Payment for loss of livelihood. This pre-existing programme was paid with an open duration but was relatively modest, providing less than the equivalent of full-time employment at the minimum wage. A new income benefit programme was set up temporarily for people not qualifying for either the Civil Defence Payment or means-tested social assistance. The Earthquake Job Loss Cover provided full-time workers whose employer had closed due to the earthquakes a benefit of NZD 400 per week for a maximum duration of six weeks and a smaller benefit to part-time workers. About 2% of the workers in the Canterbury region were receiving this benefit in March 2011.

The government also set up a range of active employment services, on top of the existing general system, to assist workers displaced due to this natural disaster. The Earthquake Support Subsidy was a time-limited employment subsidy that supported small firms in retaining workers during the disaster recovery period. Overall, this subsidy was paid to about 16% of the workers in the greater Canterbury region in March 2011. According to the 2011 Canterbury Employers Survey, 57% of workplaces that received the subsidy said that it "helped a lot" in keeping their business going. Two further labour market programmes were also introduced to assist workers whose jobs could not be saved. Jobs for a Local was a wage subsidy programme for jobseekers in the Canterbury region. The jobs created had to be full-time and permanent, and required the further development of a training plan. The second programme was an extension of the existing Straight to Work programme, where employers were encouraged to train workers to fill labour shortages.

During the rebuilding phase, when worker shortages arose, the Ministry of Social Development (MSD) also introduced a NZD 3k to Christchurch worker mobility subsidy that connected welfare beneficiaries nationwide to the Canterbury labour market by providing a non-taxable NZD 3 000 payment for applicants who need to relocate to secure sustainable, full-time employment. Applicants need a confirmed job before relocating and as of June 2015, 1 512 jobseekers were approved for NZD 3k to Christchurch incentive payments.

There do not appear to have been formal evaluations of the effectiveness of any of the earthquake policies. In large part, the lack of evaluations is due to the need for rapid responses and the temporary nature of assistance. Planning and designing evaluations under such crisis circumstances is always unlikely to be a policy priority.

Source: OECD (2017[38]), *Back to Work: New Zealand: Improving the Re-employment Prospects of Displaced Workers,* http://dx.doi.org/10.1787/9789264264434-en.

Overall, a cautious but pragmatic approach to the use of general and targeted programmes seems best. Targeted early intervention measures appear to be useful for managing mass layoffs and this type of support should be extended, as much as possible, to workers who are displaced by small-scale layoffs. Once workers are displaced, the case for setting up targeted programmes is more limited, but should not be dismissed out of hand. Finally, there should be a strong preference to organise targeted measures as options within the portfolio of ALMPs operated by the public employment service, rather than setting them up as a separate programme such as TAA.

4.4. Income support

When quick job-to-job transitions are not feasible, income support becomes a key issue for displaced workers. The most important source of public income support for displaced workers is unemployment insurance (UI) and other types of unemployment benefits (UBs). Accordingly, this section focusses on recent policy experience with providing UBs to this group. The biggest challenge for a UB system is to provide income security without undermining work incentives. While this is true for all UB recipients, the forms taken by the tension between benefit coverage and adequacy, on the one hand, and labour supply incentives, on the other, tend to be somewhat different for stable workers who experience a redundancy than for other unemployed jobseekers. While the general principles for designing and operating UI/UB systems also apply to their role in providing income support to displaced workers, there are some important nuances.

The earnings losses associated with unemployment are only one of the sources of the income losses that many displaced workers experience and this has important implications for designing income support for this group, including how extensively UBs should be supplemented by other forms of compensation. Panel A of Table 4.3, identifies four distinct sources of earnings losses for displaced workers and the different types of income support measures that are used to address each type of loss. Panel B then provides an overview of some of the policy design issues that arise for each of the six types of income support measures included in the table. As was discussed in Section 4.2, EPL can be used to require employers to provide compensation for the earnings losses suffered by workers they displace in the form of severance payments. However, any such requirement needs to be used with care because research suggests that they have a high efficiency cost – see OECD (2013[2]), for a survey of the literature. Accordingly, this section does not analyse a policy option of raising mandatory severance levels, but it does consider the implications of severance pay for the operation of public UB systems.

Table 4.3. Income support for displaced workers: Sources of income loss, types of policy measures and selected policy design issues

A. Different sources of income losses

	Types of policy measures					
Sources of income loss for displaced workers	Short-time work (STW) scheme	Unemployment insurance	Means-tested unemployment and social assistance benefits	Severance payments	Public insurance against unpaid compensation	Wage insurance
Earnings dip prior to displacement	XX		X (Especially, in-work benefits).			
Lost compensation due to insolvency of former employer					XX	
Post-displacement joblessness		XX	X	XX		
Loss of earnings once re-employed (e.g. due to loss of specific human capital or seniority wages)		X (If partial UI benefits paid to workers re-employed at low earnings).	X (Especially, in-work benefits).	X		XX

B. Policy design issues

	Types of policy measures					
Policy design issues	Short-time work (STW) scheme	Unemployment insurance	Means-tested unemployment and social assistance benefits	Severance payments	Public insurance against unpaid compensation	Wage insurance
Income targeting criteria	Earnings loss due to lower hours worked.	Earnings loss due to joblessness.	Household income falls below adequacy standard.	None (tied to end of employment relationship).	Compensation left unpaid due to employer insolvency.	Decline in earnings between pre- and post-displacement jobs.
Other targeting criteria	Meet minimum UI eligibility thresholds and employer facing temporarily low demand.	Meet minimum employment/ contribution thresholds; may be means-tested against severance payments.	Asset test(s) common, especially for social assistance.	Usually reflects tenure, sometimes also age or occupation.		Minimum hours worked on new job, sometimes limited to certain groups of displaced workers, such as those aged 50 and older.
Work availability requirement	Sometimes subject to job search or training requirements.	Conditional on work availability and active job search, but nature of activation measures varies considerably.	Conditional on work availability for some beneficiaries, but nature of activation measures varies considerably.	None.	None.	Minimum work hours on new job.
Potential sources of inefficiency and abuse	Impeding efficiency-enhancing mobility by subsidising jobs that are no longer economically viable.	Blunting of labour supply incentives leading to excessive unemployment duration and benefit dependency.	Blunting of labour supply incentives leading to excessive unemployment duration and benefit dependency.	Blunting of incentives for efficiency – enhancing mobility (pre-displacement) and labour supply (post-displacement).	Blunting of incentives for employers to pre-fund deferred compensation (and for workers/unions to insist that they do).	Blunting incentives to find a new job that pays as well as the lost job or to work full time.

	Types of policy measures					
Policy design issues	Short-time work (STW) scheme	Unemployment insurance	Means-tested unemployment and social assistance benefits	Severance payments	Public insurance against unpaid compensation	Wage insurance
Prominence of displaced workers among all beneficiaries	In principle, all beneficiaries risk displacement, but some deadweight is likely (i.e. subsidies are paid for jobs that would have been preserved in any case).	Displaced workers are one of the main groups targeted.	Persons facing longer-term disadvantages are the main target group.	Displaced workers are the main target group.	A subset of displaced workers is the target group.	A subset of displaced workers is the target group.
How widely is this policy measure used in OECD countries?	24 out of 34 OECD countries, but take-up is low in many cases.	Widespread, but not universal (e.g. Australia and New Zealand have means-tested social assistance with benefit levels that reflect family income needs, rather than the level of past earnings).	Widespread, but coverage and generosity vary considerably.	Mandatory severance in 22 out of 34 OECD countries. Collective bargaining and firm human resource policies provide for severance (or additional severance) for some workers.	Widespread, but not universal	Small programmes in only a few countries (e.g. France, Korea and the United States), but gradual benefit phase-out for UI beneficiaries accepting low-paying jobs has a similar effect and is more widespread.
Other policy issues (highly selective)	Should STW be combined with mandatory job search or training?	Should UI benefit eligibility be delayed until severance payments have been spent down?	Should there be time limits or mandatory workfare?	Should legally mandated severance take the form of portable retirement savings accounts, so as to avoid penalising voluntary labour mobility?	How should this insurance relate to bankruptcy law, where workers are only one of multiple creditors?	Affordability of a broad wage insurance scheme remains to be demonstrated.

Note: In Panel A, XX and X denote, respectively, a major and secondary policy goal of the indicated policy. UI: Unemployment insurance.

As was already emphasised in Section 4.1, the two main sources of earnings losses for displaced workers are those associated with the period of joblessness and zero earnings that follows most layoffs and the longer-term losses due to re-employment at a lower level of earnings. While these losses and the ways in which they can be compensated will be the main focus of this section, it is useful also to briefly discuss two additional sources of earnings losses for displaced workers, namely, a tendency for earnings to decline in the period immediately preceding displacement (e.g. as hours of work are reduced in a struggling firm) and the risk that a firm entering bankruptcy will fail to pay their employees all of the compensation to which they are entitled. Both short-time working schemes and in-work benefits provide some compensation for a pre-displacement dip in earnings.[63] As regards unpaid compensation, some OECD countries have established public insurance schemes to compensate such losses, such as the *Wage Earner Protection Plan* (WEPP) that the Canadian government established in 2008 (OECD, 2015[13]).[64]

4.4.1. Unemployment benefits

Benefit adequacy

A generous unemployment benefit system represents one of the most straightforward policy approaches for reducing the costs borne by displaced workers. However, governments need to carefully balance the direct benefits for workers, who are better compensated for their earnings losses and can therefore smooth their consumption over time as well as have sufficient resources to look for a job that matches their skills and expectations, against the disincentive effects on individual job search effort (moral hazard effect) as well as possible aggregate effects on labour supply, labour demand and the government budget – see e.g. Tatsiramos and van Ours (2014[39]); Schmieder and von Wachter (2016[40]); Nekoei and Weber (2017[41]). Whether or not the moral hazard effect of UI benefits is particularly large for displaced workers, as compared to other UI recipients, remains an open question. Nevertheless, the evidence suggests that there is an effect and governments need to find a middle ground between generously compensating displaced workers for their lost earnings and encouraging rapid re-employment.

Consistent with the benefit entitlement rules for UI programmes, displaced workers with a stable work history tend to have relatively high benefit levels, as compared to job losers with less continuous employment histories. Nonetheless, Figure 4.8 shows that the level of income support that results is much higher in some OECD countries than in others. Focusing on the nine countries that participated in the *Back to Work* reviews, the figure shows that average net replacement rates (NRRs) during the first year of unemployment vary from 19% in the United States to 75% in Denmark. This gap reflects both the higher initial benefit level in Denmark (net replacement rates of 75% in Denmark versus 50% in the United States) and the longer maximum duration of benefit payments (24 versus 4.6 months). Since a considerable share of displaced workers experience long spells of unemployment, the share of earnings losses due to joblessness that is compensated by UBs will be significantly lower in countries where the maximum period of benefit receipt is relatively short.[65] For example, one in four displaced workers in the United States in 2014 had exhausted their UI entitlement – OECD (2016[27]). While many displaced workers do not qualify for unemployment benefits in Australia and New Zealand, due to means testing (see below), and the initial NRRs are quite low for qualifying job losers in these countries, the absence of a time-limit on the receipt of these benefits means that the average NRRs over 5 years are substantially above the OECD average.

Given the high level of concern about the hardship experienced by displaced workers and the relatively high risk they experience long spells of unemployment, it is natural to ask whether UB rules should treat displaced workers more generously than other unemployed jobseekers. To a limited extent this is quite common. For example, eligibility rules often either deny benefits to certain groups, such as workers who voluntarily left their job, self-employed or apprentices whose contract is not renewed, or impose an additional waiting period on such applicants before they are entitled to begin receiving benefits. However, the *Employment Insurance* (EI) programme in Japan provides an example of a much more ambitious approach to providing greater income support to formerly stable workers who are displaced and then are slow to become re-employed than is available to other jobseekers (OECD, 2015[23]). The maximum duration of EI payment is significantly longer for *specific qualified recipients*, a category which mostly applies to displaced workers, than it is for *ordinary unemployed*, a category which includes most people voluntarily quitting their job or whose temporary job ended. The maximum EI payment duration also increases quite strongly with age and job tenure for *specific qualified recipients* (e.g. from 90 days for a displaced worker aged 44 years or younger with 1 to 5 years of job tenure, at the low end, up to 330 days for a displaced worker aged 45-59 with 20 or more years of tenure). Such an approach probably better aligns the level of income support with the risk of long-term unemployment, but should only be pursued if combined with more intensive activation of the groups eligible for longer duration benefit payments.

Coverage rates

How effectively UB systems compensate for the earnings losses is also influenced by the share of displaced workers who qualify to receive these benefits, that is, the effective coverage rate for this group.[66] That share appears to be quite high in seven of the review countries where the first tier UB system is organised as unemployment insurance (see Chapter 5). Nonetheless, coverage gaps are of concern for certain workforce groups. For example, effective UI coverage is relatively low among non-regular workers who are displaced in Korea and Japan. However, coverage rates are on an upward trend in Korea (as the UI system matures) and Japan experimented successfully with a temporary extension of UI eligibility to more low tenure workers during the economic crisis, possibly setting the stage for permanent measures (OECD, 2013[42]; 2015[23]). There has been a downward trend in UI coverage rates in Denmark and Sweden, where enrolment is voluntary, but only Sweden has a basic public unemployment benefit that is available to job losers who chose not to enrol in a UI fund (OECD, 2015[26]; 2016[43]). Declining coverage in Denmark is also highly concentrated in the bottom three income deciles causing lower-income displaced workers to be particularly unlikely to receive income benefits, even when they experience a lengthy spell of unemployment.[67] By far the largest gaps in UB coverage are found in Australia and New Zealand, where the first tier UB programme is designed as a safety net of last resort that provides a flat-rate payment to families whose income and liquid assets are below the minimum adequacy standards set by the government (OECD, 2016[28]; 2017[38]). This results in relatively few displaced workers qualifying for public income support following displacement, at least initially, although more become eligible eventually if they remain unemployed for an extended period and their spouse has little or no earnings. For example, only about one-third of the stock of non-employed displaced workers reported welfare benefit receipt in 2015 in New Zealand.

Interaction with other sources of income support

In assessing the adequacy of the income support that displaced workers receive from UB programmes, it is important also to take account of both the severance awards received by many displaced workers and other public programmes, especially the social assistance programmes that act as a backstop to the first tier UB scheme. Severance awards are quite widespread in some OECD countries and can be quite high. For example, long-tenure regular workers in large corporations in Japan tend to accumulate severance entitlements that exceed their maximum cumulative UI benefit entitlement (OECD, 2015[23]). However, it appears that the displaced workers with the greatest UB entitlements also tend to receive the most severance, suggesting a limited role for severance payments in plugging the most worrisome gaps in UB adequacy.[68] Another indication that severance awards and last-resort social benefits are of limited effectiveness in avoiding large uncompensated earnings losses following displacement is that the poverty risk for displaced workers appears to be quite high in some of the countries studied. For example, in the United States, two in three families with a displaced worker fall into poverty for some time (OECD, 2016[27]).

Figure 4.8. Unemployment benefit schemes are a key source of income support

Net replacement rates (NRRs)[a] for an average-income earner, calculated at three different points of time
(initially, averaged over one year and averaged over five years), 2015, percentages

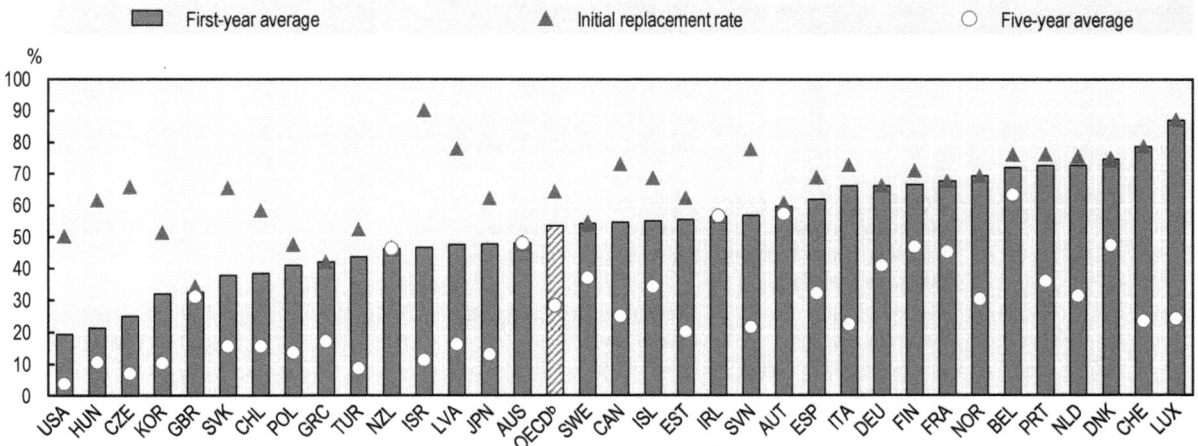

a) Net replacement rate (NRR) is the ratio of net income out of work to net income while in work. Calculations consider cash income (excluding, for instance, employer contributions to health or pension insurance for workers and in-kind transfers for the unemployed) as well as income taxes and mandatory social security contributions paid by employees. Unemployment benefits include unemployment insurance and unemployment assistance. Social assistance and housing-related benefits potentially available as income top-ups to unemployment benefits for low-income families are not included. Family benefits are included, while entitlements to severance payments are excluded. NRRs are calculated for a 40-year-old worker with an uninterrupted employment record since age 22. They are averages over four different stylised family types (single parents and one-earner couples, with and without children) and two earnings levels on the lost job (67% and 100% of average full-time wages). Due to benefit ceilings, NRRs are in most countries lower for individuals with above-average earnings.

b) Unweighted averages of the 34 OECD countries shown in Panel A above (excluding Mexico).

Source: OECD Tax-Benefit Models, www.oecd.org/els/social/workincentives.

StatLink ⟪⟫ http://dx.doi.org/10.1787/888933778326

The *Back to Work* country reviews highlighted an issue that has not received a lot of attention, namely, how unemployment benefit entitlements and severance payments should be co-ordinated. Table 4.4 summarises legal entitlements to severance pay in the reviewed countries (and several other OECD countries), as well as any rules about interactions between severance pay and UB payments. Quite often, the receipt of severance pay delays UB entitlement with this effect being particularly strong in Australia, Canada, Finland and Sweden. In Denmark and Sweden, the size of the severance payment declines as the UI benefit increases. These various off-sets may reflect judgements about the overall adequacy of the income support provided by the combination of these two types of payments. While the question how best to co-ordinate UB and severance payments is understudied and it would be premature to designate best practice principles, these examples raise several issues that merit further attention:

**Table 4.4. Characteristics of severance pay schemes for displaced workers
in selected OECD countries**

	Legal basis and eligibility conditions	Minimum amount set by statutory law	Collective bargaining coverage rate[a]	Interaction with UI entitlement
Australia	Federal statutory law and provisions in collective agreements.	**Min**: tenure < 1 year = 0, tenure ≥ 1 year and < 2 year = 4 weeks. **Max**: tenure ≥ 9 years and < 10 years = 16 weeks. Tenure ≥ 10 years = 12 weeks.	59% (2016).	Waiting period for UI benefits is increased by number of (wage) days received in severance pay.
Austria[b]	Statutory law: Access to individual accounts only if tenure over 3 years. Otherwise account carried over to next employer.	Amount depends on the capital accrued in the fund, investment income earned and capital guaranteed.	98% (2016).	None.
Canada	Federal statutory law, Provincial law, and provisions in collective agreements.	**Min (employees covered by federal law)**: tenure < 1 year = 0, tenure ≥ 1 year and < 3 years = 5 days after which tenure ≥ 3 years = 2 days for each year of tenure. **Min (Ontario)**: tenure < 1 year = 0, **Max (Ontario)**: Tenure ≥ 26 years = 26 weeks if the firm has a payroll of CAD 2.5 million or more. **Other jurisdictions**: no legislated severance pay.	28% (2016).	Waiting period for UI benefits is increased by number of (wage) days received in severance pay.
Denmark[c]	Statutory requirement for white collar workers and collective agreements ofor blue collar workers.	*White collars:* **Min**: Tenure < 12 years = 0, Tenure ≥ 12 years and < 15 years = 1 month. **Max**: Tenure ≥ 18 years = 3 months. *Blue collars:* The monthly amount of severance pay is calculated as follows: 85% of monthly salary *minus* the monthly unemployment benefit, and is payable for: 1 month > 3-year tenure; 2 months > 6-year tenure; 3 months > 8-year tenure.	84% for all workers (2015).	For blue-collar workers, the amount of severance pay is reduced by the amount of UI benefits. Indeed, since initial replacement rates are most often above 85% for low-paid workers, severance pay is rarely paid to blue collars.
Finland	No legal requirement. Provisions in collective agreements.	n.a.	89% (2015).	Waiting period for UI benefits is increased by the number of (wage) days received in severance pay.
France	Statutory law and provisions in collective agreements.	**Min**: tenure < 8 months: 0, tenure ≥ 8 months and < 10 years: 0.25 months per year of service, tenure ≥ 10 years: 1/3 month per year of service	99% (2014).	Waiting period for UI benefits is increased if severance pay exceeds legal minima, by a duration in days corresponding to the extra-amount in severance pay divided by 90 (total waiting period capped at 75 days).

	Legal basis and eligibility conditions	Minimum amount set by statutory law	Collective bargaining coverage rate[a]	Interaction with UI entitlement
Germany	Statutory law: an employee working in a firm with at least ten employees who is dismissed on the basis of compelling operational reason is entitled to severance pay if offered by the employer and the workers renounces to go to court.	Half a month's pay per year of tenure (if offered by the employer).	56% (2016).	Waiting period for UI benefits is increased by a fraction of the number of (wage) days of severance, where the fraction varies with age and job tenure and the delay is capped at 1 year.
Japan	No legal requirement. Provisions in collective agreements.	n.a.	17% (2016).	None.
Korea	No legal requirement. Provisions in collective agreements.	n.a.	12% (2015).	3-month delay in UI benefits if severance pay is KRW 100 million or more.
New Zealand[d]	No statutory requirements in the Employment Relations Act. Except under some circumstances for a very small group of "vulnerable" workers.	Paid if explicitly negotiated and included in individual or collective employment agreements.	20% (2016).	No interaction, except one week longer benefit stand-down (i.e. two weeks) if redundancy pay pushes prior annual income over the average annual income.
Sweden	No legal requirement. General provisions established in collective agreements respectively for white collars aged over 40 and for blue collars aged over 40 and with 50 months of employment over the last 5 years.	White collars: Complements UI at a max of 70% of previous wage for a period of 6-18 months depending on age. Blue collars are entitled to a lump sum increasing with age.	90% (2015).	Waiting period for UI benefits is increased by number of (wage) days received in severance pay. Severance pay amount declines with UI benefit level for white-collar workers.
United States	No legal requirement. Provisions in collective agreements.	n.a.	12% (2016).	Increased waiting period for UI benefits or reduction in the benefit amount depending on the state.

Note: UI: Unemployment insurance; n.a.: Not applicable.

a) The collective bargaining coverage rate provides an indication of the proportion of the workforce potentially covered under these agreements and therefore likely to receive higher severance packages than the legislated ones.

b) Austria: Conditions refer to workers with contracts concluded after January 2003.

c) Denmark: Conditions are regulated by collective agreements per sector for blue-collar workers and by regulation for white-collar workers.

d) New Zealand: In case of restructuring, defined as outsourcing, the employee has the right to ask for transfer to the contractor. If refused, the worker can negotiate redundancy arrangements.

Source: For statutory severance pay: *Décret n° 2017-1398 du 25 septembre 2017,* https://www.legifrance.gouv.fr/eli/decret/2017/9/25/2017-1398/jo/texte, for France, and *OECD Employment Protection Database,* 2013 update, www.oecd.org/employment/protection, for other countries; *OECD/ICTWSS Database,* https://stats.oecd.org/Index.aspx?DataSetCode=CBC, for adjusted bargaining coverage rates; and country responses to the "OECD Questionnaire on Eligibility Criteria for Unemployment Benefits and Interventions in the Unemployment Spell" for interaction with UI entitlement (rules as of June 2014).

- As was discussed in Section 4.3, delaying eligibility for UBs until severance pay has been spent down (as appears to be the logic of the offset rules used in Australia, Canada, Finland and Sweden), has important implications for the provision of re-employment support to displaced workers. In particular, a strategy is then needed to connect displaced workers to re-employment services even before they become eligible for UB payments

- If UB and severance payments are considered to represent alternative sources of compensation for the earnings losses experienced by displaced workers, then it is natural to think of them as being close substitutes and to means test eligibility for one of these payments based on how much of the other is received. However, it might be more appropriate to think of UB benefits as providing partial insurance against the earnings losses due to post-displacement unemployment, whereas severance payments provide insurance against the loss of earnings due to lower wages upon re-employment. Parsons (forthcoming[44]) provides a theoretical argument supporting the idea that a well-designed combination of UI and severance pay could represent an efficient form of "job displacement insurance". In that package, UI provides insurance against the unemployment risk while severance pay provides insurance against wage loss. From this perspective, it probably does not make sense to think of these two types of insurance as being close substitutes and to means test one against the other.

- Considered as insurance for the wage loss associated with displacement, severance pay takes the form of a scheduled (i.e. lump sum) benefit, the payment of which is triggered by displacement while the amount paid is independent of the size of the actual wage losses. An alternative design for providing wage insurance is to structure it as a public social insurance programme where eligibility to receive a benefit is conditional on re-employment at a lower wage and the size of the payment depends on *ex-post* wage losses.

4.4.2. Is there a role for wage insurance?

A major unresolved issue related to the provision of income support to displaced workers is whether and how to compensate for the part of earnings losses that sometimes persists long after they have become re-employed, because they can no longer command as high of a wage as they earned on the lost job. Particularly for long-tenure blue-collar workers, this can represent the largest part of total earnings losses in the long-run. Wage insurance (WI) is sometimes proposed as a supplement to unemployment insurance which cushions this second type of earnings loss following displacement. Similarly, to unemployment benefits, which offset a portion of the earnings losses due to post-displacement unemployment, WI pays displaced workers who accept new jobs at lower wages an earnings supplement that replaces a fraction of the difference between earnings on the old and the new job. Often, it is proposed that this supplement would be limited in duration (maybe one or two years) or limited to certain groups who are particularly at risk of experiencing a permanent loss of earnings capacity, such as older and long-tenured displaced workers, and/or workers who become re-employed within a certain period (e.g. within six months after displacement). The experience to date with WI is quite limited, but proposals to implement it on a larger scale have been a recurrent feature of employment policy discussions in North America the past several decades (OECD, 2015[13]; 2016[27]).[69]

Proponents of WI argue that it can provide a more equitable sharing of the gains from economic restructuring by reducing the adjustment costs faced by those who are hurt the most. It is also argued that WI would improve incentives for speedy re-employment, as unemployment benefits become less attractive relative to accepting a new job. But WI also comes with potential problems. *First*, the cost could be high unless the earnings supplements are tightly targeted. Tight targeting, however, would be likely to create inequities between displaced workers re-employed at lower wages who receive the WI benefit and similar workers who do not. To the extent WI speeds up re-employment, shorter unemployment spells could come at the cost of shifting workers into low-quality jobs with low wages and poor prospects for training and wage growth. *Finally*, there may be a risk of employers being able to offer lower wages than they would in the absence of such schemes.

Evaluations of two small wage insurance schemes in North America suggests that WI is an effective instrument for reducing the decline in the net incomes of displaced workers who become re-employed at a lower wage, but does not have a significant impact in speeding re-employment or affecting the post-displacement wage (Bloom et al., 2001[45]; Wandner, 2016[46]). While it seems premature to implement a large-scale wage insurance scheme in the absence of a clearly demonstrated working model, further pilot studies of WI schemes would be of considerable value given the high level of concern about the impact of displacement on worker well-being. It would also be useful for researchers to assess the comparative advantages and disadvantages of WI as compared to alternative measures that also be used to compensate displaced workers who become re-employed at a lower wage, such as a gradual phasing out of UI benefits as re-employment earnings rise, severance pay and general in-work benefit schemes.

4.5. Concluding remarks

Reconciling economic dynamism with employment and income security for workers is an important policy challenge and labour market programmes have a central role to play in meeting that challenge. This chapter has analysed how best labour market programmes can play that role by summarising the main lessons from the OECD's recent *Back to Work* reviews in nine countries. It highlights a number of effective practices that are already in place in some OECD countries, as well as a number of areas where improvement is needed. The latter include reducing both the sometimes large discrepancies in the assistance provided to different groups of displaced workers facing similar difficulties in reintegrating into the labour market as well as the sometimes long delays in connecting displaced workers with the re-employment services they require.

The chapter confirms that the starting point for improving the re-employment prospects and income security of displaced workers is to make further progress at developing a system of well-designed and adequately-resourced active and passive labour market programmes that implement an effective national activation strategy while also providing an adequate level of income security. However, the general principles of good labour market practice need to be applied in a way that addresses the particular situation of displaced workers, including both the particular barriers to successful re-employment that they face and their particular advantages in searching for a new job. From the perspective of activation policy, two of the most important differences between displaced workers and other jobseekers are the greater scope for *proactive* measures, beginning during the notice period before the layoff occurs, and the large contribution that employers can make to fostering successful mobility for workers they displace, ideally in close collaboration with trade unions and labour market authorities.

The chapter identifies a number of avenues for improving the assistance that labour market programmes provide to displaced workers, but also leaves key questions unanswered. One such question concerns spending priorities. Many of the strategies identified here for improving re-employment services and income-support for displaced workers would imply higher spending. In the context of tight budgetary constraints, expanding the resources devoted to assisting displaced workers could lead to a reduction of the resources available to help other groups (e.g. the long-term unemployed, welfare benefit recipients and people with partial disabilities), who have been a major focus of activation policy in recent years. Spending priorities will need to be set in light of specific national conditions, but the currently high level of concern about mass layoffs suggests it is timely to consider redoubling efforts to assist displaced workers. Even if it were not deemed appropriate to increase spending on assistance for this group, the chapter may provide useful guidance for using existing resources more effectively.

Notes

[1] Other terms for this group include redundant, retrenched and laid-off workers. Similarly, job displacements are often referred to as redundancies, retrenchments, layoffs and economic dismissals.

[2] The ageing of the workforce also increases the risk that rapid structural change in the labour market inflicts large costs on displaced workers, since labour market mobility is particularly difficult for older workers (OECD, 2014[64]).

[3] The potential fragility of this political support is underlined by the recent successful exploitation of widespread concerns about job losses by populist political movements in a number of OECD countries.

[4] See OECD (2013[42]) for Korea, OECD (2015[23]) for Japan, OECD (2015[13]) for Canada, OECD (2015[26]) for Sweden, OECD (2016[28]) for Australia, OECD (2016[43]) for Denmark, OECD (2016[22]) for Finland, OECD (2016[27]) for the United States, and OECD (OECD, 2017[38]) for New Zealand. The OECD Secretariat is grateful to the national authorities and many other stakeholders in the nine countries that participated in the OECD *Back to Work* reviews of policies to assist displaced workers back into suitable jobs. The analysis underlying this chapter could not have been successfully conducted without their generous support.

[5] The nine countries reviewed are quite diverse yet were found to be grappling with very similar issues in their efforts to support displaced workers. This suggests that these reviews are likely to be informative on the main policy issues that need to be addressed in other OECD countries. It should be noted, however, that no Latin American or non-Nordic European countries participated in the reviews and it is possible that the chapter's analysis fails to address specific aspects of the policy challenges facing such countries.

[6] A recent example of this genre is Amy Goldstein's book about the 2008 closing of a large General Motors plant in Janesville, Wisconsin (Goldstein, 2017[52]).

[7] For the purpose of this analysis, the term *displaced worker* refers to workers involuntarily separated from their job due to economic or technological reasons, such as layoffs related to a recession or structural economic change. Two distinct approaches were used to differentiate job displacement from other types of separations, such as voluntary quits, depending on the underlying data source in each country: i) *self-defined displacement* – when household survey data is used, the worker's assessment of the reason for the separation is used to identify displacements; and ii) *firm-identified displacement* – when linked employer-employee longitudinal data (usually from administrative sources) is used, job displacements are defined as job separations from firms that, from one year to the next, experienced a large reduction in employment. In order to focus on workers likely to have a stable attachment to their jobs, attention is restricted to workers aged 20-64 who had at least one year of job tenure prior to separating from their employer. OECD (2013[2]) provides detailed documentation of the underlying data sources and definitions.

[8] The most notable measurement issue is the use of the self-defined displacement concept and household survey data for some countries, while the firm-identified displacement concept and linked employer-employee data are used for other countries (as discussed in the previous endnote). Both types of data sources and the associated definitions have strengths and weaknesses and it is not clear *a priori* which provides the most accurate information about displacement (OECD, 2013[2]).

[9] While the majority of job displacements reflect structural, rather than cyclical, variations in labour demand, recent research analysing the costs of recessions has provided evidence that total displacement costs increase sharply during recessions, due to both higher rates of displacement and greater costs for each displaced worker due to longer durations of unemployment and an

elevated risk of re-employment in lower paying jobs (Davis and von Wachter, 2011[58]; Farber, 2017[55]).

[10] Assuming that displacement risk in each year is distributed as an independent and identically distributed random variable, an annual displacement risk of 3% implies that a worker has a 70% chance of experiencing one or more displacements over the course of a 40-year career.

[11] Moreover, some workers are also dismissed for poor job performance or fault.

[12] The estimates of total separations and displacement are based on different data sources for some of these countries and may not be fully comparable. Thus, the estimated displacement shares of total separations should be considered as providing only an approximate indication of the contribution of economic dismissals to total separations. The large cross-country differences in this ratio should also be interpreted with caution since they may reflect measurement biases.

[13] See OECD (2013[4]) for a fuller discussion of variations in the risk of job displacement.

[14] The figures shown in Figure 4.3 are lower than, and conceptually different from, the re-employment rates exactly 1 or 2 years after displacement, which are reported in a number of national studies. In order to cover a maximum number of countries, the statistics on displacement that are analysed in this section are based on panel data in which the labour market status of individuals in the sample are observed at 12 month intervals. Thus, the within-one-year re-employment rates presented in Figure 4.3 indicate the share of persons who; i) were displaced at some point between year *t*-1 and year *t*; and ii) were employed when observed in year *t*. It follows that the time since displacement can range from 1 day to a full year. Whereas the re-employment rate within 1 year was 30% in France during 2004-2008 and even lower during the crisis, the re-employment rate of displaced workers 1 year later averaged 42% during 2003-2011 (Nafilyan, 2016[50]).

[15] While some of the cross-country differences in the speed of re-employment probably reflect measurement issues or differences in business cycle conditions in the years covered, the speed of re-employment following displacement probably does vary substantially. One indication that this is the case is that the countries with low re-employment rates in Figure 4.3 also have a high incidence of long-term unemployment (e.g. the correlation between the 1-year re-employment rates of displaced workers during 2003-08 and the share of all unemployed who had been out of work for 12 months or longer was -0.8).

[16] Whereas Figure 4.1 indicated that the increase in the incidence of displacement during the crisis quickly reversed once the recovery was underway, Figure 4.3 indicates that the increased difficulty in finding a new job persisted longer, presumably because the rapid recessionary increase in the unemployment rate reversed only slowly.

[17] OECD (2013[4]) provides full documentation of the estimation equations, variable definitions and samples that were used in this analysis.

[18] Not surprisingly, the post-displacement dip in earnings is smaller in countries where re-employment is rapid, such as Finland and Sweden, than in countries where many displaced workers remain jobless for an extended period of time, such as Portugal.

[19] OECD (2013[4]) survey this research literature.

[20] For example, Farber (2004[54]) shows that the average change in weekly earnings following displacement in the United States are 1% for re-employed workers who had 1-3 years of job tenure on the lost job, -6% for workers who had 4 to 10 years of tenure, -17% for workers who had 11-20 years of tenure and -32% for workers who had 20 or more years of tenure. A study using Dutch data for the period 2000-2011 shows that the tendency for earnings losses to be larger for long-tenure displaced workers is strongest for older workers displaced from sectors where overall employment is declining (Deelen, de Graaf-Zijl and van den Berge, 2018[57]).

[21] This co-ordination is sometimes formalised in private-public partnerships to manage the impact of a mass layoff, as is exemplified by the SSI Task Force which was set up in response to the closing of the SSI Steelworks in Redcar in 2015 (SSI Task Force, 2017[48]).

[22] For example, Andrews and Saia (2017[8]) provides evidence that both direct policy measures (e.g. greater spending on ALMPs) and indirect measures (e.g. regulatory reforms lowering entry barriers in product markets) are associated with faster re-employment of workers displaced due to plant closings.

[23] This risk also exists for direct measures. In particular, inadequate income and re-employment support for displaced workers can generate political demands for excessively strict employment protection legislation that has a high efficiency cost – see Chapter 3 in OECD (2013[2]).

[24] One reason that evaluation studies rarely single out displaced workers for attention is that the administrative data that they typically rely upon rarely classifies jobseekers according to whether they were displaced from a previously stable job or became unemployed in another way. For the same reason, the staff operating ALMPs often has little idea which types of services displaced workers receive as compared with their other clients.

[25] Barnow and Smith (2015[60]) and OECD (2016[27]) survey key results from these evaluations.

[26] International research has shown that the effectiveness of ALMPs is enhanced when they are combined with systematic monitoring of compliance with benefit eligibility criteria, such as actively searching for a job, that is backed up by benefit sanctions. This form of activation is relatively weak in the United States and is likely to be especially weak for displaced workers who have already exhausted their UI eligibility (Arni, Lalive and Van Ours, 2013[61]; OECD, 2015[29]).

[27] A recent dissertation uses a regression discontinuity design to evaluate the benefits generated by an early intervention measure for blue collar workers in Sweden and concludes that workers receiving this assistance experience only slightly better re-employment outcomes (Andersson, 2017[62]). However, the policy discontinuity used to identify the effectiveness of these re-employment services allows estimating the impact only for very low-tenure workers; probably the sub-groups of displaced workers with the least need for this type of assistance.

[28] These typically include requirements that recipients meet regularly with a case worker, follow-up on job referrals from the employment office or participate in time-intensive active measures such as counselling or training, that are backed up by monitoring and the possibility of benefit sanctions – see Immervoll and Knotz (forthcoming[65]) for an overview of these requirements.

[29] The only general application of experience rating of employers' UI contributions within OECD countries comes from the United States. Nevertheless, other countries may levy specific taxes at the time of layoff to finance unemployment benefits or re-employment plans – e.g. Italy and, in the case of certain types of collective dismissals, Spain – see OECD (2013[2]). Moreover, a number of OECD countries have had considerable success in discouraging overuse of sickness benefits by requiring employers to pay some of the cost of sickness benefits (OECD, 2015[63]).

[30] One way to limit potential overuse of STW subsidies is to require employers to bear part of the cost of earnings supplements that are paid to workers while their hours of work are temporarily reduced, as is the case in both Germany and Japan.

[31] Research in the United States has shown that displaced workers receiving advanced notice spend less time unemployed than workers laid-off without advance warning – see e.g. Nord and Ting (1991[49]) and Swaim and Podgursky (1990[47]). This effect is likely to be greater when advance warning triggers early access to re-employment assistance, but evidence appears to be lacking about whether that is the case.

[32] In the case of mass layoffs, it is quite common for the PES to set-up a temporary office either at the work site or very close to it. In many cases, these temporary offices continue to function for some time after the workers are displaced and become unemployed, but workers remaining unemployed are eventually transferred to being served by the general PES system.

[33] Initiating training during the notice period often would be incompatible with the worker continuing to perform on the old job. It also makes sense to assess carefully which displaced workers require training given that this is an expensive measure that creates a substantial lock-in effect.

[34] It is possible that local labour market authorities tend to overvalue early intervention measures because these measures are most commonly used in the case of mass layoffs, when there is strong political pressure to be seen to be doing something for the workers losing their jobs.

[35] The challenge of scaling-up employment services is discussed in more detail in Section 4.3.

[36] Indeed, large Japanese employers make considerable efforts to avoid layoffs, including by arranging for staff who are no longer needed to transfer directly to another firm, often within the same business group (*keiretsu*). Industrial groups have also created a national network of Industrial Employment Stability Centres that facilitate inter-company transfers between firms that do not belong to the same business group.

[37] While the Job Security Councils in Sweden offer a very attractive model for managing layoffs, it is not a realistic choice for countries where collective bargaining coverage is low or employers and unions do not have a tradition of collaborating in the management of restructuring.

[38] Sixty days of notice is required for layoffs of 50 or more workers. However, noncompliance appears to be quite high and almost two-thirds of all displaced workers reported receiving no advance notice during 2000-14 (OECD, 2016[27]).

[39] For example, notice periods are significantly longer for white-collar workers than for blue-collar workers in Denmark, even though re-employment rates tend to be higher for more skilled workers.

[40] Employees in firms with 1 000 or more employees are entitled to outplacement leave (*congé de reclassement*) which provides both re-employment services and income support that is organised and financed by the firm and the details of which are specified in a PSE.

[41] The *Labour Mobility Subsidy* payments were only available to small and medium sized firms until 2014, when the programme was made more generous and extended to cover larger firms.

[42] As was noted above, some workers are not covered by a job security council and the intensity of the re-employment and retraining services varies considerably across the different councils, with white-collar workers in the private sector receiving significantly more intensive support than their blue-collar counterparts (OECD, 2015[26]).

[43] While there appears to be only anecdotal evidence on this point, a number of studies have found that displaced workers fare worse in regions with high unemployment. Local labour market conditions would matter less if workers displaced into a depressed local labour market responded by migrating to regions with more buoyant labour markets. While that happens to a limited degree, the geographic mobility of displaced workers is inhibited by many factors (e.g. the spouse's job, ties to the community and home ownership) and it appears to be quite low in practice.

[44] There does not appear to be any research examining whether displacement costs systematically rise with the number of workers who are displaced. However, Gibbons and Katz (1991[53]) found that US workers who were displaced when their employer closed or moved actually fared better – in the sense that they were re-employed more rapidly and experienced a smaller reduction in

earnings on the new job – than workers losing jobs as part of a partial reduction in staffing at their place of work.

[45] This situation has probably improved in recent years, as the national government has devoted increased attention to improving coordination across departments and with state and territorial governments in the management of mass layoffs.

[46] One weakness of the otherwise impressive performance of the Swedish system for providing re-employment services to displaced workers is that the PES has little knowledge of the gaps in the services offered by the Job Security Councils and, hence, is not as active as it should be in filling those gaps before workers have been out of work for an extended period of time (OECD, 2015[26]).

[47] Activation services are more difficult to deliver and tend to be less effective for displaced workers and other jobless persons of working age who do not qualify for unemployment or social-assistance benefits. This occurs because these income benefits provide the principal instrument for linking jobless people to employment services and active labour market programmes, while the risk of benefit sanctions and related warnings provide a strong incentive to effectively engage with service providers (Immervoll, 2012[51]). While most displaced workers not finding a new job before the end of their notice period are eligible for public income benefits, at least for some period of time, some exceptions occur and are discussed below.

[48] The spending data in Figure 4.7, suggests that some of the association that regression-based studies have documented between the aggregate level of ALMP spending and labour market outcomes – e.g. Bassanini and Duval (2006[59]); OECD (2017[10]) – might actually reflect the cross-country association between higher spending on ALMPs, on the one hand, and employer and union federations playing a larger role in the labour market on the other hand, including by effectively collaborating in the management of labour market restructuring. For example, Sweden's high spending on ALMPs might contribute less to its impressive re-employment statistics for displaced workers (cf. Section 4.1) than the effectiveness of its Job Security Councils (cf. Section 4.2).

[49] Since active labour market programmes (as well as UI benefit schemes) were invented, in large part, to support displaced workers, it may appear unlikely that existing activation systems would not offer services that correspond closely to the re-employment assistance needs of this group. However, the nine *Back to Work* reviews showed that many labour market stakeholders in these countries perceive that the PES is primarily focussed on improving the employment prospects of more disadvantaged groups, such as the long-term unemployed, sole parents and early school leavers.

[50] As was discussed above, the French PES has recently expanded targeted re-employment services for displaced workers who opt for intensive public re-employment services in exchange for surrendering some of their rights to contest their layoff and to receive employer-provided transition assistance. Opening a targeted re-employment track for displaced workers has made it possible to designate and train case workers who specialise in assisting this group. It has also facilitated the use of private labour market intermediaries which are able to provide customised placement services to different groups of displaced workers. For example, private placement firms with the relevant expertise and contacts have recently been engaged to run re-employment workshops for displaced managers and obtained good results (OECD, 2014[64]).

[51] It is occasionally possible for displaced workers to continue to reside in their own community while obtaining a new job in a different region. During the recent mining booms in Australia and Canada, acute labour shortages in remote and sometimes inhospitable mining areas led employers to organise "fly in, fly out" employment arrangements whereby workers who live elsewhere – including urban production workers displaced from manufacturing jobs – alternate periods of intense work at the mining site with periods living in their homes (OECD, 2016[28]).

[52] One notable exception is the United States, where a portion of the funding for ALMPs has been dedicated to "dislocated workers" since 1962. As a result, job seekers newly registering at the PES are classified according to whether they are displaced workers (OECD, 2016[27]). However, this classification exercise appears to be more a question of assigning costs to the correct budgetary category, rather than an integral part of assessing individual re-employment needs.

[53] While a tendency to target intensive ALMPs on workers with longer-standing disadvantages – rather than newly displaced workers who appear to face a difficult adjustment – appears to be widespread, this pattern is likely to be especially strong in Australia and New Zealand (OECD, 2016[28]; OECD, 2017[38]). Both countries structure income benefits for the unemployed and the associated activation regime on a social assistance model that serves families whose incomes fall below an adequacy threshold. Given this orientation, it is logical that intensive re-employment services are targeted at the benefit recipients thought most at-risk of long-term welfare dependency. At a result, relatively few displaced workers receive income benefits and, when they do receive benefits, they are often assigned to the lowest level of re-employment support, at least initially.

[54] The *Back to Work* reviews also identified a number of interesting initiatives targeting more intensive re-employment and retraining services to older long-tenure displaced workers, including the *Second Career* programme in Ontario (OECD, 2015[13]).

[55] Since unemployment benefits in Australia and New Zealand (the *New Start Allowance* in Australia and *Jobseeker Support* in New Zealand) is systematically means tested against all forms of income, many displaced workers have no access to these benefits (e.g. if they have a working spouse) or can only access these benefits after a long period of unemployment during which they deplete their savings. This design makes it particularly likely that many displaced workers never receive any public re-employment assistance or only begin receiving it after a long delay.

[56] In the United States, ALMP expenditures per displaced worker fell from around 1 500 USD in 2008 to around 500 USD in 2010 (OECD, 2016[27]).

[57] Funding for ALMPs automatically increases when the unemployment rate rises in Denmark and Switzerland, but most OECD governments rely upon discretionary policy measures to boost budgets for re-employment services during recessions. The discretionary fiscal stimulus packages that many governments enacted in 2009, in response to the global financial crisis, generally included expanded funding for re-employment services for the unemployed, as wells as measures to increase income support for this group (OECD, 2009[1]).

[58] One outcome of this experience was the development of a national inventory of mobile PES offices ("One-Stop Centers"), so as to make it easier in the future to organise interstate loans of these units.

[59] The Australian national government has recently announced a new initiative, the *Stronger Transitions Package*, that is designed to provide early support to workers in selected regions facing significant structural changes (Department of Jobs and Small Business, 2018[56]). The measure is due to start in July 2018 and will broaden the sectoral adjustment approach previously used by expanding the focus to workers in hard-hit regions.

[60] Developing new sources of comparative advantage in localities that are hard-hit by import competition or economic change more generally is an important policy goal. However, it tends to operate on too long of a time horizon to be of much help to most of the workers losing their jobs in declining sectors.

[61] Political economy concerns to build and sustain popular support for trade liberalisation appear to have played an important role in the creation of TAA, EGF and the structural adjustment programmes in Australia.

[62] The problems discussed in this paragraph appear to be much less severe, or possibly even absent, when tailored services are offered for displaced workers within the general ALMPs operated by the PES, even when those services extend beyond early intervention measures. As was discussed above, the career security contracts (CSP) in France and the dislocated worker funding track within the main ALMPs in the United States are notable examples of this approach.

[63] As was discussed above, the primary purpose of short-time working schemes is to preserve viable jobs and thus avoid permanent layoffs that do not enhance allocative efficiency. However, even in a well-designed STW scheme some of the workers receiving benefits ultimately will be displaced when it becomes clear their job is not viable in the long run.

[64] Over 58 000 WEPP claimants received compensation payments between July 2008 and March 2013, but difficulties and delays have arisen when firms close without a formal declaration of bankruptcy (so-called "walk away firms").

[65] See Chapter 5 for a comparison of maximum unemployment benefit durations in OECD countries.

[66] See Chapter 5 for an analysis of recent trends in benefit coverage which shows that coverage rates tend to be higher for displaced workers than for other unemployed persons.

[67] Almost one in five displaced workers in Denmark who are still unemployed one year later have no access to income support.

[68] Statistics on the joint distribution of these two sources of income support are very rare, but the characteristics of displaced workers receiving large severance awards accords quite closely with the profiles that imply the greatest UI entitlements (high earners with long tenure).

[69] President Obama proposed a national wage insurance scheme in his final State of the Union speech in January 2016. His proposal was essentially to expand the small wage insurance programme that has existed for older trade displaced workers since 2002 (renamed as *Reemployment Trade Adjustment Assistance* or RTAA in 2009) to cover most of the adult workforce.

References

Albrecht, J. and S. Vroman (1999), "Unemployment Compensation Finance and Efficiency Wages", *Journal of Labor Economics*, Vol. 17/1, pp. 141-167, http://dx.doi.org/10.1086/209916. [18]

Andersson, J. (2017), *Insurances against job loss and disability: Private and public interventions and their effects on job search and labor supply*, Uppsala University, http://www.nek.uu.se/digitalAssets/244/c_244210-l_3-k_josefine-andersson.pdf (accessed on 26 April 2018). [62]

Andrews, D. and A. Saia (2017), "Coping with creative destruction: Reducing the costs of firm exit", *OECD Economics Department Working Papers*, No. 1353, OECD Publishing, Paris, http://dx.doi.org/10.1787/bbb44644-en. [8]

APEC (2013), *Building Natural Disaster Response Capacity Sound Workforce Strategies for Recovery and Reconstruct*, https://www.apec.org/Publications/2014/02/Building-Natural-Disaster-Response-Capacity--Sound-Workforce-Strategies-for-Recovery-and-Reconstruct (accessed on 21 February 2018). [36]

Arni, P. (2012), *Conseil et coaching intensifs pour demandeurs d'emploi âgés : une voie pour améliorer leurs chances sur le marché du travail ?*, Université de Lausanne, Lausanne, https://works.bepress.com/patrick_arni/3/. [15]

Arni, P., R. Lalive and J. Van Ours (2013), "How effective are unemployment benefit sanctions? Looking beyond unemployment exit", *Journal of Applied Econometrics*, Vol. 28/7, pp. 1153-1178, http://dx.doi.org/10.1002/jae.2289. [61]

Autor, D., D. Dorn and G. Hanson (2016), "The China Shock: Learning from Labor-Market Adjustment to Large Changes in Trade", *Annual Review of Economics*, Vol. 8, pp. 205-240, http://dx.doi.org/10.1146/annurev-economics-080315-015041. [3]

Barnow, B. and J. Smith (2015), "Employment and Training Programs", in Robert Moffitt (ed.), *Economics of Means-Tested Transfer Programs in the United States, Volume 2*, National Bureau of Economic Research, Inc, https://econpapers.repec.org/bookchap/nbrnberch/13490.htm (accessed on 19 February 2018). [60]

Bassanini, A. and E. Caroli (2015), "Is Work Bad for Health? The Role of Constraint versus Choice", *Annals of Economics and Statistics* 119/120, pp. 13-37, http://dx.doi.org/10.15609/annaeconstat2009.119-120.13. [9]

Bassanini, A. and R. Duval (2006), "Employment Patterns in OECD Countries: Reassessing the Role of Policies and Institutions", *OECD Social, Employment and Migration Working Papers*, No. 35, OECD Publishing, Paris, http://dx.doi.org/10.1787/702031136412. [59]

Blanchard, O. and J. Tirole (2008), "The Joint Design of Unemployment Insurance and Employment Protection: A First Pass", *Journal of the European Economic Association*, Vol. 6/1, pp. 45-77, http://dx.doi.org/10.1162/JEEA.2008.6.1.45. [17]

Bloom, H. et al. (2001), "Testing a Financial Incentive to Promote Re-employment among Displaced Workers: The Canadian Earnings Supplement Project (ESP)", *Journal of Policy Analysis and Management*, Vol. 20/3, pp. 505-523, http://dx.doi.org/10.1002/pam.1005. [45]

BLS (2016), *Displaced Workers Summary*, Economic News Release, Bureau of Labor Statistics, Washington, D.C., https://www.bls.gov/news.release/disp.nr0.htm. [7]

Boeri, T. and H. Bruecker (2011), "Short-time work benefits revisited: some lessons from the Great Recession", *Economic Policy*, 10.1111/j.1468-0327.2011.271.x, pp. 697-765, http://dx.doi.org/10.1111/j.1468-0327.2011.271.x. [21]

Cahuc, P. and F. Malherbet (2004), "Unemployment compensation finance and labor market rigidity", *Journal of Public Economics*, Vol. 88/3-4, pp. 481-501, http://dx.doi.org/10.1016/S0047-2727(03)00018-5. [19]

Cahuc, P. and S. Nevoux (2017), "Inefficient Short-Time Work", *IZA Discussion Papers*, No. 11010, IZA, http://dx.doi.org/www.iza.org. [20]

Card, D., J. Kluve and A. Weber (2015), "What Works? A Meta Analysis of Recent Active Labor Market Program Evaluations", *IZA Discussion Papers*, No. 9236, IZA, http://ftp.iza.org/dp9236.pdf (accessed on 19 February 2018), http://ftp.iza.org/dp9236.pdf. [11]

DARES analyses (2017), *Le contrat de sécurisation professionnelle favorise-t-il la reprise d'emploi des licenciés économiques qui y adhèrent ?*, DARES, http://dares.travail-emploi.gouv.fr/IMG/pdf/2017-020.pdf. [14]

Davis, S. and T. von Wachter (2011), "Recessions and the Costs of Job Loss", *Brookings Papers on Economic Activity*, Vol. Fall, https://www.brookings.edu/wp-content/uploads/2011/09/2011b_bpea_davis.pdf (accessed on 19 February 2018), pp. 1-72. [58]

Deelen, A., M. de Graaf-Zijl and W. van den Berge (2018), "Labour market effects of job displacement for prime-age and older workers", *IZA Journal of Labor Economics*, Vol. 7/3, http://dx.doi.org/10.1186/s40172-018-0063-x. [57]

Department of Jobs and Small Business (2018), *Stronger Transitions*, https://www.jobs.gov.au/stronger-transitions (accessed on 28 April 2018). [56]

Diedrich, A. and O. Bergström (2006), "The Job Security Councils in Sweden", http://imit.se/wp-content/uploads/2016/02/2007_145.pdf. [24]

Duell, N. et al. (2010), "Activation Policies in Switzerland", *OECD Social, Employment and Migration Working Papers*, No. 112, OECD Publishing, Paris, http://dx.doi.org/10.1787/5km4hd7r28f6-en. [31]

European Commission (2010), *27 National Seminars on anticipating and managing restructuring*, EU Synthesis Report, http://www.employment-studies.co.uk/resource/27-national-seminars-anticipating-and-managing-restructuring-arenas. [25]

Farber, H. (2017), "Employment, Hours, and Earnings Consequences of Job Loss: US Evidence from the Displaced Workers Survey", *Journal of Labor Economics*, doi: 10.1086/692353, pp. S235-S272, http://dx.doi.org/10.1086/692353. [55]

Farber, H. (2004), "Job loss in the United States, 1981–2001", http://dx.doi.org/10.1016/S0147-9121(04)23003-5. [54]

Filges, T. and A. Hansen (2017), "The threat effect of active labor market programs: a systematic review", *Journal of Economic Surveys*, Vol. 31/1, pp. 58-78, http://dx.doi.org/10.1111/joes.12134. [16]

Fujii, M. and R. Kambayashi (2014), "Long-term effects of job displacement in Japan: A conservative estimate using the Japanese Longitudinal Survey on Employment and Fertility (LOSEF)", *Hermes-IR Technical Report*, No. 2014-10, Hitotsubashi University, https://hermes-ir.lib.hit-u.ac.jp/rs/bitstream/10086/26917/1/DP634.pdf. [5]

Gibbons, R. and L. Katz (1991), "Layoffs and Lemons", *Journal of Labor Economics*, Vol. 9/4, http://www.jstor.org/stable/2535075, pp. 351-380. [53]

Goldstein, A. (2017), *Janesville : an american story.*, Simon & Schuster, New York, NY, http://www.simonandschuster.com/books/Janesville/Amy-Goldstein/9781501102264 (accessed on 15 January 2018). [52]

Immervoll, H. (2012), "Reforming the Benefit System to 'Make Work Pay': Options and Priorities in a Weak Labour Market", *IZA Policy Papers*, No. 50, IZA, Bonn. [51]

Immervoll, H. and C. Knotz (forthcoming), "How demanding are activation requirements for jobseekers? New evidence on activity-related eligibility criteria for unemployment and social assistance benefits", *OECD Social, Employment and Migration Working Papers*, OECD Publishing, Paris. [65]

Immervoll, H. and S. Scarpetta (2012), "Activation and employment support policies in OECD countries. An overview of current approaches", *IZA Journal of Labor Policy*, Vol. 1/1, p. 9, http://dx.doi.org/10.1186/2193-9004-1-9. [30]

Kluve, J. (2010), "The effectiveness of European active labor market programs", *Labour Economics*, Vol. 17/6, pp. 904-918, http://dx.doi.org/10.1016/J.LABECO.2010.02.004. [12]

Mosley, H. (2010), *Reform of placement services - Perr Review on 'Systemic preventive integration approach (Support) for jobseekers and unemployed*, EC Mutual Learning Programme, http://ec.europa.eu/social/BlobServlet?docId=10712&langId=en. [32]

Nafilyan, V. (2016), "Lost and found?: The cost of job loss in France", *OECD Social, Employment and Migration Working Papers*, No. 194, OECD Publishing, Paris, http://dx.doi.org/10.1787/5jlsk8tzll42-en. [50]

Nekoei, A. and A. Weber (2017), "Does extending unemployment benefits improve job quality?", *American Economic Review*, http://dx.doi.org/10.1257/aer.20150528. [41]

Nord, S. and Y. Ting (1991), "The impact of advance notice of plant closings on earnings and the probability of unemployment", *Industrial and Labor Relations Review*, Vol. 44/4, pp. 681-691. [49]

OECD (2017), *Back to Work: New Zealand: Improving the Re-employment Prospects of Displaced Workers*, Back to Work, OECD Publishing, Paris, http://dx.doi.org/10.1787/9789264264434-en. [38]

OECD (2017), *OECD Employment Outlook 2017*, OECD Publishing, Paris, http://dx.doi.org/10.1787/empl_outlook-2017-en. [10]

OECD (2016), *Back to Work: Australia: Improving the Re-employment Prospects of Displaced Workers*, Back to Work, OECD Publishing, Paris, http://dx.doi.org/10.1787/9789264253476-en. [28]

OECD (2016), *Back to Work: Denmark: Improving the Re-employment Prospects of Displaced Workers*, Back to Work, OECD Publishing, Paris, http://dx.doi.org/10.1787/9789264267503-en. [43]

OECD (2016), *Back to Work: Finland: Improving the Re-employment Prospects of Displaced Workers*, Back to Work, OECD Publishing, Paris, http://dx.doi.org/10.1787/9789264264717-en. [22]

OECD (2016), *Back to Work: United States: Improving the Re-employment Prospects of Displaced Workers*, Back to Work, OECD Publishing, Paris, http://dx.doi.org/10.1787/9789264266513-en. [27]

OECD (2015), *Back to Work: Canada: Improving the Re-employment Prospects of Displaced Workers*, Back to Work, OECD Publishing, Paris, http://dx.doi.org/10.1787/9789264233454-en. [13]

OECD (2015), *Back to Work: Japan: Improving the Re-employment Prospects of Displaced Workers*, Back to Work, OECD Publishing, Paris, http://dx.doi.org/10.1787/9789264227200-en. [23]

OECD (2015), *Back to Work: Sweden: Improving the Re-employment Prospects of Displaced Workers*, Back to Work, OECD Publishing, Paris, http://dx.doi.org/10.1787/9789264246812-en. [26]

OECD (2015), *Fit Mind, Fit Job: From Evidence to Practice in Mental Health and Work*, Mental Health and Work, OECD Publishing, Paris, http://dx.doi.org/10.1787/9789264228283-en. [63]

OECD (2015), *OECD Employment Outlook 2015*, OECD Publishing, Paris, http://dx.doi.org/10.1787/empl_outlook-2015-en. [29]

OECD (2014), *Ageing and Employment Policies: France 2014: Working Better with Age*, Ageing and Employment Policies, OECD Publishing, Paris, http://dx.doi.org/10.1787/9789264207523-en. [64]

OECD (2013), *Back to Work: Re-employment, Earnings and Skill Use after Job Displacement*, OECD, Paris, http://www.oecd.org/employment/emp/Backtowork-report.pdf. [4]

OECD (2013), *Korea: Improving the Re-employment Prospects of Displaced Workers*, Back to Work, OECD Publishing, Paris, http://dx.doi.org/10.1787/9789264189225-en. [42]

OECD (2013), *OECD Employment Outlook 2013*, OECD Publishing, Paris, http://dx.doi.org/10.1787/empl_outlook-2013-en. [2]

OECD (2012), *OECD Employment Outlook 2012*, OECD Publishing, Paris, http://dx.doi.org/10.1787/empl_outlook-2012-en. [34]

OECD (2010), *OECD Employment Outlook 2010: Moving beyond the Jobs Crisis*, OECD Publishing, Paris, http://dx.doi.org/10.1787/empl_outlook-2010-en. [33]

OECD (2009), *OECD Employment Outlook 2009: Tackling the Jobs Crisis*, OECD Publishing, Paris, http://dx.doi.org/10.1787/empl_outlook-2009-en. [1]

OECD (2005), *OECD Employment Outlook 2005*, OECD Publishing, Paris, http://dx.doi.org/10.1787/empl_outlook-2005-en. [6]

Parsons, D. (forthcoming), "The simple analytics of job displacement insurance", *Journal of Risk and Insurance*, http://dx.doi.org/10.1111/jori.12216. [44]

Reserve Bank of New Zealand (2016), *The Canterbury rebuild five years on from the Christchurch earthquake*, Bulletin, Wellington, http://www.rbnz.govt.nz/email-updates. [37]

Schmieder, J., T. von Wachter and S. Bender (2016), "The Effect of Unemployment Benefits and Nonemployment Durations on Wages", *American Economic Review*, Vol. 106/3, pp. 739-777, http://dx.doi.org/10.1257/aer.20141566. [40]

SSI Task Force (2017), *SSI Task Force Legacy Report*, http://www.redcar-cleveland.gov.uk/taskforce.nsf/c7ec965d5c9e6c0b80257f930030066e/$File/SSI%20Task%20Force%20Legacy%20Report%20Two%20Years.pdf (accessed on 28 April 2018). [48]

Swaim, P. and M. Podgursky (1990), "Advance Notice and Job Search: The Value of an Early Start", *The Journal of Human Resources*, Vol. 25/2, pp. 147-178, http://dx.doi.org/10.2307/145752. [47]

Tatsiramos, K. and J. van Ours (2014), "Labor Market Effects of Unemployment Insurance Design", *Journal of Economic Surveys*, Vol. 28/2, pp. 284-311, http://dx.doi.org/10.1111/joes.12005. [39]

Venn, D. (2012), "Helping Displaced Workers Back Into Jobs After a Natural Disaster: Recent Experiences in OECD Countries", *OECD Social, Employment and Migration Working Papers*, No. 142, OECD Publishing, Paris, http://dx.doi.org/10.1787/5k8zk8pn2542-en. [35]

Wandner, S. (2016), "Wage Insurance as a Policy Option in the United States", *Upjohn Institute Working Papers*, No. 16-250, Upjohn Institute for Employment Research, Kalamazoo, MI, http://dx.doi.org/10.17848/wp16-250. [46]

Chapter 5. Unemployment-benefit coverage: Recent trends and their drivers

This chapter discusses the scope of unemployment-benefit systems, documents recent trends in the number of benefit recipients, and presents alternative measures of benefit coverage in comparative perspective. A decomposition analysis for selected countries seeks to identify key driving forces behind observed coverage trends, including labour-market and demographic changes, as well as benefit policy reforms. In most countries, only a minority of jobseekers receive unemployment benefits and while benefit receipt has increased substantially during the early post-crisis period, this has failed to arrest the longer-term trend towards falling benefit coverage documented in earlier studies. Although composition effects account for a significant share of the recent decline of benefit coverage, some of it is a result of policy reforms that have reduced unemployment-benefit generosity either in search of budgetary savings or in an effort to articulate job-search incentives for the unemployed.

The statistical data for Israel are supplied by and under the responsibility of the relevant Israeli authorities. The use of such data by the OECD is without prejudice to the status of the Golan Heights, East Jerusalem and Israeli settlements in the West Bank under the terms of international law.

Key findings

Among the range of income-support measures that countries operate, unemployment benefits have a central role in stabilising the incomes of jobseekers and in facilitating access to associated employment-support programmes. Low or declining benefit coverage among jobseekers has been one of the drivers of the long-term rise in income inequality. In addition, with the expansion of new forms of employment and potential risks of higher job displacement through automation or digitalisation there are growing concerns that demand for out-of-work support will increase but that existing benefit systems may not be able to provide effective support for all those in need.

This chapter presents different measures of the effective reach of unemployment benefits and documents how benefit coverage has evolved since before the start of the financial and economic crisis. It then employs a decomposition analysis to identify key driving forces behind the observed coverage trends for selected countries.

The main findings are:

- While unemployment benefits potentially affect job-seeking behaviours or participation, it is commonly assumed that jobseekers have ready access to such transfers. However, results in this chapter show that, in most countries, only a minority of jobseekers receive unemployment benefits, fewer than one-in-three on average across countries.

- The scope of unemployment benefit systems differs widely across OECD countries. Reflecting different national policy objectives or constraints, unemployment benefits are received by different labour-market groups, including unemployed people who are actively looking for work, but also groups who do not report active job search or have some employment.

- While benefit receipt has increased substantially during the early post-crisis period, this has failed to arrest a longer-term trend of falling benefit coverage documented in earlier studies. Coverage rates are now slightly below pre-crisis levels, on average.

- A decomposition analysis of benefit coverage trends for selected countries shows that the changing composition of the jobseeker population during the early crisis years was a major driver of increasing coverage levels. In particular, soaring job losses led to a large inflow of unemployed with sufficiently long employment histories to qualify for benefits. Policy initiatives to make benefits accessible to a larger group of jobseekers also extended coverage during this period in some countries.

- However, some or most of these increases were subsequently reversed during the post-recession years. Factors that widened the coverage gap in recent years include the growth of long-term unemployment, migration inflows, and the rising numbers of jobseekers entering the labour force without previous work experience as labour markets tightened during the recovery.

- Policy reforms also contributed to widening coverage gaps as a number of governments tightened entitlement conditions or reduced benefit durations. In some countries, measures to tackle high or growing numbers of youth who are not in employment, education or training (NEET), accelerated school-to-work transitions. While this ultimately strengthens labour-market participation, it also increased the number of jobseekers without work experience or benefit entitlements.

Introduction

Income support for jobseekers is a central pillar of social protection and labour market policies. Medium-term social and economic trends, as well as more recent labour market developments, have reinforced interest in the reach and accessibility of unemployment benefits and of related out-of-work transfers. This chapter presents evidence on recent trends in unemployment-benefit coverage, and illustrates their driving factors for selected countries. It focuses on *observed* coverage, i.e. support that is actually received by jobseekers. This is different from concepts of *implicit* coverage, such as the share of workers who have built up rights to unemployment insurance, but who may or may not claim or qualify for benefits upon unemployment.

In a rights-and-responsibilities framework, unemployment benefits have a key role in targeting employment-support and activation measures. Declining benefit coverage can erode the effective reach of job-search assistance, training and other social and employment re-integration measures. Out-of-work benefits also serve as a major instrument for countering growing income inequality. For instance, trends towards increasing inequality between the 1990s and mid-2000s have been linked to declining shares of jobseekers receiving benefits (OECD, 2011[1]). Other types of cash support may be available to those not receiving unemployment benefits. But transfers such as last-resort social assistance, disability or early-retirement benefits are less focussed on re-employment and may facilitate temporary or permanent labour-force withdrawal.

Widespread reductions in unemployment-benefit coverage prior to the global financial and economic crisis were documented in earlier OECD work (Immervoll and Richardson, 2011[2]). Since then, concerns about non-coverage have intensified, as demand for out-of-work support escalated during and after the Great Recession (OECD, 2014[3]). More recently, maintaining effective support has been a focus in the Future of Work debate as less predictable career patterns, new forms of employment and a greater risk of job displacement through automation create challenges for traditional forms of social protection (OECD, 2017[4]; forthcoming[5]). One key question in this context is whether the shortening of job tenures that is observed for some countries and groups (OECD, forthcoming[6]), or may be expected for future years, would further erode the accessibility of income support during out-of-work spells.

Aggregate trends in benefit receipt may signal a need for policy responses in order to maintain coverage at desired levels. However, the particular policy levers that are suitable for maintaining effective support for jobseekers cannot be discerned through inspection of headline beneficiary headcounts alone. For instance, the huge inflow of new jobseekers in the aftermath of the Great Recession, the subsequent rise in long-term unemployment, and ongoing demographic changes due to population ageing, have led to sizeable shifts in the composition of jobseeker populations. In turn, these *composition effects* typically produce changes in observed coverage, independently of any policy changes. In addition, the post-crisis period has seen a high density of *policy reforms*, including determined measures to extend or restrict access to benefits at different points (OECD, 2014[3]).

Because of major concurrent trends during the post-crisis period, identifying the drivers of changing benefit accessibility is challenging, but also important. Each of the drivers will generally have different sets of policy implications, and understanding them is a necessary input into policy discussions of how to keep social protection effective and accessible. For instance, governments' policy responses during the post-crisis period, together with successive waves of large flows into and out of unemployment, may have easily swamped other concurrent trends that are of policy interest, such as difficult access to unemployment protection among a rising number of workers engaged in platform work and other new or emerging forms of employment.

Section 5.1, first presents recent changes in the aggregate number of unemployment-benefit recipients drawing on OECD SOCR – the Social Benefit Recipients Database. It then examines benefit coverage among the unemployed in more detail and shows the evolution of benefit receipt patterns for different labour-market groups. Section 5.2 explores different drivers of the observed trends using an empirical approach for separating the role of composition and policy effects. The approach is illustrated using micro-data for six countries: Australia, Denmark, Poland, Spain, Sweden and the United States.

5.1. Access to unemployment benefits: Recent trends

5.1.1. Number of benefit recipients

In most OECD countries, the number of unemployment-benefit recipients rose steeply after 2008 as job losses mounted and unemployment reached historic highs (Figure 5.1). The strong rise also reflects a large inflow of benefit claimants who were at the beginning of their unemployment spell and had sufficiently long employment histories to be entitled to benefits. However, benefit receipt subsequently declined relatively quickly, while unemployment remained high, long-term unemployment increased and many unemployed exhausted their rights to benefits. For the 2007-14 period as a whole, unemployment rose more strongly than the number of benefit recipients, suggesting a decline in coverage.[1] This trend was more marked in the European Union (EU) (Panel B of Figure 5.1) than in the OECD area (Panel A).

Before the crisis, about 2.5% of the working-age population received unemployment benefits on average across OECD countries, rising to 3.5% by 2014 (Figure 5.2). By then recipient numbers varied from less than 1% of working-age individuals in Hungary, Japan, Poland, Slovak Republic, and Turkey, to more than 10% in Ireland and Finland. Changes in recipient totals have been very large over this period and the comparison between two years hides much greater swings in several countries. For instance, benefit receipt in the United States soared by 250% between 2007 and 2009, before a gradual decline between 2010 and 2014 brought totals back to their pre-crisis level. Full country details are available in the SOCR Database.[2]

5.1.2. Benefit coverage among jobseekers

Metrics of benefit coverage relate recipient numbers to a certain population of interest. Different measures are useful for different purposes and each has specific interpretations and data requirements. The simple ratio of total benefit recipients and unemployed – based on the definition of the International Labour Organization (ILO) – is commonly referred to as "pseudo-coverage rate". Depending on the intended scope of unemployment benefits and the benefit entitlement rules that are in force, not all unemployed qualify for unemployment benefits, while some individuals who are not unemployed – e.g. because they are not actively looking for work or are working a few hours per week – may receive them. Pseudo-coverage can therefore vary from very low rates to more than 100% (see Box 5.1).

Figure 5.1. Benefit receipt rose quickly at the onset of the crisis, then dropped while unemployment remained high

Unemployment benefit recipients and unemployed, headcounts 2007=100

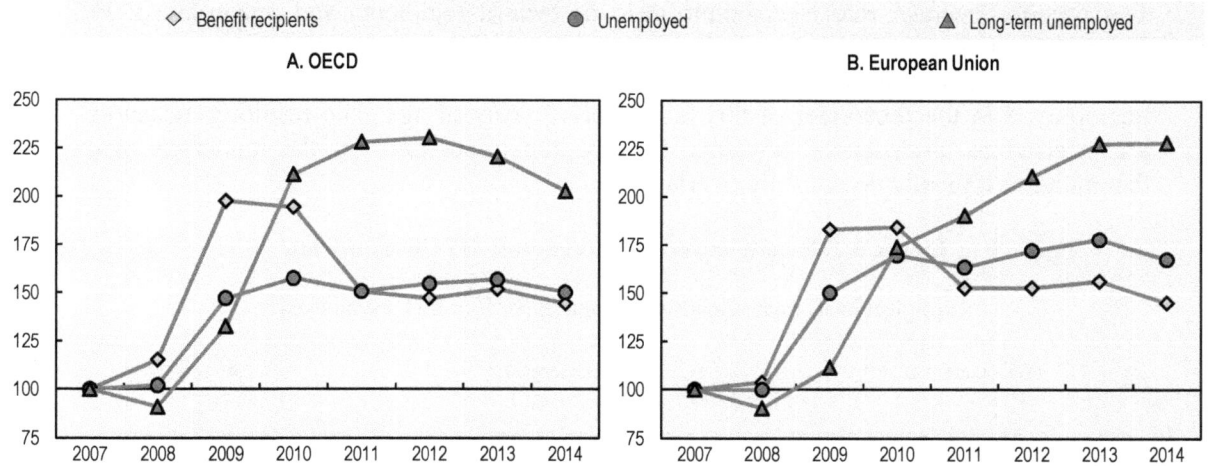

Note: Unweighted country averages. Data for Greece are missing. There is currently no unemployment benefit in Mexico. Unemployed are individuals who are not working, have actively looked for work in the previous four weeks and are available to start work within the next fortnight.
Source: OECD *Social Benefit Recipients Database (SOCR)* (www.oecd.org/social/recipients.htm) and *OECD Labour Force Statistics* (http://dx.doi.org/10.1787/lfs-data-en).

StatLink ⫘ http://dx.doi.org/10.1787/888933778421

Figure 5.2. Unemployment-benefit receipt rose following the financial and economic crisis

Recipient totals from administrative sources, in % of working-age population (ages 16-64)

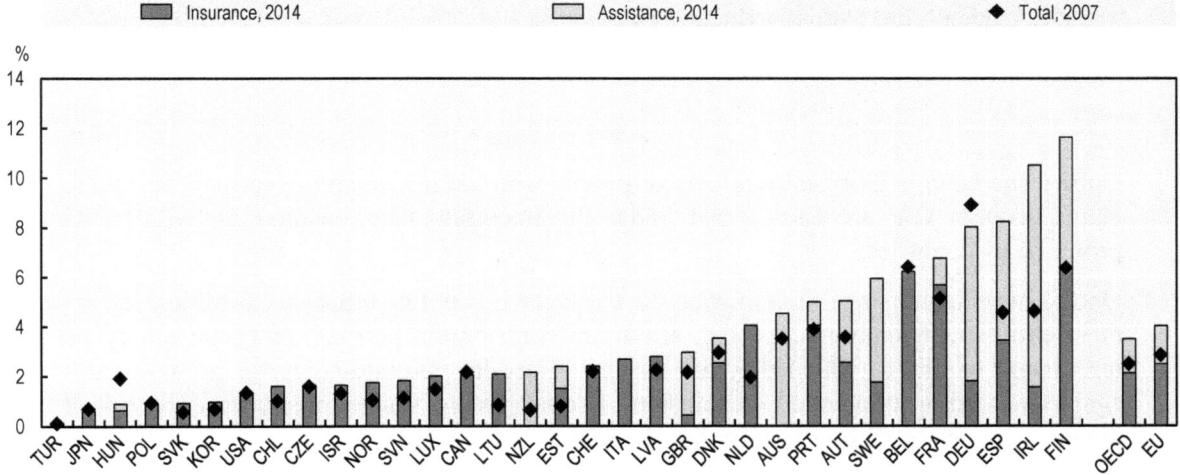

Note: Includes unemployment insurance and assistance benefits. Benefit recipients data for Greece are missing and there is currently no unemployment benefit in Mexico. 2007 data for Italy and Sweden are omitted for comparability reasons. In some countries, additional forms of income support may be available to some unemployed (e.g. for participants in certain labour-market programmes).
Source: OECD *Social Benefit Recipients Database (SOCR)* (www.oecd.org/social/recipients.htm).

StatLink ⫘ http://dx.doi.org/10.1787/888933778440

Box 5.1. Pseudo-coverage rates derived from benefit recipient totals: Construction and interpretation

The pseudo-coverage rate is a simple ratio of benefit recipients and unemployed. In Figure 5.3, the numerator is the number of beneficiaries of unemployment insurance and assistance benefits. The denominator is the number of ILO unemployed, referred to as unemployed in the remainder of this box, over 15 years of age. The resulting measures are referred to as "pseudo" coverage because the populations in the numerator and denominator typically do not fully overlap.

Figure 5.3. Pseudo-coverage rates across OECD countries

Recipient totals from administrative sources, in % of ILO unemployed

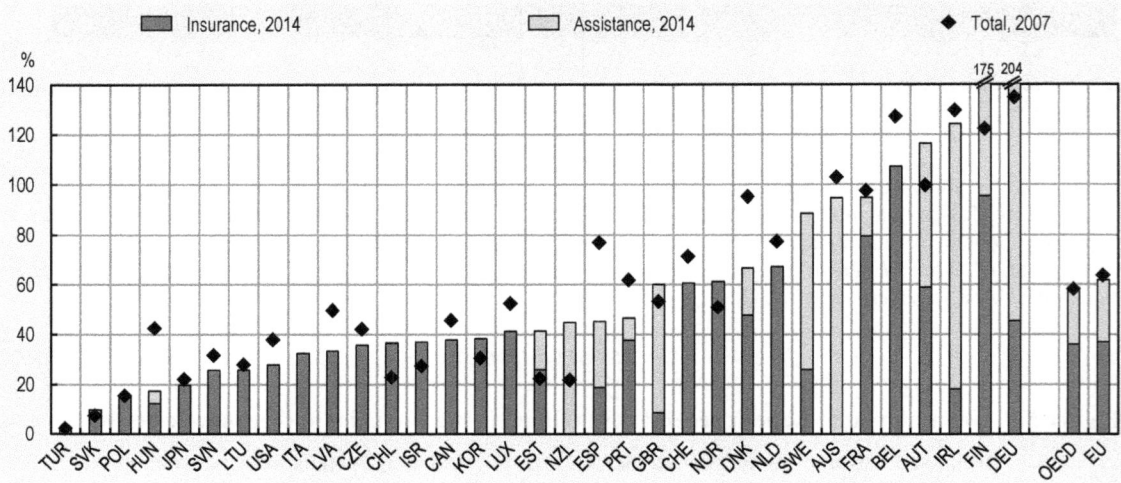

Note: See Figure 5.2. ILO: International Labour Organization.
Source: *OECD Social Benefit Recipients Database (SOCR)* (www.oecd.org/social/recipients.htm) and *OECD Employment and Labour Market Statistics* (http://dx.doi.org/10.1787/lfs-data-en).

StatLink ⟶ http://dx.doi.org/10.1787/888933778459

On the one hand, significant numbers of people who are not unemployed may be able to claim benefits that are categorised under the unemployment heading in SOCR data provided by countries.

On the other hand, some unemployed do not receive benefits, either because they do not meet entitlement requirements (e.g. minimum contribution periods) or because they do not claim benefits to which they are entitled. Very low pseudo-coverage rates signal – again intended or unintended – exclusion of some groups of unemployed from receipt of income support through unemployment benefits.

The above figure shows that pseudo-coverage in four out of five countries was below 70% in 2014 and below 20% in Turkey, Slovak Republic, Poland and Hungary. Rates above 100% in Belgium, Austria, Ireland, Finland and Germany indicate that significant shares of benefit payments go to individuals other than active jobseekers, which may be intended or unintended. On average, pseudo-coverage rates fell from 59% to 57% between 2007 and 2014. But changes were very different across countries:

Significant increases in Austria, Chile, Estonia, Finland, Germany, Israel, Korea, New Zealand and Norway contrast with marked drops in Australia, Denmark, Belgium, Canada, Hungary, Latvia, Luxembourg, the Netherlands, Portugal, Spain, Switzerland, and the United States.

Key reasons for differences in scope between the numerator and denominator in the pseudo-coverage rates include the following:

1. Benefits awarded to groups who are not unemployed according to the ILO definition. Examples of these situations are:

   o Individuals who are not actively looking for work. Recipients may be registered as jobseekers but may still not report active job search in the Labour Force Surveys if job-search and other eligibility conditions are not very demanding or are not strictly enforced (Immervoll and Knotz, forthcoming[7]).

   o Individuals close to retirement age. In some countries, job search requirements are less strict if the beneficiary is approaching retirement age. For instance, in Belgium, unemployment insurance (UI) duration is unlimited and receipt is common among older unemployed. Some categories of older unemployed are exempted from active job-search obligations.

   o Some recipients may not even be registered as jobseekers. Available recipient headcounts for some countries include sizeable groups of labour-market inactive individuals, e.g. because they are unable to work. For instance, in Germany, about 6 million people lived in households who received unemployment assistance (UA; *Arbeitslosengeld* II) in December 2016; of those, 1.6 million were not able to work and only 1.7 million unemployed (Bundesagentur für Arbeit, 2017[8]). For many UA recipients, the benefits they receive are, strictly speaking, not an unemployment benefit.

   o Individuals in work. In several countries, it is possible to combine earnings from work with unemployment benefits under certain conditions (e.g. subject to working hours or earnings). For example, in France, about 700 000 recipients of the UI benefit were in work during the second quarter 2015.

2. Different reporting units: In Germany, UA recipient stocks are reported in number of families rather than individuals. As a result, where two or more unemployed live in the same family, only one payment will be counted in the numerator.

3. Measurement period: Both recipient stocks and unemployed headcounts are in principle expressed as averages over a 12-month period. If the numerator or the denominator changes significantly during the year, annual pseudo-coverage rates can differ from instantaneous ones.

4. Double counting of different types of benefits can also push up pseudo-coverage rates in some cases. In a few countries, concurrent receipt of UI and UA is possible (e.g. the United Kingdom and Ireland), resulting in some degree of double counting when summing up recipients of the different benefit programmes.

Pseudo-coverage rates are informative as broad indicators of the scope of unemployment benefits. But they do not show the coverage for specific policy-relevant groups in the labour market, such as the unemployed, and changes over time can be difficult to interpret. A more concise coverage measure can be derived using microdata, such as labour force surveys. While benefit-receipt information is less precise in these surveys than in the administrative SOCR data, it is possible to break down unemployment-benefit recipient totals by employment status.

Although most benefits indeed go to individuals who are unemployed according to the ILO definition (henceforth "unemployed"), other groups also qualify for benefits under certain conditions (Figure 5.4). Among the countries included in Figure 5.4, individuals working and receiving unemployment benefits are relatively numerous in Australia, Austria, Belgium, Denmark, Finland, France, and Latvia. Significant numbers of "working" benefit recipients may simply be due to differences between national definitions of unemployment, which may allow for a few hours of work per week, and the ILO definition, which does not.[3] Allowing individuals to combine benefits with some work, perhaps for a limited period of time, may also reflect a policy objective to strengthen work incentives for some jobseeker groups.

In addition, significant shares of benefit recipients do not report active job search ("discouraged" and "other inactive" in Figure 5.4). This group is relatively sizeable in countries with higher benefit caseloads (Australia, Austria, Belgium, Finland, France and Spain). But it also accounts for large proportions of benefit recipients in some countries where benefits are received by small or very small shares of the working-age population (Hungary, Italy, Luxembourg and Slovenia). "Discouraged" jobseekers are those who are available for work, but have temporarily stopped looking, e.g. due to poor job-finding prospects, because participation in active labour market programmes (ALMPs) leaves little time for active job search or formally exempt participants from job-search requirements, or because some groups of benefit recipients (e.g. lone parents or older unemployed) are explicitly or implicitly exempt from some job-search obligations. Depending on national provisions, it can, however, also include some recipients who have already found work but are waiting to start the new job in the medium term.[4]

Finally, countries may operate exemptions from requirements to be immediately available for work, or their enforcement may be partial. As a result, some individuals who are neither available for work nor actively looking for it ("other inactive" in Figure 5.4) may receive benefits. As part of longer-term activation strategies, some of these recipients may have been intentionally moved onto unemployment benefits from other programmes that do not require availability for work (such as disability or lone-parent benefits).

Figure 5.5 reports coverage rates using individual-level Labour Force Surveys (LFS) data for some of these groups.[5] Results are shown both for a narrow definition of unemployed (Panel A) and for a broader definition that comprises both the "unemployed" and "discouraged" (Panel B). Since the number of "discouraged" recipients is substantial in a number of countries, the remainder of this chapter presents results for this extended group of unemployed, and refers to them as "jobseekers".

Figure 5.4. Different labour-market groups receive unemployment benefits

Recipients in % of the working-age population (ages 16-64), 2016

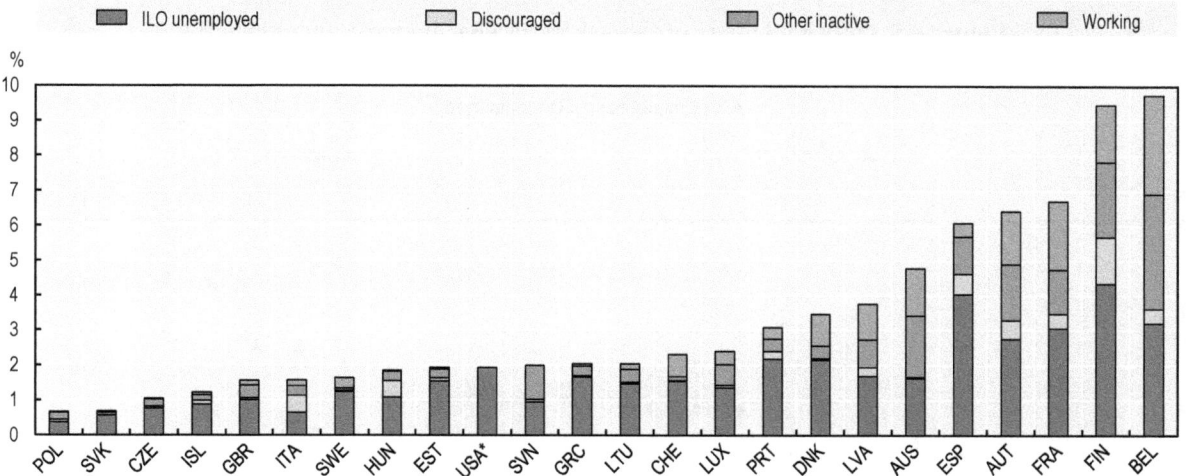

Note: Some European countries are excluded due to missing information in EU-LFS data. 2015 figures for Australia. LFS data for Sweden do not include a series of benefits that are accessible to jobless individuals who: i) are not in receipt of core unemployment benefits; and who ii) satisfy other conditions such as active participation in employment-support measures. *ILO unemployed* are out-of-work individuals who want a job, have actively sought work in the previous four weeks, and can start working within the next fortnight. Those who have made arrangements to take up paid employment or self-employment in the near future are also included in the definition of ILO unemployment. *Discouraged workers* are out-of-work individuals who want a job and are available to start working, but are not actively looking. The *Other inactive* category refers to out-of-work individuals who are not available to start employment, e.g. because they are students, retired, unable to work, e.g. due to ill-health or care responsibilities, or who prefer not to work for other reasons. ILO: International Labour Organization.
* The breakdown by employment status in the United States is not shown as information on benefit receipt and employment status in the underlying microdata refers to different time periods.
Source: Household, Income and Labour Dynamics in Australia (HILDA) for Australia; European Union Labour Force Survey (EU-LFS) for European countries; and Current Population Survey (CPS) for the United States.

StatLink ⟪⟫ http://dx.doi.org/10.1787/888933778478

The group of recipients intended by national unemployment-benefit policy may, however, differ significantly from both the broader and the narrow definition of unemployed (see also Figure 5.6 below). It may, for instance, exclude those with short employment histories (including the previously self-employed), those who are judged to have quit their job voluntarily, or those considered to be insufficiently active in their search or preparation for future employment. In addition, benefits may also be limited to an initial period of unemployment, subject to waiting periods before payments start, or limited to jobseekers living in low-income households. The coverage rates presented here reflect these provisions and can serve as metrics for the intended scope of unemployment benefits relative to countries' population of unemployed.

While the coverage levels in Figure 5.5 are naturally different from pseudo-coverage rates in Box 5.1, changes since 2007 are broadly similar. Across 24 OECD countries, fewer than one-in-three unemployed, and fewer than one-in-four jobseekers, receive unemployment benefits on average. Coverage rates for jobseekers are below 15% in Greece, Italy, Poland, Slovak Republic, Slovenia and the United States. Austria, Belgium and Finland show the highest coverage rates in 2016, ranging between approximately 45% and 60%: In countries with the highest coverage in the OECD, at least four-in-ten jobseekers still report not receiving an unemployment benefit.

Figure 5.5. Only a minority of jobseekers receive unemployment benefits

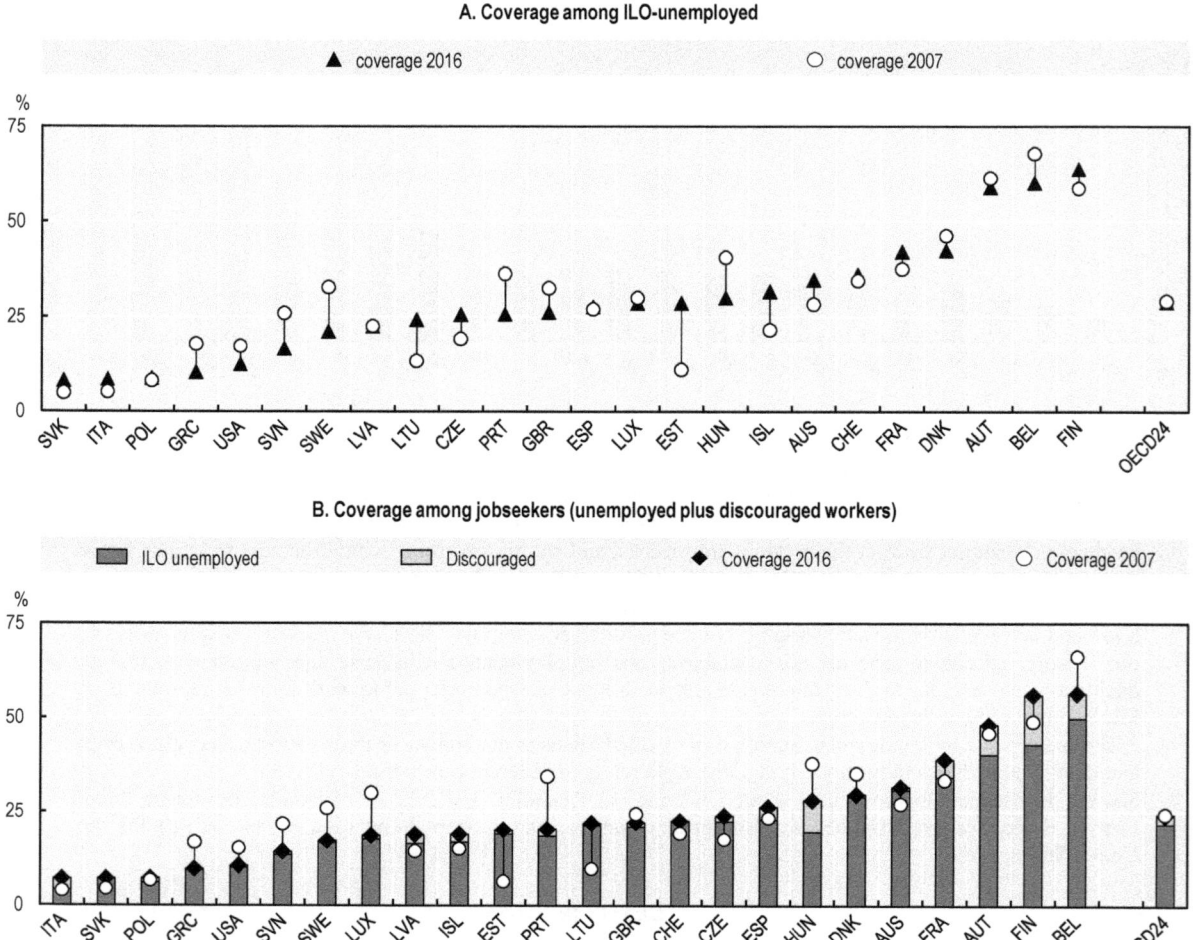

Note: Some European countries are excluded due to missing information in EU-LFS data. OECD-24 corresponds to the unweighted average of the countries shown. 2015 figures for Australia. LFS data for Sweden do not include a series of benefits that are accessible to jobless individuals who: i) are not in receipt of core unemployment benefits; and who ii) satisfy other conditions such as active participation in employment-support measures. ILO: International Labour Organization.
Source: Household, Income and Labour Dynamics in Australia (HILDA) for Australia; European Union Labour Force Survey (EU-LFS) for European countries; and Current Population Survey (CPS) for the United States.

StatLink ⎯⎯ http://dx.doi.org/10.1787/888933778497

5.2. Access to unemployment benefits: Driving factors

Coverage trends are affected by a number of policy and non-policy factors interacting with one another (Figure 5.6). Non-policy factors include demographics (e.g. ageing, migration) and labour-market conditions, although each of them may, in turn, shape policies regarding the accessibility of benefits.

Figure 5.6. Drivers of unemployment benefit coverage

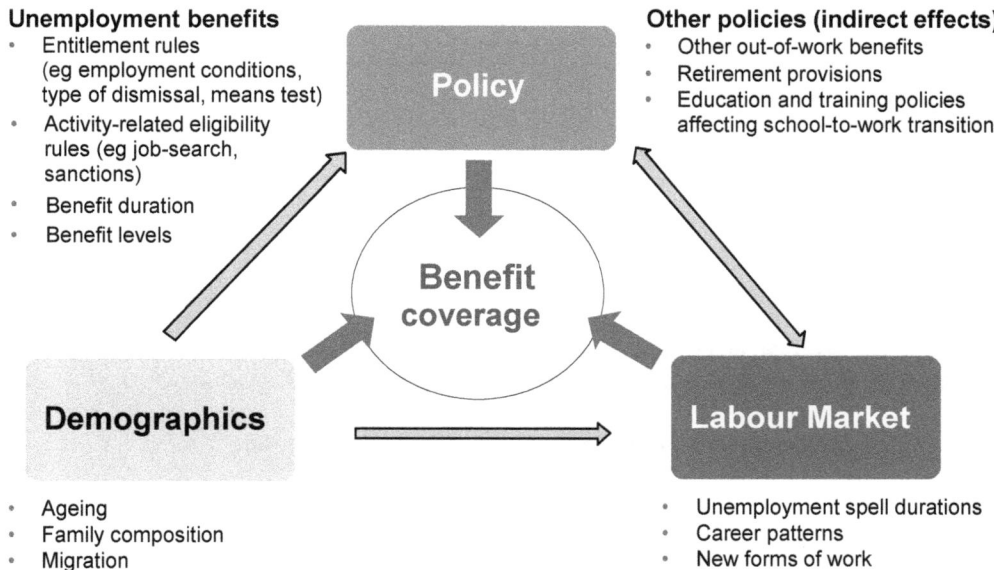

Unemployment benefits
* Entitlement rules (eg employment conditions, type of dismissal, means test)
* Activity-related eligibility rules (eg job-search, sanctions)
* Benefit duration
* Benefit levels

Other policies (indirect effects)
* Other out-of-work benefits
* Retirement provisions
* Education and training policies affecting school-to-work transitions

Demographics
* Ageing
* Family composition
* Migration

Labour Market
* Unemployment spell durations
* Career patterns
* New forms of work

5.2.1. Policy levers

The conditionality built into unemployment-benefit programmes, such as employment conditions, means-tests or activation-related behavioural requirements, are the most direct policy lever for making support more or less accessible initially, while limited benefit durations exclude longer-term unemployed from support provisions. Those who qualify for benefits may decide not to take them up if benefit levels are seen as low relative to the cost of claiming, or if other types of transfers are more generous or easier to obtain. In addition, the perceived accessibility and generosity of benefits can affect the job-search and (re-)employment decisions of unemployed individuals.[6]

Figure 5.7 presents information on three important aspects of benefit policy across OECD countries.[7] As for coverage rates, country differences in the policy parameters governing benefit accessibility are very substantial. Claimants in Slovak Republic, Turkey and Lithuania need to be employed for at least one year and a half before qualifying for unemployment benefits, while employment requirements can be less than six months in several other countries, including in Australia and New Zealand, where no previous employment is needed to qualify for means-tested assistance benefits (Panel A). Behavioural eligibility conditions, such as formal requirements to report active job search and be available for taking up employment, also vary greatly. One indicator of overall strictness suggests that requirements are tightest in Portugal, Luxembourg and Estonia, and comparatively lenient in Hungary, Czech Republic and Turkey (Panel B). For those claiming benefits successfully, maximum benefit durations are half a year or less in Hungary, the United States and Czech Republic but unlimited in Belgium and in several countries operating (means-tested) assistance benefits either as the main form of unemployment support or as a follow-up to first-tier insurance benefits (Panel C).

Figure 5.7. Benefit access provisions vary widely across countries

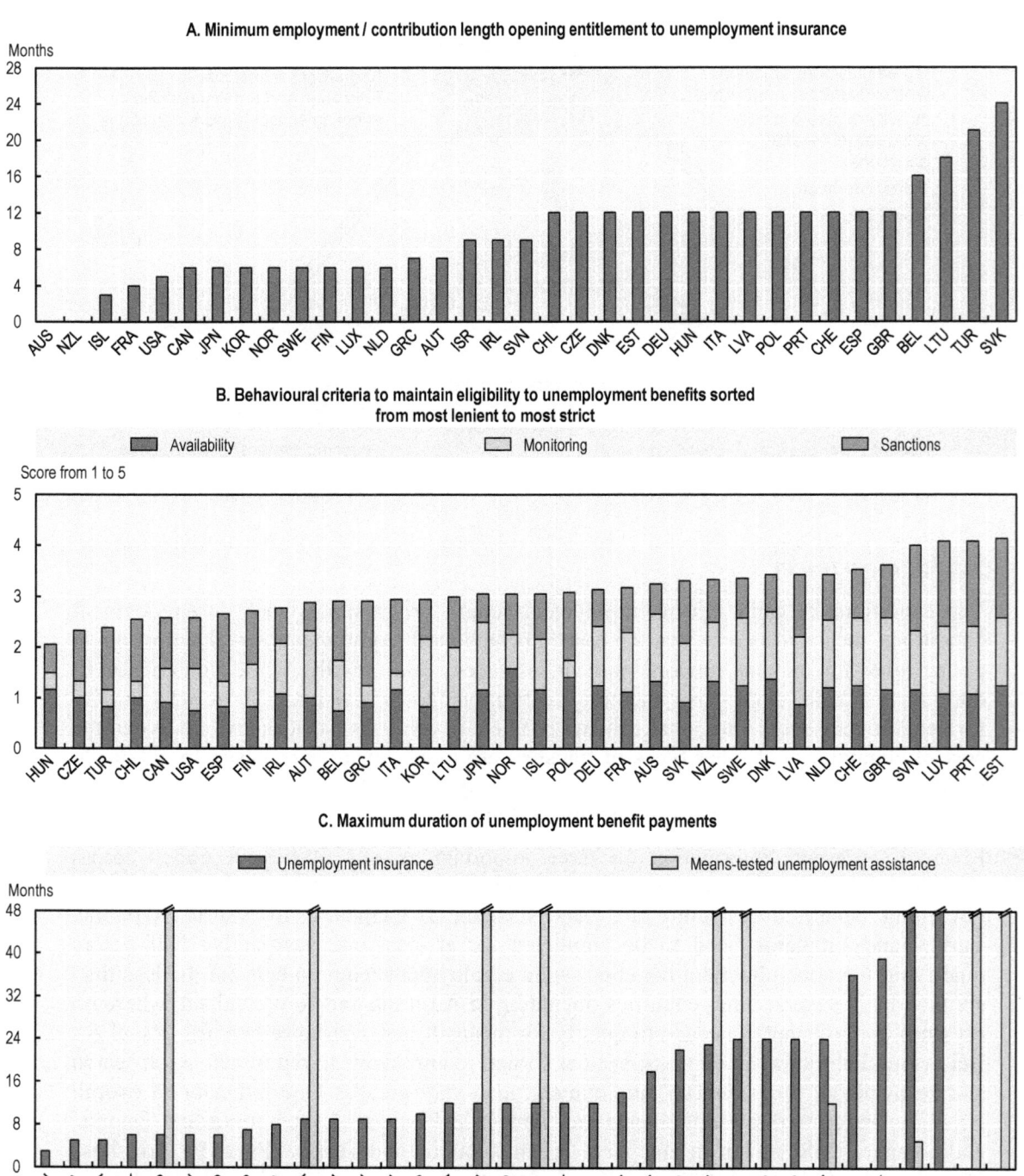

A. Minimum employment / contribution length opening entitlement to unemployment insurance

B. Behavioural criteria to maintain eligibility to unemployment benefits sorted from most lenient to most strict

C. Maximum duration of unemployment benefit payments

Note: Information for 2014 or as specified. Data are not shown for Mexico as there is no unemployment benefit. *Employment requirements*: For individuals with full-time open-ended contracts prior to employment loss. Minimum earnings/contributions requirements in the United Kingdom, the United States and Norway and are assumed to be met. *Behavioural eligibility criteria*: Scores from 1 (least strict) to 5 (most strict). See Langenbucher (2015[9]) and Immervoll and Knotz (forthcoming[7]) for content and scope of the strictness indicator. *Benefit durations*: For a 40 year-old with a "long" employment record. Unemployment-assistance durations are for individuals who have exhausted unemployment-insurance rights. Unlimited durations are shown as 48 months. Benefit durations in the United States vary by State and unemployment rate. The 20-week benefit duration in the United States refers to Michigan as at 1 July 2015. Unemployed individuals in Chile can draw unemployment insurance pay-outs provided there are sufficient assets in their individual savings account. In Sweden and in some other countries, additional unemployment support can be available for unemployed individuals participating in activation and employment support programmes.

Source: *OECD Tax-Benefit Policy Database* (www.oecd.org/els/social/workincentives); Langenbucher (2015[9]), "How demanding are eligibility criteria for unemployment benefits, quantitative indicators for OECD and EU countries", http://dx.doi.org/10.1787/5jrxtk1zw8f2-en; Immervoll and Knotz (forthcoming[7]), "How demanding are activation requirements for jobseekers? New evidence on activity-related eligibility criteria for unemployment and social assistance benefits".

StatLink ᾶᾶᵴ▰ http://dx.doi.org/10.1787/888933778516

In addition to unemployment-benefit policy, a number of indirect policy factors also have an impact on unemployment-benefit coverage, e.g. if reforms make it easier or harder to substitute other types of benefits for unemployment support. In combination, the different benefit policy parameters determine the likelihood of receiving benefits for a specific individual with a *given* set of characteristics and preferences.

5.2.2. Composition effects

Demographics and labour-market conditions, in turn, determine the *number* of jobseekers with each specific combination of characteristics and preferences. Some groups are significantly more likely to receive benefits than others (Figure 5.8) and changing sizes of different groups of jobseekers alter observed coverage rates through composition effects. For instance those with less stable temporary employment whose contracts have ended are less likely to meet relevant entitlement conditions for benefits that require a minimum duration of past employment (such as contribution-based insurance benefits). A growing share of jobseekers with less stable employment patterns will therefore tend to drive down coverage rates. By contrast, an increase in the number of older jobseekers with long previous job tenure can have the opposite effect and drive up coverage rates. The same applies to workers who were made redundant, and who typically have longer job tenure than the average job seeker (see Chapter 4).

Figure 5.9 illustrates possible magnitudes of composition effects using data for two countries. In the United States (Panel A), the share of jobseekers who were dismissed from their previous job rose sharply from 23% in 2007 to 46% in 2010 before falling back to 30% by 2016. Overall benefit coverage moved in the same direction, consistent with a positive composition effect as jobseekers dismissed in a steep labour-market downturn include large shares with sufficiently long employment histories to qualify for benefits. In Denmark, the share of young jobseekers increased between 2005 and 2008, fell between 2008 and 2010, and rose again between 2010 and 2016. Overall coverage moved in the opposite direction, consistent with a negative composition effect as youth are less likely to receive benefits than other jobseekers.

Figure 5.8. Some groups of jobseekers are more likely to receive benefits than others

Coverage rates by selected group relative to overall coverage, average across 24 OECD countries

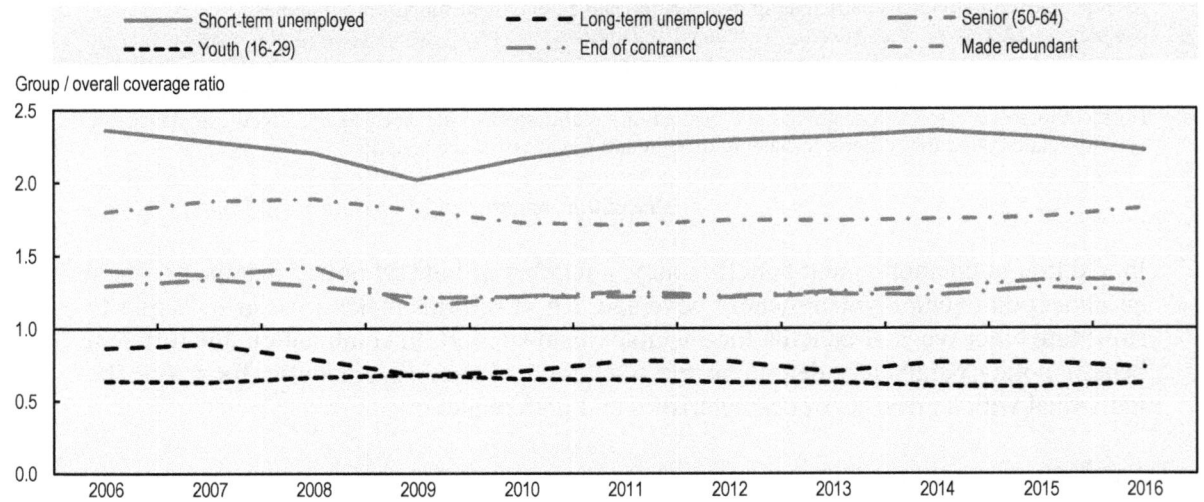

Note: "Jobseekers" include both the unemployed and discouraged workers. Country averages are for the same 24 countries as in Figure 5.5 but are not fully balanced across years due to missing data. They exclude the United Kingdom in 2010 and 2011, Denmark in 2015 and Australia in 2016.

Source: Household, Income and Labour Dynamics in Australia (HILDA) for Australia; European Union Labour Force Survey (EU-LFS) for European countries; and Current Population Survey (CPS) for the United States.

StatLink ⫘ http://dx.doi.org/10.1787/888933778535

Figure 5.9. Positive and negative composition effects: An illustration

Overall coverage rate and relative size of selected jobseeker groups, % of jobseekers

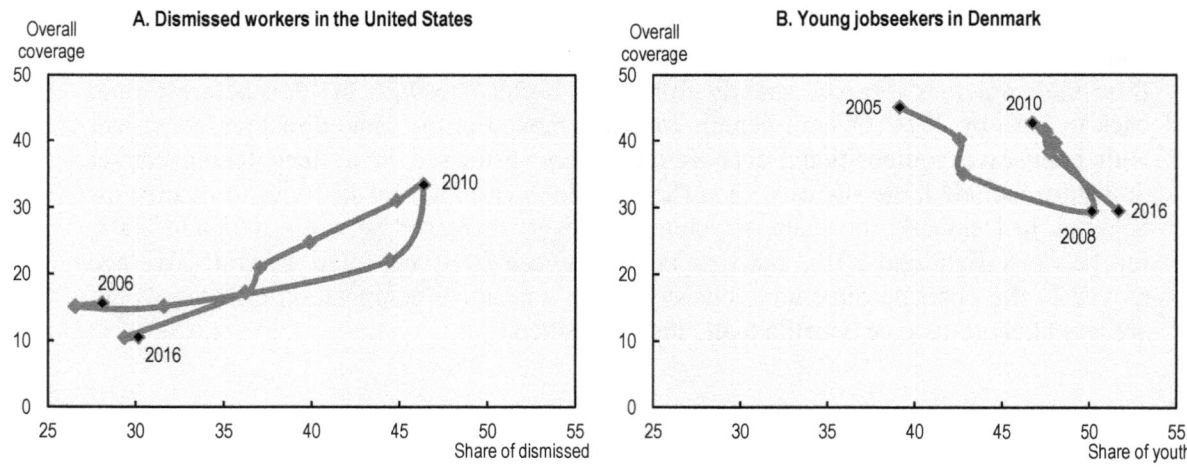

Note: "Jobseekers" include both the unemployed and discouraged workers.
Source: European Union Labour Force Survey (EU-LFS) for Denmark and Current Population Survey (CPS) for the United States.

StatLink ⫘ http://dx.doi.org/10.1787/888933778554

5.2.3. Disentangling different drivers of benefit coverage

In practice, different composition and policy effects occur in parallel and may interact. The mechanics behind observed change in overall coverage determines whether or not it may be a policy concern, and which policy responses may be suitable. For instance, stable overall coverage can hide a need for policy action if it is the result of offsetting composition effects that go in different directions (e.g. higher coverage due to ageing, and lower coverage due to increasing own-account work or shortening job tenure). Different drivers may also indicate which policy levers would be effective or appropriate for maintaining coverage at desired levels. For instance, a modest drop in coverage following tighter job-search requirements and associated sanctions might be intended or acceptable whereas a similar drop due to a surge in long-term unemployment may motivate a review of the balance between benefit adequacy and activation provisions.

This section aims to shed light on the concomitant forces that drove changes in coverage since the onset of the global financial and economic crises for six countries: Australia, Denmark, Poland, Spain, Sweden and the United States. The countries were chosen based on data availability and quality, notably the match between benefit-receipt information recorded in labour-force surveys, and the recipient totals available from administrative sources as documented in the OECD SOCR Database. The selected countries also represent different benefit-policy regimes, crisis exposures and broader labour-market contexts.

The method is adapted from common statistical decomposition techniques – see Blinder (1973[10]), Oaxaca (1973[11]) and Fairlie (2005[12]). The decomposition separates changes in observed coverage into those that can be attributed to changing characteristics of the unemployed population ("explanatory variables"), and those that are due to "structural" shifts, notably including benefit reforms, but also changes in behaviours and other factors that are not directly observed in micro-data.[8] Coverage changes and their respective drivers are assessed relative to a reference year prior to the onset of the financial and economic crisis: 2005 for Sweden and 2006 for the remaining five countries. The earlier reference year for Sweden is intended to facilitate capturing the impact of an important benefit reform that was enacted in 2006-07 (see below). OECD (2018[13]) provides details on the decomposition method, data and the criteria that were used to select explanatory variables.

The share of jobseekers receiving benefits grew in all six countries during the immediate aftermath of the crisis (Figure 5.10). But coverage trends for the core unemployment benefits over a more extended post-crisis period up until 2016 were either decreasing (Sweden, Denmark, and the United States) or stable (Australia, Poland and Spain).[9]

Changes in the composition of the unemployed population were important drivers of observed coverage trends in most of the countries (Figure 5.11). Composition effects (blue line) explain almost the entire observed trend in Australia, Denmark and Poland. But the part of the trends explained by compositional changes is smaller in Spain, the United States and Sweden, indicating that other factors, such as benefit policy changes, have shaped coverage trends in important ways.[10]

Figure 5.10. Coverage trends in selected OECD countries

Individuals who receive unemployment benefit as % of jobseekers

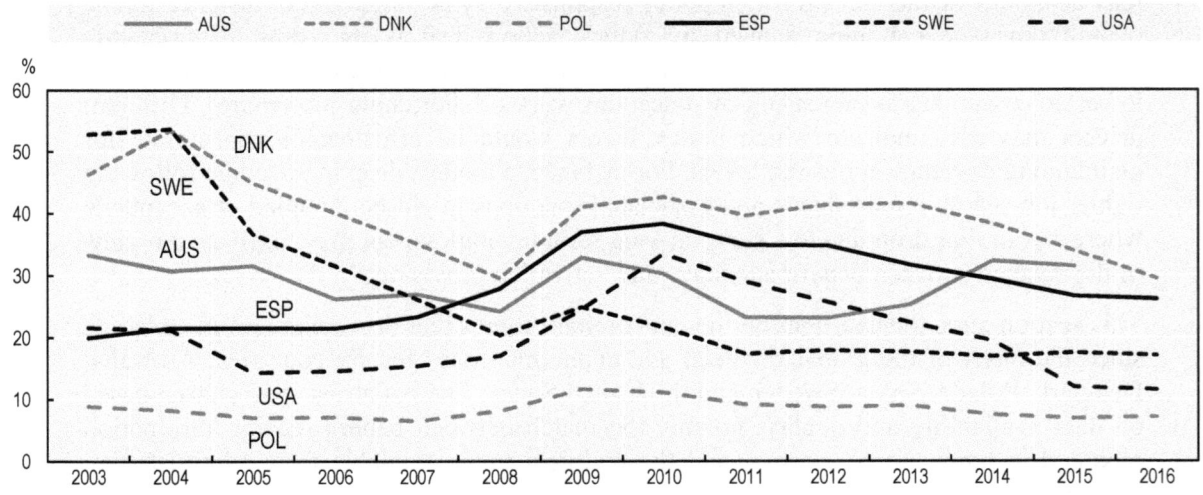

Note: The population of jobseekers includes both the unemployed and discouraged workers. Data for Sweden do not include a series of benefits for jobless individuals who: i) are not in receipt of core unemployment benefits; and who ii) satisfy other conditions such as active participation in employment-support measures. Due to data availability, results for the United States refer only to those who have been unemployed for 52 weeks or less. Records with missing values were excluded from the samples. OECD (2018[13]) provides full details, http://www.oecd.org/employment/oecd-employment-outlook-19991266.htm.
Source: Household, Income and Labour Dynamics in Australia (HILDA) for Australia; European Union Labour Force Survey (EU-LFS) for European countries; and Current Population Survey (CPS) for the United States.

StatLink ⟩⟨ http://dx.doi.org/10.1787/888933778573

The composition effect can be examined more closely by isolating the role of different characteristics, shown as stacked bars in the chart (see notes in Figure 5.11 for details). For instance, the *net* effect of changes in *out-of-work durations* on measured coverage is shown by the light-blue bars. In Spain and the United States, and to a lesser extent in Denmark and Poland, large inflows to unemployment in the aftermath of the crisis tended to push up coverage rates. Increasing shares of those experiencing long-term unemployment during the later stages of the labour-market crisis had the opposite effect.[11] The effect of "*reasons for entering unemployment*" (light-grey bars in Figure 5.11) is similar to the case of out-of-work durations. Increasing proportions of jobseekers that were recently dismissed or reached the end of a temporary employment contract pushed up measured coverage in Spain and the United States during the recession and in the first years of the recovery.[12]

Figure 5.11. Observable changes driving coverage in six OECD countries

Contribution of observable characteristics to changes in coverage among jobseekers,
relative to the baseline year

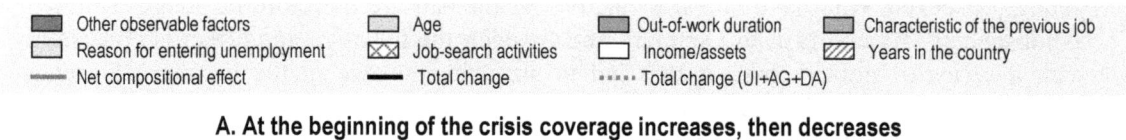

A. At the beginning of the crisis coverage increases, then decreases

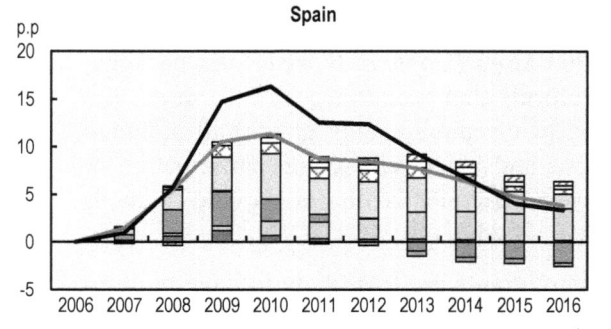
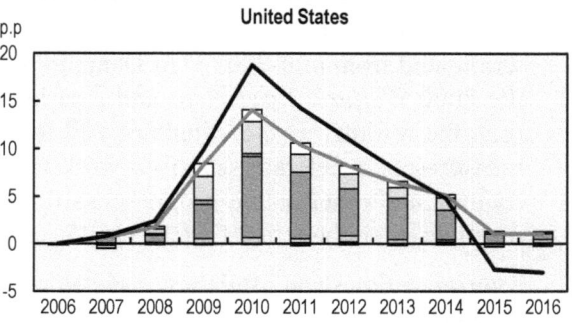

B. Coverage decreases

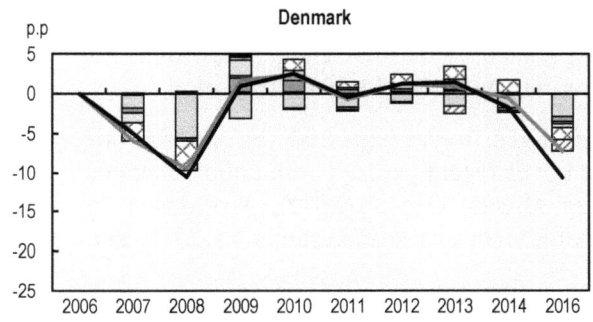
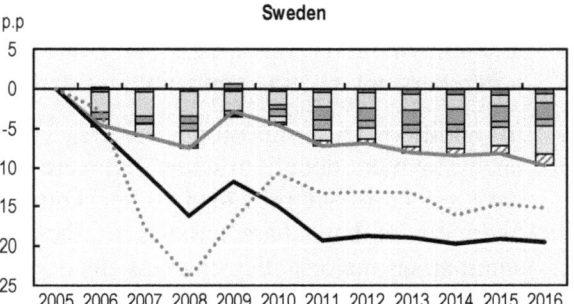

C. Changes in coverage are limited

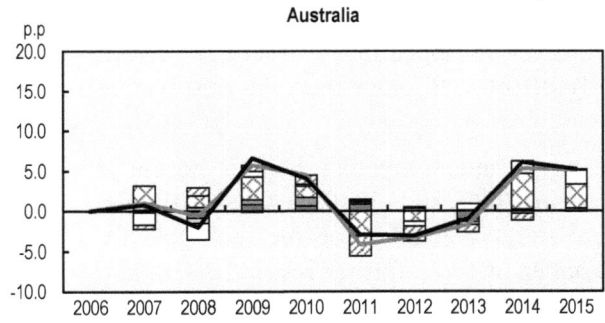
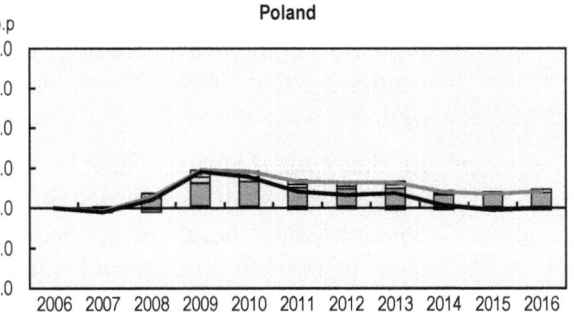

Note: The reference year is 2005 in Sweden and 2006 in Australia, Denmark, Poland, Spain and the United States. Composition effects for different groups (e.g. changes in the size of each different age group) are aggregated into broader domains (e.g. "age") to facilitate visual inspection. The additional dotted line for Sweden is an estimate of the total change in coverage after accounting for two other important activity-related benefit programmes (Activation Grant [AG] and Development Allowance [DA]) for which aggregate data were available. The estimates assume that all recipients are "jobseekers" as per definition in this chapter. Decomposition results for Sweden however are only for the core unemployment benefits reported in the European Union Labour Force Survey. p.p: percentage points. UI: Unemployment insurance.

Source: Household, Income and Labour Dynamics in Australia (HILDA) for Australia; European Union Labour Force Survey (EU-LFS) and administrative data for Sweden; European Union Labour Force Survey (EU-LFS) for other European countries; and Current Population Survey (CPS) for the United States.

StatLink 〰️📊 http://dx.doi.org/10.1787/888933778592

The *age composition* of the jobseeker population was a significant driver of coverage trends in Denmark, Sweden and Spain (grey bars). However, the underlying reasons driving these shifts differ across these countries. Spain saw an increasing proportion of young jobseekers who have become inactive NEET and are therefore no longer counted as jobseekers. By contrast, in Denmark and Sweden the negative age effect is consistent with a series of policy changes that led to sizeable increase in the number of young jobseekers with no or limited previous work experience. In Sweden, the *Adult Education Initiative* in mid-2003, which had previously taken up to 4% of the jobless out of the labour force while they acquired educational qualifications (OECD, 2004[14]) was terminated from mid-2003.[13] In Denmark the 2003 *More People in Work* reform package, the 2006 *Welfare Agreement,* and a series of reforms that took place in 2007 and 2008 (e.g. the reforms of the voluntary 10th form and of the public study grants) all included measures to accelerate school-to-work transitions and incentivise youth participation in training and other active programmes that, however, frequently do not provide rights to unemployment benefits (OECD, (2005[15]; 2006[16]; 2008[17]).[14]

Migration flows can affect coverage as recent immigrants are less likely to have built up the employment records that may be needed to qualify for benefits. Increasing shares of non-native unemployed has reduced coverage especially in Denmark and Sweden since 2013 – see also OECD (2012[18]). In Australia, a larger inflow of recent immigrants into unemployment between 2011 and 2013 is associated with increasing proportions of jobseekers not meeting applicable residence-duration conditions for benefit receipt.

In addition to composition effects, coverage rates were impacted by reforms of unemployment benefit systems that were enacted over recent years. These policy changes have either offset or added to the composition effects. OECD (2018[13]) provides an overview of key characteristics of these unemployment-benefit systems in 2016 and summarises major policy changes since 2005.[15]

- In *Spain*, a number of reforms during the earlier phase of the labour-market downturn have made benefits more accessible to long-term unemployed, but subsequent policy changes have tended to reduce coverage.[16] Results in Figure 5.11 show a declining, and ultimately disappearing, "structural" effect, suggesting that these reforms have partly offset each other over the observation period.

- In the *United States*, sizeable extensions of unemployment benefit durations explain the growing "structural" effect in 2009 and 2010.[17] After 2011, as unemployment began to decline, several states gradually became ineligible for parts of the federal extensions and a number of them further restricted standard benefit durations. The "structural" effect consequently declined and turned negative in 2014 as access to benefits became more restrictive on average than it had been in the 2006 baseline year.

- In *Denmark*, composition effects explain almost all of the coverage changes until 2013, but negative structural effects start playing a role from 2014. This is consistent with a substantial shortening of the maximum duration of unemployment insurance benefits that was approved in 2010 but only came fully into effect several years later.[18]

- In *Sweden*, composition effects explain only around one-third of the overall change in coverage levels since 2005 and unemployment-benefit reforms are therefore likely to have had a major role. Important benefit reforms implemented in Sweden during this time period include measures to shorten benefit durations or make membership in the voluntary unemployment insurance funds more costly to workers.[19] Results in Figure 5.11 suggest that these policy changes were indeed associated with a significant decline in coverage of the core unemployment benefits.[20] The full effects of some of these reforms appear to have materialised only gradually as the negative "structural" component grew significantly for several years. This was followed by a slight narrowing since 2011, consistent with a roll-back of the earlier reforms.

- Benefit coverage in *Poland* increased in the aftermath of the crisis but was back to 2006 levels by 2016, with a negative "structural" effect offsetting the positive composition effects from 2010. Maximum benefit durations were shortened in 2008/2009.[21] From 2013 onwards, unemployment rates in several regions fell below the threshold that triggered the 12-month benefit extension, contributing to the widening negative "structural" effect after 2013.

5.3. Concluding remarks

This chapter has shown evidence of a declining trend in unemployment benefit coverage since the end of the recession. This decline could be one factor making jobseekers less selective as regards job offers and, therefore, contribute to explaining the increase in lower-quality jobs that has been observed in recent years (see Chapter 1). However, the trend has been far from uniform, both across countries and over time, with sometimes temporary extensions of potential benefit durations increasing coverage in the early recovery years. Although composition effects account for a significant part of the evolution of benefit coverage in many countries, some change can also clearly be ascribed to policy reforms aimed at reducing unemployment benefit generosity either to contain public spending or in order to dampen job-search disincentives for the unemployed. In countries with generous systems and high coverage levels, a reduction in the share of unemployed receiving benefits may reflect temporary changes in the jobseeker population or more effective activation provisions without necessarily involving the weakening of its protective role. But in countries with very low coverage further reductions may cast doubts on the capacity of the unemployment benefit system to effectively contribute to labour market inclusiveness by helping people to weather negative labour-market shocks. Low coverage also fuels apprehensions about new forms of employment and a risk of job displacement through automation. Together, these labour-market developments create additional demands for out-of-work support but also challenges for maintaining effective support for all those in need (OECD, 2017[4]) (OECD, 2018[19]).

Low and declining unemployment benefit coverage rates can also be a concern for other reasons. For example, unemployment benefits provide the principal instrument for linking jobless people to employment services and active labour market programmes to improve their job prospects. In the absence of accessible unemployment benefits, it can be difficult to reach out to those facing multiple barriers to employment, who therefore risk being left behind (Immervoll, 2012[20]). In these cases, achieving good benefit coverage can be essential to make an activation strategy effective and sustainable. For this reason the new OECD Jobs Strategy calls for clear policy action to extend access to unemployment benefit within a rigorously-enforced "mutual obligation" framework, in which governments have the duty to provide jobseekers with benefits and effective services to enable them to find work and, in turn, beneficiaries have to take active steps to find work or improve their employability (OECD, forthcoming[5]).

Notes

[1] 2014 is currently the latest data available in the OECD SOCR Database.

[2] The Social benefit recipients Database - www.oecd.org/social/recipients.htm

[3] See, e.g. Knittler (2017[33]) for Austria.

[4] Those waiting to start a job in the short term are classified as ILO unemployed in Labour Force Surveys data.

[5] OECD (2018[13]) provides details on data sources and limitations.

[6] For instance, once a sanction is imposed, the cost of unemployment increases for jobseekers, creating additional incentives for finding and accepting work more quickly than they may otherwise have done – *ex-post* effect of sanctions Fredriksson and Holmlund (2006[22]), Arni, Lalive and van Ours (2013[35]), van den Berg, van der Klaauw and van Ours (2004[23]). However, positive effects of higher exit rates from unemployment, and higher re-employment rates, can also come at the cost of poorer job matches, a lower quality of post-unemployment outcomes with respect to job stability and earnings (Arni, Lalive and Van Ours, 2013[35]), or a higher probability of working in part-time jobs (van den Berg and Vikström, 2014[24]). Evidence of the effect of unemployment support on post-unemployment job quality is mixed (Tatsiramos and van Ours, 2014[34]) with some newer research finding no effect (Le Barbanchon, 2012[29]) while others document a statistically and economically significant positive effect of benefit durations on post-unemployment wages (Nekoei and Weber, 2017[21]). The latter study also reconciles disparate results by carefully accounting for the two countervailing forces of: i) reduced wages due to longer unemployment; and ii) higher wages due to a better bargaining position and more careful job search.

[7] Full details on unemployment-benefit policy, and changes since the early 2000s, is available from the OECD Tax-Benefit Policy Database (www.oecd.org/social/benefits-and-wages.htm).

[8] Decomposition analysis, in general, does not rely on the identification of structural or "causal" relationships from the data and does not explicitly reveal which policy mechanisms, if any, are driving the observed changes in coverage levels. Results therefore require careful interpretation. For instance, composition effects can themselves be a result of policy changes (e.g. the indirect policy levers depicted in Figure 5.6). For instance, a new active labour market policy for young jobseekers might increase the share of youth who are registered with the Public Employment Service and actively searching for jobs. Since young jobseekers are comparatively less likely to receive unemployment benefits, this would tend to reduce coverage.

[9] Sweden operates a series of benefits that are available to jobless individuals who: i) are not in receipt of core unemployment benefits; and who ii) satisfy other conditions such as active participation in employment-support measures. These benefits are included in the SOCR data presented in Figure 5.2 and Figure 5.3. But they are unlikely to be reported in EU-LFS survey data and thus not included in the resulting coverage measures and in the decomposition analysis. Some of these programmes existed since the 1990s, including the Activity Grant and the Development Allowance, which both provide a mix of employment and income support measures. After a decline in the 1990s and early 2000s, programme participation increased between 2008 and 2010 and fell again until 2016. In 2016, about 90 000 individuals (about 8% more than in 2005) participated in a given month, accounting for about 19% of the jobseeker population. The Introduction Benefit (not included in this study) became available in December 2010 and is intended for those who have recently arrived in Sweden. There were about 48 700 recipients in 2016 (Swedish Social Insurance Agency, 2017[28]; OECD, 2016[27]).

[10] Composition effects for different groups (e.g. changes in the size of each different age group) are aggregated into broader domains (e.g. "age") to facilitate visual inspection. Fuller granularity, as well as group definitions for each country, are available in OECD (2018[13]).

[11] For instance, the fraction of long-term unemployed (12+ months) among jobseekers in Spain increased from 34% in 2009 to 50% in 2015. Details for each country are in OECD (2018[13]).

[12] In Spain the increasing number of jobseekers from 2012 onwards who entered the labour force without any recent work experience partially reversed this positive effect on coverage. One likely explanation for this is women starting to look for work in an attempt to offset other household members' loss of earnings (the so-called "added worker effect"), a phenomenon that was common in Spain in the aftermath of the crisis (OECD, 2017[26]; Fernández, 2017[25]).

[13] The inflow of young jobseekers without previous work experience can also explain why in Sweden the overall net effect of other observable characteristics such as the "Reason for entering unemployment" is negative. For instance, the increasing number of jobseekers without previous work experience who entered unemployment for reasons "other than dismissals or terminations of temporary contract" increased significantly from 2005 onwards. As this group is less likely to qualify for unemployment insurance the overall net effect on coverage is negative.

[14] These reforms can also explain why in Denmark changes in the numbers of jobseekers reporting "active job search" (grid-pattern bars) is among the drivers of coverage trends. Between 2006 and 2008, there was a rising share of jobseekers who had not actively sought employment due to participation in training and other active labour market programmes. Such "lock-in" effects can, in part, be related to the 2006 reform that strengthened active programmes for people under 29 years old (OECD, 2008[17]).

[15] No major benefit reform occurred in Australia in the period of observation. As a result fluctuations in coverage are fully explained by composition effects (see Figure 5.11).

[16] A new temporary unemployment benefit was introduced in 2009 (*Programa Temporal de Protección por Desempleo e Inserción*, PRODI), extending benefit durations by six months for those who had exhausted entitlements to contributory unemployment benefits and were not eligible for other support. In 2011, PRODI was replaced by a programme providing up to six months of benefit support to jobseekers undertaking professional qualification (*Programa de recualificación personal de las personas que agoten su protección por desempleo*, PREPARA). In 2012, the so-called "pre-retirement" age (the age at which it is possible to receive unemployment assistance until retirement) was increased from 52 to 55 years.

[17] In addition to the 26 weeks standard benefit duration prior to the crisis, the Extended Benefits programme provides up to 20 weeks of additional entitlement during periods when a state experiences high unemployment. In addition, the federal Emergency Unemployment Compensation (EUC) enacted in 2008 extended benefit durations by 13 weeks, increasing to up to 53 weeks of federally financed additional benefits (a useful summary by state is provided by Rothstein (2011[32])). Last-resort benefits (SNAP, formerly known as the "Food Stamp" programme) also became significantly more accessible from 2007 (Immervoll and Richardson, 2013[31]).

[18] Denmark approved a reform that reduced the maximum duration of unemployment insurance from four to two years, with a clause that durations could be extended *temporarily* for six months during periods of economic downturns. This exception was applied twice, in 2011 and 2012. The impact of the shorter benefit duration was further dampened by the introduction of a series of other temporary programmes in 2012/13, such as a new education allowance and access to social assistance with more lenient means-testing following expiry of unemployment insurance entitlements.

[19] In 2007 Sweden abolished the possibility to maintain unemployment insurance benefits beyond the standard duration. In addition, two reforms in 2007 and 2008 made contributions to the voluntary unemployment insurance dependent on the rate of unemployed workers covered by each fund, raising contribution payments by 300% on average and reducing the share of workers who are fund members. The reforms were rolled back in 2014 but fund density has yet to recover to its pre-reform levels (Kolsrud, 2018[36]). In addition, a number of job-search and other activity-related eligibility conditions became more strict, see Immervoll and Knotz (forthcoming[7]) and OECD (2015[30]).

[20] See Endnote 9 for related benefit programmes extended or brought in during this period.

[21] Standard benefit duration limits were six months before the reform, with a 12-month special extension for jobseekers living in regions where the unemployment rate was more than 1.25 times the national average. In special cases, the maximum duration could be extended by up to 18 months instead of 12. The reform abolished the possibility for the 18-month extension and increased the unemployment-rate threshold for the 12-month extension.

References

Arni, P., R. Lalive and J. Van Ours (2013), "How effective are unemployment benefit sanctions? Looking beyond unemployment exit", *Journal of Applied Econometrics*, Vol. 28/7, pp. 1153-1178, http://dx.doi.org/10.1002/jae.2289. [35]

Blinder, A. (1973), "Wage Discrimination: Reduced Form and Structural Estimates", *The Journal of Human Resources*, Vol. 8/4, p. 436, http://dx.doi.org/10.2307/144855. [10]

Bundesagentur für Arbeit (2017), *Grundsicherung für Arbeitsuchende (SGB II) - statistik.arbeitsagentur.de*, https://statistik.arbeitsagentur.de/Navigation/Statistik/Statistik-nach-Themen/Grundsicherung-fuer-Arbeitsuchende-SGBII/Grundsicherung-fuer-Arbeitsuchende-SGBII-Nav.html. [8]

Fairlie, R. (2005), "An extension of the Blinder-Oaxaca decomposition technique to logit and probit models", *Journal of economic and social measurement.*, Vol. 30/4, pp. 305-316, https://content.iospress.com/articles/journal-of-economic-and-social-measurement/jem00259. [12]

Fernández, R. (2017), *Faces of Joblessness in Spain: Main Results and Policy Inventory*, OECD, Paris, http://www.oecd.org/els/soc/Faces-of-Joblessness-in-Spain-CPP2017.pdf (accessed on 15 February 2018). [25]

Fredriksson, P. and B. Holmlund (2006), "Improving Incentives in Unemployment Insurance: A Review of Recent Research", *Journal of Economic Surveys*, Vol. 20/3, pp. 357-386, http://dx.doi.org/10.1111/j.0950-0804.2006.00283.x. [22]

Immervoll, H. (2012), "Reforming the Benefit System to 'Make Work Pay': Options and Priorities in a Weak Labour Market", *IZA Policy Papers*, No. 50, IZA, Bonn, http://repec.iza.org/pp50.pdf. [20]

Immervoll, H. and C. Knotz (forthcoming), "How demanding are activation requirements for jobseekers? New evidence on activity-related eligibility criteria for unemployment and social assistance benefits", *OECD Social, Employment and Migration Working Papers*, OECD, Paris, http://dx.doi.org/10.1787/1815199X. [7]

Immervoll, H. and L. Richardson (2013), "Redistribution Policy in Europe and the United States: Is the Great Recession a 'Game Changer' for Working-age Families?", *OECD Social, Employment and Migration Working Papers*, No. 150, OECD Publishing, Paris, http://dx.doi.org/10.1787/5k44xwtc0txp-en. [31]

Immervoll, H. and L. Richardson (2011), "Redistribution Policy and Inequality Reduction in OECD Countries: What Has Changed in Two Decades?", *OECD Social, Employment and Migration Working Papers*, No. 122, OECD Publishing, Paris, http://dx.doi.org/10.1787/5kg5dlkhjq0x-en. [2]

Knittler, K. (2017), *Die Definition macht die Zahl*, Statistik Austria, Vienna, pp. 180-191. [33]

Kolsrud, J. (2018), "Voluntary unemployment insurance as an option for non-standard work: The case of Sweden", in OECD (ed.), *The Future of Social Protection: What works for nonstandard workers?*, OECD publishing, Paris. [36]

Langenbucher, K. (2015), "How demanding are eligibility criteria for unemployment benefits, quantitative indicators for OECD and EU countries", *OECD Social, Employment and Migration Working Papers*, No. 166, OECD Publishing, Paris, http://dx.doi.org/10.1787/5jrxtk1zw8f2-en. [9]

Le Barbanchon, T. (2012), *The effect of the potential duration of unemployment benefits on unemployment exits to work and match quality in france*, http://www.crest.fr/ckfinder/userfiles/files/Pageperso/Indemnisation%20Crest%20wp%202012-21.pdf (accessed on 15 February 2018). [29]

Nekoei, A. and A. Weber (2017), "Does extending unemployment benefits improve job quality?", *American Economic Review*, http://dx.doi.org/10.1257/aer.20150528. [21]

Oaxaca, R. (1973), "Male-Female Wage Differentials in Urban Labor Markets", *International Economic Review*, Vol. 14/3, p. 693, http://dx.doi.org/10.2307/2525981. [11]

OECD (2018), "Supplementary material for Chapter 5", in *OECD Employment Outlook 2018*, OECD Publishing, Paris, http://dx.doi.org/10.1787/empl_outlook-2018-14-en. [13]

OECD (2018), *The Future of Social Protection: What works for non-standard workers?*, OECD, Paris, http://dx.doi.org/www.oecd.org/employment/future-of-work.htm. [19]

OECD (2017), "Basic Income as a policy option: Can it add up?", *Policy Brief on the Future of Work*, http://dx.doi.org/www.oecd.org/employment/future-of-work.htm. [4]

OECD (2017), *OECD Economic Surveys: Spain 2017*, OECD Publishing, Paris, http://dx.doi.org/10.1787/eco_surveys-esp-2017-en. [26]

OECD (2016), *Investing in Youth: Sweden*, Investing in Youth, OECD Publishing, Paris, http://dx.doi.org/10.1787/9789264267701-en. [27]

OECD (2015), *Back to Work: Sweden: Improving the Re-employment Prospects of Displaced Workers*, Back to Work, OECD Publishing, Paris, http://dx.doi.org/10.1787/9789264246812-en. [30]

OECD (2014), "The crisis and its aftermath: A stress test for societies and for social policies", in *Society at a Glance 2014: OECD Social Indicators*, OECD Publishing, Paris, http://dx.doi.org/10.1787/soc_glance-2014-5-en. [3]

OECD (2012), *OECD Economic Surveys: Sweden 2012*, OECD Publishing, Paris, http://dx.doi.org/10.1787/eco_surveys-swe-2012-en. [18]

OECD (2011), *Divided We Stand: Why Inequality Keeps Rising*, OECD Publishing, Paris, http://dx.doi.org/10.1787/9789264119536-en. [1]

OECD (2008), *OECD Economic Surveys: Denmark 2008*, OECD Publishing, Paris, http://dx.doi.org/10.1787/eco_surveys-dnk-2008-en.   [17]

OECD (2006), *OECD Economic Surveys: Denmark 2006*, OECD Publishing, Paris, http://dx.doi.org/10.1787/eco_surveys-dnk-2006-en.   [16]

OECD (2005), *OECD Economic Surveys: Denmark 2005*, OECD Publishing, Paris, http://dx.doi.org/10.1787/eco_surveys-dnk-2005-en.   [15]

OECD (2004), *OECD Economic Surveys: Sweden 2004*, OECD Publishing, Paris, http://dx.doi.org/10.1787/eco_surveys-swe-2004-en.   [14]

OECD (forthcoming), "Are jobs becoming less stable?", *Policy Brief on the Future of Work*, OECD Publishing, Paris.   [6]

OECD (forthcoming), *Good Jobs for All in a Changing World of Work: The OECD Jobs Strategy*, OECD Publishing, Paris, http://dx.doi.org/one.oecd.org/#/document/COM/ECO/CPE/DELSA/ELSA(2017)1/en?_k= o0lyqn.   [5]

Rothstein, J. (2011), "Unemployment Insurance and Job Search in the Great Recession", *Brookings Papers on Economic Activity*, Vol. 2011/2, pp. 143-213, http://dx.doi.org/10.1353/eca.2011.0018.   [32]

Swedish Social Insurance Agency (2017), *Social Insurance in Figures 2017*, https://www.forsakringskassan.se/wps/wcm/connect/6fa0e434-a212-4e6b-8c8d-5d7a498a253d/socialforsakringen-i-siffror-2017-engelsk.pdf?MOD=AJPERES&CVID=.   [28]

Tatsiramos, K. and J. van Ours (2014), "Labor market effects of unemployment insurance design", *Journal of Economic Surveys*, Vol. 28/2, pp. 284-311, http://dx.doi.org/10.1111/joes.12005.   [34]

van den Berg, G., B. van der Klaauw and J. van Ours (2004), "Punitive Sanctions and the Transition Rate from Welfare to Work", *Journal of Labor Economics*, Vol. 22/1, pp. 211-241, http://dx.doi.org/10.1086/380408.   [23]

van den Berg, G. and J. Vikström (2014), "Monitoring Job Offer Decisions, Punishments, Exit to Work, and Job Quality", *The Scandinavian Journal of Economics*, Vol. 116/2, pp. 284-334, http://dx.doi.org/10.1111/sjoe.12051.   [24]

Supplementary material for Chapter 5

Supplementary material for Chapter 5 is available online only in English at the following DOI: http://dx.doi.org/10.1787/empl_outlook-2018-14-en.

Chapter 6. Starting close, growing apart: Why the gender gap in labour income widens over the working life

This chapter begins with an overview of women's working lives – how they differ from men's, and how those differences impact their labour income throughout the lifecycle. It then focuses on the reasons behind these different career pathways, pointing to key forks in women's professional lives that could lead to career traps, and examining the specific roles played by professional mobility, childbirth and part-time work. The chapter also provides a framework to help countries identify their country-specific sources of inequalities so as to meet the complex and multifaceted challenge of gender labour inequality. The chapter finally provides policy recommendations on how to address these country-specific sources of inequalities for further improvements of women's position in labour markets.

Key findings

The pursuit of gender equality is an uphill battle (OECD, 2017[1]). The recent OECD assessment of how well countries are doing in implementing policy measures aimed at reaching gender equality goals is crystal clear: they need to do more. In particular, despite major improvements in the education of young girls, the rising labour force participation of women and widespread laws against gender discrimination, women's position in the labour market severely lags behind that of men, and the gender gap in labour income remains a global phenomenon.

This chapter provides a more in-depth analysis of how labour market gender inequalities evolve over the career of men and women across OECD countries, by providing a life-long analysis of the gender gap in labour income (GGLI hereafter) and investigating the potential causes for the reasons why this gap increases during the working life. The GGLI is the gap between the per capita labour income of all men and women between 20 and 64 years of age and therefore provides an overall measure of women's position in the labour market relative to that of men. It takes account of gender differences in participation, as well as of hours worked and hourly earnings when employed, and consequently gives a broader picture than the traditional gender pay gap measures which concentrate on the wages of full-time employees and therefore ignore part of the female working population. This chapter also analyses the extent to which life and career events influence women's income mobility (moves up and down the earnings ladder and in and out of work), and what role these events play in gender pay gaps over the life cycle. It proposes a new framework to measure countries' performance in various dimensions of labour market gender equality, identifying the main levers of action for improvement and a set of corresponding employment policy guidelines for national governments.

Women continue to have lower labour market incomes than men, and this gap widens over the working life:

- Although it has narrowed in the past decade, the gender gap in labour income (GGLI) remains wide. The largest gaps are found in East Asian and Latin American countries (Japan, Korea, Mexico and Chile). Gender gaps are also relatively high (above 40%) in many Mediterranean countries, German-speaking countries, large English-speaking economies, the Netherlands and the Czech Republic. The smallest gaps (less than 30%) are found in many Nordic and Eastern European countries and Portugal.

- On average, gaps in employment rates explain the largest share of the GGLI (40%), while the gap in the number of hours worked by men and women accounts for a further 20%. The remainder is accounted by the gap in hourly earnings.

- The GGLI widens over the working life. Most of it is generated in the first half of the career. In a number of countries it continues to increase in the second half, although at a slower pace.

- Gaps in employment rates and working hours are the consequence of different career patterns. Women's careers are one-third shorter on average than men's, and four times as likely to involve part-time work and flexible working time arrangements. Women's professional careers are not linear, and comprise several different working lives.

- The gender gap in hourly earnings is generally widest at around 40 years of age. After 40, low-skilled women catch up, slightly closing the gap. By contrast, the hourly-earnings gap for highly-skilled women often keeps worsening in the final years of working life.

Childbirth and early career events play a crucial role in the widening of gender disparities over the life course:

- Not only do women experience slightly fewer job changes than men on average, but the nature of their labour market mobility also differs from that of men. Women do experience in-work transitions – change of employer, job or contract type – but less often than men, and they tend to have fewer in-work transitions that occur at the beginning of men's careers. By contrast, in almost all countries, women move part-time and enter inactivity more often than men, although they also exit inactivity more often too.

- The frequent job changes that occur at an early stage of both men's and women's careers have a big impact on future prospects. Women participate less intensely than men in this critical stage of career development. Fewer in-work transitions for women than men during the early years of their careers, particularly around the time of childbirth, translate into lower earnings growth.

- In most countries, childbirth leads a large proportion of young mothers to leave the labour market, either temporarily or for a longer period. In some countries, women even withdraw completely from the labour market for several years in the middle of their career in order to have and raise children. Childbirth can have long-lasting effects on a woman's career, in terms of time spent out of the labour market, lost career opportunities, limited hours of work, and earnings. On average, the gender gap in the career length of parents is more than twice as large as that of childless workers.

- Greater availability of part-time work a few years after childbirth can prevent women from withdrawing completely from the labour market. However, it can also induce significant earnings dependency on their partner, which becomes prejudicial in cases of separation or divorce. In this context, childbirth generally leads to greater income vulnerability for women in many countries. Moreover, going part-time after childbirth may make mothers miss key job opportunities, thereby resulting in less dynamic career patterns also at later stages of their working life.

Countries can use targeted measures to reduce gender inequalities:

- There is a broad policy strategy to foster gender equality that is common across countries. Key elements of this strategy include: i) family policies to improve access to childcare facilities, correct disincentives to work for second wage-earners and move towards a gender-neutral tax/benefit system; ii) measures to encourage behavioural changes among both men and women, including combating long hours, getting fathers more involved in caring, and promoting more equal forms of paid leave; and iii) fostering changes in the workplace, including increased take-up of part-time and flexible working-time arrangements.

- Countries should focus their efforts on reducing the quantitatively largest sources of the gender gap in labour income. The relative importance of each component in individual countries (e.g. women's lower labour force participation, lower working hours, or the concentration of women in lower-paid sectors and occupations) provides a valuable guideline for policy action. For example, policies should focus on increasing female labour participation at young ages in countries such as Greece, Spain and Italy, where large shares of older cohorts of women never entered the labour market. However, attention should focus more on policies to reconcile parental care responsibilities with working in Australia, Austria and a number of Eastern European countries, where a larger-than-average share of women withdraw from the labour market following childbirth, and in Germany, the Netherlands and Switzerland, where women often spend large parts of their careers in part-time jobs.

Introduction

One of the major labour market developments in OECD countries over the post-war period has been the continued progress made by women, with female labour force participation and employment expanding considerably and the wage gap relative to men narrowing almost everywhere (OECD, 2002[2])). These developments reflect changes both in the labour supply behaviour of women and on the labour demand side. On the supply side, the transfer of traditional female household tasks to the labour market (OECD, 2002[2]) and the development of time-saving electronic devices (OECD, 2017[1]) reduced the burden of unpaid work faced by women, freeing them to concentrate on different activities and giving them more options. At the same time, a broadening of employment and working-time arrangements available to women eased their transition from home activities to the labour market. On the demand side, the shift of employment from agriculture and manufacturing towards services, where women are over-represented, created new opportunities for them. The constant rise in levels of female education – with women's educational achievements now surpassing those of their male counterparts – also increased their attractiveness for employers. Nevertheless, further efforts are needed in terms of public support to ensure that women, and especially mothers, have the option of fully participating in the labour market and enjoying the same career opportunities as men.

In 2017, the OECD reviewed progress made by countries in implementing the OECD Recommendations on Gender Equality in Education, Employment and Entrepreneurship and on Gender Equality in Public Life (OECD, 2017[1]). The report concludes that in the past five years, countries have made very little progress in fostering gender equality goals, and that much remains to be done to meet the G20 target of reducing the gender gap in labour force participation between men and women by 25% by 2025. Twenty-one of the 35 OECD countries are well on track to reach this goal, but further action will be needed to enable the remaining 14 countries to cross the finishing line – see OECD (2017[1]), Figure 1.10. Promoting greater participation of women in the labour market and improving the quality of their employment will contribute to stronger and more inclusive growth, and be beneficial to society as a whole.

Much of the attention in the past has focused on increasing female labour market participation by providing better work-life balance, and redesigning tax and benefit systems to avoid unemployment traps. Strong emphasis has also been placed on reducing gender wage gaps among full-time workers, on reducing low pay for women and on ways to curb discrimination as well as occupational and industrial segregation. OECD work examining the qualitative aspects of women's professional lives showed that while unemployment rates for men and women are broadly similar, employment rates and wages are substantially lower for women but men somewhat more frequently suffer job strain (OECD, 2014[3]). A later survey providing a comprehensive picture of long-term earnings inequality and the importance of earnings mobility across 24 OECD countries, also found that long-term earnings inequalities tend to be greater among women than men. Long-term low pay indeed appears an especially prominent risk for women (OECD, 2015).

Less attention has been devoted to investigating women's professional trajectories once in the labour market or their transitions into and out of employment, and how these affect the size of the gender pay gap over the course of their careers. The purpose of this chapter is to fill this gap and draw a comprehensive set of country-specific policy recommendations to promote better career paths for women. It is important not only to remove barriers to the participation of women in paid work, but also barriers to their career progression once in work.

This chapter therefore aims at providing an overview of women's working lives, and their impact on labour income throughout the lifecycle, adopting a dynamic perspective and analysing the main reasons explaining gender gaps in career pathways, and in particular the specific roles played by professional mobility, childbirth and part-time work, which are shown to account for most of the widening of the gap during the working life. By contrast, delivering an exhaustive list of sources for gender inequalities is beyond the scope of this chapter. A complementary analysis of gender equality across OECD countries is presented in OECD (2017[1]). It examines drivers not analysed in this chapter such as: the role played by gender-related education disparities (reverse educational gender gap, under-representation of women in science, technology, engineering and mathematics – STEM – fields); gender gaps in entrepreneurship, financial literacy and financial education; health gender differences; and gender inequalities in unpaid work (childcare, care of older parents and housework obligations).

The rest of the chapter is divided into three parts. Section 6.1 provides a comprehensive overview of women's employment and earnings pathways, analysing how they differ from men's. The section also investigates how and when the gender pay gap appears over the life cycle. Section 6.2 concentrates on the reasons for these different career pathways, and identifies key turning points in women's professional lives that could lead them into career traps. Section 6.3 provides a framework to help countries identify the main sources of gender inequalities in OECD labour markets. This framework illustrates how the very diverse nature of gender labour market inequality calls for appropriate country-specific policy responses, which are then detailed in Section 6.4. The last section provides concluding remarks.

6.1. Gender differences in professional lives

Lifetime earnings differentials are largely determined in the first ten years of workers' careers (OECD, 2015). Nevertheless, very little is known about how the lifecycle component of earnings trajectories plays a role or not in generating the so-called gender gap. In all OECD countries, women are less often employed than men, and when they do have a job, work fewer hours per month (OECD, 2017[1]). They also experience more interruptions in their careers, the majority of which relating to their family situation. The effect of motherhood on wages is well documented in the literature (family penalty). However, women's professional lives are not linear and rising gender inequalities over the lifecycle might as well be the consequence of different trajectories of women over their working life.

The traditional gender wage gap for full-time employees increases with age and especially during parenthood (OECD, 2017[1]). Going beyond the wage gap for full-time employees requires focussing on a broader measure of women's position in the labour market, the gender gap in labour income (GGLI hereafter). The GGLI combines gender disparities along three dimensions: gender gaps in employment rates, hours worked and hourly wage.[1] OECD (2017[4]) shows that, in all OECD countries, the GGLI is much larger than the traditional gender wage gap for full-time employees. This difference illustrates how gender differences in employment rates and hours of work reinforce the impact of the gender wage gap in depressing the labour income of women relative to that of men. This section investigates how professional trajectories of men and women worsen the gender inequality picture as a cohort ages, by describing how employment, hours and earnings vary along the life-cycle and in correspondence with specific life events.

6.1.1. Women's employment pathways: Not linear, and shorter than men's

The early stages of a woman's career are crucial

OECD (2015[5]) has shown that the first 10-15 years in the labour market are critical for long-term career and earnings mobility, and that careers begin differently for women and men (Figure 6.1). In all OECD countries, women leave their parents' home earlier than men on average and they also become involved in a relationship (defined as living with a spouse or partner in the same household) earlier. They have children earlier and more often live with them than men. In all OECD countries except Japan, Portugal, the Netherlands and Turkey, women take shorter educational paths and leave school earlier than men – see also OECD (2018[6]).[2] Finally, in most OECD countries, women enter the labour market through temporary jobs more often than men do.

Women's professional careers in fact combine several working lives

Women's professional careers are not linear, and combine several different working lives. Figure 6.2 displays the detailed activity status of women by age, based on cross-sectional data (Box 6.1). For reference, Figure 6.2 also indicates the activity rate of men (continuous lines, to be compared with the addition of the four solid-filled layers including employed full-time, employed part-time, unpaid workers and unemployed). For both men and women in most countries, the activity rate displayed in the chart have the classical hump-shaped pattern as a function of age, since labour force participation tend to increase in the first half of the career and decrease afterwards. Yet, these simple charts underlie key moments in women's careers and the variety of their working lives across countries:

- *Employment gaps are unequally distributed over the life cycle* – Four patterns emerge as regards women's absence from employment – that is, by comparing in Figure 6.2 the sum of full-timers and part-timers for women with the solid line for men: i) women are largely under-represented in paid employment at the early stage of their career (aged 20 to 40 years) in the Czech Republic, Estonia, Hungary, Latvia, the Slovak Republic and (to a lesser extent) Finland, France, Germany, Poland and the United States; ii) women are under-represented at the middle and later stage of their life cycle in Australia, Greece, Ireland, Israel, Japan, Korea, Switzerland and, to a lesser extent, Luxembourg, the Netherlands, Spain and Portugal – their entry into the labour market resembles that of men (employment rates are similar at age 25-29) but a significant share of women then disappears from the labour market as of age 30; iii) in Austria, Belgium, Canada,

Denmark, Iceland, Norway, Slovenia, Sweden and the United Kingdom, the employment gap is constant over the life cycle; and iv) in Mexico and Turkey, and to a lesser extent in Chile and Italy, a significant share of the female population never enters the labour market.

- Women often experience a *"second working career"* – A significant share of women enter or re-enter the labour market at a second stage of life (Austria, the Czech Republic, Estonia, Finland, Hungary, Iceland, Poland, the Slovak Republic and to a lesser extent Denmark, France, Germany, Latvia, Sweden, and the United Kingdom). In these countries, starting around 30-34 years old, employment rises for women but not for men. This increase is mostly driven by permanent contracts in all countries except in Korea, where this second career of women is entirely driven by temporary contracts, self-employment and unpaid work.

- *Up to ten years before reaching the legal pension age, many women are already inactive* – Four patterns emerge: i) the share of women who are inactive but not retired ("other inactive" in Figure 6.2) is significantly larger than the same share for men in Chile, Ireland, the Netherlands, Norway, Sweden, Switzerland and to a lesser extent Austria, Denmark and Germany – see OECD (2018[6]); ii) In a second set of countries, the proportion of early leavers is high for both men and women: early retirement continues to play a large role in Belgium, Hungary, Poland and to a lesser extent Finland; iii) In a third set of countries, neither men nor women withdraw prior to reaching the legal pension age: the Czech Republic, Estonia, Iceland, Latvia, the Slovak Republic, Slovenia and the United Kingdom; iv) In Korea – where the pension system is recent compared to those in other OECD countries (OECD, 2018[7]) – and to a lesser extent in Greece, Italy, Luxembourg, Mexico, Portugal, Spain and Turkey, the proportion of women out of the labour market continuously increases with age, and a considerable share of them never ends up receiving a pension.[3] Gender inequalities in later stages of the life cycle are particularly challenging in these countries, a situation that calls for specific actions to promote women's participation in the labour market earlier in their career.

- *Part-time work* may also represent a career trap for women. Even if it helps to reconcile work life balance, part-time employment status can become permanent for many women, while it usually remains a transitory one for men. In Australia Austria, Denmark, Finland, Iceland and the Netherlands, part-time status is particularly frequent among active women aged over 45.[4]

Figure 6.1. The working lives of women start differently than those of men

Major life events at career start (percentage of the population aged 25-29 years old, except Panel D, 20-24 years old)

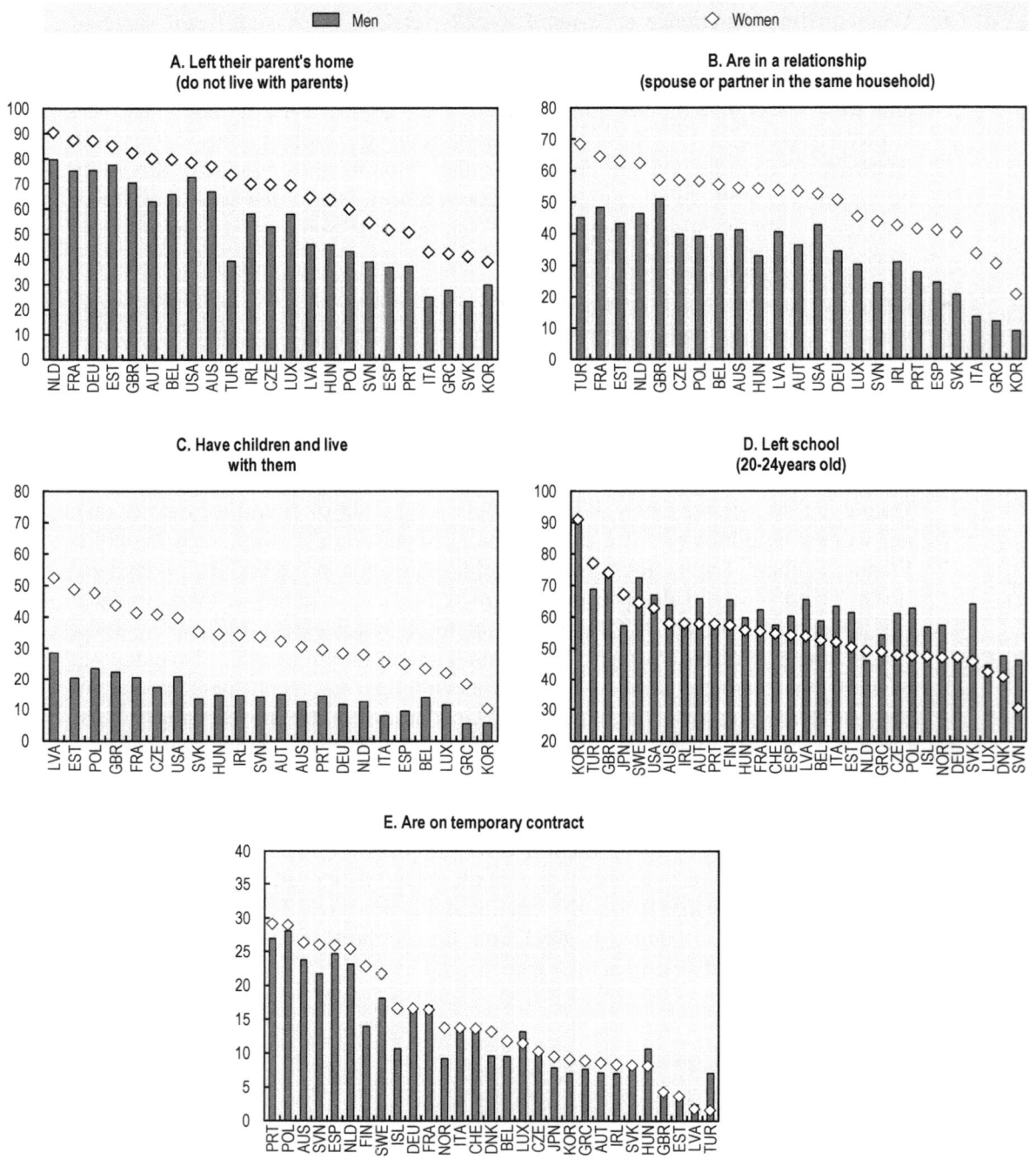

Note: Denmark, Finland, Iceland, Japan, Norway, Sweden and Switzerland are not shown in Panel A, B or C; Turkey is not in Panel C; and the United States are not shown in Panel E (data not available).
Source: Household, Income and Labour Dynamics in Australia (HILDA), 2015 for Australia; European Union Labour Force Survey (EU-LFS), 2013-15 for European countries; Labour Force Survey (LFS), 2012 for Japan; Korean Labor and Income Panel Study (KLIPS), 2010-14 for Korea; Labour Force Survey (LFS), 2013 for Turkey; and Current Population Survey (CPS), 2016 for the United States.

StatLink ⧉ http://dx.doi.org/10.1787/888933778611

**Figure 6.2. Women's professional careers are not linear
and combine several different working lives**

Detailed activity status of women and men, by age, cohort population = 100, 2015 or latest available year

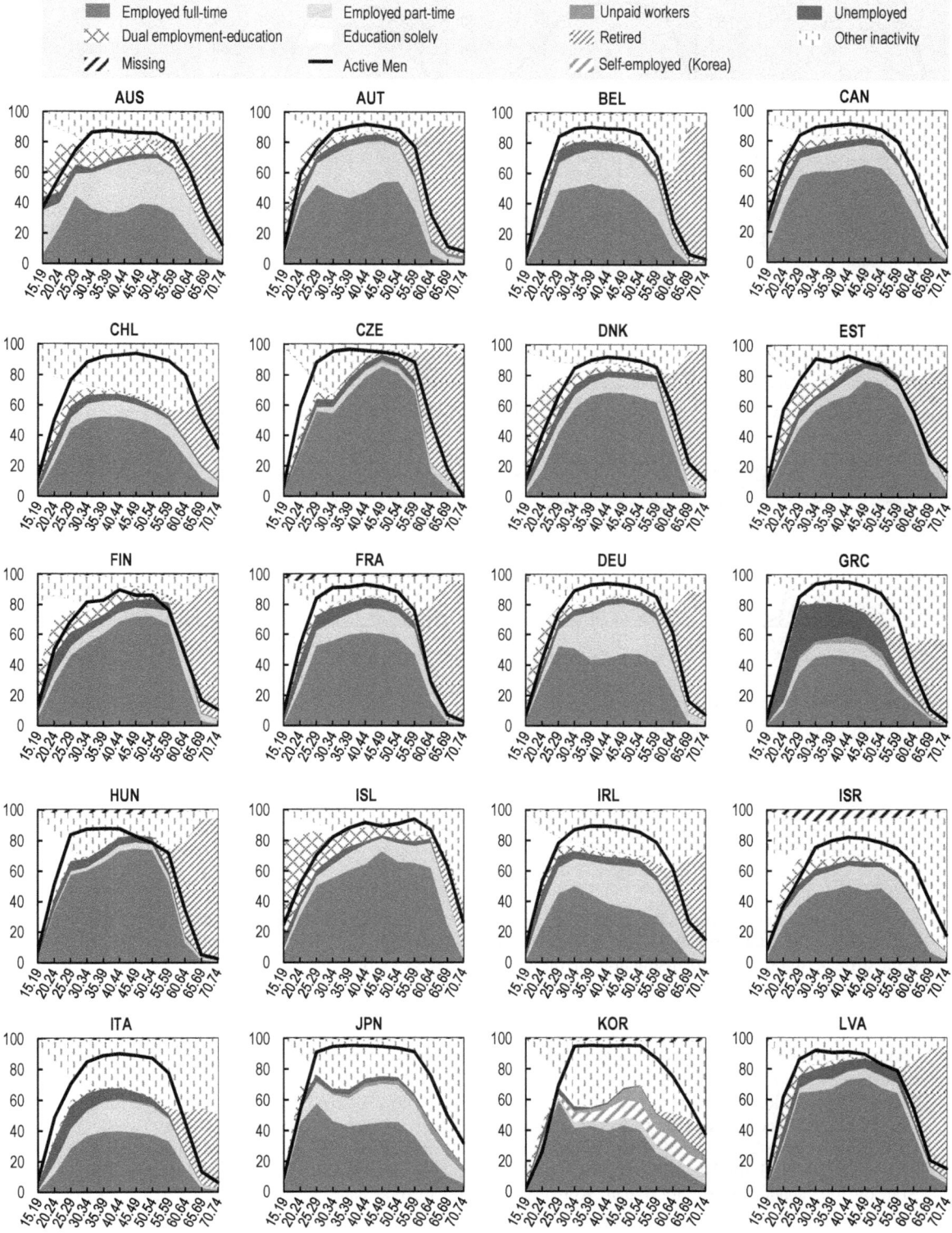

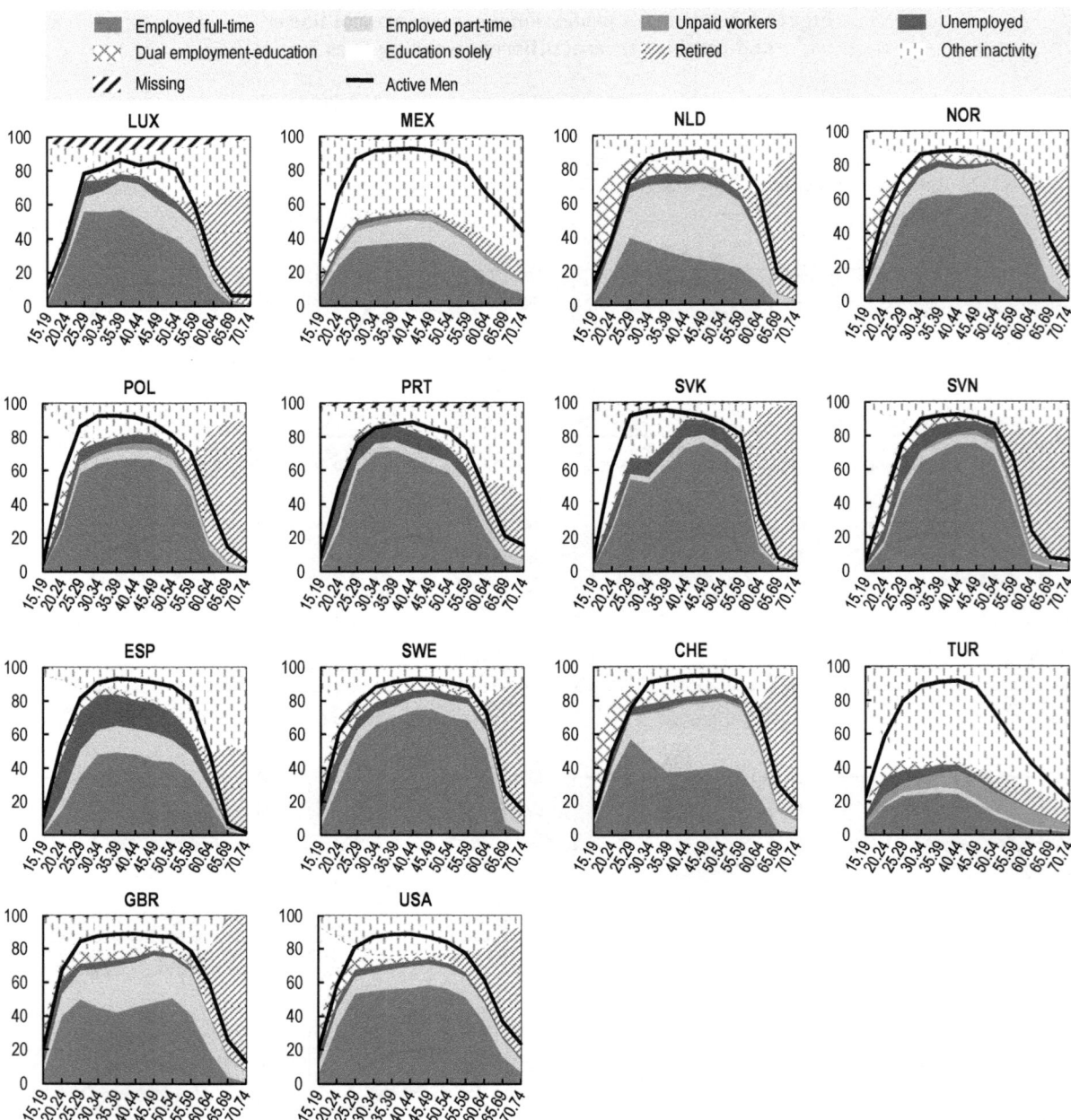

Note: The solid line displays the proportion of active men; "active" includes the categories "employed full-time", "employed part-time", "unpaid workers" and "unemployed". This activity rate for men may differ from official figures due to distinction of the separate category "dual employment-education" that helps identify how men and women enter the labour market. The activity rates presented here are in fact "activity rates with achieved education". "Part-time" is defined as less than 30 hours worked per week. For Korea, data on working hours are available for employees only; the self-employed appear as a separated category. For Canada and Japan, "retired" are included in "other inactivity". For Japan, data refer to 2012 and the unpaid workers category is in fact "family workers".

Source: Household, Income and Labour Dynamics in Australia (HILDA), 2015 for Australia; European Union Labour Force Survey (EU-LFS), 2015 data for European countries; Labour Force Survey (LFS), 2015 for Canada; *Encuesta de Caracterizacion Socioeconomica Nacional* (CASEN), 2015 for Chile; Labour Force Survey (LFS), 2011 for Israel; Kambayashi (2017[8]), "Global Change in the Structure of Employment: A Note on the Japanese Case" for Japan; Korean Labor and Income Panel Study (KLIPS), 2014 for Korea; *Encuesta Nacional de Ocupación y Empleo* (ENOE), 2016 for Mexico; Labour Force Survey (LFS), 2015 for Turkey; and Current Population Survey (CPS), 2016 for the United States.

StatLink 🔗 http://dx.doi.org/10.1787/888933778630

Box 6.1. Strengths and limitations of the available data sources

Ideally, analysing the career paths of women would involve observing their complete working lives and comparing them with the career trajectories of men. The resulting ideal data would reveal career path dependencies allowing assessing how choices made at the start of one's career continue to impact one's professional situation, earnings trajectories and well-being several years or decades later. The effects can even extend beyond retirement, as pensions depend on career length and work trajectories over the entire working life. Unfortunately such ideal data do not exist on a cross-country comparable basis, as panel data only follow individuals over a limited period. This chapter makes use of several sorts of microdata, taking advantage of their strengths while not losing sight of their limitations.

Panel data

Panel data follow individuals over time. They allow investigation of year-to-year transitions, as well as transitions occurring between two interviews (by reconstructing monthly calendars based on retrospective questions). In contrast to much of the literature (dealing with yearly transitions), this chapter concentrates on monthly professional transitions drawn from short panel data. For each year/individual, given the person's activity status in January, it considers any monthly transition that may occur over the year. Several transitions are therefore possible for the same individual from one year to the next. For a subset of countries (Australia, Germany and the United States), available panel data track people over a period of sufficient length to examine longer-term effects of career events, as well as career path dependencies. Based on these long panel data, the chapter investigates cumulative mobility over time, and how childbirth affects women's professional opportunities over the medium to long-term (seven years).

Long retrospective data

Long retrospective data are powerful alternative sources. This chapter makes use of the Survey of Health, Ageing and Retirement in Europe (SHARE), Wave 3 – SHARELIFE, which provides a rich set of information on the work and personal histories (from marriages and divorces to maternity, health and housing) of 30 000 older workers aged 50 and over in 2009 in 13 European countries (Austria, Belgium, the Czech Republic, Denmark, France, Germany, Greece, Italy, the Netherlands, Poland, Spain, Sweden and Switzerland). SHARELIFE's major limitation is memory bias: coverage is limited to spells of employment longer than six months, covers a period when the labour markets were much less mobile than they are now, and when people remained with the same company their entire lives. Even so, it is the only dataset that affords a look at entire individual trajectories of workers and non-workers over their life cycle.

Cross-sectional data

Even cross-sectional data can be very informative as regards women's situation on the labour market at different times in their career. Beyond reporting about employment, unemployment and inactivity, these data allow: i) including an in-between category ("education and work"); ii) specifying the reason for inactivity (solely in education, retirement, military services, other inactive); iii) looking at full-time/part-time/unpaid work as well as permanent/temporary/self-employed. They allow drawing a clear picture of women's activity status at different moments in their lives and make it easier to remain mindful of the orders of magnitude of the sub-population being dealt with when focusing on career events and paths. Nevertheless, using cross-sectional data, one can easily mix age, career and cohort effects, which play a crucial role in the analysis of gender-related issues (see Box 6.2).

Goldin and Mitchell (2016[9]) argue that the hump shape of labour force participation over the life cycle is disappearing in favour of the emergence of M-shaped curves prevailing for new cohorts. The explanation put forward is that birth events had always produced a temporary withdrawal from employment but are now occurring later because of the delay in marriage and childbirth – see OECD (2018[6]). In Figure 6.2, an M-shaped curve is clearly visible in Korea and Japan, suggesting that women tend to exit the labour force upon childbirth but re-enter once children have grown older. By contrast, in those countries where part-time expands at childbirth age, an M-shaped curve is visible only for the share of full-time employment (the intensive margin), while it remains hump-shaped when both full-time and part-time are taken into account. This, however, is likely due to further evolution of behaviours over time, transforming M-shaped curves on the extensive margin (including both full-time and part-time) into similar curves prevailing only on the intensive margin. For example, Blundell, Bozio and Laroque (2013[10]) found clear M-shaped curves for the United Kingdom in 1977 both on the intensive and extensive margins, and yet these remained visible only on the intensive margin in 2007.

6.1.2. Gender gaps in hourly earnings: an inverted U-curve

Full-time women still earn less than men

Beyond gaps in employment and hours worked, earnings for the same amount of hours of work represent a crucial difference between men and women's labour market success. Gender wage disparities are slowly decreasing but remain considerable.[5] On average, among OECD countries, full-time women earned 15% less than their men peers in 2014, while this gap was 16% in 2005 (Figure 6.3). The gender wage gap for full-timers is the largest in Korea (over 35%) and the smallest in Belgium (less than 5%). The latter is also the country with the largest gap reduction (almost 10 percentage points) since 2005. By contrast large increases are observable in Chile and Latvia. However, in these countries larger gaps go hand in hand with a significant increase in female participation, in particular among the low-skilled, which, by increasing the number of women at the bottom end of the wage distribution, mechanically reduce average wages among working women.

Gender wage gaps draw an inverted U-curve over the career

In many countries with sufficient data to estimate gender gaps in hourly earnings for different cohorts (Figure 6.4), these gaps show an inverted U shape over the career with most of the wage gap increase taking place from 30 to 40 years of age (e.g. Australia, Canada, Germany, Korea, Mexico, the United Kingdom and the United States). In English-speaking countries and Korea, gender wage gaps tend to shrink in the later part of the working life, while they stabilise after age 40 in Germany and Mexico. By contrast, in France and Italy, where seniority premiums play a large role in wage setting and lower professional mobility limits new job opportunities at old age (see Section 6.2 below), the gender gap continues to increase over the career.

Figure 6.3. Gender disparities in full-time earnings remain considerable

Gender gap in median earnings of full-time employees (15 years and over), 2005 and 2014

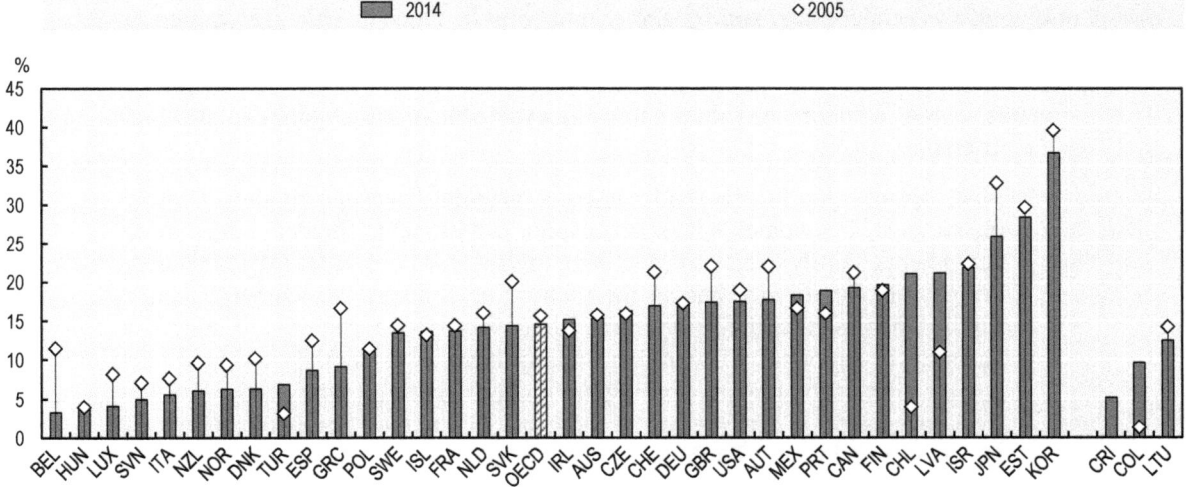

Note: Countries are sorted in ascending order representing increasingly poor performance. They are selected on the basis of data availability. Gaps computed as the difference between median earnings of men and women relative to median earnings of men. Data refer to full-time workers; to 2005 except for Chile, Estonia, Latvia, Lithuania, Luxembourg, the Netherlands, Poland, Slovenia, Switzerland and Turkey (2006), Colombia (2007) and Denmark (2008); and to 2013 except for Israel (2011), France and Spain (2012), Sweden (2013) and Chile (2015). Data for the OECD is an unweighted average.
*Source: OECD Earnings Distribution Database (*www.oecd.org/employment/emp/employmentdatabase-earningsandwages.htm*)*.

StatLink ᐧᐧᓯ᠍ᑊᐧ http://dx.doi.org/10.1787/888933778649

A narrowing gap for younger cohorts

The age-gender wage gap profiles of recent cohorts lie below those of older ones, implying that the gap tends to narrow over time. Yet, this shift does not occur homogenously in all stages of the working life and in all countries, which implies that it might also be misleading to try to infer life-cycle / career pathways by looking at labour income gaps at different ages at one point in time (Box 6.2). Arrows in Figure 6.4 illustrate how the gap evolved across cohorts.[6] Gaps are smaller for younger cohorts in Canada, France, Germany, Mexico, the United Kingdom and the United States. In the United States, the narrowing of the gender wage gap that occurred between 1975 and 2009 is largely due to cohort effects (Campbell and Pearlman, 2013[11]), but convergence has slowed since 2000 (Juhn and McCue, 2017[12]). Interestingly, while gains in female wages contributed to the decline in gender wage gaps for cohorts born before 1950 in the United States, the narrowing for later cohorts is primarily the result of male wages declining (Campbell and Pearlman, 2013[11]). In other countries (notably, France and Mexico) the narrowing of the wage gap appears more pronounced at the end of the working life. The age at which the gap starts decreasing or becomes flat has generally gone down over time for the oldest cohorts, but there are signs of inversion of this process in a few countries (e.g. Canada and the United Kingdom).

Box 6.2. Empirical biases in the analysis of the gap in hourly earnings over the life cycle

Looking at the gender wage gap by age at one point in time (in 2015, for example) can be misleading. The data indeed capture gender wage gaps of different cohorts taken at different moments in the life cycle, but they do not measure the evolution of the gender gap of a cohort over their entire life cycle. There are several explanations for the difference:

- First, composition effects render cohorts different from one another. Indeed, megatrends in women's human capital investment (higher educational attainment), family decisions (declining marriage, delays in fertility decisions, decrease in family size and in the number of children per women), labour supply (increased participation in the labour market over the past decades and changes in amounts of working hours) have considerably changed the composition of the female working population. Therefore, the gender gap for workers aged 50 in 2015 is not the same as the one their parents experienced 20 years previously. Participation in the labour market has increased significantly over the past decades; women are more educated; and they withdraw less from the labour market at childbirth. The gender gap is expected to decrease for more recent cohorts, as working men and working women are more alike now than a few decades ago.

- Second, returns to individual characteristics may differ across cohorts, gender and time (for example the effect an additional year of schooling is likely to have on individual earnings), with the result that the gender income gap evolves differently, even for similarly composed cohorts.

- Third, time variation effects have been identified through age-period-cohort analysis – see Campbell and Pearlman (2013[11]) for a detailed presentation of these models. There are three types of time-related variation: i) *age effects*: the physiological or social processes associated with ageing, such as motherhood or tenure, produce changes in wages; ii) *period effects*: certain events (the global financial crisis, for example) simultaneously affect all cohorts, but at different ages. Several other phenomena might simultaneously affect all cohorts at different moments of the life cycle, such as job polarisation or emerging new forms of work (OECD, 2017[4]); this may bias also the cohort analysis, as shocks may bias the inter-cohort comparison; iii) *cohort effects*: the timing of life and labour market experiences, such as entering the labour market during a recession, can shift career trajectories for men and women (Campbell and Pearlman, 2013[11]).

Figure 6.4 displays hourly earnings gaps between genders for all workers (full-time and part-time) by age for five cohorts. Cohorts are here defined as all individuals born within a five-year period; the periods selected are 1936-40, 1946-50, 1956-60, 1966-70 and 1976-80. Results are the same with the in-between cohorts, but the juxtaposition of too many cohort curves would make the figure unreadable. Unfortunately, this is a demanding exercise in terms of data availability, as it requires microdata over a very long period. In most countries, microdata are not available over a sufficiently long period to enable building wage gap curves by cohorts. Thus, only nine countries appear in the figure.

**Figure 6.4. The gender earnings gap grows until the middle of the career
and then stabilises or falls**

Gender gap in hourly labour earnings, by age and cohorts

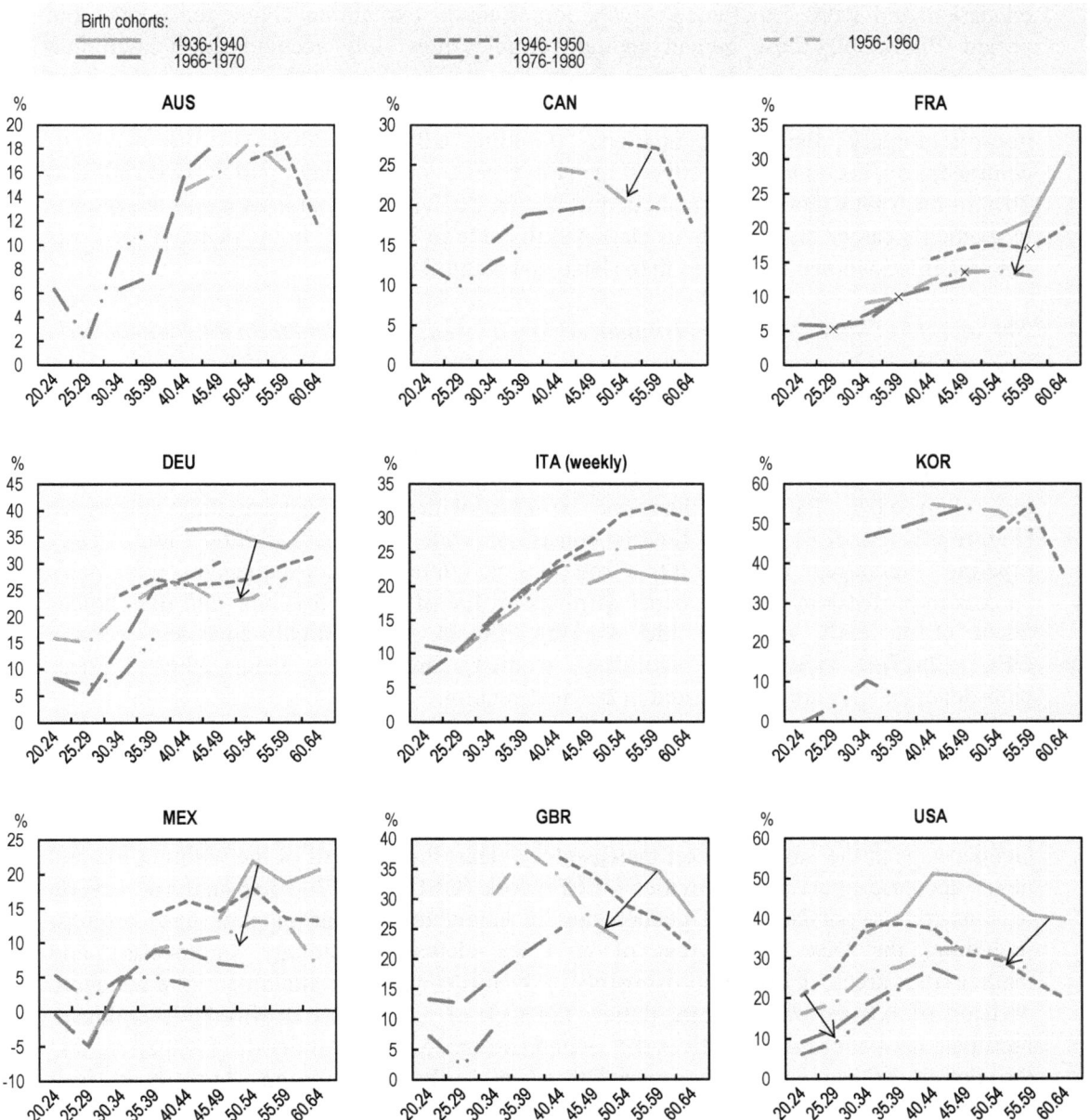

Note: Labour hourly earnings definition: Australia, Germany, the United Kingdom and the United States – yearly earnings from labour divided by the total number of hours worked during the year (for those working at least 52 hours during the year); Canada – hourly wages (of employees only); France – Net hourly earnings (break in series in 2003, identified by a cross on the curves); Italy – gross weekly earnings; Mexico – gross hourly earnings. The gender gap is defined as the difference between median earnings of men and women relative to median earnings of men. Arrows illustrates how the gender labour income gap evolved across cohorts.

Source: Cross-National Equivalent File (CNEF) for Australia (2001-14), Germany (1984-2014), the United Kingdom (1991-2008) and the United States (1970-2013); Labour Force Survey (LFS), 1997-2015 for Canada; *Enquête emploi* (1990-2012) for France; *Istituto Nazionale Previdenza Sociale* (INPS), 1985-2014 for Italy; Korean Labor and Income Panel Study (KLIPS), 1998-2014 for Korea; and *Encuesta Nacional de Ocupación y Empleo* (ENOE), 1995-2016 for Mexico.

StatLink ⸗ http://dx.doi.org/10.1787/888933778668

The main reason for narrowing wage gaps is the increase in female educational attainment for younger cohorts; young women even outperform young men in many countries, leading to the so-called reversed educational gender gap. Nevertheless, Blau and Kahn (2016[13]) find that while women's gains in market skills – measured by education and work experience – were important in explaining convergence over the period 1980-2000, these human capital variables now only account for a negligible portion of the remaining gap.[7] Other reasons for the shrinking of the gap have also been well documented in the literature and include: increasing employment of women in non-traditionally female occupations (Goldin, 2004[14]; 2006[15]); the role of contraception, accounting for 10% of the convergence of the gender gap in the 1980s and 30% in the 1990s (Bailey, Hershbein and Miller, 2012[16]); and an increase in the returns to women's career investments in market skills, due to increases in the demand for skills that benefited women relative to men (Blau and Kahn, 1997[17]).

The inverted U-curve is more pronounced for low-skilled workers than for high-skilled ones facing a glass ceiling

The inverted U shape of age-gender wage gaps is more evident in the case of low-skilled workers. In Canada, France and the United States, for example, the gender wage gap starts decreasing at younger age in the case of workers with upper secondary education or less (Figure 6.5, Panel A), than for workers with higher educational attainment (Figure 6.5, Panel B). While this is consistent with the "glass ceiling" and "leaky pipeline" literature, [8] it also points to the possible cumulative consequences on women's careers in professions with a steeper earnings profile of the professional and life choices taken at an early stage of the working life by many highly-educated women. OECD (2017[1]) notes that childless women fare better than others. These path-dependencies are investigated in the next section.

6.2. Women's professional trajectories and career path-dependency: the role of lost opportunities

Gender gaps in the labour market increase for at least the first half of the working life and never decrease afterwards. Previous OECD work (OECD, 2017[1]) has analysed several reasons for the persistence of gender gaps in labour market participation and earnings, including: the lack of progress of girls in science, technology, engineering and mathematics areas, despite improvements in overall educational attainment; the gendered division of housework and care duties; the lack of adequate and affordable childcare facilities; tax-benefit disincentives for second earners to work; gender discrimination; and the deficit of women in managerial positions. All these reasons have been well documented in the literature. Less attention, however, has been paid to women's professional trajectories and their consequences. To shed some light on this issue, this section analyses gender differences in labour mobility, consequences of a childbirth and professional choices. In particular, it investigates the medium- and long-term consequences of childbirth on women's propensity to withdrawing from the labour market, opting for part-time work or turning down better-paid job offers, as well as the implications of these labour supply responses for career progression and the gender pay gap at different ages.

**Figure 6.5. The inverted U-curve of the gender wage gap is more pronounced
for low-educated workers**

Gender gap in hourly labour earnings, by educational attainment, age and cohorts

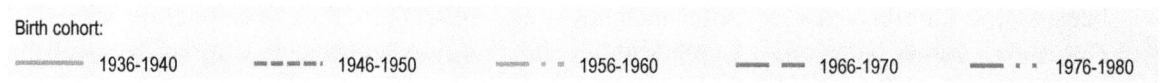

A. Workers with upper secondary education or less

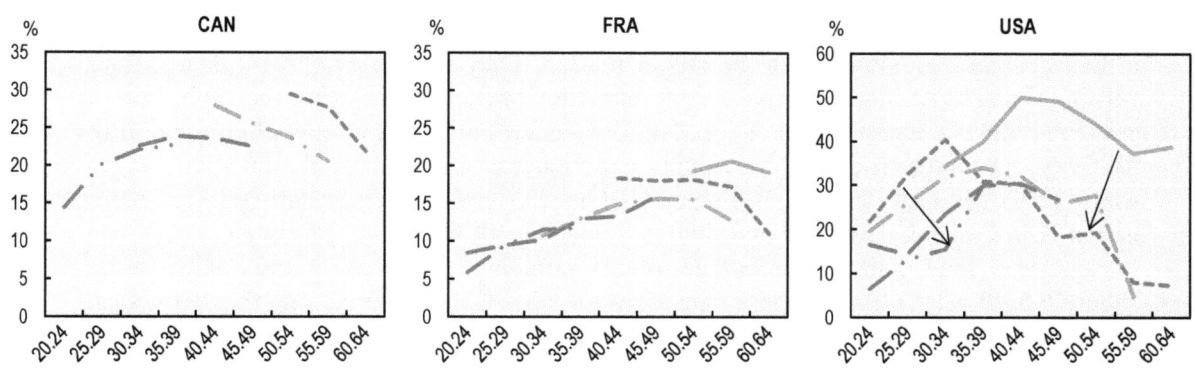

B. Workers with more than upper secondary education

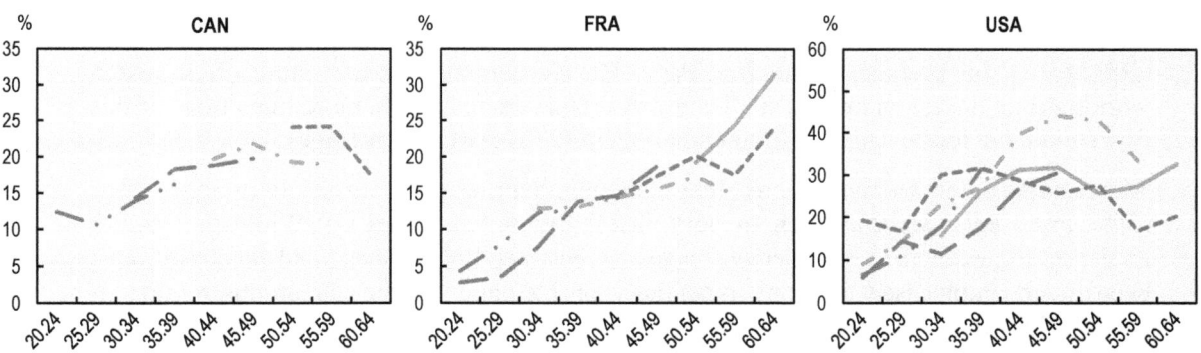

Note: Labour hourly earnings definition: CNEF – Yearly earnings from labour divided by the total number of hours worked during the year (for those working at least 52 hours during the year); Canada – Hourly wages (of employees only); France – Net hourly earnings (break in series in 2003). The gender gap is defined as the difference between median earnings of men and women relative to median earnings of men.
Arrows illustrates how the gender labour income gap evolved across cohorts.
Source: Labour Force Survey (LFS), 1997-2015 for Canada; *Enquête emploi* (1990-2012) for France; and Cross-National Equivalent File (CNEF), 1970-2013 for the United States.

StatLink 🔗 http://dx.doi.org/10.1787/888933778687

6.2.1. Women's labour mobility differs from men's

Women have fewer in-work transitions than men

Job-to-job mobility, especially early in a career, is an important source of wage growth because job mobility enables better matches – e.g. OECD (2015[5]).[9] Personal decisions that impact career paths relate to job search behaviour, job acceptance, contract type and housework. In particular, potential and actual fertility can have an effect on career events (and career events can affect fertility and the decision to have children).[10] Labour mobility can be measured in various ways (Box 6.3).

Every year in OECD countries, 16% of the working-age population experience a change in their professional situation in the labour market. They change employer, change their working time (switching from full-time to part-time or the reverse), lose their job, find (a new) one, become unemployed or inactive, or re-enter the labour market after a period of inactivity. The proportion of individuals experiencing a professional transition ranges from 12% or less in Italy, France,[11] Greece, Ireland and Portugal to more than 25% in Finland, Sweden and Iceland. Gender differences are rather small (on average less than half a percentage point) compared to cross-country differences (Figure 6.6, Panel A). Professional transitions are obviously higher among the active than the inactive population, with almost one active person out of five going through a professional change every year.

Women have on average the same number of professional transitions as men over their entire working lives – 9.6 on average in OECD countries – but they are of different nature than men's.[12] For example, with the exception of Finland, Germany and Japan, women have fewer in-work transitions (i.e. changes of employer, job or contract type) than men (20% fewer, on average, Figure 6.6, Panel B). By contrast, women more often switch working time than men in almost all countries (an average of 40% more transitions of this type) and have fewer episodes of unemployment (21% fewer on average).

Women also enter inactivity more often than men, but they also exit inactivity more often (29% more episodes than men in both cases; Figure 6.6, Panel C). While the greater tendency for women to experience transitions between employment and inactivity have been much emphasised as being potentially problematic for the career progression of women, less frequent in-work transitions may also represent an important handicap for women.

Women miss crucial professional transitions around childbirth

In-work transitions are important because they have a positive impact on income growth, particularly for younger workers (Figure 6.7, Panel A). In all OECD countries, in-work transitions have a positive impact on earnings all other things equal,[13] increasing labour income by 7.8% on average. Moreover, transitions seem to pay off more when they occur at young age than later. Job mobility in the early stages of working life has been shown to have particularly strong effects on wage growth and also helps workers to find job matches that open up career ladders.[14] OECD (2015[5]) shows, for example, that the first 10-15 years in the labour market are crucial for long-term career and earnings mobility.

Figure 6.6. Professional transitions of women are of a different nature than those of men

A. Total number of professional transitions[a] during working life for men and women

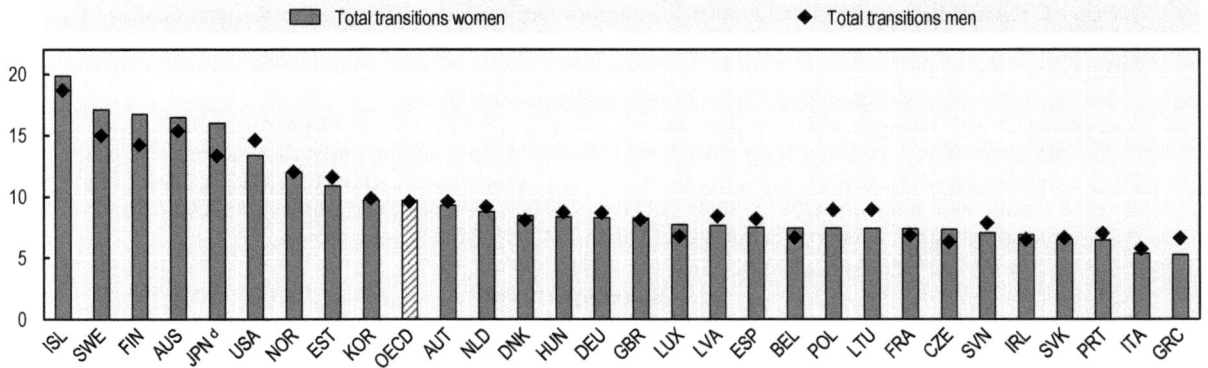

B. Ratios[b] of total number of in-work transitions and transitions through unemployment of women compared to men's

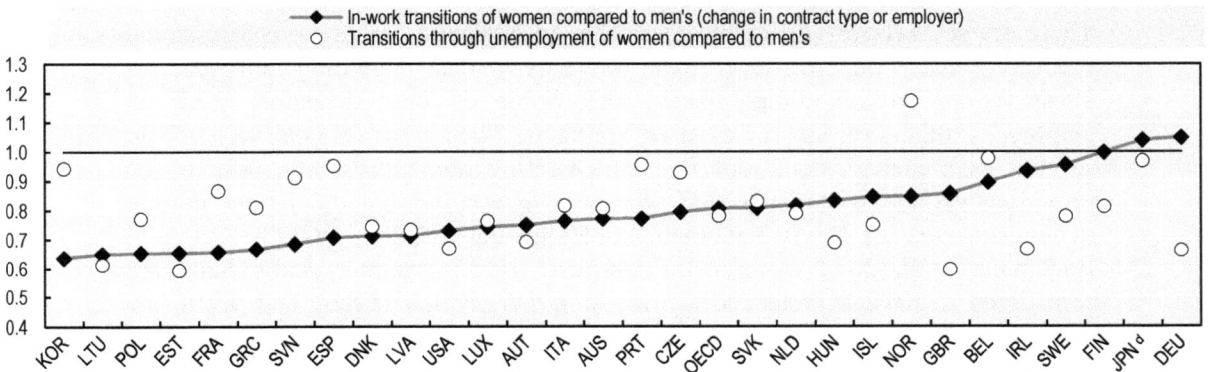

C. Ratios[c] of total number of transitions of women compared to men's through inactivity

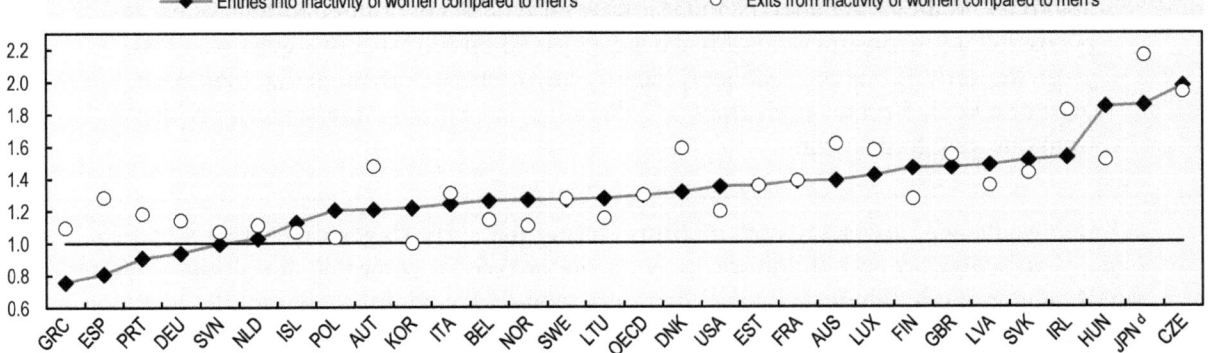

Note: Professional transitions refer to any significant professional change that might occur from one year to the next based on a monthly calendar. Individuals are considered to have experienced a professional transition if they had any change in their professional situation on the labour market, meaning that they changed employer, contract type or working time (switching from full-time to part-time or the reverse); lost their job or found (a new) one; became unemployed or inactive; or re-entered the labour market after a period of inactivity. Several transitions are therefore possible for the same individual from one year to the next. Population aged 16 to 74. The number of lifetime transitions is simulated by adding up transitions over five years of similar individuals belonging to different cohorts.

a) Transitions reported in panel A include transitions between employment, unemployment and inactivity, as well as in-work transitions (changes in contract type, working hours or change of employer).

b) Panel B reports the ratio of the total number of in-work transitions (changes in contract type, working hours or change of employer) of women to the total number of in-work transitions of men, as well as the ratio of the total number of transitions to and from unemployment of women compared to the corresponding transitions through unemployment of men.

c) Panel C reports the ratio of the total number of entries into inactivity of women to the total number of entries into inactivity of men, as well as the ratio of the total number of exits from inactivity of women to the total number of exits from inactivity of men.

d) For Japan, data refer to persons aged 20 to 74, and results are unweighted.

Source: Household, Income and Labour Dynamics in Australia (HILDA), 2005-15 for Australia; European Union Statistics on Income and Living Conditions (EU-SILC), 2005-15 for European countries; German Socio Economic Panel (GSOEP), 2005-15 for Germany; Japan Household Panel Survey (KHPS), 2009-14 for Japan; Korean Labor and Income Panel Study (KLIPS), 2005-14 for Korea; and Current Population Survey (CPS), Annual Social and Economic Supplement (ASEC), 2006-15 for the United States.

StatLink ⟰ http://dx.doi.org/10.1787/888933778706

Box 6.3. Measuring transitions in labour markets

There are several very different approaches to estimating labour or professional mobility, based on firm-level data, on survey data including retrospective questions, or on longitudinal panel data. Some of these measures focus on employees, others on jobs or even on contracts. Their ultimate goal varies from serving as a management tool for implementing human resource policies, to providing economic statistics that will help in ascertaining the labour market dynamism – see e.g. Davis, Faberman and Haltiwanger (2006[18]) OECD (2015[5]); Bachmann et al. (2014[19]). For the purpose of this chapter, individuals are considered to have experienced a *professional transition* if they had, from one year to the next, any change in their professional situation on the labour market, meaning that they changed employer, contract type or working time (switching from full-time to part-time or the reverse); lost their job or found (a new) one; became unemployed or inactive; or re-entered the labour market after a period of inactivity. With short panel data that follow individuals over three to four years, it is possible to reconstruct monthly calendars based on retrospective questions and, given the activity status in January, identify any monthly transition that may occur over one year. Several transitions are therefore possible for the same individual from one year to the next.

As a consequence, lower in-work mobility during the early stages of women's careers, and in particular around childbirth, plays a major role in enlarging the initially quite small gender gap in labour income.[15] Not only women are slightly less mobile than men on average, but they especially miss the crucial in-work transitions occurring in the early stages of men's career, which promote stronger career advancement for them. More specifically, women miss these in-work transitions immediately after childbirth. In fact, mothers with children aged three years or less are 4.2 percentage points less likely to experience an in-work transition than their partner, even conditional on working the year before (Figure 6.7, Panel B). The tendency for women to have a considerable lower share of in-work mobility around the time that they become mothers has the potential to significantly limit women's careers,[16] and contributes to the gender pay gap generated before age 40 (Section 6.2).[17]

Figure 6.7. In-work transitions have a positive impact on earnings, but mothers are missing many of these opportunities for advancement for several years after childbirth

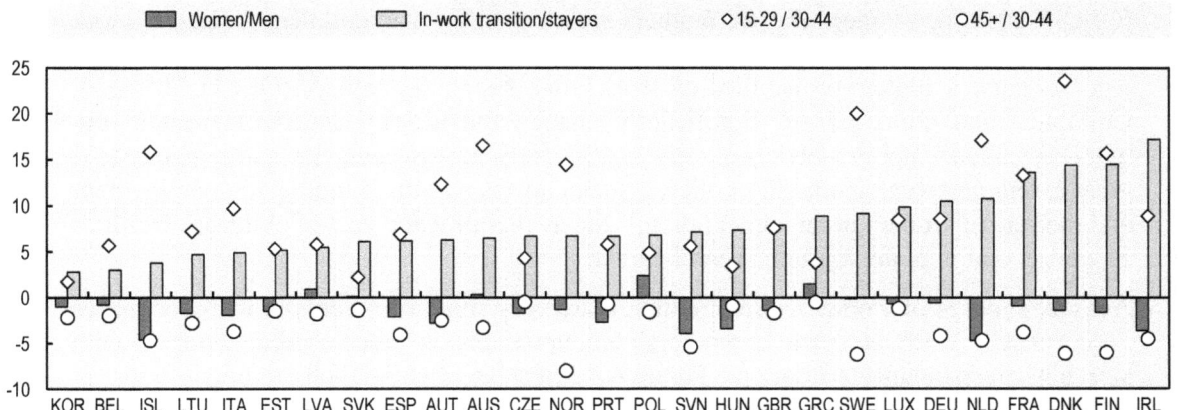

A. Expected total labour income growth conditional on working last year
Marginal effects (percentage points)

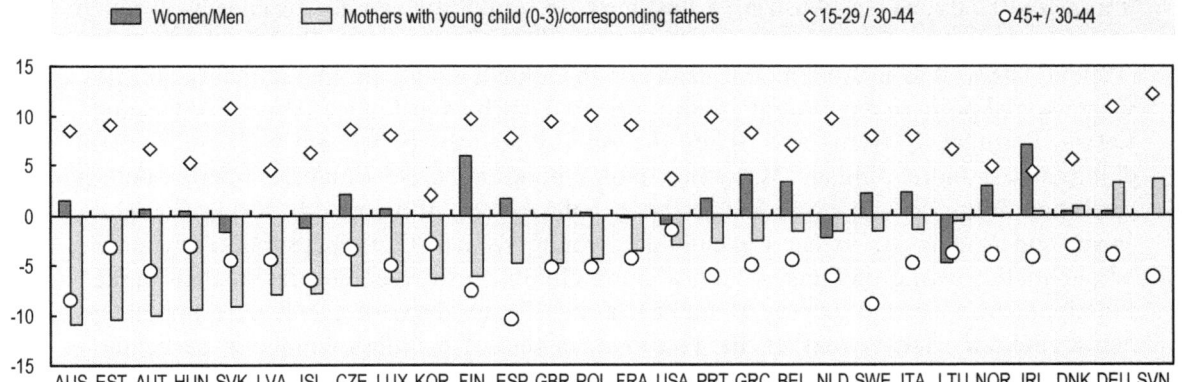

B. Probability of experiencing at least one in-work transition (change of job, of employer or contract), conditional on working last year
Marginal effects (percentage points)

Note: Panel A shows marginal effects from regressions, where the dependent variable is total labour income growth from one year to the next, conditional on having worked the year before. Results presented are marginal effects for in-work transitions (change of employer, job or contract type compared to stayers), women (compared to men), youth (15-29, compared to prime age 30-44), and older workers (45+ compared to prime age). Regressions are country specific and include controls (with female cross-effects) for the presence/age of the last child (0-3; 4-6 and 7+), education, whether the person is single, married or in a non-married partnership, whether the person has had very bad health and year dummies. Sample: persons aged 15-64 years old. Panel B shows marginal effects from probit regressions, where the dependent variable is whether or not the person experienced an in-work transition (change of employer job or contract type) during the current year, conditional on having worked the year before. Results presented are the marginal effects for women compared to men, mothers with young child (0-3) compared to corresponding fathers, youth (15-29, compared to prime age 30-44) and older workers (45+ compared to prime age). Regressions are country specific and also include controls (with female cross-effects) for the presence/age of the last child (0-3; 4-6 and 7+), education, whether the person is single, married or in a non-married partnership, whether the person has had very bad health and year dummies. Sample: persons aged 15-64 years old.
Source: Household, Income and Labour Dynamics in Australia (HILDA), 2006-14 for Australia; European Union Statistics on Income and Living Conditions (EU-SILC), 2006-14 for European countries; German Socio Economic Panel (GSOEP), 2006-14 for Germany; Korean Labor and Income Panel Study (KLIPS), 2006-14 for Korea; and Current Population Survey (CPS), Annual Social and Economic Supplement (ASEC), 2006-15 for the United States.

StatLink ᴍꜱᴾ http://dx.doi.org/10.1787/888933778725

6.2.2. *Unravelling the role of childbirth on women's careers*

Female labour supply reacts very differently to childbirth in different countries

Women's careers are disproportionately hampered by childbearing and child rearing (OECD, 2017[1]). Women who are mothers are more likely than childless women to work fewer hours, earn less than men, or opt out of the workforce entirely. By contrast, men tend to have a higher probability of work after becoming fathers (OECD, 2016[20]). Childbirth and child rearing significantly change the activity status of women, but mothers' labour supply elasticities vary significantly across countries and depends to a great extent on social and family policies; social norms regarding mothers in employment and the role of women in raising children;[18] the availability and cost of childcare facilities as well as marginal tax rates on second-earners.

Activity statuses of women without children are very similar to men's in many countries – see OECD (2018[6]) – while mothers' labour supply is much different, albeit with sizeable cross-country variation. Figure 6.8 displays the detailed activity status at different ages of women with and without children for six illustrative OECD countries. Panel A shows that in Hungary, as in the Czech Republic, Estonia, the Slovak Republic and to a lesser extent Poland and the United States, a large proportion of young mothers are inactive but they later enter (or re-enter) the labour market. Panel B illustrates that in the Netherlands as in Austria, adjustment to childbirth comes primarily through significant take-up of part-time work. A combination of both patterns appears in Germany (Panel C) as well as in Australia, Ireland and the United Kingdom. In a number countries, where social policies are strongly family oriented, such as in France (Panel D), Belgium, Latvia, Portugal, Slovenia and Spain, the activity statuses of women with and without children are more similar. However, motherhood in these countries can result in education drop-out with consequences later in the careers of women. In Korea (Panel E), Japan and to a lesser extent Luxembourg, young women participate massively in the labour market while mothers withdraw upon childbirth to re-enter later in their career. Finally, in Mexico and Turkey (Panel F), a significant share of the female population never enters the labour market: the employment rate of childless women is particularly low, despite being still twice as large as that of mothers.

Juhn and McCue (2017[12]) provide a review of academic literature focusing on the "motherhood penalty" and the "family gap" in earnings. They show that the wages of mothers are significantly lower than those of non-mothers with similar human capital characteristics. The motherhood penalty amounts to approximately 5-15 log points for mothers compared to non-mothers.[19] And it has long-lasting effects: wage gaps indeed accumulate, particularly among highly-skilled women. Wilde, Batchelder and Ellwood (2010[21]) find larger wage gaps of 17 log points at ten or more years after childbirth. Each of these studies focuses on hourly wages rather than annual earnings. Gaps in annual earnings are even larger, as mothers are significantly more likely to work part-time, part year, or not at all. Mothers' average contribution to households' overall earnings from employment and self-employment is lowest in German-speaking countries, followed by Southern Mediterranean countries, while mothers in France, Sweden and Denmark contribute over 35% of household income from their earnings on average (OECD, 2017[22]).

Using Danish administrative data, Kleven et al. (2018[23]) show that a long-run penalty in female earnings of 21% can be attributed to the arrival of children, driven in roughly equal proportions by labour force participation, hours of work, and wage rates. Childbirth has a clear long-lasting effect on occupation, promotion to manager, and "the family friendliness of the firm for women relative to men". The most striking result being that this child penalty worsened over time, as the fraction of the aggregate gender gap that can be explained by children strongly increased from 30% in 1980 to 80% in 2011, showing that non-child reasons for gender inequality have largely disappeared.

Long lasting effects of mothers' withdrawal from the labour market at childbirth

In most countries, a substantial share of women having a child reduces their labour supply. These withdrawals have long-lasting effects on the careers of women, in terms of time spent out of the labour market and lost opportunities for career advancement.[20] Figure 6.9 shows estimates of the effect of childbirth on mothers' employment, controlling for a number of individual characteristics. The estimated employment probability is presented for up to seven years after childbirth.[21] Highly diverse patterns of withdrawal are observed for the different countries analysed. The results show that the withdrawal from the labour market at childbirth is: i) large and quite persistent (more than three years) for the 10 countries shown in Panel A (Australia, Austria, the Czech Republic, Estonia, Finland, Germany, Hungary, Korea, the Slovak Republic); ii) intermediate or large initially but short-lived (only one year) in Denmark, Iceland, Latvia, Luxembourg and Norway, (see Panel B); or iii) intermediate initially but very persistent in the six countries shown in Panel C (Belgium, France, Greece, Ireland, Italy and Poland and the United Kingdom; or, iv) very limited, possibly due to the effect of social policies in preventing women from losing connection with the labour market in the six countries shown in Panel D (Lithuania, the Netherlands, Portugal, Spain, Slovenia and Sweden).

Women's in-work transitions are also affected for a very long time after childbirth. For example, Figure 6.10 shows the cumulative probability of having an in-work transition (change of employer, job or contract) over seven consecutive years, using the Household, Income and Labour Dynamics in Australia (HILDA) panel, which allows people to be tracked over an extended period (Box 6.1). If the deficit in career advancement opportunities is around 12 percentage points for a change of employer within the first year following childbirth, the cumulated effect over the next six years reaches a 25 percentage point lower probability of changing employer, and a 35 percentage point lower probability of changing contract or working hours. By contrast, childless women have in-work transition rates similar to those of men. As seen before, in-work transitions are crucial for career and wage progression. Therefore the lower frequency of these transitions after childbirth sheds light on how motherhood has a pronounced and persistent effect in limiting career opportunities for mothers.

Part-time work can prevent withdrawal from the labour market…

If some women completely withdraw from the labour market at childbirth ages, another large share adapts their professional career so as to free up enough time to meet their family obligations. A significant share of women around the ages of 30-44 years changes to part-time employment, either within the same job (with the same employer) or by switching jobs. For example Liu (2015[24]) shows that women's preference for part-time work in the United States increases with marriage and the number of children but that this is not the case for men.

Figure 6.8. Women adapt their labour supply to childbirth very differently in different countries

Detailed activity status of mothers and non-mothers in selected OECD countries (by age), cohort population = 100, 2015

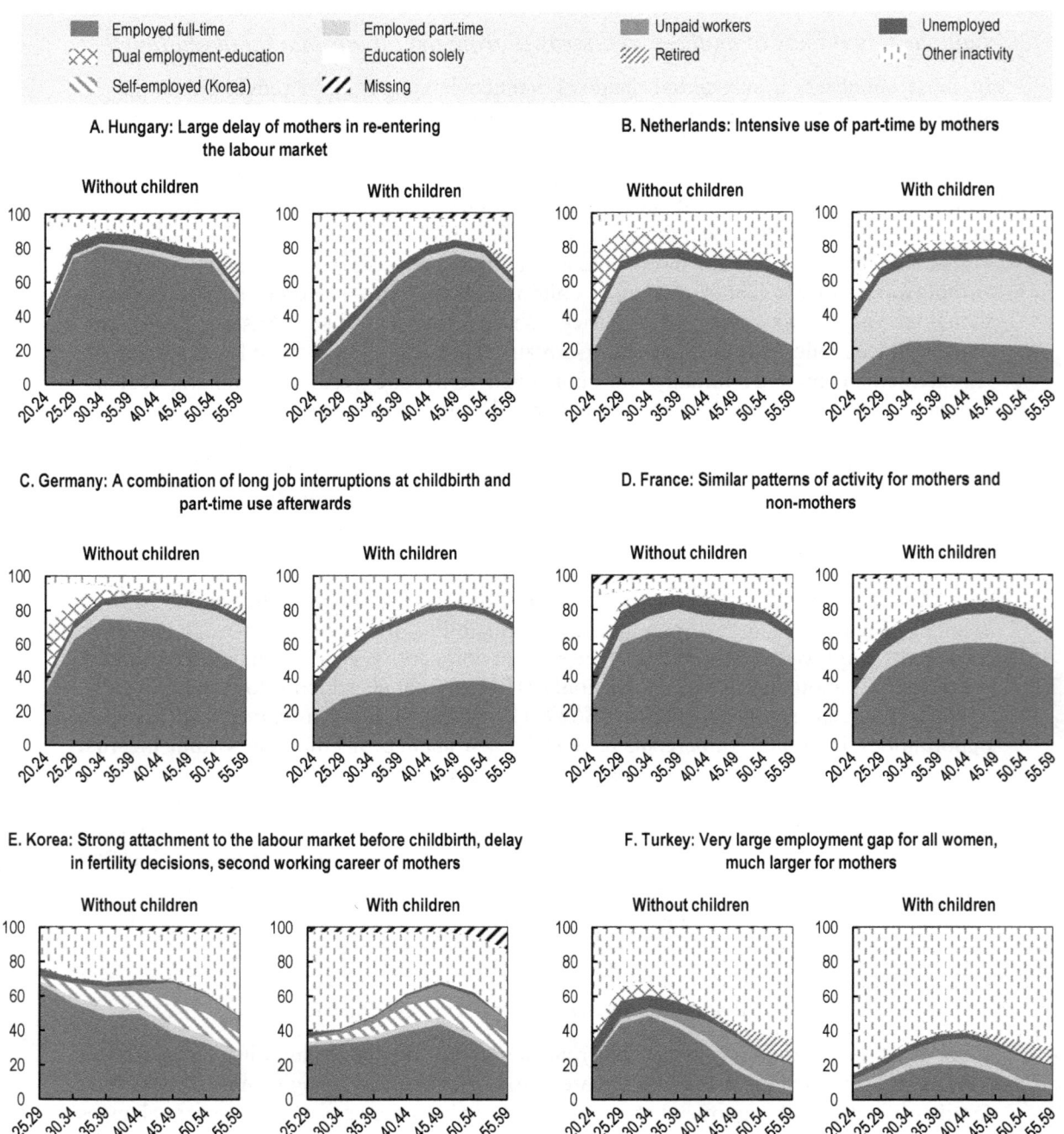

Source: European Union Labour Force Survey (EU-LFS), 2015 for France, Germany, Hungary and the Netherlands); Korean Labor and Income Panel Study (KLIPS), 2008 14 for Korea; and Labour Force Survey (LFS), 2013 for Turkey.

StatLink http://dx.doi.org/10.1787/888933778744

Figure 6.9. Withdrawal from the labour market at childbirth can have long-lasting effects on women's careers

Percentage point marginal effect of childbirth on the participation gap of mothers
(by age of their youngest child) as compared to men and non-mothers, 2006-15

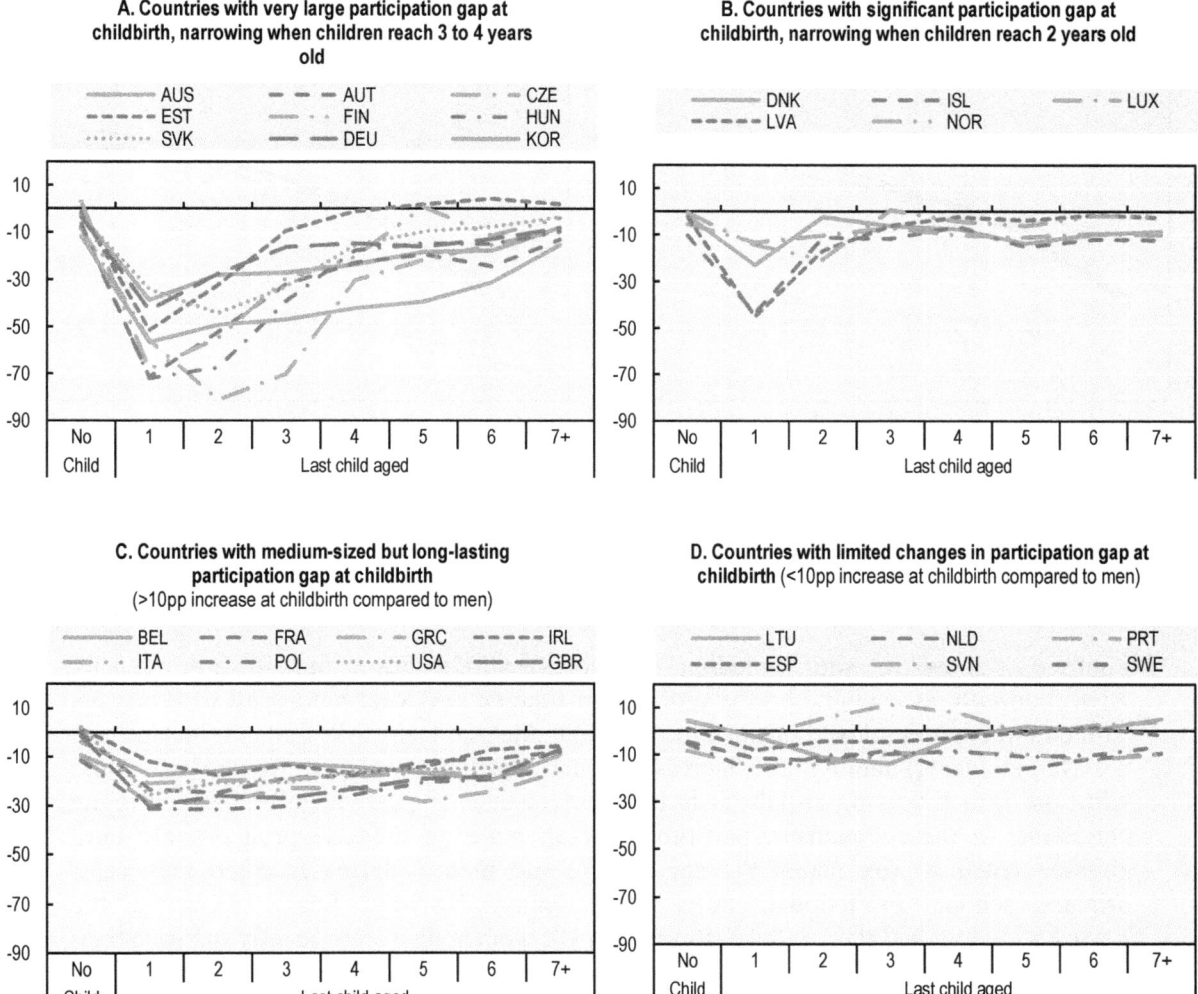

Note: The panels show marginal effects from probit regressions including female cross-effects, where the dependent variable is whether or not the person is employed. Results presented are the marginal effects for childless women and mothers considering the age of their youngest child, relative to men. Regressions are country specific and also include controls (with female cross-effects) for age categories, education, whether the person is single, married or in a non-married partnership, whether the person has had very bad health and year dummies. Sample: persons aged 20-64 years old. pp: percentage points
Source: Household, Income and Labour Dynamics in Australia (HILDA), 2006-15 for Australia; European Union Statistics on Income and Living Conditions (EU-SILC), 2006-15 for European countries; German Socio Economic Panel (GSOEP), 2006-15 for Germany; Korean Labor and Income Panel Study (KLIPS), 2006-14 for Korea; and Current Population Survey (CPS), Annual Social and Economic Supplement (ASEC), 2008-15 for the United States.

StatLink ᐧᓂᔑᓚ http://dx.doi.org/10.1787/888933778763

Figure 6.10. Long-term effect of childbirth on women's in-work transitions

Cumulative probability (expressed in percentage) of experiencing at least one in-work transition over long periods in Australia conditional on being employed before childbirth

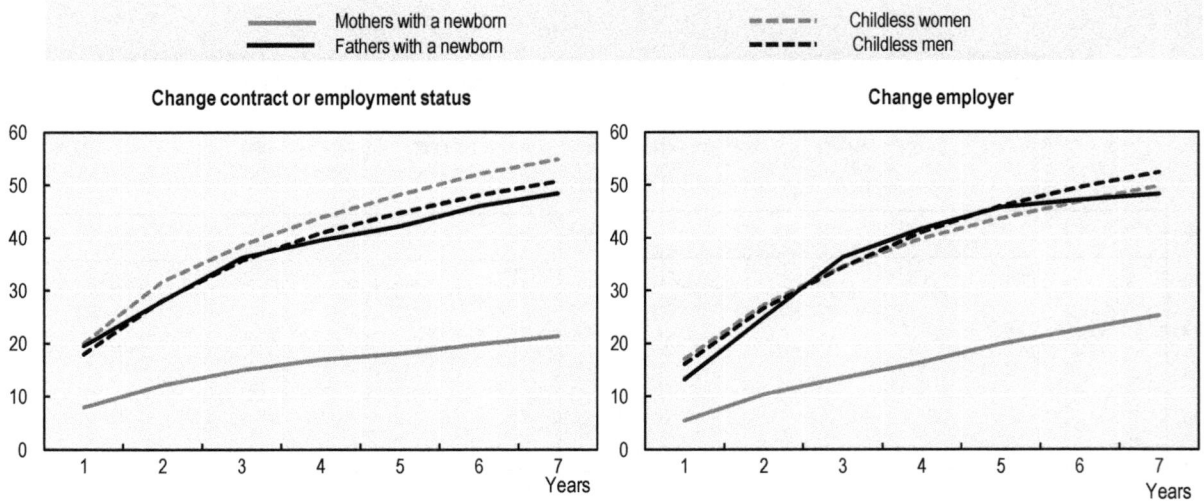

Note: For each transition (change of contract, employment status or employer), probability of having at least one transition over the next one to seven years.
Source: Household, Income and Labour Dynamics in Australia (HILDA), 2001-15.

StatLink ᎏᎏᎏ http://dx.doi.org/10.1787/888933778782

Figure 6.11 shows the short-, medium- and long-term changes in female work intensity after childbirth, as captured by the rate of part-time employment among all working-age women (whether employed or not). In Australia, Austria, Denmark, Finland, Iceland and the Netherlands (Panel A), the increase in the share of employed women who hold part-time jobs following childbirth is large (more than 10 percentage points) and quite persistent. In these countries, part-time take-up tends to increase progressively until children reach approximately the age of five and then it decreases when they enter primary school. In Estonia, Italy, Luxembourg, Norway, Spain, Slovenia, the United Kingdom and the United States (Panel B), women also significantly increase their take-up of part-time employment following childbirth (more than 4 percentage points), but this increased part-time use does not vary much with the age of the youngest child. In Belgium, France, Germany, Ireland and Sweden (Panel C), part-time take-up is not directly linked to the arrival of a child: the part-time employment gap is high relative to men even among childless women, but remains largely unchanged after childbirth. Finally, part-time take-up is rarely used as an adjustment variable by women in the Czech Republic, Greece, Hungary, Korea, Latvia, Lithuania, Poland, Portugal and the Slovak Republic (Panel D). In a few of these countries (e.g. many Eastern European countries), outright withdrawal from the labour force is the most preferred option by women upon childbirth. Since part-time employment can be an effective means to reconcile family responsibilities and paid employment, this pattern suggests that policy measures may be needed in these countries to promote part-time work and provide women with more flexible working time arrangements.

Figure 6.11. After childbirth, re-entry into the labour market can be made through part-time work

Female part-time employment gap compared to men, for childless women and mothers (by age of their youngest child), percentage point marginal effect

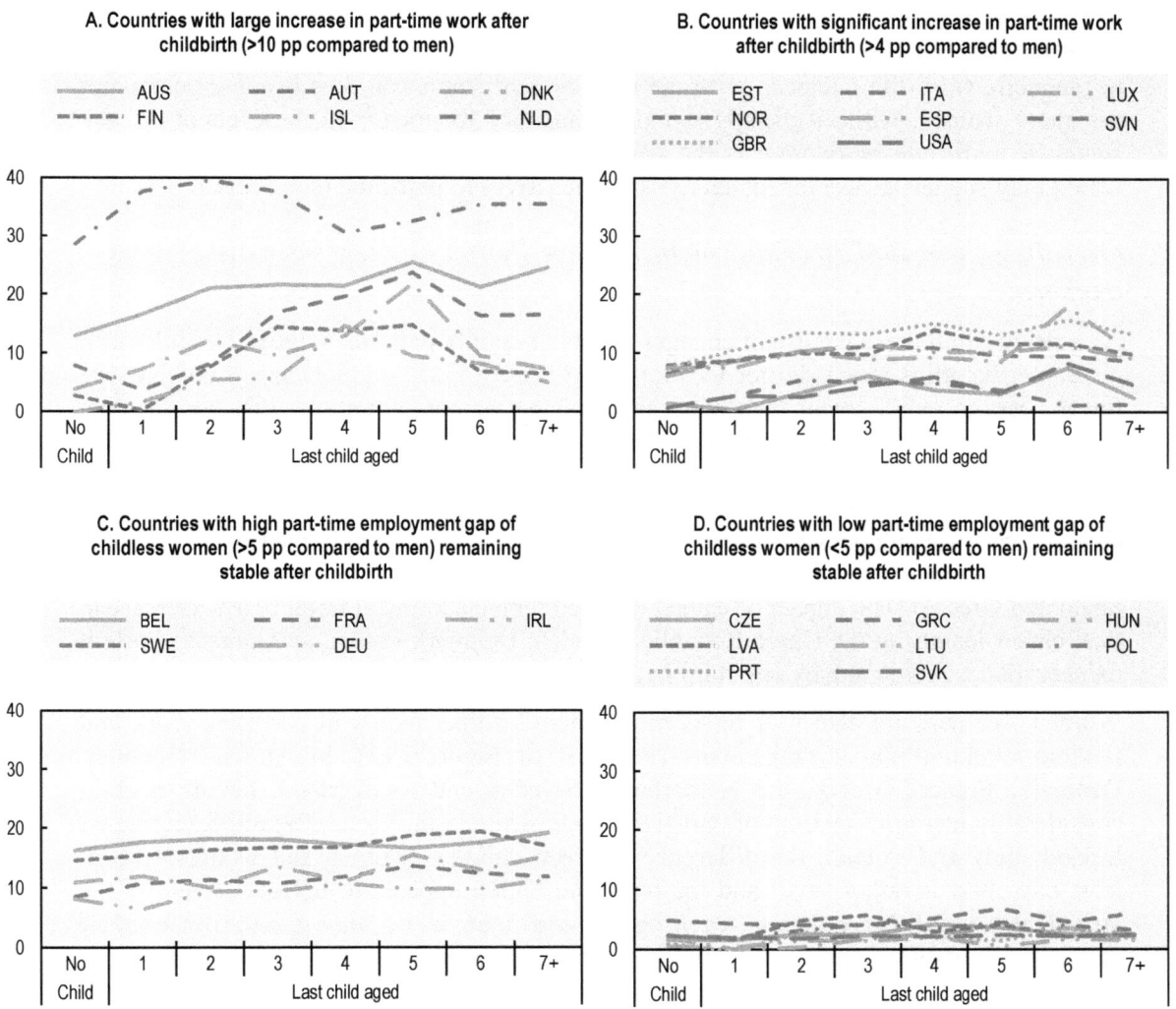

Note: The panels show marginal effects from probit regressions including female cross effects, where the dependent variable is whether or not the person is employed part-time and the sample includes all working age people whether employed or not. Results presented are marginal effects for childless women and mothers considering the age of their youngest child expressed as percentage point differences from the incidence of part-time employment for men. Regressions are country specific and also include controls (with female cross-effects) for age categories, education, whether the person is single, married or in a non-married partnership, whether the person has had very bad health and year dummies. Sample: persons aged 20-64 years old. Countries are grouped into the four panels according to the size and persistence of the post birth increase in the incidence of part-time employment for women.

Source: Household, Income and Labour Dynamics in Australia (HILDA), 2006-14 for Australia; European Union Statistics on Income and Living Conditions (EU-SILC), 2006-14 for European countries; German Socio Economic Panel (GSOEP), 2006-14 for Germany; and Current Population Survey (CPS), Annual Social and Economic Supplement (ASEC), 2008-15 for the United States.

StatLink ᐃ㎰ᕈ http://dx.doi.org/10.1787/888933778801

...but both withdrawing from the labour force or working part-time may represent career traps for women

While increased take-up of part-time work for a few years after childbirth can prevent complete labour market withdrawal in many cases, part-time work can also represent a career trap for women. Women working part-time experience significantly fewer professional transitions than men working part-time (on average 7 percentage points less), and this is likely hamper their upward mobility throughout their career. [22] Even if it helps to reconcile work-life balance, part-time employment status can thus become permanent for many women, while it usually remains transitory for men.[23] In these countries, the switch to part-time work widens the gender gap in labour income within the family, which may suggest a case for reducing fiscal incentives to part-time (see Section 6.4).

Overall, women, and especially mothers, have shorter and less intensive careers than men

As a result of all these persistent changes in labour supply patterns induced by childbirth, net career length is much shorter for mothers (Figure 6.12):[24] mothers spend indeed 46% fewer years in employment than men, and their net careers are about 20% shorter than those of childless women (Panel A).[25] However, the average gender gap in career length for parents is more than twice as large as that of childless people, suggesting that children are by far the most important factor accounting for gender differences in career length. Overall, career-length gaps between men and women are very small in the Czech Republic, Denmark and Sweden, while they are the largest in southern European countries (Italy, Spain and Greece). The impact of having children remains limited (around 10% decrease in total career length) in the Czech Republic, Sweden, Denmark Poland and Greece, while it reduces total career length by one-third in Austria, Switzerland, Ireland, Italy and Spain.

Women's careers are also four times more intensive than men's in part-time work and flexible working time arrangements (Panel B of Figure 6.12). In Austria, Belgium, Denmark, France, Greece, the Netherlands, Sweden and Switzerland, having a child considerably increases take-up of part-time work, while in the Czech Republic, Germany, Ireland, Italy and Poland, the difference between childless women and women with at least one child is rather small and the part-time option appears to be less driven by the arrival of a child. Nevertheless, even childless women spend almost one-fifth of their career on part-time work or flexible working time arrangements in Germany, the Netherlands and Switzerland, illustrating national preferences for part-time, the importance of tax-benefit disincentives and/or limited use of out-of-school care (Section 6.4).[26]

Figure 6.12. Women's careers are one-third shorter than men's and four times more intensive than men's in part-time work and flexible working time arrangements

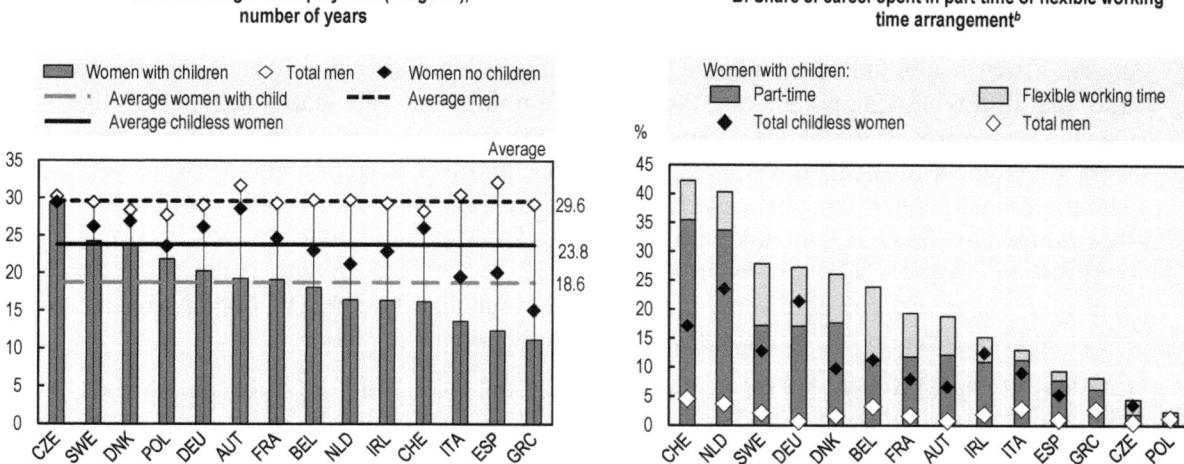

a) Career length refers to the number of years spent in employment from age 15.

b) Part-time and full-time statuses are self-defined (declaration). Flexible working time arrangement refers to years in which changes from part-time to full-time or from full-time to part-time occurred.

Note: Results presented in these figures focus on careers observed up to the age of 50. Part-time and full-time statuses are self-declared. Data collection: 2008-11.

Source: OECD calculations based on the Survey of Health, Ageing and Retirement in Europe (SHARE), Wave 3 – SHARELIFE.

StatLink ᕒᎦᒲᔞᏞ http://dx.doi.org/10.1787/888933778820

6.3. Towards a broad assessment of labour market gender equality

6.3.1. The gender gap in labour income

Gender inequality in labour markets indeed represents a multifaceted challenge for countries (OECD, 2017[1]; 2017[4]). The gender gap in labour income (GGLI), which is considered in this section, is a simple indicator that captures the key element of gender inequality in the labour market. In fact, women's lower total labour income has consequences for their bargaining power within the household, for their income in case of divorce, and for pension and living standards of widows once their partner's income ceases to play its buffering role (OECD, 2017[25]). The GGLI summarises in one number, three complementary dimensions of women's position in the labour market: the gender gap in employment rates; hours worked; and hourly earnings. As seen in the previous sections, all these dimensions may play a role in accounting for gender disparities in the labour market. Decomposing the gap into different components allows identifying the most important sources of gender labour market inequalities in each country. In the next section, tailored levers of action for policy makers are then identified depending on the source of gender differences in each country.

The size of the overall GGLI varies substantially across countries (Figure 6.13, Panel A).[27] Considering all women (without restricting the analysis to those working full-time), the largest gaps are found in East Asian and Latin American countries (Japan, Korea, Mexico and Chile). Gender gaps are also relatively high (above 40%) in many

Mediterranean countries, German-speaking countries, many large English-speaking economies as well as the Netherlands and the Czech Republic. By contrast, the gender gap in labour income is the smallest (less than 30%) in many Nordic and Eastern-European countries and in Portugal.

The GGLI is decomposable (see Box 6.4), which can help design strategies to reduce gender disparities in the labour market. The decomposition divides the overall gender gap into the following components: i) the gender employment rate gap (also called the extensive margin); ii) the gender hours gap (e.g. the more intensive take-up of part-time work by women, also called the intensive margin); and iii) the gender hourly wage gap. The traditional gender pay gaps usually published by the OECD considerably differ from those shown by the GGLI, mostly because they are based only on hourly wages and focus on full-time workers. On this basis, OECD (2017[1]) provides an interesting focus by analysing the gender gap at different points of the wage distribution. The two approaches focus on very different populations, and are therefore complementary.

Figure 6.13, Panel A presents the decomposition of the GGLI into the three components. The main drivers of gender labour inequality are by far the employment gap and the hourly wage gap (explaining both about 40% of the overall inequality). By contrast, the more intensive take-up of part-time work by women and the derived differential in the number of hours worked by men and women, accounts for 20% of overall gender labour inequality.

The GGLI has shrunk in the past decade in almost all countries, with the contraction of the employment gap being by and large also the main driver of the reduction of the labour income gap (Figure 6.13, Panel B). On average, little progress has been made in the other dimensions of the labour income gap, partly because of changes in the composition of working women (with less skilled and employable women joining the labour force and employment in recent years, sometimes ending up working part-time).

6.3.2. Gender gaps by educational attainment and age group

Low-educated women struggle the most in reaching gender equality

Low-educated women face higher gender divides in the labour market (Figure 6.14, Panel A): in almost all countries, labour income of women is much lower relative to men at low levels of education. This significant educational divide in GGLI is driven by large employment gaps (Panel B) more than counterbalancing the fact that, on average, the gender wage gap is smaller among men and women with low educational attainment (Panel D and Section 6.1.2). Low-educated women struggle the most in reaching gender equality in Belgium, Canada, Greece, Ireland, Italy, Latvia, Mexico, Poland, the Netherlands, Spain and Turkey (more than 20 percentage point difference in GGLI for women with less than upper secondary compared with tertiary-educated women).

Figure 6.13. The gender gap in labour income significantly decreased over the past decade driven by the enhanced participation of women to the labour force

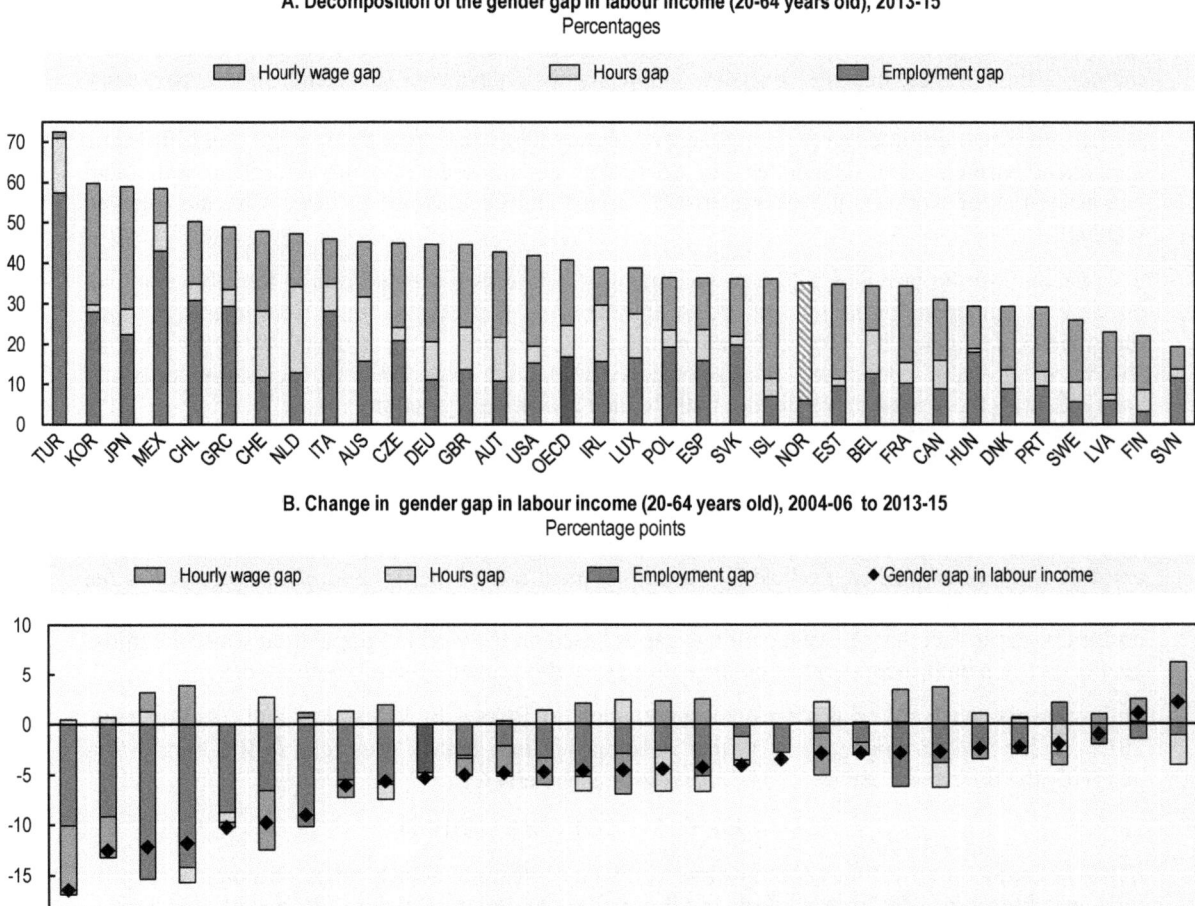

A. Decomposition of the gender gap in labour income (20-64 years old), 2013-15
Percentages

B. Change in gender gap in labour income (20-64 years old), 2004-06 to 2013-15
Percentage points

Note: For Canada and Turkey, data on earnings refer to wage and salary only. For Norway, the breakdown of hourly wage gap and hours gap is not available.
Source: Earnings and hours: Household, Income and Labour Dynamics in Australia (HILDA), 2004-06 and 2013-15 for Australia; European Union Statistics on Income and Living Conditions (EU-SILC), 2013-15 for European countries; Labour Force Survey (LFS), 2013-15 for Canada; *Encuesta de Caracterizacion Socioeconomica Nacional* (CASEN), 2006 and 2013-15 for Chile; Japan Household Panel Survey (KHPS), 2005-06 and 2013-14 for Japan; Korean Labor and Income Panel Study (KLIPS), 2005-06 and 2013-14 for Korea; *Encuesta Nacional de Ocupación y Empleo* (ENOE), 2005-06 and 2013-15 for Mexico; Labour Force Survey (LFS), 2004-06 and 2013-15 for Turkey; and Current Population Survey (CPS), Annual Social and Economic Supplement (ASEC), 2004-06 and 2013-15 for the United States. Employment gap: *OECD Employment Database* (www.oecd.org/employment/database).

StatLink ⫶⫶⫶ http://dx.doi.org/10.1787/888933778839

Box 6.4. Decomposition of the gender gap in labour income

The gender gap in per capita labour income (GGLI) is the gap between total labour income of men (based on the male population between 20 and 64 years of age) and total labour income of women (of the corresponding female population). Labour income includes monthly earnings of employees including base wages, bonuses, overtime, supplementary payments (thirteenth month payment), paid leave and cash benefits of self-employed. This global gender gap in labour income can be further decomposed into three components: employment gap, part-time effect, and full-time equivalent earnings gap. The latter can be further decomposed into the returns to individual characteristics of workers, job characteristics, sector and occupation, as well as an unexplained residual.

This decomposition provides a global assessment of women's place and role in the labour market as well as guidance for policy action. *Comprehensive*, it measures employment and earnings dimensions. *Inclusive*, it is based on all men and women and not just those working full-time. *Analytical*, it enables policy makers to compare the relative importance of each component and easily identify the most striking gender issue to tackle with policy action.

The gender gap in per capita labour income (GGLI) can be decomposed as follows:

$$GGLI = EG + (1 - EG) * Total\ Earnings\ Gap$$

Where EG is the employment gap (i.e. the difference between the employment rate of men and the employment rate of women, divided by the employment rate of men) the *total earnings gap* is the gender gap of total monthly labour income among the employed. The component $(1 - EG)$ derives from the fact that the total earnings gap is based on the working population while the initial gender gap in labour income relies on the entire population (aged 20-64 in both cases).

Following the analysis of professional segregation in France by (Chamkhi and Toutlemonde, 2015[26]), the *total earnings gap* is further decomposed into hourly wage gap (HWG) and hours gap (HG, the difference between *Total earnings gap* and HWG).

$$GGLI = EG + (1 - EG) * [HG + HWG]$$

HWG is based on an estimate of full-time equivalent incomes, which relies on country-specific full-time thresholds (40 hours a week in all countries except in Belgium [39 hours], and France [35 hours]). All labour incomes above this full-time threshold remain unchanged, while those below the threshold are converted into full-time equivalent income by multiplying the labour income by the national full-time threshold, and dividing the result by the number of hours usually worked in the reference week. The HG component is therefore the contribution of the lower number of working hours by women (intensive margin) to the overall labour income difference between men and women.

The HWG can then be further decomposed using a classic Oaxaca-Blinder decomposition between IND a component explained by the individual characteristics of workers (age, education), JOB a component explained by observable job's characteristics (firm size and contract type), and $OCCSECT$ a component explained by occupation and sector. The residual part is the unexplained component ($UNEXP$), which accounts for various unobservable factors.

$$GGLI = EG + (1 - EG) * [HG + IND + JOB + OCCSECT + UNEXP]$$

Full results of this finer decomposition are presented in OECD (2018[6]).

Figure 6.14. Low-educated women face higher gender gaps in labour income mainly driven by considerable employment gaps

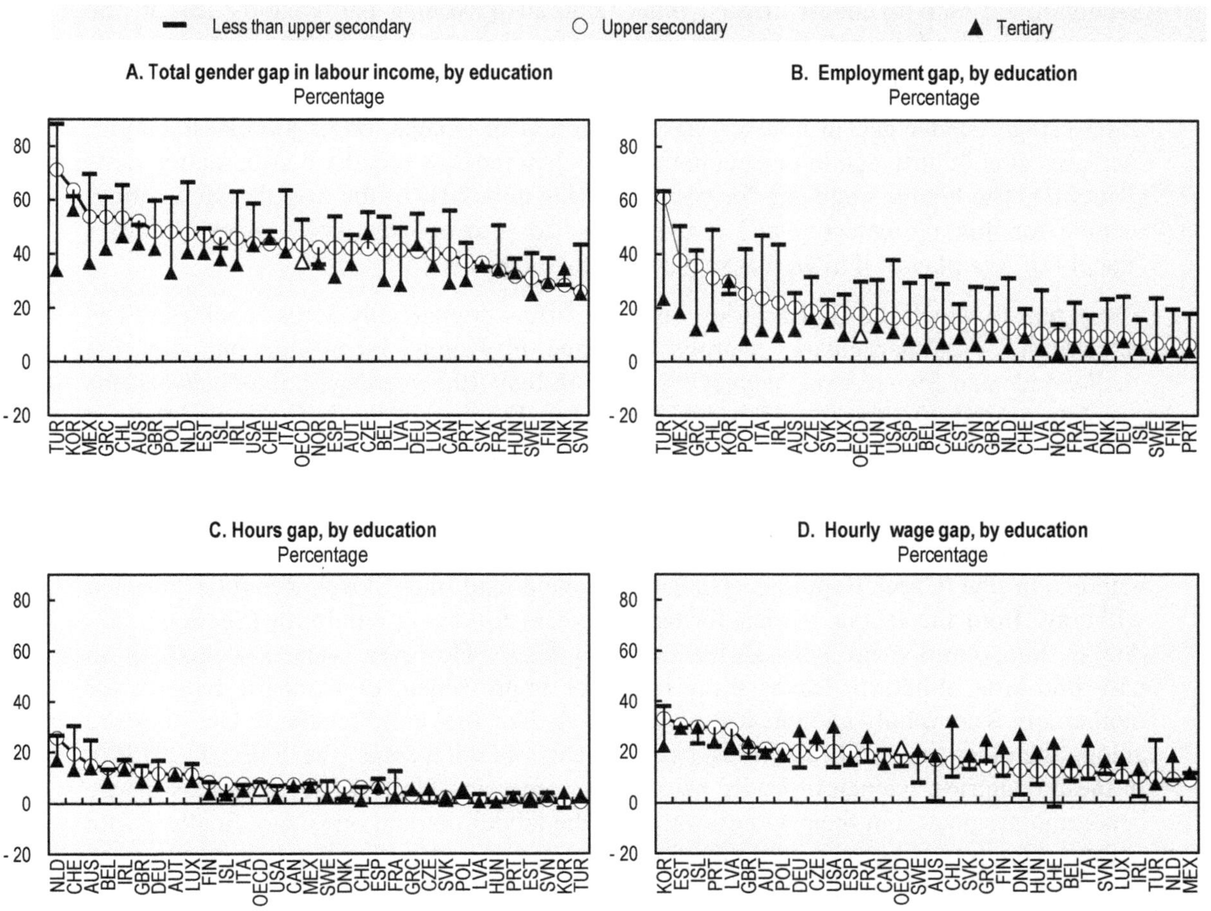

Note: For Canada and Turkey, data on earnings refer to wage and salary only.
Source: Earnings and hours: Household, Income and Labour Dynamics in Australia (HILDA), 2013-15 for Australia; European Union Statistics on Income and Living Conditions (EU-SILC), 2013-15 for European countries; Labour Force Survey (LFS), 2013-15 for Canada; *Encuesta de Caracterizacion Socioeconomica Nacional* (CASEN), 2013-15 for Chile; Japan Household Panel Survey (KHPS), 2013-14 for Japan; Korean Labor and Income Panel Study (KLIPS), 2013-14 for Korea; *Encuesta Nacional de Ocupación y Empleo* (ENOE), 2013-15 for Mexico; and Current Population Survey (CPS), Annual Social and Economic Supplement (ASEC), 2004-06 and 2013-15 for the United States. Employment gap: *OECD Employment Database* (www.oecd.org/employment/database).

StatLink 🔗 http://dx.doi.org/10.1787/888933778858

Gender labour inequality increases over the life cycle

Figure 6.15 presents the GGLI separately for three age groups and shows that gender labour inequalities sharply increase with age in a large majority of countries, confirming insights from Sections 6.1 and 6.2. Yet, as discussed, cross-sectional data in Figure 6.15 are also affected by cohort effects, which magnifies the steepness of age-labour-income-gap profiles. These profiles may appear through four possible channels: i) withdrawal from the labour market at childbirth age of a substantial share of mothers, some of whom remaining inactive for a long time or even permanently –

Section 6.1.1 and Section 6.2.2; ii) part-time employment becoming the norm at latter stages of mother's career in some countries – Section 6.1.1, Section 6.2.2 and OECD (2018[6]); iii) the age profile of the gender wage gap among full-time workers – Section 6.1.2; and iv) cohort effects: older cohorts of women participating less in the labour market and being usually much less paid than their male counterparts – see especially Section 6.1.2.

The average gender gap in hourly wage (regardless of occupation of job classification) increases at childbirth age in most countries and then remains broadly constant afterwards (Panel B). The hourly wage gap for youth explains only 20% of the overall gap in labour income for this age category and is even close to zero or negative in many countries (Panel D). Age plays a limited role in gender hours gaps.

The extent to which the GGLI varies with age differs dramatically across countries. The gender gap rises particularly sharply with age in Korea, Japan, Luxembourg, the Netherlands and Switzerland (increasing by more than 40 percentage points between the population aged 20-29 years old and 45 and over). The size of the GGLI components at different ages helps better understand the age profile of the gender income gap and why it varies so much across OECD countries. In Chile, the Czech Republic, Greece, Korea, Italy, Japan and Mexico, gender labour income inequality is driven by an extremely high employment gaps at all ages: a significant share of women is absent from the labour market. In the Czech Republic, Hungary, Poland and the Slovak Republic, women withdraw from the labour market for several years following childbirth (Section 6.2.2) due to long entitlement periods for maternal leave. However, very low take-up in part-time after childbirth leaves some room for improvement of work-life balance for mothers. In Korea, Italy and Greece, women have their first child relatively late (they are among the oldest in OECD countries, over 30 years old on average – see OECD (2018[6]). In these countries, women typically begin their career and work for several years before becoming pregnant, but their withdrawal from the labour market, once they finally start a family, often proves permanent. In the Czech Republic, on the other hand, women tend to have their children first (the average age of women at first birth was 28.1 years in 2014), and only enter the labour market for a late career once their children have entered school. The activity rate of young Czech women with children (around 20%) is among the lowest of all OECD countries, indicating barriers to the participation of mothers in the labour market.

In Australia, Austria, Belgium, Ireland, Germany, Luxembourg, the Netherlands, Switzerland and the United Kingdom, gender disparities are important but employment gaps are of medium size: the earnings that women bring home are much lower than those of men due to frequent take-up of part-time employment (see Figure 6.14). The more frequent take-up of part- time is often a way for women with children to stay in the labour market (see Section 6.2.2), but part-time work is also sizeable among childless women in Australia, Germany, Ireland, the Netherlands and the United Kingdom (at least 14%).

Finally the hourly wage gap is a key component of the large gender disparities in Japan and Korea. In the latter country, however, the wage gap is relatively contained in the case of youth and increases dramatically with age (see also Section 6.1.2). The hourly wage gap play also a key role in many Nordic countries where the overall gender gap in labour income remains contained. This is notably the case of Iceland and Norway, whose GGLI would be among the smallest if it were not for a relatively large wage gap.

Figure 6.15. Labour markets are more egalitarian at earlier stages of the career, but can become particularly gender-biased as professional paths move forward

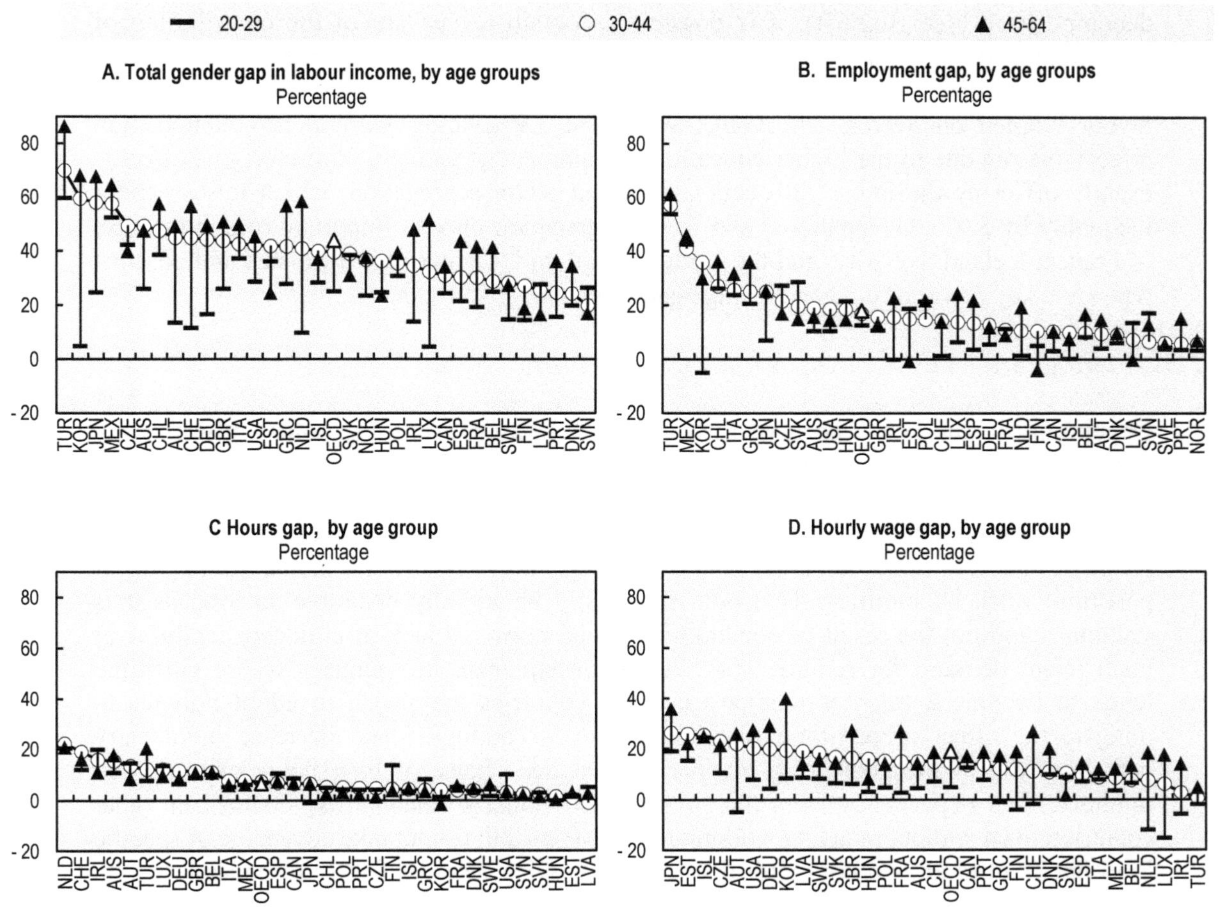

A. Total gender gap in labour income, by age groups
Percentage

B. Employment gap, by age groups
Percentage

C Hours gap, by age group
Percentage

D. Hourly wage gap, by age group
Percentage

Note: For Canada and Turkey, data on earnings refer to wage and salary only.
Source: Earnings and hours: Household, Income and Labour Dynamics in Australia (HILDA), 2013-15 for Australia; European Union Statistics on Income and Living Conditions (EU-SILC), 2013-15 for European countries; Labour Force Survey (LFS), 2013-15 for Canada; *Encuesta de Caracterizacion Socioeconomica Nacional* (CASEN), 2013-15 for Chile; Japan Household Panel Survey (KHPS), 2013-14 for Japan; Korean Labor and Income Panel Study (KLIPS), 2013-14 for Korea; *Encuesta Nacional de Ocupación y Empleo* (ENOE), 2013-15 for Mexico; and Current Population Survey (CPS), Annual Social and Economic Supplement (ASEC), 2004-06 and 2013-15 for the United States. Employment gap: *OECD Employment Database* (www.oecd.org/employment/database).

StatLink 🔗 http://dx.doi.org/10.1787/888933778877

6.3.3. Occupational segregation

Men and women remain likely to work in different sectors and occupations across OECD countries (OECD, 2017[1]): women continue to be overrepresented in the service sector, specifically within areas such as retail, health and social work: 84% of employed women worked in the services sector in 2015 (60.7% of men), 11.6% in industry (32.6% of men); and 4% in agriculture (6.3% of men). This occupational segregation derives from: i) on the supply side, the self-selection of women into certain occupations/sectors[28] (under-representation of women in STEM fields, early career choices and motherhood, gender gaps in entrepreneurship); and ii) on the demand side, the gendered preferences of employers.

Decomposing further the hourly wage gap, following a standard Oaxaca-Blinder decomposition (see Box 6.4), it is possible to obtain a measure of the contribution of individual and jobs characteristics, as well as occupation/sector gender differences to gender disparities in hourly wages.[29] Gender differences in individual characteristics favour women on average (the GGLI would be 3.9% larger without this composition effect), mainly due to the higher educational attainment of women. However, this effect is exactly offset by the impact of occupational and sector segregation, which raises gender inequality by 3.9%. Occupational and sector segregation play an important role in the case of France, Iceland, Norway, and the United Kingdom.[30] By contrast, firm-size and contract type are a key driver of the gender wage gap in Japan.

6.4. How can gender labour inequalities be overcome?

Depending on the key drivers of the GGLI in different countries, policy priorities are likely to differ, calling for policy responses that are tailored to country-specific conditions. For example, in a few countries, the main policy priority remains promoting women's participation in the labour market so as to decrease the employment gap.[31] However, success in reducing the employment gap may result in an increased take-up of part-time work by mothers. This outcome would be socially desirable so long as it is voluntary and not the result of constraining social norms, a lack of childcare facilities or insufficient demand for female work. As a consequence, in countries where part-time tends to become a trap for women's careers, countries may wish to adopt policies to mitigate the effect of part-time work on women's earnings,[32] and decrease involuntary part-time work – the goal being to give women free choice of their hours of work and minimise their dependency from the "main breadwinner's" income. By contrast, in other countries, even without reducing working time, women still cannot take advantage of specific job opportunities around childbirth due to their heavier share of family responsibilities. In these countries, policy priorities should focus on reducing this burden. In all these cases, albeit with a different combination of policy tools depending on policy priorities, policy action should focus on reducing disincentives to work for women with caring responsibilities, providing adequate services and support for families with young children, and enhancing equity of opportunities and flexibility of existing schemes, so as to provide women with greater options on the labour market and freedom for their career choices.[33] These policy tools are discussed in order:

Reduce financial disincentives to work: disincentives to work and barriers to female participation play a key role in the existing gender division of labour and in the GGLI. Therefore, providing adequate incentives for women and especially mothers to enter the labour market is key, especially for countries where the employment gap and/or the part-time component of the GGLI are high. Removing the disincentives induced by tax-benefit systems must also be a priority for those countries where raising labour market performance of mothers from lower socio-economic positions is a key priority, since these are the most affected by these disincentives.

- *Provide adequate paid leave options.* Many OECD countries provide extensive paid leave programmes for parents around the time of childbirth – see OECD (2018[6]). Maternity and parental leave are important measures that help mothers combine childcare responsibilities with their work commitments, improving the work-life balance of both women and men (OECD, 2017[1]). Paid parental leave is associated with higher female labour force participation across countries, as it provides incentives to be employed prior to giving birth (to ensure paid leave eligibility) and gives women post-birth job security (OECD, 2017[1]). Leave policies have a significant effect on the employment of mothers, although the loosened connection with the labour market may be detrimental when leave durations are overly long – see Section 6.2.2 and Olivetti and Petrongolo (2016[27]). With the exception of the United States, all OECD countries have national schemes offering mothers a statutory right to paid maternity leave.

- *Correct disincentives in the tax-benefit systems* through "make work pay" measures,[34] and individualisation of taxation. In many countries, work incentives for low-paid second-earner parents are weak due to high marginal effective tax rates for second earners when moving from non-employment to employment – the so-called *participation tax rate* – see OECD (2018[6]). After various deductions and changes in benefit entitlements, low-paid second-earner parents entering employment often take home less than 40% of their additional gross earnings. The effect of benefit withdrawal rules, and their interaction with taxes, can be significant for single parents and one-earner families. In fact, phasing-out of social assistance, as well as family and housing benefits often brings marginal effective tax rates close to 100%, particularly for families with one earner and two dependent children. Conversely, imperfect neutrality of taxation implies that in many countries sharing work equally amongst the members of the household (for example in the form of two part-time jobs with close-to-full-time hours) is more costly than unequal sharing (e.g. through one full-time and one low-intensity part-time jobs). This is particularly the case in Chile, Belgium and France for low-income households and in Germany and Switzerland for middle-income households – see OECD (2018[6]).

- *Reduce childcare costs.* Childcare costs remain very high in some OECD countries (OECD, 2018[6]), further weakening financial incentives to work and therefore reducing the attractiveness of labour force participation (OECD, 2017[1]). These high costs act as a barrier to paid employment for second earners and single parents, especially those with less-educated women with low potential earnings. Indeed, on average across European OECD countries, more than one-in-five economically-inactive mothers with a very young child report that a lack of affordable childcare prevents them from looking for work (OECD, 2016a). High childcare costs dramatically increase the marginal effective tax rate for second earners when moving from non-employment to employment – see OECD (2018[6]). But the effects on marginal tax rate are also important when increasing working hours of second earners in many countries (Eurofound, 2016[28]).

Provide adequate services and support, also by increasing the flexibility of existing schemes: in order to give women a real choice in their leave and labour supply decisions, providing them with childcare facilities is key. Indeed, time spent on housework affects time spent in the labour market, and vice versa. The large increase in female labour force participation over the past decades was associated with a decline in time spent on unpaid home and care work, but women still bear the brunt of unpaid work and fathers spend a lot less time with children than mothers. In addition, while a considerable part of eldercare work takes place outside the household, some two-thirds of the inside-household carers are women, informal care being particularly prevalent in countries with relatively few paid care workers (OECD, 2013[29]). A disproportionate burden on women to care for children can deter mothers from re-entering full-time work and can make employers less likely to hire mothers or women of childbearing age (OECD, 2017[22]). It can indeed be difficult for working-age carers to combine paid work with caring duties and carers may choose to quit paid works or reduce the work hours. This may compromise their future employability and lead to either permanent drop-out from the labour market or to lower-profile subsequent careers.

- *Increase childcare availability*[35] by providing publicly subsidised early childhood education and care (ECEC) to children as a legal right (OECD, 2016[30]).[36] Women are often involved in childcare duties, especially when care services are lacking or fail to meet the needs of full-time working parents. Indeed, those countries where the use of formal care is the lowest (such as Austria, the Netherlands, New Zealand, Switzerland or the United Kingdom) are those for which the gender gap in hours worked per worker is the greatest – see OECD (2018[6]). It is therefore necessary to provide alternatives to families caring for children at home by offering care in a form that can be reconciled with parents' working hours.

- *Provide further financial support for low-income families*, especially when childcare costs are very high (OECD, 2016[30]). Subsidising child care is all the more necessary to reduce inequalities between low- and high-skilled households. Childcare costs can indeed be prohibitively high, in particular for parents with disadvantaged backgrounds whose children are lagging behind in terms of ECEC access. This may explain the large differences in gender labour income gaps across educational levels in some countries (Figure 6.15, panel C).

- *Develop out-of-school care services*. Out-of-school-hours care services remain under-developed in most OECD countries – see OECD (2018[6]) – and explain to some extent the relatively high share of part-time work among working mothers in some countries (such as Australia and Germany). Childcare issues do not disappear once children enter pre-primary or primary school. Children in the educational system do spend a large amount of time at school, but opening hours are frequently incompatible with a full-time working week and school holidays are almost always longer than annual leave entitlements for employees. Informal care services provided by friends or relatives can help, but these are not always available and working families with school-age children often need to find additional formal solutions both before and after school, and also during school holidays. A few OECD countries have developed extensive out-of-school-hours care systems for school-age children – see (OECD, 2017[1]) for more details.

- *Enable flexible working time arrangements* to foster work-life balance. These include the availability of part-time work, working from home on an occasional or regular basis (teleworking), flexitime (allowing employees to adjust their daily working time, possibility to adapt their working time to take care of personal or family matters). OECD (2016[20]) provides an assessment of how workplace flexibility can help employees balance work and family responsibilities. The availability to choose one's working time (within employer's predefined limits) enables employees to devote their most productive hours to work, while also deal with their family responsibilities, relieving the pressure as regards family commitments. Flexitime may also decrease the tension of commuting at rush hour for both parents and childless employees. For flexible working time arrangements to be effective and not considered as "mothers' working arrangements", governments need to assure that their initiatives to promote workplace flexibility are designed so as to: i) grant all employees (and not just mothers of young child) a right to request flexible working arrangements; ii) encourage social partners to cover workplace flexibility in collective bargaining agreements; and iii) help companies change their work organisation.

- Adopt measures to *encourage men to spend more time at home* caring for their children and their dependants more generally. In that respect, fathers' leave-taking can be considerably effective. Indeed, while couples today tend to be fairly egalitarian in their division of (unpaid) household labour before children are born, things often change soon after childbirth. Women start doing much more unpaid work upon arrival of the first child, so that fathers' leave-taking around childbirth can play a crucial role in relieving this burden (OECD, 2017[1]). Promoting men's use of leave can also be achieved through the introduction or extension of "fathers-only" leave, such as paid paternity leave and longer periods of paid leave reserved for or targeted at fathers within parental leave systems (OECD, 2017[1]). These instruments can significantly contribute to promote re-entry of mothers into the labour market. However, paternity leave entitlements may not suffice if father are not encouraged to take it in their workplace. For example, Korea and Japan have generous paternity leave schemes but only 3% of fathers do take advantage of them. Governments could consider putting in place soft or hard incentives for employers to adopt effectively non-discriminatory practices against fathers taking voluntary paternity leave.

- Countries must also *strengthen support for informal carers*, particularly for the elderly – such as cash benefits, respite care, training and counselling – and ensure that these benefits reach those who need them most, in particular low-income women. To meet those needs, many countries provide employees with a right to either flexible working time or to family-caregiver leave, but often without financial compensation and little flexibility. It is also important that such leave can be granted within a short notice period given that long-term care needs are largely unpredictable.

Other interventions involving actions beyond labour and social policy:

- *Promote women's earning potential.* Improving the acquisition of valuable market skills by women and enhancing their access to vocational training are key to raise the wages women can command on the market, as well as measures to reduce occupations and sector segregation. Policies to promote female employment in high-wage sectors and occupations are particularly important in countries where women are concentrated in low-paid occupations and sectors – as is the case for two thirds of the countries, see OECD (2018[6]). Considerable progress has been made in closing the education gap, resulting in girls even outstripping boys in educational attainment in many countries. However, further efforts are required to close remaining gender gaps in education (particularly in science, technology, engineering and mathematics) – see (OECD, 2017[1]). Moreover, the returns to these human capital investments will only be realised if women are actually employed.

- *Address stereotypes, reduce discrimination and promote female leadership.* Virtually all OECD countries have put in place policies to address stereotypes and reduce discrimination through anti-discriminatory rules, anti-harassment actions and promoting change in employers' perceptions and in social norms. The evidence suggests, however, that discrimination is more frequent in career progression and access to senior management positions – see (OECD, 2017[1]). Most OECD countries have initiated policies to promote gender balance on company boards and in senior management, such as gender quota in boards. However, these actions alone are likely insufficient without investing in promoting career progression and leadership development schemes for women, also based on peer-to-peer support – such as sponsorship, mentoring, building confidence and access to networks. But it is also critical to engage men leaders in achieving gender equality. Moreover, because workplace culture is central to sexual harassment, anti-harassment laws and initiatives targeting employers show promise and should be evaluated carefully. Many countries, as part of their awareness-raising campaigns, provide employers with information on employers' obligations to prevent and respond to harassment and discrimination. Finally, ensuring that both women and men do not experience discrimination when they take leave from work to care for dependents is also key to promote the evolution of social norms (OECD, 2017[1]).

Success/failure factors:

- Cultural expectations and values concerning female employment and dominant practices in the gendered division of care and family work may undermine policies (Eurofound, 2016[28]). The ideals regarding care and who is best placed to rear children and care about dependants indeed affect take-up of childcare and the social roles of men and women (Kremer, 2007[31]). Policy reforms should therefore be accompanied by campaigns addressing these cultural factors.

- Experimenting with pilot programmes to assess the relative effectiveness of potential policy measures on different types of family households before implementing the nationwide measure should also be considered. Policies based on financial incentives or supportive interventions should be targeted based on evidence on which groups are more responsive to different types of policy actions (Eurofound, 2016[28]). This will allow clear targeting of the beneficiary population, avoid deadweight loss, and increase the effectiveness of the measure. It is also important to implement reforms intended to decrease labour supply disincentives for women gradually, so as to allow sufficient time for families to adjust to the changing incentives offered to them.

6.5. Concluding remarks

Despite sizeable improvements in the situation of women in the labour market during recent decades, gender inequalities remain a major issue for policy makers in OECD countries. This chapter has provided an overview of the working lives of women and how they compare with those of men, as well as an assessment of how those differences contribute to the persistence of significant gender gaps in labour market outcomes. This analysis confirms that the degree of gender labour inequality varies across countries, as does the form it takes and the relative importance of different types of gender gaps. The labour income gap between women and men increases over the course of their careers and is mostly the result of missed opportunities in terms of professional mobility during the early stages of women's careers, and in particular during the years immediately following the birth of their children. This chapter has also documented the many ways in which childbirth affects female labour supply across countries in terms of labour market participation and the take-up of part-time work, as well as the longer-run implications of those choices for professional mobility and, therefore, income growth. Getting onto a good career track and staying on it is a strong determinant of future income growth, and missed opportunities following childbirth are particularly prejudicial. Life events like child birth, parenting (but also caring for the elderly in the family and family responsibilities more generally) affect both wage progression and the accumulation of earnings over a lifetime, and these career breaks also reduce pension entitlements (OECD, 2017[32]). However, while childbirth and other life events significantly affect women's professional trajectories everywhere, the way they do so varies across countries. This suggests that policy can have a major impact.

This chapter proposes a framework to help governments better address the complex challenges involved in fostering gender equality by targeting their efforts on the most important gender gaps in labour market outcomes in each country. While this framework identifies the quantitatively most important sources of the overall gender gap in labour income per capita, more research is needed to identify the resulting implications for policy. In particular, new evidence is needed to better understand the respective role played by each policy measure on each of the different components of the gender labour income gap, in particular the gap in working hours. New research is also required to assess the role that collective bargaining can play in further reducing gender gaps through the setting of wages, anti-discrimination rules, and flexible working arrangements. Additional research is also needed to identify the impacts that megatrends such as digitalisation and population ageing will have on occupational segregation and gender gaps in labour markets, and how different policies can shape those impacts in order to promote greater gender equality.

Notes

[1] The gender gap in labour income is defined as the difference between average annual earnings of men and women as a percentage of those of men. Average earnings are computed by considering the whole working age population, independently of whether effectively working or not during the year. A person with no labour income, therefore, contributes to the denominator of average earnings but not to the numerator (see Section 6.3).

[2] In the latter countries, which include Australia, Denmark, Finland, Germany, Iceland, the Netherlands, Norway and Switzerland, apprenticeship plays a major role in bridging educational and professional aspects. Interestingly, in the Nordic countries and the United Kingdom, more women than men take on this dual activity at the earliest career stage. In Finland and the United Kingdom, women once again combine education and work at very late stages of their career.

[3] Retirement status is self-determined in Labour Force Surveys. While it is not possible to say whether all those who declare themselves being retired receive a retirement pension, the opposite is likely to be true.

[4] Other general gender differences include the fact at all ages, more men are self-employed than women in all countries (OECD, 2018[6]). In some countries – Australia, Austria, Switzerland, the Czech Republic, Germany and the United Kingdom – women tend to be more often self-employed during the later stages of their careers, but this late-career increase in self-employment is much lower than for men. By contrast, unemployment is not particularly gender biased.

[5] Gaps in full-time earnings are measured using hourly, weekly, monthly or annual earnings, depending on data availability. To the extent that the variability of contractual hours among full-time is limited, the gaps presented in Figure 6.3 can be assumed to proxy gaps in hourly earnings. Tests made on a limited group of countries for which both hourly and monthly earnings are available validate this assumption.

[6] Doing so risks confounding true age effects with composition effects (e.g. changing educational attainment and labour participation across cohorts), changes in returns to individual characteristics (e.g. earnings differentials of a characteristic), and time variation effects (see Box 6.2).

[7] Changes in female workforce composition (women's investment in market skills, leading more able women to select and enter into full-time employment) help explain why growing wage equality between genders coincided with growing inequality within gender (Mulligan and Rubinstein, 2008[49]).

[8] Glass ceiling is the "unseen, yet unbreachable barrier that keeps [...] women from rising to the upper rungs of the corporate ladder, regardless of their qualifications or achievements, that women confront as they approach the top of the corporate hierarchy" (United States Federal Glass Ceiling Commission, 1995[41]). The existence of a glass ceiling to women's career perspectives which excludes them from high-earnings and high-status positions has been well documented in the literature – e.g. Biewen and Seifert (2016[43]). The term "leaky pipeline" is usually employed to refer to the attrition in the number of women who advance to management levels. OECD (2017[1]) concludes that over the past decade, the glass ceiling remains intact and the "leaky pipeline" to top jobs has contributed to women making up only about one-third of managers in the OECD, though there is considerable variation across countries.

[9] Addison and Portugal (1989[34]) show that there are gender differences in match quality and changes in match quality over the course of careers: women are more often mismatched than men. This is true even for women with the best early-career matches.

[10] Based on Norwegian panel data, Kunze (2014[37]) shows that women with children are 25% less likely to be promoted than women without children; what the author calls the "family gap in

climbing the career". Analysing gender differences in job search behaviours, Kunze and Troske (2009[38]) show that displaced women take longer to find a new job than men in a comparable situation, and that these differences are driven by differential behaviour of prime-age women, whereas no significant gender difference is apparent for younger and older workers.

[11] Every year in France, 12% of the working-age population experience a professional transition and this is the case of 17% of the active population. These results are consistent with Flamand (2016[44]) who finds that in France labour transitions of the active population are relatively stable – around 16% on average each year– and evolve in line with the business and employment cycle.

[12] The cumulative number of transitions ranges from 6 in Greece, Italy, Portugal and Slovenia to more than 15 in Australia, Finland, Iceland, Japan and Sweden.

[13] The impact of in-work transitions on income is not gender biased, that is they do not significantly increase men's income any more than they do for women's income. The female coefficient presented in Figure 6.7, Panel B is the marginal effect of the female coefficient, not the cross-effect of female with in-work transition (which was not significantly different from zero in almost all countries).

[14] Alon and Tienda (2005[42]) show that unskilled women who experience frequent job changes during the first four post-school years reap positive wage returns, but turnover beyond this "shopping" period incurs wage penalties. By contrast, unequal returns to job mobility drive the gender wage gaps for skilled women. Adda et al. (2012[33]) also find that sources of wage growth differ by skill level, with learning-by-doing being an important component early on for unskilled workers, whereas job mobility is important for workers who acquire skills in an apprenticeship scheme before labour market entry.

[15] Age patterns of labour mobility (available upon request) are different for men and women, and can partly explain the gap. It emerges that women: i) experience professional transitions less often than men when they are young (in particular in-work transitions); ii) change their professional situation more often than men at prime age, due to higher entries into and exits from inactivity; and iii) less often go through a professional change than men above the age of 55 years.

[16] OECD (2015[5]) also shows that earnings mobility (defined as movements in and out the labour market and up and down the wage ladder) is not lower for women than for men, but the incidence of low long-term earnings is much higher among women than men, affecting about one in four working women as compared with only one in twenty men. Equal short-term earnings mobility associated with low long-term earnings among women reveals the role played by career path dependencies, i.e. the impact that early professional mobility have on future career success.

[17] Available evidence suggests that men and women with the same level of education tend to enter the labour market at similar wage levels, but wages begin to diverge during the early career (Fitzenberger and Kunze, 2005[45]; Manning and Swaffield, 2008[39]).

[18] The existence of inequalities before the first childbirth suggests that the arrival of a child is not the only factor – see for example Briard and Valat (2018[46]). Social norms and preconceptions about women are likely to play an important role in the formation and evolution of gender inequalities throughout their working lives, although their respective contributions cannot be assessed.

[19] 6 log points for mothers with one child and 13 log points for mothers with two children according to Waldfogel (1997[40]).

[20] Briard and Valat (2018[46]) provide a lifecycle analysis of the gender wage gap in France. Gender inequalities appear before the arrival of the first child, especially for non-graduates, and increase further after childbirth. More often than women, men reach a good professional position

before becoming parents. Inequality increases the most at the time of the first childbirth, regardless of the final number of children and continues to widen afterwards, but at a slower pace.

[21] The possible presence of other older children may impact estimates in Figure 6.9. Nevertheless, the age of the youngest child is more likely to have a direct effect on the mother's labour market attachment and work intensity.

[22] Andrén (2011[47]) also suggests the existence of an "absence penalty" of part-time work, increasing with the duration of part-time work, which could be interpreted as the effect of slower human capital accumulation for individuals working part-time. The study estimates that, in Sweden, full-time working men earn 26% more than part-time ones, and that full-time working women earn 13% more than their part-time counterparts. However, when observable factors (e.g. occupations) are taken into consideration, only men's wages are significantly affected by part-time work: the pay gap is reduced to 9% for men and 2% for women.

[23] Figure 6.11 is based on country-specific probit regressions of the dependent variable "employed part-time" with female cross effects for all controls including age categories. All marginal effects are not shown in Figure 6.11, but available upon request.

[24] As discussed in Box 6.1, while the cross-section data presented in Section 6.1.1 can provide a very detailed snapshot of gender differences in employment and hours worked for different age classes, panel data or retrospective data are necessary to examine the consequences of those employment patterns for individual careers.

[25] While career lengths are presented to age 50, the conclusions presented remain valid when looking at career lengths up to age 65. Nevertheless, due to the nature of the SHARELIFE dataset (retrospective data) used for these estimates, sample sizes are considerably reduced if the focus is solely on workers who have reached their 65th birthday at the date of the interview. Up to 65 years old, total career lengths of men, childless women and women with children are, on average, 40.3, 29.3 and 21.4 years, respectively.

[26] These figures rely on long retrospective data which have two limitations. First, there is a sizeable memory bias being based on the recollection by elderly people (at least 50 years old in 2009) of their entire work history. Most importantly, as pointed out in Box 6.1, they reflect the career experiences of a specific cohort that faced social norms about working women and labour market conditions that differ from those that later cohorts face. For example, labour mobility rates in many European countries tended to be lower than their current levels and many people used to remain with the same company for most or all of their careers (the oldest respondents entered the labour market in the 1960s). Second, women now participate much more in the labour market and for a much longer period. Therefore, gaps in career length may have changed considerably and the results reported in Figure 6.11 are unlikely to predict accurately what will happen to more recent cohorts of women. Nevertheless, when looking at the activity status of women in 2014-15 (see Figure 6.2), some of the main stylised facts identified for this older cohort are clearly visible, revealing sizeable inertia: employment gaps remain sizeable even for middle-aged women from recent cohorts in Greece, Ireland, Italy and the Netherlands. Therefore, even if career length gaps may have decreased for younger cohorts, they will remain significant in these countries.

[27] See also Chapter 1 for the latest available data.

[28] Women experience higher levels of occupational segregation than men, and are restricted in the jobs they "choose" to go into by a variety of factors, including educational background and gendered socialisation. OECD (2017[1]) provides an "index of dissimilarity" based on the number of different occupations women work in compared with men. Every country shows evidence of occupational segregation by gender, but rankings are somewhat difficult to interpret as they cannot account for factors such as self-selection or cross-country differences in female employment rates. Indeed, the Nordic countries have historically higher levels of occupational gender segregation and

Mediterranean countries lower levels, in part because increases in occupational segregation have positively correlated with growth in female labour supply (European Commission, 2009[48]).

[29] The gender pay gap for full-time employees can be further decomposed into several sub-components – see Box 6.3 and OECD (2018[6]): i) the impact of gender differences in observable individual and job characteristics (e.g. gender differences in educational attainment, employment status and contract type); ii) the impact of gender occupational segregation; and iii) the unexplained component of the hourly wage gap, which represents discrimination and the effect of other non-observed factors (e.g. field of study, attitudes, labour market experience, match quality and the number of previous jobs held). Most of the hourly wage gap nevertheless remains unexplained (38% on average).

[30] The effect of occupational segregation is likely to extend beyond hourly wage gaps, although this additional effect is not estimated here. Evans (2018[51]), for example, estimates gender pay gap for full-time and part-time workers in different occupations and finds that where the pay gap is largest (skilled trade occupations), men have a much larger share of full-time employment while where it is smallest (sales and customer service occupations), full-time employment shares are almost equal across gender. This pattern reinforces the relative importance of occupational segregation on the gender gap in annual labour income.

[31] Eurofound (2016[28]) estimates that the total cost arising from women's lower employment rate in the European Union was around EUR 370 billion in 2013, corresponding to 2.8% of the EU's gross domestic product (GDP).

[32] Adema, Clarke and Frey (2015[35]) point out that working part-time, especially when it is of a permanent rather than a temporary nature, has negative effects on career progression. The lack of flexibility within firms also means that women will disproportionately suffer because of working shorter hours or requesting a specific family-friendly work schedule. Goldin (2014[36]) shows that there is a wage penalty attached to working short hours, while in some sectors – particularly the corporate, financial, and legal sectors – many firms offer disproportionate promotions to employees working long, continuous hours at certain times of the day.

[33] See for example Adema, Clarke and Frey (2015[35]), OECD (2016[30]; 2017[1]), Eurofound (2016[28]), Fernandez et al. (2016[50]), and Olivetti and Petrongolo (2016[27]) for comprehensive assessments of gender employment and earnings gaps, as well as literature reviews on the effectiveness of labour market policies (including ALMP, tax benefit systems, flexible working time arrangements) and family policies (including childcare support measures and leave policies).

[34] Good practices to reduce these disincentives include the In-Work Credit for Lone Parents (the United Kingdom) and phasing out transferability of general tax credits (the Netherlands) – see Eurofound (2016[28]) for more details.

[35] Countries' provision of childcare facilities and subsidies and their elaboration of tax-benefit models and their resulting (dis)incentives set the overall framework to which women react in decisions regarding their working life (their labour supply and working hours). Women should be given a real choice as to whether to work or not, and this choice should not be dictated them by insufficient public provision of early-childhood services. In Denmark for example, parents are entitled to a guaranteed day care place for their children at the end of the parental leave period. Local authorities are responsible for providing places, and must cover parents' expenses for a private care scheme or a place in another local authority if they fail to do so within a four-week waiting period (Eurofound, 2016[28]). The result is that 65% of Danish children aged 0-2 years are enrolled in childcare or preschool; in this, Denmark is the best OECD performer. Disincentives for mothers to work due to excessive childcare costs and insufficient childcare provision explain in large part women's deficit in employment.

[36] OECD (2016[30]) provide an overview of childcare take-up in OECD countries. On average, only one-third of the children under age three have access to early childhood education and care (ECEC),

with significant differences across countries. In Sweden and Denmark, public childcare systems provide guaranteed access to a high-quality, flexible service at heavily-subsidised rate. In Sweden, children are guaranteed a place in formal childcare once they are one year old. The service is open to all parents and operates on a full-time basis; most facilities are open over a 12-hour period.

References

Adda, J. et al. (2012), "Career Progression, Economic Downturns, and Skills", *NBER Working Paper*, No. 18832, NBER, http://www.sole-jole.org/13330.pdf.   [33]

Addison, J. and P. Portugal (1989), "Job Displacement, Relative Wage Changes, and Duration of Unemployment", *Journal of Labor Economics*, Vol. 7/3, pp. 281-302, http://dx.doi.org/10.1086/298209.   [34]

Adema, W., C. Clarke and V. Frey (2015), "Paid Parental Leave: Lessons from OECD Countries and Selected U.S. States", *OECD Social, Employment and Migration Working Papers*, No. 172, OECD Publishing, Paris, http://dx.doi.org/10.1787/5jrqgvqqb4vb-en.   [35]

Alon, S. and M. Tienda (2005), "Job Mobility and Early Career Wage Growth of White, African-American, and Hispanic Women", *Social Science Quarterly*, Vol. 86, pp. 1196-1217, http://dx.doi.org/10.1111/j.0038-4941.2005.00342.x.   [42]

Andrén, T. (2011), "Frånvaroeffekter på lönen för kvinnor och män", *Specialstudier*, No. 27, Konjunkturinstitutet, Stockholm, https://www.konj.se/download/18.75c1a082150f472195814b95/1447232178624/Specialstudie-27.pdf (accessed on 29 April 2018).   [47]

Bachmann, R. et al. (2014), *A Study on Labour Market Transitions Using Micro-data from the Statistics on Income and Living Conditions (SILC). Final Report*, RWI, Essen, https://www.econstor.eu/bitstream/10419/111484/1/828807256.pdf (accessed on 19 April 2018).   [19]

Bailey, M., B. Hershbein and A. Miller (2012), "The Opt-In Revolution? Contraception and the Gender Gap in Wages.", *American Economic Journal. Applied Economics*, Vol. 4/3, pp. 225-254, http://dx.doi.org/10.1257/app.4.3.225.   [16]

Biewen, M. and S. Seifert (2016), "Potential Parenthood and Career Progression of Men and Women: A Simultaneous Hazards Approach", *IZA Discussion Papers*, No. 10050, IZA, http://ftp.iza.org/dp10050.pdf (accessed on 22 February 2018).   [43]

Blau, F. and L. Kahn (2016), "The Gender Wage Gap: Extent, Trends, and Explanations", *NBER Working Paper*, No. 21913, National Bureau of Economic Research, Cambridge, MA, http://dx.doi.org/10.3386/w21913.   [13]

Blau, F. and L. Kahn (1997), "Swimming Upstream: Trends in the Gender Wage Differential in the 1980s", *Journal of Labor Economics*, Vol. 15/1, pp. 1-42, http://dx.doi.org/10.2307/2535313.   [17]

Blundell, R., A. Bozio and G. Laroque (2013), "Extensive and Intensive Margins of Labour Supply: Work and Working Hours in the US, the UK and France", *Fiscal Studies*, Vol. 34/1, pp. 1-29, http://dx.doi.org/10.1111/j.1475-5890.2013.00175.x.   [10]

Briard, K. and E. Valat (2018), "À quels moments les inégalités professionnelles entre les femmes et les hommes se forment-elles ? - Ministère du Travail", *Document d'études DARES*, No. 2018-215, DARES, Paris, http://dares.travail-emploi.gouv.fr/IMG/pdf/de_no215_inegalites_professionnelles_femmes-hommes.pdf (accessed on 29 April 2018). [46]

Campbell, C. and J. Pearlman (2013), "Period effects, cohort effects, and the narrowing gender wage gap", *Social Science Research*, Vol. 42/6, pp. 1693-1711, http://dx.doi.org/10.1016/J.SSRESEARCH.2013.07.014. [11]

Chamkhi, A. and F. Toutlemonde (2015), "Ségrégation professionnelle et écarts de salaires femmes-hommes", *Dares Analyses* 082, http://dares.travail-emploi.gouv.fr/IMG/pdf/2015-082.pdf (accessed on 22 February 2018). [26]

Davis, S., R. Faberman and J. Haltiwanger (2006), "The Flow Approach to Labor Markets: New Data Sources and Micro-Macro Links", *The Journal of Economic Perspectives*, Vol. 20/3, http://www.jstor.org/stable/30033664, pp. 3-26. [18]

Eurofound (2016), *The gender employment gap: Challenges and solutions*, Eurofound, Dublin, https://www.eurofound.europa.eu/sites/default/files/ef_publication/field_ef_document/ef1638en.pdf (accessed on 22 February 2018). [28]

European Commission (2009), *Gender Segregation in the Labour Market: Root Causes, Implications, and Policy Responses in the EU, Report to the European Commission's Expert Group on Gender and Employment (EGGE)*, European Commission, Brussels. [48]

Evans, T. (2018), *Understanding the gender pay gap in the UK*, Office for National Statistics, London, https://www.ons.gov.uk/employmentandlabourmarket/peopleinwork/earningsandworkinghours/articles/understandingthegenderpaygapintheuk/2018-01-17 (accessed on 30 April 2018). [51]

Fernandez, R. et al. (2016), "Faces of Joblessness: Characterising Employment Barriers to Inform Policy", *OECD Social, Employment and Migration Working Papers*, No. 192, OECD Publishing, Paris, http://dx.doi.org/10.1787/5jlwvz47xptj-en. [50]

Fitzenberger, B. and A. Kunze (2005), "Vocational Training and Gender: Wages and Occupational Mobility Among Young Workers", *Oxford Review of Economic Policy*, Vol. 21/3, pp. 392-415, http://dx.doi.org/10.2307/23606828. [45]

Flamand, J. (2016), "Dix ans de transitions professionnelles : un éclairage sur le marché du travail français", *Document de Travail France Stratégie*, No. 2016-03, France Stratégie, http://www.strategie.gouv.fr/sites/strategie.gouv.fr/files/atoms/files/dt_dix_ans_de_transitions_professionnelles.pdf (accessed on 22 February 2018). [44]

Goldin, C. (2014), "A Grand Gender Convergence: Its Last Chapter", *American Economic Review*, Vol. 104/4, http://files/74/grand-gender-convergence-its-last-chapter.html, pp. 1091-1119. [36]

Goldin, C. (2006), "The Quiet Revolution that Transformed Women's Employment, Education, and Family", *NBER Working Paper*, No. 11953, National Bureau of Economic Research, Cambridge, MA, http://dx.doi.org/10.3386/w11953. [15]

Goldin, C. (2004), "The Long Road to the Fast Track: Career and Family", *NBER Working Paper*, No. 10331, National Bureau of Economic Research, Cambridge, MA, http://dx.doi.org/10.3386/w10331. [14]

Goldin, C. and J. Mitchell (2016), "The New Lifecycle of Women's Employment: Disappearing Humps, Sagging Middles, Expanding Tops", *NBER Working paper*, No. 22913, National Bureau of Economic Research, Cambridge, MA, http://dx.doi.org/10.3386/w22913. [9]

Juhn, C. and K. McCue (2017), "Specialization Then and Now: Marriage, Children, and the Gender Earnings Gap across Cohorts", *Journal of Economic Perspectives*, Vol. 31/1, pp. 183-204, http://dx.doi.org/10.1257/jep.31.1.183. [12]

Kambayashi, R. (2017), *Global Change in the Structure of Employment: A Note on the Japanese Case*, Hitotsubashi University Institute of Economic Research, mimeo. [8]

Kleven, H. et al. (2018), "Children and Gender Inequality: Evidence from Denmark", *NBER Working Paper*, No. 24219, http://www.henrikkleven.com/uploads/3/7/3/1/37310663/kleven-landais-sogaard_gender_jan2015.pdf (accessed on 22 February 2018). [23]

Kremer, M. (2007), *How welfare states care : culture, gender and parenting in Europe*, Amsterdam University Press, Amsterdam, https://www.jstor.org/stable/j.ctt46mvjz (accessed on 22 February 2018). [31]

Kunze, A. (2014), "The Family Gap in Career Progression.", *Dept. of Economics Discussion Paper*, No. 29, NHH, http://papers.ssrn.com/sol3/papers.cfm?abstract_id=2515878. [37]

Kunze, A. and K. Troske (2009), "Life-Cycle Patterns in Male/Female Differences in Job Search", *IZA Discussion Paper*, No. 4656, IZA, http://ftp.iza.org/dp4656.pdf. [38]

Liu, K. (2015), "Explaining the Gender Wage Gap: Estimates from a Dynamic Model of Job Changes and Hours Changes", *IZA Discussion Paper*, No. 9255, iza, http://ftp.iza.org/dp9255.pdf. [24]

Manning, A. and J. Swaffield (2008), "The gender gap in early-career wage growth", *The Economic Journal*, Vol. 118/530, pp. 983-1024, http://dx.doi.org/10.1111/j.1468-0297.2008.02158.x. [39]

Mulligan, C. and Y. Rubinstein (2008), "Selection, Investment, and Women's Relative Wages Over Time", *The Quarterly Journal of Economics*, 10.1162/qjec.2008.123.3.1061, http://dx.doi.org/10.1162/qjec.2008.123.3.1061, pp. 1061-1110. [49]

OECD (2018), *Ageing and Employment Policies in Korea – the challenge of an ageing population*, OECD Publishing, Paris, http://www.oecd.org/employment/emp/33906935.pdf (accessed on 22 February 2018). [7]

OECD (2018), "Supplementary material for Chapter 6", in *OECD Employment Outlook 2018*, OECD Publishing, Paris, http://dx.doi.org/10.1787/empl_outlook-2018-15-en. [6]

OECD (2017), *Dare to Share: Germany's Experience Promoting Equal Partnership in Families*, OECD Publishing, Paris, http://dx.doi.org/10.1787/9789264259157-en. [22]

OECD (2017), *OECD Employment Outlook 2017*, OECD Publishing, Paris, http://dx.doi.org/10.1787/empl_outlook-2017-en. [4]

OECD (2017), *Preventing Ageing Unequally*, OECD Publishing, Paris, http://dx.doi.org/10.1787/9789264279087-en. [32]

OECD (2017), *Report on the Implementation of the OECD Gender Recommendations - Some Progress on Gender Equality but Much Left to Do*, http://www.oecd.org/mcm/documents/C-MIN-2017-7-EN.pdf (accessed on 30 April 2018). [25]

OECD (2017), *The Pursuit of Gender Equality: An Uphill Battle*, OECD Publishing, Paris, http://dx.doi.org/10.1787/9789264281318-en. [1]

OECD (2016), *Be Flexible! Background brief on how workplace flexibility can help European employees to balance work and family*, OECD Publishing, Paris, https://www.oecd.org/els/family/Be-Flexible-Backgrounder-Workplace-Flexibility.pdf (accessed on 22 February 2018). [20]

OECD (2016), *Who uses childcare? Background brief on inequalities in the use of formal early childhood education and care (ECEC) among very young children*, OECD Publishing, Paris, https://www.oecd.org/els/family/Who_uses_childcare-Backgrounder_inequalities_formal_ECEC.pdf (accessed on 22 February 2018). [30]

OECD (2015), *OECD Employment Outlook 2015*, OECD Publishing, Paris, http://dx.doi.org/10.1787/empl_outlook-2015-en. [5]

OECD (2014), *OECD Employment Outlook 2014*, OECD Publishing, Paris, http://dx.doi.org/10.1787/empl_outlook-2014-en. [3]

OECD (2013), *Health at a Glance 2013: OECD Indicators*, OECD Publishing, Paris, http://dx.doi.org/10.1787/health_glance-2013-en. [29]

OECD (2002), *OECD Employment Outlook 2002*, OECD Publishing, Paris, http://dx.doi.org/10.1787/empl_outlook-2002-en. [2]

Olivetti, C. and B. Petrongolo (2016), "The Evolution of Gender Gaps in Industrialized Countries", *NBER Working Papers*, No. 21887, NBER, http://www.nber.org/papers/w21887. [27]

United States Federal Glass Ceiling Commission (1995), *A Solid Investment : Making Full Use of the Nation's Human Capital*, http://digitalcommons.ilr.cornell.edu/key_workplace (accessed on 22 February 2018). [41]

Waldfogel, J. (1997), "The Effect of Children on Women's Wages", *American Sociological Review*, Vol. 62/2, p. 209, http://dx.doi.org/10.2307/2657300. [40]

Wilde, E., L. Batchelder and D. Ellwood (2010), "The Mommy Track Divides: The Impact of Childbearing on Wages of Women of Differing Skill Levels", *NBER Working Paper*, No. 16582, National Bureau of Economic Research, Cambridge, MA, http://dx.doi.org/10.3386/w16582. [21]

Supplementary material for Chapter 6

Supplementary material for Chapter 6 is available online only in English at the following DOI: http://dx.doi.org/10.1787/empl_outlook-2018-15-en.

Annex A. Statistical annex

Sources and definitions

The tables of the statistical annex show data for all 35 OECD countries. Data for Brazil, China, Colombia, Costa Rica, India, Indonesia, Lithuania, the Russian Federation and South Africa are included in a number of tables.

In general, *Tables A* to *K* and *Table M* report annual averages of monthly and quarterly estimates, when they are available, based on labour force surveys. The remaining *Tables L, N, O, P* and *Q* are based on a combination of survey and administrative sources. Data shown for a number of European countries in *Tables B, C, D, H, I, J, K* and *Table M* are based on the European Labour Force Survey (EU LFS), which are more comparable and sometime more consistent over time than data series from national LFS.

The statistical data for Israel are supplied by and under the responsibility of the relevant Israeli authorities. The use of such data by the OECD is without prejudice to the status of the Golan Heights, East Jerusalem and Israeli settlements in the West Bank under the terms of international law.

Data on employment, unemployment and the labour force are not necessarily the same as the series used for analyses and forecasting by the OECD Economics Department that are reported in the *OECD Economic Outlook* and included in the online annex tables of Chapter 1 of this publication.

Most of the statistics shown in these tables can also be found in the OECD central data repository *OECD.Stat* (http://stats.oecd.org) accessible from the web page dedicated to employment statistics (www.oecd.org/employment/database).

The database contains both raw data and derived statistics. It contains longer time series and more detailed datasets by age group, gender, educational attainment, employee job tenure, part-time employment, involuntary part-time employment, temporary employment, duration of unemployment, and other series than are shown in this annex, such as, the distribution of employment by weekly usual hours worked intervals, potential labour force including people marginally attached to the labour force, etc. The datasets include information on definitions, notes and sources used by member countries. The online database also contains additional series on working time, earnings and features of institutional and regulatory environments affecting the functioning of labour markets. Among these are the following:

- Annual hours worked for comparisons of trends over time.

- Average gross annual wages per dependent employee in full-time equivalent unit.

- Distribution of gross earnings of full-time workers by upper earnings decile cut-offs and by sex to compute earnings dispersion measures.

- Statutory minimum wages: levels and ratio of minimum-to-median wages.

- Public expenditure on labour market programmes, number of beneficiaries and inflows into the labour market.

- Union members and employees.

- Synthetic indicators of employment protection.

Conventional signs

..   Data not available

| Break in series

()   Data based on small sample sizes

Major breaks in series

Table A: Breaks in series have been adjusted in most countries to ensure that harmonised unemployment rates are consistent over time.

Tables B to K and Table M: Most of the breaks in series in the data shown in the tables occurred for any of the following reasons: changes in survey design, survey questionnaire, survey frequency and administration, revisions of data series based on updated population census results. These changes have affected the comparability over time of employment and/or unemployment levels and to a certain extent the ratios reported in the aforementioned tables:

- *Introduction of a continuous survey producing quarterly results:* Austria (2003/04), Brazil (2011/12), France (2002/03), Germany (2004/05), Hungary (2005/06, monthly results), Iceland (2002/03), Italy (2003/04), Luxembourg (2002/03, quarterly results as of 2007) and Turkey (2013/14).

- *Redesign of labour force survey:* Introduction of a new survey in Chile since April 2010 (see below), Germany (2010/11), Ireland (2016/2017), Hungary (2002/03), Portugal (2010/11), Poland (2004/05) and Turkey (2004/05 from quarterly to monthly results). Israel (2011/12), change from quarterly to monthly survey results and a change from "civilian" to "total" labour force (including those who are in compulsory or permanent military service). New Zealand (2015/16), the survey includes non-civilian personnel. New continuous quarterly survey in Mexico since 2005 (Encuesta Nacional de Ocupación y Empleo, ENOE) with a different questionnaire from that of the previous survey.

Data for Ireland reported in *Tables B* to *D* have been backcasted (from Q1 1998 to Q2 2017) to minimise the impact of the break in series. This is, however, not the case of *Tables H* to *K* and *Table M*.

- *Change in the operational definition of employment:*

  o Neat application of the criterion of "at least one hour worked in a gainful job" in the Chilean *Nueva Encuesta Nacional de Empleo* (NENE), a quarterly continuous survey, from April 2010 onward.

- *Change in the operational definition of unemployment regarding:*

  o Active job-search methods: in particular a change from registration to contact with the public employment service: France (2002/03) and Spain (2000/01).

  o Duration of active job search: In Australia (2014/15) the duration of unemployment has been replaced by duration of job search. In Belgium (2010/11), the duration of job search has been changed from an unlimited duration to previous four weeks including the survey reference week. In Chile (2009/10), the duration of active job search has been shortened from last two months to previous four weeks including the survey reference week.

  o Availability to work criterion: In Sweden (2004/05), the work availability criterion changed from the reference week to two weeks from the reference week to be consistent with the operational definition in other EU countries. In Chile, the work availability criterion did not exist prior to 2010 in the *Encuesta Nacional de Empleo* (ENE) and has been introduced in the *Nueva Encuesta Nacional de Empleo* (NENE) since April 2010. It has been fixed to two weeks from the end of the reference week.

  o Persons on lay-off considered as employed instead of unemployed: Norway (2005/06).

  o Other minor changes: Australia (2000/01) and Poland (2003/04).

- *Changes in the questionnaire with impact on employment and unemployment estimates:* Germany (2010/11): new questionnaire design ensures better coverage of small jobs. This leads to higher than normal annual employment increase. Impact on employment and unemployment statistics in New Zealand (2015/16) with the inclusion of army personnel. Spain (2004/05): impact on employment and unemployment and impact on unemployment estimates in Norway (2005/06) and Sweden (2004/05).

- *Change from seasonal to calendar quarters:* Switzerland (2009/10) and the United Kingdom (2005/06). However, there is no break in series between 2005 and 2006 for the United Kingdom as calendar-quarter-based historical series are available since 1992.

- *Introduction of new EU harmonised questionnaire:* Sweden (2004/05) and Turkey (2003/04).

- *Change in lower age limit from 16 to 15 years:* Iceland (2008/09), Norway (2005/06) and Sweden (2006/07).

- *Change in lower age limit from 15 to 16 years:* Italy (2007/08).

- *Change in data collector in Denmark since the first quarter of 2017*: the LFS response rate has increased and has resulted in a significant break in series between 2016 and 2017.

- In Norway, since 2006, age is defined as years reached at the survey reference week, instead of completed years at the end of the year, as in previous years.

- *Inclusion of population controls based on census results in the estimation process:* Mexico (2009/10) and Turkey (2006/07).

- In Japan, data for 2011 exclude three prefectures (Iwate, Miyagi and Fukushima) due to the temporary suspension of the labour force survey operation following the Great East Japan earthquake.

Colombia, Costa Rica and Lithuania are currently undergoing an accession process.

Table A. Harmonised unemployment rates in OECD countries
As a percentage of civilian labour force

Percentage

	1991	1995	2000	2006	2007	2008	2009	2010	2011	2012	2013	2014	2015	2016	2017
Australia	9.6	8.5	6.3	4.8	4.4	4.2	5.6	5.2	5.1	5.2	5.7	6.1	6.1	5.7	5.6
Austria	..	4.2	3.9	5.3	4.9	4.1	5.3	4.8	4.6	4.9	5.4	5.6	5.7	6.0	5.5
Belgium	6.4	9.7	6.9	8.3	7.5	7.0	7.9	8.3	7.2	7.6	8.5	8.5	8.5	7.9	7.1
Canada	10.3	9.5	6.8	6.3	6.1	6.1	8.4	8.1	7.5	7.3	7.1	6.9	6.9	7.0	6.3
Chile	8.2	7.3	9.7	7.8	7.1	7.8	9.7	8.2	7.1	6.4	5.9	6.4	6.2	6.5	6.7
Czech Republic	..	4.0	8.8	7.1	5.3	4.4	6.7	7.3	6.7	7.0	7.0	6.1	5.1	4.0	2.9
Denmark	7.9	6.7	4.3	3.9	3.8	3.5	6.0	7.5	7.6	7.5	7.0	6.5	6.2	6.2	5.7
Estonia	..	..	14.5	5.9	4.6	5.5	13.6	16.7	12.4	10.0	8.6	7.4	6.2	6.8	5.8
Finland	6.6	15.4	9.8	7.7	6.9	6.4	8.2	8.4	7.8	7.7	8.2	8.7	9.4	8.8	8.6
France	9.6	12.0	9.6	8.8	8.0	7.4	9.1	9.3	9.2	9.8	10.3	10.3	10.4	10.1	9.4
Germany	5.5	8.3	8.0	10.3	8.5	7.4	7.6	7.0	5.8	5.4	5.2	5.0	4.6	4.1	3.8
Greece	..	..	11.2	9.0	8.4	7.8	9.6	12.8	17.9	24.5	27.5	26.6	25.0	23.6	21.5
Hungary	..	..	6.3	7.5	7.4	7.8	10.0	11.2	11.1	11.0	10.1	7.7	6.8	5.1	4.2
Iceland	..	..	..	2.9	2.3	3.0	7.2	7.6	7.1	6.0	5.4	5.0	4.0	3.0	2.8
Ireland	14.8	12.3	4.5	4.8	5.0	6.8	12.7	14.6	15.4	15.5	13.8	11.9	9.9	8.4	6.7
Israel	..	6.9	8.8	8.4	7.3	6.1	7.5	6.6	5.6		6.9	6.2	5.9	5.2	4.8	4.2
Italy	8.5	11.2	10.1	6.8	6.1	6.7	7.8	8.4	8.4	10.6	12.1	12.7	11.9	11.7	11.2
Japan	2.1	3.2	4.7	4.1	3.8	4.0	5.1	5.1	4.6	4.4	4.0	3.6	3.4	3.1	2.8
Korea	2.5	2.1	4.4	3.5	3.3	3.2	3.6	3.7	3.4	3.2	3.1	3.5	3.6	3.7	3.7
Latvia	..	..	14.3	7.0	6.1	7.7	17.6	19.5	16.2	15.0	11.9	10.9	9.9	9.6	8.7
Luxembourg	1.7	2.9	2.2	4.6	4.2	4.9	5.1	4.6	4.8	5.1	5.9	6.1	6.5	6.3	5.6
Mexico	2.7	6.3	2.5	3.6	3.7	4.0	5.5	5.4	5.2	5.0	4.9	4.8	4.4	3.9	3.4
Netherlands	5.7	8.4	3.7	5.0	4.2	3.7	4.4	5.0	5.0	5.8	7.2	7.4	6.9	6.0	4.9
New Zealand	10.6	6.5	6.2	3.9	3.6	4.0	5.8	6.2	6.0	6.4	5.8	5.4	5.4	5.1	4.7
Norway	5.5	4.9	3.2	3.4	2.6	2.7	3.3	3.7	3.4	3.3	3.8	3.6	4.5	4.8	4.2
Poland	..	..	16.1	14.0	9.6	7.0	8.1	9.7	9.7	10.1	10.3	9.0	7.5	6.2	4.9
Portugal	4.2	7.2	5.1	8.9	9.1	8.8	10.7	12.0	12.9	15.8	16.5	14.1	12.7	11.2	9.0
Slovak Republic	..	..	18.9	13.5	11.2	9.6	12.1	14.5	13.7	14.0	14.2	13.2	11.5	9.7	8.1
Slovenia	..	..	6.7	6.0	4.9	4.4	5.9	7.3	8.2	8.9	10.1	9.7	9.0	8.0	6.6
Spain	15.5	20.8	11.9	8.5	8.2	11.3	17.9	19.9	21.4	24.8	26.1	24.5	22.1	19.7	17.2
Sweden	3.1	8.8	5.6	7.0	6.1	6.2	8.3	8.6	7.8	8.0	8.0	7.9	7.4	7.0	6.7
Switzerland	..	..	..	..	..	..	..	4.8	4.4	4.5	4.7	4.8	4.8	4.9	4.8
Turkey	..	..	..	8.8	8.8	9.7	12.6	10.7	8.8	8.2	8.7		10.0	10.3	10.9	10.9
United Kingdom	8.6	8.5	5.4	5.4	5.3	5.6	7.6	7.8	8.1	7.9	7.6	6.1	5.3	4.8	4.4
United States	6.8	5.6	4.0	4.6	4.6	5.8	9.3	9.6	9.0	8.1	7.4	6.2	5.3	4.9	4.4
OECD[1]	..	..	6.2 e	6.1 e	5.6 e	6.0 e	8.1 e	8.3 e	8.0 e	8.0 e	7.9 e	7.4 e	6.8 e	6.3 e	5.8 e

.. Not available; | Break in series; e Estimated value

Note: The OECD harmonised unemployment rates are compiled for 35 OECD member countries and conform to the International Labour Office (ILO) guidelines. In so far as possible, the data have been adjusted to ensure comparability over time. All series are benchmarked to labour-force-survey-based estimates. Data for the European Union member countries, Norway and Turkey are produced by the Statistical Office of the European Communities (Eurostat) and data for the remaining OECD countries are produced by the OECD. Methodological notes: www.oecd.org/std/labourstatistics/44743407.pdf.

1. Weighted average.

Source: OECD Employment Database, www.oecd.org/employment/emp/onlineoecdemploymentdatabase.htm.

http://dx.doi.org/10.1787/888933778896

Table B1. Employment/population ratios by selected age groups - Total
As a percentage of the population in each age group

Percentage

	Total (15-64)				Youth (15-24)				Prime age (25-54)				Older population (55-64)			
	2000	2007	2016	2017	2000	2007	2016	2017	2000	2007	2016	2017	2000	2007	2016	2017
Australia	69.1	72.8	72.4	73.0	61.7	64.1	58.3	58.4	76.2	79.9	79.7	80.2	46.1	56.5	62.5	63.6
Austria	68.3	69.9	71.5	72.2	52.8	53.8	51.0	50.6	82.5	82.9	83.6	84.1	28.3	36.0	49.2	51.3
Belgium	60.5	62.0	62.3	63.1	29.1	27.5	22.7	22.7	77.4	79.7	79.1	79.5	26.3	34.4	45.4	48.3
Canada	70.9	73.5	72.6	73.4	56.2	59.5	55.4	56.5	79.9	82.2	81.4	82.3	48.1	57.0	61.6	62.2
Chile[1]	54.5	57.6	62.2	62.7	29.0	29.0	29.2	28.3	65.6	70.1	74.8	74.9	47.7	54.8	63.8	65.3
Czech Republic	65.2	66.1	72.0	73.6	38.3	28.5	28.6	29.1	81.6	83.5	85.7	86.7	36.3	46.0	58.5	62.1
Denmark	76.3	77.0	74.9	74.2	66.0	65.3	58.2	56.3	84.2	86.1	82.5	81.7	55.7	58.9	67.8	68.9
Estonia	60.6	69.6	72.0	74.1	34.9	34.6	38.6	41.6	74.4	84.6	82.4	83.8	42.8	59.4	65.1	67.9
Finland	67.5	70.5	69.2	70.1	42.9	46.4	43.3	44.1	80.9	83.3	79.9	80.6	42.3	55.0	61.4	62.5
France	61.1	64.3	64.6	65.2	23.2	31.2	28.2	29.1	78.3	82.1	80.3	80.6	34.3	38.2	49.9	51.4
Germany	65.6	69.0	74.7	75.2	47.2	45.9	45.8	46.5	79.3	80.3	84.0	84.2	37.6	51.3	68.6	70.1
Greece	56.5	60.9	52.0	53.5	27.6	24.0	13.0	14.1	70.5	75.4	66.0	67.4	39.0	42.7	36.3	38.3
Hungary	56.0	57.0	66.5	68.2	32.5	21.1	28.1	29.0	73.0	74.7	82.2	83.7	21.9	32.2	49.8	51.7
Iceland[2]	84.6	85.7	86.3	85.8	68.2	74.3	77.1	75.3	90.6	89.4	89.6	89.6	84.2	84.9	84.4	83.4
Ireland	68.0	71.7	66.4	67.4	61.0	62.3	43.0	41.0	75.5	78.7	75.3	77.2	45.3	54.1	57.1	58.9
Israel[3]	62.1	64.5	68.6	69.0	48.1	46.4	44.3	44.8	71.3	74.0	79.2	79.7	46.5	57.1	66.5	66.8
Italy[2]	53.9	58.6	57.2	58.0	27.8	24.5	16.6	17.1	68.0	73.4	68.8	69.4	27.7	33.7	50.3	52.2
Japan	68.9	70.7	74.3	75.3	42.7	41.4	42.5	42.5	78.6	80.2	83.3	84.1	62.8	66.1	71.4	73.3
Korea	61.5	64.1	66.1	66.6	29.4	26.3	26.9	27.2	72.3	74.1	76.2	76.3	57.8	60.6	66.2	67.5
Latvia	57.3	68.1	68.7	70.1	29.2	38.1	33.0	33.0	73.5	82.1	79.7	81.2	35.9	58.0	61.4	62.3
Luxembourg	62.7	64.2	65.6	66.3	31.8	22.5	25.7	25.8	78.2	81.9	82.5	83.7	27.2	32.0	40.4	39.9
Mexico	60.1	61.0	61.0	61.1	48.9	44.9	40.8	40.8	67.4	70.0	71.2	71.3	51.7	54.5	55.0	54.9
Netherlands	72.1	74.4	74.8	75.8	66.5	65.5	60.8	62.3	81.0	84.4	82.9	83.5	37.6	48.8	63.5	65.7
New Zealand	70.3	75.1	75.6	76.9	54.2	58.0	54.3	55.4	78.2	81.8	83.1	84.1	56.9	71.8	76.1	78.2
Norway[2]	77.9	76.9	74.4	74.1	58.1	55.1	49.2	48.8	85.3	85.8	82.7	82.4	67.1	69.0	72.6	71.9
Poland	55.0	57.0	64.5	66.1	24.5	25.8	28.4	29.6	70.9	74.9	80.3	81.4	28.4	29.7	46.2	48.3
Portugal	68.3	67.6	65.2	67.8	41.8	34.4	23.9	25.9	81.8	80.9	80.2	82.5	50.8	51.0	52.1	56.2
Slovak Republic	56.8	60.7	64.9	66.2	29.0	27.6	25.2	26.9	74.7	78.0	80.0	80.0	21.3	35.7	49.0	53.0
Slovenia	62.8	67.8	65.8	69.3	32.8	37.6	28.6	34.7	82.6	85.3	83.5	86.1	22.7	33.5	38.5	42.7
Spain[2]	57.4	66.8	60.5	62.1	36.3	43.0	20.5	22.9	68.4	77.1	71.5	73.2	37.0	44.5	49.1	50.5
Sweden[2]	74.3	74.2	76.2	76.9	46.7	42.1	44.3	44.8	83.8	86.1	85.9	86.3	65.1	70.1	75.6	76.6
Switzerland	78.3	78.6	79.6	79.8	65.0	62.6	62.5	63.1	85.4	86.1	86.3	86.2	63.3	67.2	71.5	72.2
Turkey	48.9	44.6	50.6	51.5	37.0	30.2	34.1	34.3	56.7	53.2	60.0	61.1	36.4	27.1	33.4	34.4
United Kingdom[2]	72.3	72.4	74.3	75.0	61.4	56.4	53.7	54.0	80.3	81.4	83.0	83.8	50.8	57.3	63.5	64.0
United States[2]	74.1	71.8	69.4	70.1	59.7	53.1	49.4	50.3	81.5	79.9	77.9	78.6	57.8	61.8	61.8	62.5
OECD[4]	65.4	66.5	67.0	67.8	45.4	43.5	41.1	41.6	75.9	77.0	77.1	77.8	47.8	53.4	59.2	60.4
Colombia	..	60.2	67.2	66.9	..	38.0	43.8	43.3	..	72.0	78.3	78.0	..	51.9	62.8	62.8
Costa Rica	59.6	64.1	58.7	59.8	44.9	46.3	33.2	33.6	69.1	74.6	71.6	72.4	46.4	54.8	50.8	53.3
Lithuania	58.8	65.0	69.4	70.4	25.2	24.8	30.2	30.4	75.0	82.2	82.7	83.3	40.3	53.2	64.6	66.1
Brazil	..	67.4	61.3	60.7	..	52.9	39.4	39.0	..	76.1	72.4	71.8	..	53.8	48.1	47.9
China[5]	79.3	..	..	..	61.9	..	..	..	88.0	..	..	..	59.2	..	..	..
India[5]	58.2	..	..	..	41.3	..	..	..	67.4	..	..	..	54.1	..	..	..
Indonesia	65.0	62.0	65.4	66.1	41.5	39.5	38.9	39.7	75.6	71.4	75.3	75.9	67.8	66.9	68.4	68.5
Russian Federation	63.3	68.5	70.0	70.3	34.6	33.7	31.5	29.6	80.2	84.7	86.1	86.8	34.8	52.0	48.2	47.7
South Africa	..	44.4	43.0	43.4	..	15.7	12.3	12.5	..	60.6	57.5	57.4	..	42.2	39.5	41.1

.. Not available

Note: Please refer to the Box entitled "Major breaks in series" in the introduction to the Statistical Annex.

1. New labour force survey since April 2010. To remove the break, data prior to 2010 are spliced using *new-to-old* chaining coefficients based on data of fourth quarter of 2009.
2. The lower age limit is 16 instead of 15. For Iceland up to 2008, Italy after 2007, Norway up to 2005 and Sweden up to 2006.
3. Redesigned monthly labour force survey since January 2012. To remove the break, data prior to 2012 are spliced using *new-to-old* chaining coefficients between monthly and quarterly surveys based on data of fourth quarter of 2011.
4. Weighted average.
5. Data up to 2010 for China and up to 2012 for India can be found in the database.

Source: OECD Employment Database, www.oecd.org/employment/emp/onlineoecdemploymentdatabase.htm and www.oecd.org/els/emp/lfsnotes_sources.pdf.

http://dx.doi.org/10.1787/888933778915

Table B2. Employment/population ratios by selected age groups - Men
As a percentage of the male population in each age group

Percentage

	Men (15-64)				Youth (15-24)				Prime age (25-54)				Older population (55-64)			
	2000	2007	2016	2017	2000	2007	2016	2017	2000	2007	2016	2017	2000	2007	2016	2017
Australia	76.9	79.5	77.5	77.9	62.6	65.0	57.9	58.1	85.6	88.1	86.5	86.6	57.6	65.7	68.5	69.6
Austria	77.3	76.3	75.4	76.2	57.6	57.0	52.9	52.1	91.4	89.0	86.6	87.2	40.5	46.0	57.6	60.1
Belgium	69.5	68.7	66.5	67.5	32.8	29.9	24.0	24.4	87.3	87.0	83.8	84.4	36.4	42.9	50.7	53.8
Canada	76.2	77.0	75.4	76.3	56.7	59.2	54.1	55.4	85.8	86.2	85.0	86.0	57.4	63.5	66.4	66.6
Chile[1]	72.4	72.9	72.4	72.5	37.5	36.0	33.6	31.8	86.4	88.0	86.2	85.9	70.6	76.0	81.6	82.8
Czech Republic	73.6	74.8	79.3	80.9	42.8	32.8	33.8	33.8	89.3	91.7	92.7	93.7	51.7	59.6	68.2	71.7
Denmark	80.8	80.8	77.7	76.9	68.5	66.5	56.5	55.3	88.5	89.8	86.4	85.2	64.1	64.9	71.9	72.8
Estonia	64.1	73.2	75.6	77.4	40.8	39.1	41.1	45.0	75.8	89.4	87.6	88.4	51.0	58.1	63.5	66.3
Finland	70.5	72.4	70.8	71.6	45.7	47.9	43.3	44.3	84.1	85.9	83.0	83.3	43.7	55.1	59.8	61.7
France	68.1	69.2	68.0	68.9	26.6	34.2	30.2	31.5	87.1	88.4	84.7	85.5	38.5	40.5	51.6	52.8
Germany	72.9	74.7	78.5	78.9	49.7	48.2	47.0	47.4	87.2	86.4	88.1	88.4	46.4	59.4	73.7	75.0
Greece	71.5	74.2	61.0	62.7	32.7	29.1	14.7	15.9	88.5	90.1	76.0	77.5	55.2	59.1	46.2	49.6
Hungary	62.7	63.7	73.0	75.2	36.0	24.4	31.5	32.9	79.2	81.6	88.2	90.1	32.8	40.1	59.7	62.6
Iceland[2]	88.2	89.5	89.0	88.1	66.1	73.6	76.6	74.5	95.1	94.2	92.8	92.1	94.2	89.6	89.4	88.4
Ireland	79.7	80.4	71.6	72.6	66.6	66.2	43.2	40.5	88.5	87.9	81.4	83.7	63.3	67.8	65.4	66.9
Israel[3]	68.9	70.1	72.0	72.5	51.2	49.3	44.9	45.3	79.6	80.6	83.4	83.8	56.9	65.1	73.4	74.4
Italy[2]	68.2	70.6	66.5	67.1	33.2	29.4	19.2	20.1	84.9	87.4	79.3	79.9	40.9	45.0	61.7	62.8
Japan	80.9	81.7	82.5	82.9	42.5	41.3	42.0	42.0	93.4	92.8	92.5	92.7	78.4	81.5	83.5	85.0
Korea	73.2	74.9	75.9	76.3	24.6	21.3	23.0	23.1	88.0	87.3	87.9	87.7	68.6	74.8	79.1	80.4
Latvia	61.1	72.7	70.0	71.9	34.3	43.8	34.0	35.0	74.4	86.0	81.4	83.5	48.1	64.3	61.3	62.4
Luxembourg	75.0	72.3	70.5	69.9	35.3	26.5	24.9	27.0	92.8	92.2	88.5	87.4	37.9	35.6	47.7	45.5
Mexico	82.8	80.8	78.6	79.0	64.7	58.5	53.1	53.2	93.8	92.7	91.1	91.6	78.1	78.3	75.8	76.4
Netherlands	81.2	81.1	79.6	80.4	67.9	66.9	59.6	61.0	91.4	91.4	88.1	88.4	49.7	60.0	72.8	74.8
New Zealand	77.8	82.0	80.7	81.9	56.2	60.3	56.5	57.3	87.0	90.0	89.8	90.4	67.9	80.7	81.7	84.4
Norway[2]	81.7	79.7	75.8	75.7	61.0	54.0	48.1	48.2	88.8	89.2	84.5	84.3	73.1	73.9	75.7	75.0
Poland	61.2	63.6	71.0	72.8	27.3	29.2	32.8	33.9	77.6	81.1	86.1	87.3	36.7	41.4	55.7	58.3
Portugal	76.3	73.6	68.3	71.1	47.3	38.5	25.5	27.6	90.0	87.2	83.0	85.6	62.2	58.7	58.5	63.0
Slovak Republic	62.2	68.4	71.4	72.0	29.8	30.9	31.9	32.4	79.6	85.0	86.3	86.3	35.4	52.6	55.1	56.6
Slovenia	67.2	72.7	68.9	72.5	35.7	43.2	31.1	38.6	85.7	88.1	85.6	88.5	32.3	45.3	43.6	48.0
Spain[2]	72.7	77.3	65.8	67.6	43.2	48.6	21.8	23.8	85.6	87.5	77.4	79.2	55.2	59.6	55.7	57.8
Sweden[2]	76.3	76.5	77.5	78.3	47.9	41.9	42.9	43.8	85.9	89.0	88.0	88.4	67.7	73.1	77.6	78.5
Switzerland	87.3	85.6	83.7	84.3	66.5	65.4	61.8	63.9	95.2	93.6	91.2	91.1	77.0	76.4	77.2	78.6
Turkey	71.7	66.8	70.0	70.7	49.7	41.5	44.9	45.3	85.0	80.7	83.1	83.8	51.9	40.5	49.1	50.6
United Kingdom[2]	79.0	78.7	79.1	79.6	63.6	57.9	53.2	54.1	87.5	88.3	89.1	89.5	60.0	66.0	69.3	69.6
United States[2]	80.6	77.8	74.8	75.4	61.9	54.4	50.1	50.8	89.0	87.5	85.0	85.4	65.7	67.4	67.5	68.4
OECD[4]	76.1	75.9	74.9	75.5	50.1	47.4	44.1	44.7	88.2	87.9	86.3	86.8	59.5	63.8	67.8	69.1
Colombia	..	75.2	79.2	78.9	..	47.9	52.5	51.9	..	88.9	91.0	90.5	..	72.8	79.9	80.6
Costa Rica	80.1	81.4	72.8	74.2	58.6	58.3	41.9	42.4	92.5	94.1	88.0	89.0	74.3	79.3	69.8	70.9
Lithuania	60.1	68.2	70.0	70.6	28.3	29.4	32.5	32.3	73.8	84.2	82.6	83.1	49.9	60.7	66.8	67.2
Brazil	..	79.7	71.9	70.7	..	63.0	46.1	45.4	..	89.0	83.8	82.4	..	70.1	63.9	62.6
China[5]	84.6	..	..	..	61.8	..	..	..	94.2	..	..	..	70.4	..	..	..
India[5]	81.1	..	..	..	57.2	..	..	..	93.8	..	..	..	78.7	..	..	..
Indonesia	80.7	78.2	79.7	80.0	48.8	48.7	46.6	46.8	95.0	91.1	92.5	92.9	83.6	82.8	82.5	82.5
Russian Federation	67.6	72.0	75.2	75.6	38.2	36.6	35.2	33.1	82.7	87.0	89.8	90.5	46.8	63.9	59.0	58.9
South Africa	..	52.2	49.2	49.1	..	18.8	15.0	14.9	..	71.3	65.1	64.3	..	55.3	47.2	49.7

.. Not available

Note: Please refer to the Box entitled "Major breaks in series" in the introduction to the Statistical Annex.

1. New labour force survey since April 2010. To remove the break, data prior to 2010 are spliced using *new-to-old* chaining coefficients based on data of fourth quarter of 2009.
2. The lower age limit is 16 instead of 15. For Iceland up to 2008, Italy after 2007, Norway up to 2005 and Sweden up to 2006.
3. Redesigned monthly labour force survey since January 2012. To remove the break, data prior to 2012 are spliced using *new-to-old* chaining coefficients between monthly and quarterly surveys based on data of fourth quarter of 2011.
4. Weighted average.
5. Data up to 2010 for China and up to 2012 for India can be found in the database.

Source: OECD Employment Database, www.oecd.org/employment/emp/onlineoecdemploymentdatabase.htm and www.oecd.org/els/emp/lfsnotes_sources.pdf.

http://dx.doi.org/10.1787/888933778934

Table B3. Employment/population ratios by selected age groups - Women
As a percentage of the female population in each age group

Percentage

	Women (15-64)				Youth (15-24)				Prime age (25-54)				Older population (55-64)			
	2000	2007	2016	2017	2000	2007	2016	2017	2000	2007	2016	2017	2000	2007	2016	2017
Australia	61.3	66.1	67.4	68.1	60.8	63.2	58.8	58.7	67.0	71.9	73.1	74.0	34.2	47.3	56.7	57.9
Austria	59.4	63.5	67.7	68.2	48.1	50.6	49.0	49.0	73.6	76.7	80.6	81.0	16.8	26.5	41.1	42.8
Belgium	51.5	55.3	58.1	58.7	25.4	25.0	21.4	20.9	67.2	72.3	74.3	74.6	16.6	26.0	40.2	42.8
Canada	65.6	69.9	69.7	70.6	55.7	59.8	56.8	57.6	73.9	78.2	77.8	78.6	39.1	50.7	56.9	57.9
Chile[1]	36.8	42.3	52.0	52.8	20.2	21.7	24.1	24.3	45.0	52.3	63.8	64.1	26.6	35.1	47.0	48.6
Czech Republic	56.9	57.3	64.4	66.2	33.6	23.9	23.2	24.3	73.7	74.9	78.4	79.3	22.4	33.5	49.3	53.0
Denmark	71.6	73.2	72.0	71.5	63.3	64.0	60.0	57.3	79.8	82.3	78.5	78.1	46.6	52.9	63.6	65.2
Estonia	57.3	66.1	68.5	70.8	28.5	29.8	36.0	38.1	73.2	79.9	77.0	79.1	36.5	60.5	66.4	69.2
Finland	64.5	68.5	67.6	68.5	39.9	44.7	43.3	43.8	77.6	80.7	76.7	77.9	40.9	54.8	63.0	63.4
France	54.3	59.6	61.4	61.7	19.8	28.1	26.3	26.8	69.6	76.1	75.9	75.8	30.3	36.0	48.3	50.1
Germany	58.1	63.2	70.8	71.5	44.6	43.5	44.5	45.5	71.2	74.0	79.8	80.0	29.0	43.4	63.6	65.4
Greece	41.7	47.7	43.3	44.4	22.4	18.8	11.3	12.4	52.7	60.9	55.9	57.2	24.3	27.0	27.2	28.0
Hungary	49.6	50.7	60.2	61.3	28.8	17.7	24.6	24.8	66.9	67.9	76.2	77.2	13.1	25.8	41.5	42.4
Iceland[2]	81.0	81.7	83.4	83.3	70.5	75.0	77.7	76.1	86.0	84.1	86.4	86.9	74.4	80.0	79.3	78.4
Ireland	56.1	62.8	61.3	62.3	55.2	58.3	42.8	41.6	62.4	69.3	69.3	70.9	27.0	40.1	49.0	51.0
Israel[3]	55.5	59.0	65.2	65.6	44.8	43.4	43.6	44.3	63.5	67.7	75.1	75.7	36.8	49.3	60.0	59.5
Italy[2]	39.6	46.6	48.1	48.9	22.1	19.5	13.7	13.9	50.9	59.6	58.5	59.0	15.3	23.0	39.7	42.3
Japan	56.7	59.5	66.1	67.4	43.0	41.5	42.9	42.9	63.6	67.4	73.9	75.3	47.9	51.2	59.6	61.9
Korea	50.1	53.4	56.1	56.9	33.6	30.8	30.7	30.9	56.1	60.5	63.8	64.5	48.0	46.9	53.6	54.8
Latvia	53.8	63.9	67.6	68.4	23.8	32.2	31.9	30.9	72.6	78.4	78.1	79.0	26.8	53.4	61.4	62.1
Luxembourg	50.0	56.1	60.4	62.5	28.3	18.4	26.5	24.5	63.0	71.7	76.4	79.8	16.8	28.6	32.9	34.0
Mexico	39.6	43.6	45.1	44.9	34.0	32.2	28.4	28.3	44.3	50.6	53.6	53.5	27.7	33.1	37.1	36.4
Netherlands	62.7	67.5	70.1	71.3	65.1	64.0	62.1	63.6	70.3	77.3	77.8	78.6	25.5	37.5	54.2	56.6
New Zealand	63.1	68.6	70.7	72.0	52.1	55.6	52.0	53.3	69.9	74.2	76.9	78.2	46.1	63.2	70.9	72.5
Norway[2]	74.0	74.0	72.8	72.4	55.0	56.3	50.3	49.5	81.6	82.3	80.8	80.4	61.2	64.0	69.5	68.7
Poland	48.9	50.6	58.1	59.5	21.8	22.4	23.7	25.2	64.3	68.8	74.5	75.3	21.4	19.4	37.6	39.3
Portugal	60.5	61.8	62.4	64.8	36.1	30.2	22.2	24.1	73.9	74.8	77.6	79.7	40.9	44.3	46.3	50.2
Slovak Republic	51.5	53.0	58.3	60.3	28.2	24.1	18.2	21.1	69.8	71.0	73.5	73.4	9.8	21.2	43.5	49.6
Slovenia	58.4	62.6	62.6	65.8	29.7	31.4	26.1	30.4	79.3	82.4	81.2	83.5	13.8	22.2	33.4	37.5
Spain[2]	42.0	56.0	55.1	56.5	29.0	37.2	19.2	22.0	51.0	66.3	65.6	67.1	20.1	30.2	42.8	43.5
Sweden[2]	72.2	71.8	74.8	75.4	45.4	42.2	45.9	45.8	81.7	83.0	83.7	84.1	62.4	67.2	73.6	74.6
Switzerland	69.3	71.6	75.4	75.2	63.4	59.7	63.2	62.4	75.6	78.5	81.3	81.2	50.1	58.1	65.8	65.8
Turkey	26.2	22.8	31.2	32.2	24.8	19.3	23.2	23.0	27.6	25.6	36.7	38.3	21.5	14.6	18.1	18.7
United Kingdom[2]	65.7	66.3	69.5	70.4	59.1	54.9	54.1	53.8	73.2	74.6	76.9	78.2	41.8	48.8	58.0	58.7
United States[2]	67.8	65.9	64.0	64.9	57.4	51.8	48.8	49.9	74.2	72.5	71.1	72.1	50.6	56.6	56.5	57.1
OECD[4]	55.0	57.3	59.4	60.1	40.6	39.4	38.0	38.5	63.8	66.3	68.1	68.9	36.9	43.7	51.1	52.2
Colombia	..	46.0	55.7	55.5	..	28.2	35.0	34.7	..	56.3	66.1	66.0	..	33.4	48.1	47.5
Costa Rica	38.8	46.3	44.3	45.0	30.2	33.3	22.7	24.1	45.7	55.2	55.3	55.6	20.3	31.2	33.3	37.4
Lithuania	57.5	62.0	68.8	70.2	22.1	20.0	27.8	28.4	76.1	80.2	82.9	83.6	33.0	47.5	62.8	65.2
Brazil	..	55.9	51.3	51.4	..	42.7	32.5	32.4	..	64.3	61.8	61.9	..	39.5	34.7	35.3
China[5]	73.8	..	..	..	62.1	..	..	..	81.6	..	..	..	47.1	..	..	..
India[5]	34.5	..	..	..	24.1	..	..	..	40.4	..	..	..	29.5	..	..	..
Indonesia	49.5	45.6	50.9	52.1	34.4	29.8	31.0	32.2	56.3	52.0	58.1	59.1	52.4	49.4	54.1	54.3
Russian Federation	59.3	65.3	65.2	65.5	30.9	30.8	27.5	26.0	77.8	82.5	82.6	83.3	25.9	43.1	40.1	39.3
South Africa	..	37.4	37.0	37.7	..	12.6	9.6	10.1	..	51.2	50.0	50.5	..	31.8	33.1	34.0

.. Not available

Note: Please refer to the Box entitled "Major breaks in series" in the introduction to the Statistical Annex.

1. New labour force survey since April 2010. To remove the break, data prior to 2010 are spliced using new-to-old chaining coefficients based on data of fourth quarter of 2009.
2. The lower age limit is 16 instead of 15. For Iceland up to 2008, Italy after 2007, Norway up to 2005 and Sweden up to 2006.
3. Redesigned monthly labour force survey since January 2012. To remove the break, data prior to 2012 are spliced using new-to-old chaining coefficients between monthly and quarterly surveys based on data of fourth quarter of 2011.
4. Weighted average.
5. Data up to 2010 for China and up to 2012 for India can be found in the database.

Source: OECD Employment Database, www.oecd.org/employment/emp/onlineoecdemploymentdatabase.htm and www.oecd.org/els/emp/lfsnotes_sources.pdf.

http://dx.doi.org/10.1787/888933778953

Table C1. Labour force participation rates by selected age groups - Total
As a percentage of the population in each age group

Percentage

	Total (15-64)				Youth (15-24)				Prime age (25-54)				Older population (55-64)			
	2000	2007	2016	2017	2000	2007	2016	2017	2000	2007	2016	2017	2000	2007	2016	2017
Australia	73.8	76.2	76.9	77.4	70.2	70.8	66.8	66.9	80.3	82.7	83.4	83.9	48.2	58.1	65.2	66.3
Austria	70.8	73.5	76.2	76.4	55.7	59.4	57.5	56.1	85.2	86.5	88.4	88.7	29.8	37.2	51.7	53.6
Belgium	65.1	67.1	67.6	68.0	35.3	33.9	28.5	28.1	82.4	85.3	85.1	84.8	27.1	35.9	48.1	51.3
Canada	76.2	78.3	78.1	78.5	64.4	67.0	63.7	63.9	84.8	86.6	86.5	87.0	50.9	60.0	65.8	66.0
Chile[1]	61.0	63.0	66.8	67.4	38.6	37.0	34.6	34.1	71.5	75.1	79.6	79.9	51.3	57.6	66.4	68.0
Czech Republic	71.6	69.8	75.0	75.9	46.1	31.9	32.0	31.7	88.4	87.8	88.9	89.1	38.2	48.2	60.8	63.6
Denmark	80.0	80.1	80.0	78.8	70.7	70.6	66.2	63.3	87.9	88.9	87.4	86.2	58.2	61.0	70.6	71.6
Estonia	71.1	73.0	77.4	78.8	44.8	38.4	44.3	47.1	86.6	88.3	87.6	88.5	48.3	61.6	70.8	72.0
Finland	74.9	75.7	76.0	76.9	53.8	55.0	53.5	54.5	87.9	88.0	86.3	86.8	46.6	58.8	66.4	67.8
France	68.0	69.7	71.7	71.8	29.3	38.4	37.2	37.2	86.2	87.9	87.8	87.7	37.3	40.0	53.7	54.9
Germany	71.1	75.6	78.0	78.2	51.5	52.0	49.3	49.9	85.3	87.2	87.4	87.3	42.9	57.2	71.3	72.6
Greece	63.8	66.5	68.2	68.3	39.0	31.0	24.6	25.0	78.1	81.8	85.5	85.0	40.5	44.2	44.9	46.7
Hungary	59.9	61.6	70.1	71.2	37.2	25.7	32.3	32.4	77.3	80.1	86.1	86.9	22.6	33.7	52.1	53.6
Iceland[2]	86.6	87.8	89.0	88.3	71.6	80.1	82.5	81.7	92.2	90.6	91.9	91.3	85.7	85.7	86.3	85.0
Ireland	71.5	75.7	73.1	72.5	66.3	69.5	52.7	48.9	78.8	82.1	81.9	81.9	46.6	55.4	61.2	62.3
Israel[3]	69.9	71.2	72.1	72.1	58.2	55.5	48.5	48.3	78.7	80.3	82.7	82.8	50.9	61.2	69.2	69.1
Italy[2]	60.3	62.4	64.9	65.4	39.5	30.8	26.6	26.2	74.3	77.5	77.5	77.9	29.0	34.5	53.4	55.4
Japan	72.5	73.6	76.9	77.5	47.0	44.9	44.8	44.5	81.9	83.3	86.0	86.6	66.5	68.4	73.6	75.3
Korea	64.5	66.4	68.7	69.2	33.0	28.8	30.2	30.3	75.2	76.5	78.8	79.1	59.6	61.9	68.1	69.1
Latvia	67.0	72.6	76.3	77.0	37.4	42.6	39.4	39.7	85.5	87.1	87.8	88.6	39.8	60.7	67.6	67.9
Luxembourg	64.2	66.9	70.0	70.2	34.0	26.5	28.5	30.5	79.8	84.7	87.2	88.0	27.6	32.7	40.4	41.0
Mexico	61.7	63.4	63.6	63.4	51.5	48.4	44.2	43.8	68.6	72.0	73.7	73.5	52.4	55.6	56.1	56.0
Netherlands	74.3	77.1	79.7	79.7	70.8	70.4	68.2	68.3	83.1	86.8	86.9	86.7	38.5	50.8	68.4	69.5
New Zealand	75.0	78.1	79.9	80.9	62.7	64.5	62.6	63.4	82.0	84.0	86.5	87.2	59.7	72.9	78.6	80.5
Norway[2]	80.7	78.9	78.2	77.4	64.7	59.4	55.3	54.4	87.6	87.5	86.4	85.7	68.0	69.7	74.1	73.3
Poland	65.8	63.2	68.8	69.6	37.8	33.0	34.5	34.8	82.4	81.7	84.9	84.9	31.3	31.8	48.3	50.1
Portugal	71.2	73.9	73.7	74.7	45.7	41.3	33.2	34.0	84.8	87.7	89.1	89.6	52.5	54.6	58.5	61.5
Slovak Republic	69.9	68.2	71.8	72.1	46.0	34.5	32.4	33.2	88.4	86.8	87.5	86.6	24.3	38.8	53.9	56.4
Slovenia	67.5	71.3	71.6	74.2	39.2	41.8	33.7	39.1	87.4	89.3	90.5	91.9	24.0	34.6	41.2	45.6
Spain[2]	66.7	72.8	75.4	75.1	48.5	52.5	36.9	37.3	78.0	83.1	87.4	87.0	40.9	47.4	59.2	59.6
Sweden[2]	79.0	79.1	82.0	82.5	52.9	52.1	54.7	54.4	88.2	90.0	90.9	91.2	69.3	73.0	79.8	80.6
Switzerland	80.5	81.6	83.9	84.0	68.3	67.4	68.4	68.7	87.4	88.9	90.6	90.4	65.1	69.3	74.3	75.1
Turkey	52.4	49.8	57.0	58.0	42.5	37.7	42.4	43.3	59.6	58.2	66.5	67.6	37.2	28.3	35.6	36.8
United Kingdom[2]	76.4	76.5	78.1	78.5	69.6	65.7	61.9	61.2	83.9	84.5	86.1	86.7	53.0	59.2	65.9	66.4
United States[2]	77.2	75.3	73.0	73.3	65.8	59.4	55.2	55.5	84.0	83.0	81.3	81.7	59.2	63.8	64.1	64.5
OECD[4]	69.9	70.6	71.7	72.1	51.7	49.4	47.2	47.3	80.2	81.0	81.9	82.1	50.3	55.7	62.1	63.0
Colombia	..	68.0	74.3	74.1	..	48.8	53.7	53.2	..	79.1	84.8	84.8	..	55.2	66.5	66.4
Costa Rica	62.8	67.2	65.0	65.9	50.4	51.9	43.2	43.4	71.4	76.8	77.2	77.9	47.7	56.0	53.3	55.4
Lithuania	70.5	67.9	75.5	75.9	36.2	27.1	35.3	35.0	88.8	85.6	89.3	89.3	45.4	55.3	70.0	71.3
Brazil	..	73.5	69.4	69.8	..	63.6	54.1	55.0	..	81.1	79.4	79.7	..	55.4	50.6	50.9
China[5]	82.3	..	..	..	67.9	..	..	..	90.5	..	..	..	59.4	..	..	..
India[5]	60.9	..	..	..	45.9	..	..	..	69.4	..	..	..	55.0	..	..	..
Indonesia	69.4	68.7	69.4	70.0	51.8	52.8	47.9	48.3	77.8	75.8	77.8	78.5	68.1	68.4	69.6	70.0
Russian Federation	70.9	72.9	74.1	74.2	43.6	39.4	37.6	35.3	88.3	89.2	90.5	90.9	37.5	53.7	50.0	49.6
South Africa	..	57.2	58.7	59.8	..	29.3	26.4	26.9	..	74.5	75.8	76.7	..	44.8	43.4	45.4

.. Not available

Note: Please refer to the Box entitled "Major breaks in series" in the introduction to the Statistical Annex.

1. New labour force survey since April 2010. To remove the break, data prior to 2010 are spliced using *new-to-old* chaining coefficients based on data of fourth quarter of 2009.
2. The lower age limit is 16 instead of 15. For Iceland up to 2008, Italy after 2007, Norway up to 2005 and Sweden up to 2006.
3. Redesigned monthly labour force survey since January 2012. To remove the break, data prior to 2012 are spliced using *new-to-old* chaining coefficients between monthly and quarterly surveys based on data of fourth quarter of 2011.
4. Weighted average.
5. Data up to 2010 for China and up to 2012 for India can be found in the database.

Source: OECD Employment Database, www.oecd.org/employment/emp/onlineoecdemploymentdatabase.htm and www.oecd.org/els/emp/lfsnotes_sources.pdf.

http://dx.doi.org/10.1787/888933778972

Table C2. Labour force participation rates by selected age groups - Men
As a percentage of the male population in each age group

Percentage

	Men (15-64)				Youth (15-24)				Prime age (25-54)				Older population (55-64)			
	2000	2007	2016	2017	2000	2007	2016	2017	2000	2007	2016	2017	2000	2007	2016	2017
Australia	82.3	83.0	82.3	82.6	71.9	71.8	67.2	67.4	90.2	90.8	90.2	90.3	60.9	67.7	71.9	72.8
Austria	79.9	80.0	80.7	81.0	60.6	62.9	60.2	58.4	94.0	92.5	91.8	92.3	42.8	47.6	61.2	63.0
Belgium	73.7	73.6	72.3	72.8	38.7	36.1	30.7	30.6	91.8	92.5	90.4	90.0	37.5	44.4	53.6	56.9
Canada	81.9	82.4	81.8	81.9	65.8	67.4	63.5	63.8	91.0	91.1	90.9	91.1	60.7	67.0	71.4	71.0
Chile[1]	80.1	78.5	77.4	77.6	47.6	44.0	39.2	37.7	93.5	93.0	91.4	91.3	76.8	79.8	84.8	86.2
Czech Republic	79.4	78.1	82.2	82.9	51.3	36.7	37.5	36.5	94.9	95.0	95.4	95.7	54.5	62.4	70.9	73.2
Denmark	84.2	83.7	82.6	81.5	73.4	72.0	65.0	62.5	91.7	92.3	90.8	89.6	66.7	66.9	74.9	75.6
Estonia	76.3	77.5	81.7	82.6	52.1	44.3	48.1	51.6	89.2	93.2	93.3	93.2	60.0	62.4	70.2	71.7
Finland	77.6	77.4	77.9	78.7	56.4	56.3	53.8	54.8	90.7	90.3	89.7	89.8	48.1	59.2	65.1	67.5
France	74.4	74.7	75.6	75.9	32.6	41.9	40.0	40.6	94.2	94.1	92.7	92.9	41.7	42.5	56.0	56.8
Germany	78.9	81.8	82.2	82.4	54.7	54.9	51.0	51.3	93.4	93.8	92.0	91.9	52.4	65.8	76.9	77.9
Greece	77.4	78.4	76.2	76.4	41.7	34.4	26.4	26.2	94.4	94.6	93.2	93.0	57.3	60.9	57.3	59.8
Hungary	67.5	68.6	76.9	78.2	41.8	29.5	36.1	36.5	84.4	87.2	92.4	93.3	34.1	42.1	62.4	64.5
Iceland[2]	89.8	91.6	91.8	90.8	70.1	80.0	82.0	81.5	96.1	95.3	94.9	93.8	94.7	90.4	91.9	90.2
Ireland	83.6	84.7	79.5	78.7	72.3	74.5	54.5	49.6	92.2	91.5	89.1	89.4	64.9	69.4	70.8	70.7
Israel[3]	77.5	77.0	75.6	75.6	61.9	58.3	49.0	48.5	87.5	87.0	86.9	87.0	63.5	70.3	76.8	77.4
Italy[2]	74.3	74.3	74.8	75.0	44.6	36.0	30.2	30.0	90.6	91.0	88.2	88.5	42.7	46.2	65.9	67.0
Japan	85.2	85.2	85.4	85.5	47.4	45.1	44.6	44.1	97.1	96.3	95.5	95.5	84.1	84.9	86.4	87.5
Korea	77.2	77.9	78.9	79.3	28.5	24.0	25.8	26.1	92.2	90.5	91.2	91.0	71.3	76.8	81.7	82.7
Latvia	72.3	77.9	78.8	79.8	43.4	49.2	43.3	42.8	87.8	91.6	90.2	91.8	53.9	67.6	69.4	69.1
Luxembourg	76.4	75.0	75.1	74.0	37.4	30.6	28.8	32.6	94.2	94.9	93.1	91.8	38.6	36.4	47.7	46.7
Mexico	84.7	83.8	81.8	81.8	67.7	62.6	57.2	56.7	95.2	95.2	94.2	94.2	79.3	80.2	77.8	78.2
Netherlands	83.2	83.8	84.4	84.2	71.6	71.4	67.2	67.0	93.2	93.5	91.7	91.3	50.9	62.6	78.2	79.0
New Zealand	83.1	84.9	85.0	85.7	65.8	67.1	64.9	65.4	91.1	92.1	92.9	93.1	71.9	81.9	84.3	86.8
Norway[2]	84.8	81.8	80.3	79.4	67.5	58.6	55.1	54.5	91.4	90.9	88.9	87.9	74.4	74.7	77.8	77.0
Poland	71.7	70.0	75.7	76.6	40.9	36.5	39.8	39.7	88.3	87.9	90.8	91.1	40.4	44.8	58.6	60.8
Portugal	78.9	79.2	77.2	77.9	50.5	44.7	35.0	35.6	92.5	92.9	91.9	92.3	64.5	63.2	67.0	69.2
Slovak Republic	76.8	75.8	78.3	78.2	49.4	38.7	39.8	39.6	93.9	93.0	93.5	93.1	41.0	56.9	60.1	60.0
Slovenia	71.9	75.8	74.5	77.1	41.7	47.6	36.8	42.9	90.6	91.3	92.0	93.4	34.6	46.7	47.1	51.8
Spain[2]	80.4	82.6	80.5	80.2	53.6	57.3	38.9	39.3	93.0	92.5	92.5	92.0	60.5	62.8	67.0	67.9
Sweden[2]	81.5	81.4	83.9	84.3	54.4	51.5	54.0	53.8	90.7	92.9	93.3	93.6	72.6	76.4	82.6	83.3
Switzerland	89.4	88.2	88.2	88.5	70.5	70.2	67.8	69.5	96.7	95.8	95.5	95.2	79.3	78.4	80.7	82.1
Turkey	76.9	74.4	77.6	78.2	57.6	51.6	54.3	55.2	89.5	88.1	90.8	91.2	53.4	42.9	53.0	54.8
United Kingdom[2]	84.1	83.3	83.3	83.4	73.3	68.7	62.6	62.4	91.9	91.7	92.3	92.4	63.4	68.8	72.5	72.6
United States[2]	83.9	81.7	78.8	79.0	68.6	61.5	56.5	56.7	91.6	90.9	88.5	88.6	67.3	69.6	70.2	70.6
OECD[4]	80.9	80.4	80.0	80.2	56.9	54.1	50.9	51.0	92.6	92.2	91.4	91.4	62.8	66.6	71.4	72.3
Colombia	..	82.6	85.4	85.2	..	58.2	61.3	60.5	..	95.2	96.3	96.1	..	77.7	85.1	85.3
Costa Rica	83.8	84.2	79.2	80.4	64.7	63.6	51.7	52.3	95.2	95.7	93.4	94.1	76.3	80.9	73.8	74.4
Lithuania	74.3	71.3	77.1	77.4	41.6	31.6	38.7	37.8	89.7	87.7	90.2	90.4	57.9	63.3	73.6	73.3
Brazil	..	84.9	80.2	79.9	..	72.3	60.5	61.0	..	92.8	90.7	90.2	..	72.3	67.5	67.0
China[5]	87.8	..	..	..	68.0	..	..	..	96.8	..	..	..	70.8	..	..	..
India[5]	84.9	..	..	..	63.6	..	..	..	96.7	..	..	..	80.0	..	..	..
Indonesia	85.8	85.6	84.7	84.8	60.8	63.6	57.2	56.9	97.6	95.9	95.9	96.1	83.9	84.8	84.1	84.4
Russian Federation	75.9	76.9	79.8	79.9	47.5	42.7	41.8	39.1	91.4	92.0	94.4	94.8	50.6	66.3	61.7	61.6
South Africa	..	64.3	65.4	66.1	..	32.0	29.3	29.4	..	84.0	83.6	84.1	..	59.1	53.2	55.5

.. Not available

Note: Please refer to the Box entitled "Major breaks in series" in the introduction to the Statistical Annex.

1. New labour force survey since April 2010. To remove the break, data prior to 2010 are spliced using *new-to-old* chaining coefficients based on data of fourth quarter of 2009.
2. The lower age limit is 16 instead of 15. For Iceland up to 2008, Italy after 2007, Norway up to 2005 and Sweden up to 2006.
3. Redesigned monthly labour force survey since January 2012. To remove the break, data prior to 2012 are spliced using *new-to-old* chaining coefficients between monthly and quarterly surveys based on data of fourth quarter of 2011.
4. Weighted average.
5. Data up to 2010 for China and up to 2012 for India can be found in the database.

Source: OECD Employment Database, www.oecd.org/employment/emp/onlineoecdemploymentdatabase.htm and www.oecd.org/els/emp/ lfsnotes_sources.pdf.

http://dx.doi.org/10.1787/888933778991

Table C3. Labour force participation rates by selected age groups - Women
As a percentage of the female population in each age group

Percentage

	Women (15-64)				Youth (15-24)				Prime age (25-54)				Older population (55-64)			
	2000	2007	2016	2017	2000	2007	2016	2017	2000	2007	2016	2017	2000	2007	2016	2017
Australia	65.3	69.4	71.6	72.3	68.5	69.7	66.4	66.3	70.5	74.8	76.9	77.7	35.3	48.6	58.8	60.1
Austria	61.8	67.1	71.7	71.8	50.8	56.0	54.6	53.7	76.3	80.5	84.9	85.0	17.6	27.5	42.7	44.5
Belgium	56.4	60.4	62.9	63.2	31.8	31.6	26.2	25.4	72.7	78.0	79.8	79.6	17.1	27.5	42.8	45.8
Canada	70.4	74.2	74.4	75.0	62.9	66.5	64.0	64.0	78.5	82.1	82.2	82.9	41.4	53.3	60.3	61.1
Chile[1]	42.1	47.6	56.1	57.1	29.4	29.7	29.2	29.8	49.7	57.3	68.2	68.8	27.8	36.8	49.0	50.6
Czech Republic	63.7	61.5	67.6	68.7	40.6	26.9	26.2	26.6	81.8	80.3	82.1	82.1	23.7	35.2	51.2	54.5
Denmark	75.6	76.4	77.2	76.1	67.8	69.1	67.3	64.1	84.0	85.3	83.8	82.7	49.0	55.1	66.4	67.6
Estonia	66.3	68.8	73.1	75.0	37.1	32.1	40.2	42.3	84.1	83.4	81.6	83.6	39.4	61.0	71.3	72.3
Finland	72.1	73.9	74.1	74.9	51.1	53.7	53.2	54.2	85.0	85.6	82.8	83.6	45.2	58.3	67.6	68.2
France	61.7	64.9	67.9	67.9	26.0	34.9	34.3	33.7	78.4	82.0	83.1	82.8	33.0	37.6	51.5	53.1
Germany	63.3	69.4	73.6	74.0	48.2	49.0	47.4	48.3	76.9	80.6	82.7	82.5	33.5	48.9	65.9	67.5
Greece	50.5	54.8	60.4	60.3	36.2	27.5	22.9	23.9	62.0	69.2	77.7	77.0	25.4	28.2	33.6	34.9
Hungary	52.6	54.9	63.5	64.2	32.5	21.8	28.2	28.2	70.5	73.2	79.8	80.4	13.3	26.9	43.5	44.3
Iceland[2]	83.3	83.6	86.2	85.7	73.2	80.1	83.0	81.9	88.2	85.4	88.8	88.7	76.8	80.7	80.5	79.7
Ireland	59.3	66.4	66.8	66.4	60.1	64.4	50.9	48.2	65.4	72.5	74.9	74.7	28.0	41.2	51.8	54.0
Israel[3]	62.5	65.5	68.6	68.7	54.3	52.5	48.0	48.0	70.3	73.9	78.5	78.8	39.1	52.4	61.8	61.4
Italy[2]	46.3	50.6	55.2	55.9	34.3	25.4	22.8	22.1	57.9	64.1	66.8	67.3	16.1	23.4	41.7	44.5
Japan	59.6	61.9	68.1	69.4	46.6	44.7	44.9	44.9	66.5	70.1	76.3	77.5	49.7	52.5	61.0	63.3
Korea	52.1	54.9	58.3	59.0	37.0	33.2	34.3	34.3	57.8	62.0	65.9	66.6	48.8	47.5	54.8	55.9
Latvia	62.1	67.8	74.0	74.3	31.2	35.8	35.4	36.5	83.3	82.8	85.5	85.4	29.2	55.7	66.1	66.9
Luxembourg	51.7	58.9	64.7	66.2	30.6	22.3	28.2	28.3	64.9	74.7	81.1	84.0	16.8	29.1	32.9	34.9
Mexico	41.0	45.4	47.0	46.7	36.3	35.1	31.2	30.8	45.4	52.3	55.5	55.3	28.0	33.4	37.5	36.8
Netherlands	65.2	70.4	75.0	75.2	70.0	69.4	69.2	69.7	72.7	79.9	82.2	82.0	25.9	38.9	58.5	60.2
New Zealand	67.2	71.5	74.9	76.2	59.5	61.9	60.0	61.3	73.4	76.5	80.5	81.6	47.8	64.1	73.2	74.5
Norway[2]	76.5	75.9	75.9	75.3	61.8	60.3	55.5	54.4	83.5	84.0	83.9	83.3	61.6	64.6	70.4	69.5
Poland	59.9	56.5	62.0	62.6	34.8	29.3	28.9	29.7	76.5	75.6	79.0	78.7	23.7	20.6	39.0	40.5
Portugal	63.8	68.7	70.5	71.6	40.9	37.8	31.3	32.3	77.3	82.7	86.6	87.0	42.0	47.0	51.0	54.6
Slovak Republic	63.2	60.7	65.3	65.9	42.6	30.1	24.7	26.5	82.9	80.5	81.4	79.8	10.7	23.3	48.2	53.0
Slovenia	62.9	66.6	68.6	71.2	36.4	35.4	30.6	34.9	84.2	87.3	88.9	90.3	14.1	23.1	35.2	39.5
Spain[2]	52.9	62.8	70.2	69.9	43.3	47.5	34.9	35.2	62.8	73.3	82.3	82.0	22.6	32.7	51.7	51.8
Sweden[2]	76.4	76.8	80.2	80.6	51.2	52.6	55.4	55.1	85.6	87.1	88.4	88.7	65.9	69.6	76.9	77.9
Switzerland	71.6	75.0	79.5	79.3	66.0	64.5	69.0	67.8	78.0	81.9	85.5	85.5	51.3	60.3	67.9	68.0
Turkey	28.0	25.7	36.2	37.6	28.1	24.4	30.4	31.1	28.9	28.0	42.0	43.8	21.6	14.8	18.6	19.3
United Kingdom[2]	69.0	69.8	73.0	73.6	65.8	62.7	61.1	59.9	76.1	77.5	80.0	81.0	43.1	49.9	59.7	60.4
United States[2]	70.7	69.1	67.3	67.9	63.0	57.2	53.8	54.3	76.7	75.4	74.3	75.0	51.9	58.3	58.4	58.9
OECD[4]	59.2	61.0	63.6	64.0	46.4	44.8	43.4	43.5	68.0	70.1	72.6	73.0	38.6	45.4	53.3	54.3
Colombia	..	54.2	63.6	63.6	..	39.5	46.0	45.8	..	64.2	73.9	74.0	..	35.2	50.4	50.2
Costa Rica	41.6	49.7	50.4	51.1	35.2	39.2	32.9	33.7	47.7	57.8	61.1	61.5	21.0	31.9	34.5	38.2
Lithuania	67.1	64.9	73.9	74.6	30.5	22.3	31.9	32.2	87.9	83.6	88.5	88.1	35.9	49.2	67.2	69.6
Brazil	..	62.8	59.3	60.3	..	54.7	47.4	48.8	..	70.2	68.9	70.0	..	40.6	36.3	37.1
China[5]	76.7	..	..	..	67.8	..	..	..	84.0	..	..	..	47.2	..	..	..
India[5]	36.0	..	..	..	26.9	..	..	..	41.5	..	..	..	30.0	..	..	..
Indonesia	53.2	51.7	53.9	55.1	43.1	41.7	38.2	39.1	58.1	56.2	59.8	61.0	52.6	50.5	54.8	55.3
Russian Federation	66.2	69.2	68.9	69.0	39.7	36.0	33.2	31.3	85.3	86.6	86.7	87.2	27.8	44.2	41.3	40.6
South Africa	..	50.8	52.2	53.6	..	26.6	23.6	24.3	..	66.2	68.0	69.3	..	33.3	35.3	37.1

.. Not available

Note: Please refer to the Box entitled "Major breaks in series" in the introduction to the Statistical Annex.

1. New labour force survey since April 2010. To remove the break, data prior to 2010 are spliced using *new-to-old* chaining coefficients based on data of fourth quarter of 2009.
2. The lower age limit is 16 instead of 15. For Iceland up to 2008, Italy after 2007, Norway up to 2005 and Sweden up to 2006.
3. Redesigned monthly labour force survey since January 2012. To remove the break, data prior to 2012 are spliced using *new-to-old* chaining coefficients between monthly and quarterly surveys based on data of fourth quarter of 2011.
4. Weighted average.
5. Data up to 2010 for China and up to 2012 for India can be found in the database.

Source: OECD Employment Database, www.oecd.org/employment/emp/onlineoecdemploymentdatabase.htm and www.oecd.org/els/emp/lfsnotes_sources.pdf.

http://dx.doi.org/10.1787/888933779010

Table D1. Unemployment rates by selected age groups - Total
As a percentage of the total labour force in each age group

Percentage

	Total (15-64)				Youth (15-24)				Prime age (25-54)				Older population (55-64)			
	2000	2007	2016	2017	2000	2007	2016	2017	2000	2007	2016	2017	2000	2007	2016	2017
Australia	6.4	4.4	5.9	5.8	12.1	9.4	12.6	12.6	5.0	3.4	4.5	4.4	4.5	2.7	4.3	4.1
Austria	3.5	4.9	6.1	5.6	5.1	9.4	11.2	9.8	3.1	4.2	5.4	5.1	5.2	3.4	5.0	4.2
Belgium	7.0	7.5	7.9	7.1	17.5	18.8	20.1	19.3	6.1	6.6	7.1	6.2	3.0	4.2	5.7	5.9
Canada	6.9	6.1	7.1	6.4	12.7	11.2	13.1	11.6	5.7	5.1	6.0	5.4	5.5	5.1	6.4	5.8
Chile[1]	10.7	8.7	6.8	7.0	25.0	21.6	15.6	16.8	8.2	6.6	6.0	6.3	7.0	4.7	3.9	4.0
Czech Republic	8.8	5.4	4.0	2.9	17.0	10.7	10.5	7.9	7.7	4.9	3.5	2.7	5.2	4.6	3.8	2.4
Denmark	4.6	3.8	6.3	5.9	6.7	7.5	12.0	11.0	4.2	3.1	5.5	5.2	4.4	3.4	4.0	3.7
Estonia	14.8	4.7	6.9	5.9	22.2	9.9	12.8	11.6	14.0	4.2	5.9	5.3	11.5	3.6	8.1	5.7
Finland	9.8	6.9	8.9	8.8	20.3	15.7	19.1	19.1	8.0	5.3	7.4	7.1	9.4	6.5	7.5	7.8
France	10.1	7.7	9.8	9.2	20.7	18.8	24.1	21.6	9.2	6.6	8.6	8.2	7.9	4.4	7.1	6.3
Germany	7.8	8.7	4.2	3.8	8.4	11.7	7.0	6.8	7.0	8.0	3.9	3.5	12.3	10.3	3.9	3.4
Greece	11.6	8.5	23.7	21.7	29.2	22.7	47.3	43.6	9.7	7.8	22.8	20.7	3.9	3.4	19.2	18.1
Hungary	6.4	7.5	5.1	4.2	12.7	18.0	12.9	10.7	5.7	6.9	4.5	3.7	3.0	4.4	4.4	3.6
Iceland[2]	2.3	2.3	3.1	2.9	4.7	7.2	6.5	7.9	1.7	1.3	2.5	1.9	1.7	0.9	2.2	1.8
Ireland	5.0	5.2	9.3	7.0	8.0	10.3	18.4	16.1	4.2	4.2	8.1	5.8	2.8	2.4	6.7	5.5
Israel[3]	11.2	9.4	4.9	4.3	17.3	16.3	8.6	7.3	9.4	7.8	4.2	3.8	8.7	6.8	3.8	3.4
Italy[2]	10.6	6.2	11.9	11.4	29.7	20.4	37.8	34.7	8.5	5.3	11.1	10.9	4.5	2.4	5.7	5.8
Japan	5.0	4.1	3.3	3.0	9.2	7.7	5.1	4.6	4.1	3.7	3.1	2.8	5.6	3.4	2.9	2.6
Korea	4.6	3.4	3.8	3.8	10.8	8.7	10.7	10.3	4.0	3.1	3.4	3.5	2.9	2.2	2.8	2.4
Latvia	14.5	6.2	9.9	8.9	22.1	10.6	16.4	17.0	14.0	5.7	9.3	8.3	9.6	4.5	9.2	8.3
Luxembourg	2.4	4.1	6.3	5.5	6.4	15.2	10.0	15.4	2.0	3.4	5.3	4.9	1.4	2.1	0.0	2.7
Mexico	2.6	3.8	4.0	3.6	5.1	7.2	7.7	6.9	1.8	2.9	3.4	3.0	1.4	1.9	2.1	1.9
Netherlands	3.1	3.6	6.1	4.9	6.1	7.0	10.8	8.9	2.5	2.8	4.6	3.7	2.1	4.0	7.2	5.5
New Zealand	6.2	3.8	5.3	4.9	13.5	10.1	13.2	12.7	4.7	2.6	3.9	3.5	4.7	1.4	3.1	2.8
Norway[2]	3.5	2.6	4.9	4.3	10.2	7.3	11.0	10.3	2.6	1.9	4.4	3.8	1.3	1.0	2.0	1.9
Poland	16.4	9.7	6.2	5.0	35.2	21.7	17.7	14.8	13.9	8.4	5.4	4.2	9.4	6.8	4.4	3.7
Portugal	4.2	8.5	11.5	9.2	8.6	16.7	28.0	23.8	3.5	7.7	10.0	7.9	3.2	6.5	11.0	8.6
Slovak Republic	18.8	11.0	9.7	8.2	37.0	20.1	22.2	18.9	15.5	10.1	8.6	7.6	12.3	8.1	9.0	6.0
Slovenia	6.9	5.0	8.1	6.7	16.3	10.1	15.2	11.2	5.6	4.5	7.7	6.3	5.3	3.3	6.5	6.4
Spain[2]	13.9	8.3	19.7	17.3	25.3	18.1	44.4	38.6	12.3	7.2	18.2	15.9	9.4	6.0	17.0	15.3
Sweden[2]	5.9	6.2	7.1	6.8	11.7	19.2	18.9	17.8	4.9	4.4	5.5	5.3	6.1	3.9	5.3	5.1
Switzerland	2.7	3.7	5.1	5.0	4.8	7.1	8.6	8.1	2.3	3.1	4.7	4.7	2.7	3.1	3.8	3.8
Turkey	6.7	10.5	11.1	11.2	13.1	20.0	19.6	20.8	4.9	8.5	9.7	9.5	2.1	4.3	6.2	6.5
United Kingdom[2]	5.4	5.3	5.0	4.5	11.7	14.2	13.2	11.8	4.3	3.8	3.7	3.3	4.2	3.3	3.6	3.5
United States[2]	4.0	4.7	4.9	4.4	9.3	10.5	10.4	9.2	3.1	3.7	4.2	3.8	2.5	3.1	3.6	3.1
OECD[4]	6.4	5.8	6.5	5.9	12.2	12.1	12.9	11.9	5.4	4.9	5.8	5.3	5.0	4.0	4.6	4.2
Colombia	..	11.5	9.5	9.7	..	22.2	18.4	18.6	..	9.0	7.7	8.0	..	5.9	5.5	5.4
Costa Rica	5.2	4.6	9.7	9.2	11.0	10.8	23.1	22.6	3.2	2.8	7.2	7.1	2.8	2.0	4.7	3.7
Lithuania	16.7	4.3	8.1	7.3	30.2	8.4	14.5	13.3	15.6	4.0	7.4	6.6	11.2	3.7	7.7	7.3
Brazil	..	8.3	11.7	13.0	..	16.8	27.1	29.0	..	6.1	8.8	9.9	..	2.9	5.0	5.9
China[5]	3.7	..	..	..	8.8	..	..	..	2.8	..	..	..	0.4	..	..	..
India[5]	4.4	..	..	..	10.1	..	..	..	2.9	..	..	..	1.6	..	..	..
Indonesia	6.3	9.8	5.7	5.6	19.9	25.3	18.7	17.8	2.9	5.9	3.2	3.3	0.4	2.2	1.7	2.1
Russian Federation	10.7	6.1	5.6	5.2	20.7	14.4	16.3	16.1	9.2	5.1	4.8	4.5	7.3	3.1	3.7	3.9
South Africa	..	22.3	26.7	27.4	..	46.5	53.3	53.4	..	18.6	24.1	25.1	..	5.6	9.0	9.5

.. Not available

Note: Please refer to the Box entitled "Major breaks in series" in the introduction to the Statistical Annex.

1. New labour force survey since April 2010. To remove the break, data prior to 2010 are spliced using *new-to-old* chaining coefficients based on data of fourth quarter of 2009.
2. The lower age limit is 16 instead of 15. For Iceland up to 2008, Italy after 2007, Norway up to 2005 and Sweden up to 2006.
3. Redesigned monthly labour force survey since January 2012. To remove the break, data prior to 2012 are spliced using *new-to-old* chaining coefficients between monthly and quarterly surveys based on data of fourth quarter of 2011.
4. Weighted average.
5. Data up to 2010 for China and up to 2012 for India can be found in the database.

Source: *OECD Employment Database*, www.oecd.org/employment/emp/onlineoecdemploymentdatabase.htm and www.oecd.org/els/emp/ lfsnotes_sources.pdf.

http://dx.doi.org/10.1787/888933779029

Table D2. Unemployment rates by selected age groups - Men
As a percentage of the male labour force in each age group

Percentage

	Men (15-64)				Youth (15-24)				Prime age (25-54)				Older population (55-64)			
	2000	2007	2016	2017	2000	2007	2016	2017	2000	2007	2016	2017	2000	2007	2016	2017
Australia	6.6	4.1	5.8	5.7	12.9	9.5	13.8	13.7	5.1	3.0	4.1	4.1	5.3	2.8	4.8	4.4
Austria	3.3	4.6	6.6	6.0	5.0	9.3	12.1	10.8	2.8	3.8	5.7	5.5	5.4	3.4	5.9	4.6
Belgium	5.8	6.7	8.1	7.2	15.3	17.1	21.7	20.2	4.9	5.9	7.3	6.3	3.0	3.6	5.4	5.3
Canada	7.0	6.5	7.8	6.9	13.8	12.3	14.8	13.3	5.7	5.3	6.5	5.6	5.5	5.2	7.0	6.3
Chile[1]	9.7	7.2	6.4	6.6	21.2	18.2	14.4	15.7	7.6	5.4	5.7	5.9	8.0	4.8	3.8	4.0
Czech Republic	7.4	4.3	3.4	2.4	16.7	10.6	9.9	7.4	6.0	3.5	2.8	2.0	5.0	4.5	3.8	2.0
Denmark	4.1	3.5	6.0	5.7	6.8	7.6	13.1	11.4	3.5	2.7	4.8	4.9	3.9	3.0	4.0	3.8
Estonia	16.0	5.5	7.5	6.3	21.7	11.8	14.6	12.9	15.0	4.2	6.2	5.2	15.0	6.9	9.5	7.5
Finland	9.1	6.5	9.2	9.0	18.9	14.8	19.6	19.0	7.2	4.8	7.5	7.3	9.3	6.9	8.2	8.7
France	8.5	7.3	10.1	9.2	18.4	18.3	24.6	22.5	7.5	6.1	8.6	7.9	7.6	4.7	7.9	7.1
Germany	7.6	8.6	4.5	4.2	9.2	12.2	7.8	7.6	6.6	7.8	4.2	3.9	11.5	9.7	4.1	3.7
Greece	7.6	5.3	19.9	17.9	21.6	15.5	44.3	39.3	6.2	4.7	18.4	16.7	3.7	2.9	19.3	17.2
Hungary	7.1	7.2	5.2	3.8	13.8	17.4	12.9	9.7	6.2	6.5	4.5	3.4	3.7	4.8	4.3	3.0
Iceland[2]	1.8	2.3	3.1	3.0	5.7	8.0	6.6	8.6	1.1	1.2	2.2	1.8	0.5	0.9	2.8	2.0
Ireland	4.7	5.1	10.0	7.7	7.8	11.1	20.7	18.5	4.0	3.9	8.6	6.4	2.5	2.3	7.7	5.5
Israel[3]	11.1	9.0	4.8	4.2	17.3	15.3	8.2	6.7	9.1	7.4	4.0	3.7	10.4	7.4	4.5	3.8
Italy[2]	8.2	5.0	11.1	10.6	25.4	18.4	36.5	33.0	6.3	4.0	10.1	9.7	4.4	2.6	6.4	6.3
Japan	5.1	4.1	3.4	3.0	10.4	8.3	5.7	4.7	3.9	3.6	3.2	2.9	6.8	4.1	3.4	2.8
Korea	5.1	3.8	3.9	3.9	13.5	11.1	11.0	11.2	4.5	3.6	3.5	3.6	3.9	2.7	3.2	2.8
Latvia	15.5	6.7	11.2	9.9	20.9	11.0	21.4	18.3	15.3	6.1	9.8	9.0	10.7	4.9	11.8	9.7
Luxembourg	1.8	3.6	6.0	5.6	5.7	13.5	13.6	17.2	1.4	2.8	5.0	4.8	2.0	2.3	0.0	2.7
Mexico	2.3	3.5	4.0	3.5	4.4	6.6	7.2	6.3	1.5	2.7	3.3	2.8	1.5	2.4	2.5	2.3
Netherlands	2.5	3.2	5.6	4.5	5.3	6.3	11.4	9.0	1.9	2.3	4.0	3.2	2.5	4.2	7.0	5.3
New Zealand	6.4	3.5	5.0	4.5	14.5	10.0	13.1	12.4	4.6	2.2	3.4	2.9	5.5	1.5	3.2	2.9
Norway[2]	3.6	2.6	5.6	4.8	9.5	7.9	12.6	11.6	2.9	1.9	5.0	4.0	1.8	1.1	2.7	2.6
Poland	14.6	9.1	6.2	5.0	33.3	20.0	17.4	14.6	12.1	7.8	5.1	4.1	9.1	7.4	5.1	4.1
Portugal	3.3	7.0	11.5	8.8	6.3	13.8	27.2	22.4	2.7	6.1	9.7	7.3	3.6	7.1	12.6	9.0
Slovak Republic	19.0	9.8	8.8	8.0	39.7	20.3	19.8	18.1	15.2	8.6	7.7	7.3	13.5	7.7	8.4	5.6
Slovenia	6.6	4.1	7.6	5.9	14.6	9.4	15.6	9.9	5.4	3.4	6.9	5.2	6.6	3.0	7.5	7.3
Spain[2]	9.6	6.5	18.2	15.8	19.4	15.2	44.0	39.5	8.0	5.5	16.3	13.9	8.6	5.0	16.9	14.8
Sweden[2]	6.3	6.0	7.5	7.1	12.1	18.6	20.5	18.7	5.3	4.1	5.6	5.5	6.8	4.3	6.1	5.7
Switzerland	2.3	3.0	5.0	4.8	5.6	6.8	8.8	8.1	1.6	2.3	4.5	4.3	3.0	2.6	4.3	4.2
Turkey	6.8	10.2	9.8	9.6	13.7	19.6	17.4	17.8	5.0	8.5	8.5	8.1	2.9	5.4	7.3	7.7
United Kingdom[2]	6.0	5.6	5.1	4.6	13.2	15.8	15.0	13.3	4.7	3.7	3.4	3.1	5.2	4.1	4.3	4.1
United States[2]	3.9	4.8	5.0	4.5	9.7	11.6	11.5	10.3	2.9	3.7	4.0	3.6	2.4	3.2	3.8	3.1
OECD[4]	5.9	5.6	6.4	5.8	12.0	12.3	13.3	12.2	4.8	4.6	5.5	5.0	5.3	4.2	5.0	4.5
Colombia	..	8.9	7.3	7.4	..	17.8	14.3	14.3	..	6.6	5.4	5.8	..	6.3	6.2	5.5
Costa Rica	4.4	3.3	8.1	7.7	9.3	8.3	18.9	19.0	2.8	1.7	5.8	5.5	2.6	2.0	5.4	4.7
Lithuania	19.1	4.3	9.3	8.8	32.1	7.0	15.9	14.6	17.7	3.9	8.4	8.1	13.7	4.1	9.2	8.4
Brazil	..	6.1	10.3	11.5	..	12.9	23.8	25.6	..	4.2	7.6	8.6	..	3.0	5.4	6.5
China[5]	3.6	..	..	..	9.2	..	..	..	2.7	..	..	..	0.6	..	..	..
India[5]	4.5	..	..	..	10.1	..	..	..	2.9	..	..	..	1.6	..	..	..
Indonesia	5.9	8.6	5.9	5.7	19.7	23.3	18.6	17.7	2.7	5.0	3.5	3.3	0.4	2.3	1.9	2.2
Russian Federation	10.9	6.4	5.8	5.4	19.5	14.5	15.7	15.6	9.6	5.4	4.9	4.5	7.5	3.5	4.4	4.4
South Africa	..	18.8	24.7	25.7	..	41.1	48.6	49.2	..	15.1	22.1	23.5	..	6.4	11.3	10.4

.. Not available

Note: Please refer to the Box entitled "Major breaks in series" in the introduction to the Statistical Annex.

1. New labour force survey since April 2010. To remove the break, data prior to 2010 are spliced using *new-to-old* chaining coefficients based on data of fourth quarter of 2009.
2. The lower age limit is 16 instead of 15. For Iceland up to 2008, Italy after 2007, Norway up to 2005 and Sweden up to 2006.
3. Redesigned monthly labour force survey since January 2012. To remove the break, data prior to 2012 are spliced using *new-to-old* chaining coefficients between monthly and quarterly surveys based on data of fourth quarter of 2011.
4. Weighted average.
5. Data up to 2010 for China and up to 2012 for India can be found in the database.

Source: OECD Employment Database, www.oecd.org/employment/emp/onlineoecdemploymentdatabase.htm and www.oecd.org/els/emp/lfsnotes_sources.pdf.

http://dx.doi.org/10.1787/888933779048

Table D3. Unemployment rates by selected age groups - Women
As a percentage of the female labour force in each age group

Percentage

	Women (15-64)				Youth (15-24)				Prime age (25-54)				Older population (55-64)			
	2000	2007	2016	2017	2000	2007	2016	2017	2000	2007	2016	2017	2000	2007	2016	2017
Australia	6.1	4.8	5.9	5.8	11.2	9.2	11.4	11.5	4.9	3.9	5.0	4.8	3.2	2.6	3.6	3.7
Austria	3.8	5.4	5.6	5.1	5.2	9.6	10.2	8.7	3.5	4.7	5.1	4.7	4.7	3.5	3.8	3.7
Belgium	8.7	8.5	7.6	7.1	20.3	20.9	18.2	18.0	7.6	7.4	6.9	6.2	2.9	5.3	6.0	6.5
Canada	6.7	5.7	6.3	5.9	11.4	10.1	11.3	9.9	5.8	4.8	5.4	5.2	5.5	4.9	5.6	5.2
Chile[1]	12.7	11.1	7.3	7.5	31.3	26.9	17.6	18.5	9.4	8.7	6.4	6.7	4.3	4.6	4.2	3.9
Czech Republic	10.6	6.8	4.8	3.6	17.4	11.0	11.4	8.7	9.9	6.7	4.5	3.4	5.4	4.8	3.8	2.9
Denmark	5.3	4.2	6.8	6.0	6.7	7.4	10.9	10.7	5.0	3.6	6.4	5.5	5.1	4.0	4.1	3.6
Estonia	13.5	3.9	6.3	5.5	23.0	7.2	10.6	10.0	12.9	4.2	5.6	5.3	7.5	0.9	6.9	4.3
Finland	10.6	7.3	8.7	8.5	21.8	16.8	18.6	19.3	8.8	5.8	7.4	6.9	9.4	6.0	6.9	7.0
France	11.9	8.1	9.6	9.1	23.7	19.5	23.5	20.6	11.1	7.2	8.6	8.5	8.3	4.1	6.2	5.6
Germany	8.1	8.9	3.8	3.4	7.5	11.1	6.1	5.8	7.5	8.1	3.5	3.1	13.6	11.2	3.6	3.1
Greece	17.5	13.0	28.3	26.3	38.2	31.7	50.7	48.2	15.1	12.0	28.1	25.6	4.3	4.3	19.0	19.7
Hungary	5.7	7.8	5.1	4.6	11.2	18.9	12.9	12.1	5.0	7.3	4.5	4.0	1.6	3.9	4.5	4.3
Iceland[2]	2.8	2.4	3.2	2.8	3.6	6.3	6.4	7.1	2.4	1.6	2.8	2.0	3.2	0.9	1.5	1.6
Ireland	5.4	5.4	8.4	6.2	8.2	9.5	15.9	13.6	4.5	4.5	7.5	5.0	3.5	2.6	5.4	5.5
Israel[3]	11.2	9.9	5.0	4.4	17.4	17.3	9.1	7.8	9.7	8.4	4.4	3.8	6.0	6.0	3.0	3.0
Italy[2]	14.6	7.9	12.9	12.5	35.4	23.3	39.6	37.3	12.1	7.1	12.5	12.3	4.7	2.1	4.8	5.0
Japan	4.7	3.9	3.1	2.8	7.9	7.1	4.5	4.5	4.4	3.9	3.1	2.8	3.6	2.4	2.3	2.2
Korea	3.8	2.8	3.7	3.6	9.1	7.2	10.5	9.7	3.0	2.4	3.2	3.3	1.6	1.3	2.1	1.9
Latvia	13.4	5.7	8.6	7.9	23.7	10.0	9.9	15.4	12.8	5.3	8.7	7.5	8.0	4.1	7.1	7.1
Luxembourg	3.2	4.7	6.6	5.5	7.3	17.5	6.1	13.2	2.9	4.0	5.8	5.0	0.0	1.7	0.0	2.7
Mexico	3.4	4.1	4.1	3.7	6.2	8.2	8.8	8.0	2.4	3.2	3.4	3.1	0.9	1.0	1.2	1.2
Netherlands	3.9	4.1	6.5	5.3	7.0	7.8	10.3	8.8	3.3	3.3	5.4	4.2	1.5	3.8	7.4	5.8
New Zealand	6.0	4.0	5.7	5.4	12.4	10.2	13.4	13.0	4.8	3.0	4.5	4.2	3.6	1.3	3.1	2.8
Norway[2]	3.2	2.5	4.1	3.8	10.9	6.6	9.3	9.0	2.3	2.0	3.7	3.5	0.7	0.8	1.3	1.0
Poland	18.4	10.4	6.3	5.0	37.3	23.8	18.0	15.1	16.0	9.1	5.7	4.4	9.7	5.7	3.5	3.1
Portugal	5.2	10.1	11.5	9.6	11.6	20.3	28.8	25.5	4.4	9.5	10.4	8.5	2.6	5.8	9.1	8.1
Slovak Republic	18.6	12.6	10.8	8.5	33.8	19.9	26.3	20.2	15.8	11.9	9.7	8.0	8.7	9.1	9.7	6.4
Slovenia	7.2	6.0	8.7	7.6	18.5	11.2	14.7	13.0	5.8	5.6	8.7	7.5	2.5	3.8	5.1	5.3
Spain[2]	20.6	10.7	21.5	19.1	32.9	21.7	44.9	37.4	18.9	9.5	20.3	18.2	11.3	7.7	17.2	15.9
Sweden[2]	5.4	6.5	6.7	6.5	11.3	19.8	17.2	16.8	4.5	4.7	5.3	5.2	5.4	3.5	4.4	4.3
Switzerland	3.2	4.6	5.1	5.2	3.9	7.4	8.4	8.0	3.1	4.1	4.9	5.1	2.3	3.8	3.1	3.3
Turkey	6.5	11.3	14.0	14.4	11.9	20.8	23.7	26.1	4.6	8.8	12.6	12.5	0.5	1.1	2.9	3.1
United Kingdom[2]	4.7	5.0	4.8	4.3	10.2	12.5	11.3	10.3	3.8	3.8	3.9	3.4	2.8	2.2	2.8	2.8
United States[2]	4.1	4.6	4.8	4.3	8.9	9.4	9.3	8.1	3.3	3.8	4.3	3.9	2.5	3.0	3.3	3.1
OECD[4]	7.0	6.1	6.6	6.1	12.4	11.9	12.5	11.5	6.2	5.3	6.1	5.7	4.5	3.7	4.1	3.9
Colombia	..	15.1	12.4	12.7	..	28.6	23.9	24.3	..	12.3	10.5	10.8	..	5.0	4.7	5.4
Costa Rica	6.7	6.9	12.2	11.8	14.2	15.1	31.1	28.7	4.2	4.6	9.5	9.6	3.3	2.1	3.4	2.0
Lithuania	14.3	4.4	6.8	5.9	27.5	10.4	12.6	11.7	13.5	4.0	6.4	5.1	8.1	3.4	6.5	6.4
Brazil	..	11.0	13.5	14.8	..	21.9	31.5	33.5	..	8.5	10.3	11.5	..	2.7	4.3	5.0
China[5]	3.8	..	..	..	8.4	..	..	..	2.9	..	..	..	0.2	..	..	..
India[5]	4.2	..	..	..	10.2	..	..	..	2.6	..	..	..	1.6	..	..	..
Indonesia	7.0	11.7	5.5	5.5	20.1	28.4	18.8	17.8	3.2	7.5	2.8	3.2	0.4	2.1	1.3	1.8
Russian Federation	10.4	5.7	5.3	5.1	22.2	14.4	17.1	16.8	8.8	4.8	4.7	4.4	7.1	2.6	2.9	3.2
South Africa	..	26.4	29.1	29.6	..	52.8	59.3	58.5	..	22.6	26.5	27.1	..	4.5	6.3	8.3

.. Not available

Note: Please refer to the Box entitled "Major breaks in series" in the introduction to the Statistical Annex.

1. New labour force survey since April 2010. To remove the break, data prior to 2010 are spliced using *new-to-old* chaining coefficients based on data of fourth quarter of 2009.
2. The lower age limit is 16 instead of 15. For Iceland up to 2008, Italy after 2007, Norway up to 2005 and Sweden up to 2006.
3. Redesigned monthly labour force survey since January 2012. To remove the break, data prior to 2012 are spliced using *new-to-old* chaining coefficients between monthly and quarterly surveys based on data of fourth quarter of 2011.
4. Weighted average.
5. Data up to 2010 for China and up to 2012 for India can be found in the database.

Source: *OECD Employment Database*, www.oecd.org/employment/emp/onlineoecdemploymentdatabase.htm and www.oecd.org/els/emp/lfsnotes_sources.pdf.

http://dx.doi.org/10.1787/888933779067

Table E. Employment/population ratios by educational attainment, 2016
Persons aged 25-64, as a percentage of the population in each gender

Percentage

	Total			Men			Women		
	Below upper secondary education	Upper secondary and post-secondary non-tertiary education	Tertiary education	Below upper secondary education	Upper secondary and post-secondary non-tertiary education	Tertiary education	Below upper secondary education	Upper secondary and post-secondary non-tertiary education	Tertiary education
Australia	58.1	78.2	83.5	66.7	84.8	89.3	50.2	69.9	78.8
Austria	53.9	75.9	86.2	60.5	79.4	88.5	49.9	72.0	83.8
Belgium	46.4	73.0	85.2	54.6	79.5	87.5	37.5	65.5	83.2
Canada	54.6	73.6	81.8	63.1	78.6	85.6	43.3	67.1	78.9
Chile[1]	62.2	71.8	84.4	83.6	85.9	91.0	43.9	59.6	78.8
Czech Republic	45.1	80.7	85.6	56.6	87.6	93.4	37.9	73.1	78.3
Denmark	63.5	81.1	85.9	71.7	84.8	88.7	53.8	76.8	83.8
Estonia	61.4	76.9	84.9	66.7	81.8	91.3	51.4	70.8	81.1
Finland	53.7	73.2	83.1	60.2	75.8	85.4	43.5	69.9	81.5
France	51.3	72.9	85.0	58.6	76.3	88.1	44.7	69.2	82.3
Germany	59.4	81.0	88.3	68.4	84.4	91.3	52.0	77.7	84.6
Greece	48.5	58.1	70.4	60.9	70.7	76.4	35.0	45.8	65.2
Hungary	51.7	76.1	85.0	62.2	82.9	91.2	43.6	68.2	80.5
Iceland	78.8	88.4	93.6	84.3	92.3	96.8	73.0	82.5	91.4
Ireland[1]	48.8	68.9	82.1	61.1	77.8	86.8	33.2	59.9	78.4
Israel	48.1	72.7	87.0	63.1	77.7	90.4	31.7	66.8	84.3
Italy	51.2	70.6	79.7	66.0	80.7	85.5	35.1	60.6	75.4
Japan[2]	..	..	..	..	..	..	..	..	..
Korea	65.5	72.5	77.3	76.4	84.3	89.0	58.3	60.7	63.4
Latvia	58.8	71.2	87.2	64.5	75.0	88.7	49.4	66.8	86.4
Luxembourg	59.6	70.5	85.7	69.7	76.2	89.2	49.7	64.1	82.0
Mexico	64.8	70.5	79.8	88.6	88.9	88.0	44.4	54.6	71.6
Netherlands	60.7	79.4	88.4	72.9	84.8	91.3	49.3	73.8	85.5
New Zealand	71.7	82.1	87.3	78.9	89.5	92.2	65.0	74.1	83.3
Norway	61.7	80.2	88.8	67.1	83.1	89.5	55.7	76.5	88.1
Poland	40.7	68.4	87.5	51.8	77.5	92.0	29.3	57.9	84.4
Portugal	65.5	79.4	85.1	71.8	82.1	86.8	58.8	76.8	83.9
Slovak Republic	37.7	74.3	81.3	43.8	80.8	87.4	33.1	66.9	76.7
Slovenia	46.1	71.0	85.2	53.7	74.9	86.5	39.6	65.7	84.3
Spain	53.9	69.2	79.8	63.1	75.9	83.5	43.5	62.5	76.7
Sweden	65.9	85.3	89.6	72.4	87.5	90.4	58.6	82.3	88.9
Switzerland	67.6	81.9	88.5	75.2	86.8	91.9	61.6	77.5	84.2
Turkey	51.4	61.9	75.0	75.1	80.9	84.0	28.2	32.9	63.3
United Kingdom[3]	61.6	80.3	84.8	72.3	86.0	88.9	51.7	74.3	80.9
United States	56.6	68.8	81.6	68.4	75.0	86.9	43.2	62.3	77.1
OECD[4]	56.7	74.7	84.2	66.9	81.5	88.8	46.5	67.2	80.1
Colombia	72.0	76.5	82.5	89.5	89.0	89.1	54.3	64.6	77.4
Costa Rica	61.7	71.1	80.6	82.3	88.2	88.6	40.4	54.1	74.0
Lithuania	49.3	72.6	91.0	53.2	76.0	92.6	41.7	68.9	90.0
Brazil[1]	65.0	73.9	83.4	80.6	85.8	89.9	49.1	63.7	78.9
Russian Federation[1]	51.0	72.4	82.2	58.8	80.0	88.6	41.6	63.2	77.8
South Africa[1]	46.5	62.3	82.7	55.4	70.8	86.2	38.1	53.8	79.7

.. Not available

Note: Data refer to ISCED 2011, except for Brazil and the Russian Federation (ISCED-97). See the description of the levels of education in www.oecd.org/els/emp/definitions-education.pdf.

1. Year of reference 2015.
2. Education levels are grouped somewhat differently. Data can be found in the database.
3. Includes completion of intermediate upper secondary programmes. See notes to Table A5.1 of *Education at a Glance 2017*, http://dx.doi.org/10.1787/eag-2017-en.
4. Unweighted average.

Source: OECD (2017), *Education at a Glance*, Indicator A5, www.oecd.org/edu/education-at-a-glance-19991487.htm.

http://dx.doi.org/10.1787/888933779086

Table F. Labour force participation rates by educational attainment, 2016
Persons aged 25-64, as a percentage of the population in each gender

Percentage

	Total			Men			Women		
	Below upper secondary education	Upper secondary and post-secondary non-tertiary education	Tertiary education	Below upper secondary education	Upper secondary and post-secondary non-tertiary education	Tertiary education	Below upper secondary education	Upper secondary and post-secondary non-tertiary education	Tertiary education
Australia	63.1	81.5	86.3	72.0	87.9	92.3	54.9	73.5	81.4
Austria	61.1	80.1	89.3	70.8	84.0	91.8	55.2	75.7	86.6
Belgium	54.2	78.5	88.5	63.6	85.2	90.7	44.1	70.6	86.6
Canada	61.2	79.1	86.1	70.8	85.0	90.2	48.4	71.5	82.8
Chile[1]	66.0	76.7	88.9	87.8	91.3	95.9	47.5	64.1	82.9
Czech Republic	55.8	83.4	87.2	68.9	90.0	94.8	47.6	76.1	80.0
Denmark	68.0	84.9	90.3	75.8	88.0	92.9	58.7	81.1	88.3
Estonia	69.3	83.2	88.1	74.6	88.3	95.1	59.4	76.8	84.0
Finland	60.8	79.8	88.1	67.0	82.5	90.9	51.1	76.5	86.0
France	61.0	80.1	89.5	69.9	83.6	92.7	52.9	76.3	86.9
Germany	66.0	84.0	90.3	77.1	87.9	93.3	56.9	80.3	86.5
Greece	65.7	76.6	85.1	80.0	87.1	87.8	50.1	66.3	82.6
Hungary	58.6	79.4	86.4	70.5	86.4	92.7	49.5	71.4	81.8
Iceland	81.0	91.2	95.2	86.4	95.1	98.2	75.4	85.1	93.1
Ireland[1]	58.0	76.5	86.6	74.0	87.4	91.9	37.8	65.5	82.4
Israel	51.8	76.5	89.9	67.7	81.4	93.4	34.4	70.7	87.1
Italy	59.7	77.5	85.4	76.2	87.3	90.3	41.9	67.7	81.7
Japan[2]	..	..	..	..	..	..	..	..	..
Korea	67.4	75.0	80.0	79.5	87.5	92.1	59.5	62.6	65.6
Latvia	71.8	80.2	90.8	78.2	84.4	92.7	61.3	75.5	89.8
Luxembourg	64.1	74.7	89.1	74.7	80.1	92.9	53.5	68.8	85.0
Mexico	66.6	73.2	83.4	91.0	92.3	92.3	45.6	56.8	74.6
Netherlands	65.7	84.2	91.5	78.0	89.3	94.2	54.2	79.0	88.8
New Zealand	75.7	85.3	89.6	83.2	92.2	94.5	68.9	78.0	85.7
Norway	66.7	83.1	91.5	73.0	86.5	92.9	59.7	78.7	90.2
Poland	46.7	72.7	90.2	59.5	81.9	94.5	33.5	62.0	87.2
Portugal	74.0	88.7	91.9	81.5	90.5	93.5	66.2	87.1	90.9
Slovak Republic	53.1	81.0	85.6	61.4	87.1	91.5	46.9	74.1	81.2
Slovenia	53.6	76.9	90.7	61.8	80.3	91.6	46.6	72.1	90.0
Spain	72.9	83.5	89.6	82.5	88.5	92.1	62.0	78.4	87.5
Sweden	76.0	89.1	93.1	82.8	91.4	94.7	68.2	86.0	91.9
Switzerland	75.0	85.6	91.5	83.4	91.0	94.9	68.4	80.8	87.3
Turkey	56.7	68.8	82.8	82.5	87.8	90.5	31.5	39.9	72.8
United Kingdom[3]	65.8	83.2	87.1	76.9	89.2	91.1	55.4	77.0	83.3
United States	61.6	73.0	83.9	74.0	79.7	89.3	47.6	65.9	79.2
OECD[4]	64.0	80.2	88.3	75.2	87.0	92.7	52.8	72.7	84.2
Colombia	76.4	83.5	90.8	93.5	94.9	96.3	59.2	72.6	86.6
Costa Rica	67.1	76.1	84.7	88.5	92.1	91.6	45.0	60.1	78.8
Lithuania	65.5	80.3	93.6	71.2	84.1	95.4	54.5	76.2	92.4
Brazil[1]	69.6	80.5	87.4	85.1	91.7	93.6	53.6	70.9	83.1
Russian Federation[1]	58.0	77.1	85.0	67.1	85.0	91.6	46.9	67.5	80.4
South Africa[1]	63.1	79.2	89.5	73.2	86.9	92.8	53.6	71.4	86.7

.. Not available

Note: Data refer to ISCED 2011, except for Brazil and the Russian Federation (ISCED-97). See the description of the levels of education in www.oecd.org/els/emp/definitions-education.pdf.
1. Year of reference 2015.
2. Education levels are grouped somewhat differently. Data can be found in the database.
3. Includes completion of intermediate upper secondary programmes. See notes to Table A5.1 of *Education at a Glance 2017*, http://dx.doi.org/10.1787/eag-2017-en.
4. Unweighted average.
Source: OECD (2017), *Education at a Glance*, Indicator A5, www.oecd.org/edu/education-at-a-glance-19991487.htm.

http://dx.doi.org/10.1787/888933779105

Table G. Unemployment rates by educational attainment, 2016
Persons aged 25-64, as a percentage of the population in each gender

Percentage

	Total			Men			Women		
	Below upper secondary education	Upper secondary and post-secondary non-tertiary education	Tertiary education	Below upper secondary education	Upper secondary and post-secondary non-tertiary education	Tertiary education	Below upper secondary education	Upper secondary and post-secondary non-tertiary education	Tertiary education
Australia	7.5	4.5	3.2	7.6	3.8	3.0	7.3	5.5	3.4
Austria	11.7	5.2	3.4	14.5	5.5	3.6	9.5	4.9	3.2
Belgium	14.5	7.0	3.7	14.2	6.8	3.5	14.9	7.3	3.9
Canada	10.9	7.0	4.9	11.2	7.6	5.0	10.2	6.1	4.8
Chile[1]	5.8	6.4	5.0	4.8	5.9	5.1	7.5	7.0	5.0
Czech Republic	19.2	3.2	1.8	17.8	2.7	1.4	20.5	3.9	2.2
Denmark	6.6	4.4	4.9	5.4	3.7	4.5	8.4	5.3	5.1
Estonia	11.5	7.6	3.7	10.6	7.4	4.0	13.5	7.8	3.5
Finland	11.7	8.1	5.9	9.4	8.3	6.2	16.4	7.9	5.6
France	15.9	9.0	5.1	16.1	8.8	4.9	15.5	9.2	5.2
Germany	10.0	3.7	2.2	11.3	4.1	2.2	8.6	3.2	2.2
Greece	26.2	24.2	17.2	23.9	18.9	13.0	30.2	31.0	21.2
Hungary	11.8	4.2	1.7	11.7	4.1	1.7	11.8	4.4	1.7
Iceland	2.8	3.0	1.7	2.4	3.0	1.4	3.2	3.1	1.9
Ireland[1]	15.9	9.9	5.1	17.4	10.9	5.5	12.1	8.6	4.8
Israel	7.1	4.9	3.2	6.9	4.5	3.2	7.7	5.6	3.2
Italy	14.3	8.8	6.6	13.4	7.6	5.1	16.0	10.4	7.7
Japan[2]	..	..	..	..	..	..	..	..	..
Korea	2.8	3.4	3.3	3.8	3.6	3.3	1.9	3.0	3.3
Latvia	18.1	11.3	4.0	17.5	11.1	4.3	19.4	11.5	3.8
Luxembourg	6.9	5.7	3.8	6.7	4.8	4.0	7.2	6.7	3.4
Mexico	2.6	3.8	4.4	2.7	3.7	4.6	2.5	3.9	4.1
Netherlands	7.6	5.7	3.4	6.6	5.0	3.1	9.1	6.5	3.7
New Zealand	5.4	3.9	2.6	5.2	3.0	2.5	5.6	5.0	2.7
Norway	7.5	3.4	3.0	8.2	3.9	3.7	6.7	2.8	2.4
Poland	12.8	5.8	3.0	12.8	5.3	2.7	12.8	6.5	3.2
Portugal	11.6	10.5	7.4	11.9	9.2	7.1	11.2	11.8	7.6
Slovak Republic	29.0	8.3	5.1	28.7	7.3	4.4	29.4	9.7	5.6
Slovenia	14.0	7.6	6.0	13.1	6.8	5.6	15.0	8.8	6.4
Spain	26.1	17.0	10.9	23.5	14.2	9.4	30.0	20.3	12.3
Sweden	13.2	4.3	3.8	12.6	4.2	4.4	14.2	4.4	3.3
Switzerland	9.9	4.4	3.3	9.9	4.6	3.2	9.9	4.2	3.6
Turkey	9.3	10.1	9.4	8.9	7.8	7.2	10.4	17.6	13.1
United Kingdom[3]	6.3	3.5	2.6	6.0	3.6	2.4	6.6	3.5	2.9
United States	8.1	5.7	2.7	7.5	5.8	2.7	9.2	5.5	2.7
OECD[4]	11.6	6.9	4.6	11.3	6.4	4.3	12.2	7.7	4.9
Colombia	5.8	8.4	9.1	4.3	6.2	7.5	8.2	11.0	10.6
Costa Rica	8.0	6.5	4.8	7.0	4.3	3.4	10.2	9.9	6.2
Lithuania	24.8	9.6	2.7	25.3	9.6	2.9	23.5	9.6	2.6
Brazil[1]	6.5	8.2	4.6	5.4	6.4	3.9	8.5	10.2	5.1
Russian Federation[1]	12.0	6.1	3.2	12.4	5.9	3.3	11.3	6.4	3.2
South Africa[1]	26.3	21.3	7.6	24.3	18.6	7.0	28.9	24.6	7.8

.. Not available

Note: Data refer to ISCED 2011, except for Brazil and the Russian Federation (ISCED-97). See the description of the levels of education in www.oecd.org/els/emp/definitions-education.pdf.

1. Year of reference 2015.
2. Education levels are grouped somewhat differently. Data can be found in the database.
3. Includes completion of intermediate upper secondary programmes. See notes to Table A5.1 of *Education at a Glance 2017*, http://dx.doi.org/10.1787/eag-2017-en.
4. Unweighted average.

Source: OECD (2017), *Education at a Glance*, Indicator A5, www.oecd.org/edu/education-at-a-glance-19991487.htm.

http://dx.doi.org/10.1787/888933779124

Table H. Incidence and composition of part-time employment
Persons aged 15 and over, percentages

Percentage

	Part-time employment as a proportion of total employment												Women's share in part-time employment			
	Total				Men				Women				2000	2007	2016	2017
	2000	2007	2016	2017	2000	2007	2016	2017	2000	2007	2016	2017				
Australia[1]	..	23.7	25.9	25.7	..	12.3	15.1	15.0	..	37.7	38.3	38.0	..	71.5	68.9	69.0
Austria	11.7	17.3	20.9	20.9	2.4	5.6	8.6	8.6	23.9	31.4	34.7	34.8	88.6	82.4	78.3	78.2
Belgium	19.3	18.1	17.8	16.4	6.9	6.4	6.9	6.5	35.5	32.2	30.0	27.8	79.5	80.7	79.4	78.9
Canada	18.1	18.3	19.2	19.1	10.3	11.1	12.6	12.7	27.2	26.3	26.4	26.2	69.2	68.0	65.6	65.2
Chile	4.7	8.0	17.4	17.6	3.1	5.2	12.2	12.5	8.7	13.9	25.0	24.9	53.9	56.9	58.6	58.1
Czech Republic	3.2	3.5	4.9	5.4	1.6	1.7	2.6	2.7	5.4	5.9	8.0	8.7	72.5	72.3	70.9	71.5
Denmark	15.3	17.3	21.7	20.4	9.1	11.9	17.3	16.0	22.4	23.4	26.7	25.3	68.1	63.3	57.7	58.5
Estonia	7.2	6.8	8.7	8.1	4.6	3.6	5.6	5.0	10.0	10.1	11.9	11.4	67.9	73.2	67.2	68.3
Finland	10.4	11.7	14.0	14.0	7.1	8.2	10.6	10.9	13.9	15.5	17.7	17.4	63.8	63.7	60.8	59.8
France	14.2	13.3	14.2	14.3	5.3	4.9	7.0	7.0	24.3	22.8	22.0	22.2	80.1	80.5	74.7	74.5
Germany	17.6	22.0	22.1	22.2	4.8	7.8	9.1	9.4	33.9	39.1	36.9	36.8	84.5	80.7	78.1	77.4
Greece	5.3	7.7	11.0	11.0	3.0	4.1	7.2	7.1	9.4	13.3	16.1	16.3	65.0	67.7	61.9	62.5
Hungary	3.2	3.1	4.0	3.6	1.7	1.8	2.6	2.3	4.7	4.5	5.5	5.1	71.2	68.6	64.8	65.4
Iceland[1,2]	20.2	15.8	17.1	17.1	9.1	7.9	10.8	10.8	32.8	25.3	24.2	24.4	76.0	72.8	66.4	66.0
Ireland	18.1	19.9	22.8	22.0	7.3	7.4	11.9	11.5	32.0	35.0	34.8	33.8	77.1	79.8	72.4	72.2
Israel	15.6	16.1	15.5	15.3	7.4	8.1	9.1	9.0	25.4	25.3	22.8	22.4	74.5	73.3	68.5	68.7
Italy[2]	11.7	15.3	18.6	18.5	5.4	5.5	8.5	8.3	22.5	29.8	32.6	32.4	70.9	78.2	73.6	74.1
Japan[3]	15.9	18.9	22.8	22.4	7.1	9.2	11.9	11.5	29.0	32.6	37.1	36.7	73.7	71.5	70.3	70.9
Korea[3]	7.0	8.8	10.8	11.4	5.1	6.2	6.8	7.3	9.8	12.4	16.4	16.9	57.6	58.9	63.7	62.7
Latvia	8.8	5.4	7.3	6.5	6.3	3.4	4.8	4.0	11.4	7.4	9.7	8.8	64.6	67.5	67.7	69.4
Luxembourg	13.0	13.1	13.6	14.2	2.1	1.4	4.9	4.1	28.9	27.6	24.1	25.9	90.4	93.9	80.4	84.5
Mexico	13.5	17.8	17.7	17.2	7.1	11.4	12.0	11.5	25.6	28.5	26.9	26.4	65.1	60.0	58.1	58.5
Netherlands	32.1	35.9	37.7	37.4	13.1	16.1	18.7	18.9	57.3	59.9	59.8	58.7	76.7	75.5	73.3	72.9
New Zealand	22.2	21.9	21.2	21.1	10.9	11.0	11.6	11.6	35.7	34.5	32.1	31.7	73.2	73.2	71.3	70.8
Norway[2]	20.2	20.4	19.2	18.8	8.7	10.5	12.0	11.8	33.4	31.6	27.2	26.7	77.0	72.9	67.1	67.0
Poland	12.8	10.1	6.0	6.1	8.8	6.0	3.4	3.4	17.9	15.0	9.0	9.5	61.7	67.0	68.2	69.6
Portugal	9.3	10.0	9.1	8.5	4.9	6.3	6.8	6.1	14.7	14.4	11.5	11.0	70.9	66.7	62.5	63.9
Slovak Republic	1.9	2.4	5.8	5.8	1.0	1.1	4.2	4.1	2.9	4.0	7.6	7.9	70.6	74.0	59.0	61.3
Slovenia	4.9	7.8	8.0	8.8	3.9	6.3	5.2	6.1	6.1	9.7	11.1	11.8	56.8	56.2	64.8	62.4
Spain[2]	7.5	10.5	14.1	13.8	2.6	3.6	7.1	6.7	16.1	20.1	22.3	22.1	78.3	80.0	72.8	73.9
Sweden[2]	14.0	14.4	13.8	13.8	7.3	9.5	10.1	10.4	21.4	19.7	17.8	17.5	72.9	65.0	61.8	60.4
Switzerland	23.0	26.8	25.9	26.7	8.4	10.1	10.4	11.2	42.7	47.1	43.7	44.6	79.2	79.4	78.6	77.5
Turkey	9.4	8.1	9.5	9.6	5.7	4.4	5.8	5.9	19.3	18.6	17.8	17.9	55.4	59.6	57.4	57.6
United Kingdom[2]	23.3	22.9	23.8	23.5	8.5	9.7	11.6	11.5	40.7	38.2	37.5	37.0	80.2	77.2	74.1	74.3
United States[2,4]	12.6	12.6	12.9	12.5	7.7	7.6	8.5	8.2	18.0	17.9	17.6	17.1	68.1	68.4	65.8	66.0
OECD[5]	13.9	15.4	16.7	16.5	6.7	7.8	9.4	9.2	23.7	25.3	25.8	25.5	72.4	71.5	68.8	68.9
Colombia	..	14.5	15.9	15.9	..	9.2	8.5	8.5	..	22.8	26.1	26.1	..	61.3	69.0	68.7
Costa Rica	..	..	15.6	16.5	..	..	9.7	10.1	..	..	25.8	27.5	..	..	60.6	61.1
Lithuania	10.6	6.1	6.9	7.0	7.7	3.6	4.4	4.6	13.5	8.6	9.3	9.3	64.5	69.9	70.2	69.2
Brazil	..	18.3	..	..	..	10.3	..	..	..	29.1	..	..	..	67.6	..	..
Russian Federation	7.4	5.1	4.3	3.5	4.9	3.5	3.1	2.4	10.0	6.6	5.6	4.6	66.0	64.8	62.9	64.2
South Africa	..	..	9.0	9.0	..	..	5.6	5.9	..	..	13.3	12.8	..	..	64.6	62.9

.. Not available

Note: Part-time employment refers to persons who usually work less than 30 hours per week in their main job.
   Please refer to the Box entitled "Major breaks in series" in the introduction to the Statistical Annex.
1. Part-time employment based on hours worked at all jobs.
2. The lower age limit is 16 instead of 15. For Iceland up to 2008, Italy after 2007, Norway up to 2005 and Sweden up to 2006.
3. Data are based on actual hours worked.
4. Data are for wage and salary workers only.
5. Weighted average.
Source: OECD Employment Database, www.oecd.org/employment/emp/onlineoecdemploymentdatabase.htm and www.oecd.org/els/emp/lfsnotes_sources.pdf.

http://dx.doi.org/10.1787/888933779143

Table I. Incidence and composition of involuntary part-time employment
Persons aged 15 and over, percentages

Percentage

	Involuntary part-time employment as a propotion of total employment												Involuntary part-time employment as a proportion of part-time employment			
	Total				Men				Women				2000	2007	2016	2017
	2000	2007	2016	2017	2000	2007	2016	2017	2000	2007	2016	2017				
Australia	6.3	6.6	8.9	9.1	4.3	4.5	6.6	6.7	8.8	9.3	11.5	11.9	23.8	23.5	28.0	28.7
Austria	1.8	2.7	3.6	3.4	0.9	1.0	2.0	2.0	3.0	4.6	5.3	5.0	11.1	11.8	12.4	11.8
Belgium	4.6	3.2	2.2	1.9	1.7	1.5	1.3	1.2	8.4	5.5	3.2	2.7	22.1	14.6	8.8	7.7
Canada	4.6	4.0	4.8	4.6	2.8	2.6	3.5	3.3	6.6	5.6	6.2	6.1	25.4	22.0	25.0	24.2
Chile	..	..	9.7	9.9	..	..	7.6	7.9	..	..	12.9	12.7	..	..	48.1	48.1
Czech Republic	1.4	0.8	0.9	0.8	0.3	0.3	0.4	0.3	2.9	1.4	1.6	1.4	27.1	16.4	13.9	10.9
Denmark	2.9	3.1	3.6	3.5	1.1	1.3	2.0	2.1	5.1	5.0	5.4	5.0	13.8	13.0	13.1	13.4
Estonia	..	1.2	0.9	0.8	..	0.7	0.6	0.5	..	1.8	1.2	1.0	..	15.3	9.2	9.2
Finland	3.5	2.9	4.3	4.2	1.5	1.3	2.6	2.4	5.7	4.6	6.1	6.1	28.7	20.7	26.3	25.2
France	4.6	5.2	7.9	7.9	2.3	1.8	3.6	3.8	7.3	9.0	12.5	12.3	27.0	29.9	42.1	42.0
Germany	2.3	5.3	3.1	3.0	0.8	2.7	1.7	1.7	4.2	8.4	4.7	4.5	12.0	20.3	11.2	10.6
Greece	1.9	2.4	6.8	6.6	1.2	1.2	5.1	4.9	3.2	4.3	9.2	9.1	42.9	42.7	70.1	69.5
Hungary	0.7	1.1	1.4	1.2	0.4	0.7	1.1	0.9	1.2	1.6	1.9	1.5	19.0	26.3	27.3	24.0
Iceland[1]	2.2	1.1	3.1	3.0	0.8	..	1.2	1.3	3.8	2.5	5.3	5.0	8.5	5.0	12.8	12.6
Ireland	2.7	1.8	7.0	4.7	2.2	1.3	6.0	4.1	3.4	2.6	8.3	5.4	16.4	10.3	31.6	22.9
Israel	3.6	4.2	2.4	2.3	1.6	1.9	1.3	1.3	6.1	6.8	3.7	3.5	15.9	17.6	10.9	10.7
Italy[1]	3.2	5.2	11.7	11.4	1.8	2.4	6.5	6.4	5.4	9.5	19.1	18.3	37.1	38.3	62.5	60.8
Japan	..	4.5	4.4	4.0	..	2.6	2.5	1.9	..	7.1	7.0	6.7	..	23.6	19.5	17.7
Korea	..	..	..	..	..	..	..	..	..	..	..	..	..	..	..	..
Latvia	..	1.4	3.1	2.7	..	1.0	2.3	1.3	..	1.8	3.8	4.1	..	22.2	36.1	34.4
Luxembourg	0.8	0.8	2.3	2.6	0.2	0.4	0.4	0.4	1.7	1.3	4.7	5.2	6.8	4.4	12.5	13.8
Mexico	..	..	..	..	..	..	..	..	..	..	..	..	..	..	..	..
Netherlands	1.4	2.1	4.2	3.5	0.9	1.1	3.0	2.7	2.2	3.3	5.6	4.4	3.6	4.6	8.7	7.1
New Zealand	5.9	3.8	5.2	5.4	3.4	2.4	3.2	3.2	8.9	5.3	7.6	8.0	26.1	17.1	24.5	25.5
Norway[1]	1.6	1.5	1.7	1.4	0.8	0.7	1.2	0.9	2.6	2.3	2.3	1.9	6.4	5.6	6.6	5.5
Poland	..	2.0	1.6	1.4	..	1.3	0.9	0.8	..	2.8	2.4	2.1	..	21.3	23.5	19.4
Portugal	2.5	3.3	4.5	4.1	1.0	1.5	2.8	2.6	4.3	5.4	6.3	5.7	22.4	26.8	37.6	36.6
Slovak Republic	0.7	0.9	3.8	3.3	0.2	0.3	3.1	2.5	1.3	1.6	4.8	4.2	33.5	33.8	63.7	53.2
Slovenia	..	0.4	1.3	1.1	..	0.3	0.6	0.6	..	0.6	2.1	1.7	..	4.6	13.7	10.8
Spain[1]	1.8	3.9	9.4	9.3	0.6	1.4	5.0	5.3	3.8	7.4	14.7	14.0	22.1	33.6	61.9	62.0
Sweden[1]	3.4	7.7	5.9	5.5	1.7	4.3	4.4	4.1	5.3	11.5	7.5	7.0	16.0	32.4	26.3	24.7
Switzerland	1.3	1.8	2.9	3.0	0.8	0.8	1.5	1.6	1.9	3.1	4.5	4.7	4.4	5.7	8.0	8.2
Turkey	..	0.6	1.1	1.2	..	0.5	1.1	1.2	..	0.7	1.1	1.3	..	7.3	11.5	12.9
United Kingdom[1]	2.4	2.3	3.8	3.5	1.8	1.8	3.0	2.7	3.2	3.0	4.7	4.3	9.7	9.3	14.4	13.3
United States[1]	0.7	0.8	1.3	1.1	0.5	0.6	1.1	0.9	0.9	1.0	1.6	1.3	4.1	4.8	7.3	6.3
OECD[2]	2.0	2.7	3.5	3.3	1.1	1.5	2.2	2.1	3.1	4.3	5.1	4.9	11.6	14.8	17.1	16.4
Colombia	..	7.6	6.8	6.5	..	5.4	4.6	4.5	..	11.0	10.0	9.4	..	52.1	43.1	41.2
Lithuania	..	2.4	2.3	2.4	..	2.0	1.8	1.8	..	2.9	2.8	3.0	..	26.6	31.3	30.2
Russian Federation	0.3	0.1	0.2	0.2	0.3	0.1	0.2	0.1	0.4	0.2	0.3	0.3	3.0	1.9	3.2	2.9

.. Not available

Note: Involuntary part-time employment refers to part-time workers who could not find full-time work. Part-time employment is based on national definitions.

Please refer to the Box entitled "Major breaks in series" in the introduction to the Statistical Annex.

1. The lower age limit is 16 instead of 15. For Iceland up to 2008, Italy after 2007, Norway up to 2005 and Sweden up to 2006.
2. Weighted average.

Source: OECD Employment Database, www.oecd.org/employment/emp/onlineoecdemploymentdatabase.htm and www.oecd.org/els/emp/lfsnotes_sources.pdf.

http://dx.doi.org/10.1787/888933779162

Table J. Incidence and composition of temporary employment
As a percentage of dependent employment in each age group

Percentage

	Total (15+)				Youth (15-24)				Prime age (25-54)				Women's share in temporary employment			
	2000	2007	2016	2017	2000	2007	2016	2017	2000	2007	2016	2017	2000	2007	2016	2017
Australia	..	6.3	5.4	5.3	..	6.0	6.0	5.5	..	6.4	5.5	5.5	..	52.3	52.2	53.1
Austria	7.9	8.8	9.0	9.2	33.0	34.8	33.9	34.7	3.8	4.3	5.5	5.9	47.1	47.5	49.1	48.3
Belgium	9.1	8.7	9.2	10.4	30.8	31.6	39.0	47.4	6.9	6.6	7.4	8.4	58.3	57.3	52.9	51.7
Canada	12.5	13.0	13.3	13.7	29.1	28.9	30.7	31.9	8.8	9.2	9.9	10.3	51.0	51.8	52.3	51.7
Chile	..	..	28.7	27.7	..	..	45.6	45.3	..	..	27.5	27.0	..	..	37.6	38.5
Czech Republic	9.3	8.6	10.2	10.0	19.6	17.4	32.4	31.0	5.2	5.6	8.4	8.4	46.6	54.3	55.1	56.5
Denmark	9.7	9.1	13.6	12.9	27.4	22.5	33.6	37.9	6.6	6.9	10.6	9.0	54.8	55.7	54.1	52.8
Estonia	3.0	2.1	3.6	3.0	6.4	6.6	13.1	10.6	2.6	1.6	3.1	2.5	27.4	37.6	46.4	45.4
Finland	16.5	16.0	15.9	16.1	45.6	42.4	43.3	43.7	13.0	13.2	13.2	13.3	60.3	61.8	59.3	59.2
France	15.4	15.1	16.2	16.9	55.1	53.6	58.6	58.0	11.6	11.1	12.8	13.5	49.6	52.5	51.3	51.3
Germany	12.7	14.6	13.1	12.9	52.4	57.4	53.3	52.6	7.5	9.1	9.7	9.6	46.2	46.7	48.1	47.8
Greece	13.5	11.0	11.2	11.4	29.5	26.5	31.0	29.1	11.6	10.0	10.5	10.8	46.5	50.9	49.7	52.6
Hungary	7.1	7.3	9.7	8.8	13.9	18.9	20.2	17.6	5.9	6.5	8.8	8.0	43.8	44.0	49.2	50.0
Iceland[1]	12.2	12.4	11.9	10.7	28.9	32.0	29.5	25.3	7.5	8.9	8.9	8.3	53.3	53.8	53.1	54.2
Ireland	6.0	8.5	8.2	9.2	15.9	21.2	29.3	30.8	3.0	5.6	6.2	5.9	55.1	56.6	52.1	51.6
Israel	..	..	..	..	..	..	..	..	..	..	..	..	..	..	..	..
Italy[1]	10.1	13.2	14.0	15.4	26.6	42.2	54.7	61.9	8.5	11.4	13.3	14.5	48.1	51.7	47.1	46.8
Japan[2]	14.5	13.9	7.2	7.0	24.9	26.4	13.4	12.7	9.5	10.9	4.9	4.7	61.7	65.1	60.5	60.6
Korea	..	24.7	21.9	20.6	..	30.0	25.7	22.8	..	21.3	16.3	15.1	..	44.3	48.6	48.7
Latvia	6.6	4.1	3.7	3.0	10.9	9.0	8.3	6.5	6.0	3.5	3.4	2.8	33.6	33.8	40.3	42.2
Luxembourg	3.4	6.8	9.0	9.1	14.5	34.1	40.4	41.5	2.3	5.3	7.2	7.0	54.0	49.9	46.3	48.3
Mexico	20.5	..	..	..	25.7	..	..	..	17.8	..	..	..	19.7	..	..	..
Netherlands	13.7	18.1	20.8	21.8	35.5	45.1	55.6	56.8	9.1	12.9	15.2	16.3	53.7	51.1	51.0	51.0
New Zealand	..	..	..	..	..	..	..	..	..	..	..	..	..	..	..	..
Norway[1]	9.3	9.5	8.7	8.4	28.5	27.3	27.9	26.4	6.9	7.4	6.8	6.8	58.8	59.8	57.8	55.8
Poland	..	28.2	27.5	26.2	..	65.7	70.7	68.2	..	24.0	25.0	23.6	..	45.9	47.4	48.2
Portugal	19.9	22.3	22.3	22.0	41.4	53.1	66.3	65.9	16.4	19.7	20.7	20.3	50.0	49.1	50.9	50.5
Slovak Republic	4.8	5.1	10.1	9.6	10.5	13.7	25.4	23.2	3.4	3.7	8.9	8.2	44.6	48.3	48.7	49.8
Slovenia	13.7	18.5	17.1	17.9	46.3	68.3	74.0	72.5	9.4	12.9	13.7	13.9	51.3	52.4	51.2	51.1
Spain[1]	32.2	31.6	26.1	26.7	68.3	62.7	72.9	73.3	27.7	29.3	25.7	26.3	40.7	45.4	48.4	49.4
Sweden[1]	15.2	17.5	16.7	16.9	49.5	57.3	54.3	53.8	11.9	13.0	11.9	12.1	57.6	56.9	54.7	54.6
Switzerland	11.5	12.9	13.2	13.4	47.0	50.3	50.7	50.9	5.1	6.4	7.8	7.9	50.1	47.1	47.6	47.2
Turkey	20.3	11.9	13.6	13.3	23.7	12.4	29.1	25.3	18.6	11.3	10.4	10.4	12.1	21.6	25.8	26.4
United Kingdom[1]	7.0	5.8	6.0	5.7	14.2	13.4	15.2	14.6	5.4	4.2	4.3	4.2	54.4	53.9	53.7	53.2
United States	..	..	..	..	..	..	..	..	..	..	..	..	..	..	..	..
OECD[3]	11.7	12.2	11.2	11.2	24.3	25.6	24.6	24.6	8.9	10.0	9.3	9.3	45.9	47.5	46.3	46.4
Colombia[4]	..	29.7	28.3	28.2	..	42.3	38.5	40.0	..	27.9	27.1	26.8	..	44.3	48.4	47.4
Costa Rica	..	..	9.4	8.0	..	..	14.7	13.1	..	..	8.2	7.0	..	..	27.5	25.8
Lithuania	4.4	3.8	1.9	1.7	9.4	10.5	7.8	6.8	4.1	3.1	1.5	1.3	38.0	33.0	47.7	42.4
Russian Federation	5.5	12.3	8.4	8.3	14.5	23.1	17.7	18.2	4.2	11.2	7.8	7.7	36.5	41.9	36.8	37.0

.. Not available

Note: Temporary employees are wage and salary workers whose job has a pre-determined termination date as opposed to permanent employees whose job is of unlimited duration. To be included in these groups are: i) persons with a seasonal job; ii) persons engaged by an employment agency or business and hired out to a third party for carrying out a "work mission"; iii) persons with specific training contracts (including apprentices, trainees, research assistants, probationary period of a contract, etc.). Country-specific exceptions to this generic definition may be found in (PDF) www.oecd.org/els/emp/lfsnotes_sources.pdf.

Please refer to the Box entitled "Major breaks in series" in the introduction to the Statistical Annex.

1. The lower age limit is 16 instead of 15. For Iceland up to 2008, Italy after 2007, Norway up to 2005 and Sweden up to 2006.
2. Japan applies a maximum duration threshold of one year to classify jobs as temporary employment. As a result, a regular employee with a fixed-term contract lasting more than one year is not included in temporary employment.
3. Weighted average.
4. The data cover only salaried employees who reported a written labour contract.

Source: OECD Employment Database, www.oecd.org/employment/emp/onlineoecdemploymentdatabase.htm and www.oecd.org/els/emp/lfsnotes_sources.pdf.

http://dx.doi.org/10.1787/888933779181

Table K1. Incidence of job tenure, less than 12 months - Total
As a percentage of total employment in each age group

Percentage

	Total (15-64)				Youth (15-24)				Prime age (25-54)				Older population (55-64)			
	2000	2007	2016	2017	2000	2007	2016	2017	2000	2007	2016	2017	2000	2007	2016	2017
Australia	..	23.6	20.4	20.7	..	47.7	42.1	43.5	..	20.1	17.9	18.3	..	10.2	9.4	8.2
Austria	..	15.5	15.4	15.9	..	39.7	40.4	41.6	..	12.3	13.2	14.0	..	5.0	5.1	4.9
Belgium	13.2	13.0	11.6	11.9	50.8	48.8	50.0	52.4	10.1	10.7	10.2	10.4	2.4	2.7	2.4	2.7
Canada	21.4	21.0	18.3	18.6	54.0	53.2	48.9	50.0	16.2	16.1	14.9	15.0	8.0	8.3	7.1	7.6
Chile	..	..	28.4	27.2	..	..	60.1	58.7	..	..	26.8	26.1	..	..	15.9	15.2
Czech Republic	..	10.7	10.4	10.8	..	35.0	38.9	39.3	..	8.8	9.3	9.9	..	7.6	5.3	5.4
Denmark	22.5	26.0	23.5	22.8	53.5	56.4	50.3	51.1	18.9	23.3	21.0	20.0	6.5	10.2	9.4	9.8
Estonia	..	15.1	16.2	17.4	..	42.5	52.3	50.4	..	12.7	14.3	15.9	..	7.9	8.3	8.7
Finland	20.6	20.3	19.1	20.1	65.2	62.6	60.3	61.1	16.1	16.8	16.1	17.2	5.8	6.3	6.8	7.8
France	15.8	15.4	13.6	14.4	56.7	55.0	54.6	55.2	12.6	12.3	11.4	12.3	3.6	4.6	4.1	4.3
Germany	14.9	14.9	13.9	14.0	38.8	40.9	40.9	40.6	13.0	12.7	12.8	13.0	4.7	4.9	4.8	4.6
Greece	9.5	8.4	9.7	10.1	31.0	28.8	41.0	39.8	7.7	7.5	9.2	9.6	2.8	3.1	4.0	4.5
Hungary	11.7	11.7	14.3	13.6	29.7	39.1	43.9	40.9	9.3	10.3	12.9	12.3	4.5	5.3	8.0	7.6
Iceland[1]	25.4	22.5	20.4	20.9	59.1	53.1	49.4	49.3	20.0	18.3	16.8	17.7	6.1	7.2	6.4	6.4
Ireland	19.4	18.0	15.9	17.0	46.8	45.0	52.1	50.4	13.6	14.1	13.9	14.2	5.7	4.6	5.5	5.7
Israel	..	..	..	..	..	..	..	..	..	..	..	..	..	..	..	..
Italy[1]	10.6	11.6	10.5	10.9	36.8	41.1	43.5	47.1	8.9	10.3	10.2	10.4	3.3	3.7	3.7	3.8
Japan	..	14.1	..	..	..	41.2	..	..	..	10.3	..	..	..	6.3	..	..
Korea[2]	..	40.0	30.3	29.5	..	72.0	68.6	68.3	..	35.6	25.3	24.6	..	46.4	33.9	32.3
Latvia	..	19.3	14.0	15.5	..	50.1	47.8	46.7	..	15.7	12.2	14.1	..	10.2	8.2	9.6
Luxembourg	11.6	10.6	12.1	13.2	40.4	44.0	45.2	50.0	9.6	9.0	10.5	11.4	0.5	1.9	5.4	4.7
Mexico	..	24.1	21.9	22.0	..	45.7	45.1	45.6	..	19.3	18.1	18.3	..	10.4	9.3	8.9
Netherlands	..	9.8	16.8	17.5	..	34.3	46.9	47.4	..	8.2	12.9	13.7	..	2.5	4.8	5.2
New Zealand	..	..	..	..	..	..	..	..	..	..	..	..	..	..	..	..
Norway[1]	..	20.9	14.6	14.9	..	52.5	40.0	42.0	..	18.1	12.8	12.8	..	4.9	3.6	3.8
Poland	13.7	15.7	11.9	11.7	41.2	47.3	40.3	41.6	11.0	12.8	10.7	10.3	6.0	6.9	5.2	5.2
Portugal	14.1	13.1	14.9	15.2	39.2	40.0	56.3	55.3	11.4	11.7	13.8	14.1	3.2	3.6	5.0	5.8
Slovak Republic	..	11.8	12.3	12.7	..	35.7	41.7	40.6	..	9.5	10.9	11.2	..	6.3	6.9	8.3
Slovenia	..	13.9	11.4	14.1	..	51.1	47.6	51.1	..	10.5	9.7	12.2	..	2.8	3.8	5.2
Spain[1]	21.2	21.9	17.2	17.9	54.5	55.5	63.5	64.7	17.8	19.8	16.8	17.3	6.5	6.1	6.0	6.1
Sweden[1]	15.8	20.4	20.5	21.2	49.4	65.4	59.1	58.2	14.0	17.0	17.7	18.9	4.6	6.5	8.0	8.1
Switzerland	16.5	15.3	16.2	17.6	44.6	41.4	40.6	43.4	13.4	12.7	14.4	15.9	3.9	4.2	5.3	5.6
Turkey	..	19.6	27.1	27.1	..	41.6	57.4	58.0	..	15.7	22.5	22.6	..	6.4	14.3	13.8
United Kingdom[1]	19.8	17.9	16.6	16.7	48.5	46.0	43.8	43.8	16.1	14.5	13.9	14.1	8.1	7.2	7.3	7.4
United States[1,2]	27.1	..	23.3	..	61.8	..	56.5	..	21.7	..	19.7	..	11.2	..	10.2	..
OECD[3]	19.5	19.9	18.8	19.3	48.7	49.6	50.1	50.7	15.5	16.2	15.8	16.4	7.4	8.3	8.5	8.6
Colombia	..	37.4	37.1	35.9	..	65.0	65.0	63.0	..	32.6	33.2	32.4	..	19.6	19.1	18.0
Costa Rica	..	..	26.6	26.8	..	..	51.9	51.7	..	..	23.7	24.3	..	..	14.2	14.8
Lithuania	14.2	15.0	19.4	18.4	37.1	45.3	56.9	56.6	12.7	13.1	17.3	16.5	5.7	6.7	12.0	10.8
Brazil	..	18.8	..	..	..	37.6	..	..	..	14.7	..	..	..	6.5	..	..

.. Not available

Note: Please refer to the Box entitled "Major breaks in series" in the introduction to the Statistical Annex.

1. The lower age limit is 16 instead of 15. For Iceland up to 2008, Italy after 2007, Norway up to 2005 and Sweden up to 2006.
2. Data cover dependent employment.
3. Weighted average.

Source: OECD Employment Database, www.oecd.org/employment/emp/onlineoecdemploymentdatabase.htm and www.oecd.org/els/emp/lfsnotes_sources.pdf.

http://dx.doi.org/10.1787/888933779200

Table K2. Incidence of job tenure, less than 12 months - Men
As a percentage of male employment in each age group

Percentage

	Men (15-64)				Youth (15-24)				Prime age (25-54)				Older population (55-64)			
	2000	2007	2016	2017	2000	2007	2016	2017	2000	2007	2016	2017	2000	2007	2016	2017
Australia	..	22.2	20.1	20.9	..	45.6	42.0	43.9	..	19.0	17.6	18.7	..	9.9	10.3	8.9
Austria	..	14.7	14.7	15.6	..	39.8	38.1	39.7	..	11.6	12.8	14.1	..	5.0	4.4	5.1
Belgium	12.8	12.5	11.6	12.0	49.3	46.2	46.6	50.0	9.9	10.4	10.4	10.7	2.5	2.8	2.5	3.1
Canada	20.6	20.8	18.1	18.9	53.8	52.8	48.1	50.5	15.6	16.2	15.0	15.5	8.2	8.7	7.7	8.1
Chile	..	..	28.8	27.8	..	..	59.2	58.5	..	..	27.5	26.9	..	..	16.0	15.4
Czech Republic	..	9.5	8.8	9.0	..	34.3	36.3	36.1	..	7.5	7.5	7.8	..	6.0	4.5	4.4
Denmark	20.7	24.1	22.4	22.6	49.5	51.6	49.0	50.9	17.5	21.7	20.2	20.1	6.1	9.8	9.1	9.5
Estonia	..	14.6	15.7	16.6	..	39.2	46.8	49.2	..	11.9	13.5	14.4	..	7.7	10.3	9.4
Finland	19.5	18.9	18.1	19.1	62.5	60.2	60.2	60.9	15.3	15.2	15.0	16.0	5.8	6.9	7.3	8.2
France	15.7	15.2	13.6	14.2	56.7	53.3	52.3	53.3	12.4	12.1	11.3	11.9	4.1	4.5	4.2	4.3
Germany	13.8	14.4	13.5	13.5	37.9	39.7	39.6	39.0	12.0	12.4	12.4	12.6	4.1	4.9	4.8	4.5
Greece	8.6	7.6	9.2	9.1	29.0	26.5	37.4	36.1	7.1	6.8	8.8	8.7	2.5	3.2	4.2	4.5
Hungary	11.8	11.9	13.4	13.1	29.1	38.2	41.3	39.2	9.6	10.4	12.1	11.8	4.5	6.2	7.2	7.2
Iceland[1]	23.9	21.1	19.9	19.7	58.0	52.1	49.7	47.7	19.4	17.1	15.8	16.5	2.8	6.4	5.4	4.9
Ireland	17.1	16.3	15.9	16.8	44.0	40.8	52.3	50.0	12.2	13.2	14.0	14.2	4.9	4.2	6.1	6.3
Israel	..	..	..	..	..	..	..	..	..	..	..	..	..	..	..	..
Italy[1]	9.6	10.4	9.6	10.3	36.2	38.7	41.5	44.8	8.0	9.0	9.1	9.7	3.2	3.5	3.7	3.9
Japan	..	10.7	..	..	..	39.6	..	..	..	7.1	..	..	..	6.3	..	..
Korea[2]	..	36.3	27.4	27.5	..	81.9	75.0	73.2	..	32.3	22.8	23.1	..	42.3	31.9	31.5
Latvia	..	20.8	15.3	16.1	..	47.7	45.3	47.7	..	16.9	13.5	13.9	..	12.3	9.7	12.3
Luxembourg	10.3	10.0	11.8	13.5	41.2	43.8	46.5	51.8	8.3	8.2	10.1	11.7	0.8	1.3	6.8	4.2
Mexico	..	22.5	20.9	20.5	..	43.1	42.7	43.0	..	17.9	16.9	16.5	..	9.9	8.9	8.2
Netherlands	..	9.3	15.9	16.6	..	31.5	45.5	45.9	..	8.1	12.5	13.4	..	2.6	5.0	5.5
New Zealand	..	..	..	..	..	..	..	..	..	..	..	..	..	..	..	..
Norway[1]	..	20.2	13.9	14.3	..	51.1	38.9	41.0	..	17.9	12.2	12.2	..	5.1	3.8	4.5
Poland	14.6	15.8	11.7	11.5	40.3	45.5	37.7	39.3	12.2	13.1	10.3	10.0	6.2	7.6	5.9	5.6
Portugal	14.0	13.0	15.2	15.2	38.6	38.4	51.7	51.2	11.1	11.5	14.3	14.2	3.7	3.5	5.5	6.3
Slovak Republic	..	11.6	12.1	12.2	..	34.8	40.2	38.9	..	9.5	10.1	10.3	..	5.3	7.8	8.7
Slovenia	..	13.5	10.8	13.9	..	49.4	46.3	48.4	..	9.9	9.1	11.9	..	3.1	2.9	5.5
Spain[1]	19.4	20.4	17.1	17.3	52.8	53.2	62.9	63.5	16.3	18.6	16.6	16.7	6.2	5.7	6.5	6.6
Sweden[1]	16.0	20.3	19.7	20.5	46.2	62.7	55.9	55.3	14.7	17.3	17.2	18.6	4.7	7.3	8.0	7.7
Switzerland	15.2	13.8	14.8	16.3	41.8	39.2	38.7	39.5	12.6	11.3	13.2	14.9	4.2	3.6	4.7	5.3
Turkey	..	19.7	27.2	27.1	..	43.3	59.1	59.3	..	15.9	22.6	22.6	..	7.2	14.4	14.1
United Kingdom[1]	18.7	17.3	15.9	16.0	47.1	44.4	42.5	42.9	15.1	14.1	13.3	13.5	8.6	7.8	7.2	7.3
United States[1,2]	25.9	..	22.6	..	59.4	..	55.1	..	20.6	..	19.1	..	11.3	..	10.6	..
OECD[3]	18.0	18.8	18.1	18.4	46.6	47.9	48.7	49.2	14.2	15.3	15.1	15.4	7.3	8.2	8.7	8.7
Colombia	..	35.5	34.4	33.3	..	62.1	61.8	59.8	..	30.7	30.2	29.6	..	19.4	16.9	16.6
Costa Rica	..	..	27.3	27.1	..	..	53.7	51.1	..	..	23.7	24.3	..	..	15.2	16.2
Lithuania	16.4	16.7	20.8	20.2	36.4	45.7	54.3	53.5	14.9	14.4	18.6	18.2	7.8	8.5	13.2	13.3
Brazil	..	18.0	..	..	..	35.3	..	..	..	14.1	..	..	..	6.4	..	..

.. Not available

Note: Please refer to the Box entitled "Major breaks in series" in the introduction to the Statistical Annex.
1. The lower age limit is 16 instead of 15. For Iceland up to 2008, Italy after 2007, Norway up to 2005 and Sweden up to 2006.
2. Data cover dependent employment.
3. Weighted average.
Source: OECD Employment Database, www.oecd.org/employment/emp/onlineoecdemploymentdatabase.htm and www.oecd.org/els/emp/lfsnotes_sources.pdf.

http://dx.doi.org/10.1787/888933779219

Table K3. Incidence of job tenure, less than 12 months - Women
As a percentage of the female population in each age group

Percentage

	Women (15-64)				Youth (15-24)				Prime age (25-54)				Older population (55-64)			
	2000	2007	2016	2017	2000	2007	2016	2017	2000	2007	2016	2017	2000	2007	2016	2017
Australia	..	25.4	20.7	20.4	..	50.1	42.2	43.0	..	21.4	18.3	17.9	..	10.6	8.3	7.4
Austria	..	16.3	16.3	16.3	..	39.6	43.0	43.7	..	13.1	13.6	13.9	..	5.1	6.0	4.6
Belgium	13.8	13.6	11.7	11.8	52.7	52.0	53.9	55.4	10.4	10.9	9.9	10.2	2.2	2.7	2.0	2.2
Canada	22.3	21.2	18.5	18.3	54.2	53.6	49.7	49.6	16.9	16.1	14.8	14.6	7.6	7.8	6.6	7.0
Chile	..	..	27.7	26.4	..	..	61.6	59.0	..	..	25.9	25.0	..	..	15.6	14.8
Czech Republic	..	12.3	12.4	13.2	..	36.1	42.9	43.8	..	10.5	11.6	12.4	..	10.1	6.3	6.7
Denmark	24.6	28.2	24.7	23.1	58.1	61.7	51.6	51.3	20.4	24.9	21.9	19.9	7.2	10.7	9.8	10.1
Estonia	..	15.7	16.8	18.2	..	46.9	58.4	51.7	..	13.5	15.1	17.5	..	8.1	6.4	7.9
Finland	21.7	21.9	20.2	21.1	67.9	64.9	60.6	61.3	17.0	18.5	17.4	18.5	5.8	5.8	6.5	7.5
France	15.9	15.6	13.5	14.7	56.7	57.2	57.4	57.6	12.8	12.6	11.4	12.8	2.9	4.6	3.9	4.4
Germany	16.4	15.5	14.4	14.5	39.8	42.2	42.5	42.5	14.2	13.0	13.3	13.5	5.8	4.9	4.9	4.8
Greece	11.0	9.6	10.3	11.5	34.0	32.6	45.6	44.5	8.9	8.5	9.7	10.9	3.2	3.1	3.6	4.5
Hungary	11.5	11.5	15.4	14.2	30.4	40.3	47.3	43.2	9.0	10.2	14.0	13.0	4.5	4.2	9.0	8.2
Iceland[1]	27.1	24.2	21.1	22.2	60.1	54.2	49.0	51.1	20.7	19.7	17.8	19.1	10.1	8.2	4.7	5.5
Ireland	22.6	20.3	15.9	17.2	50.2	49.8	51.9	50.8	15.7	15.1	13.8	14.2	7.7	5.4	4.7	5.0
Israel	..	..	..	..	..	..	..	..	..	..	..	..	..	..	..	..
Italy[1]	12.4	13.5	11.7	11.6	37.7	44.7	46.3	50.7	10.4	12.2	11.6	11.4	3.3	4.0	3.8	3.8
Japan	..	18.6	..	..	..	42.9	..	..	..	14.5	..	..	..	6.4	..	..
Korea[2]	..	45.2	34.0	32.1	..	65.7	64.2	65.0	..	40.7	28.7	26.7	..	53.1	36.4	33.4
Latvia	..	17.7	12.7	14.9	..	53.4	50.7	45.2	..	14.4	10.9	14.4	..	8.3	7.0	7.5
Luxembourg	13.6	11.4	12.5	12.9	39.4	44.4	44.0	48.0	11.5	10.1	10.9	11.0	..	2.6	0.4	2.2
Mexico	..	26.8	23.5	24.4	..	50.3	49.8	50.6	..	21.6	19.8	20.9	..	11.4	9.9	10.2
Netherlands	..	10.5	17.8	18.4	..	37.7	48.3	48.9	..	8.3	13.4	14.1	..	2.3	4.4	4.9
New Zealand	..	..	..	..	..	..	..	..	..	..	..	..	..	..	..	..
Norway[1]	..	21.7	15.3	15.5	..	53.9	41.1	43.1	..	18.3	13.4	13.5	..	4.5	3.3	3.1
Poland	12.7	15.5	12.2	12.0	42.4	49.9	44.0	44.8	9.7	12.5	11.1	10.7	5.8	5.6	4.3	4.6
Portugal	14.2	13.3	14.6	15.2	39.9	42.1	61.7	60.3	11.8	11.8	13.2	14.0	2.5	3.7	4.5	5.2
Slovak Republic	..	12.1	12.6	13.2	..	37.0	44.4	43.2	..	9.5	11.9	12.2	..	8.6	5.9	7.8
Slovenia	..	14.3	12.1	14.4	..	53.5	49.7	55.5	..	11.1	10.3	12.6	..	2.3	4.4	4.8
Spain[1]	24.3	23.9	17.4	18.5	57.0	58.5	64.2	66.1	20.4	21.5	17.0	17.9	7.3	6.8	5.3	5.5
Sweden[1]	15.7	20.5	21.4	21.9	52.7	68.3	62.3	61.3	13.3	16.6	18.3	19.2	4.4	5.6	8.0	8.5
Switzerland	18.2	17.1	17.7	19.2	47.6	43.8	42.6	47.5	14.5	14.3	15.7	17.0	3.5	5.0	6.0	5.9
Turkey	..	19.5	26.9	27.1	..	38.2	54.1	55.2	..	15.1	22.2	22.7	..	4.3	13.8	13.0
United Kingdom[1]	21.1	18.6	17.5	17.5	49.9	47.6	45.1	44.8	17.3	15.0	14.6	14.9	7.3	6.3	7.4	7.6
United States[1,2]	28.4	..	24.0	..	64.2	..	57.9	..	22.9	..	20.4	..	11.2	..	9.8	..
OECD[3]	21.4	21.2	19.7	20.4	51.2	51.6	51.7	52.5	17.2	17.4	16.7	17.4	7.7	8.6	8.3	8.4
Colombia	..	40.2	40.9	39.4	..	69.7	69.8	67.7	..	35.4	37.2	36.1	..	19.9	22.3	20.1
Costa Rica	..	..	25.5	26.3	..	..	48.1	52.8	..	..	23.8	24.2	..	..	12.2	12.3
Lithuania	12.0	13.1	18.1	16.6	38.0	44.7	60.1	60.2	10.6	11.8	16.1	14.9	3.3	4.9	10.9	8.7
Brazil	..	19.7	..	..	..	41.0	..	..	..	15.5	..	..	..	6.7	..	..

.. Not available

Note: Please refer to the Box entitled "Major breaks in series" in the introduction to the Statistical Annex.

1. The lower age limit is 16 instead of 15. For Iceland up to 2008, Italy after 2007, Norway up to 2005 and Sweden up to 2006.
2. Data cover dependent employment.
3. Weighted average.

Source: OECD Employment Database, www.oecd.org/employment/emp/onlineoecdemploymentdatabase.htm and www.oecd.org/els/emp/lfsnotes_sources.pdf.

http://dx.doi.org/10.1787/888933779238

Table L. Average annual hours actually worked per person in employment
National accounts concepts unless otherwise specified

Hours per person per year

	Total employment								Dependent employment							
	1979	1983	1990	1995	2000	2007	2016	2017	1979	1983	1990	1995	2000	2007	2016	2017
Australia	1 832	1 779	1 788	1 799	1 780	1 723	1 672	1 676	..	..	..	..	..	..	..	..
Austria	..	..	..	1 774	1 798	1 725	1 609	1 613	..	..	..	1 455	1 509	1 526	1 419	..
Belgium	1 727	1 675	1 663	1 585	1 595	1 577	1 546	..	..	..	..	1 447	1 459	1 448	1 424	1 426
Canada	1 841	1 779	1 797	1 775	1 779	1 741	1 706	1 695	1 812	1 761	1 782	1 768	1 773	1 740	1 715	1 706
Chile	..	..	2 422	2 338	2 263	2 128	1 974	1 954	..	..	..	..	2 318	2 168	2 049	..
Czech Republic	..	..	..	1 858	1 896	1 784	1 778	1 776	..	..	..	1 987	2 018	1 914	1 833	1 805
Denmark	1 564	1 546	1 441	1 419	1 466	1 433	1 414	1 408	1 470	1 469	1 381	1 366	1 407	1 390	1 416	..
Estonia	..	..	..	..	1 978	1 998	1 855	1 857	..	..	..	..	..	..	..	..
Finland	1 869	1 823	1 769	1 776	1 742	1 691	1 635	1 628	..	..	1 666	1 672	1 638	1 594	1 602	1 601
France	1 787	1 671	1 629	1 591	1 550	1 530	1 503	1 514	1 643	1 533	1 514	1 482	1 445	1 437	1 423	..
Germany	..	..	..	1 528	1 452	1 424	1 363	1 356	..	..	..	1 442	1 360	1 346	1 298	..
Greece	..	2 186	2 084	2 111	2 108	2 111	2 030	2 018	..	1 760	1 761	1 785	1 818	1 780	1 726	..
Hungary[1]	..	..	..	1 820	1 845	1 795	1 759	1 740	..	1 829	1 710	1 765	1 795	1 778	1 819	1 799
Iceland	..	..	..	..	..	..	..	..	..	..	..	..	..	..	..	..
Ireland	..	..	..	..	1 826	1 763	1 739	1 738	..	..	..	..	..	..	..	..
Israel	..	..	..	1 995	2 017	1 931	1 889	1 885	..	..	..	..	..	..	..	..
Italy	..	..	..	1 856	1 851	1 818	1 724	1 723	..	..	..	1 680	1 696	1 652	1 577	1 578
Japan[2]	2 126	2 095	2 031	1 884	1 821	1 785	1 714	1 710	..	..	..	1 910	1 853	1 808	1 724	1 721
Korea	..	..	..	..	..	..	2 071	2 024	..	..	..	..	..	..	2 052	2 014
Latvia	..	..	..	..	1 976	1 878	1 902	1 875	..	..	..	..	..	1 869	1 674	..
Luxembourg	..	..	..	1 593	1 603	1 566	1 519	1 518	..	..	..	1 593	1 605	1 570	1 515	1 514
Mexico	..	..	..	2 294	2 311	2 260	2 255	2 257	..	..	..	2 360	2 360	2 337	2 348	2 348
Netherlands	1 556	1 524	1 451	1 479	1 462	1 430	1 437	1 433	1 512	1 491	1 434	1 424	1 394	1 359	1 359	1 359
New Zealand	..	..	1 809	1 841	1 836	1 774	1 752	1 753	..	..	1 734	1 766	1 777	1 754	1 740	1 751
Norway	1 580	1 553	1 503	1 488	1 455	1 426	1 424	1 419	..	..	..	..	..	..	..	..
Poland	..	..	..	..	1 988	1 976	1 928	1 895	..	..	..	..	1 963	1 953	1 890	1 861
Portugal	2 017	1 971	1 959	1 893	1 917	1 900	1 865	1 863	..	..	1 830	1 778	1 729	1 731	1 679	..
Slovak Republic	..	..	..	1 853	1 816	1 791	1 740	1 714	..	..	..	..	1 768	1 774	1 680	..
Slovenia	..	..	..	1 755	1 710	1 655	1 667	1 655	..	..	..	..	1 606	1 593	1 617	1 608
Spain	1 954	1 848	1 763	1 755	1 753	1 704	1 701	1 687	1 864	1 769	1 696	1 686	1 705	1 662	1 653	1 639
Sweden	1 530	1 546	1 575	1 640	1 642	1 612	1 626	1 609	..	..	..	..	..	..	..	..
Switzerland[3]	..	..	..	1 720	1 713	1 669	1 590	1 570	..	..	..	..	..	..	..	..
Turkey	1 964	1 935	1 866	1 876	1 937	1 911	..	..	..	..	..	..	..	..	..	..
United Kingdom	1 813	1 711	1 765	1 731	1 700	1 677	1 670	1 681	1 747	1 649	1 700	1 695	1 680	1 658	1 660	1 669
United States	1 833	1 821	1 833	1 840	1 832	1 796	1 781	1 780	1 833	1 828	1 835	1 844	1 831	1 797	1 787	1 786
OECD[4]	1 923	1 900	1 879	1 863	1 841	1 802	1 765	1 759	..	..	..	..	..	..	..	..
Costa Rica	..	..	2 358	2 345	2 362	2 387	2 205	2 179	..	..	..	..	..	..	2 244	2 246
Lithuania	..	..	..	1 729	1 897	1 903	1 885	1 844	..	..	..	..	1 915	1 906	1 882	1 840
Russian Federation	..	..	..	1 891	1 982	1 999	1 974	1 980	..	..	..	1 886	2 000	2 020	1 996	1 994

.. Not available

Note: Total hours worked per year divided by the average number of people in employment. The data are intended for comparisons of trends over time; they are unsuitable for comparisons of the level of average annual hours of work for a given year, because of differences in their sources and method of calculation. Part-time and part-year workers are covered as well as full-time workers.

1. Data for dependent employment refer to establishments in manufacturing with five or more employees.
2. Data for dependent employment refer to establishments with five or more regular employees.
3. OECD estimates on hours per worker are obtained by dividing total hours worked by SPAO-based average employment, both according to domestic concept taken from FSO website .
4. Weighted average.

Source: OECD Employment Database, www.oecd.org/employment/emp/onlineoecdemploymentdatabase.htm and www.oecd.org/employment/emp/ANNUAL-HOURS-WORKED.pdf.

http://dx.doi.org/10.1787/888933779257

Table M1. Incidence of long-term unemployment, 12 months and over - Total
As a percentage of total unemployment in each age group

Percentage

	Total (15+)				Youth (15-24)				Prime(25-54)				Older population (55+)			
	2000	2007	2016	2017	2000	2007	2016	2017	2000	2007	2016	2017	2000	2007	2016	2017
Australia	25.9	15.4	23.7	23.5	14.9	9.9	18.2	17.1	30.7	17.2	24.4	25.2	45.6	30.5	38.5	35.9
Austria	25.8	27.2	32.3	33.4	12.7	13.4	18.1	15.2	25.5	30.2	34.0	35.6	49.7	58.1	53.4	55.6
Belgium	54.2	50.4	52.0	50.0	29.1	29.7	31.4	26.8	61.9	54.8	53.4	52.7	79.4	80.3	83.2	72.9
Canada	11.2	7.0	11.6	12.1	4.0	1.5	4.9	5.4	14.0	8.9	12.3	12.6	18.6	12.3	19.6	20.0
Czech Republic	48.8	53.4	43.2	36.0	37.8	33.6	24.5	19.8	53.3	58.3	45.2	38.3	45.6	51.7	54.6	43.2
Denmark	21.7	16.1	22.5	22.9	2.1	4.2	8.2	6.5	24.7	16.6	26.9	27.0	41.2	38.3	39.2	44.9
Estonia	45.1	49.8	31.6	33.5	26.3	30.5	20.4	15.1	49.4	52.7	30.0	34.4	52.5	73.5	43.9	47.2
Finland	29.0	23.0	26.6	24.9	8.8	5.5	8.0	6.1	34.0	25.9	30.5	28.3	56.5	47.6	44.8	44.7
France	42.6	39.9	44.4	44.0	20.6	24.6	27.7	27.5	45.3	43.0	46.3	45.9	69.7	67.7	66.8	65.2
Germany	51.5	56.6	41.2	41.9	23.5	32.2	21.9	22.8	51.0	57.5	41.3	42.4	69.1	76.9	57.9	58.7
Greece	54.7	49.7	72.0	72.8	50.2	41.4	53.3	54.2	56.9	51.5	73.0	73.6	56.2	59.5	83.3	84.7
Hungary	48.9	47.5	47.3	41.3	37.8	36.6	28.1	22.6	52.6	49.6	48.6	43.2	57.9	54.3	68.0	58.5
Iceland[1,2]	11.8	8.0	8.8	9.2	..	..	1.2	5.6	17.0	8.6	10.1	9.0	33.0	56.8	23.5	22.7
Ireland	37.3	30.0	55.3	47.0	19.9	21.0	35.0	28.5	44.9	33.5	57.6	50.7	47.6	42.4	75.6	66.3
Israel	12.0	24.9	13.5	11.6	6.1	13.2	5.2	5.4	13.5	27.3	13.3	12.3	21.8	41.6	30.1	19.2
Italy[2]	61.8	47.5	58.3	58.8	57.5	41.1	52.4	53.8	63.8	49.4	59.3	59.4	63.7	53.4	63.8	63.7
Japan	25.5	32.0	39.5	36.7	21.5	20.0	34.6	21.7	22.5	33.1	41.7	41.1	36.0	39.6	36.2	33.3
Korea[1]	2.3	0.6	0.9	1.3	0.9	0.4	0.5	0.2	2.8	0.7	1.1	1.7	2.9	..	0.7	1.0
Latvia	58.6	27.1	42.6	38.5	43.4	11.1	29.4	13.4	61.3	30.6	42.7	40.8	67.5	38.4	52.1	45.7
Luxembourg[1]	22.4	28.7	39.5	42.6	14.3	23.0	11.4	14.7	24.9	29.9	41.5	45.1	26.4	43.7	82.2	89.3
Mexico	1.2	1.9	2.0	2.0	0.9	0.9	1.4	1.2	1.2	2.1	2.1	2.3	4.3	6.8	4.2	2.8
Netherlands	..	39.4	42.7	40.7	..	12.6	17.1	13.9	..	44.1	44.6	42.4	..	74.4	69.5	69.9
New Zealand	19.9	6.0	14.1	15.6	9.8	2.4	6.5	6.5	23.1	8.6	17.4	20.3	44.8	15.8	29.0	31.8
Norway[1,2]	5.3	8.8	12.5	15.6	1.3	2.6	3.8	6.7	7.3	11.8	14.9	18.7	14.1	19.5	27.3	27.7
Poland	37.9	45.9	35.0	31.0	28.0	30.0	24.5	21.4	41.5	50.6	36.8	32.5	44.2	57.0	45.6	42.2
Portugal	42.2	47.2	55.4	50.0	21.2	27.4	29.4	26.5	47.9	49.6	57.6	51.4	68.5	67.8	75.4	71.3
Slovak Republic	54.6	70.8	56.6	58.8	43.1	53.9	44.7	41.8	59.9	74.5	58.6	61.6	60.1	82.6	61.8	66.8
Slovenia	61.4	45.7	54.5	48.4	42.4	29.2	47.4	33.6	67.9	49.8	52.4	47.9	86.2	57.4	83.4	66.8
Spain[2]	41.7	20.4	48.4	44.5	29.3	10.1	28.9	26.5	45.0	21.2	48.6	44.1	58.0	46.8	69.2	65.9
Sweden[2]	26.4	12.8	16.8	16.8	8.9	3.5	3.9	4.5	26.6	16.4	20.5	19.6	49.3	27.8	32.0	33.0
Switzerland	29.0	40.8	39.4	37.9	..	..	..	..	..	..	..	..	..	..	..	..
Turkey	21.1	30.3	20.6	21.9	19.8	26.6	14.3	14.7	21.8	32.2	22.2	24.2	31.4	41.0	36.0	35.1
United Kingdom[2]	26.7	23.8	27.2	26.0	12.3	15.7	17.0	15.7	32.9	28.4	30.2	29.4	43.4	35.5	44.6	40.6
United States[2]	6.0	10.0	17.0	15.1	3.9	6.5	10.4	8.1	6.6	11.1	18.4	16.2	11.9	14.3	24.2	23.1
OECD[3]	31.0	28.2	32.4	31.0	19.7	16.2	18.5	17.0	34.3	31.7	35.3	34.0	43.1	40.5	43.1	41.5
Colombia	..	12.0	7.3	8.4	..	8.4	4.3	5.0	..	14.2	8.6	9.8	..	16.3	12.5	14.1
Costa Rica	..	..	16.7	14.7	..	..	14.2	12.8	..	..	18.4	15.9	..	..	18.2	17.2
Lithuania	49.8	32.4	38.6	38.1	43.1	21.1	14.4	12.7	51.4	33.0	40.6	39.5	52.0	45.6	49.9	49.6
Russian Fed.	46.2	40.6	29.6	30.4	32.6	28.6	20.3	18.4	50.2	45.9	32.1	33.2	62.8	44.2	34.8	37.1
South Africa	..	57.7	58.8	60.4	..	36.2	35.1	36.0	..	61.8	61.4	63.1	..	80.5	70.9	70.7

.. Not available

Note: For country details related to data on unemployment by duration of job search, see www.oecd.org/els/emp/lfsnotes_sources.pdf. Persons for whom no duration of unemployment was specified are excluded from the total used in the calculation.

Please refer to the Box entitled "Major breaks in series" in the introduction to the Statistical Annex.

1. Data based on small sample sizes.
2. The lower age limit is 16 instead of 15. For Iceland up to 2008, Italy after 2007, Norway up to 2005 and Sweden up to 2006.
3. Weighted average.

Source: OECD Employment Database, www.oecd.org/employment/emp/onlineoecdemploymentdatabase.htm and www.oecd.org/els/emp/lfsnotes_sources.pdf.

http://dx.doi.org/10.1787/888933779276

Table M2. Incidence of long-term unemployment, 12 months and over - Men
As a percentage of male unemployment in each age group

Percentage

	Men (15+)				Youth (15-24)				Prime(25-54)				Older population (55+)			
	2000	2007	2016	2017	2000	2007	2016	2017	2000	2007	2016	2017	2000	2007	2016	2017
Australia	28.8	16.4	24.9	25.0	15.6	10.0	19.9	18.4	33.9	18.9	25.2	27.2	49.5	30.7	37.9	36.8
Austria	28.1	26.9	34.3	33.7	10.0	14.0	20.5	16.5	27.2	29.2	35.6	35.3	56.4	57.1	53.4	55.4
Belgium	54.1	49.3	52.7	52.2	27.2	30.1	30.7	30.7	62.8	53.0	55.0	54.6	75.1	80.2	85.3	77.5
Canada	12.3	8.1	12.5	13.0	4.4	1.5	5.4	5.8	15.6	10.8	13.4	13.9	20.4	11.7	20.1	20.5
Czech Republic	47.5	51.7	42.8	36.2	37.2	35.4	24.7	18.7	53.3	56.5	45.0	40.1	45.2	54.9	54.2	42.0
Denmark	21.0	15.6	23.2	24.0	0.9	3.3	8.1	7.2	25.2	17.6	29.7	28.8	38.8	35.4	38.0	43.8
Estonia	47.1	53.3	32.8	36.0	31.3	33.8	17.6	16.6	51.2	55.2	32.2	35.4	51.3	80.4	47.6	56.9
Finland	32.2	26.5	29.0	27.9	8.8	5.9	10.3	8.4	39.1	30.2	33.7	32.5	58.3	52.4	44.5	43.2
France	41.2	40.2	46.4	45.7	20.0	28.8	30.2	29.3	43.8	42.1	48.0	47.8	68.7	66.8	69.8	67.8
Germany	50.1	56.7	43.1	43.8	23.7	33.5	23.8	25.1	49.1	57.9	43.9	44.5	69.0	76.2	58.8	60.3
Greece	48.0	41.5	71.2	70.8	42.9	32.8	54.3	54.7	49.9	42.5	71.2	70.7	55.8	58.0	84.3	83.4
Hungary	51.1	47.2	46.5	41.8	40.7	38.0	30.8	28.4	54.4	48.9	47.0	42.5	62.9	54.7	67.4	59.0
Iceland[1,2]	8.7	9.5	9.5	8.7	..	..	..	2.3	17.1	14.3	12.9	11.3	..	..	..	..
Ireland	46.7	35.4	61.5	51.5	21.5	24.8	39.0	31.4	56.1	39.6	64.2	55.5	58.5	44.8	79.8	73.0
Israel	13.5	28.9	14.6	11.9	8.1	15.7	5.2	4.8	13.7	31.0	13.3	12.1	25.5	44.4	32.6	21.0
Italy[2]	61.8	45.6	58.1	59.7	56.7	41.0	52.9	55.2	64.0	46.7	58.6	60.0	67.0	54.2	64.7	65.4
Japan	30.7	40.3	49.6	47.1	26.3	24.0	40.0	25.0	29.4	43.0	54.8	54.7	35.6	44.7	42.4	39.3
Korea[1]	3.1	0.7	1.1	1.3	1.4	0.3	0.1	0.1	3.5	0.9	1.3	1.6	3.4	..	1.1	1.2
Latvia	58.8	30.1	46.1	41.6	46.7	11.6	33.6	22.4	61.1	37.2	47.2	44.1	64.8	29.3	54.2	45.8
Luxembourg[1]	26.4	35.4	42.7	48.6	20.4	30.5	..	16.1	28.7	36.5	46.6	53.1	..	..	..	..
Mexico	0.6	2.0	2.2	1.9	..	0.8	1.5	1.4	0.5	2.1	2.4	2.0	5.3	7.5	3.9	3.0
Netherlands	..	41.8	43.5	40.4	..	12.2	18.1	14.4	..	45.9	45.1	40.7	..	75.3	69.5	68.9
New Zealand	23.7	6.6	14.9	16.9	12.1	2.3	7.1	6.7	27.4	10.0	19.0	23.3	47.6	18.2	29.2	34.8
Norway[1,2]	6.9	10.2	13.5	17.2	1.3	3.1	4.6	8.7	9.3	14.4	16.2	20.1	16.6	18.5	24.7	26.3
Poland	34.1	45.8	35.8	31.9	25.5	31.0	25.4	23.5	37.3	49.9	37.6	32.9	43.3	57.2	46.6	42.0
Portugal	43.9	47.6	57.4	50.6	20.3	26.2	32.6	27.4	47.5	50.1	59.3	51.4	73.9	66.6	74.9	71.3
Slovak Republic	54.1	72.3	59.1	62.1	43.9	57.8	48.4	48.7	59.2	75.6	62.0	65.4	59.3	86.5	59.4	63.8
Slovenia	62.8	45.3	55.2	53.8	41.7	27.8	46.1	40.8	68.9	51.1	52.6	51.2	86.8	57.9	81.0	75.9
Spain[2]	35.3	17.4	46.1	42.5	25.5	8.6	29.2	27.1	35.9	17.4	45.5	41.4	58.9	42.3	67.5	64.1
Sweden[2]	29.3	14.2	17.8	18.8	11.0	3.3	4.5	5.8	30.1	18.9	21.7	21.2	48.6	28.1	32.7	36.4
Switzerland	28.2	37.9	38.4	36.4	..	..	..	..	..	..	..	..	..	..	..	..
Turkey	18.1	27.0	17.3	17.5	16.0	23.3	12.3	11.6	19.0	28.3	17.4	18.1	31.4	40.4	35.3	34.8
United Kingdom[2]	32.6	28.5	30.4	28.8	14.6	18.9	19.1	18.6	40.2	34.7	34.6	33.4	49.0	39.6	48.3	40.4
United States[2]	6.7	10.7	18.6	15.5	4.5	7.6	12.2	8.7	6.7	11.4	19.7	16.6	15.6	16.8	26.5	24.4
OECD[3]	29.9	28.3	32.5	30.8	18.8	16.8	19.5	17.6	32.7	31.3	35.0	33.5	43.2	41.3	43.8	41.9
Colombia	..	10.8	6.3	7.1	..	8.3	4.2	4.0	..	12.0	6.5	7.8	..	16.0	11.7	13.9
Costa Rica	..	..	10.1	9.8	..	..	11.0	6.5	..	..	8.8	11.2	..	..	13.0	16.4
Lithuania	51.4	34.9	37.8	37.9	50.2	22.9	17.6	15.7	52.0	34.6	40.2	39.7	49.2	53.3	47.5	49.0
Russian Fed.	42.7	39.1	28.6	29.9	31.2	28.4	20.1	19.0	45.7	43.7	30.7	32.3	59.2	44.4	35.1	37.0
South Africa	..	52.6	53.7	56.6	..	34.2	31.2	33.7	..	55.5	55.8	58.9	..	80.7	70.4	69.5

.. Not available

Note: For country details related to data on unemployment by duration of job search, see www.oecd.org/els/emp/lfsnotes_sources.pdf. Persons for whom no duration of unemployment was specified are excluded from the total used in the calculation.

Please refer to the Box entitled "Major breaks in series" in the introduction to the Statistical Annex.

1. Data based on small sample sizes.
2. The lower age limit is 16 instead of 15. For Iceland up to 2008, Italy after 2007, Norway up to 2005 and Sweden up to 2006.
3. Weighted average.

Source: OECD Employment Database, www.oecd.org/employment/emp/onlineoecdemploymentdatabase.htm and www.oecd.org/els/emp/lfsnotes_sources.pdf.

http://dx.doi.org/10.1787/888933779295

Table M3. Incidence of long-term unemployment, 12 months and over - Women
As a percentage of female unemployment in each age group

Percentage

	Women (15+)				Youth (15-24)				Prime(25-54)				Older population (55+)			
	2000	2007	2016	2017	2000	2007	2016	2017	2000	2007	2016	2017	2000	2007	2016	2017
Australia	21.9	14.4	22.4	21.8	14.1	9.9	15.9	15.6	26.4	15.6	23.5	23.3	33.9	30.2	39.6	34.5
Austria	22.8	27.6	29.7	33.1	16.5	12.8	14.9	13.3	23.5	31.1	31.9	36.0	31.7	59.6	53.5	55.9
Belgium	54.3	51.4	51.2	47.5	30.8	29.3	32.5	21.2	61.3	56.6	51.4	50.5	89.1	80.3	81.0	68.0
Canada	9.8	5.7	10.3	10.9	3.5	1.4	4.1	4.7	12.1	6.6	10.9	10.9	15.8	13.1	18.9	19.3
Czech Republic	49.8	54.7	43.7	35.8	38.5	31.1	24.3	21.1	53.3	59.4	45.2	37.0	46.3	46.6	55.2	44.3
Denmark	22.4	16.6	21.8	21.7	3.5	5.3	8.4	5.7	24.4	15.8	24.6	25.2	43.9	41.0	40.6	46.2
Estonia	42.6	44.4	30.1	30.3	19.4	22.8	25.2	12.6	47.3	49.9	27.2	33.3	54.9	29.6	39.8	33.9
Finland	26.2	19.5	23.8	21.4	8.8	5.0	5.4	3.6	29.6	21.8	26.8	23.4	54.5	42.2	45.1	46.5
France	43.7	39.7	42.2	42.2	21.1	19.9	24.7	25.0	46.5	43.9	44.5	44.1	70.7	68.8	62.9	61.9
Germany	53.1	56.5	38.5	39.2	23.2	30.4	18.9	19.3	52.9	57.0	37.9	39.3	69.1	77.8	56.8	56.5
Greece	59.2	54.4	72.7	74.5	55.1	46.7	52.3	53.8	61.2	56.3	74.4	75.9	57.0	61.6	81.7	86.5
Hungary	45.7	47.9	48.3	40.8	33.1	34.7	24.6	16.2	50.1	50.3	50.4	43.8	37.5	53.6	68.7	58.1
Iceland[1,2]	14.1	5.7	8.1	9.9	..	..	2.6	10.7	16.9	2.7	7.7	6.5	..	..	..	..
Ireland	23.0	21.7	45.0	41.3	18.1	15.5	29.0	24.4	26.2	23.9	47.1	44.5	19.9	37.2	65.3	57.8
Israel	10.4	20.9	12.4	11.2	4.2	11.2	5.3	6.0	13.2	23.8	13.3	12.6	12.4	36.3	25.8	16.3
Italy[2]	61.8	49.2	58.6	57.8	58.3	41.1	51.7	51.9	63.6	51.5	60.0	58.8	56.1	51.6	62.2	60.8
Japan	17.1	19.4	24.1	21.9	14.8	15.0	27.3	18.2	13.8	20.6	24.1	22.9	37.5	20.0	21.4	21.4
Korea[1]	0.8	0.3	0.7	1.3	0.5	0.5	0.7	0.3	0.9	0.2	1.0	1.8	1.1	..	..	0.6
Latvia	58.3	23.4	38.0	34.6	39.3	10.4	16.6	..	61.5	22.8	37.6	36.7	72.0	47.2	49.3	45.6
Luxembourg[1]	18.8	22.3	36.2	36.2	8.4	14.8	21.1	12.7	21.9	24.0	36.3	37.2		..	..	..
Mexico	2.0	1.7	1.6	2.1	2.1	1.1	1.4	0.9	1.9	2.1	1.6	2.7	..	2.9	5.6	1.7
Netherlands	..	37.1	42.0	40.9	..	13.0	16.0	13.5	..	42.7	44.2	43.8	..	72.8	69.6	71.2
New Zealand	14.9	5.4	13.4	14.5	7.0	2.4	5.7	6.2	18.1	7.5	16.1	18.1	37.5	12.5	28.8	28.6
Norway[1,2]	3.3	7.1	10.9	13.5	1.4	2.0	2.6	4.0	4.4	9.2	13.0	16.8	9.3	21.4	33.5	30.9
Poland	41.3	46.0	34.0	30.0	30.7	29.0	23.3	18.6	45.1	51.3	36.1	32.0	45.7	56.7	43.5	42.5
Portugal	41.0	46.9	53.4	49.4	21.8	28.3	25.9	25.6	48.2	49.3	56.1	51.3	58.6	69.6	76.4	71.2
Slovak Republic	55.1	69.4	54.2	55.1	42.0	48.5	40.1	32.1	60.5	73.5	55.3	57.3	63.3	75.8	64.2	69.6
Slovenia	59.8	46.1	53.8	43.6	43.0	31.1	49.2	25.8	66.9	48.9	52.1	45.4	82.9	56.7	89.1	50.1
Spain[2]	46.3	22.8	50.6	46.4	32.4	11.3	28.6	25.7	50.8	24.0	51.3	46.3	56.3	52.2	71.2	67.9
Sweden[2]	22.8	11.3	15.6	14.4	6.4	3.7	3.3	2.9	22.1	14.0	19.1	17.8	50.3	27.3	31.1	28.3
Switzerland	29.7	43.0	40.6	39.4	..	..	..	..	..	..	..	..	..	..	..	..
Turkey	29.8	38.9	25.5	28.0	28.5	32.9	17.0	18.5	31.3	43.8	29.2	32.5	..	50.0	40.9	37.5
United Kingdom[2]	18.1	17.6	23.4	22.7	9.4	11.2	13.9	11.8	22.6	21.4	25.8	25.5	28.3	25.7	39.0	40.9
United States[2]	5.3	9.0	15.2	14.6	3.1	5.1	7.9	7.3	6.4	10.7	16.9	15.8	7.4	11.2	21.4	21.7
OECD[3]	32.3	28.2	32.2	31.1	20.8	15.3	17.2	16.3	36.0	32.2	35.6	34.5	42.8	39.3	42.0	40.8
Colombia	..	13.1	8.1	9.4	..	8.6	4.3	5.9	..	16.1	10.0	11.2	..	17.4	14.2	14.6
Costa Rica	..	..	23.8	20.0	..	..	17.9	19.8	..	..	27.2	20.0	..	..	36.2	21.1
Lithuania	47.7	29.9	39.7	38.4	31.4	19.3	8.0	6.4	50.7	31.5	41.1	39.1	58.0	36.3	53.0	50.2
Russian Fed.	50.0	42.4	30.6	31.0	34.2	28.7	20.4	17.6	55.1	48.3	33.5	34.2	67.4	43.9	34.4	37.2
South Africa	..	62.3	64.6	64.9	..	38.3	39.8	38.6	..	66.9	67.7	67.9	..	79.8	72.2	72.6

.. Not available

Note: For country details related to data on unemployment by duration of job search, see www.oecd.org/els/emp/lfsnotes_sources.pdf. Persons for whom no duration of unemployment was specified are excluded from the total used in the calculation.

Please refer to the Box entitled "Major breaks in series" in the introduction to the Statistical Annex.

1. Data based on small sample sizes.
2. The lower age limit is 16 instead of 15. For Iceland up to 2008, Italy after 2007, Norway up to 2005 and Sweden up to 2006.
3. Weighted average.

Source: OECD Employment Database, www.oecd.org/employment/emp/onlineoecdemploymentdatabase.htm and www.oecd.org/els/emp/lfsnotes_sources.pdf.

http://dx.doi.org/10.1787/888933779314

Table N. Real average annual wages and real unit labour costs in the total economy
Annualised growth rates

	Average wages in 2017 USD PPPs[3]	Average wage (%)[4]					Unit labour costs (%)[4]				
		2000-07	2007-17	2007	2016	2017	2000-07	2007-17	2007	2016	2017
Australia	49 126	1.2	0.5	2.8	0.1	-1.0	1.0	-0.2	2.2	-0.7	-0.5
Austria	50 349	0.8	0.5	0.5	1.3	0.0	-1.1	0.4	-1.1	1.1	-1.6
Belgium	49 675	0.2	0.2	-0.5	-0.4	-0.7	-0.5	0.0	-1.0	-1.6	-0.5
Canada	47 622	1.6	1.1	2.4	-0.6	0.5	0.9	0.3	2.4	-0.8	-0.3
Chile[1]	25 879	1.1	2.0	0.4	1.8	-1.3	-0.6	1.5	1.7	0.5	1.3
Czech Republic	25 372	4.7	1.5	3.0	4.1	4.3	0.8	0.3	-0.1	2.8	1.0
Denmark	51 466	1.7	0.9	1.1	1.4	-0.7	1.1	0.0	3.6	0.6	-0.4
Estonia	24 336	8.1	1.4	16.1	4.8	1.7	1.8	0.8	7.6	2.5	-0.8
Finland	42 964	1.9	0.4	1.5	0.6	-0.4	-0.1	0.2	-1.5	-1.2	-2.5
France	43 755	1.2	1.0	0.4	1.1	1.2	0.1	0.5	-0.5	0.7	-0.2
Germany	47 585	0.2	1.2	-0.2	1.5	1.0	-1.9	1.0	-2.2	1.3	0.1
Greece	26 064	2.6	-2.2	0.0	0.0	-1.0	1.6	-0.4	0.4	1.2	-0.1
Hungary	22 576	4.5	0.4	-1.5	4.5	8.4	0.8	-0.3	-0.9	4.8	3.4
Iceland[1]	61 787	3.0	1.0	2.6	8.4	10.1	1.1	0.1	-0.5	3.0	7.5
Ireland	47 653	3.0	0.2	3.1	0.8	1.5	1.2	-3.2	1.6	-0.4	-3.5
Israel	35 067	-0.3	0.7	1.9	3.2	2.9	-0.5	0.1	-0.2	1.8	2.3
Italy	36 658	0.5	-0.2	-0.1	0.7	-1.0	0.6	0.3	0.0	1.3	-0.4
Japan	40 863	-0.2	0.1	-0.2	1.7	0.4	-1.0	0.2	-0.6	2.2	0.2
Korea	35 191	2.5	0.9	1.7	3.4	1.8	0.5	0.0	-0.1	1.2	-0.6
Latvia	23 683	9.2	1.9	23.4	5.3	4.2	2.4	0.2	15.0	2.7	0.5
Luxembourg	63 062	1.1	0.9	2.6	0.2	1.6	0.7	1.6	-1.6	0.7	2.0
Mexico[1]	15 314	1.2	-0.7	0.4	-0.5	-0.6	-1.7	-1.5	-4.6	-3.6	-1.3
Netherlands	52 877	0.8	0.5	1.1	0.2	-0.8	-0.7	-0.1	0.0	0.0	-1.0
New Zealand[1]	40 043	2.7	0.8	5.9	3.1	0.9	2.1	0.1	2.7	-0.1	0.6
Norway	51 212	3.1	1.3	4.3	-1.6	0.8	2.3	1.4	6.5	-2.6	0.0
Poland	27 046	0.9	2.3	2.5	4.9	4.5	-1.6	0.6	1.7	3.1	1.0
Portugal	25 367	-0.3	-0.2	0.7	0.8	0.0	-0.7	-0.4	-1.7	1.6	0.6
Slovak Republic	24 328	3.5	1.9	6.1	3.4	2.2	-2.6	0.4	-2.9	2.1	1.8
Slovenia	34 933	2.9	0.8	2.2	3.1	0.6	-0.3	-0.1	-1.2	2.4	-1.5
Spain	38 507	0.1	0.5	1.3	-0.4	-1.8	0.5	-1.0	1.3	-0.3	-1.5
Sweden	42 393	1.9	1.2	3.2	1.7	0.6	0.2	0.8	2.6	0.9	0.2
Switzerland	62 283	1.1	0.6	1.5	-0.2	-0.1	0.2	1.0	0.0	0.0	-0.3
Turkey	..	..	..	..	..	..	..	..	..	..	..
United Kingdom	43 732	2.4	-0.3	2.9	1.3	0.0	1.2	-0.6	1.6	0.8	0.3
United States	60 558	1.2	0.5	2.0	0.0	-0.2	-0.4	-0.2	0.9	0.1	-0.7
OECD[2]	45 056	1.1	0.5	1.3	0.9	0.3	-0.5	0.0	0.3	0.5	-0.5
Lithuania	24 287	9.0	2.6	10.2	5.3	7.6	-0.2	0.3	-0.4	0.8	-0.4

.. Not available

Note: Average annual wages per full-time equivalent dependent employee are obtained by dividing the national-accounts-based total wage bill by the average number of employees in the total economy, which is then multiplied by the ratio of average usual weekly hours per full-time employee to average usual weekly hours for all employees. For more details, see: http://www.oecd.org/employment/emp/average_wages.pdf.

1. Real compensation per employee (instead of real wages).
2. The OECD average wages and real wage growth are a weighted average based on dependent employment weights in 2017 for the countries shown.
3. Average wages are converted in USD PPPs using estimated 2017 USD PPPs for private consumption.
4. Average annual wages and unit labour costs are deflated by a price deflator for private final consumption expenditures in 2017 prices.

Source: OECD Employment Database, www.oecd.org/employment/emp/onlineoecdemploymentdatabase.htm and www.oecd.org/els/emp/lfsnotes_sources.pdf.

http://dx.doi.org/10.1787/888933779333

Table O. Earnings dispersion and incidence of high and low pay

| | Earnings dispersion[3] | | | | | | Incidence of | | | |
| | 9th to 1st earnings deciles Ratio | | 9th to 5th earnings deciles Ratio | | 5th to 1st earnings deciles Ratio | | Low pay %[4] | | High pay %[5] | |
	2006	2016	2006	2016	2006	2016	2006	2016	2006	2016
Australia	3.26	3.32	1.90	1.99	1.71	1.67	15.2	15.7	..	..
Austria	3.30	3.27	1.92	1.95	1.72	1.68	15.8	15.4	20.2	20.9
Belgium	2.43	2.36	1.74	1.72	1.39	1.37	6.3	4.6	12.8	13.5
Canada	3.74	3.71	1.87	1.88	2.00	1.97	22.5	22.3	11.0	8.5
Chile	4.76	4.32	2.78	2.71	1.71	1.59	13.0	11.9	27.5	26.4
Czech Republic[1]	3.45	3.46	1.83	1.82	1.88	1.90	19.7	19.8	..	..
Denmark	2.43	2.57	1.71	1.75	1.43	1.46	7.6	8.2	2.5	2.9
Estonia	4.39	3.78	2.14	1.97	2.05	1.92	22.9	22.1	25.8	22.7
Finland	2.47	2.50	1.73	1.75	1.43	1.43	7.5	7.1	16.1	16.6
France	2.96	3.06	2.00	2.04	1.48	1.50	7.6	9.1	19.2	19.1
Germany	3.35	3.33	1.78	1.82	1.88	1.84	18.3	18.9	18.1	18.0
Greece	3.33	3.27	1.94	1.95	1.71	1.68	20.0	15.8	19.8	20.2
Hungary	4.56	3.73	2.34	2.22	1.94	1.68	23.1	19.6	..	..
Iceland	3.10	2.99	1.77	1.78	1.75	1.68	17.1	14.9	16.7	17.1
Ireland	3.92	3.79	2.05	2.00	1.91	1.89	21.2	22.5	..	..
Israel	..	7.22	..	2.75	..	2.63	..	26.4	..	30.2
Italy	2.31	2.25	1.59	1.50	1.45	1.50	9.3	7.7	12.1	9.0
Japan	3.11	2.85	1.86	1.82	1.67	1.56	16.1	12.7	..	..
Korea	5.12	4.50	2.42	2.36	2.12	1.91	24.9	23.5	..	..
Latvia	5.99	4.00	2.45	2.15	2.44	1.86	31.6	26.0	30.8	25.4
Luxembourg	3.22	3.15	1.99	2.07	1.62	1.52	14.8	12.2	22.3	24.4
Mexico	4.00	3.33	2.13	1.94	1.88	1.72	16.3	16.1	23.1	19.5
Netherlands	2.88	3.02	1.78	1.86	1.62	1.62	14.0	14.5	18.8	19.2
New Zealand	2.84	2.86	1.78	1.88	1.60	1.53	14.6	11.2	..	..
Norway	2.15	2.55	1.46	1.52	1.48	1.68	..	..	..	..
Poland	4.32	3.81	2.11	2.05	2.05	1.86	23.5	21.7	..	..
Portugal	4.29	3.95	2.67	2.57	1.60	1.54	15.6	11.4	26.8	28.4
Slovak Republic	3.51	3.49	2.01	1.99	1.75	1.76	18.0	19.0	..	..
Slovenia	3.73	3.33	2.08	2.00	1.79	1.67	19.6	19.2	24.6	23.2
Spain	3.10	3.12	1.99	1.94	1.56	1.61	12.3	14.6	23.6	22.8
Sweden	2.31	2.28	1.67	1.67	1.38	1.36	..	..	..	..
Switzerland	2.70	2.65	1.80	1.78	1.50	1.49	11.4	10.2	..	..
Turkey	4.10	3.53	3.56	2.85	1.15	1.24	0.5	0.8	33.5	28.9
United Kingdom[1]	3.62	3.42	1.99	1.96	1.82	1.74	20.7	19.3	..	..
United States	4.84	5.05	2.30	2.41	2.10	2.10	24.2	24.9	..	..
OECD[2]	3.52	3.42	2.03	2.01	1.72	1.69	16.4	15.7	20.3	19.9
Colombia	7.04	4.51	2.99	2.71	2.35	1.67	26.9	24.2	22.1	12.7
Costa Rica	5.38	5.00	2.80	2.93	1.92	1.71	18.1	14.7	27.6	26.1
Lithuania	4.58	3.78	2.22	2.11	2.06	1.79	27.2	21.3	27.7	25.8

.. Not available

Note: Estimates of earnings used in the calculations refer to gross earnings of full-time wage and salary workers. Country-specific variations from this definition as well as national data sources and earnings concepts can be found at: http://stats.oecd.org//Index.aspx?QueryId=18974.

1. For the Czech Republic and the United Kingdom, there are breaks in the series. In both cases, data were spliced from new-to-old series to remove the breaks.
2. Unweighted average for the above countries.
3. Earnings dispersion is measured by the ratio of 9th to 1st deciles limits of earnings, 9th to 5th deciles and 5th to 1st deciles. Year 2006 refers to 2007 for Colombia and 2010 for Costa Rica. Year 2016 refers to 2013 for Sweden; to 2014 for Estonia, Latvia, Lithuania, Luxembourg, the Netherlands, Slovenia, Spain and Turkey; and to 2015 for Belgium, Chile, France, Iceland, Israel and Norway.
4. The incidence of low pay refers to the share of workers earning less than two-thirds of median earnings. See note 1. for countries with different time periods, with the addition of France for which 2016 refers to 2014, and Switzerland for which 2006 refers to 2008.
5. The incidence of high pay refers to the share of workers earning more than one-and-a-half times median earnings. See note 1. for countries with different time periods, with the addition of France for which 2016 refers to 2014.

Source: OECD Earnings Distribution Database, www.oecd.org/employment/emp/employmentdatabase-earningsandwages.htm.

http://dx.doi.org/10.1787/888933779352

Table P. Relative earnings: Gender, age and education gaps

Percentage

	Gender[2]		Age[3]				Education/Skills[4]			
	Women/Men		15-24/25-54		55-64/25-54		Low/Medium		High/Medium	
	2006	2016	2006	2016	2006	2016	2005	2015	2005	2015
Australia	17	14	40	40	0	-5	12	12	-36	-40
Austria	22	16	36	33	-17	-22	..	24	..	-52
Belgium	10	5	30	35	-26	-28	10	13	-32	-36
Canada	21	18	42	42	-3	-1	23	16	-34	-32
Chile	6	21	44	42	-10	3	..	30	..	-133
Czech Republic	15	16	35	33	-2	2	..	25	..	-80
Denmark	10	6	36	40	-2	-2	..	11	..	-25
Estonia	30	28	17	28	19	19	15	11	-24	-27
Finland	19	16	32	31	-6	-3	4	1	-43	-34
France	14	13	36	36	-32	-18	..	11	..	-46
Germany	18	16	46	41	-9	-10	..	21	..	-54
Greece	12	4	35	40	-31	-27	..	22	..	-35
Hungary	0	9	37	36	-17	0	..	25	..	-95
Iceland	12	10	37	38	2	-1	..	..	..	..
Ireland	14	11	46	54	-6	-13	17	2	-72	-56
Israel	..	19	..	73	..	-16	..	26	..	-62
Italy	8	6	32	24	-29	-20	..	17	..	-40
Japan	33	25	44	41	-1	0	..	..	..	..
Korea	40	37	44	43	10	9	9	19	-33	-45
Latvia	11	21	19	21	12	17	..	11	..	-45
Luxembourg	8	3	40	41	-34	-27	..	26	..	-59
Mexico	19	16	23	29	-3	0	..	36	..	-110
Netherlands	16	14	49	48	-14	-11	13	14	-47	-47
New Zealand	9	8	36	40	3	2	19	19	-23	-28
Norway	9	7	32	35	-5	-8	12	14	-26	-20
Poland	11	9	43	30	-20	1	..	16	..	-62
Portugal	14	14	42	37	-14	-21	35	26	-77	-69
Slovak Republic	18	14	31	32	4	7	27	26	-42	-69
Slovenia	7	5	36	34	-31	-14	..	20	..	-71
Spain	14	12	34	34	-22	-17	17	20	-35	-42
Sweden	15	13	28	30	-10	-8	..	17	..	-16
Switzerland	21	15	38	37	-10	-13	..	23	..	-43
Turkey	3	7	41	36	-60	-27	..	26	..	-66
United Kingdom	22	17	49	47	5	3	..	23	..	-48
United States	19	18	47	49	-8	-11	..	28	..	-71
OECD[1]	15	14	37	38	-11	-7	..	19	..	-53
Colombia	1	7	45	40	-10	-19	..	31	..	-124
Costa Rica	5	2	38	37	-18	-29	..	24	..	-108
Lithuania	16	12	20	27	3	5	..	11	..	-68

.. Not available

1. Unweighted average for the above countries.
2. See note to Table O. The gender wage gap is unadjusted and is calculated as the difference between median earnings of men and women relative to median earnings of men. Year 2006 refers to 2007 for Colombia and 2011 for Costa Rica. Year 2016 refers to 2013 for Sweden; to 2014 for Estonia, Latvia, Lithuania, Luxembourg, the Netherlands, Slovenia, Spain and Turkey; and to 2015 for Belgium, Chile, France, Iceland, Israel and Norway.
3. Age wage gaps are calculated as the difference between mean earnings of 25-54 year-olds and that of 15-24 year-olds (respectively 55-64 year-olds) relative to mean earnings of 25-54 year-olds. Data refer to 55-year-olds and over for Hungary and Norway. Year 2006 refers to 2009 for the Slovak Republic, 2010 for Costa Rica and Greece, and 2011 for Colombia. Year 2016 refers to 2014 for Austria, Estonia, France, Iceland, Latvia, Lithuania, Luxembourg, the Netherlands, Slovenia, Spain and Turkey; and to 2015 for Belgium, Chile, Israel and Norway.
4. Earnings by skill (or education) levels refer to mean annual full-time earnings of 25-64 year-old employees. Earnings gaps by skill levels are calculated as the difference between mean earnings of medium-skilled employees and low- (respectively high-) skilled employees relative to mean earnings of medium-skilled employees. The skill levels are based on the International Standard Classification of Education (ISCED, 2011), except for Korea which refers to ISCED, 1997. *Low skills* correspond to less than upper secondary; *Medium skills* to upper secondary and post-secondary non-tertiary; and *High skills* to tertiary education. For Korea, tertiary education refers to ISCED, 1997 Levels 5 and 6. Year 2005 refers to 2006 for Korea. Year 2015 refers to 2013 for France and Italy; and to 2014 for Canada, Denmark, Finland, Lithuania, Luxembourg, the Netherlands, Portugal and Spain.

Source: OECD Earnings Distribution Database, www.oecd.org/employment/emp/employmentdatabase-earningsandwages.htm for earnings gap by gender and age; and OECD (2017), *Education at a Glance 2017: OECD Indicators*, OECD Publishing, http://dx.doi.org/10.1787/eag-2017-en for earnings gaps by skills or education levels. For Korea, data on earnings by education are provided by national authorities.

http://dx.doi.org/10.1787/888933779371

STATISTICAL ANNEX

Table Q. Public expenditure and participant stocks in labour market programmes in OECD countries

Percentage

| | Public expenditure (% of GDP) | | | | | | | | Participant stocks (% of labour force) | | | |
| | Total | | Active programmes | | of which: Active measures not including PES and administration | | Passive programmes | | Active measures not including PES and administraion | | Passive programmes | |
	2015	2016	2015	2016	2015	2016	2015	2016	2015	2016	2015	2016
Australia	0.91	0.89	0.23	0.24	0.09	0.09	0.68	0.65	2.22	2.18	6.59	6.51
Austria	2.23	2.29	0.74	0.77	0.57	0.59	1.49	1.53	3.41	3.51	7.84	7.79
Belgium	2.43	2.31	0.72	0.73	0.52	0.53	1.71	1.58	6.91	8.59	14.13	13.17
Canada	0.86	0.90	0.24	0.25	0.12	0.12	0.62	0.65	0.52	0.57	2.80	2.89
Chile	0.53	0.57	0.17	0.17	0.13	0.14	0.36	0.40	..	..	2.08	2.03
Czech Republic	0.62	0.54	0.43	0.36	0.31	0.25	0.19	0.18	1.68	1.45	1.92	1.83
Denmark	3.33	3.22	2.05	2.07	1.66	1.66	1.28	1.15	6.63	7.10	5.16	4.53
Estonia	0.64	0.78	0.22	0.32	0.10	0.18	0.43	0.46	0.61	0.71	2.20	2.28
Finland	2.94	2.84	1.00	0.99	0.85	0.85	1.93	1.85	4.63	4.71	11.85	11.82
France	2.98	..	1.01	..	0.76	..	1.98	..	6.54	..	13.78	..
Germany	1.51	1.45	0.63	0.63	0.27	0.26	0.88	0.82	2.92	1.81	6.37	6.00
Greece	..	..	..	..	0.24	..	0.49	..	..	..	..	..
Hungary	1.14	1.18	0.90	0.94	0.83	0.88	0.25	0.24	5.48	5.74	4.05	3.85
Iceland	..	..	..	..	..	..	..	..	..	..	..	..
Ireland	1.83	1.57	0.58	0.50	0.49	0.42	1.25	1.07	4.25	3.49	14.40	12.42
Israel	0.68	0.63	0.16	0.16	0.14	0.14	0.52	0.47	4.00	4.11	4.63	4.24
Italy	1.80	..	0.51	..	0.42	..	1.29	..	..	..	5.21	5.43
Japan	0.32	0.30	0.14	0.14	0.08	0.08	0.17	0.16	..	..	..	..
Korea	0.68	0.70	0.36	0.37	0.32	0.33	0.32	0.33	..	..	..	..
Latvia	0.56	0.64	0.14	0.19	0.10	0.14	0.41	0.45	0.77	1.02	3.70	3.80
Luxembourg	1.34	1.41	0.66	0.80	0.59	0.74	0.68	0.61	8.70	10.02	3.90	3.82
Mexico	0.01	0.01	0.01	0.01	0.00^{n}	0.01	0.00^{n}	0.00^{n}	..	..	..	..
Netherlands	2.60	2.40	0.77	0.72	0.52	0.49	1.82	1.68	3.99	3.84	9.56	9.39
New Zealand	0.67	0.62	0.33	0.30	0.15	0.14	0.35	0.32	2.09	1.87	2.66	2.51
Norway	0.97	1.06	0.52	0.53	0.39	0.38	0.46	0.53	1.93	1.88	2.42	2.72
Poland	0.74	0.69	0.46	0.45	0.39	0.37	0.27	0.24	3.68	3.77	2.39	2.20
Portugal	1.91	1.68	0.55	0.48	0.48	0.41	1.36	1.21	5.60	4.18	7.14	6.39
Slovak Republic	0.53	0.60	0.20	0.26	0.16	0.21	0.34	0.35	2.10	2.57	1.93	2.00
Slovenia	0.76	0.74	0.24	0.24	0.16	0.16	0.53	0.50	1.15	0.80	2.12	2.10
Spain	2.52	..	0.60	..	0.45	..	1.92	..	8.20	..	9.56	..
Sweden	1.82	1.73	1.27	1.17	1.01	0.90	0.55	0.55	5.22	4.73	5.18	5.21
Switzerland	1.25	1.33	0.59	0.62	0.48	0.51	0.65	0.71	1.29	1.35	2.62	2.74
Turkey	..	..	..	..	..	..	..	..	..	..	..	..
United Kingdom	..	..	..	..	..	..	..	..	..	..	..	..
United States	0.28	0.27	0.10	0.11	0.08	0.09	0.18	0.16	..	..	..	..
OECD	1.33	1.31	0.53	0.54	0.40	0.40	0.79	0.77	3.78	3.79	5.78	5.59
Lithuania	0.53	0.52	0.31	0.30	0.25	0.24	0.23	0.22	1.60	1.42	2.41	2.34

.. Not available

Note: The data shown are not strictly comparable across countries or through time, since data may differ from standard definitions and methods and certain programmes or programme categories are not always included in the data for participants stocks. OECD average has variable country coverage. OECD average for 2016 is calculated using the latest available data. Fiscal years for Australia, Canada, Japan, New Zealand, the United Kingdom and the United States.

n) Nil or less than 0.005

Source: For European Union countries and Norway, European Commission (2018), Labour Market Policy, http://ec.europa.eu/eurostat/web/labour-market/labour-market-policy/database and detailed underlying data supplied to the OECD by the European Commission with certain Secretariat adjustments. For other countries: OECD Database on Labour Market Programmes, http://dx.doi.org/10.1787/data-00312-en.

http://dx.doi.org/10.1787/888933779390

ORGANISATION FOR ECONOMIC CO-OPERATION AND DEVELOPMENT

The OECD is a unique forum where governments work together to address the economic, social and environmental challenges of globalisation. The OECD is also at the forefront of efforts to understand and to help governments respond to new developments and concerns, such as corporate governance, the information economy and the challenges of an ageing population. The Organisation provides a setting where governments can compare policy experiences, seek answers to common problems, identify good practice and work to co-ordinate domestic and international policies.

The OECD member countries are: Australia, Austria, Belgium, Canada, Chile, the Czech Republic, Denmark, Estonia, Finland, France, Germany, Greece, Hungary, Iceland, Ireland, Israel, Italy, Japan, Korea, Latvia, Luxembourg, Mexico, the Netherlands, New Zealand, Norway, Poland, Portugal, the Slovak Republic, Slovenia, Spain, Sweden, Switzerland, Turkey, the United Kingdom and the United States. The European Union takes part in the work of the OECD.

OECD Publishing disseminates widely the results of the Organisation's statistics gathering and research on economic, social and environmental issues, as well as the conventions, guidelines and standards agreed by its members.

OECD PUBLISHING, 2, rue André-Pascal, 75775 PARIS CEDEX 16
(81 2018 16 1 P) ISBN 978-92-64-30178-8 – 2018